THE MYSTERIES OF PARIS AND LONDON

Victorian Literature and Culture Series
Karen Chase, Jerome J. McGann, and Herbert Tucker
General Editors

Daniel Albright
> Tennyson: *The Muses' Tug-of-War*

David G. Riede
> Matthew Arnold and the Betrayal of Language

Anthony Winner
> Culture and Irony: *Studies in Joseph Conrad's Major Novels*

James Richardson
> Vanishing Lives: *Style and Self in Tennyson, D. G. Rossetti, Swinburne, and Yeats*

Jerome McGann, Editor
> Victorian Connections

Antony Harrison
> Victorian Poets and Romantic Poems: *Intertextuality and Ideology*

E. Warwick Slinn
> The Discourse of Self in Victorian Poetry

Linda K. Hughes and Michael Lund
> The Victorian Serial

Anna Leonowens
> The Romance of the Harem
> Edited and with an Introduction by Susan Morgan

Alan Fischler
> Modified Rapture: *Comedy in W. S. Gilbert's Savoy Operas*

Barbara Timm Gates, Editor
> *Journal of Emily Shore*, with a new Introduction by the Editor

Richard Maxwell
> The Mysteries of Paris and London

THE
MYSTERIES OF
PARIS AND
LONDON

Richard Maxwell

UNIVERSITY PRESS OF VIRGINIA
Charlottesville and London

THE UNIVERSITY PRESS OF VIRGINIA
Copyright © 1992 by the Rector and Visitors
of the University of Virginia

First published 1992

Library of Congress Cataloging-in-Publication Data

Maxwell, Richard, 1948–
    The mysteries of Paris and London / Richard Maxwell.
        p.   cm. — (Victorian literature and culture series)
    Includes bibliographical references (p.   ) and index.
    ISBN 0-8139-1341-1
    1. Dickens, Charles, 1812—1870—Knowledge—England—London.
2. Detective and mystery stories—Histories and criticism.   3. Hugo, Victor,
1802–1865—Knowledge—France—Paris.   4. Literature, Comparative—
English and French.   5. Literature, Comparative—French and English.
6. City and town life in literature.   7. Cities and towns in literature.
8. London (England) in literature.   9. Paris (France) in literature.   I. Title.
II. Series.
PR4592.L58M38   1992
823'.8—dc20   91-36789
                                                                                                          CIP

Printed in the United States of America

Contents

Illustrations

Preface

In 1845 a writer for *Bentley's Miscellany* observed gleefully that "mystery-mania has crossed the channel." He was mocking a fashion in fiction that included, by that time, Eugène Sue's *Mystères de Paris* (1842–43) and G. W. M. Reynolds's *Mysteries of London* (1844–48), best-sellers both. The success of Sue or Reynolds must have seemed no more than a topic of the moment; mystery-mania, however, had deeper roots than most people suspected as well as greater staying power. *All the Year Round* in 1860, *Punch* in 1880, could refer to the conventions of the genre as casually as *Bentley's* during the mid-forties.[1] And some of the century's finest novelists were deeply conversant with it: above all, Victor Hugo and Charles Dickens, both of whom wrote in this vein at regular intervals, to the shocked or bemused commentary of their contemporaries.

The novel of urban mysteries, as I shall call it, is well known to historians of popular culture. Most of the better works it produced or influenced have already been enshrined in various canons. To study this line of books, to insist on its continuity, might therefore seem a pastime for antiquarians. I believe, on the contrary, that working from Hugo's *Notre-Dame de Paris* to Dickens's novels of the early 1840s, from them to *Les Mystères de Paris* and its imitations, and from them to the later novels of Dickens and Hugo provides a fresh understanding of the novel's ability to produce and present social knowledge, to analyze the relationship between that mysterious artifact the modern city and its often disoriented citizens.

My inquiry into the novel of urban mysteries proceeds from two assumptions. I suppose that a city dweller lacking appropriate figures of speech "could have no verbal representations of his own or any other city."[2] I suppose, further, that without such representations the city dweller would be left in a position of baffled, paralyzed silence. These premises suggest why the novelists in this line occupied

themselves so intensely with certain persistent figures for city
life and why a massive audience—sometimes working-class,
sometimes middle-class, occasionally both together—
responded so eagerly to their efforts. Hugo, Dickens, and the
others wrote of labyrinths, crowds, panoramas, or paperwork
(to name four crucial examples). These subjects were pursued
so ardently that they came to have a significance larger than the
literal realities named. It was implied, on occasion stated, that
understanding a figure meant understanding the city with
which it was linked. This double riddle was the mystery posed,
and in some cases solved, by the novel of urban mysteries.

The work that defined such concerns was *Notre-Dame,* first
published in 1831. Seldom has a literary fashion begun this
ominously. Hugo's flair for tinkering with figures helped him
evoke an urban dilemma typical of his time: he dramatized the
intricate kinds of confusion that occurred in a city where many
different sorts of people were forced together; where because of
class limitations, newly obvious cultural divisions, and changes
in the structure of knowledge, nobody could claim—much less
act upon—an inclusive understanding of society. Despite its
author's evident virtuosity, *Notre-Dame* refused to affirm the
positive use of figures; in its concluding chapters, any chance
for public knowledge, knowledge based on common
assumptions, seemed to disintegrate along with the corpse of
Quasimodo. Some readers who got this far recoiled; others
wrote books in response, taking issue with Hugo or finding
within the ghastliest scenes of his novel possibilities of renewal.
Notre-Dame described a perplexity from which a myriad of
works sought a release.

The release was accomplished by means of allegory.
Allegory was originally a technique for using enigmatic figures
to reveal an invisible world. By the middle of the nineteenth
century, London or Paris was that world: visible enough in its
particulars, perhaps, but as a whole unimaginable . . . unless it
could be apprehended through figures that suggested its full
significance. Where *Notre-Dame* hinted at this approach, then
emphasized its dangers or futility, subsequent works took a
different direction. Under the aegis of allegory, figures were
used to create and communicate knowledge: knowledge in part
negative, since it rejected the uncritical acceptance of absolutes;

knowledge in part positive, since it included social facts otherwise difficult to define. Both nineteenth- and twentieth-century theorists of allegory have doubted the feasibility of combining negative with positive knowledge (I will consider their denials in my opening chapter); the conscious, determined practice of the novelists shows, to the contrary, how it could be accomplished.

The core of my book is its study of figures and their use within a particular group of nineteenth-century novels. This topic requires the reader to keep in mind several different orders of information. It is important to know something of illustration and its conventions. As often in allegory, words elicit images and images reveal new twists in the words that called them forth. The work of George Cruikshank, Phiz (Hablôt Browne), and Charles Meryon can illuminate the interaction between word and image; so can Albrecht Dürer's *Melencolia I,* an allegory of frustrated and paralyzed knowledge that haunts the nineteenth century. Conventions of scientific inquiry, of the quest after facts and principles, often clarify the city novelist's undertaking; see my studies of "singularity" in *Martin Chuzzlewit* or *Les Travailleurs de la mer,* as well as of "curiosity" in *The Old Curiosity Shop.* Journalistic practice is equally instructive: figural methods of presenting the city are often developed within Dickens's fact-obsessed magazines, then transferred to the novels—where, as a rule, they undergo substantial modification or revision. For this reason Dickens's own nonfiction prose, as well as work by journalists like George Sala and Andrew Wynter, enters the argument; so, more broadly, do forms of topographical description developed in newspapers and guidebooks. Wynter's psychiatric work, along with the *Arabian Nights,* suggests yet another source of allegorical rhetoric prominent in the novel of urban mysteries: folklore, fairy tales, and dreams, studied here as they were transformed into writing about London. Last, there are the serials of Reynolds and Sue (along with obscurer derivatives, such as W. H. Ainsworth's *Auriol*); I will demonstrate that each of these books has its special logic and that each in its way conditions the success of the now-canonical authors. This point is perhaps most significant with respect to Reynolds, a man remembered mainly by those who love or hate his politics. He deserves wider recognition (and a good biography), not just because he was one of the best-selling authors of mid-Victorian England but because his Chartist polemics make possible a historically grounded appreciation of Dickens. If one want to see how the eminent novelist used the figures of the mysteries novel to get outside the bounds of his own experience, then one can do so by judging him against Reynolds, who writes on a similar subject but for a (largely) different audience and with different motives.

I have tried to allow for the variety and scope needed in any investigation of urban figures; on the other hand, one contrast, one pairing of authors, tends to dominate. The affinities between Hugo and Dickens are fairly obvious, though less remarked in our century than in their own. Both are realists of a peculiarly extravagant kind, makers of myth committed to lifelong explorations of imperial cities. Both, furthermore, combine the sentimental and the cruelly bizarre in a manner at once marketable (socially acceptable among middle-class readers) and perennially disturbing. A historical accident adds to the interest of this juxtaposition. French romanticism culminated about the same time that English Victorian culture became firmly established. Hugo influenced Dickens in rather specific ways, especially during the 1840s and in his late novel (1870) *The Mystery of Edwin Drood,* but did so through a sort of cultural time warp. *Notre-Dame* emerges from a moment when the last great national movement of romanticism was approaching its height (it still had a decade to go, expiring only with Hugo's *Les Burgraves,* in 1843); on the other side of the channel, *Notre-Dame* reaches a literary culture settling into staider habits of workaday social concern. When Dickens tries to adapt the story of Quasimodo and his cathedral, he seeks the Victorian accommodation of romantic strengths and faults. A death-obsessed view of the city, a flirtation with sorrowful and self-pitying solipsism, must be absorbed by a broader system of values. Paris or London can be known; this knowledge may be communicated, even though a descent into the abyss (Hugo's image) is first necessary. *Les Misérables,* several decades later, is an effort along the same lines. A compromise where morbidity and public-mindedness mingle is never less than difficult: so far as it is achieved, it contributes to that other reconciliation—between the negative and positive features of allegory—which marks the outstanding novels in this tradition.

My chapters will be most informative pursued in sequence and as contributions to an overall argument. One strand in that argument shows why *The Mysteries of Paris and London* has taken its present shape. I have come to believe that *Notre-Dame* is an exemplary book as well as an excellent one. It is as rich in its implications—in what it gives other writers—as, say, *Waverley* or *Madame Bovary;* it belongs in the first rank of nineteenth-century fiction, not just for specialists in nineteenth-century French literature or specialists in popular culture but for everyone who cares about novels. Perhaps this suggestion is substantial enough to justify a book in itself. On the other hand, it remains elusive unless followed through in connection with *Notre-Dame*'s pervasive influence: the line of urban mysteries is vigorous for most of the nineteenth century and into the first years of the twentieth. The genre, in turn, can hardly be given its due until it is studied with reference to a larger question; it is important because it illuminates, or more precisely activates, the relation between allegory and social knowledge. To sum up the attraction of *Notre-Dame* and of the books that responded to it: sooner or later, through a widening circle of contexts, a student of these works must inquire after the kinds of truth with which fiction is concerned. No nineteenth-century writer ever produced a work like that compelling potboiler perused by Oliver Twist, a tale whose "terrible descriptions were so real and vivid, that the sallow pages seemed to turn red with gore" [*OT,* 20, 196]. But the pages of *Bleak House* or *Les Misérables*—pages black with ink— can bring the persistent inquirer closer to the city than might have been anticipated. *The Mysteries of Paris and London* chronicles the developments in urban culture and urban writing by which this turn of events became possible.

Acknowledgments

Leo Steinberg once did a parody of acknowledgments pages. He thanked a rich and bizarre cast of characters, each of whom had a name that was an anagram of his own. It is possible that the following venture in acknowledgment is not quite so self-promoting as the one imagined by Steinberg. So I hope.

My thanks to those friends and colleagues who read all of *The Mysteries of Paris and London* in draft, some of them more than once: Stuart Tave, Keith Cushman, Megan Wolfe, Wendy Olmsted, William Olmsted, Edward Eigner, Jerome McGann, John Sutherland, Cecil Lang. My thanks also to those who commented on individual sections or discussed my ideas with me: Jonathan Arac, Robert Caserio, Gregory Alles, Frederick Niedner, Mark Schwehn, James Chandler, Lawrence Porter, Kathryn Grossman, René Steinke. One way or another, each of these people helped improve the manuscript. Whatever virtues it now possesses are in large part attributable to them.

Some of the chapters in this book derive from previously published essays. (These sections have, without exception, been revised.) Parts of chapter 8 appeared in *Nineteenth-Century Fiction* 32, no. 2 (September 1977): 188–213 (© 1977 by the Regents of the University of California); of chapters 3 and 6 in *Comparative Literature* (1978); of chapter 5 in *The Journal of English and Germanic Philology* (1979); of chapter 12 in *ELH* (1979); and parts of chapter 9 are reprinted by permission from the *Romanic Review* 73, no. 3 (1982): 314–30 (© 1982 by the Trustees of Columbia University in the City of New York). My thanks to the editors of these journals not only for permission to reprint but for advice given and—as a general rule—taken. Along the same lines, I am grateful to Robert Newsom, who gave me an opportunity to present my thoughts on Dickens and the *Arabian Nights* (chapter 11 of the current volume) at the 1980 meeting of the Modern Language Association. A related talk (the basis for chapter 2 of this book) was given at Vanderbilt University's Nineteenth-Century French Literature conference (1985), as part of a Hugo panel chaired by Patricia Ward.

I am grateful to the New York Public Library, the British Library, the Southwark Local Studies Library, and the interlibrary loan service of Valparaiso University, for providing me with many otherwise difficult-to-find resources: books, parts-issue versions of novels, maps, pamphlets, catalogs, directories, and in one especially illuminating case a scrapbook.

Financial support for this project was given by Valparaiso University and my father and mother. In addition, my father spent several months (on and off) helping me get photographs of plates. I thank Margaret Maxwell and Bela and Klari Erdoss for hospitality of unstinted lavishness on trips to New York City.

At the University Press of Virginia, Nancy Essig more than once helped me out beyond the call of duty and Cynthia Foote was rigorous in her editing. In Valparaiso, Indiana, Tracy Inskeep did an enormous amount of work double-checking quotations, references, and hundreds of other textual details; I thank her for this assistance and also for some excellent discussions of *Notre-Dame*.

Works Frequently Cited

Charles Dickens

I have quoted from the Oxford Illustrated Edition (Oxford:
Oxford University Press, 1947–58), 21 vols., which includes all
the fiction, as well as much of the journalism, and is almost
universally available. The text of this series is based on the
Charles Dickens edition (1867–68), not a sensible choice: see
Philip Collins, "Dickensian Errata." Other editions of the
novels, published by Clarendon Press, Penguin Books, and
Norton Books, often provide better texts. They also have been
consulted and—where noted—quoted in preference to Oxford
Illustrated. I have identified quotations by chapter and page.
Several novels by Dickens—*Little Dorrit, A Tale of Two Cities,
Our Mutual Friend*—are divided into books; *The Chimes* is
divided into "quarters." In these cases, I have identified
quotations by book (or "quarter"), chapter, and page.
Abbreviations are as follows.

AN: American Notes and Pictures from Italy (1843, 1846)
BH: Bleak House (1852–53)
BR: Barnaby Rudge (1841)
CS: Christmas Stories (1871)
DS: Dombey and Son (1846–48)
ED: The Mystery of Edwin Drood (1870)
GE: Great Expectations (1860–61)
HT: Hard Times (1854)
LD: Little Dorrit(1855–57)
MC: Martin Chuzzlewit (1843–44)
MHC: Master Humphrey's Clock (1840–41).

> *Master Humphrey's Clock* contains materials not reprinted
> in *The Old Curiosity Shop;* though Oxford Illustrated
> includes a volume largely devoted to these materials, I
> have quoted instead from the three-volume bound

edition of *Master Humphrey's Clock,* published by
Chapman and Hall in 1840. Here Dickens's words and
the wood engravings provided by his artists can be seen
in logical conjunction with one another.

NN: Nicholas Nickleby (1838–39)
OCS: The Old Curiosity Shop (1840–41)
OMF: Our Mutual Friend (1864–65)
OT: Oliver Twist (1838)
SB: Sketches by Boz (1836–37)
TC: The Chimes (in *Christmas Books*) (1844)
TTC: A Tale of Two Cities (1859)

Other frequently cited Dickensian materials include the
following:

AYR: All the Year Round
Essays that first appeared in this weekly magazine edited
by Dickens are cited by the date of publication: such
dates are often important to my argument. In *Dickens'*
"All the Year Round": Descriptive Index and Contributor List
(Troy, N.Y.: Whitston Publishing Company, 1984), Ella
Ann Oppenlander identifies some contributors to *AYR*
(many of these essays remain unattributed); her
identifications are incorporated into my references.
Essays in the "Uncommercial Traveller" series later
appeared in *The Uncommercial Traveller,* sometimes under
different titles.

Collins: Philip Collins, *Dickens: The Critical Heritage* (New
York: Barnes and Noble, 1971).

Forster, *Life:* John Forster, *The Life of Charles Dickens,* 2 vols.,
new edition with notes and an index by A. J.
Hoppé and additional author's footnotes (London:
Dent, 1966).

HW: Household Words
Essays that first appeared in this weekly magazine edited
by Dickens are cited, as with *AYR* references, by the date
of publication. In *Household Words: A Weekly Journal 1850–*
1859 Conducted by Charles Dickens (Toronto: University of
Toronto Press, 1973), working from the *HW* office book,
Anne Lohrli identifies contributors to *HW;* her
identifications are incorporated into my references.

Pilgrim Edition: The Letters of Charles Dickens, edited by
        Madeline House, Graham Storey, and Nina
        Burgis, 6 vols. (Oxford: The Clarendon Press,
        1965–).

Victor Hugo

The comprehensive edition of Hugo edited by Jean Massin is a
world in itself: *Oeuvres complètes,* 18 vols., Paris: Le Club
Français du Livre, 1967–70. I have been grateful for the texts,
prefaces, annotations, and illustrations provided by Massin and
his many collaborators; however, citations from Hugo's novels
are keyed to more widely available editions. Hugo had a
particular fondness for dividing his novels into sections: *Notre-
Dame* is divided into books and chapters, *Les Misérables* and *Les
Travailleurs de la mer* into parts, books, and chapters. My
citations include references to these units, followed by page
numbers.

DJ: Le Dernier Jour d'un condamné, précédé de Bug-Jargal, with
    preface and commentaries by Roger Borderie (Paris:
    Gallimard, 1970; first published 1829).
LM: Les Misérables, with commentaries by Bernard Leuilliot, 3
    vols. (Paris: Le Livre de Poche, 1972; first published 1862).
LT: Les Travailleurs de la mer, edited by Yves Gohin (Paris:
    Gallimard, 1980; first published 1866).
ND: Notre-Dame de Paris 1482, with preface and commentaries
    by Léon Cellier (Paris: Garnier-Flammarion, 1967; first
    published 1831; expanded edition published 1832).
P: Poésie, edited by Bernard Leuilliot, 3 vols. (Paris: Aux
    Editions du Seuil, 1972).
PC: Préface de Cromwell, in Hugo, *Oeuvres complètes,* edited by
    Jean Massin, vol. 3 (Paris: Le Club Français du Livre, 1967;
    first published 1827).
PS: Promontorium somnii, in Hugo, *Oeuvres complètes,* edited by
    Jean Massin, vol. 12 (Paris: Le Club Français du Livre,
    1967; manuscript of *PS* dated 1863).
WS: William Shakespeare, in Hugo, *Oeuvres complètes,* edited by
    Jean Massin, vol. 12 (Paris: Le Club Français du Livre,
    1967; first published 1864).

Other Frequently Cited Sources

ML: G. W. M. Reynolds, *The Mysteries of London,* 4 vols. (London: George Vickers, 1846).

MP: Eugène Sue, *Les Mystères de Paris,* nouvelle édition, revue par l'auteur. 4 vols. (Paris: Librairie de Charles Gosselin, 1843).

Simmel: Georg Simmel, *The Sociology of Georg Simmel,* translated, edited, and with an introduction by Kurt Wolff (New York: The Free Press, 1950).

Quotations from Hugo are presented in both the original and a translation, mine unless otherwise indicated. On a few occasions where I have thought it useful, this form of double quotation is accorded other authors; otherwise I have simply provided a translation, mine unless otherwise indicated.

THE MYSTERIES OF PARIS AND LONDON

I

———◦◦◦◦◦∞◦◦◦◦———

Introductory

In the handsome street, there are folks asleep who have dwelt there all their lives, and have no more knowledge of these things than if they had never been, or were transacted at the remotest limits of the world—who, if they were hinted at, would shake their heads, look wise, and frown, and say they were impossible, and out of Nature—as if all great towns were not.

Dickens,
*Master
Hum-
phrey's
Clock*

1. Allegory and City Life

ON MY SHELF STAND four tall red volumes (size, Royal Octavo), titled *The Mysteries of London*. No author is mentioned on the spines, but prices are clearly indicated: the successive volumes of *Mysteries* sold for six shillings and sixpence apiece. Above the announcement of price, each spine is dominated by an ornament, half abstract pattern, half manic tendril: what a Renaissance painter would have called a grotesque, after the sort of design one found in grottoes. While three of these volumes have worn well for their age (almost a hundred and fifty years), the spine of the fourth is ripped down the top, revealing the wastepaper used as backing beneath it. Where MYS and LON should be, the first group of letters above the second, I can make out a few words in smaller type, lengthways: *plans of London*. A closer look reveals that such a plan is being advertised for sale, and that it is—or was—six feet, six inches in length.

Maps have at least the appearance of reliability, of stern fact recorded for the viewer's instruction. Fiction's relation to social actualities is more elusive. Early nineteenth-century literature manifests confusion and unease about what it might mean to know a city. The adjective *knowing* is often applied during the period to a sort of character who wrongly claims great knowledge. To use a familiar idiom, the knowing character gets around: such a person collects trivia or retreats within an expertise that substitutes for any broader perspective. Relied on exclusively, knowingness becomes a bogus form of understanding. It is displayed by many memorable novelistic creations, among whom Dostoyevsky's Lebedyev (from *The Idiot*) may stand as an example. Although knowingness is usually associated with the lower or lower-middle classes, it is a quality traceable through many stations of life—including, incidentally, that of novelist.[1]

Disguising one's own ignorance is a common activity, but the situation of the city dweller in the 1830s and 1840s retains its special pathos. An irreversible process seems to be occurring. Greatest among artifacts, the metropolis eludes the grasp of the human mind; to revise a traditional dictum, the maker no longer knows what he has made.[2] At the same time, some urbanites prove less paralyzed than others. A few inquisitive people step outside their usual lives and try to grasp their environment from a fresh perspective. Not all these experimenters compose fiction. There are the compilers of blue books, those formidable parliamentary reports, there is the indefatigable interviewer Henry Mayhew, there are the social workers. But my present concern is with novelists, especially those who worked under the disreputable auspices of the mysteries tradition.[3]

The novelist of urban mysteries turns his attention to moments when the articulation of facts, the words in which they are stated, becomes a central issue: he confronts social dilemmas that are also figures of speech.[4] So described, his effort might seem to anticipate one of those schemes for "metafiction" worked out in our own century by such masters as Gide, Nabokov, and Borges. The mysteries novelist, however, has special reasons for taking this approach. When Gringoire finds his hackneyed allegorical pageant abandoned by its audience and strays out into the allegory of Paris (*Notre-Dame*); when Master Humphrey enters a crowded London shop and discovers that it is, of all things, an allegory (*The Old Curiosity Shop*); when Allegory itself points from the ceiling of Mr. Tulkinghorn's chambers and finds its gesture taking on new meaning (*Bleak House*)— when these and similar events occur, the novelist sets in motion an extraordinary revival: he finds a way to combine the aspirations of realism with a venerable allegorical rhetoric. Out of this union emerges a means for imagining the city and deciding what lives it might allow its inhabitants.

New Allegories for Old

A rhetorical figure is a turn in language, a departure from normal usage that "predisposes us to a desired interpretation of the facts conveyed." Figures shape an understanding of realities whose nature is uncertain; they can also be problematic on their own account. It is these "dark figures" (Bunyan's phrase) that are especially associated with the allegorical literature of the Middle Ages and the Renaissance. A product of inspiration, dark figures may not be comprehensible even to the person who articulates them. In any case their meaning is never evident all at once. Two premises ensure the value of obscure words about the ineffable. It is assumed that multiple figures, multiple perspectives, are aspects of a divinely ordained unity. (Cf. Edgar Wind on "composite gods" and "mythological compounds" in the Renaissance.) It is also assumed that dark figures contain eternal wisdom. These assumptions have consequences: as a group the figures are understood to harmonize, whatever their apparent discrepancies; separately, they are made to undergo a process of "incessant, cumulative transformation" through which their implications can unfold. Thus understood, figures seem to reveal the psyche, the cosmos, and divinity. A vision of this sort, in which the study of words takes the interpreter all the way to absolute Truth (at which point words will seem inadequate, will fall away like emptied husks), "must have been as absolute and shattering as death."[5]

The description just outlined is crucial to everything that follows; I don't expect anyone to be completely comfortable with it. Although one knows how allegory was supposed to work, a question remains: What did this ambitious and intricate form actually accomplish? An answer is proposed by Angus Fletcher. Somewhat perversely, Fletcher waits until the last sentence of his work on the subject to note that "allegories are the natural mirrors of ideology." His observation makes sense, however tardy. A political or social order that wants to validate itself could do worse than to call on the allegorist, whose dazzling forms of expression are useful *because* they claim a more-than-human authority. In other words, allegory's tendency to implicate its reader in a search for hieratic, unified knowledge easily coincides with a society's attempt to represent its identity, structure, and goals as unquestionable.[6]

Fletcher's claim is not that all allegories are mirrors of ideology, only that allegory invites such a use. Furthermore, the linguistic assumptions that allowed the interpretation of figures to seem like a journey toward irresistible Truth dissipated after the Renaissance; if these assumptions persisted here and there, then they did so eccentrically.[7] The nineteenth-century allegorical revival, often remarked in recent years,[8] may thus open up fresh possibilities. The late Paul de Man, who did much to rehabilitate the term *allegory* for readers of romantic and Victorian literature, suggested one possible change of emphasis. De Man's "The Rhetoric of Temporality" postulates a close bond between allegory and irony; allegorist and ironist "are . . . linked in their common demystification of an organic world postulated in a symbolic mode of analogical correspondences or in a mimetic mode of representation."[9] Writing in the years before World War II, Walter Benjamin made a related claim; his unfinished magnum opus on the Paris of Baudelaire underlines the "corrosive" effects of allegorical thought, which is said to clear away delusions, to anticipate the apocalyptic purification of a corrupt bourgeois world, and ultimately to become a "mimesis of death."[10] Though De Man's essay and Benjamin's more extended study differ on many points, both imply that certain nineteenth-century allegories are *anti*-ideological: as though allegory's energies had been turned against themselves—as though a great authoritarian tradition had been changed from the inside out, charged with a terrifying negativity.

Subsequent chapters will substantiate this kind of case; I will insist, however, upon a large qualification. It is true that once allegory is separated from a supernatural theory of language it may well display anti-ideological tendencies; however, the new allegory is not exclusively the reverse of the old. If the allegorist's interrogation of dark figures becomes an assault on established social assumptions, then the assault is seldom a self-justifying end. Ideologies are shaken up—never, on the other hand, eliminated.[11] This process underlies the expression of positive knowledge: that is, of knowledge presented by a public, consensual, and potentially deceptive means but maintaining a persistent relation with actual social conditions (as distinguished from ideologies—that is, from fantasies about those conditions).[12]

The new allegory, destructive and constructive both, did not come into being easily. It had to be formulated step by step; moreover, the challenge of applying it to city life was sobering even at the best of times. Before focusing directly on fiction, I will consider two nineteenth-century thinkers who face these awkwardnesses with unusual theoretical explicitness. Goethe writes around the beginning of the mysteries tradition, Ruskin a few years after the end of its greatest period. The two of them share a conviction that there must be some relation between the negative and positive impulses of modern allegories; trying to read *Notre-Dame,* trying to read the novel of urban mysteries, they fail to see how and why this relation can be sustained. The negative prevails (*Notre-Dame* becomes a handbook for sadists); the possibility of positive knowledge evaporates.

Goethe, Metamorphosis, and Nature

Goethe's most famous comments on allegory occur in the *Maximen* of 1822: allegory is said to use the particular as an example of the universal, whereas symbols display the universal in the particular. A related distinction comes up further on. Allegory changes a visible appearance into a concept, a concept into an image; the concept is fully expressed by the image. The symbolic mode accomplishes a similar transformation, but in such a way that "die Idee im Bild immer unendlich wirksam und unerreichbar bleibt" (the idea remains always infinitely active and unapproachable).[13] One might be a little disturbed that Goethe's symbols are identified first with particularity and then with incommensurability, but there is no contradiction. The implication is that symbols belong to the realm of experience: the concrete, living, and sensate world that Goethe calls Nature. Allegory is different from symbolism because it depends on abstraction or distancing (for example, in such devices as personification).[14] It is a rational form that attempts to systematize Nature, to render it static, whereas symbols reveal a much more immediate logic in experience—the logic of unceasing development that for Goethe can be identified with the natural.

The old allegory is perhaps closer to what Goethe calls symbolism than to what he calls allegory; however, it answers exactly to neither definition. Why does the sage of Weimar insist on his polemical and somewhat skewed distinction? This contrast is present in much earlier works by Goethe, where it springs from the demands of romantic doctrine. A good example is the scene in *Faust* called *Nacht* (Night), written during the 1770s. Here the scientist-philosopher communes with magical *Zeichen* (signs) from which he conjures up spirits or visions. The first of these signs is allegorical in Goethe's special sense; the second, symbolic:

1.   The sign of the macrocosm yields a vision of "wirkende Natur vor meiner seele liegen" (creative Nature open to my soul). Creative Nature is presented by means of a traditional image, Jacob's Ladder: angels go up and down the ladder, passing golden ewers ceaselessly. Faust is moved by the image but finds it unsatisfactory because it is so pat: a spectacle only, uninvolving for the viewer.
2.   He turns to the sign of the earth spirit, from which he releases an overwhelming presence—a bullying, fiery force so close that it threatens to consume him. Faust thinks that the earth spirit is just what he has been looking for, but the creature finds him insignificant and departs.[15]

Both signs are unsatisfactory. The macrocosm is too far away, the earth spirit too near; the macrocosm too available, the earth spirit not available enough. Contemplative abstraction (Goethe's allegory) offers no succor to Faust. Burning, symbolic immediacy cannot be absorbed by the human spirit, at least not all at once. With his need to escape his study, to get into the fields and experience Nature directly, Faust has lost out two ways at once—like Goethe himself, many years later in the *Maximen*. If Faust is to resolve his difficulties, he must combine the powers of Goethe's allegory and Goethe's symbolism. In the terms of *Nacht,* he must learn to treat the earth spirit as less a reality, more a figure, thus achieving some analytical distance from it. Alternately, he must learn to treat the macrocosm as less a figure, more a reality—and thus get more actively involved with it. Faust needs figures that are real or a reality that yields to figurative interpretation. He gets the extremes but not the middle ground.

Faust begins in the exaltation of experience and action over analysis and interpretation; then it becomes clear that the two contrarieties have to be combined. Goethe comes nearer to accomplishing this goal in *Faust* than in the *Maximen* or other mainly philosophical works. Most importantly, during the first act of part 2—in a scene that parallels the evocation of the macrocosm and the earth spirit—Faust summons the spirit of Helena. It disappears before he can possess it, much as the earth spirit had disappeared. Faust must now attempt to recover this lost vision.

He first approaches Helen through the classical Walpurgis night, whose proliferating mythological creatures (the Sphinx, griffins, Chiron, etc.) must be understood as *Antezedentien* (antecedents) to the lady. Each in its own way, these fantastical figures foreshadow her advent: Faust struggles towards Helena by confronting the Sphinx and others, by learning to see in them what he will later meet head-on. Metamorphosis, a fundamentally natural process, becomes a movement of mind: Goethe can feel it "der schönste Besitz, solche werte Bilder oft in der Einbildungskraft erneute zu sehen, da sie sich denn zwar immer umgestalteten, doch, ohne sich zu verändern, einer reineren Form, einer entschiednern Darstellung entgegenreiften" (my fondest possession to find such precious images often renewed in my imagination, where, to be sure, they were in a constant state of transformation and yet, remaining intrinsically unchanged, ripened towards a purer form, a more definite representation).[16]

Helena actually appears in the section of *Faust*, part 2, sometimes called the *Helena*, which Goethe classified as a classical-romantic phantasmagoria, and Carlyle even more aptly as a "Phantasmagory." A pressing issue throughout is her reality or lack of it. Is she a phantasm only? Given her apparent lack of substance, how can she enter the world of generation where Faust wants to establish her? Hidden meaning is revealed to the attentive "durch einander gegenübergestellte und sich gleichsam in einander abspielgelnde Gebilde" (by images placed in juxtaposition and so reflecting one another). Under these circumstances, Helena achieves a certain palpability; "ein beginnendes Vorbild" (the germ of an image) flowers.[17] Helena is more compelling than the sign of the macrocosm, more malleable than the sign of the earth spirit. Though she fades away and her son by Faust perishes, some other members of her entourage—also summoned by Faust—linger on permanently. Faust does not achieve the marriage of classicism and romanticism, a union he desired, but his attempt to do so has made a change or two in the world around him. Interpretation is also a form of creation, and creation of action.

Goethe insisted that his phantasmagory was more objective than anything in part I of *Faust,* an assertion that readers have tended to take on faith or (like G. H. Lewes) to reject by throwing the author's own attack on allegory back at him.[18] But allegory in these later parts of the work is no longer the purely abstract, rationalizing form condemned by the *Maximen.* It is not that Goethe has reverted to medieval thought. He embraces no literal belief that words in themselves contain truth. If Faust (or his creator) is enlightened by holy runes, then they are the runes of Nature rather than those of an actual book. Fortunately, Nature, with her rules of metamorphosis, is sufficient to guarantee allegory's coherence. Goethe's symbol and allegory unite (theirs is the real marriage); out of this union emerges the old allegory, revivified.

Goethe did not approve of all he had set in motion. He loathed *Notre-Dame,* whose dependence on his own masterwork is conspicuous. Just four years after the publication of his classical-romantic phantasmagoria, he abandoned Hugo's novel: he could never finish reading it. He told Karl Friedrich Zelter that he, Goethe, had tried all his life to cultivate a natural sense, a judgment based on Nature. He was not willing to corrupt himself with literature that mixed the beautiful and the ugly. (By implication this mixture is unnatural.) If *Notre-Dame* displayed "dem entscheidenen historisch-rhetorischen Talent" (a definite historical-rhetorical talent), it was used, alas, to produce abominations. Dwelling on the impossible and the unbearable, books like *Notre-Dame* produce a strange realism that can only corrupt a civilized sensibility.[19]

One is likely to begin by dismissing Goethe's criticisms. He was a very old man when he made them, and seeing the new French romanticism arise so long after the German romanticism that he himself had outgrown must have been perturbing. Moreover, *Notre-Dame* is now such a familiar book: it is hard to recapture the impact it had on first appearance. Hugo has picked up motifs and techniques from Goethe (among others), then modified them in consonance with principles of his own. To take one representative example, his shrunken and tortured Faust—Claude Frollo—enters a "fantasmagorie" induced by obsessive love of an elusive, beautiful woman [*ND*, 9.1]. However, there is no sense of playfulness or of progressive enlightenment in Frollo's adventure. All around him an abyss opens up; eventually he takes a fall. Goethean objectivity is not the issue—not even a by-product—of this unfortunate life.

Something in *Notre-Dame* blocks a judgment based on Nature. Might the something be Paris? For the last fifty years of his life, Goethe resided in Weimar, a different kind of city than the great metropolises then developing all over Europe. Weimar (notes Martin Green) "had a little of everything, but nothing in such demanding dimensions that it could impose itself as an ineluctable life-task."[20] However artificial, Weimar never became an enveloping and all-demanding world; human will was neither dwarfed by the city nor cut off from that logic of Nature that Goethe thought underlay human development. Paris was different. Paris set up its own standards. It was this contrast, I suspect, that most disturbed Goethe. Human consciousness had turned toward the greatest creation of human will and discovered it to be an object more mysterious, more sinister, than anything in that larger cosmos that Faust had presumed to explore. This object calls out for the powers of the old allegory—even while it implicitly denies their pertinence.

Sincerity and the Symbolical Grotesque in Ruskin

In a well-known essay, "Of the Real Nature of Greatness of Style," Ruskin puts a high value on the comprehensive representation of reality. Since the visible world is saturated with divine truth, to grasp it whole is to participate in that truth. The artist's participation is termed "sincerity," defined as the expression of "the largest possible quantity of Truth in the most perfect possible harmony." An artist of the highest stature unites the greatest number of observations into "one great system of spacious truth," "subduing all his powers . . . to the arbitrement of a merciless justice, and the obedience of an incorruptible verity."[21]

It is admitted in Ruskin's account of sincerity that human beings can only grasp so much at a time. "There are, indeed, certain facts of mystery, and facts of indistinctness, in all objects, which must have their proper place in the general harmony."[22] Some things cannot be scrutinized without obscuring an understanding of the whole. Though Ruskin is writing about physical appearances, the principle is implied to have a broader application. Just a few years before he published *Modern Painters,* volume 3 (where "Greatness of Style" appears as chapter 3), Ruskin had discussed at length this problem of human capacity and its relation to comprehensive truth.

Studying Venice's "Grotesque Renaissance" (*The Stones of Venice,* 1853), Ruskin finds himself in a dilemma. He must discuss a group of art works he has characterized as grotesque. Some of them he admires and some he hates. A principled distinction must be made between the two groups. Ruskin makes it this way:

Most men's minds are dim mirrors, in which all truth is seen, as St. Paul tells us, darkly; this is the fault most common and most fatal. . . . we can in some sort allow for the distortion of an image, if only we can see it clearly. And the fallen human soul, at its best, must be as a diminishing glass, and that a broken one, to the mighty truths of the universe round it; and the wider the scope of its glance, and the vaster the truths into which it obtains an insight, the more fantastic their distortion is likely to be. . . . Now, so far as the truth is seen by the imagination in its wholeness and quietness, the vision is sublime; but so far as it is narrowed and broken by the inconsistencies of the human capacity, it becomes grotesque.[23]

Ruskin acknowledges that the soul is fallen; it follows that comprehensive representation of a serene and perfectly balanced kind will not often be attained. On many occasions one must make do with another sort of art, an uneasy compromise. Grotesque art works by means of fantastic distortions, a disturbing method. Ruskin has to decide when grotesqueness is an acceptable artistic strategy.

His answer, in effect, is that the grotesque is justified by its link with a special variety of figurative interpretation. One example is Jacob's Ladder, which he calls the "narrowed and imperfect intimation" of a truth too large or obscure for the human mind. Understanding the vision of Jacob means first looking into oneself, then recognizing through this "diminishing glass" the universe. Just for a moment, knowledge and experience become one. Such images express the Terrible or Symbolical Grotesque. These two categories are virtually indistinguishable, for "even if the symbolic vision itself be not terrible, the sense of what may be veiled behind it becomes all the more awful in proportion to the insignificance or strangeness of the sign itself." Ruskin thus renders usable those "melancholy or majestic" superstitions connected with the Symbolical Grotesque: "the wraith and foreboding phantom; the spectra of second sight; the various conceptions of avenging or tormented ghost, haunting the perpetrator of crime . . . the presence of death itself." Each of these forms suggests the "trembling of the human soul in the presence of death" and the world beyond it. The grotesque may be trivialized or debased—it may become a dim mirror—but not in cases like this. "The grotesque which we are examining arises out of that condition of mind which appears to follow naturally upon the contemplation of death, and in which the fancy is brought into morbid action by terror, accompanied by the belief in spiritual presence, and in the possibility of spiritual apparition."[24] Wholeness and quietness are hard to achieve when the artist aims at rendering so

comprehensive a fact. Under these conditions, expressive distortion becomes an acceptable tool; distortion enables people to imagine the unimaginable, to perceive through imperfect means their own identities and
that of a divinely wrought cosmos.

The Symbolical Grotesque is Ruskin's name for allegory. His account
is sympathetic: it catches the essential progress of allegorical vision,
through necessarily insufficient figures to a deathlike confrontation that
transforms—transfigures—a sense of one's place in the world. At the
same time, the Symbolical Grotesque has some telltale Victorian characteristics. It concentrates on the appalling distance between Truth and any
possible artistic rendering. God is a long way off. Ruskin is very anxious.
In reading his description of the Symbolical Grotesque, I constantly feel
that allegory is about to fail, that it could not possibly catch the nature of
self or world. Whether or not this is true of Renaissance art, Ruskin feels it
to be the case with certain modern productions aspiring to the grotesque.
Take Dickens, for instance: "The classical and Renaissance manufactures
of modern times having silenced the independent language of the [work-
ing-class] operative, his humour and satire pass away in the word-wit
which has of late become the especial study of the group of authors headed
by Charles Dickens."[25] Formerly Dickens's extravagant grotesqueries
would have found their outlet in the sculpture of the cathedrals. Now
"word-wit" drifts free, uncontrolled, and trivialized—no longer symbolic, except that it signifies an irresistible process of decay.

Ruskin resumes the critique of Dickens some thirty years after *The
Stones of Venice*, in his lectures on "Fiction, Fair and Foul" (1880–81). Here
he identifies the mysteries tradition exactly, with *Notre-Dame* its "effectual
head," *Bleak House* its crowning product, and the Paris morgue its spiritual
home.[26] Once this line of fiction comes centrally into view, it demands a
firm rejection—and not just in passing. Ruskin seeks to identify the causes
of this peculiar fashion, to situate it authoritatively in the category of dim
vision. He does so by describing and analyzing the landscape of Croxted
Lane ("between the hostelry of the Half-moon at the bottom of Herne
Hill, and the secluded College of Dulwich"):

> *A deep-rutted, heavy-hillocked cart-road, diverging gatelessly into vari-
> ous brickfields or pieces of waste; and bordered on each side by heaps of—
> Hades only knows what!—mixed dust of every unclean thing that can
> crumble in draught, and mildew of every unclean thing that can rot or rust
> in damp: [Here commences a magnificent Dickensian catalogue, cul-
> minating in] cinders, bones, and ordure, indescribable; and variously*

kneaded into, sticking to, or fluttering foully here and there over all these,
remnants, broadcast, of every manner of newspaper, advertisement or big-
lettered bill, festering and flaunting out their last publicity in the pits of
stinking dust and mortal slime.

For anyone who grows up with only Croxted Lane as a country walk, "the
ultimate power of fiction to entertain him is by varying to his fancy the
modes, and defining for his dulness the horrors, of Death."[27] The Renaissance artist depicted death as the "revealer of secrets."[28] Croxted Lane—a
boundary line where the city overtakes the natural world—makes death
itself the secret.

Where Jacob's Ladder implies a tense equilibrium between "Divine
message" and dedicated interpreter, the modern grotesque parodies this
balance or dissolves it altogether. Part of Ruskin's resentment about Croxted Lane is personal—this, he confesses, is where he had thought out part
of *Modern Painters* many years before. From the desecration of the landscape, both memory and society will suffer. Within the wasteland of
Croxted Lane nothing keeps its identity. Corrupted human dreams—
compare the list of "melancholy or majestic" superstitions in *The Stones of
Venice*—are of "truncated and Hermes-like deformity," "death by falling,
or sinking, as in delerious sleep," "petrifaction or loss of power." The very
idea of a shaping intention undergoes progressive debasements: God's
hand gives way to man's, and then human intention peters out in the
random intersection of many conflicting aims.[29] Once city dwellers start
thinking about Croxted Lane, much less living along it, they have in an
important sense yielded to its influence. They are scientists of a sort,
systematically cataloging "modes of mental ruin"—exclaiming over them
much as the botanist might over a new lichen. And then they go beyond
this mock science; they slip from taxonomy to a morbid, compulsive
poetry, creating new visions of horror and corruption to satisfy the appetite that Croxted Lane has raised. The pathos in Ruskin's description of
the cursed locality is that he feels himself on the verge of the fate he
describes. Trying to write what he has seen in the city, he confronts
unbearable fantasies, dreams that possess him rather than he them. His
conclusion seems inescapable. Once the dilemma of Croxted Lane is
generalized—once multiplied by the force of mass communication and the
market economy—then literature becomes just one more manifestation of
urban pathology. Language sinks abandoned into the dust, flaunting out
its last publicity. London's modes of ruin dominate.

Might Croxted Lane be treated as the object of a revived and modernized allegory: might one find in it figures that can be interpreted? Now and then Ruskin hints that this is the case. His account of J. W. M. Turner in *Modern Painters* introduces, potentially, a hero of modern life. Ruskin's Turner is a master allegorist; he is fascinated by the rise and fall of imperial cities; his paintings turn on *death* in the nineteenth century. These points, however, do not add up. Ruskin is almost afraid to imagine how a modern allegory might work. Facts are no good without God—or at least His created world—to hold them together: the allegorical method appropriate to exploring a divine reality could not be borrowed to make sense of city experiences. At the end of *Modern Painters* Ruskin looks back at his studies and comments, "Full of far deeper reverence for Turner's art than I felt when this task of his defence was undertaken . . . I am more in doubt respecting the real use to mankind of that, or any other transcendent art; incomprehensible as it must always be to the mass of men." Such devices as allegory could never be adapted to an urbanized civilization. For Ruskin this is an insoluble difficulty.[30]

Solving the Insoluble

According to Goethe and Ruskin, allegory can be preserved for modern times; according to them also, the city is the place of all places where allegory shouldn't work. This logical snarl is unavoidable. Though these sages update traditional allegorical methods with considerable boldness, they carry over substantially unaltered an archaic concept of knowledge; they suppose that an understanding of human life and human environments must be dependent on dictums delivered unconditionally from above. It matters little whether one's unalterable rule is called God or Nature. In either case the compromise fails; if knowledge is absolute and the metropolis overwhelms absolutes, then the yearnings of Faust will lapse into decadence, the grotesques of the cathedral run wild. Under these circumstances, a synthesis between the negative and positive aspects of allegory becomes impossible.

So Goethe, so Ruskin. The novelists they critiqued understand the situation differently. In whatever way their fascination with allegory may have gotten started—as a holdover from romanticism, as a nostalgic throwback to preindustrial times, as the expression of a longing for ritual and the sacred in a context where divine inspiration seems impossible—it persists because they avoid the snarl just described. Their modernization of allegory, unlike that of the sages, includes new criteria for what it means to know a city. Goethe's grudging praise of *Notre-Dame,* that it displays a definite historical-rhetorical talent, thus acquires a new meaning. As adapted in the novel of urban mysteries, allegory links history and rhetoric. It opens up rhetorical claims to historical, as opposed to timeless or transcendent, understanding; it demarcates a probable and provisional order rather than an eternal one; it replaces divination with . . . urbanation. On these terms knowledge is conceived as uncertain but not unusable. "The gods hid within lying figures." For Dickens and Hugo it is the city that hides, the city that must be revealed.[31]

Subsequent chapters pursue two ways of describing this project. First, I argue that the figures of city life were endowed with a special kind of coherence; taken together, they were treated, not as a closed system, certainly not as a harmonious one, but as an open and overlapping order by which urgent social questions could be publically framed. Second, I argue that individual figures were interpreted by a formalized, almost a ritualized means; they were considered enigmas that could be *gradually* unraveled, in more or less discrete stages. Both these approaches recall the form of traditional allegory; in this respect they are much like the updatings of Goethe and Ruskin. Both, however, admit a less absolute concept of knowledge than either of the sages could accept.[32]

The matter of coherence and the matter of interpretation are closely linked; for the most part, it will be convenient to discuss them concurrently. All the same, each deserves a separate introduction. I begin with coherence. As Dickens had it, the "phase[s]" of London's "immensity" are inexhaustible [*DS*, 33, 480]. The metropolis is a theater, a prison, a wilderness, a mouth that swallows up multitudes, an anthill or a beehive, a great wen, Hell. Paris does not have the same kind of geographical history—it has always been a more contained city than its sister across the Channel—but is equally rich in the figures it has inspired. Choices among these possibilities must to some extent be arbitrary; however, within the line of urban mysteries, four figures prove particularly rich—and particularly wrapped up with one another.

1. *Labyrinths* have long been a subject of allegorical works, such as *The Faerie Queene*. The widespread tendency to see cities as mazes is a related but more recent phenomenon, a product, I would guess, of historical memory. Once Paris and London begin to be modernized— once streets are widened and straightened to facilitate the circulation of traffic—the older, usually poorer neighborhoods exert a new fascination. Here there are many narrow, winding alleys; here traffic easily gets itself into knots; here, the visitor who is not a native may well feel mystified. Sometimes this experience is initially treated as charming or quaint, as when Mr. Pecksniff enters the maze of

Todgers's [*MC*, 8, 122]. But mixed in with the charm is a more problematic element. The labyrinth signifies information that is specialized, even secretive. When mazes are assimilated by the novel of mysteries, they retain an element of nostalgia, Washington Irving-style, but become preeminently figures of initiation into hidden knowledge. It is not only Gringoire who passes through a sinister urban maze to reach a proscribed territory. This motif is used by Dickens throughout his career (I will study in special detail the case of *Oliver Twist,* where the labyrinth's relation to the criminal underworld is an obsessive concern, where mazes *lead* to ropes); it reappears in the opening chapters of *Les Mystères de Paris, The Mysteries of London,* and offshoots from Sue or Reynolds; it is developed further in Hugo's later fiction, especially *Les Misérables.* As the above list suggests, the secrecy of the labyrinth often signifies crime. Hugo's novels also insist on identifying labyrinths with women. This theme is initiated in *Notre-Dame,* where Esmeralda is worshipped by the criminals who inhabit the Court of Miracles; like crime, femininity figures as a terrifying but ultimately illuminating Other (a similar idea is contrastingly developed in *Les Travailleurs de la mer*). In each of the novels I have mentioned, one can learn from an initiation into the maze only if one survives it; one can survive it by understanding the nature of the struggle between the poor and those outside the realm of poverty. Initiation, in other words, is not just a matter of achieving some exclusive, secret status but also of learning to find a way among places, classes, or genders. The city as labyrinth is a realm of hidden but real connections.

2. *Crowds* pouring through the city streets, especially at night, have often been described as phantasmagorias. The original phantasmagorias were magic-lantern slide shows, those "loud-gibbering Spectral Realities" that impressed so many visitors to Paris and later London. Scott calls London a "phantasmagorical place" (1828, cited in *OED*); *Howitt's Journal* describes posters on city walls as creating "a phantasmagoria of scenes as rapid in their progression as they are brilliant in their character"; Hazlitt writes of the Cockney that he "sees hundreds and thousands of gay, well-dressed people pass—an endless phantasmagoria." From Hazlitt it is only a step to the elaborate literary usages of Hugo, Dickens, Baudelaire, and many others—down to recent explorers of city life, like Thomas Pynchon. As might be expected from such a miscellaneous list, the implications of the phantasmagoria are diverse. In its abundance, the phantasmagoric crowd

can seem either a nightmarish onslaught or a generous overflow: both alternatives are explored in *The Old Curiosity Shop*. It can serve a policing function (*Oliver Twist, Martin Chuzzlewit*) as well as a revolutionary one (*Notre-Dame, Les Misérables*). However, while the crowd lacks fixed iconographic meaning, it tends through these varied contexts to suggest an abiding dilemma. It moves through the street, also through minds. It has the compelling immediacy of the flashing images in the dark room; it also has their evanescence, their ghostliness. (The image of this ghostliness is presented effectively in the frontispiece to the 1845 Chapman and Hall translation of Sue's *Mystères,* where a nocturnal crowd surges forth from behind a theatrical curtain, held by a wizard—see fig. 1.) To quote Hugo, a confrontation with the crowd generates "la poussée obscure d'une rencontre inexprimable qui s'évanouit" (the obscure pressure of an unutterable encounter—which vanishes). The crowd is a collectivity that often seems just close enough to grasp but then, phantasmagorically, withdraws. It thus confirms the pedestrian's isolation, even while taunting him with his complicity in an order that he has failed to fathom. Little wonder that the urban crowd haunts the novelist of urban mysteries.[33]

3.   *Panorama* is also a coinage of popular culture. Dolf Sternberger and Richard Altick have traced the panorama's development as a visual display, in which the simulation of a 360-degree vista by painting and other illusionistic means drew fascinated audiences.[34] The panorama promises comprehensive survey, a seductive but dangerous prospect. The perils of the panorama are recognized before *Notre-Dame,* in Hugo's *Le Dernier Jour d'un condamné,* where the condemned man remembers looking out over Paris from the great cathedral, hearing its bells ring, and feeling a vertiginous panic. To survey the city with the bells banging away becomes a premonition of the death he will soon face. While the condemned man's position might seem a rather special one, such difficulties recur in subsequent novels. A famous early chapter of *Notre-Dame* describes a "bird's-eye view" of Paris: Frollo later falls from the cathedral, *into* the view whose grand coherence he has lost by focusing exclusively on Esmeralda. A view of everything prepares a narrowing into nothing. Among those who rethink Hugo's cautionary tale are W. H. Ainsworth, Charles Meryon, and J. K. Huysmans. However, it is Dickens who most frequently chronicles urban panoramas and their lure. An especially elaborate example is the view from Todgers's (*Martin Chuzzlewit*),

THE

MYSTERIES OF PARIS.

BY

EUGÈNE SUE.

VOL. I.

LONDON:
CHAPMAN AND HALL, 186 STRAND.
M.DCCC.XLV.

1. Title page to Eugène Sue, *The Mysteries of Paris* (London, 1845). (From a copy in a private collection.)

where the novelist describes the appeal of enigmatic fragments: it took a gypsy dancer to distract Frollo, but Dickens's viewer is shaken by a glimpse of a man at a window or a pair of chimney pots signaling to each other. Odd details seem to dominate the vista. The view demands a centrality no one possesses, while eliciting a sort of detective work all too closely related to paranoia. Knowledge of London or Paris will not spontaneously emerge from the dazzling expanse that seems to promise it.

4.   From *Notre-Dame* onward, the novel of urban mysteries emphasizes the role of paper and *paperwork*. Allegory has always been associated with "the book of the world"; the notion that city life constitutes a "close and blotted" text is a less traditional idea but, by the mid-nineteenth century, a familiar one: Carlyle, always a wonderful phrasemaker, dubbed modern times the Paper Age.[35] Some recent commentaries have helped me explore the significance of this idea, most especially the connections between cities and paper. Henri Lefebvre asserts that the city begins as writing on the ground; Lévi-Strauss suggests that "the only phenomenon with which writing has always been concomitant is the creation of cities and empires, that is, the integration of large numbers of individuals into a political system, and their grading into castes or classes."[36] Even if one doesn't go all the way with Lévi-Strauss and decide that writing's main function is to facilitate slavery, these comments can be helpful. They suggest that paperwork is connected with certain kinds of power typically available within cities, a link picked up by many nineteenth-century novelists. *Notre-Dame* initiates much of the discussion on this point by contrasting the writing on stone of the cathedral with the printed book produced from movable type. The conversation is broadened by the contributions of Sue, Reynolds, and other serialists, for whom documents are objects of terror: What incriminating secrets might this or that scrap of paper contain! Into whose hands might stray a scrap of information thus reified! *Bleak House* synthesizes these ideas, suggesting that writing is a point of exchange between public and private modes of communication, subjective understanding and accumulated information. Especially in this novel and in Hugo's *Les Misérables,* writing is not just a sociological or aesthetic phenomenon within the city but a force analogous to it. The book/city puts all ages, all cultures, all interpretations within reach, only to propose the further dilemma of how this mass of material could possibly be used. Both Dickens and Hugo find ways for their characters to come to terms

with paper and more paper: thus Jean Valjean's descent into the sewers (an antiliterate version of Paris that turns out to mirror the Paris above, a city suffused with documents); thus Esther Summerson's relinquishment of manipulative control over written secrets (she writes in order to let her writing go); thus Dickens's fascination in later novels yet with information that forms an ordered whole but exists on paper or in some other material form rather than in a particular mind.

Allegorical figures are supposed to signify an ultimate harmony. The figures listed above can be mixed, no doubt, but the mixture makes sense only under very peculiar conditions. At times a sequence is discernible: the secretive labyrinth leads to the spectacular vision of panorama or crowd (occasionally it leads to both); though spectacle sometimes appears to explain the labyrinth, it is overtaken by a concern for paper and paperwork, a figure that tends to supersede all the others; in certain borderline cases, paperwork also opens up access to a natural world outside the artificial city: the book of the metropolis once again becomes the book of the world. This pattern might seem to constitute a master myth of the sort described in Northrop Frye's criticism; I prefer to consider it a contingent chain of associations, defined by and occasionally defining a long-term literary fashion. Passing from figure to figure, the allegorist works towards the truths of city life.

Coherence is half my subject; the other half is interpretation. Interpretive questions always come up in discussions of allegory—even where their pertinence is denied.[37] Perhaps this is only just. The darkness of allegorical figures encourages a corresponding desire for light; seeing in a glass darkly creates the expectation of seeing face to face. Of course, such expectations have their problematic side: a progress from mystery to revelation is likely to turn back on itself; if mystery implies revelation, the converse may also be true. This qualification admitted, I have recognized three stages by which individual figures are clarified in the novel of urban mysteries. The first of these is associated with narrative, the second with heroes and heroic action, the third with the autonomy of knowledge:

1. Interpretation originates in a moment when a figure is recognized as a potential source for a narrative. This recognition requires an uncommon talent. As Aragon once observed, the city's unrecognized sphinxes will never "stop the passing dreamer to ask him life and death questions unless he directs his distracted meditations towards them."[38] The challenge is to sustain such a confrontation. If the allegorist returns many times to a chosen "allegorical fancy" [*HT,*

2.10, 201], he ends up telling a story from which a figure's meanings—the lies it has been used to tell, the truths it may possibly communicate—are gradually produced. He thus achieves his own version of traditional allegory's incessant transformations or of Goethe's "ripening" metamorphoses: without, however, any ideal or transcendent goal in mind.

2. Interpretation develops through an encounter, an identification, with a protagonist of a special sort. Acting as a surrogate for the author and his largely metropolitan readership,[39] the hero of the mysteries novel tends to be a bit panicked; at times, panic, a kind of half-annihilated identity, is the hero's whole raison d'être. *A Tale of Two Cities* suggests why this should be the case: "the vision of a drowning man, or of any human creature at any very great pass, could see a world if it were there" [3.2, 249]. Dickens's remark catches perfectly the problem of agents in allegory: overwhelmed by social formations almost as formidable as God but without His benevolence, struggling to take responsibility for their own words and actions, achieving responsibility at the moment when they seem to be doomed, they hover between nonexistence and unforgettable presence; the closer they come to "drowning," the closer they come to gauging their place in the world. One might say: In allegory, will substitutes for nature.[40]

3. Interpretation culminates in the comprehension of a social formation, the modern city, which nobody (hero or otherwise) could possibly comprehend. This seeming paradox requires a word of explanation. The city embodies what we know—where *we* denotes the understanding held in common by an urban civilization rather than by any one individual. This understanding is autonomous because it doesn't belong to anybody; it exists as a thing in itself. Thus emerges a perennial difficulty: if there is no person *in particular* who can grasp the whole of London or Paris, how is knowledge of these cities to be made usable?[41] More precisely yet: how is positive understanding, as distinguished from fantasies about people and locales, to become the basis of purposive action? The novel of urban mysteries suggests a solution. It shows that the incomprehensible can remain incomprehensible without necessarily garbling human intentions. Will survives the autonomy of knowledge.

In conceiving the connections among narrative, hero, and knowledge, I emphasize cause and effect. That is, if you tell a story about figures, there must be actions in it and these actions must have someone to act them out; once specified, the story's hero, typically a stand-in for author and reader, will prove to have a limited, human understanding; such limits make collective artifacts like cities appear arbitrary, inaccessible, even incomprehensible—until the new allegory can be brought to bear on them, brought to bear by that same circumscribed agent for whom the city is an intimidating riddle. Note that there are conflicting currents here, potentially a kind of vicious circle. Narrative makes agency visible, underlines its importance; knowledge, a vast, impersonal force, slaps it back into place, even at times annihilates it. The agent is caught between narrative and knowledge. The agent must sooner or later create a solution to the difficulty that, by his nature, he precipitates.

I noted earlier that I would discuss coherence and interpretation concurrently. The reasoning behind this decision can now be spelled out. For many city dwellers, the lure of direct, personalized experience has been irresistible; they have wanted to perambulate through London or Paris for hours, sometimes days, at a time: Dickens is especially notorious for his indulgence of this habit. In themselves, however, such activities produce no more than "knowingness." The wanderer, the flaneur, may sustain an appetite for compelling urban vignettes encountered on the street or in the market, but vignettes are seldom a suitable basis for knowledge. Indeed, an appetite directed toward them may reflect primarily their unsatisfactoriness: I can never have enough of this sort of thing precisely because it is thin; an hour later I'm hungry once more and have to go on the prowl again. (The thinness of random urban encounters is evident even in certain undeniable masterpieces—for instance, Baudelaire's Hugolian "Les Sept Vieillards.")

What then supplements, at times replaces, the lure of direct experience? One powerful tradition of sociological writing suggests that the discontinuities and shocks of urban life might tempt city dwellers to adopt a blasé attitude; they could ultimately react to city life by turning away from flaneurlike promenades, by learning to block out experience and substitute for it an order of knowledge embodied by such institutions as the newspaper. Substitutions of this kind are usually considered unfortunate; rather than embracing an abstract frame of reference provided by writing, the metropolitan citizen is supposed to seek out older traditions of knowledge where memory and tradition stabilize or deepen the flimsy experiential surfaces provided in the city.[42] I make quite a different argument. Discussing coherence, I praise paper and paperwork: writing conceived as an extension or abstraction of all that can be immediately observed. Discussing interpretation, I affirm the usability of knowledge—even (or especially) when knowledge is conceived as autonomous. These

two affirmations are close to each other. Chapter 12 will go a step further
and show that they are equivalent, but their near equivalence will be
evident long before. In either frame of reference I am arguing against an
excessive reliance on the experiential understanding conjured up from
one's own life. My interest is directed toward those conditions that make it
possible for a particular person to *extend* experience through the mediation
of books and similar tools. In summation: urban allegory suggests the
virtues of an indirect, intricate approach to matters that most people want
to meet head-on—to conceive by way of that nebulous entity "common
sense." Allegory's virtue is that it works to make sense genuinely common, genuinely shared.

I have stated a big idea quickly. Nonetheless, at this point the reader
knows enough to benefit from a picture of the urban allegorist at work.
During the brief reign of the Newgate Novel, *Punch* published a picture of
"The Literary Gentleman" (see fig. 2, from *Punch, or the London Charivari* 2
[January–June 1842]: 68). This illustration is not quite the summarizing
emblem I seek; it comes near, though. The Literary Gentleman is shown
sitting in a housecoat, puffing on a pipe from which emerge ghostly
forms. In front of him, on a table, is a sheaf of papers (his novel, presumably); directly behind the papers looms a miniature gallows with an inkwell underneath it. The writer stares at this absurd model, one eye cocked.
He confronts the generative device of his tale, seeming to find it something
of a riddle even as he relies upon it for inspiration. An accompanying
"valentine" evokes his predicament:

> Illustrious scribe! whose vivid genius strays
> 　'Mid Drury's stews to incubate her lays,
> 　And in St. Giles's slang conveys her tropes,
> Wreathing the poet's lines with hangmen's ropes.

Do ropes make practicable tropes? *Punch* concludes that they do not. The
writer's posture, his play with the toy death machine, his humiliating
abasement before such a sordid figure, exemplifes folly. To dwell on the
twisting, turning gallows is an exploitative pastime, yielding profits
rather than understanding. (Shades of Croxted Lane.) On the other
hand—if this seedy entrepreneur could become an allegorist, then a contemplation of the mock scaffold would open up other possibilities. Inves-
tigating the rope; dwelling on it to what might seem the point of morbidity or madness; treating the toy seriously or treating the nightmare that
it miniaturizes playfully; imagining, sooner or later, a frantic crowd
running about beneath that charismatic noose or imagining the dangerous

2. Alfred Crowquill [Alfred Henry Forrester], *The Literary Gentleman*. Wood engraving from "Punch's Valentines" (*Punch* 2 [January–June 1842, valentine supplement]: pp. 62 ff.) (From a copy in the Special Collections Department, William R. Perkins Library, Duke University.)

view from above it: these approaches would help him grasp a city's social and physical geography. The novelist would be able to *write* the city: to state for a large, often-exploited audience how and on what basis the metropolis holds together.

Thus—in small—the novel of urban mysteries: a genre as disreputable as it was, in its time, essential. I turn now to the book that founded the tradition, founded it less by setting an example than by issuing a challenge that proved irresistible. Enter *Notre-Dame*.

2. The Labyrinths of Notre-Dame

A LABYRINTH IS "an endlessly repeated meander or spiral line . . . [which] leads surely, despite twists and turns, back to the beginning"; this figure is associated with the founding of a legendary city, sometimes called "Troy town." How should we conceive a meandering that can institute a metropolis? The mythographer C. Kerenyi gives two related answers. The labyrinth is either a palace or a dance ground; in the first case it houses the Minotaur; in the second it suppports the weaving of a knot. Both functions, observes Kerenyi, imply the ritual celebration of a community's cohesiveness.[1]

Something of these meanings can be traced through *Notre-Dame*. Esmeralda dances her way in and out of Parisian crowds, thus tying the city together. The cathedral, house of Quasimodo as well as of God, articulates the city in another way, clarifying the entanglement of streets by presenting it from a stable architectural point. Dance and house are mediators in a theological and also in a secular sense: Both personify the labyrinth over which they preside; both intercede on behalf of those they protect at moments of great peril; both insist that the discontinuities of Paris can be bridged without any loss of an articulating social order. Influenced by Esmeralda or Notre-Dame, people have no trouble living harmoniously within a city whose diversities of culture and custom might otherwise kill them—or simply break down their confidence in the fabric of everyday life.[2] This reliance on a mediating maze/virgin, this catholicizing of a Greek myth, can be attributed to more than one writer's predilections. Worship of the Virgin Mary had revived in the post-revolutionary and post-Napoleonic years, a trend to be discussed later in this chapter. Nonetheless, despite their currency and all their evident strengths, *nos dames,* our ladies, our protectors, eventually run out of power. After a certain stage, neither can any longer stand between Parisians and Paris; neither can shield her subjects from the city yet simultaneously reveal it to them.

In the plot of *Notre-Dame,* this unfortunate development is explained largely by relations among characters. However, I will treat another kind of explanation as having a prior claim. If we want to know why Esmeralda and the cathedral lose their power to guide us through the maze, we had best take a look at Hugo's theory of history. The *Préface de Cromwell*, published some three years before *Notre-Dame*, posits successive ages of mankind: lyric, epic, dramatic. The lyric is "cette vie pastorale et nomade par laquelle commencent toutes les civilisations" (the pastoral, nomadic life from which all civilizations begin). At such periods man's thought "ressemble au nuage qui change de forme et de route, selon le vent qui le pousse" (resembles the clouds that change form and direction with the wind that impels them). There follows an epic or aristocratic stage, where everything is of a monumental character. "Le camp fait place à la cité, la tente au palais, l'arche au temple" (The camp yields to the city, the tent to the palace, the arch to the temple). "Tout s'arrête et se fixe" (Everything is fixed in place). Under the influence of Christianity a third dispensation comes into being, reaching perfection no earlier than Shakespeare but still sustained in the 1830s by the genius of Victor Hugo. Literature can now "mêler . . . sans pourtant les confondre, l'ombre à la lumière, le grotesque au sublime . . . le corps à l'âme, la bête à l'esprit" (mix . . . yet not confound, darkness with light, the grotesque with the sublime . . . the body with the soul, the beast with the spirit). This difficult act of synthesis is meditative: even when accomplished on a public stage, it remains associated with introspection and privacy. Hugo calls his third age dramatic or melancholic [*PC,* 45–50].

Systems of this sort were proposed by many of Hugo's contemporaries—e.g., Comte. Even at their most attractive, they are open to a charge of fallacy. In Robert Nisbet's words: "An array of differences . . . is not in itself a change: merely an array of differences. But if this array of peoples and cultures is appropriately arranged, and if to the array there is added the intuitive vision of some powerful, if unprovable, unverifiable, *vis genetrix,* some principle of constant, continuous, *development,* then the illusion of motion is made complete."[3] From an arrangement of the sort described by Nisbet, *Notre-Dame* will gradually diverge. Hugo holds to a belief in the inexorable march of civilization, but Paris and *Notre-Dame* produce so many unexpected juxtapositions that this conviction must be reformulated. At the nomadic Court of Miracles, Esmeralda sustains a vision of the whole. At the summit of Notre-Dame, the cathedral itself reveals the city's unity. Such reassuring visions disintegrate when our ladies are felt to exert equally compelling claims. The virgin that one worships should be unique; when there are conflicting mediators, each projecting or enacting a vision of the maze, history seems to be taking place all at once—as though different periods had been superimposed on each other.

Frollo and Quasimodo struggle with the conflicts that result. Each seeks a Paris that could reconcile Esmeralda, Notre-Dame, and much more. Quasimodo comes closer than Frollo to discovering it: He stumbles upon the realm of melancholy, finding there a principle of mixing that unites not only the grotesque and the sublime, according to the *Cromwell* program, but all of Paris and its "historical" stages.[4] This accomplishment proves dubious. The site on which things mix is the notorious Montfaucon, whose scaffold and charnel house thrived just outside Paris. Mingling too many mysteries—trying to mediate among mediators—brings the urban explorer face-to-face with a modern labyrinth, more inclusive than its medieval predecessor and also more problematic; it proves to be an engulfing tomb, a living death available right at home. In the conclusion to his novel, Hugo has constructed a disturbing yet stimulating trap that he and his followers will try many times to escape.

Gringoire Enters the Maze

Hugo's initial account of the labyrinth and its powers of integration occurs in the first two books of *Notre-Dame*. He begins in what seems a monumental city, conducts Gringoire to a lyric or nomadic one, then strives to make sense of this perilous transition. Gringoire's adventure is played as comedy but prepares for the lurid events to follow, introducing the novel's attempt to conceive a city as a whole.

The difficulty of recreating medieval Paris occupies Hugo from the beginning of *Notre-Dame*. His instinct is to start with a vast, splendid space—the Great Hall in the Palace of Justice—whose later destruction by fire he immediately anticipates. Not surprisingly, the chapters that follow initiate a process of disruption and inundation. A swelling audience blots out the "saillies"—the protrusions, the ledges, perhaps the *wit*—of the Palace [*ND*, 1.1, 43]. As Paris awaits Gringoire's "mystère"—composed in celebration of a royal marriage and featuring a learned personification allegory—Hugo searches for the moment when even the infinitely spacious hall will start to cramp its inhabitants: bring them together in unexpected ways or expel them from accustomed habits altogether.

The Great Hall contains an immovable slab of marble on which is erected a wooden stage. Here the mystery, which celebrates a great official marriage, is about to be performed. The play and the hall are curiously interdependent, not only because one is literally based on the other but also because the play's subject mirrors the conflicts of the audience. In both places the conflict of labor and clergy, of aristocrat and merchant, are acted out. Unfortunately, the play's version of the conflict is rather tame, whereas the audience enacts its rivalries of class vigorously and entertainingly. As a consequence, the pageant is constantly interrupted—by a beggar's cry for charity, by the jibes of students, by the entrance of dignitaries. Anything provides occasion for dispute. The author, Gringoire, finally "commença à crier, en se confondant le plus possible avec la foule: Recommencez le mystère! recommencez!" (began to yell, blending as best he could with the audience, "Begin the mystery play again! Begin again!") [*ND*, 1.4, 68]. According to Gringoire the play cannot suffer interruption: once it is disrupted it must circle back to its beginning. Is there something odd about Gringoire's logic? No matter—he is ignored. The Flemish visitor Jacques Coppenole proposes a wholesale abandonment of the production in favor of a Feast of Fools, whereupon the audience erupts: "Il n'y avait plus ni écoliers, ni ambassadeurs, ni bourgeois, ni hommes, ni femmes. . . . Tout s'effaçait dans la licence commune" (There were no longer students, ambassadors, burghers, men, women. . . . All distinctions were obliterated in common license) [1.5, 73]. Social and artistic decorum are sacrificed to pandemonium. The play's erstwhile audience elects a Fool's Pope, the hunchback Quasimodo, then marches after him in a sort of carnival procession. Gringoire's play continues. It is cut short once and for all when a popular street dancer appears outside. Someone steals the ladder connecting stage and dressing room in order to view her performance from the window. This is the last straw. None of the actors can get on or off the stage. As Gringoire retreats, he mutters "je veux que le diable m'écorche si je comprends ce qu'il veulent dire avec leur Esmeralda!" (I wish that the devil may flay me if I understand what they mean by their Esmeralda!) [5.1, 80].

Gringoire has good reason for his puzzlement. Esmeralda is a vagrant, a gypsy, or as he himself later puts it, "une espèce de femme abeille, ayant des ailes invisibles aux pieds, et vivant dans un tourbillon" (a species of female bee, with invisible wings for feet, and living in a whirlwind) [*ND*, 7.2, 277]. Her agility is a challenge, not just to the mystery play, but to the culture it supposedly affirms. The Paris of 1482 has appeared to be monumental, at least in its official guise, but the intrusion of a nomadic stranger defies this order. Gringoire depends on the carpenter (who takes precedence over him in the records of the play); Esmeralda merely rolls out her Persian carpet, "dont les arabesques s'effaçaient . . . sous le dessin capricieux de sa danse" (whose arabesques seemed to efface themselves . . . under the capricious patterns of her dance) [7.2, 274]. This performance asserts its autonomy; in its elusive arabesques, it rejects the need for monumental support. No marble tables, gargantuan or otherwise—even the table disappears. Esmeralda works on her own. Her dance establishes its own community and therefore its own space, unlike that ill-fated drama that foundered on a missing ladder.

No one ever again will attend to Gringoire's painstakingly composed personification allegory—no one but Victor Hugo, and he just to make fun of it. "Comme on s'en doute bien, les quatre personnages allégoriques étaient un peu fatigués d'avoir parcouru les trois parties du monde. . . . Je déclare que cette métaphore hardie est admirable, et que l'histoire naturelle du théâtre, un jour d'allégorie et d'épithalame royal, ne s'effarouche aucunement d'un dauphin fils d'un lion" (One could hardly doubt that the four allegorical personages were a bit fatigued by traveling over three parts of the earth. . . . I declare that this bold metaphor is admirable, and that the natural history of the theater, on a day of allegory and of a royal epithalamium, should hardly be shocked by a dolphin who is the son of a lion) [*ND*, 1.2, 57–58]. However, though personification allegory can be dismissed, there are allegorical figures and actions that *Notre-Dame* takes seriously. Another kind of mystery than Gringoire's silly play might evoke or sustain the Paris of *Notre-Dame*. This is the attraction of Esmeralda.

It is hard to say precisely what ancient labyrinth dances were like, but traditions about them illuminate Esmeralda's power. I have already cited Kerenyi on mazes; Hugo would have gotten his guidance from classical sources. Perhaps the best-known description of a labyrinth dance occurs in the fifth book of the *Aeneid*, where, during the Trojan games, boys on horses execute an elaborate series of maneuvers:

> And, as the *Cretan* Labyrinth of old,
> With wand'ring Ways, and many a winding fold,
> Involv'd the weary Feet, without redress,
> In a round Error, which deny'd recess;
> So fought the *Trojan* Boys in warlike Play,
> Turn'd and return'd, and still a diff'rent way.
> Thus Dolphins, in the Deep, each other chase,
> In Circles, when they swim around the wat'ry Race.
> This Game, these Carousels *Ascanius* taught;
> And, building *Alba,* to the *Latins* brought:
> Shew'd what he learn'd: The *Latin* Sires impart,
> To their succeeding Sons, the graceful Art:
> From these Imperial *Rome* receiv'd the Game;
> Which *Troy,* the Youths the *Trojan* Troop, they name.[5]

The labyrinth dance is connected with images of weaving (Dryden's "many a winding fold" translates Virgil's "parietibus textum caecis iter," more literally "a path woven with blind walls"), festivity, and graceful play ("Thus Dolphins, in the Deep, each other chase"). Above all it is evoked in an overlapping group of double actions: fathomless intricacy creating its own resolution, destructive conflict mimicked by an ordered and bloodless drill, war transformed to peace. These movements are confirmed by systematic repetitions (another kind of doubling); each tends, through turns and counterturns, toward the celebration of a city built in common. Philip West notes the association of the labyrinth with the *labrys,* the twoheaded axe. "The *labrys* is the way through the labyrinth. . . . the two entities unite in the concept of the legitimacy of the Minoan state."[6] The lore passed down by Virgil and others emphasizes this legitimizing function of the labyrinth dance, whose seemingly needless complications are ultimately revealed as a means of establishing political and cultural unity.[7]

Esmeralda's dance reveals its similarly labyrinthine nature soon after the failure of Gringoire's play. Plodding away from the failed production in the Great Hall, the poet searches for oblivion. Everything reminds him of the day's disaster, so he goes to the place de Grève, rediscovering there the convolutions of Esmeralda. Up close, her act charms him. Gringoire belongs to that "race précieuse et jamais interrompue de philosophes auxquels la sagesse, comme une autre Ariane, semble avoir donné une pelote de fil qu'ils s'en vont dévidant depuis le commencement du monde à travers le labyrinthe des choses humaines. . . . toujours selon tous les temps" (precious and uninterrupted race of philosophers, to whom wisdom, like another Ariane, seems to have given a ball of thread that they have gone on unwinding from the beginning of the world through the whole labyrinth of human affairs. . . . always adapting themselves to the age) [*ND,* 1.3, 59]. Soon after losing himself in Esmeralda's dance, he loses himself in the streets of Paris—as though the second kind of disorientation inevitably followed the first and were, in fact, a logical extension of it. "Gringoire, philosophe pratique des rues de Paris, avait remarqué que rien n'est propice à la rêverie comme de suivre une jolie femme sans savoir où elle va" (Gringoire, practical philosopher of the streets of Paris, had observed that nothing is more conducive to reverie than following a pretty woman without knowing where she is going) [2.4, 96]. He "s'était engagé, à la suite de l'égyptienne, dans ce dédale inextricable de ruelles, de carrefours et de culs-de-sac, qui environne l'ancien sépulcre des SaintsInnocents, et qui ressemble à un écheveau de fil brouillé par un chat. — Voilà des rues qui ont bien peu de logique! disait Gringoire, perdu dans ces mille circuits qui revenaient sans cesse sur eux-mêmes, mais où la jeune fille suivait un chemin . . . bien connu" (had become involved, while following the gypsy, in that inextricable labyrinth of alleys, courts, and dead-end streets which surround the ancient sepulchre of the Holy Innocents, and which resemble a skein of yarn entangled by a cat. "These streets don't make much sense!" said Gringoire, lost in a thousand windings that always kept coming back to their beginnings, but through which the girl followed a path . . . well known) [2.4, 98].[8]

The poet had innocently or perhaps compulsively asked that his play return to its beginning. The crowd's irreverent interruptions should have prepared him for his present dilemma. Within the maze created by Esmeralda, Gringoire really does double back to his beginnings. Frightened by pursuing beggars, he attempts a retreat; however, "toute cette légion s'était refermée derrière lui, et ses trois mendiants le tenaient. Il continua donc, poussé à la fois par ce flot irrésistible, par la peur et par un vertige qui lui faisait de tout cela une sorte de rêve horrible" (the whole legion had closed in behind him, and the three beggars grabbed at him. He went on, therefore, impelled all at once by the irresistible flood, by fear, and by a vertigo which made all this seem like a horrible dream) [ND, 2.6, 105]. Gringoire has arrived at the Court of Miracles, "cercle magique où les officiers du Châtelet et les sergents de la prévôté qui s'y aventuraient disparaissaient en miettes; cité des voleurs, hideuse verrue à la face de Paris" (magic circle where the officers of the Chatelet and the sergeants of the provosty who ventured there disappeared like crumbs; the city of thieves, a hideous wart on the face of Paris) [2.6, 106]. He faces alone a Walpurgis night in which "les limites des races et des espèces semblaient s'effacer dans cette cité comme dans un pandémonium. . . . chacun y participait de tout" (the boundaries of race and species seemed to be effaced in that city as in a pandemonium. . . . everybody did everything) [2.6, 106]. Esmeralda's dance has transported him to a city apart, a doubling not only of the Great Hall but of Paris. The court is a magic circle and also a hideous wart: it is both enchanted and damned. Thus people from the morning's celebration reappear in startling metamorphoses. When taken before the King of Thieves, "Gringoire tressaillit. Cette voix, quoique accentuée par la menace, lui rappela une autre voix qui le matin même avait porté le premier coup à son mystère en nasillant au milieu de l'auditoire: *La charité, s'il vous plaît!* Il leva la tête. C'était en effet Clopin Trouillefou" (Gringoire trembled. This voice, though marked by menace, reminded him of another voice which that very morning had given the first blow to his mystery play by whining out in the middle of the auditory, "*Charity, I beg you!*" He raised his head. Sure enough, it was Clopin Trouillefou [literally: funky crazy, daft shirker]) [2.6, 109]. Clopin threatens to hang Gringoire. Now it is the poet who must find the words for charity.

If Gringoire is not to hang, he must join the kingdom of argot. Easy enough, he supposes: "*et omnia in philosophia, omnes in philosopho continentur*" (*and philosophy contains all things, the philosopher all men*) [*ND,* 2.6, 113]. Latin, however, is not so universal a tongue as he had surmised. Clopin takes it for "argot de juif de Hongrie" (the argot of a Hungarian Jew); unable to clarify this misapprehension, Gringoire is left with an unsettling perspective on his beloved classical learning. In the Court of Miracles, Latin is (or might as well be) a mere subspecies of argot, thieves' language.[9] It is the main branch of this tongue—Clopin's, of course—by which Gringoire must now endeavor to live. The poet accustoms himself as quickly as possible to this abrupt reshuffling of values and hierarchies: He offers to relinquish all suspect bourgeois standards; he will join the argotized company of the court; he will become a Truand, a vagrant. A test of resilience follows his bid. An initiate enters argot by picking the pockets of a mannequin decked out in bells. Gringoire has little success in this delicate undertaking. "Il voulut machinalement s'appuyer au mannequin, perdit l'équilibre, et tomba lourdement sur la terre, tout assourdi par la fatale vibration des mille sonnettes du mannequin" (He mechanically tried to support himself against the dummy, lost his equilibrium, and fell heavily to the ground, deafened by the fatal vibration of the dummy's thousand bells) [2.6, 115]. He tries to beg for mercy, but everyone is laughing; his words die on his lips. It seems increasingly doubtful that philosophy contains all things.

Gringoire needs help: just in time it arrives. For the second time in the Court of Miracles he hears a familiar name. That morning he had asked the devil to strangle him if he understood what "Esmeralda" meant. Upon her appearance in the Court, "La Esmeralda! dit Gringoire, stupéfait, au milieu de ses émotions, de la brusque manière dont ce mot magique nouait tous les souvenirs de sa journée" ("Esmeralda," said Gringoire, stupefied, in the midst of his emotions, by the abrupt manner in which this magic word knotted together the memories of his day) [*ND,* 2.6, 118]. This is the saving moment of Gringoire's adventures. It will not be necessary for the devil or anyone else to cut off his wind. He has understood the name—and the name has *abruptly* clarified his day, rendered suddenly sensible what seemed to be a kind of deadly mystification. Appropriately Esmeralda marries Gringoire, saving him from hanging. He eludes the knot of the noose by tying the knot of marriage (though Esmeralda refuses his sexual invitation, thereby—one supposes—preserving another knot).

Notre-Dame is a closely organized novel: it is packed almost too tightly with ironies, symmetries, cross-references, the whole pack of them threatening to burst the book open—something like the audience in the Great Hall. "Mon mauvais génie! mon bon ange!" (My evil spirit! my good angel!) remarks Gringoire of Esmeralda [*ND,* 2.7, 120]. He could say the same of that labyrinth in which he is caught. Starting out from the articulated spaciousness of the Great Hall, he moves through the maze of a dance that is also a city, then circles back to the audience of the morning revealed in its nighttime truth. The reader may wonder how his own identity, his own sense of self, has been marked by these changes. He loses a career, risks death, and perhaps even changes class, undergoing, in each case, a major public humiliation. Nonetheless, after a brief period of shock, the poet is his usual self. "Il y avait dans ce mariage à la cruche cassée quelque chose de naïf et d'antédiluvien qui me plaisait" (There was in this marriage of the broken pitcher something naive and antediluvian which pleased me) [2.7, 127]. What tickled his fancy? He cannot quite put a finger on the source of his pleasure, but a retrospective glance suggests an excellent reason. Just at the moment when his play was ruined, he found himself pitched into its plot. The search for the most beautiful bride in the world culminated in his meeting her, marrying her . . . and becoming her mountebank assistant. These symmetries content him. The labyrinth snatched away the Hall of Justice but provided the Court of Miracles. It disrupted a majestic theatrical betrothal, then enforced an unconsummated marriage of thieves. The gypsy's appearance in the court thus reconciles a sequence of disorienting recognitions, insisting on the aesthetic harmony of Gringoire's delirious journey through Paris. There is no loss for him—how could there be?in proceeding from the Great Hall to "l'industrie que vous me connaissez. . . . Porter des pyramides de chaises sur mes dents" (that skill of mine which you already know. . . . To carry pyramids of chairs in my teeth) [10.1, 405–6]. Indeed, "je suis un philosophe pyrrhonien . . . et je tiens tout en équilibre" (I am a Pyrrhonean philosopher . . . and I hold everything in equilibrium) [10.1, 405]. He takes too much credit for an equilibrium determined by someone else, but at least knows how to benefit from it. Having discovered the Parisian carnival, the city turned upside down, he finds he can live by its rules as well as by any others. Throughout subsequent chapters, Gringoire is occupied with balancing chairs (dubiously and to the detriment of cats), courting

Esmeralda's goat, and compiling a rhetorical handbook of regular and irregular figures.

A View from Above

Gringoire's position as the central character of *Notre-Dame* ends with book 2. During book 3 his place is taken by an anonymous tourist. This person, effectively the reader's representative within the novel, subjects himself to the influence of a maze different from Esmeralda's but just as powerful in its general effect. If I describe the structure of book 3 quickly, it is only because it follows the precedents already established. Like Gringoire, the tourist-reader is shocked by dizzying possibilities but ultimately reassured, even edified.

Once more Hugo begins with the verbal reconstruction of an ancient building. One of the curious facts about his description of the cathedral is that it mentions Quasimodo not at all. It is hardly possible to forget the hunchback, characterized on his introduction [*ND*, 1.5, 73] as a monstrosity, a broken giant, and a Cyclops, or to pass over the striking information that this creature dressed in a costume of bells is the deaf bell ringer of Notre-Dame. All the more striking that he remains unmentioned throughout book 3's elaborate tribute to the cathedral and to Paris. Like the Holmesian dog that did nothing in the night, Quasimodo is conspicuous by his absence. The monster of the labyrinth house is an implied presence—or if he does receive explicit recognition, it is in his original form as a god, the divinity to which the first maze was devoted. By putting his description in a theological frame, Hugo underlines the cathedral's communal and cultic significance rather than its bizarre or eccentric potentialities.[10] The Notre-Dame of book 3 is going to be seen as a structure that serves a collective function and supports communal values.

Notre-Dame's reconciling energies are expressed in its tolerantly eclectic architecture: each of the building's details is "ralliés puissamment à la tranquille grandeur de l'ensemble. . . . Tout se tient dans cet art venu de lui-même" (assembled powerfully in the tranquil grandeur of the whole. . . . Everything has its place in this self-created art) [*ND*, 3.1, 132]. However, the cathedral's maze like powers come clearest when Hugo describes what he calls its principal beauty—"la vue du Paris qu'on découvrait alors du haut de ses tours" (the view of Paris one then discovered from the top of its towers) [3.2, 139]. We reach this view through a mazelike route—"tatonné longtemps dans la ténébreuse spirale qui perce perpendiculairement l'épaisse muraille des clochers" (groping for a long

time in the dark spiral [staircase] which bores perpendicularly the thick
wall of the bell towers) [3.2, 139]. Then we emerge on the roof. Here
Hugo proposes a panorama, a "vol d'oiseau,"[11] which presents the city
below as one great architectural unity—"un spectacle *sui generis* . . .
entière, complète, homogène" (a spectacle *sui generis* . . . whole, complete,
homogeneous) [3.2, 139]. In describing this spectacle, the novelist masters
a problem at once technical and philosophical. Verbal description builds
up a picture successively, calling on the reader's memory, powers of
synthesis, and willingness to reread. The labyrinth of words evokes the
labyrinth of the Paris streets: these crossings and recrossings knit together
a picture ("un tricot inextricable," an inextricable knitting or weaving) in
our minds. At the same time, Hugo warns, the spectator may be overwhelmed by the originality that calls from all sides for attention. Many
times the description of the view seems on the point of collapsing—of
getting lost in what the novelist calls an entanglement. Yet this never
happens for long: Hugo counters his own excesses with précis. This
technique is especially well used at the end of the bird's-eye view proper,
where he writes, "Entre la Courtille et Saint-Laurent votre oeil avait déjà
remarqué au couronnement d'une hauteur accroupie sur des plaines dé-
sertes une espèce d'édifice qui ressemblait de loin à une colonnade en ruine
debout sur un soubassement déchaussé. Ce n'était ni un Parthénon, ni un
temple de Jupiter Olympien. C'était Montfaucon" (Between Courtille
and Saint-Laurent, your eye had already noticed on the crown of a little hill
that squatted upon a deserted plain, a kind of edifice which resembled
from far away a ruined colonnade over a basement with an exposed
foundation. This was neither a Parthenon, nor a temple of Olympian
Jupiter. This was Montfaucon) [3.2, 154]. Much later in *Notre-Dame,*
Montfaucon's narrative significance will become clear; at this stage Hugo's
awkward and elaborate sentence, with its peculiar mixed figures (a crown
squats; the Parthenon has a basement), appears distracting. Montfaucon
thus exists not only at the edge of what can be seen (or should be seen) as
Paris but also at another edge, where the unity of the author's verbal tour
de force is in danger of breaking down. Shifting to a new paragraph, Hugo
immediately acknowledges and repairs this possible flaw. "Maintenant, si
le dénombrement de tant d'édifices, quelque sommaire que nous l'ayons
voulu faire, n'a pas pulvérisé, à mesure que nous la construisions, dans
l'esprit du lecteur, l'image générale du vieux Paris, nous la résumerons en
quelques mots" (Now, if the enumeration of so many edifices, succinct as
we have tried to be, has not pulverized in the reader's mind the general

image of old Paris as fast as we have constructed it, we will sum it up in a few words) [3.2, 154]. This clarity depends on a balance between order and disorder, the hierarchical and the free, much as in the church. Hugo implies that his style (in this passage) can reproduce or mime the controls of monumental culture; he also claims that these controls were once concentrated in the extraordinary play between cathedral and view.

From the gypsy girl, whom "toute sa tribu . . . tient en vénération singulière, comme une Notre-Dame" (all her tribe . . . hold in singular veneration, like Our Lady), it is a sudden and drastic step to Notre-Dame itself [*ND,* 7.2, 277]. All the same, what Esmeralda accomplishes by grace or impulse, Notre-Dame manages in a heavier fashion. Architecture can perform the gypsy's act of synthesis, something we would never have suspected if remembering only the scene in the Great Hall. As the *Préface de Cromwell* puts it, "on y déroule de vastes spectacles. . . . tout porte un caractère monumental" (vast spectacles are unrolled. . . . everything takes on a monumental character) [*PC,* 47]. Notre-Dame reveals Paris monumentally. "Un beau tableau . . . se déroulait à la fois de toutes parts sous vos yeux" (A beautiful picture . . . unrolled itself all at once in every part, under your eyes) [*ND,* 3.2, 139]. The cathedral is an epic, organizing energy, an impression confirmed by the concluding passage in Hugo's bird's-eye view. "Il semble qu'en certains instants l'oreille aussi a sa vue" (It seems that in certain moments the ear also sees) [3.2, 158–59]. These moments are summoned up, even in the culturally debased days of 1831, when all the bells in Paris ring together. Listening to them, we enter an eloquence become music: "une masse de vibrations sonores qui se dégage sans cesse des innombrables clochers, qui flotte, ondule, bondit, tourbillonne sur la ville, et prolonge bien au délà de l'horizon le cercle assourdissant de ses oscillations" (a mass of sonorous vibrations, breaking loose endlessly from the innumerable steeples, that float, undulate, leap, whirl over the city, and sustain beyond the horizon the deafening circle of its oscillations) [3.2, 159]. This ringing spreads across Paris "comme une broderie de toutes sortes de sons charmants" (like an embroidery of all sorts of delightful sounds) [7.3, 281]. There are hints that the huge noise is overwhelming. Sooner or later, however, we end up feeling secure rather than deafened. The circle of oscillations has proclaimed an order that is finally manageable. Hugo's description of the miracle is confirmed in an evocation of its aural counterpart: music, language, and vision work toward an organized act of glorification. From many labyrinthine windings he produces an exhilarating sense of a vast view grasped instantly: "à la fois" (all at once) [3.2, 139].

Frollo's Divorce

Each of our ladies—the dancer, the house—has her own way of celebrating Paris's unity. Each offers guidance, a way of keeping the peace while one moves through the city and its perilous entanglements. Esmeralda is never juxtaposed with the cathedral until the novel is well under way. This development is experienced by linked protagonists, Quasimodo and his master, Claude Frollo. Quasimodo is introduced during the Feast of Fools, on the eventful evening of January 6. As noted above, the crowd elects him Fools' Pope—but after a brief appearance in this role he is dethroned by Frollo and dragged away. The next time Quasimodo and Frollo show up in the narrative, they try to kidnap Esmeralda. Quasimodo is captured by the guard, while Frollo slinks off. These are largely peripheral events, whose function becomes clear only after the descriptive digression on the cathedral. Immediately following that set piece, Hugo gives a retrospective account of Frollo and Quasimodo, summed up in an explicit comparison of the two [*ND*, 4.5].

They are connected by strong links to Notre-Dame. Gringoire's reliance on monumental culture was presented as a sort of joke; when the playwright cast off his allegiance to the Great Hall and joined the Court of Miracles, the consequences were minimal. Gringoire drifts; Frollo and Quasimodo do not. The one is committed to *reading* the cathedral; he treats it as a page of magic written in stone, or even more precisely as a palimpsest (a document with many layers). The other grasps it as an encompassing harmony expressed in the ringing of bells. Each understands one aspect of the cathedral and its bird's-eye view. Both are involved in a worship of the monument Notre-Dame from which only the most drastic challenge could turn them.

Since it is Frollo's actions and desires that get the plot moving, best to begin with him and then consider Quasimodo's response. The priest is a magus in the occult tradition of late medieval Europe. For the magus— who draws on the hermetic lore of Egypt—interpretation is a learned, difficult art, so that the cathedral "semblait un énorme sphinx à deux têtes assis au milieu de la ville" (seemed an enormous two-headed sphinx seated in the midst of the city) [*ND*, 5.1, 197]. The same chapter suggests that Notre-Dame is a hieroglyph, another Egyptian import in which enigmas and riddles figure. To answer the riddle of the hieroglyph is to achieve a special kind of victory. Glossing Plotinus, Marsilio Ficino declared that "the Egyptian Priests did not use individual letters to signify mysteries, but whole images of plants, trees and animals; because God had knowledge of things *not* through a multiplicity of thought processes, but rather as a simple and firm form of the thing."[12] Frollo is in search of a magical language, but for other ends than courtly display. He wants to see as God sees. He also wants the power of God. The flash of divine knowledge, he thinks, would allow him to rule the world. Frollo moves toward an intellectual version of the great panorama, except that he digs rather than climbs. "Pour entreprendre ce voyage à travers les choses mystérieuses" (To undertake the journey through all these mysterious things), the magus must descend into "les innombrables embranchements de la caverne sans apercevoir" (the innumerable windings of the unseeable cavern). He might be exploring "les chambres sépulcrales des pyramides" (the sepulchral chambers of the pyramids): "je rampe encore; je m'écorche la face et les genoux aux cailloux de la voie souterraine" (I am still crawling; I am scraping the skin off my face and knees on the stones of the subterranean tunnel) [5.1, 194–96]. His groping recession through ancient darkness is in the service of ultimate enlightenment. Enlightenment, however, remains distant. "Selon la mode des hermétiques" (In the hermetic manner) [7.4, 286], Frollo has carved mysterious inscriptions into the walls of his cell and thus of Notre-Dame. This rendering of wisdom as stone looks at first sight like a celebratory ritual of the magus, an enshrinement of knowledge in architecture. Then Hugo describes the inscriptions, which are not what might have been expected: they overflow "au hasard, celles-ci sur celles-là, les plus fraîches effaçant les plus anciennes, et toutes s'enchevêtrant les unes dans les autres comme les branches d'une broussaille, comme les piques d'une mêlée" (at random, one upon another, the more recent effacing the more ancient, and all mixed up with each other like branches of brushwood, like pikes in a melee) [7.4, 286]. The Egyptian associations of secrecy, hieroglyphs, subterranean caverns, and sphinxes define a philosophy of knowledge within a monumental civilization, but these pikes in a melee suggest another possibility: a melee, as Hugo would have known from reading *Ivanhoe* (chap. 12), is that moment in a feudal tournament when the rigors and ceremonies of chivalry give way to something very much like a free-for-all. Hugo wants us to see Frollo as a formidable sorcerer, far more capable than the other intellectuals of Paris. He also suggests that Frollo is the sorcerer's apprentice. The magus has set in motion a process he no longer controls. He experiences a mixture, conflict, or melee whose location and chronology are altogether uncertain.

In one of the central chapters of *Notre-Dame,* "Ceci tuera cela" (This will kill that), Frollo struggles to make the appropriate distinctions—to define his own failing quest against the movements of what he takes to be history. "Le livre tuera l'édifice," he announces: the book will kill the edifice [*ND*, 5.2, 198]. Frollo's prophecy (to a disguised Louis XI) cues a chapter-long commentary in which Hugo speaks on behalf of his sorcerer. The book, he predicts, will kill the edifice because printing effectively replaces architecture as the central means of embodying human knowledge. As long as the cathedral remains a central cultural symbol, its communal authority and solidity make room for the most vital elements in the thought of a given period. Once knowledge takes the form of print, it explodes into a hundred diverse incarnations. To use the terms of the *Préface de Cromwell:* the book is the typical medium of a dramatic or melancholic culture, creating its own dispersed and elusive unity, distinct from that of either dance or house.

Hugo borrows this argument from Walter Scott's *Quentin Durward* (chap. 13), where it is presented to Louis XI by the astrologer Martivalle. Prompted by the developing logic of his novel—and perhaps by the crisis of the monarchy in 1830–31[13]—Hugo makes the idea his own. Not only does he expand Scott's succinct paragraph to an extensive essay, he situates this essay in a context—a book—where questions about different kinds of unity are constantly being raised. Hugo understands all too well that the novel he is writing is part of the dilemma described by Frollo and himself. In the "Note ajoutée à l'édition définitive" (Note added to the definitive edition, 1832), where he justifies the addition of seemingly new passages to *Notre-Dame* (*including* the chapter "Ceci tuera cela"), he claims: "Un roman . . . naît, d'une façon en quelque sorte nécessaire, avec tous ses chapitres; un drame naît avec toutes ses scènes. Ne croyez pas qu'il y ait rien d'arbitraire dans le nombre de parties dont se compose ce tout, ce mystérieux microcosme que vous appelez drame ou roman. . . . Une fois la chose faite, ne vous ravisez pas, n'y touchez plus" (A novel . . . is born, in a sense necessarily, with all its chapters; a drama is born with all its scenes. Do not believe that there is anything arbitrary about the number of parts that make up this whole, this mysterious microcosm that you call a drama or a novel. . . . The thing accomplished, you do not change your mind or revise, you no longer touch what you have done) [*ND*, p. 31]. Here, as elsewhere in Hugo's work, the pose of semidivine creator cannot be easily relinquished. All the same, creating—or understanding—*all at once* may be a more problematic notion than this small manifesto is willing to admit. Hugo protests vigorously against arguments that his novel, in Frollo's person, articulates. In an era of the book, the inclusive harmonies of

Gothic Paris disintegrate (as may, to some extent, the possibility of the vatic, divinely authorized poet), giving way to a new kind of coherence and with it a new kind of community.

How does Frollo fare under these evolving circumstances? "Ceci tuera cela" sums up one analysis of his dilemma. This tag acknowledges that reading is no longer an act confined to hermetic philosophers and their ilk. Instead of being controlled and shaped by monumental culture, the book gains autonomy, a fact that Frollo laments. The old formulas fail in a world where inscriptions run mad; the intricate palimpsest becomes just another form of Babel. It is typical of *Notre-Dame* that this analysis should twist back on itself most curiously. While Frollo feels threatened by the future, he is also disturbed by a regression into the nomadic past. The book comes between him and the cathedral; between him and the book [*ND*, 8.4, 344] comes Esmeralda.

"La double voie tortueuse" (the double twisted path [of fate]) has already entangled the priest with the gypsy dancer [*ND*, 9.1, 372]. Midway through *Notre-Dame*, he looks out over the city to the spot where she is dancing. Her dance and the great view from the cathedral are shown to be mutually exclusive: he cannot see at once both dancer and panorama [*ND*, 7.2, 273]. It is far easier to operate inside a system than to acknowledge that it has aspects that don't quite fit with one another. Such is Frollo's emerging difficulty. The more closely he observes Esmeralda, the less he can comprehend the view and the less he can pursue his hermetic studies. He is no longer capable of relying on the firm ministrations of monumental culture—yet a complete reversion to nomadic culture is unthinkable. Where then might Frollo and Esmeralda meet on friendly terms?

Frollo's search for a world in which he might grasp Esmeralda, embrace her physically and mentally, begins to dominate his energies. As the "Egyptian" cathedral gives way to the gypsy dance he becomes a vagrant, a wanderer like a gypsy, yet he never leaves off attempting to behave monumentally. Having experienced the disturbing force of absolute erotic desire he tries first to expel it, then to place it: to stop it from moving around. A law is passed forbidding dancing in the streets. Esmeralda dances all the same. Her incessant whirling sends him back to his libraries, where he can look up everything ever recorded about dancing witches with goats. Of her goat, an outstanding talent may be noted: the beast understands the principle of movable type but is able with its letter blocks to form only one word, the name of Esmeralda's beloved Phoebus [*ND*, 7.2, 279]. Djali's automatic repetition in a medium designed for rational flexibility suggests something of Frollo's own dilemma. Magic, literacy, and love cross one another hopelessly, so that nothing is used or perceived as he intends. This deadlock continues until he is able to follow the clue of that irksome anagram. *Phoebus* proves to be, not a philosophical, but an erotic talisman. It points toward the identity of Esmeralda's unknown lover. From this initial insight Frollo tracks down the real Phoebus—a dandified military officer—spies on his assignation with Esmeralda, stabs him in the back, and frames the gypsy girl for his presumed murder.

Now follows a pivotal decision: having arranged for Esmeralda's incarceration, Frollo decides to visit her. He has spent years crawling about among the windings of philosophical caverns. Paris has its caverns also. They can neither be danced through freely nor surveyed from above, but after Esmeralda's arabesques and the panoramic view, they too articulate the labyrinthine order of the city.[14] More precisely, they mirror it. As Hugo informs us, the Paris of *Notre-Dame* is almost as much under ground as above it. Notre-Dame itself represents an intriguing exception: the novelist accurately observes that the cathedral has no basement proper but is built upon piles [*ND*, 8.4, 336]. The multiplicity harmonized by this edifice does not, therefore, include an underground. Elsewhere in Paris, the situation is different: Dungeons, sepulchers, and other gloomy haunts branch out interminably, like landscapes seen upside down in the waters of a lake [8.4, 337]. This topsy-turvy Paris is where Esmeralda regains consciousness after her trial for witchcraft. Oppressed and confused, she can barely remember her name, until suddenly Frollo arrives. Then—in a great rush—she recalls who she is. Almost in the same moment he promises that she is going to know everything, that he will tell her things he has scarcely dared tell himself.

Like the other labyrinths of the novel, this one knots together clues and hints into a sudden outburst, a revelation that "revinrent à la fois" (returned all at once) [*ND*, 8.4, 341]. The claustrophobic atmosphere remains, however. Frollo has affirmed that if ice is buried for a thousand years it becomes rock crystal; burying a ray of the sun might produce even more striking results—though one couldn't open the vault for eight thousand years [5.1, 194; 7.4, 287]. Neither of these ingenious techniques are going to work under the present circumstances. Esmeralda buried remains Esmeralda, except that she is subjected to an incomprehensible confessional monologue. Something about this labyrinthine darkness forbids the kind of union that Frollo craves. The priest has brought together the gypsy world and the Egyptian one, he has tried to found a city centered on both Esmeralda and Notre-Dame. His straining toward an ever-greater inclusiveness issues in secrecy and isolation.

Shortly after her dialogue with Frollo in the dungeon, Esmeralda is sentenced to be hung. Frollo flees the metropolis but cannot escape it: he confronts in his mind's eye the gallows and the Tower of Babel upside-down (another vision of inverted, underground Paris). He then flies to the cathedral where "il se jeta avidement sur le saint livre" (he cast his eyes eagerly upon the sacred book)only to read of a hair-raising spirit passing in the wind [ND, 9.1, 379]. It has become all too probable that his bookish world *is* the world of darkness, that it pushes him back toward that underground which Notre-Dame itself lacks. This realization is far from comforting. Frollo has sought the melancholic Paris anticipated by his own prediction, "Ceci tuera cela." He has not exactly found it, close though he may have come. Instead of locating a place where troublesome oppositions can be reconciled, he experiences a collapse of necessary and useful distinctions. All the objects before him melt together into a private apocalypse. Even the line between life and death is momentarily erased.

Harmony and Discord

Hugo initially emphasizes two points about Quasimodo, his ugliness (what seems a grimace is his normal expression) and his defective consciousness of self. Both these traits are presented as vulnerabilities—and so they are, until seen in the context of Notre-Dame. There is (Hugo claims) a preexisting affinity between the monster and his house [ND, 4.3, 171]. His ugliness is a mysterious harmony founded on his lack of consciousness and revealed most graphically in his love for the bells of Notre-Dame. When he rides them he seems "une espèce d'Astolphe horrible emporté sur un prodigieux hippogriffe de bronze vivant" (a sort of horrible Astolfo, carried away on a prodigious hippogriff of living bronze) [ND, 4.3, 176]. Such images suggest that Quasimodo and the cathedral belong together, that (at least toward the beginning of the novel) they form a single being or move toward a single purpose.

Dostoyevsky believed that "Quasimodo is the personification of an oppressed and despised French people of medieval times, deaf and disfigured, gifted only with a terrible physical strength, but in whom there finally awaken love and thirst for justice, and together with these, both consciousness of its own truth and yet untapped endless strength."[15] For Dostoyevsky, *Notre-Dame* is essentially about the redemption, the awakening to consciousness, of an oppressed and outcast people. This idea can indeed be traced through the novel, but in uneasy conjunction with other demands. At issue here is the nature of Quasimodo's awakening, whose inception is depicted in a telltale tear. Having been arrested for the attempted kidnapping of Esmeralda, the hunchback is flogged at the pillory and then left to bake in the sun. A hostile crowd jeers at his cries for water, all except Esmeralda. When Quasimodo has finished drinking from the gourd she offers him, and has wept that single tear, he offers to kiss her hand. Her antipathy may be to his supposed viciousness or then again to his deformity. She moves lightly, efficiently, and just outside the circle of his reach. She treats him as an animal, although he no longer is one [*ND*, 6.4, 254].

Soon after the scene at the pillory, Quasimodo is able to soliloquize, to dream, to decide. To use Dostoyevsky's phrase again, "love and a thirst for justice" finally awaken in him, but awaken at a price: spying Esmeralda from his perch in the belfry of Notre-Dame, "Il s'arrêta, tourna le dos au carillon" (He stopped, turning his back on the bells) [*ND*, 7.3, 282]. Like Frollo, Quasimodo experiences his love for Esmeralda as a disturbing deflection of attention. Up to this point in his life the cathedral has used him; now he will use the cathedral, first merely to watch Esmeralda, then at a moment of crisis created by Frollo to snatch her from the scaffold. Quasimodo's metamorphosis implies an accession of power: he transforms Notre-Dame into a field for heroic action. By the same token he separates himself from it. Whether monster, god, scapegoat, or all three, he is no longer an unthinking extension of the cathedral but has assumed an identity apart from it.

According to the *Préface de Cromwell,* "Le beau n'a qu'un type; le laid en a mille. C'est que le beau, à parler humainement, n'est que la forme considérée dans son rapport le plus simple, dans sa symétrie la plus absolue, dans son harmonie la plus intime avec notre organisation. Aussi nous offre-t-il toujours un ensemble complet, mais restreint comme nous. Ce que nous appelons le laid, au contraire, est un détail d'un grand ensemble qui nous échappe, et qui s'harmonise, non pas avec l'homme, mais avec la création tout entière. Voilà pourquoi il nous présente sans cesse des aspects nouveaux, mais incomplets" (The beautiful has but one form, the ugly a thousand. To speak in human terms, beauty is nothing but form considered most simply, in absolute symmetry and intimate harmony with our organizing structure. Moreover, it always offers us completeness and comprehensiveness, but is limited like us. On the other hand, what we call ugly is a detail in a huge whole that escapes us, and that harmonizes, not with man, but with the entire creation. For this reason, it unceasingly presents new aspects, but incomplete ones). Hugo goes on to declare that (in Shakespeare's time and by implication in his own day) "le moment est venu où l'équilibre entre les deux principes va s'établir" (the moment has arrived when the equilibrium between the two principles is going to be established) [*PC,* 55, 57]. A good example would be the fairy tale of "La Belle et La Bête," in which, however, Beauty and the Beast are reconciled through the hero's transformation (beautification). Such victories are not often won: after all, the beautiful and the ugly or the grotesque require different kinds of understanding. So do Quasimodo and Esmeralda. They have in common their agility, their capacity to animate. Both are enliveners who remain in tune with their worlds by the very fact of social isolation. Each speeds through a complicated man–made space, thus winning it back from obscurity or chaos—but here the comparison founders, for where the beautiful exists independently, even within a space it illuminates or clarifies, the grotesque is one detail of a great whole that passes our comprehension. When Quasimodo falls in love with Esmeralda, he discovers a mirror in which he can contemplate his own deformity. She constantly reminds him of his ugliness. He is no longer unthinkingly at home with cathedral and bells, since the beautiful has intervened. Quasimodo waits patiently for the gypsy and the cathedral to become one indistinguishable object of desire. This cannot happen, even when the two of them have been brought so closely together.

Frollo drags Esmeralda downward, Quasimodo upward. Morally Quasimodo's action seems preferable, but it is no more effective than his master's. A rhetorical vocabulary can pinpoint the hunchback's shift of desire. Quasimodo is associated with Notre-Dame because he is part of it: the relationship is called synecdoche. Esmeralda is associated with the cathedral because she is like it: she performs the same function as Notre-Dame but performs it on her own, an alternate version of the guiding Ariadne who helps us through the labyrinth. Her relationship to the cathedral is therefore that of metaphor. The lines between synecdoche and metaphor are not entirely clear; each at times merges into metonymy, another of rhetoric's prominent figures.[16] Quasimodo is not so far off when he gets them confused. The problem is that he relates them falsely: he is wishful rather than logical. As a consequence, he ends up holding two conflicting viewpoints: he thinks of himself and Esmeralda as the same kind of being; he also thinks that he can live in her as he did in Notre-Dame. Neither of these opinions is accurate and together their influence is disastrous. On the strength of the first idea, it is only natural for Quasimodo to turn to the gypsy girl through an apparent line of equivalences. This "surprising interchangeability between the epitomes of the sublime and the grotesque" pushes him inevitably toward her.[17] The second view is attractive to the Truands as well as to Quasimodo; from their lair in the Court of Miracles, they also understand Esmeralda as a kind of Notre-Dame. On this assumption, it transpires, the grand climax of the novel is based.

The battle of Notre-Dame takes several chapters to prepare, for it involves a number of converging forces. Frollo has been busily scheming during Quasimodo's courtship of Esmeralda; the hunchback won't let him anywhere near her, however, and so he has to work from a distance. Meanwhile Parliament decrees her execution. It now becomes necessary to get the girl out of the cathedral before she is taken by law. Under urging from Frollo, Gringoire works up a strangely convoluted scheme. The Truands will do the job for them, sacking Notre-Dame and rescuing Esmeralda all at once. The plan is so intricate as to be unbelievable. This is the weakest link in Hugo's plot, yet it makes a kind of sense. Frollo, the fearful prophet of democracy, is responsible for rousing the mob. The mob sets out to dismantle the former object of his studies. Such transformations suggest a delicate irony. Frollo almost becomes that archetypal figure of modern history, the intellectual who discovers (or thinks he discovers) his links with the masses and so foments revolution. Almost, not quite. His dizzying historical jumps—regressing one moment, anticipating the next—cancel any notion of orderly cultural evolution. In a recapitulation of the novel's general movement, history is redistributed within the space of the city, which now appears a battlefield, a zone where many cultural or historical possiblities can be realized and so all are in frequent conflict. (Perhaps not by coincidence the reader is treated once more to pikes in a melee—*ND,* 10.7, 467.) This state of affairs is emphasized by an expository interruption, just before the attack proper, when the narrator considers the legalities of the whole affair. The only reason the Truands can threaten the cathedral so boldly is the "façon bizarre" (bizarre fashion) by which medieval Paris is governed. "Le vieil échafaudage des juridictions féodales resta debout; immense entassement de bailliages et de seigneuries se croisant sur la ville, se gênant, s'enchevêtrant, s'emmaillant de travers, s'échancrant les un les autres; inutile taillis de guets, de sous-guets et de contre-guets, à travers lequel passaient à main armée le brigandage, la rapine et la sédition" (The old scaffolding of the feudal jurisdictions remained standing; immense accumulation of bailiwicks and seigneuries intersecting across the city, obstructing and entangling each other, getting bound up together wrongly, mutually intruding: a useless thicket of lookouts, underlookouts, and counterlookouts, through which brigandage, rapine, and sedition passed in arms" [10.4, 425]. Previously this feudal framework has been presented only in its positive guise: it allows Notre-Dame to exist as a legal sanctuary, a point of rest within the dangers of Paris. Now the same logic is turned against the cathedral, whose vulnerability is emphasized. Frollo continues to operate secretly and compulsively—but his mental state has apparently spilled over into Paris, through the unlikely medium of Gringoire and the Court of Miracles.

Hugo allows many of his representative figures—Gringoire, Clopin, Jacques Coppenole, Louis XI—to argue the significance of the Truands' attack, even as it progresses. In each of these minds the assault is understood differently, so that it portends, for example, absolutism or democracy, defeat for the rabble or the stirrings of revolution. In the case of Quasimodo, perhaps the crucial one, it has a less abstract meaning. As the hunchback surveys Paris one night, "une cohue de morts" (a crowd of the dead) appears to rise against the cathedral. "Il lui semblait voir s'avancer vers lui un brouillard plein d'hommes, voir remuer des ombres dans l'ombre" (He thought he saw advancing toward him a mist full of people, saw, as they stirred, shadows within a shadow) [*ND*, 10.4, 423]. The Truands, citizens of the Court of Miracles, have come to rescue Esmeralda—or is it to sack the building? "Si ton église est sacrée, notre soeur l'est aussi; si notre soeur n'est pas sacrée, ton église ne l'est pas non plus. C'est pourquoi nous te sommons de nous rendre la fille si tu veux sauver ton église, ou que nous reprendrons la fille et que nous pillerons l'église. Ce qui sera bien" (If your church is sacred, our sister is too; if our sister is not sacred, neither is your church. This is why, if you would save your church, we summon you to give up the girl; or we shall take the girl and pillage the church. This would be good) [10.4, 426]. Quasimodo, who cannot hear any of Clopin's threats, reasons that "il y avait une haine populaire sur [Esmeralda] comme il y en avait une sur lui" (There was popular hatred of Esmeralda, much as of himself") [10.4, 422]. One can't quite tell, in the battle that follows, just whom the hunchback is defending. Subjected to an assault he can't fully comprehend—and which is in its source one of his master's schemes, part of his master's madness—he makes one last effort to resolve his multiplying confusions. The result has a fine inevitability. The Truands' attack is from their point of view on Esmeralda, from Quasimodo's on the cathedral; Quasimodo can only attend to one of our ladies at a time. He concentrates by necessity on a defensive bewitching of Notre-Dame, so that the building seems to be defending itself. While he is absorbed in this task Esmeralda disappears—

spirited away by Frollo. When he realizes that she has gone, he searches every corner of Notre-Dame [11.2, 500]. Alas, the church and Esmeralda have separated forever, leaving Quasimodo to a gigantic architectural void.

As the twentieth-century reader approaches the morbidly sentimental conclusion of *Notre-Dame,* the extravagances of the book may seem so absurd as to be more and more easily dismissed. All the same, here as elsewhere in Hugo's work, it is the most extravagant ideas that answer most closely to events of the author's time. I noted above that worship of the Virgin (bordering, in fact, on Mariolatry) was widespread just before *Notre-Dame,* specifically in the fifteen-year span that includes the restoration of the Bourbons and the subsequent installation of Louis-Philippe's bourgeois monarchy. Nicholas Perry and Loreto Echeverría have written pointedly on this subject:

> *Catholicism was once more the state religion in France. . . . The most remarkable aspect of the revival was the proliferation and scope of organizations consecrated to Notre-Dame. . . . Recipients of the munificence of aristocratic benefactors, these foundations constituted a fundamental part of the framework that would sustain the apparitions and subsequent devotions, Marian "science" and papal dogmas. Through them millions were conditioned to an obedient life "under her mantle" and found consolation amidst the miseries of the age. Refuge of Sinners, Mother of Mercy, Suppliant Omnipotent, Mary stood in diametrical opposition to Marianne, the allegorical figure who simultaneously personified the republic and was the mother of it. "Virgin of Liberty, deliver us from King and Popes! Virgin of Equality, deliver us from aristocrats!" Shamelessly parodying the Ave Maria, revolutionaries sang, "Hail Marianne, full of strength, the People are with thee, Blessed is the fruit of thy womb, the Republic!"*[18]

It is unlikely that the opposition between Notre-Dame and Esmeralda is specifically intended to parallel that between Mary and Marianne. All the same, the analogy is instructive: the early 1830s were a time when clashing mediators, rival virgins, one authoritarian and one democratic, one monumental and one nomadic, could define the course of a society. Consider, as a point of reference, the most famous painting produced in 1830: Delacroix's *La Liberté guidant le peuple* (Liberty guiding the people, exhibited in the first salon of the July Monarchy, 14 April 1831; *Notre-Dame* had been published on 16 March). Here, an unforgettable bare-breasted Liberty, tricolor in her right hand and musket in her left, is juxtaposed with Notre-Dame, looming up out of smoke and barricades off to the right. Delacroix is more optimistic than Hugo: Liberty leads the people and wins the day; the cathedral has been subordinated to her, for the tricolor flies on one of its western towers. There is no great cognitive or historical mixup. However, there remains a crucial similarity between *La Liberté guidant le peuple* and *Notre-Dame*. In both works the movement of history is imagined through mediating figures that answer the same need but answer it differently. Hugo's effort to evoke rival systems thus belongs to a way of thinking, of conceptualizing the situation of France, which the politics of Delacroix could also accommodate.

Tales of the Crypt

Notre-Dame ends with two tableaux. The first sets Quasimodo against Frollo; the second unites him with Esmeralda, then separates them once more. Together these scenes define a new state of affairs, the descent into an abyss—a literal abyss, an abyss also of understanding—from which no quick release is possible. We come to understand that we share Quasimodo's dilemma.

For Ruskin ("Fiction, Fair and Foul") *Notre-Dame* is epitomized and self-condemned by the moment in which Quasimodo watches Esmeralda's execution. "The effectual head of the whole cretinous school [of urban Gothic fiction] is the renowned novel in which the hunchbacked lover watches the execution of his mistress from the tower of Notre-Dame."[19] Why single out this chapter, among all the others? The reader must see the scene as Quasimodo sees it. "Tout à coup l'homme repoussa brusquement l'échelle du talon, et Quasimodo qui ne respirait plus depuis quelques instants vit se balancer au bout de la corde, à deux toises au-dessus du pavé, la malheureuse enfant avec l'homme accroupi les pieds sur ses épaules. La corde fit plusieurs tours sur elle-même, et Quasimodo vit courir d'horribles convulsions le long du corps de l'égyptienne" (All at once the man pushed back the ladder with his heel, and Quasimodo, who for several moments no longer breathed, saw dangling at the end of the rope, about two fathoms up from the ground, the unfortunate child with the man squatting on her shoulders. The rope twisted round several times, and Quasimodo saw horrible convulsions run along the gypsy's body) [*ND*, 11.2, 504]. Hugo duplicates a common classical link between hanging and the sexual violation of virgins.[20] This archaic tradition is adapted to his own peculiar purposes. Earlier, the disappearance of a ladder signaled Esmeralda's triumph; now it signals her death. Earlier, in this same square, she danced the arabesques of the labyrinth; now she *dances upon nothing.*[21] Earlier, Esmeralda knotted Paris together; now the twists of the rope tighten the knot around her neck. Earlier Esmeralda was the fly threatened by the spider; now she looks like a spider dangling from its string, an object of aggression obscenely identified with the aggressor.[22] These echoes and puns are directed sotto voce to the thoughtful reader. The most terrible pun is visual, and significant for its importance to Quasimodo. In the hangman crouched on Esmeralda's shoulders, the hunchback faces a travesty of himself.[23] When Quasimodo rode the great bells, they pierced through his deafness (the deafness they had helped create) and he seemed to speak with their voices; he heard his own voice, as did all Paris. The hangman rides Esmeralda to suffocate her. The music of the bells is set against a final cutting off of breath.

There is more. Just in front of Quasimodo and oblivious to him, Frollo also watches. Hugo gives at this juncture a last account of the great panorama, including one discordant detail: the smoke of chimneys rises as through the fissures of a sulphur mine. For Frollo the panorama no longer exists: his gaze is fixed only on one spot. For Quasimodo—despite his long sight—there is little of Paris to be seen, since the sun is rising and the city appears to catch on fire. While Esmeralda struggles, a laughing Frollo is given a furious push by Quasimodo. The priest stops his descent by grabbing a protruding gargoyle: At this moment the view becomes "un abîme" (an abyss) [*ND,* 11.2, 505]. We are asked once more to think in terms of analogies. Following the example of the hangman—whose actions seemed to parody his own—Quasimodo, too, has become an executioner. He kills not only Frollo (who eventually falls the rest of the way down) but the panorama itself. And he does so, bizarrely enough, by means of the cathedral that made the panorama possible. How is this turnabout possible? Notre-Dame no longer defines his world: it merely encloses an emptiness. From an instrument for saving Esmeralda, therefore, the building can become without difficulty an instrument of execution, a scaffold like the one on which the gypsy perishes.

So much for Hugo's first tableau. It is almost immediately succeeded by a second, also featuring a formidable cathedral/scaffold. A few years following the events "qui terminent cette histoire" (that end this tale), the charnel house at Montfaucon (described previously in Hugo's chapter on the bird's-eye view—see above) is opened up and searched [*ND,* 11.4, 509]. Last of the scenes we are asked to imagine ("se figure"), the vault at Montfaucon is covered by a gibbet: "un édifice de forme étrange, qui ressemblait assez à un cromlech celtique, et où il se faisait aussi des sacrifices" (an edifice of strange form, somewhat resembling a Celtic cromlech, and where sacrifices were made) [11.4, 508]. The movement of *Notre-Dame* is summed up by this structure, which rises in hieratic majesty, then—as Hugo's description continues—sinks downward into a mass of putrefying bodies. From this resting-place of political and religious miscreants is plucked the intriguer Oliver le Daim, allowed church burial by favor of a new king. While exhuming Oliver, workmen discover Esmeralda; embracing her corpse is the corpse of Quasimodo. The curious explorers attempt to separate these bodies. Over their shoulders, as it were, the reader is allowed to observe the hunchback's dissolution. The concluding sentence of the novel ends with the words "il tomba en poussière" (he fell into dust).

At this concluding moment, Hugo finally describes the realm of melancholy, the realm where bits and pieces of everything are mingled and where modernity emerges from a vision of history in ruins. Like Astolfo visiting the moon,[24] a visitor is liable to find here many sorts of lost items: a bit of the dance (strangled); a chip from the house (turned into dust); innumerable fragments rejected by official historymakers, since the people buried at Montfaucon all suffered governmental displeasure. This is the place that Frollo was looking for and could not find when he had Esmeralda incarcerated underground. Quasimodo has discovered the location where Esmeralda can be possessed.

His achievement is dubious, to say the least. Describing a cell inhabited by Esmeralda's mother, the unlucky Sachette, Hugo attributed to his medieval Parisians a useful knack: they could "prenait la chose en bloc" (take the thing as a whole), no matter how strange it seemed [*ND*, 6.2, 226]. The attitude thus celebrated is casual, seemingly spontaneous, often cruel. It relies on common assumptions, work already done. It is someone else's creation . . . Esmeralda's, perhaps, or Notre-Dame's. Montfaucon is a further labyrinthine entanglement. There is nothing virginal about it— and yet, like its predecessors it has a feminine identity (being presented as a concealing, sheltering cavity) and might well seem to sustain a mediation, a providential knotting together through which a desired unity is achieved. However, for the inquiring visitor to this place there is much more work to do than in any previous labyrinth of *Notre-Dame*. The novel has created ever more claustrophobic versions of an inclusive, labyrinthine unity. Montfaucon is a sort of reductio ad absurdum. On what terms is it possible to confront an obsession that disappears whenever it is exposed, that is not only inclusive but invisible? We confront the colossal drama of an open sepulchre, a mixture of all mysteries at once.[25] The mixture seems to ensure an endlessly futile act of interpretation, the pursuit of a figure that is hidden away and revealed and hidden again. "It is most melancholy to see the mind drifting in helmless hopelessness among the chimeras of a diseased brain, and endeavouring to realise substance out of such impalpable wild shadows."[26]

What do we do while we drift?

1. First, we might scream. The appropriate model here is Hugo's "La Pente de la rêverie" (The slope of reverie), published, like *Notre-Dame,* in 1831. This poem narrates a nightmarish descent into an underground Babel—an inverted tower of dreams, hardly less threatening than Montfaucon itself. In a phrase familiar from the novel, this subterranean world contains "tout à la fois" (everything at once). "Ainsi j'embrassais tout / . . . Le passé, le présent; les vivants and les morts" (Thus, I embraced all / . . . The past, the present, the living and the dead) [*P,* 1: 301–2, ll. 59, 97, 99]. Ultimately the only possible response to this descent is "un cri terrible, / Ebloui, haletant, stupide, épouvanté" (a cry terrible, / Dazzled, gasping, stupid, terrified) [ll. 142–43]—in other words, a scream that fulfills in its very helplessness and panic "the dream of unmediated communication."[27]

2. At the other end of the emotional spectrum, a second solution to the riddle of Montfaucon has its own attractions. Surely, it might be argued, the hunchback's fate is clarified by the novel that precedes it: even if the clumsy workmen don't understand why Quasimodo is there, others do. "That knowledge is the unique possession of story-tellers, audiences, and the gods."[28] Perhaps, then, the point is to read *Notre-Dame* the way Gringoire wanted people to watch his allegorical mystery play: By persisting—despite disruptions—in returning to beginnings. Even if such a return involves us only in another march to the scaffold, at least we would get there on knowledgeable terms. The novel, then, would be not a self-negating but a self-revealing device, pulling itself up out of nothingness by its own bootstraps.

These two responses—panicked terror on the model of "La Pente de la rêverie" or the crazily optimistic, do-it-yourself formalism associated with Gringoire—are to some extent included within *Notre-Dame.* Each qualifies the other; neither necessarily dominates that last chapter. While it is risky to argue from omissions or silences, one silence on Hugo's part seems to me crucial. As shown above, he includes Montfaucon in his bird's-eye view without specifying its function; he *presumes* a certain knowledge among his readers but fails to make it explicit. His attempt to create a complicity based on an unstated understanding is reenacted in the account of Quasimodo's marriage. Hugo defers detailing the medieval significance of Montfaucon until the last chapter of his novel. He defers explaining the modern significance altogether—but this too was widely known. The custom of bringing criminals' bodies to Montfaucon continued up until the Revolution; more important, the businesses that developed there after the fifteenth century sustained its notoriety as "the setting of horror par excellence." Year after year, the abiding theme of the place was waste disposal and waste reclamation: it was at or near Montfaucon that (beginning in 1761) the city's primary garbage dump was established, that human excrement from cesspools was transformed into fertilizer (*poudrette*), that the settling basins where the *poudrette* was refined were searched by "totally nude men" for "objects of value" (e.g., spoiled mackerel), that horses were slaughtered on an industrial scale, that tanners came for their hides, that rats in proliferating numbers thrived on carrion, that "an enormous reef, fifteen feet deep, of fat white worms [was] watered by an untarrying stream of blood." In 1832, A. J. B. Parent-Duchâtelet, the best-known authority on the subject, wrote that "the reservoirs of this cesspool cover an area of 32,000 square meters, not to speak of 12 acres given over to dry refuse and horse butchers' yards; some 230 to 244 square meters of human excreta are carted there daily and most of the corpses of 12,000 horses and 25,000 to 30,000 smaller animals are left to rot on the ground. . . . if you then imagine the kind of gases likely to be given off by piles of carcasses with much of the offal still clinging to them, as well as the emanations generated from a soil soaked for years with blood and animal sweat and urine, and from the blood itself left to clot in some yard or other with no drain, and from the waste matter from the gut-dressing works and skin dryers' shops nearby . . . you will get only a faint idea of the truly repugnant reek." Or as Dr. Louis Roux noted (1844): "never have the most hideous conceptions of novelists of the charnel house of the Innocents ever produced anything as repulsive." The Revolution, the Empire, the Restoration, the July Monarchy: under each of these regimes public reports execrated Montfaucon. All of them, taken together, confirmed and ensured the fame of this site where a group of ugly duties were systematically carried out, where the liabilities of city life seemed to be concentrated in a truly poisonous fashion.[29]

The reader who takes the trouble to recover this frame of reference is in a position to draw an important conclusion. The name *Montfaucon,* as used in the last chapter of *Notre-Dame,* helps to shift one's sense of what the book is, of what it intends to do. Georg Lukács thought that the invention of historical fiction prepared the ground for novels set in a uniquely

realized present, novels where *now* is itself a historically imagined moment.[30] *Notre-Dame* works toward such a turn (identified by Lukács with
Balzac's *Comédie humaine*) in a special, perhaps paradoxical way. The last
chapter may require from us something of Gringoire's obsessive, half-
mocking cleverness and something of the panic described by "La Pente,"
but it preserves the possibility of an undertaking, a project of inquiry, set
apart from both of these alternatives. Hugo's gesture is a bold one: It risks
corniness; it shoots for the moon. Imagine a historical novelist of the 1990s
ending a tale with the discovery and destruction of an aboriginal burial
mound at a site that later became Chernobyl, Love Canal, or the stretch of
steel mills just to the east of Gary, Indiana. A scene like this might bring a
reader up short. Similarly, *Montfaucon* becomes a sort of dizzying and
dazzling geographical pun; so far as we grasp the pun, we enter a world of
increasingly rationalized administration—death and waste organized on a
vast scale in a effort to support the dense human population of Paris—but
we enter it without ever leaving the archaic chamber of death where
Quasimodo hid himself after Esmeralda's execution. There are, no doubt,
different ways of handling this pun. One might decide that Quasimodo's
pathetic embrace of the gypsy seems insignificant in comparison with the
saga of urban resource management, the epic of life and death systematically—collectively—intertwined, that *Montfaucon* represented in 1830; or
one might decide that the hunchback's wedding gains in significance when
considered as a sort of harbinger leading toward this impressively palpable
fulfillment. I prefer the latter interpretation. In either case, a full understanding of *Montfaucon* changes the import of *Notre-Dame*'s last chapter.
Evoking a charnel house that bridges a gap between ages and incorporates
a rivalry between virgins, Hugo takes pains to locate himself on a boundary line. The novelist has been reconstructing a lost world ever since his
opening scene in the Palace of Justice (where justice includes the possibility
of living up to things verbally—of doing them justice in words). His
reconstructions have led him toward Paris, 1831. The marriage of Quasimodo and Esmeralda resists the sun's light, resists inquiring hands, and
crumbles into dust. So, at first, it seems. Perhaps, however, it crumbles
into something else, something susceptible to public investigation. *Montfaucon* could be the subject of a novel, but also the subject of bureaucratic
reports. It was a locale where dust, *poussière,* might be the aftermath of a
strange and secret history, but also a locale where *poudrette,* fertilizer,
might be the aftermath of certain living conditions and the prelude to
undoubted agricultural fertility. Sometime around 1863, Hugo wrote
these words: "L'allégorie extravague, attentivement écoutée par la logi-

que. La mythologie, insensée et délirante en apparence, est un récipient de réalité. Histoire, géographie, géométrie, mathématique, nautique, astronomie, physique, morale, tout est dans ce réservoir, et toute cette science est visible à travers l'eau trouble des fables" (Allegory raves, attentively heard by logic. Mythology, seemingly insensate and delirious, is a container of reality. History, geography, geometry, mathematics, nautical science, astronomy, physics, morality: all are in this reservoir, and all this science is visible through the troubled water of fables) [*PS,* 466]. The conclusion of *Notre-Dame* anticipates this extraordinary occasion, on which allegory and logic, mythology and reality, cooperate amicably and constructively. By encompassing many meanings, *Montfaucon* prompts a consideration of facts in their relation to myth, story, and fabulation; of literal truth in relation to lying figures.

For many decades, directly or indirectly, *Notre-Dame* served as a continuing provocation. Further works of fiction tried to complete what it had started; the novel's characters were resurrected, experiencing their confusions freshly and newly clarifying them in a city of present-day mysteries. Hugo, I have suggested, not only left open the possibility of this development but encouraged it, both in his choice of Montfaucon—a cathedral for the nineteenth century—as the last "edifice" to be reconstructed by his literary efforts, and in his decision to have the hunchback and the gypsy disintegrate under its templelike colonnade. If there were ever a tale that seeks to reveal a literary and historical space beyond itself, to *point* through a matrix of death and waste at a realm of common and commonly held meanings—meanings, furthermore, given a corporeal form and attached, no matter how fantastic, to the everyday world of the writer's own moment—*Notre-Dame* is the one. Urban allegory—so it would seem from Hugo's concluding chapter—would not only demand interpretation (surely all allegories do): it would make this demand on grounds conceivable only by an interpreter who was also a moral, political, and social historian.

Notre-Dame *and the Novel of Urban Mysteries*

The opportunities afforded by *Notre-Dame* were often ignored or circumvented. The most literal-minded pastiches of the novel—e.g., the anonymous *The Hunchback of Old St. Paul's; Or, a Romance of Mystery*—are significant mainly as cultural souvenirs: they demonstrate the pervasiveness of *Notre-Dame,* its adaptability as a children's story, a set of picturesque scenes, an opera libretto or a manual for the aspiring sadist, depending on taste and demand.[31] Emma Bovary named her dog "Djali" and tried to model her maternal conduct after Sachette's; Flaubert's considerable respect for Hugo could not prevent this dig at *Notre-Dame*'s inescapable but often idiotic cultural power.[32]

Living up to this novel, doing something with it rather than merely echoing it, was a demanding business. All the same, among those books that respond to the culminating mystery at Montfaucon several rise (or descend) to the occasion. They include *Les Misérables* (which centers on a narration of the events of 1832, that is, of the Paris in which *Notre-Dame* appeared) and *Les Travailleurs de la mer:* it was these two novels that Hugo himself designated as *Notre-Dame*'s successors.[33] They also include *Oliver Twist, The Old Curiosity Shop,* and *Martin Chuzzlewit,* three Dickens novels of the late 1830s and early 1840s—a time when Boz felt Hugo's impact most immediately; *Bleak House* (compared here with *Les Misérables*); *The Mystery of Edwin Drood* (Dickens's late reversion to the cathedral novel, compared with *Les Travailleurs*); Reynolds's *Mysteries of London* and Sue's *Mystères de Paris,* both popular derivations from *Notre-Dame*.[34] As suggested by my Introduction, I will have two related things to say about these works: they attempt a kind of figural interpretation controlled by a narrative, embodied in a hero, directed toward knowledge; they share a loosely coherent figural discourse, where different figures meet, all contributing toward a common truth. Each of these points can now be refined in relation to *Notre-Dame.*

The scene at Montfaucon suggests a triple problem with figural interpretation: this narrative has become unfinishable, this hero has become invisible, the knowledge sought by narrative and hero alike has become unattainable. Interpretation is blocked at every step. Among nineteenth-century works derived from *Notre-Dame,* I have singled out three remarkable failures, all of them illuminating Quasimodo's enigmatic marriage. W. H. Ainsworth's novel *Auriol* is notable for its self-consciousness on the subject of city narratives and its failure to complete such a narrative. Dickens's Christmas story *The Chimes* is striking for its flailing efforts to imagine a particular type of urban protagonist—a modern Quasimodo. Charles Meryon's etching *Le Stryge* entices the viewer into a form of paranoia, as if knowledge of the city had become a self-enclosed madness. Each of the central sections in *The Mysteries of Paris and London* begins by treating one of these cases—treating it as a half intentional, half out-of-control fantasia derived from its author's reading of *Notre-Dame.* I thus establish a frame of reference for studying narrative, intent, and knowledge in urban allegory: these categories are emphasized successively.

The question of coherence can also be studied with reference to *Notre-*

Dame. So far as I can judge, no novel of urban mysteries duplicates that novel's special achievement: none makes so sustained an effort at drama-tizing the destructiveness of conflicts among figures. Hugo's own ten-dency in subsequent works is to imagine a place where figures mingle, a mixed realm like Montfaucon but increasingly open to understanding: thus the sewers of *Les Misérables,* thus the oceanic grotto of *Les Tra-vailleurs.* Dickens often takes a different approach; for him the question of coherence arises before a particular figure is interpreted or after. He often begins his exploration of the city with the enumeration of a highly mis-cellaneous world suggesting a myriad of allegories (think of the old curiosity shop to which Nell leads Master Humphrey). On occasion, he ends with a similar sort of moment: once a figure is solved, once its meaning is revealed, other figures assert their presence—rather like a band of creditors rushing in to make claims. Any such development will seem something of an emergency; still, not all emergencies turn out badly. In *Notre-Dame,* when figures suggest conflicting forms of truth, the result is mental and physical disaster for its characters; the only possible resolution is death. In subsequent novels of mystery, the act of traversing figures, of moving among them, occasionally of combining them, as Quasimodo tried to combine Esmeralda with Notre-Dame, can be a more positive liberation.[35]

According to Adèle Hugo's well-known anecdote, "Le 14 Janvier, [*Notre-Dame*] était fini. La bouteille d'encre que M. Victor Hugo avait achetée le premier jour était finie aussi; il était arrivé en même temps à la dernière ligne et à la dernière goutte; ce qui lui donna un moment l'idée de changer son titre et d'intituler son roman: *Ce qu'il y a dans une bouteille d'encre*" (On 14 January, [*Notre-Dame*] was finished. The bottle of ink that M. Victor Hugo had bought the first day was finished also; he had arrived in the same moment at the last line and at the last drop; this gave him, in that moment, the idea of changing his title and calling his novel: *What There Is in a Bottle of Ink*).[36] The joke has its serious side. In a city like London or Paris there will be many mediators. Labyrinth, crowd, and view continue to be crucial. The old myths rise again, taking on new forms. Nonetheless, the most influential mediator for the denizen of a mixed, melancholic world like Montfaucon (perhaps we should not say *mediator* but *go-between*) turns out to be paper.[37] To put the point dif-ferently, among all the urban figures, it is paperwork whose connection with knowledge proves strongest. How the knowledge that emerges from paper can rightly be called melancholic; how, despite its lack of resem-blance to a divine, all-protecting virgin, it might helpfully stand between us and the metropolis; how, despite its tendency to generate lies or indulgence in fantasy and caprice, it might communicate truths; how it might offer some support to that peculiar concept, progress, and yet accomodate innumerable figments of the past; how it might be at once hermetic (self-contained) and public (owned collectively, seldom or never individually); how it might open up abstract kinds of thought and yet might also come into close conjunction with *poussière* or *poudrette,* dust or manure, transforming these substances and being transformed by them: These topics become permanent items on the agenda of the novelist of urban mysteries.

The last few paragraphs have spelled out a crucial tenet, a proposition implicit in every line of my argument but requiring as much emphasis as I can give it. More than Quasimodo's marriage is uncovered beneath the scaffold. More than his corpse disintegrates there. What Hugo denies in the last chapter of *Notre-Dame* is the possibility of achieving usable knowledge within an archaic way of thought. *Notre-Dame* is its author's glorification of a medieval order that may or may not have existed; it is also his farewell to that order's promised securities. New forms of knowledge must be found; a forbidden underground world displays them, but in a manner as yet obscure. The novel of urban mysteries is an effort to reenact that terrible exhumation at Montfaucon; to see it in a new and ultimately a positive light; to treat Hugo's discovery of a *melancholic* world defined by the book and its powers as the basis for an understanding of urban culture.

II

Figures and Stories

Il n'avait plus que deux images distinctes dans l'esprit: la Esmeralda et la potence. Tout le reste était noir. Ces deux images rapprochées lui présentaient un groupe effroyable, et plus il y fixait ce qui lui restait d'attention et de pensée, plus il les voyait croître selon une progression fantastique.

He had but two clear images left in his mind: Esmeralda and the gallows. Everything else was black. Together these two images made a frightful group, and the more he concentrated on them with what remain to him of alertness and thought, the more he saw them grow according to a fantastic progression.

Hugo,
Notre-
Dame de
Paris

3. Ainsworth's Revelations: Failed Narrative

NARRATIVE THINKING and critical thinking have sometimes appeared to be at odds with one another. For instance, a number of recent thinkers have scorned storytelling on the grounds that it is associated with "the illusion of a static (unchanging) equilibrium in the service of an impression of homogeneity, wholeness, and plenitude."[1] Almost by definition, any such illusion would obscure either the possibility or the desirability of change. For my own part I will be glad to admit that stories sometimes have this kind of effect, so long as I am not committed to supposing that they are *always* conservative, mythic, and eternal. One of narrative's fundamental properties—its ability to range events within a common frame of reference so that they may be compared—can be used to highlight other, more bracing possibilities. An illustration is afforded by the history of urban allegory: particularly, I will suggest, by an early phase of that history, when the example of *Notre-Dame* had recently made itself felt across the Channel.

First, a word on the context of Hugo's influence. His historical novel did not arrive alone on English shores; it came as part of an invasion. I use the latter word advisedly. French literature—unlike German, in the hands of Coleridge and Carlyle—arrived without much acceptable cultural sponsorship; soon it came to embody a threat considerably more serious than Teutonic obscurity.[2] By 1836 a *Quarterly Review* essay by J. W. Croker could condemn a whole range of Gallic authors, including Hugo, Paul de Kock, Dumas, Balzac, Michel Raymond, Michel Mason, and George Sand, as corrupters of bourgeois morality.[3] At about the same time as the *Quarterly*'s attack, socialist movements achieved new prominence in both France and England. Under these circumstances, French literary fashions took on added significance; they suggested political as well as moral dangers, a development anticipated by the *Quarterly*.[4] Even Hugo, a monarchist at the time he wrote *Notre-Dame*, attracted radical, republican, and freethinking followers: Sue read of the Court of Miracles and wrote *Les Mystères de Paris,* a book first translated, then solemnly condemned, by Thackeray.[5] Meanwhile—after investing (and losing) a small fortune in newspapers on both sides of the Channel—G. W. M. Reynolds adapted *Les Mystères* for English consumption.[6]

An underlying difference between French and English literary culture will be assumed during the following discussion. Sue could write for the working classes and still be read by all; more abstractly he could continue to be a presence in the mainstream of public discourse even while directly appealing to people outside that mainstream. This sort of compromise was difficult in England, where someone working in the mode of Hugo and Sue became either a social outcast or a figure of circumscribed respectability.[7] Reynolds, persona non grata from the start of his career, will be considered in my chapter on *Bleak House*. However, I want to begin by looking at the other approach, that of assimilating the French influence while trying to appeal to a middle-class English readership. An especially clear case of a writer who wanted to keep his respectability but learn from Hugo and Sue was W. H. Ainsworth. Ainsworth's ingenious, finally disastrous, experiments with narrative à la *Notre-Dame* suggest what might have happened to Charles Dickens when he in his own manner worked with similar precedents.

The preface of Ainsworth's first novel, *Rookwood* (1834), cites Hugo's *Le Dernier Jour d'un condamné* as a precedent for "flash" songs (i.e., ballads written in a kind of criminal slang). Seven years later Ainsworth published *Old Saint Paul's*, which reads like a loving but superficial gloss on *Notre-Dame*. Writing in the eminently respectable *Sunday Times*, he simplified Hugo's ideas and plot, sometimes to the point of absurdity. Frollo disappears. Esmeralda is split into two women. Quasimodo's defiance of the Truands from the towers of Notre-Dame inspires Solomon Eagle's defiance of Charles II from the towers of Old Saint Paul's—but the hunchback's distinctive character is lost, and lost with it his place in the original novel. The obligatory city panorama also fails to convince. No longer does it play a life-or-death role in the narrative: it is mainly there to be viewed, somewhat as one might view a tourist attraction.[8] Most disappointingly of all, Hugo's problematic dispersion of history is reduced to praise of the rising middle classes, an exemplary group opposing wicked courtiers. Ainsworth's mild populism is seldom terribly threatening. *Old Saint Paul's* is an antiquarian exercise, an exercise in the nostalgic and the picturesque appropriate for the tamest company.

A few years later, Ainsworth attempted another adaptation of *Notre-Dame*.[9] The title of his serial is *Revelations of London*, an obvious reference to Sue and Reynolds: the bound edition, from which I will quote, was published years later and is called, more sedately, *Auriol.*[10] A point of reference for Ainsworth is *Notre-Dame* 7.4, where Hugo gives a description of Frollo's cell:

> *C'était . . . un réduit sombre et à peine éclairé. Il y avait . . . un grand fauteuil et une grande table, des compas, des alambics, des squelettes d'animaux pendus au plafond, une sphère roulant sur le pavé, des hippocéphales pêle-mêle avec des bocaux où tremblaient des feuilles d'or, des têtes de mort posées sur des vélins bigarrés de figures et de caractères, de gros manuscrits empilés tout ouverts sans pitié pour les angles cassants du parchemin, enfin, toutes les ordures de la science, et partout, sur ce fouillis, de la poussière et des toiles d'araignée.*

[ND, 7.4, 285]

> *This . . . cell was gloomy and barely lighted. There was . . . a large armchair and table, compasses, alembics, animal skeletons hanging from the ceiling, a sphere rolling on the floor, horsebrains[?!] pell-mell with casks where bits of gold leaf trembled, skulls sitting on sheets of vellum mottled with figures and letters, huge manuscripts piled up, all open, without regard for the brittle corners of the parchment, in short all the rubbish of science, and everywhere on the muddled piles of papers dust and spiderwebs.*

Hugo compares this scene to Rembrandt's etching of Dr. Faustus gazing at a luminous cabalistic sun. (The same etching may have contributed to Goethe's invention of the earth spirit.[11]) Frollo, as the novelist notes, is granted no vision. He lacks the understanding of general laws, not to mention the centuries of life, which would be necessary to finish his foremost intellectual project: to change the sun's light into gold. Mircea Eliade observes that the successful alchemist "substitutes himself for Time," speeding up changes that would otherwise be impossibly long in coming.[12] Obsessed with a vision of Esmeralda that blocks all other thoughts, Frollo will never be able to produce such dazzling results. Betraying his powerlessness, his study is marked by an atmosphere of conflict (*mêlée*) and spooky incoherence.

Notre-Dame is hardly unusual in its fascination with the occult. A hermetic strain runs through the novel of urban mysteries, never predominant, never quite fading either.[13] The overtones of alchemical lore—of magic on the point of becoming science—are attractive to urban writers for a myriad of reasons, one of which seems to me foremost. The alchemist's inevitable failure could perhaps become a success if his endeavors were transferred to another domain. Where the alchemist accomplishes

little, the allegorist—another student of transformation through time—
might triumph. [14] What cannot be accomplished in the metamorphosis of
materials might nonetheless be accomplished in the metamorphosis of
images or figures. Such hopes are articulated for the nineteenth century in
the second part of Goethe's *Faust* (see my comments on *Faust* and metamorphosis in chapter 1, above). Despite his love for the novel as a mainly
antiquarian undertaking, Ainsworth is provoked by Goethe and Hugo to
take a few risks: to strive toward those transforming powers promised by
alchemy, to find them in the allegorist's narrative capabilities.

The grounds for this discovery are established by the Prologue to
Auriol. "The Sixteenth Century drew to a close." As its last hours tick
away, Doctor Lamb, an alchemist, steps out on his balcony "near the top
of a picturesque structure situated at the southern extremity of London
Bridge" [5]. Having rescued a badly wounded youth who proves to be
his great-grandson Auriol, Lamb retires to his laboratory. (See fig. 3.)
"An ancient and grotesque-looking brass lamp, with two snake-headed
burners, lighted the room. From the ceiling depended a huge scaly sea-
monster, with outspread fins, open jaws, garnished with tremendous
teeth, and great goggling eyes. Near it hung a celestial sphere. The
chimneypiece, which was curiously carved, and projected far into the
room, was laden with various implements of hermetic science" [*Auriol,*
Prologue, 13]. Under these picturesque circumstances—and there is much
more to the extravagantly disordered magician's den—Lamb has succeeded in brewing the elixir of life. Just before he can imbibe it, Auriol
snatches it from him. The young man drinks, the old man expires. On the
verge of losing consciousness, Auriol sees the skeletons grin and gibber,
the deceased alchemist shake his fist, etc. When he wakes, the room has
returned to its deathly fixity. He surveys at his leisure "the populous and
picturesque city stretched out before him, and bathed in the moonlight."
"A hundred years hence," he thought, "and scarcely one soul of the
thousands within those houses will be living, save myself. A hundred
years after that, and their children's children will be gone to the grave. But
I shall live on—shall live through all changes—all customs—all time.
What revelations I shall then have to make, if I should dare to disclose
them!" [*Auriol,* Prologue, 22–23]. What revelations indeed! Dr. Lamb's
grandson/double anticipates the pleasures of infinite human experience,
of a city which can be *lived* over many centuries and thus mastered. It is
clear that Auriol won't have as much fun as he thinks—Ainsworth has
included too many premonitions of doom—but in the event of his sufferings, he may still provide understanding for others. The magician's den is

3. Phiz [Hablôt Browne], *The Elixir of Long Life*. Etching for W. H. Ainsworth, *Auriol, or the Elixir of Life,* prologue. (From a copy in the Special Collections Department, William R. Perkins Library, Duke University.)

a figure that can be expanded into a story, thus becoming an epistemological tool. Auriol's failure is used as a premise for exploring the mysteries of London.

Ainsworth jumps from 1700 to 1830. He is now to reveal how Auriol has fared. While the novel adopts certain mannerisms associated with Sue,[15] the important reference point remains *Notre-Dame* and the image of the alchemist's study. This continuing interest is declared when a pair of wandering criminals arrive in an abandoned, ruinous neighborhood, an area off Vauxhall Road that has been used as a dumping ground by riverside industry, including a shipbreaking yard. Working from real-life models, Ainsworth delights in mixing past and present, the debris of myth and technology with political and pastoral icons (see fig. 4):

4. Phiz [Hablôt Browne], *The Ruined House in the Vauxhall Road*. Etching for W. H. Ainsworth, *Auriol, or the Elixir of Life*, chap. 1. (From a copy in the Special Collections Department, William R. Perkins Library, Duke University.)

[*Auriol*, 1.1, 31]

Looking around [they] beheld huge mill-stones, enormous waterwheels, boilers of steam-engines, iron vats, cylinders, cranes, iron pumps of the strangest fashion, a gigantic pair of wooden scales, old iron safes, old boilers, old gas pipes, old water pipes, cracked old bells, old birdcages, old plates of iron, old pulleys, ropes, and rusty chains, huddled and heaped together in the most fantastic disorder. In the midst of the chaotic mass frowned the bearded and colossal head of Neptune, which had once decorated the forepart of a man-of-war. Above it, on a sort of framework, lay the prostrate statue of a nymph, together with a bust of Fox, the nose of

the latter being partly demolished, and the eyes knocked in. Above these,
three garden divinities laid their heads amicably together. On the left
stood a tall Grecian warrior minus the head and right hand. The whole
was surmounted by an immense ventilator, stuck on the end of an iron rod,
ascending, like a lightning-conductor, from the steam-engine pump.[16]

The chaos of the magician's den has become the ruin of London. In a sense
this transformation must be disturbing; it is as though Auriol's nightmare
had spread to society at large (cf. Frollo's crazed wanderings through the
"fantasmagorie" of Paris, *ND*, 9.1, 375). Impressions of this kind are
confirmed when Auriol himself appears above the rubble heap, walking
somnambulistically on a plank and talking with invisible devils. If the
present is a ruin of the past—if the magician's den has collapsed into this
rubble—then Auriol's trancelike state is all too comprehensible: he is a
zombie of sorts, animated by the perilous means of the elixir and without
genuine volition. (Phiz's superb illustration suggests the same conclusion.)

    On the other hand there are advantages to such a change—not for
Auriol, perhaps, but for writer and reader. The rubble heap makes explicit
what was only obscurely implied by the cluttered laboratory: that having
taken the elixir, Auriol comes to carry the past with him; that the city he
inhabits mingles many times and places, which is to say many cultures
difficult of reconciliation (note that this is an appropriately Hugolian
mixture). There is no reason as yet to identify Auriol's nightmare with a
failure on the part of his author. Just the reverse. Auriol's confusion (so it
appears) has become a fictional mechanism for the exploration of London
here and now. The house, Ainsworth observes, is in Chancery. More
generally, the crazy melodrama of sleepwalking on a plank is appropriate
to the England of the forties. That discarded bust of Fox, with "the eyes
knocked in," speaks a rueful farewell to Regency dandyism—Ainsworth
himself had begun as a dandy—and also to the Whig triumphs of the early
thirties. A decade and a half after the passage of the first Reform Bill, the
past often did seem irrecoverable, the present—despite Peel's attempted
compromises—a dangerous stroll over shattered possibilities. *Notre-Dame*
ends with a knotty and mysterious image. Ainsworth has begun from
such an image, but shows every sign of subjecting it to expansive scrutiny.
It appears that he is about to explore it by means of a sustained narrative
analysis: to understand it by telling a story about it.

    Then something goes wrong. Up to this moment—and despite the
sillier flourishes in his melodrama—Ainsworth has been able to focus his

endeavors. Suddenly, however, his capacity for narrative invention and organization gives out. In the later sections of *Auriol,* Auriol spends all his time chasing about London attempting to deal with Rougemont, a Mephistophelian oppressor, and a group of subsidiary villains largely under his command. The heroine is harder pressed—she is eventually murdered and her soul captured for Hell. The dwarf Flapdragon, Doctor Lamb's erstwhile assistant, reappears on the scene. He too has partaken of the elixir, but he labors under the same curse that bedevils Auriol even though he has not committed Auriol's crimes. A few minor characters wander about in catacombs underneath the city, not to much effect.

Together the novelist and his hero become progressively confused. Neither ever makes it out of the catacombs, not really. Having made a mess of his nineteenth-century existence, Auriol wakens to find himself in a cell. His costume is Elizabethan. Seemingly he has been transported back to 1599:

> "What can this mean?" he cried. "Have I endured a long and troubled dream, during which I have fancied myself living through more than two centuries? . . .
>
> "How else, if I were not mad, could I have believed that I had swallowed the fabled elixir vitae? And yet, is it a fable? for I am puzzled still. Methinks I am old—old—old—though I feel young, and look young. All this is madness. Yet how clear and distinct it seems! I can call to mind events in Charles the Second's time. Ha!—who told me of Charles the Second? How know I there was such a king? The reigning sovereign should be James, and yet I fancy it is George the Fourth. Oh! I am mad—clean mad!"

[*Auriol,* 2.2, 195–96]

As this soliloquy progresses, the hidden Rougemont makes diabolical comments that imply that Auriol is the victim of a hoax. Later Flagdragon appears and conducts the muddled captive to the same alchemist's den where *Auriol* began. "It was the laboratory precisely as he had seen it above two centuries ago. The floor was strewn with alchemical implements— the table was covered with mystic parchments inscribed with cabalistic characters—the furnace stood in the corner" [2.4, 204]. The novel has come full circle—in a frustrated rather than purposeful manner, however. When the good Doctor Lamb makes an appearance, it is only to reassure Auriol that he has been the victim of a dream. The last words of Ainsworth's narrative confirm this note of uncertainty: "He persuaded himself, also, that he could distinguish through the gloom the venerable Gothic pile of Saint Paul's Cathedral on the other side of the water . . . he returned from the window, and said to his supposed grandsire, 'I am satisfied. I have lived centuries in a few nights' " [2.4, 207]. The tentative language confirms that the protagonist has been hoodwinked, but it never becomes clear what could motivate such a deception. All that can be deduced is what is already known, that Auriol's sense of time has collapsed, leaving his mind in the state of that house on Vauxhall Road. More important, perhaps, Ainsworth's nerve has failed. *Auriol* is incapable of sustaining a move toward allegory and allegorical analysis. The rubble heap yields no significant revelations, despite its early promise. Urban tropes are not in any sense shaped or reshaped by this tale, which is stranded between picturesque, nostalgic romance and a sort of critical mythmaking without making a full commitment to either. Instead of using time as a means toward knowledge, Ainsworth finds himself trapped within it.

When Mr. Loftus, the eccentric amateur historian of *Auriol,* tries to examine the statue of Charles II at Charing Cross, he is taunted by "ragged urchins," not to mention "a street-sweeper, rather young in the profession, a ticket-porter, a butcher's apprentice, an old Israelitish clothes-man, a coalheaver, and a couple of charity-boys" [1.10, 112]. For Ainsworth, too, people like this were finally a distraction more than a stimulant. The city could not be lived after all—nor could it, nor need it, be explored while the soothing pastime of antiquarianism was available. Ainsworth thus limited himself so drastically that his work became of consequence to hardly anyone, not even the middle-class readers at whom he was aiming (some twelve-year-old boys may have been grateful, but they formed a constituency of limited influence). "I recall a pleasant dinner at Frederick Chapman's [wrote Percy Fitzgerald] . . . where were Forster and Browning. When the latter said casually, 'I met a strange, shabby creature to-day, which on examination resolved itself into Ainsworth,' Forster merely said in his most casual way, 'No, really, did you? God bless me!' and added nothing more."[17]

No one ever dismissed Dickens that casually. One tends to take it for granted that nobody could have, but creative exhaustion and conceptual confusion threatened him on numerous occasions. It won't do simply to observe that Dickens was brighter and more enterprising than Ainsworth, that he made the grade. This is not a Horatio Alger story. How then conceive his success: his ability to extend the tradition of the city novel in about the same social context where Ainsworth failed? To put the question differently, what gave one middle-class, respectable novelist the ability to *narrate* London when another lacked it?

I begin as I did for the author of *Revelations,* by noting some points of

contact with the French and especially with Hugo. In 1847 Dickens visited
Paris, where he haunted the morgue; mingled with Sue, Gautier, Lamar-
tine, and Scribe; attended a sale after the death of Marie Duplessis "who
had led the most brilliant and abandoned of lives" (Sue bought her prayer
book; her admirer, young Dumas, celebrated her as the Lady of the
Camellias in a volume more thoroughly necrophiliac than even *Notre-
Dame*); and wrote home to John Forster about "rather a good book
announced in a bookseller's window as *Les Mystères de Londres par Sir
Trollop*."[18] After meeting Hugo, Dickens observed that the great man's
family "made a most romantic show [looking] like a picture out of one of
his own books." The backdrop of this show ("grim old chairs and tables,
and old canopies of state from old palaces") makes it probable that Boz was
thinking of *Notre-Dame*.[19] The book had been published in English as early
as 1833, when no less than three editions appeared almost simultaneously;
one of the translators was William Hazlitt, Jr., a colleague of Dickens's on
the *Morning Chronicle*. Perhaps Dickens read Hugo's novel then; there was
a considerable fuss about Hazlitt's edition, partly on political grounds.[20]
By 1847, at all events, he was able to affirm confidently that the French-
man was a genius and to state that "of all the literary men I saw [in Paris], I
like Victor Hugo best." This impression seems to have persisted: a note of
four years later, on Hugo's son Charles, has Dickens declaring: "I have the
honor of knowing his father, whose genius I hold in the profoundest
admiration, and for whom I entertain great personal respect."[21]

It's tricky to dwell on Dickens's sympathy for Hugo.[22] The French-
man is the writer who composed a systematic philosophical epic about
God and then—at the last minute—added one final voice to the discussion, an owl whose monologue is a triumph of Miltonic style and whose
skepticism, in any other poet's work, might seem to have threatened the
elegant structure surrounding it. Among Dickens's contemporaries there
is no one else like this: no one who assumes the vocation of poet with such
a combination of genius and theatricality, no one who confronts nothingness in such an *accomplished* manner, no one whose novels are so fully
informed by literary traditions much older than the novel. How could
Dickens, transcriber of parliamentary speeches, lifelong journalist, comic
novelist, compulsive worker in prose—his greatest poem is his "Ode to an
Expiring Frog"—learn from this anomalous personality?

Apparently something got through to him. Fresh from a reading of
Notre-Dame ("a more sublime *poem,* than anything which our Scott ever
performed"), Elizabeth Barrett wrote "that Charles Dickens has medi-
tated deeply and not without advantage upon Victor Hugo,—and that

some of his very finest things . . . are taken from Victor Hugo." She cited the chapter in *Oliver Twist* describing Fagin's last hours—which does indeed resemble *Le Dernier Jour,* though direct influence would be hard to prove. Closer yet are parallels in works of the early forties: *The Old Curiosity Shop,* where Quilp is a malevolent Quasimodo, or *The Chimes,* which pays another homage to *Notre-Dame* while clarifying further links with Hugo in *Martin Chuzzlewit.*[23]

A flurry of contacts: arguably just a sign of the times. It was as hard for Dickens as for Ainsworth to avoid French influence at the juncture of the late thirties and early forties. The difference, at least the initial difference, is that Dickens mastered storytelling, persevering precisely where Ainsworth lost his nerve. This is not to say that he ever stopped pursuing the favors of the bourgeois audience dominant during the nineteenth century. But he seldom lapsed into the cozy nostalgia by which Ainsworth attempted to build a refuge for himself. And though (like everyone else) he was bound in his perceptions by class and circumstance, he managed to use the rigors of literary form as a means toward reconceiving social knowledge. As will be seen in the next three chapters, he came closest to imitating Hugo at moments when he doubted his understanding of a city. The imitation, or allusion, helped him think his way through, spurred him to make up tales that were forms of historical and rhetorical inquiry rather than cognitive dead ends. A figure that was allowed to generate a story could be analyzed, explored, and questioned. Trying to escape the confusion experienced in *Revelations,* Dickens discovered the allegorical narrative demanded by *Notre-Dame.*

4. Knotting the Maze in Oliver Twist

Illustrious scribe! whose vivid genius strays
'Mid Drury's stews to incubate her lays,
And in St. Giles's slang conveys her tropes,
Wreathing the poet's lines with hangmen's ropes. "The
Literary
Gentle-
man,"
Punch
(1842)

HOW IS SOCIETY POSSIBLE? What links people into a determinate social whole? Put this way, the question elicits an answer "in reference to phenomena which bind" such as ropes, ties, cords, and knots. Many cultures have used such images. The Vicar of Wakefield orates on "the cords of society," the Atuot of the Southern Sudan on the ropes which tether cattle. Both discourses establish the obligations of an individual within a larger group; both explore what it means to belong, or to feel that one belongs.[1]

Against this background, the England of *Oliver Twist* (1837–39) presents a problematic case. The impression is registered—by John Bayley and Stephen Marcus among others—that the nation Dickens describes has no sense of its nationhood, that its people burrow in dens like solitary animals, that its social formations are dismally Benthamite and Malthusian, each individual locked in an isolated struggle for existence.[2] Admitting this quality of the novel, and perhaps of the years when it was written, there is nonetheless one tie, one rope that counts. The London evoked by Dickens is organized around the socializing influence of the gallows.

Oliver goes to London looking for friends. He discovers what E. V. Walter has called the dreadful enclosure, a forbidden and fearsome slum—or in figurative terms, a labyrinth knotted together by the hangman's rope. The gallows-labyrinth is a hidden but powerful influence on London. It is a part that tries to dominate the whole by promoting a kind of coziness and hospitability otherwise unavailable. It beckons its victim onward; it also threatens death. Dickens repeats this dilemma in its ghastly or funny details until—at the end of the novel—he is able to transform it. From an unifying and synthesizing object of terror, the gallows becomes an instrument of analysis.

Oliver Enters the Dreadful Enclosure

A rope can be terrifying, even if it is not explicitly associated with punishment. "Sauntering among the ropemaking [at Chatham Dockyard], I am spun into a state of blissful indolence, wherein my rope of life seems to be so untwisted by the process as that I can see back to very early days indeed, when my bad dreams—they were frightful, though my more mature understanding has never made out why—were of an interminable sort of ropemaking, with long minute filaments for strands, which when they were spun home together close to my eyes, occasioned screaming."[3] The sentence is designed to induce a state both fearful and strangely pleasant. Caught unawares—so he claims—Dickens is "untwisted" back to defenseless, receptive childhood, whereupon there begins a twisting in reponse. To be the witness of this coerced unity, determined by overwhelming, seemingly omnipotent forces, is to desire escape.

The scream of terror is not Dickens's only response to rope. There is also the opposite extreme: a detached facetiousness, emphasizing verbal quibbles and generally explaining too much where the other mode explains little. This stance is exemplified by several passages from Dickens's early prose. Describing the slum of Seven Dials, he writes: "Look at the construction of the place. The gordian knot was all very well in its way: so was the maze of Hampton Court: so is the maze at the Beulah Spa: so were the ties of stiff white neckcloths, when the difficulty of getting one on was only to be equalled by the apparent impossibility of ever getting it off again. But what involutions can compare with those of Seven Dials?" ["Seven Dials," *SB,* 69]. The passage seems a bit of nervous chattering, its only likely function its irrelevance—as though to reassure a middle-class audience that the author too knows classical allusions or that his dandyish clothing safely separates him from the cockneys and Irish of the Dials. Dickens's talk of knots allows him a certain safety. The only connection with hanging is an implied one, Seven Dials being the locale where "dying speeches" of criminals are published.

Would it be possible to combine the nightmare and the joke, the pun and the scream? *Oliver Twist*'s first effort in this direction occurs shortly after Oliver asks for more gruel. A member of the offended workhouse board—a gentleman in a white waistcoat—predicts that the boy will be hung, a remark often reiterated during these preparatory chapters and appropriate to Oliver's name if not his nature.[4] Dickens adds the following speculation: "As I purpose to show in the sequel whether the white-waistcoated gentleman was right or not, I should perhaps mar the interest of this narrative (supposing it to possess any at all), if I ventured to hint just yet, whether the life of Oliver Twist had this violent termination or no" [*OT*, 2, 13]. The tease extends to the beginning of the next installment, where Dickens picks up the same idea. If Oliver "had entertained a becoming feeling of respect for the prediction of the gentleman in the white waistcoat, he would have established that sage individual's pro-phetic character, once and for ever, by tying one end of his pocket-handkerchief to a hook in the wall, and attaching himself to the other" [3, 14]. Two obstacles prevent Oliver from this otherwise efficient form of self-execution. On the one hand, "pocket-handkerchiefs being decided articles of luxury, had been, for all future times and ages, removed from the noses of paupers by the express order of the board, in council assem-bled." On the other hand, Oliver is very young; he can only cry bitterly or sleep. Because of his social status he lacks the materials even for hanging. Because of his temperament he lacks the will. Dickens's ironies suggest a horrible deadlock.

For just a moment, nightmare and joke merge. The novelist needs a way to sustain and develop this synthesis; he finds it in the lore of the dreadful enclosure.[5] The notion of a forbidden urban space, a carefully demarcated territory where crime is the norm and human beings are beasts, flourishes throughout nineteenth-century literature. The most frankly fantastic version of the motif occurs in *Notre-Dame,* when Grin-goire strays to the beggar's kingdom, the notorious Court of Miracles. He just barely survives his labyrinthine journey and his initiation by hanging. The whole affair is treated as a comedy, yet the comedy—puns and horrors alike—anticipates the novel's gruesome climax. Dickens imagines an enclosure no less suggestive. At Fagin's den on Saffron Hill, the power of hanging is expressed through handkerchiefs, knots, cravats, mazes—all kinds of ties. This system of equivalences will define Oliver's entrap-ment.[6]

The following discussion includes many references to George Cruik-shank's illustrations for *Oliver Twist,* which I treat as crucial evidence for the novel's fascination with mazes. A prefatory word should clarify this choice. Sometime around the end of the eighteenth century, several experiments expanded the possibilities of the illustrated book: Blake, Goya, and Bewick helped define new ways in which word and image could illuminate one other. Their accomplishments would be extended in the Victorian era not just by the relatively high-toned Pre-Raphaelites but by more popular artists, such as Cruikshank himself.[7] *Oliver Twist* has been understood as a conflict of will between illustrator and writer, each struggling for ascendancy. While acknowledging the justice of this interpretation, I wish to modify it somewhat. Especially with regard to the book's labyrinths, the Dickens-Cruikshank collaboration is more fruitful than either of its participants may have wanted to admit. Each responds in turn to the other's formulations; word and image together create an allegorical premise that will be developed over an extended narrative.

First it is Dickens's turn. On the outskirts of London, Oliver meets the Artful Dodger. The route they take is marked out carefully. The boys "crossed from the Angel into St. John's Road"—and so on, through an intricate, meandering route that mingles the familiar with the obscure [*OT,* 8, 55]. This part of London is full of landmarks: a little to the west the Inns of Court, a little to the east the markets. Smithfield Market will be a principal point of reference once Fagin switches his headquarters across Farringdon Road. Above all, there is Newgate. Any experienced Londoner would grasp the general drift of Dodger's route—yet the passage's overall effect remains disorienting. The names come fast ("scudding" at Dodger's speed, "a rapid pace"); some of them seem chosen for mystification: "the classic ground which once bore the name of Hockley-in-the-Hole," an obscure place referred to knowingly, on the odd assumption that everyone will recognize it. Dodger and Oliver are not only going somewhere. They are getting there in a particular way: sneaky and overly elaborate. To quote from a later description of Dodger's movements, he lengthens "the distance, by various circumlocutions and discursive staggerings" as though, despite his rapid pace, to put off arriving just a little longer [12, 82].

A similar atmosphere is created when Oliver enters the thieves' den. Making his way among "little knots of houses, where drunken men and women were positively wallowing in filth," he becomes scared. Just before he can make up his mind to run, he finds himself pushed inside a doorway. "Is Fagin upstairs?" asks the Dodger. The answer comes, "Yes, he's a sortin' the wipes." Stepping into the upstairs room, Oliver sees Fagin dressed "in a greasy flannel gown, with his throat bare." He is said to divide his attention between his frying dinner "and a clothes-horse, over which a great number of silk handkerchiefs were hanging." Fagin's pupils look on while the Dodger makes introductions. Fagin observes to Oliver, "Ah, you're a-staring at the pocket-handkerchiefs! eh, my dear! There are a good many of 'em, ain't there? We've just looked 'em out, ready for the wash" [*OT,* 8, 55–57]. Everyone shouts boisterously at this joke. What's important is not only its content but the mood it generates: a tense sociability, a desire to share some unstated subject while avoiding its implications.

Can the unstated principle of the dreadful enclosure be pinned down? It will not do simply to say that Dodger is a thief, nor that Fagin exploits him and the other boys, nor even that the gang huddles together by reason of its dishonesty. Another *something* remains less accessible until our glance strays to George Cruikshank's accompanying plate. In Cruikshank's conception of *Oliver introduced to the respectable Old Gentleman* (see fig. 5), Oliver stands hesitantly at the right, his coat collar turned up against the cold, a walking stick in one hand, a handkerchief filled with belongings in the other. He searches but does not yet find the meaning of his surroundings. Several clues are conspicuous. The first is the boy's handkerchief, bound neatly at the top where he holds it. The second is the Dodger's kerchief, here and in subsequent plates knotted around his neck. The third is Fagin's knotted scarf, perched merrily on his head: Cruikshank next shows it there when the old man awaits execution. The fourth is a broadsheet over the fireplace, depicting in blotted silhouette three criminals hanging side by side from a gallows. The broadsheet is a Hogarthian emblem, a moral comment on the scene that it decorates. It is also something more. From the knot in Oliver's handkerchief to the knot in the Dodger's kerchief to the knot of Fagin's headscarf to the upper lefthand corner of the gallows there could be drawn a diagonal line. This association is there for the eye to catch, with the handkerchiefs hung out directly behind.

Cruikshank specifies the bonds that hold the gang together. The Dodger's rapidity-procrastination and the tense sociability of Saffron Hill are both included in what he depicts, a sequence of knots leading on toward the gallows. This community demands a peculiar, precarious attention to hanging. The thieves know what their ultimate fate will be— witness the print on the wall. They also assume that indefinite postponements are possible—witness the fact that they not only remain in their seats but continue their festivities. From the perspective of someone who looks at the plate, their attitude will seem stupid and deluded, so clearly is the progression of knots mapped. From their own perspective it seems

5. George Cruikshank. *Oliver introduced to the respectable Old Gentleman.*
Etching for *Oliver Twist,* chap. 8. (From a copy in the Special Collections
Department, William R. Perkins Library, Duke University.)

quite sensible. The trick is to steal a handkerchief without facing a rope; to
live with a kerchief around one's neck while avoiding the noose (the
"hempen cravat") that might replace it. The gang's unity depends on this
delicate separation of meanings that are almost but not quite indistinguishable.

I have insisted on a difference between the viewer's perspective and
the perspective of the characters in the plate. Oliver's viewpoint is ambiguous. Does the boy belong in this world or does he not? It is unclear from
his posture whether he is backing away or moving in; he almost seems to
do both. He examines the scene somewhat as the reader-viewer does, yet
compositionally he is an integral part of it. To resist a system that he
has entered—however inadvertently—that he affects by his presence, to
whose meaning he is essential, may prove a difficult challenge.

Cruikshank is often berated for his unfaithfulness to Dickens's text.

Here, at least, he has recreated the spirit of the words more vividly, more intelligently, than any other interpreter of *Oliver Twist*. His interpretation has a unique advantage. It can point up possibilities to the author as well as the reader; it can enter into the making of the work on which it comments. Dickens's likely receptiveness is suggested by two passages quoted above, the divagation on knots in "Seven Dials" and the satirical connection between handkerchiefs and hanging in the parish scenes of *Oliver Twist*. These references had no more than passing significance. How odd it must have been for Dickens to see his own conceits return upon him—used, in *Oliver introduced,* to such startling effect. The issue is not so much whether Cruikshank consciously applied the earlier passages (possible, though it is, that he did so) but whether the picture looks that way (it does). Two little associative strings combine to illustrate a lasting and systematic dilemma. They gain a fresh significance through the artist's mediation, defining both a world and our hero's problematic relation to it.

Dickens can immediately assimilate and develop the insights of *Oliver introduced;* more specifically, he can apply them to narrative. He does so in chapter 9 of *Oliver Twist,* the first he wrote after approving Cruikshank's plate. Oliver wakes up the morning after his arrival, sleepy but strangely alert. He watches Fagin make breakfast; at the same time he is "mentally engaged . . . with almost everybody he had ever known" [*OT*, 9, 58]. Why has Dickens endowed his hero with this extraordinary aptitude (these "mighty powers," 9, 58) at this particular moment? In order, it would seem, to witness an unwitting revelation from Fagin. Caressing a gold watch, the old man speaks as follows: "Clever dogs! Clever dogs! Staunch to the last! Never told the old parson where they were. Never peached upon old Fagin! And why should they? It wouldn't have loosened the knot, or kept the drop up, a minute longer. No, no, no! Fine fellows! Fine fellows!" Fagin is talking to himself. He describes his betrayal of previous accomplices, who died in silence because they did not realize that they had been betrayed. The speech narrates a deception of others; it also accomplishes a self-deception. The silenced accomplices are fine fellows, clever dogs. Fagin has it both ways, praising the rules that turn the criminal world in on itself, that keep it safe from violation, but obscuring one exception to this criminal code (his own violation of it). At the moment when Fagin struggles with the contradictions of hanging, he spies Oliver watching him. "The recognition was only for an instant—for the briefest space of time that can possibly be conceived" [9, 59]. This juxtaposition points up the contrast between them. Fagin's advantage is the power to whisper away the obvious, then replace it with a smaller and neater reality of his own making. Oliver's advantage is that his mind can still range freely, that he is in the dreadful enclosure but not of it. To maintain his equivocal position, he needs whatever "mighty powers" he can get. Dickens contrasts a mind struggling to squeeze itself into as small a space as possible with a mind struggling to break free, despite its possessor's naïveté and physical imprisonment. Though the innocent wanders among dangers, he is blessed with a kind of spiritual invulnerability.

In one more contrast from chapter 9, Oliver's struggle with the criminal maze is further defined. Once the eavesdropping affair is over, the boys come back: Dodger and Charley Bates, the latter introduced for the first time. Charley offers some stolen handkerchiefs to Fagin, who asks Oliver, "You'd like to be able to make pocket-handkerchiefs as easy as Charley . . . wouldn't you, my dear?" Oliver responds so enthusiastically that Charley chokes on his laughter and nearly undergoes "premature suffocation." Fagin "change[s] the subject by asking whether there had been much of a crowd at the execution that morning?" [*OT,* 9, 61]. Fagin has not changed the subject—far from it. Dickens emphasizes by this conversation the close relation between handkerchiefs and hanging. Dickens supplies another aspect of that connection, since executions were reputed to be among the best places for pickpockets to work. Once more Oliver is caught up in a network of implications he does not comprehend, the subject of the gallows coming and going elusively. His confusion is intensified when everyone plays a curious "game" of pick-the-pocket, Fagin impersonating a well-attired but absentminded gentleman and the others divesting him of his possessions. Oliver is induced to pick his first pocket. He imitates the boys, who in turn play themselves at work. His mistake could almost but not quite be classed with theirs. They link the game to its immediate referent—their labors at the execution—while suppressing its association with the execution itself. Oliver links the game to no referent at all. He assumes that it is an autonomous activity, self-contained and self-justifying. His mistake is less culpable than theirs, but nonetheless perilous.[8] If the emphasis a few paragraphs above was on Oliver's peculiar strength, now it is on his weakness. As in Cruikshank's plate of *Oliver introduced,* we are not quite sure whether the boy belongs to the system he confronts—but with Dickens this ambiguity becomes a principle of storytelling, of a perilously maintained and melodramatic suspense.

The Maze Repeats Itself

Gradually, Dickens and Cruikshank have specified a social world. It begins to be clear how the dreadful enclosure can be absorbed, taken into the lives of young fools like Dodger and Charley, old fools like Fagin, or even—in a more limited way—goodhearted fellows like Oliver Twist. There are suggestions by Dickens and many more by his critics that Fagin's gang embodies some principle of all-embracing evil. More to the point, it embodies the possibility of group behavior in a world generally asocial; only under the shadow of the gallows can such a group function at all. The gallows makes the gang real, endowing it with a force of attraction, a presence, that no one can overlook. It is as though crime and guilt could be located, geographically and morally. They are confined to a certain sort of neighborhood, which then—by a process of figurative elaboration—exerts an almost supernatural influence, linking an unwary protagonist with a network of miscreants.

Dickens seeks a shorthand to describe this elaborate premise. He starts to write of "the labyrinth" or "the maze." The notion of the dreadful enclosure as a maze is implied in chapter 8, when Dodger and Oliver describe their sinuous path; it is also implied by the many references to knots, for as established in "Seven Dials" or *Notre-Dame* a maze is a kind of knot. References to maze and labyrinth become frequent and explicit, however, only after Oliver realizes his danger. To write of the maze is to understand London from the boy's panicked perspective. He wants out of that tight entanglement in which a geographical knotting anticipates the knotting of the noose. He does get out—but is always drawn back and so must flee once more. He is vulnerable, cannot be touched, is vulnerable . . . Dickens, and Cruikshank in support, push this repetitive plot to extraordinary lengths. Oliver's struggle with a labyrinth of complicity remains for some time the principal subject of the novel.

It is not difficult to provide a general classification of Dickens's schema. Umberto Eco writes, "In a contemporary industrial society . . . everything can be summed up under the sign of a continuous load of information which proceeds by way of massive jolts. . . . Narrative of a redundant nature would appear in this panorama as an indulgent invitation to repose."[9] Eco instances *Les Mystères de Paris* or the Superman comic books—to which can be added the example of *Oliver Twist*. Oliver gets back to safety, no matter how great his peril; peril threatens no matter how great his safety. The labyrinth provides an insoluble but attractive dilemma, from which a story is spun and spun and spun. Eco's "sinusoidal structure" would seem to provide the perfect model for the popular storytelling used in the novel.

And so it does—up to a point. By focusing on several moments of charged, sickening, and wittily described horror—moments elaborated by both artist and novelist—I can substantiate Eco's thesis. Oliver draws back; the gang coaxes or pushes him on; a maze of streets, knots, or nooses enwraps them all. Following these confrontations, however, a change occurs. Dickens may well have begun with a repetitive, saved-in-the-nick-of-time narrative, but he finds a use for it that Eugène Sue or the creators of Superman could not have achieved.

The first scene to be discussed shows *Oliver amazed at the Dodger's mode of "going to work."* In its prelude, Oliver spends "many days" picking marks out of handkerchiefs and playing the pickpocketing game. Fagin promises him that if he goes "on, in this way," he will be "the greatest man of the time" [*OT,* 9, 63]. Dodger and Charley take Oliver further along the path to greatness. One day their young innocent goes out on the prowl with them. "What was Oliver's horror and alarm as he stood a few paces off, looking on with his eyelids as wide open as they would possibly go, to see the Dodger plunge his hand into [Mr. Brownlow's] pocket, and draw from thence a handkerchief!" [10, 66]. In Cruikshank's accompanying illustration, Brownlow has reached the moment where he is about to turn (see Dickens's cue in the text, "in the very instant when Oliver began to run, the old gentleman . . . turned sharp round" [10, 66], and compare with fig. 6). The handkerchief is just emerging from the pocket of the stout rich man, its bottom held up slightly per Fagin's recommended technique. As Charley and Dodger close in on Brownlow—pickpocketing is a matter of teamwork—Oliver shies away. He has lifted a handkerchief from Fagin in precisely this manner; he has been amused by the make-believe, so natural did it seem. Never did he understand the game's purpose. Now "the whole mystery" rushes upon his mind. He stands in a classic Cruikshank pose of amazement, facing the viewer with his right hand held in the air, his left extended forward, his body poised for flight but his eyes still fixed on the horror before him.

What could follow Oliver's frozen panic? First it seems that looking itself is an act of complicity. Dickens reinforces this impression when he lets his reader witness—through Brownlow's eyes—Oliver "scudding away at such a rapid pace." The term *scudding* was used earlier of Dodger when he led his recruit through the maze. Oliver now threads a maze on his own, turning this way and that, picking up many pursuers until he is laid low. "Must go before the magistrate now, sir," replies Oliver's captor to the sympathetic Brownlow: "Now, young gallows!" [*OT,* 11, 69]. From handkerchief to gallows has proven a short journey. Oliver is entangled by his looking and all that follows from it; he is saved by a counteracting look, that of the bookstall keeper. This man is depicted at the far left of Cruikshank's plate. Where Brownlow sees merely his book,

6. George Cruikshank. *Oliver amazed at the Dodger's mode of "going to work."* Etching for *Oliver Twist,* chap. 10. (From a copy in the Rare Book Collection, UNC Library, Chapel Hill.)

where Dodger and Charley see merely Brownlow, where Oliver sees merely the guilty act, the bookseller witnesses the whole affair. He testifies at the magistrate's court that Oliver was "perfectly amazed" when he observed the pickpocketing [11, 74]. Oliver's amazement produces his release; his little companions slink back into "a most intricate maze of narrow streets and courts" full of "circumlocutions and discursive stagger-ings" [12, 82].

Similar tensions inform a second scene, titled *Oliver's reception by Fagin and the boys.* (See fig. 7.) While attempting to return some books, Oliver strays into a Clerkenwell maze where Nancy and Sikes waylay him. They drag him through "a labyrinth of dark narrow courts" to the gang's new hideout [*OT,* 15, 108]. Here he is greeted by Dodger, Charley, and Fagin, each of whom receives him characteristically while Sikes and

7. George Cruikshank. *Oliver's reception by Fagin and the boys.* Etching for *Oliver Twist,* chap. 16. (From a copy in the Rare Book Collection, UNC Library, Chapel Hill.)

Nancy look on. According to Dickens's 1841 Preface, it is a sinister "knot of associates" that threatens Oliver, "the great black ghastly gallows closing up their prospect, turn them where they might" [Preface, xv]. In illustrating *Oliver's reception,* Cruikshank anticipates these phrases: he displays the link between fellowship and the gallows. The Dodger—an elaborate cravat-kerchief holding up his collar—searches the boy. In the center Charley, less conspicuously kerchiefed, holds the candle and leans back toward Fagin, leering "Look at his togs! Superfine cloth, and the heavy swell cut! Oh, my eye, what a game! And his books too! Nothing but a gentleman, Fagin!" Directly above Charley leers Sikes, his "dirty belcher handkerchief" (introduced with much fanfare in chapter 13) looped around his neck. Cruikshank does this disgusting article justice, for he locates kerchief (and neck) near the center of his plate. Fagin, meanwhile, bows on the right, "knitting his shaggy eyebrows into a hard knot" when he reveals to Oliver what his protectors will suppose. "They *will* think you have stolen [the books]. Ha! ha!" [16, 112–13].

The gallows knots these associates together. Each must keep silent about the others or a whole system of complicity breaks down and all will hang. The boy must be absorbed into this world—not just because Monks, his brother, is paying Fagin but also because Oliver's honesty imperils social cohesiveness among the thieves. The strain of the situation shows immediately when Oliver tries to escape. Fagin drags him back, then begins beating him with "a jagged and knotted club" [*OT*, 16, 114]. Nancy throws a fit, dashing Fagin's weapon into the fire. "I won't stand by and see it done, Fagin . . . Let him be—let him be—or I shall put that mark on some of you, that will bring me to the gallows before my time" [16, 115]. To arrive at the gallows before one's time is to renounce the maze and its postponements: to put a frightening responsibility on oneself alone. Out of a merry celebration emerges death. The knot of sociability becomes the knot of the noose.

In a third scene, *Master Bates explains a professional technicality*, Oliver has been set to shining the Dodger's boots. (See fig. 8.) The Dodger and Charley lecture him meanwhile on crime. They are all prigs, down to the dog. "He wouldn't so much as bark in a witness-box, for fear of committing himself." Thieving is better than being "dependent on your friends." Loyalty together with independence: no one could ask for more. Finally Charley brings up the matter of hanging.

> "It's naughty, ain't it, Oliver?" inquired Charley Bates [referring to the Dodger's carefree attitude]. "He'll come to be scragged, won't he?"
> "I don't know what that means," replied Oliver.
>
> [*OT*, 18, 131–32]
>
> "Something in this way, old feller," said Charley. As he said it, Master Bates caught up an end of his neckerchief; and, holding it erect in the air, dropped his head on his shoulder, and jerked a curious sound through his teeth: thereby indicating, by a lively pantomimic representation, that scragging and hanging were one and the same thing.

Oliver says little during Charley's demonstration. He reproaches the boys for deserting him in the fiasco at the bookstall but is afraid to commit himself much further. Cruikshank's illustration situates him more vividly than Dickens's words. On the left stands Charley, his knees bent outward, a toothy smile on his lips, his neck inclined to Oliver. He holds his pipe in his left hand, his neckerchief in his right. Flanking Oliver on the other side is the Dodger, sitting "on a table in an easy attitude" [18, 129] as Dickens

8. George Cruikshank. *Master Bates explains a professional technicality.* Etching for *Oliver Twist,* chap. 18. (From a copy in the Rare Book Collection, UNC Library, Chapel Hill.)

specifies. Oliver looks up at Charley, while continuing to clean the Dodger's boots. His open shirt and lack of a collar contrast with Master Bates's medium-sized kerchief and the Dodger's magnificent, flowing one. This plainness of costume suggests Oliver's distance from the gang. He "stares" at the pantomime of hanging, grasping all too clearly what it represents.

Oliver's clearness of sight is set against Charley's powerful delusions. Confronting Oliver at his *reception,* Charley declared "What a game!" Where Oliver gets over his confusion about what is a game and what isn't, Charley sinks deeper into his. The "erect" kerchief, the tugging and panting, the exciting sensation of constriction: Dickens underlines the appropriateness of the epithet "Master Bates." In Charley's "lively pantomimic representation," death is the self-inflicted climax to a pleasurable criminal career. By this choking off of speech, the individual sacrifices his life for a community and a code. Charley's emphasis is not on sacrifice, however. Like masturbation or game playing, hanging becomes one more sign of the thief's supposed freedom within the interlinked world of the dreadful enclosure. It may not be clear whose death Charley mimes: maybe his own, maybe the Dodger's. At all events he demonstrates that scragging combines fun, glory, and the lure of the forbidden. It's naughty, isn't it?

Escaping the Maze

Following Oliver's introduction to Fagin, *Oliver Twist* conveys a whole catalog of evasions, denials, and confusions. Thieves learn how to live inside a maze, to live, that is, with nooses around their necks, and yet to present the perfect image of "freedom and independence" [*OT,* 18, 129]. Oliver alone eludes this fate. He will never habituate himself to knots, neither the knot of fellowship nor of the gallows; he remains amazed at what his companions take for granted; his honesty provokes Nancy to her faux pas, when she insists on a premature forcing of meanings that everyone else would put off. Oliver will never be twisted into the maze, into those dirty paths that end at "the very gallows-foot" [51, 397], but at each refusal the plea is made once more, his complicity staged again. The naughty and knotty world of crime continues to threaten his integrity, even as he relentlessly holds it off.

Long after the fight for Oliver's freedom has come to seem endless and irresolvable, the story of the labyrinth continues. [10] The boy's apparent release from captivity makes little difference to the pattern. If anything, Fagin and the gang become more sinister than before. Dickens is capable of seemingly endless variation on the one essential situation, variations that evade the fact that nothing important has changed. The dreadful enclosure is not escaped easily. Many readers of *Oliver Twist* have wondered if it is ever escaped or whether the nightmare becomes a perpetual indulgence. [11] However, while Dickens's sinusoidal narrative seems infinitely extendable, there is one way in which it does prepare a resolution. The nuances of the maze—so lovingly accumulated—can be turned against themselves, can be made to effect a transformation from within.

There is just a hint of this development in chapter 20, when Fagin tries to stimulate Oliver by giving him a Newgate novel to read. This evidently much-thumbed volume tells of murderers who "yelled for the gibbet to end their agony. . . . The terrible descriptions were so real and vivid, that the sallow pages seemed to turn red with gore" [*OT,* 20, 146]. The idea that a book could implicate Oliver in crime has some basis: the boy was recaptured by Nancy and Sikes while returning and paying for books at that same bookstall where he originally got into trouble; subsequently, Mr. Brownlow and his friends were forced to assume that Oliver was, indeed, a thief. Nonetheless, Fagin's present tactic shows a serious mis-judgment; as has already been emphasized, the old man is entangled in the mystique he has taught his pupils. Even for him, the canniest of all the gang, the world of the dreadful enclosure has become self-enclosed, so that gore always seems fictional no matter how real it may be. Oliver's perception is different. The Newgate novel opens things up for him. The fantasy gallows seems on the point of yielding to the real one, as though the instrument itself could come forth from the page. Might a reading of a novel by Dickens yield a similar result?

Dickens further tests such possibilities in a passage from *Nicholas Nickleby,* begun while he was finishing *Oliver Twist.* It is common for adjacent works by the novelist to comment on each other. The overflow of energy has its uses. Seldom are they more evident than in the first serial installment of *Nickleby,* which appeared while *Twist* had Oliver relaxing at Chertsey in a respectable middle-class home. If the earlier book has stalled—or worse yet, threatened to continue forever—then the newer one can suggest a fresh approach to the gallows and the dreadful enclosure.

When Nicholas arrives at Snow Hill (i.e., in the immediate vicinity of Newgate), Dickens works up to describing a criminal execution. "Snow Hill! What kind of a place can the quiet town's-people who see the words emblazoned, in all the legibility of gilt letters and dark shading, on the north-country coaches, take Snow Hill to be? All people have some undefined and shadowy notion of a place whose name is frequently before their eyes, or often in their ears. What a vast number of random ideas there must be perpetually floating about regarding this same Snow Hill" [*NN,* 4, 29].[12] How could anyone imagine a place from a name, even a familiar one? Dickens allows his reader the momentary pleasure of fantasy. London is treated as though it were names alone, the reality a personal extrapolation. He goes so far as to suggest that Snow Hill is a gloomy wilderness "where desperate robbers congregate" by night. Then he describes the reality, which claims after all its own irrefutable existence. Snow Hill is placed "at the very core of London," where

> *stemming as it were the giant currents of life that flow ceaselessly on from different quarters and meet beneath its walls: stands Newgate; and in that crowded street on which it frowns so darkly—within a few feet of the squalid tottering houses—upon the very spot on which the vendors of soup and fish and damaged fruit are now plying their trades—scores of human beings, amidst a roar of sounds to which even the tumult of a great city is as nothing, four, six, or eight strong men at a time, have been hurried violently and swiftly from the world, when the scene has been*

rendered frightful with excess of human life; when curious eyes have glared from casement, and house-top, and wall and pillar; and when, in the mass of white and upturned faces, the dying wretch, in his all-comprehensive look of agony, has met not one—not one—that bore the impress of pity or compassion.

An extraordinary sentence: it doesn't so much do away with those desperate robbers as situate them newly. They are swept out of a gloomy retreat—a dreadful enclosure par excellence—into the center of a massive and immediate tumult where suddenly it is the criminal's vantage point from which we grasp London. This is the transformation enacted in the climactic chapters of *Oliver Twist*. Dickens reprises his old theme, the shocked wanderer intruding in a robber's den. Then the intruder becomes a criminal fugitive, the robber's den the scene of an execution. These reversals completed, the novel goes forward to that consummation that the criminal maze has blocked.

Several late chapters prepare *Oliver Twist*'s great hanging scene. Having fled from their employer, Noah and docile Charlotte proceed through "the obscurity of the intricate and dirty ways, which, lying between Gray's Inn Lane and Smithfield, render that part of the town one of the lowest and worst that improvement has left in the midst of London" [*OT*, 42, 319]. Their labyrinthine route leads them to Fagin, who promptly enrolls Noah in the gang. Fagin explains to his new recruit the ethos of thieves and thievery. "In a little community like ours, my dear . . . we have a general number one; that is, you can't consider yourself as number one, without considering me too as the same, and all the other young people. . . . we are so mixed up together, and identified in our interests, that it must be so." Noah fails to understand; Fagin must further specify his meaning. "You've done what's a very pretty thing, and what I love you for doing; but what at the same time would put the cravat round your throat, that's so very easily tied and so very difficult to unloose—in plain English, the halter!" Noah puts his hand to his handkerchief, as if it were a noose; Fagin warns him that the gallows "points out a very short and sharp turning," then enjoins him once more that the gang must not "go to pieces in company" [43, 327–28].

Fagin seems in control, but after this summary of the social dynamic that *Oliver Twist* has explored, his machinations begin to work against him; the labyrinth of complicity disentegrates at the very moment when Noah goes out on his first big job. He has been sent to spy upon Nancy. When she comes to a midnight meeting with Mr. Brownlow and Rose

Maylie, Noah is just around the corner. Dickens images the four of them close together "in this lonely place," with "the palace, the night-cellar, the jail, the madhouse; the chambers of birth and death, of health and sickness, the rigid face of the corpse and the calm sleep of the child" around them [*OT*, 46, 348–49]. Their actions are going to wake up the enormous circle of metropolitan sleepers.

The vital contrast in the scene is less between Nancy and the respectable folk than between Nancy and Noah. It is she who upholds the "mutual trust" [*OT*, 42, 328] on which Fagin has recently claimed that thievery is founded. She will not betray Fagin nor Sikes—only Monks, who does not belong to the gang. Against her selective betrayal is set Noah's unthinking loyalty. Once he tells Fagin what he knows about Nancy, Fagin cannot keep the information bottled up. He must tell Sikes, who murders Nancy, thus scattering his comrades far and wide. Noah learned too well the lesson Fagin taught him. He confirms his entrance to the gang by assuring Nancy's exit. The soon-to-be-traitorous recruit and the traitor who is actually loyal just barely meet in passing.

The moral dilemmas involved in "peaching," in telling and not telling, have become very delicate. The criminal and the respectable worlds are so involved one can hardly be distinguished from the other, especially in such slippery intermediaries as Nancy and Noah. How appropriate that Nancy should beg (and receive) Rose Maylie's handkerchief; like everyone else in the gang, she extracts these delicate appurtenances from rich folk—but does so on her own peculiar terms, and with unique consequences.[13] It is as though Oliver's ambiguous position—neither fish nor fowl—is spreading to other characters in the novel. Dickens thus prepares for the crucial case, which is of course Bill Sikes's.

After Sikes murders Nancy, he, his dog, Brownlow, the remnants of the gang, a pack of spies, an angry mob, and—yes—Nancy's eyes converge on Jacob's Island: "the filthiest, the strangest, the most extraordinary of the many localities that are hidden in London." While Jacob's Island may have been "wholly unknown, even by name, to the great mass of [London's] inhabitants," Dickens claims to locate it precisely: "beyond Dockhead in the Borough of Southwark . . . surrounded by a muddy ditch, six or eight feet deep and fifteen or twenty wide when the tide is in" [*OT*, 50, 381]. The more locating he does, the less it is going to stay put. To quote from a Victorian account: "The numerous wharfs, and docks, and watercourses, and ditches, which bound and intersect so considerable a portion of it, seem but so many memorials of the once potent element."[14] The sense of place runs in and out like the tide. Reporting "Evictions at

Dockhead," the *South London Chronicle* observed of a condemned building in Jacob's Island that "there is an immediate cellar underneath the tenement, and it is stated that a subterranean passage leads out of it by which Greenwich may be reached. . . . The upstairs rooms are remarkable for the number of doors, they contain, affording convenient means of entry and exit in cases of emergency."[15] It is stated—but not exactly proven. It is not even clear whether the reporter went and looked. This willful mixing of rumor and fact is typical of Jacob's Island, a freak socially marginal to the great city yet strangely insistent, pulling the wanderer toward it.

In the narration of Sikes's death, such labyrinthine evasions finally collapse. "To reach this place [writes Dickens in *Oliver Twist*], the visitor has to penetrate through a maze of close, narrow and muddy streets, thronged by the roughest and poorest of waterside people, and devoted to the traffic they may be supposed to occasion." Dickens keeps this pedestrian anonymous. He "makes his way with difficulty along, assailed by offensive sights and smells . . . deafened by the clash of ponderous waggons." Somehow or other he arrives at Jacob's Island proper, where "his utmost astonishment will be excited by the scene before him." Bereft of character, of psychology, of a Dodger to lead him on, of anything but his implied vulnerability, our visitor must nonetheless go to the island— must face its destitution head-on and be astonished. Dickens concludes, "The houses have no owners; they are broke open, and entered upon by those who have the courage; and there they live, and there they die" [*OT*, 50, 381–82]. The outsider has invaded on his own the forbidden maze of crime. At this cue begins a countermovement. Having followed an outsider in, during this suspension of narrative, the novel turns to an insider shunned and cast out.

Dickens briefly describes the breakup of the gang, whose last few members "go to pieces in company," much as predicted by Fagin. Facing Sikes in the thieves' house on Jacob's Island, none of them feel anymore the old exciting complicity. Charley Bates, his coyness gone, provokes a scene by yelling for help. Suddenly a mob collects around the house. When Sikes steps out on the roof, away from the quailing thieves, he discovers that everything in London has changed. "The murderer emerged at last on the house-top. . . . a loud shout proclaimed the fact to those in front, who immediately began to pour round, pressing upon each other in an unbroken stream. . . . The water was out, and the ditch a bed of mud. . . . [the crowd] raised a cry of triumphant execration to which all their previous shouting had been whispers. . . . it seemed as though the whole city had poured its population out to curse him. . . . there were tiers and tiers of faces in every window; cluster upon cluster of people clinging to every house-top. Each little bridge (and there were three in sight) bent beneath the weight of the crowd upon it" [*OT*, 50, 389]. Dickens does not satisfactorily establish where all these people have come from. They are spies or agents of Brownlow. They have followed Sikes's dog. They have responded to Charley's cries. Somehow they constitute "the whole city." Sikes has passed out of that mazelike world where imagining the gallows creates a treacherous complicity among thieves. He finds himself faced with a different situation, honest London assaulting a criminal stronghold, eager to revile *him,* the guilty one. Sikes assumes the position that Oliver previously held; he becomes the panicked fugitive caught on an ambiguous boundary line.

There is no plausible reason why the murder of an obscure prostitute should assemble the metropolis. Only on one occasion could a nineteenth-century Londoner anticipate a scene of this sort. The overflow of eager faces, the people crowded at windows, the vast shout: the scene Dickens sets is much like the executions described in *Nickleby* or contemporary newspaper reports.[16] Bill is then the man about to be hung, except that Dickens insists on his relative power of action; there is no executioner attending him. Surrounded by enemies, some shying back, some streaming forward to capture him, he stands against them all. He is defiant, playing up to the audience that only he can properly survey; he is afraid, cowed by its anger; he is thoughtful, noticing its quick increase. "The cries and shrieks of those who were pressed almost to suffocation . . . were dreadful" [*OT*, 50, 390]. By the same logic that brings it together and constantly increases it, the crowd begins to destroy itself. (It is as unstable in its way as the gang in the house.) Perhaps, Sikes thinks, he can escape after all, stealing away through the general chaos. He prepares the rope to lower himself, persisting even when it is clear that the tide is out and that he must drop directly into the mob.

It is this moment that Cruikshank represents. Dickens was reluctant for any moment from chapter 50 to appear in illustrated form. He warned his artist that the action was "so very complicated, with such a multitude of figures, such violent actions and torch-light to boot, that a small plate could not take in the slightest idea of it."[17] While his author was out of town Cruikshank went ahead and drew the scene anyway. The artist made no attempt to represent the mob below. He did show some faces at windows, along with laundry hung out to dry (cf. Fagin's vision, two chapters on, of hanged men turning to "dangling heaps of clothes"—*OT*, 52, 407). He did depict Sikes's mongrel Bull's-eye: "the downiest one of

9. George Cruikshank. *The Last Chance*. Etching for *Oliver Twist,* chap. 50. (From a copy in the Rare Book Collection, UNC Library, Chapel Hill.)

the lot!" [18, 130], the cleverest dog and staunchest to the last despite his unwitting betrayal of his master.[18] The emphasis, however, is on Sikes and his *Last Chance*. (See fig. 9.) In conversation with Nancy [16, 110], Bill had marked out rope as his chosen instrument of escape. Now he gets thirty-five feet of it to work with, fifteen more than he had specified as necessary for an escape from Newgate. He looks down from a steep roof, his rope secured by the chimney, then looped around one hand from which it falls into a gutter. In Cruikshank's original watercolor sketch, Sikes's neck-erchief droops; in the plate it blows upwards, erect like Charley's in the *professional technicality*. The plate anticipates Sikes's slip, the running up of the rope, the shock of the broken neck. Cruikshank relies on implication and suggestion—except in one detail. At the rope's end is the noose itself, depicted directly for the first time in *Oliver Twist*. Cruikshank proposed in *Oliver introduced* a system of hints pointing toward the gallows but never quite reaching it. *The Last Chance* explodes that system, replacing it with a world where the gallows must at last make its appearance—where in fact it is the only appropriate center to the crowd's shifting commotion.

The title of chapter 50 is "The Pursuit and Escape." Pursued by the crowd, Sikes escapes into death. Since the murder of Nancy there has been no other way out for him. In retrospect he seems to have been waiting for the right moment, the time when he can be hung but not by others. Nancy's gaze reappears just when the crowd's is distracted; it is part of Sikes, so accomplishes what the crowd cannot on its own. In the "darkness and confusion" described by Dickens Sikes achieves a blotting out of consciousness so abrupt, so unexpected, that it must seem merciful. In effect, he has yelled for the gibbet and received it. There is no more Sikes; there is merely a swinging obstruction outside a window, pushed away in order that Charley may ask to be taken out. This last obstruction removed, we can survey both labyrinth and crowd—and understand the relationship between them.

Twisting the Night Away

Dickens does not destroy the myth of the dreadful enclosure. His point (as he later commented) is precisely that such awful places exist [Preface to the Cheap Edition, 1850]. The reality of Jacob's Island, however, is larger than the reality of Saffron Hill. The enclosure is shown to contain its own antithesis; the criminal labyrinth produces its mirror image in the crowd that overwhelms it. This last-minute expansion of meaning produces new possibilities of knowledge (if not for Bill Sikes, then for the rest of us). Evil is no longer easily localized, for the more the cursed place is described, the more it will prove to contain everyone. The crowd trembles in anticipation no less than the gang did. The rope ties together not just the criminals but the city. One begins to understand why Dickens screamed in terror when those twisting filaments spun before his eyes. How is the impressionable young person to meet a world where social unity takes the forms it does in *Oliver Twist*? If the fantasy of the noose creates one nightmare of society's cohesion, the reality creates another even more awful. The impressionable young person can take his pick.

It is tempting to ignore the reversal of the enclosure and rush on to the ending that Dickens provides, where Mr. Brownlow "link[s] together" a happier "little society" than any experienced before [*OT*, 53, 412], but the novel interpolates two other possibilities: two other spaces for thought.

One is established in chapter 52, a vivid account of Fagin's trial and last days. Dickens writes in a mode largely established by Hugo and later used by Dostoyevsky.[19] A condemned prisoner's last hours are described, mostly from his own viewpoint. The reader suffers with him up to the verge of his death. Dickens uses this format to review a series of familiar frissons. At the beginning of the chapter, "The court was paved from floor to roof, with human faces. . . . [Fagin] seemed to stand surrounded by a firmament, all bright with gleaming eyes" [52, 404]. His mind is restless. "Then, he thought of all the horrors of the gallows and the scaffold—and stopped to watch a man sprinkling the floor to cool it—and then went on to think again" [52, 405]. A little later, when Oliver and Mr. Brownlow visit the prisoner, they proceed through "dark and winding ways." Far within they find their man, his countenance that of a "snared beast." "His mind was evidently wandering to his old life" [52, 409]. He mutters about Oliver, then about the necessity of cutting Noah's throat all the way through. When he realizes that Oliver is present, he confides to him the secret location of Monks's papers. Oliver promises to pray with him until dawn, whereupon Fagin becomes delirious once more and supposes that Oliver can help him sneak past the gallows. Oliver and Brownlow retreat. Outside the prison "a great multitude" has assembled. "The windows were filled with people, smoking and playing cards to beguile the time; the crowd were pushing, quarrelling, joking. Everything told of life and animation, but one dark cluster of objects in the centre of all—the black stage, the cross-beam, the rope, and all the hideous apparatus of death" [52, 411].

This accumulation of motifs evokes a mind lost between worlds. Fagin thinks himself back in his hideout—but no, the gallows has lost its power to enforce complicity. Fagin recoils from crowd to maze and maze to crowd, living fully in neither, resisting neither fully. He inhabits a limbo, a dreadful enclosure, whose identity fluctuates. This stranding of consciousness is the old man's punishment, far more than is the death that Dickens omits.

Considered in itself, the chapter institutes a little hell where Fagin can agonize eternally, and the reader with him. (Cf. Cruikshank's famous illustration of *Fagin in the Condemned Cell,* the perfect pictorial equivalent—*OT,* 52, facing 410.) Considered in relation to preceding chapters, it has quite a different effect. It speaks to the reader as reader, shaping a sense of the novel's resolution. Sikes, it will be recalled, suffers the latter half of an execution, where the criminal appears before his audience and takes the drop. Fagin suffers the first half: the part where the criminal sits in a cell and waits for his moment to arrive. This penultimate fragment follows its appropriate sequel, so that the narration of an execution is at once completed and—so to speak—left hanging.

Like Fagin the reader ends in a limbo of sorts. Unlike Fagin the reader is thereby freed. The mixup confirms a release from this novel's knotty obsessions. It is not just that the dreadful enclosure has been demystified—shown to embody the horror of persecuted guilt as well as that of persecuted innocence—but also that the possibility of detachment has been established. We move from maze to crowd each time we read *Oliver Twist,* always with the backward jog of chapter 52 fitted into just the wrong place. This moment completes a picture of a city and an execution—completes it so that its flaw is evident. So far from absorbing victims into an unthinking unity, the hangman's noose allows a moment for analysis, prompting the analyzer to move among different versions of the whole, to take none of them for granted, to rest with none. The rope that unified a maze and then a crowd becomes the means toward a usable alienation. It is finally the reader of *Oliver Twist* who takes up the charmed position of the outsider.

5. Creating the Crowd in
The Old Curiosity Shop

"WE SHOULD OWE HIM MUCH," wrote William Howitt of Dickens, "if our debt was only that of enjoyment derived from the affluent list of his admirable literary creations." A quarter of a century later, when Dickens died, this comment had become a leitmotif. Books like *Pickwick* were judged by "the creation of individual character: . . . the raising up and embodying of a number of original human beings in so substantial a form, and endowed with such living feelings and passions, and acting in so real and natural a manner, that they immediately become visibly, personally, and intimately known to us." An illustration from the time of Dickens's second visit to America shows him disembarking, followed by a mass of his own characters. Robert William Buss painted *Dickens's Dream* as a tribute to the novelist's powers, while shortly after Dickens's death appeared Luke Fildes's *The Empty Chair,* in which tiny specters of memorable characters still hover in the abandoned workroom. Written obituaries take much the same tack. What the memorialists remember about Dickens—what they are grateful for—is "a genius . . . rich to overflowing in the creation of English types of humour." According to the *Sunday Times,* "The creations of his genius were our companions . . . The CHEERYBLE brothers, LITTLE NELL, TOM PINCH, DORA, PEGGOTY, PICKWICK, and a crowd of other most human creatures . . . seem now to gather about the soul, stricken with the mystery of the death of our friend their father."[1]

All this is quite genial, quite straightforward too—until that last, resonating comment. The crowd described by the *Sunday Times* gathers about a mystery, a death; it is death, apparently, that draws crowds together and thus defines their meaning. In *The Old Curiosity Shop,* associations like these prove crucial. The crowd is used to evoke the bursting life of Dickens's novel. It is also identified with occasions of mortality: most particularly, I will suggest, with London, whose crowded streets are understood as possessing a morbid and persecuting energy. What then is the relation between these two versions of the crowd? The created multitude in Dickens's mind and the London multitude out there on the streets might not have any true connection at all—unless, by some sinister logic, they both feed on death, both exploit it.

The Old Curiosity Shop confronts such uneasy speculations. This most accidental of Dickens's books examines the reverse side of cheerful images, happy crowds; it reveals—what any Dickensian reader might already have suspected—that the novel of London, no matter how creative, is also the novel of mortality. But the author's explorations do not end here. One can finish a book like *Oliver Twist* convinced that the city is best avoided. *Twist*'s escape into a detached and analytical horror discourages a return to London (returning is after all the act of a murderer, drawn toward the scene of his crime). By contrast, *The Old Curiosity Shop* marks a moment when Dickens affirms the city's positive vitality, affirms it *despite* the ugly things he knows or discovers about novelistic creativity in this Victorian metropolis. Once the novelist faces the nightmares of the crowd, once he pursues them through a series of charged allegorical images, he can learn how to look at London all over again. In brief: this is a story where curiosity is rewarded.

Melancholy and Its Aftermath

Among those allegories where knowledge, artistic creativity, and crowd-edness are associated, perhaps the first is Dürer's *Melencolia I* (1514; see fig. 10). Dürer recalls a convention whereby knowledge, most particularly geometric knowledge, is personified; he also recalls a convention whereby Saturnine melancholy, one of the four humors, is illustrated as a slovenly housewife or a reader asleep over a book.[2] In Dürer's version we see a winged female figure who broods, head on hand, amid a clutter of unused tools. She holds in her lap a compass as well as a closed book. Nearby a bony dog drowses. A fat putto on a millstone at the center of the engraving seems relatively perky: sitting in a position that echoes the winged woman's, he is busy writing. Floods begin in the distance, while a batlike creature flutters overhead, holding up a banner that reads "MELEN-COLIA I." The whole scene is enveloped in an oddly luminous darkness.

The winged woman is clearly the protagonist of the engraving. Beyond this point there is room for argument. Does Dürer mean to damn melancholy or to praise it? Is he depicting the artistic spirit in a state of paralysis—cowed by the very instruments that should have brought her power—or does he mean to suggest that this spirit is about to break through her apparent deadlock? If she *is* about to break through, what will happen when she finally begins her long-delayed act of creation? Over the

10. Albrecht Dürer, *Melencolia 1*. Engraving, 1514. (Rosenwald Collection. National Gallery of Art, Washington, D.C.)

centuries, historians and connoisseurs have answered these questions variously. Among the many possible valuations of melancholy and *Melencolia I,* one of particular interest for my purposes was developed during the later eighteenth century, receiving its most memorable embodiments in works from England and Spain.[3] The English work is Henry Fuseli's painting *The Nightmare,* whose best-known version (1781) shows a woman sleeping on her back with head and arms hanging down over a couch. (See fig. 11.) On her stomach sits a dwarf-demon, bulbous eyes wide open; a preternatural horse pushes headfirst through a curtain. Like *Melencolia I, The Nightmare* exploits the contrast between a diminutive male figure full

11. Henry Fuseli, *The Nightmare*. Oil on canvas, 1781. (Gift of Mr. and Mrs. Bert L. Smokler and Mr. and Mrs. Lawrence A. Fleischman. The Detroit Institute of Arts.)

of vitality and a monumental female figure caught in a trance; like Richard Burton's *The Anatomy of Melancholy*, it suggests that sleeping on one's back produces bad dreams.[4] Fuseli underlines the erotic side of the situation he depicts. The male figure is an incubus or *marra* (from which, "nightmare"): a materialization of the sleeper's dream and—if Hazlitt can be believed—a dead ringer for the artist himself. There may be autobiographical motivations behind the inclusion of this bizarre self-portrait. More striking is Fuseli's presentation of the rigidly anxious dreamer.[5] Here is a figure who is paralyzed and active at the same time—a perverse variation, but not an insensitive one, on the peculiar emotional state visualized by the German artist centuries before. A few years later, Goya's forty-third *capricho* (1797–98), *El sueño de la razòn produce monstruos* (The sleep [dream] of reason produces monsters), suggests a similar paradox. (See fig. 12.) A human figure representing Goya—or Reason?—is shown with his head down on a desk, his pen laid aside, his face hidden. To the right a large cat perks up its ears; from behind the human figure owls and

12. Francisco Goya y Lucientes, *El sueño de la razòn produce monstruos* (The sleep of reason produces monsters). Etching and aquatint, 1799. Working proof. (Gift of Mr. and Mrs. Burton S. Stern, Mr. and Mrs. Bernard S. Shapiro and the M. and M. Karolik Fund. Courtesy, Museum of Fine Arts, Boston.)

bats crowd forth, swarming within that strange, dusky light familiar from Dürer's print. *El sueño* recalls a poem by Juan Antonio Meléndez Valdés, "A Jovino: El melanchólico" (To Jovino: The melancholic). It also echoes Goya's own portrait of Gaspar Melchor de Jovellanos, the Jovino of Meléndez Valdés's poem and perhaps the outstanding representative of the Enlightenment in late-eighteenth- and early-nineteenth-century Spain. Perhaps most important, *El sueño* draws on a venerable image of melancholy, the sleeping reader (as Erwin Panofsky mentions, also an influence on Dürer, though in *Melencolia I* it is the dog that slumbers).[6] However, the protagonist of *El sueño* is busy despite his apparent passivity. No less than Fuseli's dreamer, this victim seems to create his own victimizers; he is both inspired and tortured.[7]

The Fuseli-Goya variation on *Melencolia I* suggests that inspiration is a fascinating but terrible curse; the sleeping mind and the mind of the artist (forces ambiguously linked) are confronted with demonic powers that they themselves have released from a long captivity. Fuseli and Goya depict a romanticized melancholy: this fabricated emotion would remain popular for several decades, both in art and life.[8] Eventually, Dürer himself would be rediscovered and reinterpreted according to the same darkly romantic values.[9] Even as this was happening, however, a counterinterpretation began to gain favor, its primary exponent the English illustrator George Cruikshank.

Cruikshank published at least two travesties of *The Nightmare:* In 1814 a depiction of *Napoleon Dreaming in His Cell at the Military College* (see fig. 13), in 1823 a satirical portrait of Louis XVIII. Both treat Fuseli's composition loosely. The figures become much smaller in proportion to the frame; there is a greater variety of fantastic objects, including in one case a whole miniature army; the general effect is bustling and energetic rather than pathological. (Napoleon, notably, is imagining glory rather than defeat: he "dreamt that he was wondr'rous grand, / And had the world at his command."[10]) With work of this kind, Cruikshank discovered possibilities that were to fascinate him throughout his life. He returned again and again to virtuoso etchings in which an incredible number of objects and persons were crowded together, often—though not invariably—as products of a cheerfully vigorous creativity, a mind in control and also represented within the image. Long after he had given up mocking Fuseli or imitating *The Nightmare* specifically, Cruikshank persevered in visualizing such scenes. *De Omnibus Rebus et Quibusdam Aliis* (*Of All Such Things and Other Such Things*) [the *Omnibus*, May 1840] represents Queen Victoria presiding over a teeming earth, whose crowded inhabitants implicitly defer to her rulership. Victoria has in no sense created these people, but by her position at the top of the earth she appears to dominate them: they are ranged about and around her commanding presence. Perhaps the most celebrated of Cruikshank's endeavors in this direction (nearer, compositionally, to Goya's *El sueño* than to Fuseli's painting but in spirit far from either) is *The Triumph of Cupid, a Reverie!* [*George Cruikshank's Table Book,* January 1845—see fig. 14]. Here the themes of rulership and imagination meet, as they had thirty years before in *Napoleon Dreaming:* a triumphal procession headed by Cupid himself and including dozens, if not hundreds, of figures spirals from the pipe of the artist, who meditates comfortably before his fireplace: he is king of all

13. George Cruikshank, *Napoleon Dreaming in His Cell at the Military College.* Colored engraving for Dr. Syntax [William Combe], *The Life of Napoleon* (1815), canto 1. (From a copy in a private collection.)

14. George Cruikshank, *The Triumph of Cupid, a Reverie!* Etching for *George Cruikshank's Table Book* (1845). (From a copy in the Rare Book Collection, UNC Library, Chapel Hill.)

he can sketch or all he can smoke. (Though this picture putatively illustrates the universal dominion of love, it also celebrates an infinitely fertile
meerschaum: the Latin tag beneath the scene reads *Ex Fumo dare Lucem*
(*From Smoke, Light*) and a miniature Cruikshank, left center, paints, not
Cupid, but the smoking Cruikshank. Perhaps it is in the image, to the
right, of a crackling fireplace with a speared heart roasted over it, that the
themes of smoking and Eros most effectively meet).[11] Only a few months
after illustrating Cupid's triumph, Cruikshank moved on to *A Young
Lady's Vision of "the London season"* [*George Cruikshank's Table Book,* April
1845]. Such images remind us that the theme of blissful dreaming can
perhaps be overdomesticized by Cruikshank's approach; however, his
productions continue to be virtuosic and vigorous. (Their energy often
outstrips their putative subject matter.) Cruikshank's last major exercise in
the mode he had done so much to establish—eight years before his
death—is an illustration for *The Ingoldsby Legends* [new edition, 1870].
The artist-dreamer is in this case Richard Barham (author of the *Legends*),
who writes away industriously with a knight, a witch, hordes of goblins,
and an alarm clock whose arms are pendulums circling about him. He
remains unfazed by these visitations; in fact he seems to gain strength from
them.

Although Cruikshank popularized the crowded tribute to imagination, he did not work in this mode exclusively; many of his best plates
from the late thirties and forties (see my comments on the *Oliver Twist*
illustrations, chapter 4 above) are quite different. However, there is little
doubt that his splendid crowds impressed his contemporaries. The image
of creator with creatures was embraced as the perfect image of all that
made art worthwhile. Imagination becomes a domestic impulse; its fanciful projections seem to arise from familiar stimuli—a pipe, an easy chair, a
good dinner—to the end of delight. Putting aside images directly connected with Dickens, I would single out Phiz's *Our Christmas Dream* [the
Illustrated London News, 4 January 1845], an imitation of *The Triumph of
Cupid* that rivals its evident model (Phiz's darker work on *Revelations* is
from almost the same period—but there, of course, he worked at Ainsworth's prompting). Just as fine in its way is Benjamin Roubaud's caricature of Victor Hugo [*Le Charivari,* 1841], where the brooding writer so
dwarfs his own fantasies—not to mention the cathedral of Notre-Dame—
as to make his dominance of them obvious. Roubaud flirts with the
Goyesque possibilities of his theme—is that a witches' Sabbath preparing
itself in the vicinity of Hugo's high forehead, or merely a conference of
jinns?—but the possibilities established by Cruikshank win the day.[12]

Cruikshank's transformation of melancholy and (at several removes) of *Melencolia I* might seem to contradict everything that Dürer expressed in his original engraving—but then, to make this judgment is to see Dürer through romantic eyes. *The Triumph of Cupid* and similar images not only look a good deal like *Melencolia I* but possess as valid a claim to have caught Dürer's drift as do the macabre works discussed above. In fact, recent interpretations suggest that Cruikshank may have come closer to the intended spirit of *Melencolia I* than his predecessors did.[13] What the English caricaturist cannot provide is an image or series of images that *work through* a fear of melancholy and its products toward a moment of affirmation—and that cast off, along the way, the pleasure in fantasies of self-victimization shared by Goya and Fuseli. It is this more sophisticated, more dramatic, and more affecting version of Cruikshank's idea, Cruikshank's transformed melancholy, that Dickens offers in the pages of *The Old Curiosity Shop*.

Does a project so elaborate, even abstruse, seem impossible for a popular and often sentimental work produced to please a wide range of mid-Victorian readers? After this paragraph, I will concentrate exclusively on *Curiosity*. Nonetheless, I want to emphasize in passing that other works of the time parallel the accomplishment I will be describing. To mention one outstanding instance: La Motte Fouqué's romantic tale *Sintram and His Companions* (widely published and translated in the England of 1830–70) is a fantasia about the exorcism of melancholy. Fouqué's narrative grows from the Dürer engraving *The Knight, The Devil, and Death* (a companion piece to *Melencolia,* almost as widely celebrated, and eventually the subject of a poem by Hugo). In English editions, at least, *The Knight* is generally included as a frontispiece to the tale, which is thus placed as a verbal commentary—a verbal reaction—to the enigmatic image produced by the artist (Fouqué takes pains to point out in his introduction that the meaning of *The Knight* "has never been ascertained"; it is the mystery that compels him to write, evidently). The point is that quite ordinary people loved this sort of thing. In Charlotte Yonge's ubiquitous *Heir of Redclyffe* (1853), "Nothing has affected [Guy Morville] so much as Sintram. . . . I never saw anything like it. He took it up by chance, and stood reading it while all those strange expressions began to flit over his face, and at last he fairly cried over it so much, that he was obliged to fly out of the room. How often he has read it I cannot tell. I believe he has bought one for himself; and it is as if the engraving had a fascination for him; he stands looking at it as if he was in a dream." It is no surprise to learn that Guy is "a great mystery" nor that he is fated to die after experiencing, like Sintram and presumably like Dürer's knight, "a strife with the powers of darkness; the victory, forgiveness, resignation, death." *The Old Curiosity Shop,* as I will now proceed to argue, had and perhaps still has the sort of appeal represented by this passage and this kind of "melancholy history."[14]

Curious Humphrey

The Old Curiosity Shop is the most accidental of Dickens's novels; it developed from *Master Humphrey's Clock,* a periodical whose genesis is described by John Forster:

> *He had persuaded himself it might be unsafe to resume in the old way, believing the public likely to tire of the same twenty numbers over again. There was also another and more sufficient reason for change, which naturally had great weight with him; and this was the hope that, by*
>
> [Forster, *invention of a new mode as well as kind of serial publication, he might be*
> Life, 1: 111] *able for a time to discontinue the writing of a long story with all its strain on his fancy, or in any case to shorten and vary the length of the stories written by himself, and perhaps ultimately to retain all the profits of a continuous publication, without necessarily himself contributing every line that was to be written for it.*

Fearing the strain on his public's interest and on his own powers of invention, Dickens was reluctant to return to the publication in parts of a lengthy novel. Instead, he would become the editor of a miscellaneous magazine—something nearer his heart's desire than *Bentley's,* whose editorship he had abandoned a few years previously. Soon the plan became more concrete: "I shall call the book either *Old Humphrey's Clock* or *Master Humphrey's Clock;* beginning with a wood cut of old Humphrey and his clock and explaining the why and wherefore" [Forster, *Life,* 1: 111, 116]. Humphrey is to be a caretaker of sorts: protector of the old clock, out of which will appear fascinating manuscripts. Dickens puts particular emphasis on the initial woodcut, which, however, turns out to have no portrait of Humphrey at all: there is merely the clock, Saturnian emblem of melancholy time, in a spacious room with empty chairs around a table.[15] (See fig. 15.) This seems puzzling until one searches around a little and sees that the idea had already been put into effect. *Master Humphrey's Clock* was heralded—and it is now possible to appreciate the fact—by a grandiloquent Chapman and Hall advertisement (see fig. 16). Here Phiz depicts his miracle-working collaborator as opening an old clock, out of which fly the predictable hordes of creatures (Mr. Pickwick is discernible in the lower center, underneath the clock). Dickens refuses Humphrey the

15. George Cattermole, Master Humphrey's chimney corner. Wood
engraving for *Master Humphrey's Clock.* 1: 1. (From a copy in the Special
Collections Department, William R. Perkins Library, Duke University.)

distinction of such a portrait; it is Boz, instead, who has his portrait taken
with the clock—taken, despite a confessed exhaustion, as the generous
creator.

I have said something already of this image's general cultural significance; what does it mean to Dickens in particular? Writing from Lausanne
in 1846, he lamented "the absence of streets and numbers of figures. . . .
For a week or a fortnight I can write in a retired place (as at Broadstairs),
and a day in London sets me up again and starts me. But the toil and labour
of writing, day after day, without that magic lantern, is IMMENSE!!" To
sum up, "*My* figures seem disposed to stagnate without crowds about
them."[16] The creative powers of the novelist are tied up with the life of the
streets. Without the one, Dickens cannot have the other.

Understood against this background, Humphrey seems reserved for
a peculiar role. He begins his narrative as a surrogate for Dickens the
wandering Londoner, but a surrogate of a special kind. He is ugly, deformed, and timid (not much like his creator). He lives among odd,
forlorn fragments of Dickensian fancy. He fraternizes with a few other
lonely people, imagines himself among ghosts ("conjuring up a number of

NEW WORK BY "BOZ,"

IN WEEKLY NUMBERS, PRICE THREEPENCE.

NOW WOUND UP AND GOING,

PREPARATORY TO ITS STRIKING,

On Saturday, the 4th of April, 1840,

MASTER HUMPHREY'S CLOCK.

MAKER'S NAME—"BOZ."

THE FIGURES AND HANDS

BY GEORGE CATTERMOLE AND HABLOT BROWNE.

MASTER HUMPHREY earnestly hopes, (and is almost tempted
to believe,) that all degrees of readers, young or old, rich or

16. Phiz [Hablôt Browne], advertisement announcing that *Master Humphrey's Clock* will begin publication on 4 April 1840. Wood engraving for Chapman and Hall. (Henry W. and Albert A. Berg Collection. The New York Public Library. Astor, Lenox, and Tilden Foundations.)

fanciful associations with the objects that surround me," *MHC* 1: 49), or summons up the past in antiquarian fragments. He meets Mr. Pickwick, not to mention Sam Weller, and we are reminded that Dickens already had a line of books behind him. A mediator between the novelist and a loosely fictional-historical world, Humphrey becomes a weak version, almost a mockery, of the inventive Boz displayed in that wonderful prospectus. The mockery, I would guess, is more useful to the author than to his readers: it takes a bit of pressure off a man obsessed with living up to an impossible and exhausting picture of himself; it allows him an indulgent sort of self-pity, as though he were to say, "I am *this* as well as the other thing, you know."

Humphrey could have been left as a sentimental and rather mild invention; Dickens found a more striking role for him when he wrote the opening paragraphs of what was to become *The Old Curiosity Shop*.[17] "Night," Humphrey notes, "is generally my time for walking. . . . because it favours my infirmity, and because it affords me greater opportunity of speculating on the characters and occupations of those who fill the streets"[18] [*MHC,* 1: 37]. As the novelist soon acknowledges, Humphrey's taste for night walking puts him in an awkward position. Humphrey needs the crowds, but unlike Dickens he can neither face them steadily nor derive inspiration from them. To say "that is a child" or "that is a beggar" is at least the beginning of imaginative contact with London, and to recognize this variety—to be able to hold it in one's mind—should be humanizing. Humphrey thus talks himself into paying attention. He speculates feverishly. One might say that he thereby opens his heart. On the other hand, his protectiveness of self seems unlikely to lead toward any palpable contact with other people. He is caught in a vicious circle. His fantasies push him away from sociability toward a solipsism whose flimsiness he admits. "Night is kinder . . . than day, which too often destroys an air-built castle at the moment of its completion, without the least ceremony or remorse" [*OCS,* 1, 1]. He cannot look; he does not want to be seen. The upshot is that Humphrey hides himself—half from the crowds, half in them. It is almost as though he were not there at all, as though the people he dared not face had become more real than he. This possibility occurs to him in the following extraordinary fantasy:

> *Think of a sick man, in such a place as Saint Martin's Court, listening to*
> *the footsteps, and in the midst of pain and weariness, obliged, despite*
> [OCS, 1, 1]   *himself (as though it were a task he must perform) to detect the child's step*
> *from the man's, the slipshod beggar from the booted exquisite, the*
> *lounging from the busy. . . . think of the hum and noise being always*

present to his senses, and of the stream of life that will not stop pouring on, on, on, through all his restless dreams, as if he were condemned to lie, dead but conscious, in a noisy churchyard, and had no hope of rest for centuries to come!

Dead but conscious: the impression of a constant tread from which he cannot escape, which he strains to hear in a claustrophobic darkness, to which he attends passively but compulsively, burdens poor Humphrey.

I have noted the contrasting presences of the fertile novelist and the paralyzed melancholic who is tortured by his own, awful nightmares; Dickens now presents an image more elusive than either of these familiar motifs, though recalling both. This development is prepared when Humphrey meets Little Nell and accompanies her to the old curiosity shop. For once, at this moment, he cannot see enough: "I observed that every now and then she stole a curious look at my face as if to make quite sure that I was not deceiving her, and that these glances (very sharp and keen they were too) seemed to increase her confidence at every repetition. . . . my curiosity and interest were, at least, equal to the child's" [*OCS*, 1, 3]. Humphrey responds to Nell's "sharp and keen" glances by scrutinizing her closely in return. The word *curiosity,* to which Dickens will frequently return, is prominent in his account. It is given twice (in variant forms), echoing the title of the novel and the name of the place where Nell lives. Humphrey is curious about Nell in the sense that he wants to know more about her. The objects in the shop are curiosities because, like Nell, they have an air of strangeness about them. "There were suits of mail standing like ghosts in armour, here and there; fantastic carvings brought from monkish cloisters; rusty weapons of various kinds; distorted figures in china, and wood, and iron, and ivory; tapestry, and strange furniture that might have been designed in dreams" [1, 4–5]. As it appears in the illustrations, the shop's dream furniture has an air of obsessive elaboration. This aspect of nineteenth-century taste brings us to a third sense of curiosity: an object is curious if crafted intricately and in detail. Curious things demand to be looked at closely, with sharp and keen glances.

Curiosity in its several senses focuses Humphrey's mental powers; to be curious is to rise from the living death of voluntary self-burial, to concentrate on an object of knowledge, an object that elicits full and sustained exploration. His curiosity aroused, Humphrey is becoming a more energetic character; this process reaches its turning point when he actually enters the shop:

> *A part of this door was of glass, unprotected by any shutter; which I
> did not observe, at first, for all was very dark and silent within. . . . When
> she had knocked twice or thrice, there was a noise as if some person were
> moving inside, and at length a faint light appeared through the glass
> which, as it approached very slowly—the bearer having to make his way
> through a great many scattered articles—enabled me to see, both what
> kind of person it was who advanced, and what kind of place it was through
> which he came.*

[CS, 1, 4]

> *He was a little old man with long grey hair. . . . Though much
> altered by age, I fancied I could recognise in his spare and slender form
> something of that delicate mould which I had noticed in the child.*

Much as in certain theatrical effects, Dickens creates a sensation of blending and changing. Nell and Humphrey are neither here nor there. They are
outside in the street, and yet the room behind the glass door becomes ever
more vivid, as does the man (old like Humphrey, featured like Nell) who
lights it up. This moment of entering and of first perceptions is slowed
nearly to a standstill: literally to a standstill in George Cattermole's excellent illustration, preceding the story at *MHC*, 1: 37 and functioning as a
frontispiece to many subsequent editions of the novel. Under the guidance
of Dickens and Cattermole, the reader meditates, wondering where Humphrey is going before he has gotten there.

After this slow-motion moment, Humphrey and Nell cross the
threshold of the shop. Humphrey is granted admission to a world hidden
away from the city, yet a city in itself. He establishes here a transformed
memory of himself in the streets. Hovering, as it were, outside his own
situation, he perceives Nell in the clutter of curious things. "I called up all
the strange tales I had ever heard, of dark and secret deeds committed in
great towns and escaping detection for a long series of years. Wild as many
of these stories were, I could not find one adapted to this mystery, which
only became the more impenetrable. . . . Occupied with such thoughts as
these, and a crowd of others all tending to the same point, I continued to
pace the street for two long hours" [*OCS*, 1, 12].

In the context of the novel that follows, this passage does not quite
make sense. Dickens is leading his reader to expect a story that will move
toward a revelation about Nell. However, the "mystery," such as it is, is
explained in the ninth chapter. After the secret of the old man's compulsive
gambling is out, the only obscure point left is the identity of the Single
Gentleman. Evidently realizing the problem, Dickens offset these false

expectations when he prepared *The Old Curiosity Shop* for hardcover publication. A few lines below the passage describing the "impenetrable mystery," he added four paragraphs (from "I sat down in my easy-chair" to "and court forgetfulness"), the most striking of which is the second:

[OCS, 1, 13]

> *We are so much in the habit of allowing impressions to be made upon us by external objects, which should be produced by reflection alone, but which, without such visible aids, often escape us, that I am not sure I should have been so thoroughly possessed by this one subject, but for the heaps of fantastic things I had seen huddled together in the curiosity-dealer's warehouse. These, crowding on my mind, in connection with the child, and gathering round her, as it were, brought her condition palpably before me. I had her image, without any effort of imagination, surrounded and beset by everything that was foreign to its nature. . . . she seemed to exist in a kind of allegory.*

John Harvey argues that these notions were in Dickens's mind from the beginning; the added paragraphs, according to Harvey, only articulate what is latent in the original text.[19] However, there is one vital difference between versions of this passage in the serial *Master Humphrey's Clock* and the separate issue *The Old Curiosity Shop* published the next year. The serial has Humphrey speculating wildly but not getting anywhere with his speculations. While a solution may be latent in the text, that does the narrator little good; he cannot make sense of Nell's situation. In the added paragraphs, written with retrospective knowledge, "the theme was carrying me along with it at a great pace," "it would be a curious speculation," "it would be curious to find——." Humphrey now passes over the question of why the old man goes out at night, a minor enigma that in fact will soon be solved. The emphasis is on Nell, curiously asleep among curiosities. Humphrey remarks, "I had, ever before me, the old dark murky rooms . . . and alone in the midst of all this lumber and decay and ugly age, the beautiful child in her gentle slumber, smiling through her light and sunny dreams" [1, 14]. At Dickens's behest, Samuel Williams illustrated the scene so described; like Humphrey, then, readers of *The Old Curiosity Shop* contemplate an image "before" them. (See fig. 17.) *MHC* locates it at the bottom of page 46, directly before the final paragraph of chapter 1, "But, all that night . . ."; Williams's carefully placed woodcut matches, in some sense completes, Cattermole's of Humphrey entering the shop.[20] That entrance has accomplished much. Unlike the press of traffic "passing and repassing," the vision of Nell stays put: it can be interrogated. To be

17. Samuel Williams, Nell asleep amid curiosities. Wood engraving for *Master Humphrey's Clock*, 1: 46. (From a copy in the Special Collections Department, William R. Perkins Library, Duke University.)

sure, the crowd reappears in the chaos of evocative things jumbled on every side of the sleeping girl. No longer, however, does it move past so relentlessly. The press is stopped, Nell in its midst serving as a passive but ordering center. She provides "a kind of allegory" [1, 13] from which Humphrey's (and Dickens's) subsequent narrative can develop.

A Kind of Allegory

Boz was radiant among crowds, Humphrey, tortured by them. Nell is both: on the one hand, she takes the role of a victim for whom one may well anticipate some unfortunate end; on the other, she is in harmony with the creatures that gather round her—her dreams are light, she smiles through them, Dickens coaxes his reader to relish this mass of curiosities among which his heroine is so disturbingly at home. The picture of Nell asleep is neither a Cruikshankian triumph of imagination nor a romantic depiction of the artist tortured by his own dreams. This *curious* resting point cannot but be understood as an enigmatic, unstable synthesis.

An early and privileged member of Dickens's audience provides a hint as to how interpretation must now proceed. According to Forster,

[Forster,
Life, 1: 124–
25]

from the opening of the tale to that undesigned ending; from the image of little Nell asleep amid the quaint grotesque figures of the old curiosity warehouse, to that other final sleep she takes among the grim forms and carvings of the old church aisle: the main purpose seems to be always present. . . . The hideous lumber and rottenness that surround the child in her grandfather's home, take shape again in Quilp and his filthy gang. . . . And when at last Nell sits within the quiet church where all her wanderings end, and gazes on those silent monumental groups of warriors . . . the associations among which her life had opened seem to have come crowding on the scene again, to be present at its close. But, stripped of their strangenesss; deepened into solemn shapes by the suffering she has undergone; gently fusing every feeling of a life past into hopeful and familiar anticipation of a life to come.

Forster equivocates a little: the ending was "undesigned"; at the same time, "the main purpose seems to be always present." So puzzling is the image of Nell that not even Dickens, when he first describes it, is sure what it means. And yet—according to Forster—there is only one way in which her story can arrive at a satisfactory conclusion.[21] Nell's death is necessary because it pushes to an end point the image of the child among curiosities. By itself, that image is ambiguous; it comes out of the old man's wanderings through the streets, then hovers on the edge of some further implication. To articulate meanings—to see that Nell is invulnerable because she is dead, that she really does reside in the dimension of death and belonged there all along: this is like solving a difficult—but finally comprehensible—riddle.[22] Humphrey fathoms Nell's situation by telling the story it implies and thus interpreting the original emblem. He reveals that Nell's triumph is equivalent to her death. It is death that "strips" the grotesque of its "strangeness." It is death that permits the substitution of "solemn shapes" for "hideous lumber and rottenness," so providing the shelter, the invulnerability, which Nell in the curiosity shop only appeared to have.

I think that Forster has correctly gauged the spirit of *The Old Curiosity Shop*. According to the novel's ethos, if you're going to be dead, it is best to be really dead, not "dead but conscious" like Humphrey in his morbid fantasies of burial under the street. (Cf. "The Widow's Son": "Mother! dear, dear mother, bury me in the open fields—anywhere but in these dreadful streets. . . . these close crowded streets; they have killed me," *SB,*

46.) Given the circumstances of city life as experienced by Dickens's melancholy narrator, the obliteration of consciousness becomes a kind of good, a sad but somehow joyful culmination [cf. *OCS*, 53, 398]. In Humphrey's formulation, the important thing is to strive for a death that is complete, that allows rest. This death accomplished, Dickens can imagine a new version of Humphrey's relation to London—and perhaps a new version of his own relation to his audience and his books. He returns to the image of the genial creator, but returns to it with an understanding of all that lies within or perhaps behind it. [23]

Quilp as a Red Herring

Nell's progress toward death begins in earnest with the threat posed by Daniel Quilp. I don't want to make heavy weather of Quilp's derivation from Quasimodo, any more than from other dwarfish monsters. Quasimodo and Quilp both yearn for a lovely maiden—but, of course, this is the old beauty-and-the-beast idea, evident in many traditional tales (J. R. Planché's *Beauty and the Beast* was given at the Theater Royal, Covent Garden, 1841, Quilp's and little Nell's heyday). [24] The opening *Qu* suggests a more specific link between Dickens's creature and Hugo's: so does the fixed smile, a characterizing feature by which both characters are initially identified, and so does their common affinity for Gothic architecture (it is as if both were animated gargoyles). What counts—once these resemblances are grasped—is the sinister change that has come over Hugo's hunchback. Despite diminutive stature, Quasimodo and Quilp seem like giants; they are strong men whose strength emerges from their instinctive sympathy with a larger whole, outcasts somehow living at the heart of society. The hidden centrality of Quasimodo—who rings the bells of Notre-Dame and thus articulates the unity of a culture—is emphasized by his resemblance to the gargoyles among whom he perches. Quasimodo is part of the cathedral and also its animating spirit. Quilp is another monstrosity who comes to embody a way of life. But where his predecessor draws strength from Notre-Dame, he gets his from the streets, of which he is a kind of monstrous imitation. Humphrey asks us to "think of a sick man . . . listening to the footsteps . . . the stream of life that will not stop, pouring on, on, on, through all his restless dreams, as if he were condemned to lie, dead but conscious" [*OCS*, 1: 1]. Quilp is a passing crowd in himself, oppressing his victims much as the experience of the crowded streets did Humphrey: "He treated her [his wife] with a succession of such horrible grimaces, as none but himself and nightmares had the power of assuming" [4, 36: note how the fixed smile adopted from

Quasimodo has given way to specifically Quilpian powers]. "With a grin upon his features altogether indescribable, but which seemed to be compounded of every monstrous grimace of which men or monkeys are capable, the dwarf slowly retreated" [48, 358]. "Quilp . . . approached again, again withdrew, and so on for half-a-dozen times, like a head in a phantasmagoria" [48, 362].[25] Such behavior can hardly be explained psychologically, even if one works with the melodramatic psychology of something like *Richard III*. At such moments as these, Quilp is an animated idea used to advance a premise: that London is typified by persecuting energies.[26] These energies are compacted into a single character, horribly vivid, no doubt, but in its workings fundamentally abstract, denying all the other ideas of London that might want to exist along with it.

This impression of the dwarf—heavily pressed by Dickens—encourages a reading according to Forster's scheme, where Nell is persecuted by "Quilp and his filthy gang" or by some related form of the city crowd. An approach of this kind makes most sense applied to the day of Nell's actual exit from London. Quilp has taken possession of the curiosity shop. She must steal the key that will let her escape. Entering the room where the dwarf lies asleep, she stands "transfixed with terror at the sight of Mr. Quilp . . . who . . . in one of his agreeable habits, was gasping and growling with his mouth wide open, and the whites (or rather the dirty yellows) of his eyes distinctly visible" [*OCS*, 12, 96]. Here is the quintessence of the horror that she flees, the heart—and mouth and eyes—of the ghastly liveliness that must be abolished. Quilp's key possessed, "forth from the city, while it yet slumbered, went the two poor adventurers [Nell and her grandfather], wandering they knew not whither" [12, 97]. Dickens describes their departure from London ambiguously, emphasizing at one moment the city's liveliness, at another its deadness: the city gives the same mixed signals as does Quilp when he sleeps with his eyes open. Finally the travelers can feel "clear of London." The novelist now observes, "the freshness of the day, the singing of the birds . . . [are] joys to most of us, but most of all to those whose life is in a crowd or who live solitarily in great cities." And in case we haven't yet gotten the message, he has Nell comment to her grandfather that "I feel as if we were both Christian, and laid down on this grass all the cares and troubles we brought with us" [15, 117].

Nell is not quite correct in this last judgment. It is true that she has left London forever, but her escape goes on for many pages yet. The allegory is far from finished. Dickens makes one half-committed effort to suggest that Quilp is still pursuing our heroine and thus remains the motive force of the journey [*OCS*, 27, 207]; so thoroughly, however, is the dwarf identified with an idea of London that he makes no sense at all away from the city. Quilp remains in the city, retreating from it no further than his "summer-house" in a decayed tavern by the Thames [21, 162]; the fugitives must contend with a memory of him rather than with any actual pursuer—or if there is a pursuer, it is the Single Gentleman, a character later revealed to be Humphrey himself! Under these somewhat disorienting circumstances, a shift of attention is bound to occur, and it does. Quilp's prying aggressiveness (his own brand of the novel's omnipresent "curiosity"—see 48, 359 and 50, 373) is directed to the feckless boy Kit, Dick Swiveller, or the Brasses rather than to Nell. It is no longer the energetic dwarf who seems to be pressing Nell toward her death; it is Humphrey and his style of allegorical narration—which proves to be diffused through the length and breadth of Great Britain, meeting Nell everywhere she turns, associated with ever calmer crowds and an ever more serene victim, as though allegory would squelch Quilp and soothe Nell, the victimizer and victim, simultaneously. Which, in fact, allegory does.

Stories, Crowds, and Death

With Quilp receding as a threat, the relations among stories, crowds and death are probed over the course of three episodes:

1. At Mrs. Jarley's waxworks Nell figures as "an important item of the curiosities," even to sleeping among them [*OCS*, 28, 211]. Mrs. Jarley deputes to her the job of lecturing on the exhibited figures. She memorizes lectures with the assistance of her employer: "When Nell knew all about Mr. Packlemerton, and could say it without faltering, Mrs. Jarley passed on to the fat man, and then to the thin man . . . the old lady who died of dancing at a hundred and thirty-two" [28, 214]. The possession of these histories turn out to be an evanescent accomplishment. When Mrs. Jarley has to cater to an audience of little girls, Mary Queen of Scots becomes Lord Byron. The little girls scream with delight, demonstrating that sex is in the eye of the beholder. So is history, at least at Jarley's waxworks.
2. Nell again sleeps among terrors when she and her grandfather wander into a large industrial city. They find refuge for the night in a steel factory, a murky, fiery underworld of a place where their host is an eccentric workman. In the middle of the night, Nell wakes, "and

glancing at their friend saw that he sat in exactly the same attitude, looking with a fixed earnestness of attention towards the fire. . . . 'It's like a book to me . . . the only book I ever learned to read; and many an old story it tells me. . . . It's my memory, that fire, and shows me all my life' " [44, 330–31].

3.   In the Welsh village where Nell spends her last days, the curiosity shop reappears in another form: as the old church, full of ancient monuments. Here the storytelling figure is the Bachelor. "In a word, he would have had every stone, and plate of brass, the monument only of deeds whose memory should survive. All others he was willing to forget. They might be buried deep in consecrated ground, but he would have had them buried deep, and never brought to light again. . . . from the lips of such a tutor . . . the child learnt her easy task" [54, 401].

The idea of death runs as an undercurrent through all these scenes, but comes into increasing prominence. The curiosities seem to have been pilfered from tombs; on the other hand they come to life easily, taking the form of Quilp and others. The waxworks, Stephen Marcus points out, exists in some hazy region between the living and the dead.[27] It is still associated with Quilp, "who throughout [Nell's] uneasy dreams was somehow connected with the wax-work, or was wax-work himself . . . or was himself, Mrs. Jarley, wax-work, and a barrel-organ all in one, and yet not exactly any of them either," but presented this way even the dwarf's manic energies have come to seem rather . . . waxy [*OCS,* 27, 209]. At the end of Nell's journey, the old church is a literal burying place (here she will rest). The crowd has thus been reimagined as an artifact of the narrative; it is completely under the sway of Humphrey's allegory, with its ever more relentless insistence that statues stay where they are supposed to stay—that they *never,* above all, break out like manic dwarves—and that Nell in such a peaceful place is capable of winning through to the Good Death.

The shift in tone and emphasis is confirmed by the kind of stories told throughout the stages of Nell's progress. The objects in the curiosity shop are a promise. They seem to imply a progression, an increasing liveliness and open-endedness. But as Nell travels toward her death, the storyteller's activity becomes rigid and exclusive. In the first chapter, the story Humphrey tells (or begins to tell) has no definable ending; one doesn't yet know what will happen to Nell. Even Dickens is not quite sure. By the time the Bachelor appears on the scene, all art aspires to the condition of the epitaph, which not only defines a person's life but defines it selectively, so that biography is the construction of a moral ideal. Mrs. Jarley and the "lonely watcher" of the steel mill embody attitudes along the way: commitments to memory or to opportunistic and enjoyable sensationalism. But storytelling, for these two, is still open-ended in one way or another; the fire can absorb any amount of experience, and the waxworks can masquerade as anybody. This fluidity is rejected by the Bachelor. His wanderings among the tombs have tenderness, yet the tenderness is marmoreal, a tribute to the unchanging marble surfaces that cover the decay of the dead. The Bachelor tells stories in the elegiac vein favored by Humphrey himself when he writes of Nell.

Dickens did not plan in advance the progression I have been describing; there was no time for that. And there is at least one relapse or recovery, depending on one's point of view, where the crowd surges back toward Quilpian energy: see chapter 45, with its description and illustration of urban, working-class riots. Still, as the novelist draws nearer to his conclusion, art and rigidity (which is to say art and death) become intertwined. "I must have that dream . . . no more" Nell exclaims [*OCS*, 44, 327]; in light of such sentiments, descriptions of death as a dreamless sleep take on a special significance [52, 388; 54, 407: contrasting with Dickens's denial of the sleep-death analogy at 12, 92]. Quilp may have started Nell on her journey—but it is allegory that delivers up the oblivion she both fears and desires (while turning the dwarf's energies to the accomplishment of his own well-deserved extinction, 67, 510). The Gothic world where Nell gives up the ghost—so serenely illustrated by George Cattermole throughout the last third of *The Old Curiosity Shop*—is purged of all restlessness. Her corpse lies "so beautiful and calm, so free from trace of pain, so fair to look upon" [71, 538–39]. (See fig. 18.) (Quilp's at the equivalent moment still twitches a little but he's certifiably gone.) Nell's grandfather briefly supposes that she is still alive: he has a moment like Lear's over Cordelia's body, then, "when he had put the lamp upon the table, he took it up, as if impelled by some momentary recollection or curiosity, and held it near his face. . . . as if forgetting his motive in the very action, he turned away and put it down again" [71, 534]. With hope comes a brief stirring of "curiosity": recall Humphrey's initial entrance into the shop, where there were similar tricks with a lamp. Nonetheless, Nell is dead. Curiosity, narrative and otherwise, seems to be exhausted. "And now the bell—the bell she had so often heard, by night and day, and listened to with solemn pleasure almost as a living voice—rung its remorseless toll, for her, so young, so beautiful, so good. Decrepit age, and vigorous life, and blooming youth, and helpless infancy, poured forth . . .

18. George Cattermole, Nell dead. Wood engraving for *Master Humphrey's Clock*, 2:210. (From a copy in the Special Collections Department, William R. Perkins Library, Duke University.)

to gather round her tomb" [72, 542]. This crowd assembles to mourn the girl: not to threaten her and certainly not to demand further signs of life. This bell, though a "living voice," announces only her end.

London's Heart

The "impenetrable mystery" of Nell in the shop must be followed through to the formal and moral resolution of Nell among the graves. Quilp's—or London's—culpability is to this extent secondary, included within the allegory rather than the motive force behind it. There is another craving for death in the book: Dickens's, maybe the reader's. "What draws the reader to the novel is the hope of warming his shivering life with a death he reads about."[28] One does not have to leave the inner level of the book—the tale within the tale—to observe Dickens opening up other, less oppressive options for the city dweller. A likely path is suggested by the comic cockney ne'er-do-well, Dick Swiveller. While working for the Brasses, Swiveller meets the Marchioness (Quilp's bastard). He notes the little girl peering at him through a keyhole (an eye "gleaming and glistening," observant like Nell's) and hauls her into the room. He christens her with an aristocratic title, teaches her to play cards, and finds himself entranced with his discovery: " 'This Marchioness,' said Mr. Swiveller, folding his arms, 'is a very extraordinary person—surrounded by mysteries, ignorant of the taste of beer, unacquainted with her own name (which is less remarkable), and taking a limited view of society through the keyholes of doors—can these things be her destiny, or has some unknown person started an opposition to the decrees of fate? It is a most inscrutable and unmitigated staggerer!' " [*OCS*, 58, 432]. Swiveller establishes an identity for the servant girl, pulling her up from the underground where she has hitherto made her home and endowing her with name, skills, and purpose. This act of speculation, of creation, has no terminal point, as Humphrey's seems to. "For half the night, or more" after the mystery has worked its way into his mind, Swiveller plays the same tune over and over on his flute (the air, appropriately, is "Away with melancholy"), "never leaving off, save for a minute or two at a time to take breath and soliloquise about the Marchioness" [58, 433]. Thus he seems to have "exhausted his several subjects of meditation." Not really, though. The Marchioness returns Dick's compliment by saving his life. Swiveller's mastery of the doubletake returns full force: " 'It's an Arabian Night; that's what it is,' said Richard. 'I'm in Damascus or Grand Cairo. The Marchioness is a Genie.' . . . Not feeling quite satisfied with this explanation, as, even taking it to be the correct one, it still involved a little mystery and doubt, Mr. Swiveller raised the curtain again, determined to take the first favourable opportunity of addressing his companion" [64, 475–76]. This imaginative game can always be renewed. At the end of the novel, when Dick renames the Marchioness, "he decided in favour of [the name] Sophronia Sphynx, as being euphonious and genteel, and furthermore indicative of mystery" [73, 551].

Dick's fascination with the Marchioness (she is "surrounded by mysteries" [*OCS*, 58, 432], her identity and fate are an unfathomable enigma) parodies Humphrey's obsession with Nell. The parody becomes the basis for a reversal, a swivel away from death. One might even suppose that the values of *The Old Curiosity Shop* come to reside in the Swiveller-Marchioness romance, a position Garrett Stewart has argued at length.[29] There is reason to be cautious here. Dickens is no doubt fond of his eccentric lovers, but the protest implied by his regard for them would need further development to claim as much weight as Nell's excruciating, novel-long demise. It is not until the return to Humphrey, at the very end of the narrative, that Dickens's descent into death finally corrects itself.

"It remains . . ." writes Dickens in his "Chapter the Last," "to dismiss the leaders of the little crowd who have borne us company upon the road" [*OCS,* 547]. He dismisses not only the crowd but the structure that originally made possible an interpretation of it. The curiosity shop disappears "like a tale that is told"; even its location is forgotten, lying somewhere under the route of a "fine broad road" [555]. Though the urban crowd, with this road, seems to achieve a rather brutal dominance, neither characters nor shop are any longer necessary as a protection from it. The last inset woodcut of the novel shows Nell wafted to Heaven by a surrounding company of angels, the most idealized crowd that Dickens has yet proposed. Tucked into the bottom, left-hand corner of this vignette is the ecclesiastical and picturesque village where Nell expired. Even this last semblance of architectural support is left behind.

Turn the page, however: in *Master Humphrey's Clock,* though not in the single-issue *The Old Curiosity Shop,* there appears an epilogue where the shop is replaced by a grander mediating structure and a connection with urban realities is thus confirmed. Humphrey and his friends hear "the deep and distant bell of St. Paul's," then fall into conversation on it. The old man tells of a recent visit to this "great machine" (both bell and clock). He imagines Wren, musing "as I did now, upon his work, and [losing] himself amid its vast extent." What does the creator feel, dwarfed by his own creation? "I imagined [Wren] far more melancholy than proud, and looking with regret upon his labour done." Humphrey, too, continues to be melancholy; he is recognizably the same character as when the book began, but the telling of his tale has altered his perspective on London. Ascending to the bell, he hears its "regular and never-changing voice, that one deep constant note, uppermost amongst all the noise and clatter in the streets below—marking that, let that tumult rise or fall, . . . it still performed its functions with the same dull constancy. . . . Calm and unmoved amidst the scenes that darkness favours, the great heart of London throbs in its Giant breast" [*MHC,* 2: 225–26: Cf. the bell that tolled for Nell, a sign of death rather than of life].

One might say: Humphrey is able to experience the city as something other than a phantasmagoric nightmare because he is higher up than he was at the book's beginning, because the crowd is subsumed within a panorama. The figure of the crowd is not so much mastered, then, as simply abandoned; no longer personified in Quilp, the passing faces that haunted the pedestrian are now dispersed through the sleeping city. This is part of the truth, I think; however, there is another side to Dickens's argument.[30] Humphrey in the opening chapters had only two choices: either to linger with his fantasies of burial alive ("dead but conscious"—as in *OCS*, 1, 1) or to push those fantasies on to Nell sleeping in the shop and Quilp leering over her. Once he gets through the pursuit of Nell's death, a third possibility opens up. The symbiosis of victim and victimizer seems less pertinent than before. Humphrey can live in London without yielding to a need for total control. He fails to achieve an occult harmony with city and cathedral—even Wren felt St. Paul's a thing apart from him—he does not become a good Quasimodo to counter Quilp's bad one, but neither does his morbidity shut him off from the world. He will "have some thought for the meanest wretch that passes"—which is to say, the act of looking that began in curiosity must go on, must continue from this point, must bring him back to the world he wanted to escape, or from which he only wanted to express his distance. The allegory that denied London is finally used to affirm it.

Peripheries are important. This epilogue to *The Old Curiosity Shop* proper—Humphrey standing inside the clock-bell—recalls (with a difference) the image that announced *Master Humphrey's Clock,* where Boz opened the timepiece of the title. Boz was able to allow his creations their autonomy without feeling terrorized: he released them into the world. Humphrey, conversely, allows the autonomous and alien presence of London to enter his mind until he no longer feels the need to resist it. When he returns home, he nods off by the fireplace—inspiring a last plate and a proof of the reconciliation between novelist and narrator. (See fig. 19.) "An illustration deserving special examination is the tailpiece for the chapter immediately following the end of 'The Old Curiosity Shop,' where the artist [Phiz] has depicted Master Humphrey in his arm-chair, surrounded by Lilliputian figures, among which can be recognized some of the principal actors in the story."[31] Humphrey shares at last in the triumph of the original prospectus. The willful and active creator before the novel is complemented by the dreamer after it, and dreamer, conversely, by creator. These two personages are reconciled at last, brought together by the narration of Nell's death and its London aftermath.

Which is not to say that the novel has arrived at a definitive resolution. In the Preface to the first bound edition of *Master Humphrey's Clock,* Dickens avers that during the excitement of his labors he "has forgotten that like one whose vision is disordered he may be conjuring up bright figures where there is nothing but empty space" [*MHC*, 1: iii]. The creator with creatures wonders if the novel is not after all a phantasm: a meaningless dream rather than a figure for that world which lies outside his imagination. In other words, if Humphrey is like him, then he may be more like Humphrey than he would wish.[32] This flash of doubt is more

19. Phiz [Hablôt Browne], Humphrey dreaming. Wood engraving for
Master Humphrey's Clock, 2:228. (From a copy in the Special Collections
Department, William R. Perkins Library, Duke University.)

than a staged announcement; it is part of that same indecision (see Forster's
description) that led to the creation of Humphrey in the first place. City
and mind are powers that answer to one another, but not without the most
delicate adjustments. And none of these adjustments will last for good.
Dickens acknowledges the worries that were earlier transferred to Humphrey; he admits them as a necessary part of his endeavor in writing
novels. There will be other imagined deaths; he, and his readers with him,
will seek once again to warm their hands. The death of Paul Dombey is
just a few years away. The pursuit of the crowd continues indefinitely,
extended through a realm that lies between rhetoric and the material
world.

It is possible to be impatient with this sort of thing: "What modern
European artist, Sinyavsky implies the question, takes art *really seriously?*
The cozy bourgeois picture that shows Dickens surrounded by his 'creations' reveals how little he really believed in them. An icon of Gogol
terrified by the homunculi he saw crawling from his imaginative retort
would be a very different matter."[33] Cozy bourgeois pictures can indeed

be superficial, decorative mystifications of a cruel world—but when they are pictures of Dickens, or pictures associated with him, one should perhaps think twice about their uses. Pace Sinyavsky, Russian novelists have no monopoly on suffering or authenticity. And even the coziest pictures can have pleasures beyond their apparent ones. In *The Old Curiosity Shop,* above all, the creator with creatures is an image earned: it is taken apart, then reassembled, grasped as it never could have been if the writer had only dreamed it in its nightmare form and jumped back screaming. Courbet called his *Studio of the Painter* (another depiction of the melancholic creator) a "real allegory." I would say of Dickens that he creates a real allegory but an allegory nonetheless, and that in this apparent contradiction there lies the significant power of his work.

6. Repeating the Singular in *Martin Chuzzlewit*

IN THE 1820S AND 1830S, advanced social thinkers struggled toward a way to imagine society's interdependence, the participation of its members in some kind of overall agreement. Philosophers like Comte and Mill called their versions of this idea "consensus."[1] It is possible to trace the lure of consensus through all sorts of elevated circles, including Mill's *Westminster Review,* but my concern here will be with a less rarefied milieu. As recent writers have noted, consensus is often embodied in the artifacts of popular culture; it is figured, for instance, by urban panoramas.[2] Thomas Hornor's Panorama of London—perhaps the best-known example—allowed the viewer to look out over the metropolis, surveying London effortlessly from the height of a simulated St. Paul's.[3] This spectacle demonstrates two ways in which views can become images of consensus. Hornor places his viewer centrally (Where better to see the city than just here?); he insists that the parts of the view form a whole accessible to observation.[4] A spectator can inspect this London so thoroughly *because* it is presented consensually, its center universally acknowledged, its peripheral elements thriving in orderly subordination.

Politically, the late 1820s and early 1830s were shaped by consensus: Hornor's Panorama, in other words, was very much a creature of its cultural moment. The succeeding period, the 1840s, showed little evidence of widespread agreement on any level. Great Britain was governed in these years through a series of alliances and rivalries more bizarre, less stable, than any other political dispensations during Dickens's life. "The surface of a single constitution masked diversities of institutions and manners for which a confederation were better suited."[5] To put this statement in terms of consensus and the panorama: there was no agreed-upon center from which to see or speak, nor did the fragments of the political order cohere in any very reassuring or plausible way.

Under such circumstances, the status of panoramas was bound to be called into question. In the early forties it was Dickens who did so most effectively. *Martin Chuzzlewit* (1843–44) affords an outstanding example of a consensual view that is mocked (on the roof of Todgers's boarding-house), then reconstructed (at the death of Jonas Chuzzlewit). My goal is to trace the narrative progress from one of these moments to the other, with special emphasis on a pun often favored by English-language writers. A crazily anarchic urban panorama expresses, in Wordsworth's phrase, "the strife of singularity"—the strife, that is, of a city whose parts have no clear relation to a whole and whose more aggressive inhabitants all claim to inhabit a central position.[6] Dickens gets past such potential blocks to consensus; he proposes that *the singular can be repeated.* Enacted by linked characters—Jonas and Mrs. Gamp—the repetition of the singular produces a fresh panorama of London, also a fresh approach to political and social agreements.

A Singular Sort of Place

I will start with a brief history of singularity, anticipating ways in which the singular might subvert or support—might in either case transform—the method of consensus formation described above: Then we can turn to the description of Todgers's in *Chuzzlewit,* where Dickens's experiments with singularity and the panorama start taking shape. The scientific use of the singular is first established by Bacon, whose *Novum organum* proposes a "particular natural history" of that "which is new, rare, and unusual." Such "Singular Instances"—phenomena "of an apparently extravagant and separate nature"—are important because they prevent scientists from generalizing at too early a stage of inquiry. The *playfulness* of the singular, its joking quality, invites sustained investigation. It is only after extensive empirical study that the singular can be "reduced and comprehended under some Form or fixed Law"; once such laws are established, they will have greater validity than those more glibly proposed. Note that agreement is thus a matter of uncovering lots of data and working by a logical means toward generalizations.[7]

If we believe that facts are discrete fragments of experience that precede and shape theories, Bacon's singularities are the first facts. This cabinet-of-curiosities approach to science doesn't last long, but the lure of singularity survives the Renaissance. One place where singularity retains something of its importance is among eighteenth-century aesthetic terms: *the sublime, the grotesque, the picturesque, the beautiful,* and so forth. Barbara Stafford has argued that the singular becomes one of these categories; she shows that it signifies an aspect of human experience "rooted in the phenomenal world, which possesses its own vitality, vividness and intensity." Stafford emphasizes several types of singularity: pieces, lumps or heaps, and fragments. Each is remarkable for being located within a landscape while *standing out* from it. This is an adaptation—not a very drastic one, it seems—of a Baconian idea, but there is one respect in which the new singularities are more problematic than Bacon's. As in Bacon, the inquirer intuits the presence and principles of a vital material world; he grasps a reality apart from the psychology of self, explicable on the basis of logic and law. In order to get this far, however, he allows himself to become absorbed in what he sees "to such a point that the obliteration of his own identity results." The point, then, is not just that singularities compel a determined investigation of the material world but also that this investigation occurs under peculiarly difficult conditions and at the cost of individual consciousness: that is, of subjectivity as a governing principle of knowledge.[8]

The new singularity, where psychology is first crucial, then heavily at risk and possibly irrelevant, does not completely replace the Baconian tradition. Throughout *The Origin of Species* (1859), Darwin is struck by "singular facts in nature," facts often associated with "singular . . . laws." Darwin's play with the singular is in many respects reminiscent of the *Novum organum,* privileging the same techniques of generalization from a wide field of data (note the carefully chosen citations of Whewell and Bacon, opposite the title page of the *Origin*).[9] However, while Darwin's move from fact to theory compelled widespread assent—here, if anywhere in the nineteenth century, is an instance of popular scientific rhetoric establishing a new consensus[10]—his accomplishment could not be replicated in every field. Dickens, most particularly, dwells on situations that produce facts plentiful to the point of inexhaustibility, yet because of their plentifulness uncertain; the status of facts is at issue, as well as the connection between original data and a wider view. There are moments at which Dickens wants to dismiss facts altogether: *Hard Times* (1854) offers a strange instance, to whose complexities I cannot do justice here. Elsewhere—perhaps most interestingly—Dickens faces facts. A singularity becomes important to him so far as it performs two related functions. Singularity is a way of emphasizing the brute, material, irreducible nature of the factual; it is a way of confirming the *existence* of facts at a moment when their status begins to seem like a difficulty. Bacon invented facts; Dickens wants to *reinvent* them. At the same time, singularities offer reassurance that so far as one is willing to pay a price—to stop making subjectivity, individual experience, a priority—there might still be a way of getting from the singular to the general. One needs facts because they form the best, perhaps the only, stable basis for agreement. A consensus based on singularities could turn out to be more valid and more durable than a consensus based on ideology. The danger is that the maneuvers necessary for moving from singularity to consensus might involve a debilitating irrationality: in other words, the joke might get out of hand, facts and fear might genuinely consort together. This point will be taken up again later on.

"Surely there never was"—begins chapter 9 of *Chuzzlewit*—"in any other borough, city, or hamlet in the world, such a singular sort of place as Todgers's. And surely London, to judge from that part of it which hemmed Todgers's round . . . qualified to be on terms of close relationship and alliance with hundreds and thousands of the odd family to which Todgers's belonged" [*MC*, 9, 127]. This statement is slippery. Todgers's seems to be singular in all the standard dictionary senses: it is unusual, unique, and considered as an individual. Then come a series of classifications and reclassifications. Todgers's belongs to London, or rather to a particular part of London, and that part, or rather London, is worthy of Todgers's, or rather of Todgers's "family." If Dickens begins by reasoning on the individuality of Todgers's, he ends by reasoning on the metropolis at large. When the singular Todgers's multiplies, its vital relation to the whole is thereby confirmed. Todgers's can be pursued through many shifting contexts. The final result is that it blends into the city of which it is part without losing its celebrated eccentricity. It draws attention to itself and it also reveals London. So, at least, Dickens seems to promise.

Before his apparent promise can be confirmed, he must find his way to Todgers's through the neighborhood that surrounds it. This enterprise becomes a kind of preparation, for it enables the novelist to focus on one oddity after another, where each is treated as though it is singular yet plural. There are "strange solitary pumps . . . hiding themselves for the most part in blind alleys, and keeping company with fire-ladders" [*MC*, 9, 128]. Entering this "labyrinth," "you" are lost; you keep going up dead ends and encountering there these eccentric exhibitions. The experience is frustrating, but it has its attractions. The association of pumps and fire ladders is tinged with strangeness, yet it makes good, everyday sense—not the least because it is treated as multiple. If you find a solitary pump, it will keep company with a fire ladder. The singular is placed under a generalization. Dickens is able to play up the wonder of the neighborhood and yet to imply that this wonder can be reasoned out. By concentrating on an apparently peripheral freak, the intrepid explorer finds the clue to a whole. Here is one modest way in which the workings of singularity can clarify London.

After many such moments, Dickens reaches Todgers's. The boardinghouse figures among those singularities that stand out from the whole
but also reveal it. This point is not unacknowledged by its inhabitants. Mr.
Jinkins notes that Todgers's can be true to itself, can come out as strong as
its neighbors. He prides himself on the singularity of Todgers's, even
while admitting that the boardinghouse resembles certain other establish-
ments, including "a somewhat similar [one] in Cannon Street" [*MC*, 9,
148]. "That noun of multitude or signifying many, called Todgers's" [9,
133] is both singular and typical, as were so many things on the way to its
doors.

All these points about Todgers's are reassuring—the singularities are
no less and no more problematic than those of the *Novum organum*—but
Dickens's emphasis is elsewhere: on the scrambled view from the top of
the boardinghouse. I have already suggested that this notorious survey of
London needs to be seen in the context of its historical moment—a
moment when the panorama was still recognized as a cultural icon but was
rapidly diminishing in authority. There are many memorables images
with which Dickens's description could be compared—from Hornor's
great view to a splendid 1843 daguerrotype in the *Illustrated London News*
(issued just when *Chuzzlewit* was appearing).[11] However, the most telling
comparison—the one that defines best what Dickens was rejecting—is
with the literary bird's-eye view of *Notre-Dame*. Although the English
novelist presents his view in not much more than a paragraph and Hugo
sustains his over a long chapter, three stages mark both: a first, evasive
glance; a consideration of special features (each enumerated in its turn);
and a final circling back to the whole, now perceived by ear as well as eye.
At every stage in the sequence, Dickens denies a possibility affirmed by
Hugo:

1. Both Hugo's panorama and Dickens's burst upon the viewer after a
   challenging climb. The spectator of medieval Paris confronts "un
   éblouissement de toits, de cheminées, de rues, de ponts, de places,
   de flèches, de clochers" (a dazzlement of roofs, chimneys, streets,
   bridges, squares, spires, bell towers); the spectator of Victorian London is overwhelmed with "steeples, towers, belfries, shining vanes,
   and masts of ships." In the one case "tout vous prenait aux yeux à la
   fois" (everything struck the eye at once); in the other there is "smoke
   and noise enough for all the world at once" [*ND*, 3.2, 143; *MC*, 9,
   130]. Despite these similarities, *Notre-Dame*'s view promises another
   issue than *Chuzzlewit*'s. Hugo anticipates a rationalization of the

view: it will come clear, its shape will eventually be seen. The only reassurance Dickens gives assumes a peculiar form. He conjures up the man on the Monument, "close beside you, with every hair erect upon his golden head, as if the doings of the city frightened him" [*MC*, 9, 130]. Those erect hairs are stylized representations of fire; they contribute to an elaborate allegorical structure commemorating the Great Fire and London's rebuilding. Dickens's joke is to misinterpret the allegory—as though its significance had irrevocably changed, altered from the builder's intention.

2. After his preliminary survey of Paris, Hugo notes: "Le regard se perdait longtemps à toute profondeur dans ce labyrinthe, où il n'y avait rien qui n'eût son originalité, sa raison, son génie, sa beauté, rien qui ne vînt de l'art" (The gaze long lost itself in the depths of this labyrinth, where everything had its originality, its rationale, its genius, its beauty, everything had proceeded from art) [*ND*, 3.2, 144]. The viewer's bewilderment is due to conflicting bids for attention; such conflicts stem, however, from the aesthetic integrity of all that can be seen. Confusion on these terms is hardly to be feared; order pervades this embarassment of riches, for "c'était une ville homogène" (it was an homogenous city) [3.2, 155]. Medieval buildings submit, as it were, to remain subordinate features within a whole. A good cross-reference is afforded by a Hugo text of 1841, a description of a coat of arms: "des détails singuliers commencèrent à se détacher de cet ensemble mêlé et obscur, . . . curiosité s'éveilla vivement, l'attention qui se fixe est comme une lumière, et la tapisserie, se débrouillant peu à peu, finit par . . . apparaître dans son entier" (singular details began to detach themselves from this mixed and obscure whole, . . . curiosity awoke sharply, the power of attention that focuses itself is like a light, and the tapestry, clearing up little by little, finished by appearing in its entirety).[12] In the view of the medieval city, as in the inspection of the medieval coat of arms, singularity contributes to a sense of wholeness. Furthermore, even if the parts of *Notre-Dame*'s Paris were to be more assertive or distinct, the viewing platform posited by Hugo would remain the most powerfully integrative building imaginable. Very little confidence, by contrast, can be derived from a vantage point like Mrs. Todgers's boardinghouse. Dickens's choice of Todgers's as a point of observation is one of the great comic gestures in his fiction: as though he were asking, "Now what can I learn by ascending to *this* ridiculous location?"—not, however, in a condescending, but in a genuinely explor-

atory way.[13] His initial answers are appropriately alarming. "After the first glance, there were slight features . . . which sprung out from the mass without any reason." Three such manifestations are mentioned—the chimney pots whisper to each other or maliciously block out the prospect; a man mending a pen at the window retires, leaving "a blank in it, ridiculously disproportionate" [*MC*, 9, 130]; the gambols of a piece of cloth distract us from the crowd. As in the walk below, trivial details (instead of harmonious artworks) demand attention. Their singularity is insisted on more than ever—except that they now compete with one another. They do not imply or signify the whole, but merely distract from it. The conspiratorial chimney pots, the gamboling cloth, and, perhaps most maddeningly, the blank left by the man at the window are appearances that express themselves alone.[14]

3. Hugo's great bird's-eye view ends with a tirade against modern Paris: a tirade to be developed in Frollo's prophecy, "Ceci tuera cela." All the same, Hugo concludes, there is one aspect of the view that has survived. His bird's-eye view culminates in the Parisian symphony of bells, pealing out on the morning of a church festival. The move from seeing to hearing, the novelist implies, is a movement from reason to faith. He claims that there are moments when the ear itself seems to see.[15] This dispensation is celebrated by the bells, "ce tumulte de cloches et de sonneries," "ce tutti des clochers" (this tumult of bells and chimes; this tutti of bell towers) [*ND*, 3.2, 159–60]. Yes: Hugo is depending on an historical nostalgia that his novel will not sustain. However, that complication barely enters into this particular section. Though Paris's visible unity has long since been lost, for the moment it lives again—a repetition constructed in tolling or chiming "vibrations sonores." No such thing happens at Todgers's, despite a plethora of churches and bells in the immediate vicinity.[16] There is an immediate collapse of decipherable appearances. "Even while the looker-on felt angry with himself [for his irrational interest in singularities] and wondered how it was, the tumult swelled into a roar" [*MC*, 9, 130]. A tumult (Hugo's word also) is both seen and heard. Let it go unattended while one studies singularities and it becomes a roar. The viewer shifts from eye to ear—and then back to eye, objects thickening and expanding all around, a visual accompaniment to the roar. Their multiplication is different than the one offered by Hugo's chiming bells. Far from returning a spectator to the whole, the view from Todgers's reveals further singularities—each of which insists on re-

maining independent from any larger pattern. One might say: This is the negative side of consensus. The parts must be somehow related, since it is the concentration on one fragment that calls forth the others—and yet the pattern, the meaning, of this interdependence remains obscure; any sense of a totality is destroyed. Unsuspecting tourists may well end up hurling themselves into the street (so suggests a half-facetious prediction by Dickens's "looker-on," 9, 130). Otherwise they will retreat, no better informed than previously.[17]

Retrospectively, Dickens's early success at confronting singularities (solitary fire pumps, etc.) appears little more than a trick. He is unable to complete a survey of singular fragments or a survey from a singular perspective. One demand on attention leads to others, a process that ends badly. However, though the unfortunate tourist may retire, the novelist does nothing of the sort. He is persistent about studying this kind of landscape, a point expressed by a document closely connected with *Chuzzlewit.* The Preface to the novel's "Charles Dickens edition" (1867) asserts that "what is exaggeration to one class of minds and perceptions, is plain truth to another. That which is commonly called a long-sight, perceives in a prospect innumerable features and bearings non-existent to a short-sighted person" [*MC,* xiv].[18] Dickens is committed to the merits of long sight, even if long sight remains unsupported—unstabilized—by the weight of communal synthesis or established authority, as at Saint Paul's and Notre-Dame. When he acts on this commitment, he has one advantage that his suicidal view seeker lacks. If Dickens remains attracted to a freakish vantage point of the kind represented by Todger's; if he feels the need to torment himself with undecipherable but weirdly compelling fragments, like the disappearing man in the window; if he chooses this droll point of view and this absurd, apparently disastrous means of relating parts to whole; then there is still a path toward rendering the view usable. The vista observed from Todgers's already contains one allegorical element, Wren's marker of the Great Fire (a devastation that necessitated the building of a new city). After the collapse of the panorama in chapter 9, Dickens argues that the view itself can be treated as a figure—can be subjected to an allegorical reading that prepares for his own reconstruction of London. Allegory becomes a means for situating singularities within a view—and thus of defining the conditions, the grounds, of consensus.

Dickens's reconstructive allegory gains momentum slowly; indeed, there are moments in which to admit the singularity of an action or a character is to stop discussion rather than to stimulate it: e.g., when

Martin calls his grandfather a "singular character" [*MC*, 14, 244], he is using the adjective as a way of avoiding reflection on his own, dubious behavior. Singularity can function as a joke, a freak, that doesn't need explaining. Nonetheless, an allegory of the singular becomes the representative accomplishment in *Chuzzlewit*. Dickens explores the relation of part and whole by reference to Jonas Chuzzlewit, the determination that any place can be a center by reference to Sarah Gamp. I will begin with Jonas, whose narrative and allegorical function is fairly easy to establish, then show how Gamp's dilemmas, which often appear extraneous, become entangled with his. There will be reminiscences of Todgers's—windows, fires, blanks, tumults—throughout. The novelist keeps harking back to his singular panorama while he explores the energies involved in relating parts to wholes and in keeping oneself centrally positioned. Then he combines those energies; he arranges for Jonas to form a partnership with Gamp.[19] The occult sympathy between these two—they virtually switch identities—prepares the way for other people to function on the basis of shared assumptions, common agreements. It also produces a survey of London, a *chimed* panorama like *Notre-Dame*'s, though Dickens's bells have another source than church towers.

Jonas's Singular Inquiry (Part and Whole)

Jonas begins his career as a decoder of singularities in the novel's eighth installment. This section of *Martin Chuzzlewit* starts with these words:

> *Change begets change. Nothing propagates so fast. If a man habituated to a narrow circle of cares and pleasures, out of which he seldom travels, step beyond it, though for never so brief a space, his departure from the monotonous scene on which he has been an actor of importance, would seem to be the signal for instant confusion. As if, in the gap he had left, the wedge of change were driven to the head, rending what was a solid mass to fragments, things cemented and held together by the usages of years, burst asunder in as many weeks. . . .*
>
> *Most men, at one time or other, have proved this in some degree. The extent to which the natural laws of change asserted their supremacy in that limited sphere of action which Martin had deserted, shall be faithfully set down in these pages.*
>
> *"What a cold spring it is!" whimpered old Anthony, drawing near the evening fire. "It was a warmer season, sure, when I was young!"*
>
> *"You needn't go scorching your clothes into holes, whether it was or*

[*MC*, 18, 298]

not," observed the amiable Jonas, raising his eyes from yesterday's newspaper.

A compressed but crucial passage: it links the view from Todgers's with a principle of plot; it insists that the protagonist of that plot is Jonas rather than young Martin. I will expand on each of these points.

First, Dickens not only recollects but tries to rationalize the urban panorama described in chapter 9.[20] From Todgers's the tourist could see a man who mended a pen at a window, leaving on his disappearance an "exorbitant blank." Following a scrutiny of the blank and other singularities, he found that the view returned—but returned, unfortunately, as an overwhelming, inarticulate roar. Perhaps, Dickens now implies, a "natural law" could render this kind of collapse less inexplicable than it seems. Most especially: by *narrating* a survey of singularities, setting it down as a sequence of events rather than as a virtually simultaneous spectacle, one might come to comprehend it in terms of governing rules; one might grasp it as something other than an incoherent medley of details that self-destructs for no apparent reason.

Second, Dickens initially insists that events in England are the result of Martin's departure for America. There follows an account of Anthony Chuzzlewit's death, *not* an effect of Martin's departure but another blank in the scene with its own effects. Dickens continues to pursue the American side of his story, which features Martin's Bunyanesque progress toward self-knowledge; at the same time, Jonas's less traditional progress operates independently of it. Pecksniff responds to a question from Jonas, "what a very singular inquiry!"—to which his prospective son-in-law replies, "Now, don't you mind whether it's a singular inquiry or a plural one" [*MC*, 20, 326]. His pun portends his future. He repeats a singular inquiry till he reaches a knowledge of plural (ultimately, consensual) realities.[21]

There are three main phases in the narrative by which Jonas learns to understand city views. Each is concerned with the Todgers's-like riddle of a man in a window; each leads toward that deathly understanding typical of urban allegory. The first phase begins when Jonas puts poison in the desk of his father, Anthony, hoping that the old man will take it accidentally. On the morning when Anthony seems to be dying from poison, Jonas pretends that everything is normal. Everything is not normal. The hours are shot through with bizarre omens, culminating in "an apparition . . . so ghastly to the view that Jonas shrieked aloud." Anthony hobbles before them, "gabbling in an unearthly tongue," his appearance expressing "one word—Death." In the concluding sentences of the chapter, "they put [Anthony] in his easy-chair and wheeled it near the window," much as though he were a convalescent [*MC*, 18, 308–9]. Anthony's presence near the window with fresh breezes blowing over him, only emphasizes his failing powers. The window offers a bigger world outside, but offers it too late. Death cannot be denied, neither by the father nor the son, nor even by the faithful retainer Chuffey. This singularity demands attention and gets it, in Jonas's shriek, in his increasing anxiety once the body has been removed, in his need for anybody—Pecksniff even—to stay with him until the funeral is over.

The second phase of Jonas's progress emerges indirectly from the first but takes much longer to develop. It starts when Jonas goes to buy his wife an insurance policy and discovers that he is dealing with an old acquaintance, the con man Montague Tigg.

> "*Well, never mind him,*" *said Jonas [of his father].* "*He's dead, and there's no help for it.*"
>
> "*Dead, is he!*" *cried Tigg.* "*Venerable old gentleman, is he dead! You're very like him.*"
>
> *Jonas received this compliment with anything but a good grace; . . . [Tigg] perceived it, and tapping him familiarly on the sleeve, beckoned him to the window. From this moment, Mr. Montague's jocularity and flow of spirits were remarkable.*

[MC, 27, 444]

Anthony is dead, and Jonas is very much like him. Jonas does not take kindly to this insight. He is as yet unprepared to grasp its truth. An intermediary is needed, a dead man between the father's death and the son's. Unintentionally Montague steps into this role. He has discovered that he is not to talk about Anthony, that Anthony has become a forbidden subject. As if on cue he becomes a man in a window who compels the fascinated scrutiny of Jonas Chuzzlewit. "Jonas stared at him in amazement. . . . Jonas looked at him harder and harder," etc., while Montague calls attention to the "crowded street," "the multitude without," tempting Jonas to invest in his company and thus exploit the city [27, 444–45]. Surely (it might be objected) Montague's move to the window right after he drops the forbidden subject is only a coincidence. A thousand-page novel is likely to contain many windows and even more characters. There is no reason to suppose that Montague will die, merely because he has strayed in front of a convenient aperture where Jonas Chuzzlewit stares at him, nor that his death will have any link with Anthony's. On the other hand, this arbitrariness suits the spirit of the novel and especially the spirit of the view from Todgers's. A singularity absorbs the mind whether one will or no. A singularity is initially inexplicable, and therefore it puts the viewer in a mood where any explanation is a relief. Jonas may refuse to think about Anthony. In that case he will have to think about Montague and indeed about the London of which there are tantalizing glimpses outside the window. One process of inquiry is assumed into a second, more powerful form.

Once Montague thus diverts Jonas's attention, he finds ways to keep it diverted. Montague makes sure of his new partner's loyalty by blackmailing him. They both believe that Jonas has killed his father; Montague threatens to publish this fact. If Jonas wants Montague to remain quiet, he must invest heavily in the firm and bring other investors along with him. Jonas hates his persecutor. By a series of agonizing mental steps he decides on murdering him. He was able to work toward his father's death without giving a name to the deed and without actually doing anything, aside from buying poison and planting it. Montague's end is not accomplished so easily. Both murderer and victim are obsessed with the blank that Anthony made, but the real issue, barely disguised, is the blank that will follow on Montague's removal. This death is attained through a series of visions whose goal is less surprising than the landscape along the way. One part of Jonas works his motives out of the other part. When he and Montague drive together through a thunderstorm, "the eye, partaking of the quickness of the flashing light, saw in its every gleam a multitude of objects which it could not see at steady noon in fifty times that period. Bells in steeples, with the rope and wheel that moved them; ragged nests of birds in cornices and nooks; faces full of consternation in the tilted waggons that came tearing past" [*MC*, 42, 646]. In a sort of freeze-frame, Montague discovers Jonas "making as if he would aim a blow at his head." Jonas's guilty secret flashes out of him like lightning. His suppressed aggression envelops the scene, revealing itself to Montague, who then wants to suppress his new knowledge just as Jonas might. This is the oddest part: for both of them Jonas's murderous desires become "a secret which [they] knew, and yet did not know" [42, 652]. Montague has good reason to suspect Jonas, but the victim, like his murderer-to-be, cannot acknowledge the truth.

A singularity has become plural: Anthony's death has engendered the necessity of Montague's. This repetition is articulated by bells. Under the lightning, Jonas and Tigg see "bells in steeples, with the rope and wheel that moved them" [*MC*, 42, 646]. At an inn, after the storm, Montague dreams that "the secret was discovered": when he wakes to find Jonas standing over him he pulls "the bell-rope violently." Jonas stutters that "there's—there's no bell in my room" [42, 653]. A little later, when Jonas is still nearer to murder, he hears "the ringers . . . proclaim it in a crowd of voices to all the town!" [46, 718–19]. Finally, Jonas dreams of bells. He is in "a strange city, where the names of the streets were written on the walls in characters quite new to him; which gave him no surprise or uneasiness, for he remembered in his dream to have been there before. Although these streets were very precipitous, insomuch that to get from one to another it was necessary to descend great heights by ladders that were too short, and ropes that moved deep bells, and swung and swayed as they were clung to, the dangers gave him little emotion beyond the first thrill of terror" [47, 721]. Down Jonas goes, clutching the insufficient ladders and the ropes that move "deep" bells. Their deepness is in tone but also implies a mixed-up sense of direction, as though the bells were beneath Jonas. The strangely muted ringing in the bell city assembles "great crowds." Jonas stands in a porch, "fearfully surveying the multitude." He has a companion who is "constantly changing, and was never the same man two minutes to-gether"; eventually he fixes on a "struggling head" amidst the crowd, closing on him in a deadly confrontation. Once again the figure—so fixed, so concentrated upon despite all the weird metamorphoses of the dream—will leave a blank. This time Jonas says the meaning of the blank and glories in the saying. He is roused to a more vivid state of consciousness than in his previous attempt at homicide. "Aye! He made no compromise, and held no secret with himself now. Murder. He had come to do it" [47, 722]. Jonas is ready to murder Montague Tigg.

A Singular Old Female (Centrality)

When Jonas repeats a singularity, he strains toward his own identification with it. Eventually he himself will become the man in the window, effecting a blank within it by the efficient means of suicide. However, before he reaches this third phase of his progress, another character modi-fies his fate. Jonas's actions alone will not illuminate the atmosphere of agreement so ominously hinted at in the dream city, where fragments fly together instead of apart; to an understanding of his struggle must be added an understanding of Mrs. Gamp's. To sum up in advance the contrast between them: he is obsessed by a singularity and must therefore repeat it. She is a singularity already; she repeats herself. He moves toward a moment of illumination, where consciousness and conscience will sur-prise him. She blots out as much of her mind as she can, becoming an object more than a subject, a problem for others to deal with. He hears bells and feels guilt. She does neither, clinging to a hard-won lack of conscience. Dickens occasionally hints that the opposition could collapse, that Gamp could become like Jonas (and vice versa), but this won't happen until the novel's last chapters. Meanwhile Jonas and Gamp remain an opposed pair, each allowing the other wonderful opportunities to manifest his nature.

Gamp's special qualities are evident from her first appearance. Each time she comes on the scene, she acts out her identity with admirable, maddening thoroughness: evoking piously "this Piljian's Projiss of a mortal wale"; reciting Mrs. Harris's ecstatic praise of her, meditating on her deceased husband's wooden leg; describing the precise amount of liquor she takes "when I am indisposged" [*MC*, 25, 404–6]. Dickens hardly needs to point out that this is "a carefully regulated routine." Mrs. Gamp's primary function in life is to generate business and more business, a feat accomplished by publicity in the form of carefully directed repetitions. (Cf. the endeavors of the Anglo-Bengalee Insurance Company, a kind of institutionalized Mrs. Gamp.[22]) Faulkner said in an interview that he approved of Mrs. Gamp because she "coped with life, didn't ask any favors, never whined."[23] To which it might be replied: she copes with life by strategic whining. A character who dwells on her own "minutest singularities" (H. F. Chorley's phrase, echoing, as will be seen, one of Dickens's) might well possess an advantage over others. Because she fabricates endless variations on a few set themes, because she is able to appear "strikingly characteristic," Mrs. Gamp is perfectly adapted to the city where she prevails.[24]

Dickens articulates the antithesis between public, unflappable Gamp and secretive, guilty Jonas throughout a memorable series of scenes. The first occurs in the second half of chapter 25, where Mrs. Gamp displays an unusual vulnerability. Sarah makes her way to the Bull in Holborn, where her extra job, approved by Mould, awaits her. "She groaned her admiration so audibly, that they [the proprietor and others] all turned around. Mrs. Gamp felt the necessity of advancing, bundle in hand, and introducing herself." She gives what she regards as her "inauguration address," establishing her qualifications. Then she sweeps up to the room of her patient, the feverish Lewsome, where she is subjected to some unexpected pressures. As Dickens has taken some pains to observe, there is a "little cracked bell" in the shop where Sarah has her lodgings. The bell rouses neighbors or a caged sparrow. Everyone mistakes it for a fire alarm, except Mrs. Gamp. She invariably sleeps through it. She has no fear, no consciousness, of possible disaster—and yet, on this particular night, she is "glad to see a parapidge, in case of fire, and lots of roofs and chimney-pots to walk upon" [*MC, 25, 411*]. Whatever the source of this uneasiness—perhaps Old Chuffey, left all alone in the City—there now commences a remarkable counterpoint.

Gamp orders dinner (and "moralises" about cucumbers), then settles in for the evening. "Oh, weary, weary hour! Oh, haggard mind, groping darkly through the past." This apostrophe produces a little frisson, for it follows immediately upon the description of Mrs. Gamp's bedtime ablutions and seems a description of her dreams. No such thing. Within seven or eight lines a "he" is mentioned—Lewsome. Lewsome knows that Jonas attempted Anthony's murder; he would tell if he could but he can't. He begins babbling to invisible companions, occasioning interjections by Mrs. Gamp:

> *"What's the matter now?" said Mrs Gamp.*
>
> *"They're coming four abreast, each man with his arm entwined in the next man's, and his hand upon his shoulder. What's that upon the arm of every man, and on the flag?"*
>
> *"Spiders, p'raps," said Mrs Gamp.*
>
> *"Crape! Black crape! Good God! why do they wear it outside?"*
>
> *"Would you have 'em carry black crape in their insides?" Mrs Gamp retorted. "Hold your noise, hold your noise."*

[*MC, 25, 414–15*]

Mrs. Gamp has heard this sort of thing often. She has no particular interest in it. Let the marchers carry black crape wherever they want (even in their insides: what an absurd idea!). No matter how endlessly they stream on, they will not bother *her*. And yet, Lewsome's ravings do register somewhere in her mind. When Mrs. Gamp dozes off once more, she is awakened by Lewsome's cry of "Chuzzlewit." She expects "to find the passage filled with people, come to tell her that the house in the City had taken fire [cf. the man on the Monument with his flamelike hair]. . . . She opened the window, and looked out. Dark, dull, dingy, and desolate house-tops." The view lies inert. Only the "ringing" in her ears creates a disturbance. "It seemed to make the wery bottles ring." She imagines herself to have been dreaming of "that dratted Chuffey." Lewsome's guilty dreams about Jonas have prompted a fantasy that belongs to Mrs. Gamp: will Chuffey go up in flames while she is away and an accusing crowd appear to tell her of this disaster? The thought is passing, for "a pinch of snuff, and the song of the steaming kettle, quite restored the tone of Mrs. Gamp's nerves, which were none of the weakest." Though Lewsome again cries "Chuzzlewit" and again she starts, by morning she can dismiss the night's terror. " 'But

Betsey Prig:' speaking with great feeling, and laying her hand upon her arm: 'try the cowcumbers, God bless you!'" [25, 415–17].

In chapter 25 Mrs. Gamp is drawn toward the dilemma of Jonas Chuzzlewit. Her potential vulnerability is underlined by several devices of plot: she has just come from taking care of Chuffey, who knows how Anthony died; she arrives to nurse Lewsome, who thinks he knows how Anthony died; between her anxiety over the one and her restless night with the other, she begins to show a degree of apprehension. Suppressing her guilt about Chuffey, she finds the cityscape turned to a series of malignant omens. London hovers on the verge of becoming a dream in which she will be threatened with an accuser, thus facing the dilemma of how to blot out her deeds. The process never gets this far, however. Mrs. Gamp is not a woman to carry black crape in her insides or to heed an internal warning bell. What is the means by which she keeps a hold on herself? "Cowcumbers, God bless you!" Mrs. Gamp lives by cucumbers—and Mr. Gamp's wooden leg, that memorable organ, and Mrs. Harris, and all the fetishes that she calls upon in her daily round. Todgers's-like touches such as the chimney pots may start to take on a portentous significance, but they cannot compete with Mrs. Gamp's unforgettable self. If a scream of "Chuzzlewit" intrudes on her mind, it will be promptly repulsed by cucumbers or perhaps some other charm.

The implications of the contrast between Gamp and Jonas are further explored some fifteen chapters on, where half the major characters or more meet down at the London docks. Jonas is doing his best to flee the country; Mrs. Gamp is stalking his pregnant wife (a potential customer); Nadgett the detective lurks in the background; Tom Pinch and his sister Ruth just happen to be strolling by. Everybody is abruptly brought together. The scene begins with Tom enjoying the chaos of the harbor. Mrs. Gamp elbows and umbrellas her way to a place beside them, then commences an "apostrophe" to the steamboat on which Jonas and Merry Chuzzlewit are embarking. At the moment when Gamp is pointing out Merry to Ruth, the detective prevails on Tom to deliver a message for Jonas. There follows the most striking development of all. Cowed by the letter he has received, Jonas drags his wife back to shore where his blackmailer, Montague Tigg, is waiting for him. "'Here is a very singular old female dropping curtseys on my right,' said Montague, breaking off in his discourse, and looking at Mrs. Gamp, 'who is not a friend of mine. Does anybody know her?'" [*MC*, 40, 630]. Mrs. Gamp begins a story about Mrs. Harris, the upshot being that Jonas entrusts her with Merry.

Tom has ended up running Gamp's errand as well as Nadgett's—the success through repetition of a singular old female. Montague (watched by Nadgett) escorts Jonas away from the docks. A barely conceivable multiplicity of events fulfills Mrs. Gamp's aspirations—while thwarting Jonas's.

The next time Mrs. Gamp appears, the antithesis is pushed even further. At Jonas's house, she celebrates the meeting "among the packages down London Bridge," then commences a new campaign. "She added daily so many strings to her bow, that she made a perfect harp of it; and upon that instrument she now began to perform an extemporaneous concerto" [*MC*, 46, 703]. Among the high points of this composition: her choking of Chuffey, her praise of the ladies present, her consumption of available rations while she pretends to make tea for the others. Mrs. Gamp's energies thus reconfirmed, Jonas enters and goes through his own routine. He snarls at the assembled party; he throws out Tom Pinch; he upbraids his wife, who protests in these terms:

> "No, indeed! I have no knowledge of these secrets, and no clue to their meaning. I have never seen [Tom] since I left home but once—but twice—before to-day."
>
> [46, 713– 14]
>
> "Oh!" sneered Jonas, catching at this correction. "But once, but twice, eh? Which do you mean? Twice and once perhaps. Three times! How many more, you lying jade? . . . How many more times?" he repeated. . . . He was about to retort upon her, when the clock struck. He started, stopped, and listened: appearing to revert to . . . a secret within his own breast.

One last time the old oppositions are confirmed. Mrs. Gamp repeats herself publicly, boldly, and to her own profit; she organizes the city around her, meanwhile suppressing any glimmers of guilt or indeed of recognizable human consciousness. Jonas, on the other hand, is lured by repetition from secret to secret; he tries to remain out of public sight while descending further into his own nasty mind and motives.

At the end of this delightful gathering, these perfect partners are planning a further venture, Chuffey's suppression. Jonas leaves Mrs. Gamp "in the act of repeating all she had been told," and repeating also the name of Mrs. Harris [*MC*, 46, 717]. As might be guessed from this curious mixture, Gamp is about to become like Jonas, Jonas like Gamp. She will experience a parodic version of his excruciating self-persecution through the medium of sinister fragments, he a nightmare version of her ability to attract attention. This mixture accomplished, Jonas will confront a *third* man in a window.

The Other Woman Appears

Just after the tea party, Jonas has his dream of bells and deep streets, following which he kills Tigg. Three chapters later, Dickens describes the "inexplicable terrors" of Mrs. Gamp's apartment—terrors to the visitor, not to the apartment's tenant. Mrs. Gamp thrives on the tokens of self that surround her: the tent bed, the elbow chairs, the perennial umbrella; portraits of herself, Mrs. Harris, and Mr. Gamp complete with wooden leg. "Towards these objects Mrs. Gamp raised her eyes in satisfaction" [*MC*, 49, 749]. A moment after, "There's the little bell a-ringing now," said Mrs. Gamp; it is not Betsey Prig, though, but Mr. Sweedlepipe. When she sees him "white as chalk," Mrs. Gamp wonders whether the Thames might be "a-fire." Sweedlepipe announces that young Bailey has passed from this earth. Gamp takes his end philosophically, though she expresses curiosity about Jonas. If bells and fire signify no more than Bailey's removal from the scene, then Sarah Gamp remains comfortably untouched.

At this point the little bell rings again, subjecting Mrs. Gamp to a harder test. Betsey Prig not only arrives but proves unaccountably hostile. Mrs. Gamp determines to set her straight by describing the exact nature of their upcoming job. She claims that Jonas had *pleaded* with her to nurse Chuffey round the clock—but no, she adds, she would do as much only for Mrs. Harris. Such immeasurable services are far too valuable to be squandered on Chuffey. Along with the previous association of bells and fire, this astonishing fantasy can be traced back to Mrs. Gamp's abandonment of Chuffey for Lewsome—the only moment so far when conscience has bothered her. Mrs. Gamp justifies her actions to herself and then to Betsey. She rules out any incipient guilt; she establishes once again her dominance over circumstances. Then Mrs. Prig upsets all these rationalizations. "Bother Mrs. Harris! . . . I don't believe there's no sich a person!' [*MC*, 49, 756]. Betsey leaves in such an indignant flurry that the bullfinch in the shop below thinks "it [is] Fire"—which this time, perhaps, it is. Mrs. Gamp finds herself incapable of speech. She stares at nothing: the blank Mrs. Harris once filled.[25] We could hardly say that Mrs. Harris has died. The guilt of the murderer is not Mrs. Gamp's. All the same, Sarah enters the ominous world so long inhabited by Jonas. Far from holding her steady, repetition pushes her toward an undesired knowledge and an undesired reckoning.

In the concluding paragraphs of chapter 49, Dickens prepares Mrs. Gamp's future: her shift from Jonas's antithesis to his likeness. Particularly striking is her reaction to the questions of Martin the younger. Martin and his friends decide that the way to the truth about Jonas is through Chuffey and that the way to Chuffey is through Sarah Gamp. "Here was a new way out, developed in a quarter until then overlooked" [*MC*, 48, 745]. In one sense this supposition seems idle, almost pointless, for Mrs. Gamp has been rightly overlooked. She knows nothing incriminating (hint though she may at some unspeakable secret). Nonetheless, Martin elicits from Gamp an instructive response. She babbles in an alcoholic trance. How could Mrs. Prig deny Mrs. Harris, when "that dear woman is expecting of me at this minnit, Mr. Westlock, and is a-lookin' out of the window down the street" [49, 759]? A bizarre touch. Sarah knows that her friend is looking out of window, can practically see her there. On the other hand, Mrs. Harris can no longer convincingly fill a window, even a fictional one, a point that must bother Sarah. Now that Prig has proven unworthy, how will Mrs. Gamp find another assistant? She returns to the subject with which she is already occupied, murmuring "the well-remembered name which Mrs Prig had challenged—as if it were a talisman against all earthly sorrows."

This conversation serves one obvious narrative function; it lets the community of good people know precisely when Chuffey is to be handed over to Gamp. ("'From nine to ten,' said John [Westlock], with a significant glance at Martin," *MC*, 49, 760). But why should this information be so important? The meeting of Jonas and Gamp is hardly a crucial event—not unless the two of them are now so mixed up together in the very weave of the story that their presence in the same place and time has taken on a sort of occult significance. Dickens gives one last clue that a mixture of this sort has indeed been accomplished. When Gamp dozes off, "her nap was . . . broken at intervals, like the fabled slumbers of Friar Bacon, by the dropping of the other patten, and of the umbrella" [49, 760]. Friar Bacon is the Renaissance magus who manufactured a brazen head. The head was designed to "tell out strange and uncouth aphorisms, / And girt Fair England with a wall of brass" (a national defense strategy anticipating Star Wars). The tale is told most familiarly in Robert Greene's *Friar Bacon and Friar Bungay*. While the friar snored, exhausted from his labors, the head perked up, intoning "Time is . . . Time was . . . TIME IS PAST," then exploded when no one came to tend it.[26] Dickens's reference to the tale is charmingly confused. Its relevance is uncertain, unless Mrs. Harris is a brazen head with similarly urgent demands. If this is the case, the Gamp-Jonas rendezvous could have extraordinary reverberations. Martin and John—at this juncture agents of the novelist more than characters—are then correct in assuming that they must reach Jonas's establishment at precisely the right moment. "Time is," the time of a panoramic present, rapidly approaches.

Gamp's nervousness is mentioned several times when she appears on Jonas's doorstep. She speaks "with uncommon tenderness" of her patient, an anomaly indeed. Even Jonas notices "the change . . . exhibited in her new-born tenderness to her charge" [*MC,* 51, 777–78]. Jonas has many other things to think about. "With murder on his soul, and its innumerable alarms and terrors dragging at him night and day, he would have repeated the crime, if he had seen a path of safety stretching out beyond. . . . The very deed that his fears rendered insupportable, his fears would have impelled him to commit again" [51, 773]. His mind "fixed and fastened" [51, 774] on waiting for the discovery of Montague's corpse, he is nonetheless curious enough to inquire the name of Mrs. Gamp's partner, "the other woman." "It was extraordinary how much effort it cost Mrs. Gamp to pronounce the name she was commonly so ready with." A few moments later, Mrs. Gamp gives "three or four gasps" before she can again say "Harris" [51, 778].

To repeat Mrs. Harris's name has been a way of getting through the world. Under present circumstances, "Mrs. Harris" has a new meaning. Jonas feels as though condemned to bear a body in his arms "and lay it down to recognition at the feet of everyone he met" [*MC,* 51, 774]. Mrs. Gamp is condemned to bear Mrs. Harris, a burden neither dead nor alive, but no less threatening in its way than the corpse that burdens the murderer. Say that Mrs. Harris doesn't appear: in this case Mrs. Gamp is revealed to be a fraud. Say that Mrs. Harris does appear. This turn of events would be even more fearsome. It would confront Sarah with the star witness to her own advertised goodness. It would force her to live up to Mrs. Harris's testimony, for Mrs. Harris would be right on the spot. Time is . . . Time was . . . reckoning is imminent, whether the myth of Harris is confirmed or exploded. Mrs. Gamp's only hope is that she can muddle through without Jonas insisting on seeing "the other woman."

Jonas has his own reasons for pressing this apparently minor issue. His repetitions and Sarah's are now inextricable. Dickens emphasizes the equivalence by switching back and forth between the two troubled minds. A moment before Mrs. Gamp arrived, Jonas had been watching a shop across the way. "The tradesman and a customer were reading some printed bill together across the counter." As Mrs. Gamp takes Chuffey away, prior to "introducing" Mrs. Harris, Jonas looks again:

[MC, 51, 778]

> *A dispute or discussion seemed to arise among them, for they all looked up from their reading together, and one of the three, who had been glancing over the shoulder of another, stepped back to explain or illustrate some action by his gestures.*
>
> *Horror! how like the blow he had struck in the wood!*
>
> *It beat him from the window as if it had lighted on himself. As he staggered into a chair he thought of the change in Mrs. Gamp, exhibited in her new-born tenderness to her charge. Was that because it was found?—because she knew of it?—because she suspected him?*

To Gamp's discovery of inner life and inner uncertainty—black crape on the insides—corresponds Jonas's discovery of a world waiting outside: a world where his crime is public knowledge, acted out from street to street through the quick dissemination of the printed word. Under these circumstances, Gamp appears another suspicious onlooker. Jonas forces his crisis—which crisis, his or hers, can hardly be said. He asks once and then again to see her assistant, "the other woman." "But the ghastly change in Jonas told her that the other person was already seen. Before she could look round towards the door, she was put aside by old Martin's hand" [51, 779].

The steps by which Jonas has become a citywide center of attention might at this point be summarized. He began by brooding over the blank that Anthony made, then found his worries directed to Montague Tigg. Both these preoccupations are now superseded. Jonas's intent to murder his father is proved by Lewsome, his technical innocence by Chuffey. There was no need to worry about covering up Anthony's death; there was no need to silence Montague. If the first mistake led to the second, together they turn us to a third man in a window. His identity is revealed upon Nadgett's abrupt arrival.

[MC, 51, 787]

> *Hawkers burst into the street, crying it up and down; windows were thrown open that the inhabitants might hear it; people stopped to listen in the road and on the pavement; the bells, the same bells, began to ring: tumbling over one another in a dance of boisterous joy at the discovery (that was the sound they had in his distempered thoughts), and making their airy playground rock.*
>
> *"That is the man," said Nadgett. "By the window!" . . .*
>
> *The sounding street repeated Murder; barbarous and dreadful Mur-*

der; Murder, Murder, Murder. Rolling on from house to house, and echoing from stone to stone, until the voices died away into the distant hum, which seemed to mutter the same word!

They all stood silent: listening, and gazing in each other's faces, as the noise passed on.

Jonas has not lost his obsessive urge toward pursuing the meaning of singular fragments; he has reached its end, and through this repetition of the singular has become a singularity himself: an ordering hub of attention, far more than Mrs. Gamp ever has been or ever will be. Having acquired her talents without exactly losing his own, he finds himself confronting a long-prepared view. He experiences a sweeping panorama *heard* more than seen as windows open, the traffic stops, and the ringing bells blend into a distant hum. This synthesis recalls *Notre-Dame* and its bell vista; on the other hand Dickens establishes his harmonies differently than Hugo. The ringing begins inside Jonas's mind, a manifestation of his hidden guilt; only later, by the unfolding repetitions of singularity, can it be presented as though independent from any particular mind. A character like Jonas will always be close to fatalistic self-destruction; a character like Gamp to impermeable self-dramatization. The novelist's accomplishment is to combine these energies without circling back to the breakdown at Mrs. Todgers's boardinghouse. He establishes the advantages of long sight, no matter how hallucinatory or erratic it may at first seem. Far from blocking the establishment of knowledge that can be generalized, the singular helps create it. On these terms one gains access to the city, indeed to the "whole commonwealth" [xiv] pursued by Charles Dickens.

There remains a difficulty. So far as he concentrates on Jonas, Mrs Gamp, and their apocalyptic rendezvous, Dickens seems to have reverted to the literary equivalent of magic—something like the ritualistic mumbo jumbo described by René Girard when he claims that social harmony is based on the collective persecution of a scapegoat.[27] We all hate Jonas together. Agreeing, we can hear if not see things in common. The bells that originated in Jonas's guilty dreams speak or sing, ratifying our faith— a more elusive faith, I would suspect, than the one that Hugo is trying to restore. All the same, if Dickens has indulged in magic, he has emphasized its analytic rather than its regressive side: he *studies* a movement toward consensus rather than simply affirming its triumph. Baudelaire later wrote of dioramas that their "magic brutale et énorme sait m'imposer une utile illusion" (brutal and enormous magic can impose upon me a useful illusion).[28] The magic of a comprehensive view is brutal and enormous; the illusion it imposes, nonetheless usable. Dickens admits both sides of this problematic truth. He craves singularities that are facts, and on which, therefore, a long-term consensus could be based. He struggles through a fantasy of facts to a spectacle whose utility and cruelty are equally acknowledged.

A good summation of his divided attitude occurs in the concluding chapters of *Chuzzlewit*. Here he offers contrasting accounts of how an achieved social agreement might be valued. So far as they treat Jonas, these chapters affirm the social harmonies established by repeating the singular. Within a matter of minutes the exposed murderer has joined Anthony and Montague: Jonas has become, in a manner of speaking, his own last victim. On the way to prison his corpse is discovered, its hand clasping a bottle of poison "with that rigidity of grasp with which no living man, in full strength and energy of life, can clutch a prize he has won." Jonas finally fixes the identity of the singular man in the window. He discovers the only rigidity that can give the repetitions their definitive form, not "Murder, Murder, Murder," but more simply "Dead, dead, dead," the last words of chapter 51 and the end of Jonas's allegorical progress [*MC*, 51, 795].

"The crowding in of all these incidents"—"their very intensity and the tumult of their assemblage" [*MC*, 52, 796]—underlies the solidarity of the novel's officially virtuous characters. Mrs. Gamp sidles over to the winning team long before the outcome is announced. Can she therefore be restored to her former self, to those repetitions which imply that any part—any at all—can become an organizing center? Dickens answers this question during Sarah's last appearance. Just after Mr. Sweedlepipe has produced the miraculously resurrected Bailey and made "a favourable impression," Gamp determines to get her share of the attention. She "struggled to the front, therefore and stated her business":

> "Which, Mr Chuzzlewit," she said, "is well beknown to Mrs Harris as has one sweet infant (though she do not wish it known) in her own family by the mother's side, kep in spirits in a bottle; and that sweet babe she see at Greenwich Fair, a-travelling in company with the pink-eyed lady, Prooshan dwarf, and livin' skelinton, which judge her feelins when the barrel organ played, and she was showed her own dear sister's child, the same not bein' expected from the outside picter, where it was painted quite contrairy in a livin' state, a many sizes larger, and performing beautifully upon the Arp, which never did that dear child know or do: since breathe it never did, to speak on, in this wale!"

[52, 813–14]

She narrates the sad tale of an infant whose miraculous resurrection was promised but not delivered. The implication is that her auditors shouldn't look at Bailey (hardly resurrected at all, no better than a pickled embryo) but at her, the real thing. Gamp has always spoken to get attention. Now she speaks about attention too. More than ever before, she lives within a circle of repetitions that will save her from any unfortunate blanks in the scene. When old Martin responds to her speech by chastizing her, she exits this book where she entered it, with an appeal to the bottle on the chimneypiece "and let me put my lips to it, when I am so dispoged!" [52, 814].

Jonas and Gamp become the same person for a moment. Afterwards, it is once again their differences that count. Jonas is absorbed by the system of meanings he pursues. Gamp breaks out of it. Her centrality is revealed to be a carefully cultivated illusion. This is a delicate point. Her monologues establish little dramas, fleeting stories through which she can appear essential. The appearance is only that—and happily so. Mrs. Gamp maintains her freedom, escaping the disciplines of meaning, in fact of consensus and comprehensive survey. Having participated in the panorama, she nonetheless remains herself. It is one of the novel's most striking accomplishments to insist on the necessity of panoramic knowledge, of interpretation and centrality combined, while allowing Mrs. Gamp a final irrelevance untouched by the elder Chuzzlewit's judgment. Mrs. Gamp is an irreducible singular, a fact that escapes the whole: whose meaning *is* its irrelevance and whose cry of "look at me" can never therefore be satisfied or sated.

III

Figures and Heroes

"I would have stern talks with myself. 'Se-
myavin, it's only a temporary lapse away from
reality. A small aberration, nothing to worry
about. Act as you always have—strength of character, good mental health. Courage, Seman-
yavin. Soon all will be back to normal.' But do
you know what?"
"Let me guess."
A tragic sigh. "Information. What's wrong with
dope and women? Is it any wonder the world's
gone insane, with information come to be the only
real medium of exchange?"

Thomas
Pynchon,
*Gravity's
Rainbow*

7. The Hunchback of Saint Dunstan-in-the-West: Failed Heroism

I HAVE EMPHASIZED THE POWER of narrative as an interpretive device: to *narrate* a figure is eventually to understand it—but to understand it at a cost; a maze snaps into a noose, a crowd becomes a tomb, a view is reorganized as a fatal consensus. A further means for interpreting figures emerges from this journey toward a deathlike consummation. Narratives must sooner or later posit specific actors, focusing on their identity as well as their ultimate effectiveness (one might say, on their heroism or lack of it).[1] It is these actors who supply a much-needed representation of purposefulness in the face of annihilation, a crucial matter for the allegorist. I turn, then, from the role of narrative to the role of narrative agents in urban allegory.

Over the last two centuries, people have quarreled at length about "the interaction of structure and agency."[2] More precisely: Do individuals create societies and social formations or are they created by them? The classical political economists treat autonomous individuals as prior to society. Marx, by contrast, suggests that they emerge only at a specific historical crossroads: the "idea" of the individual comes into being when feudalism goes to seed and new productive technologies arise. According to the *Grundrisse,* it is social structures that endow individuals with power, that permit them (in various ways) to *act* as agents, that endow their acts with meaning.[3] The novel of urban mysteries tends toward this latter position, though it does not on this account deny the significance of agency. The agents of urban allegory are heroes who continually face the threat of moral and psychological extinction. If they survive their confrontation with metropolitan pressures—if they learn to speak or do what they mean, rather than what the city would speak or do for them—it is because they grasp the limits of identity and how to work within them.

I will make this kind of case for several midcareer novels of Dickens and Hugo, novels where the question of agency is treated with particular force. My starting point is a Dickensian Christmas tale whose attempt to imagine a hero is instructively botched. *The Chimes* (conceived during summer of 1844) looks back not only on *Chuzzlewit* but on *The Old Curiosity Shop, Oliver Twist,* and *Notre-Dame.*[4] It recapitulates these works for an excellent reason. Each of them strives not only to narrate a figure but to imagine a viewpoint from which this narration could be usable— could, as it were, transform a life rather than snuff it out. *The Chimes* moves a step further toward naming such a perspective: it revives a character long dead even if briefly exhumed every now and then; it reintroduces a hero through whom the novel of mysteries will achieve perhaps its finest moments. Though *The Chimes* is far from a success, it sets the terms on which subsequent books will succeed.

Dickens begins his tale with fantastic speculations on what it would be like to spend the night alone in a church steeple, "far above the light and murmur of the town and far below the flying clouds that shadow it" [*TC*, 1, 82]. The character whom *The Chimes* reserves for this fate is one Trotty Veck, an aged London messenger susceptible to the chidings of his betters. Trotty's betters are an obnoxious group. They include Alderman Cute, who means to put down all cant about the starvation and suffering of the poor; Mr Filer, a Gradgrindian worshipper of statistics, who has reduced his distaste for the poor to a "mathematical certainty"; a red-faced gentleman nostalgic for feudal times; and Sir Joseph Bowley, an MP who conceives himself to be the "Poor Man's Friend" [1, 93–103; 2, 105]. These four have in common a weakness for arbitrary assertion based on simple-minded intellectual formulae and a corresponding inability to understand what is in front of them. The well-intentioned Trotty, by contrast, has direct experience of what it is like to be poor but no way at all of getting his situation into perspective or even of stating it to himself. Worrying about his daughter, "he couldn't finish [her] name. The final letter swelled in his throat, to the size of the whole alphabet" [2, 102]. For this reason, Trotty tends to take seriously the harangues of Cute and his associates.

The chimes of the title soon enter this conflict. They are located in a London church (Saint Dunstan-in-the-West, according to the illustrations by Daniel Maclise). Although anonymous—no one has known their names since the time of Henry VIII—they have "clear, loud, lusty, sounding voices . . . sometimes known to beat a blustering Nor' Wester" [*TC*, 1, 82]. Their outstanding quality is thus that they can be heard. The world of Alderman Cute, a world of parliamentary reports, newspapers, and statistics, consistently depresses Trotty, driving him to the notion that the poor are extraneous and should be eradicated from the earth. At such moments as these, the chimes seem to speak to him and encourage him. His reading—reading is dangerous for naive Trotty—drives him to despair; then the voices pick him up again.

For this struggle to be resolved, Trotty must hear the voices of the chimes more clearly than before: he must learn to speak through them, to make their anonymous voices his named one. The moment of crisis that will lead to this outcome arrives when Trotty peruses a horrible newspaper story about infanticide. The chimes interrupt his despair. He is drawn by them to the church tower where they ring. He hears them "again, again, and yet a dozen times again. 'Haunt and hunt him, haunt and hunt him, Drag him to us, drag him to us!' Deafening the whole town!" [*TC*, 2, 117].

"Black are the brooding clouds," observes the novelist; "and troubled the deep waters, when the Sea of Thought, first heaving from a calm, gives up its Dead. Monsters uncouth and wild, arise in premature, imperfect resurrection; the several parts and shapes of different things are joined and mixed by chance" [*TC*, 3, 120]. It is this "Great Mystery," in Dickens's words, which *The Chimes* proceeds to describe. Ascending the towers through dark and intricate ways, Trotty confronts a crowd of "dwarf phantoms": "clambering from him, by the ropes below; looking down upon him, from the massive iron-girded beams; peeping in upon him, through the chinks and loopholes in the walls; spreading away and away from him in enlarging circles, . . . Stone, and brick, and slate, and tile, became transparent to him as to them" The spirits are the voices of the chimes but voice blends into vision: when the chimes speak, their speaking creates a power of sight shared by Trotty. This dizzying cycle—sound and sight reinforcing one another—continues throughout the scene. When the chimes stop, the spirits disappear ("the last of all was one small hunchback, who had got into an echoing corner, where he twirled . . . a long time") to be replaced by "watchful figures" within the bells themselves. Flinching under their "darksome and unwinking watch" through architectural "entanglements, intricacies and depths," Trotty has a sudden desire to throw himself off the steeple but cannot move. He is paralyzed by "being high, high, high, up there, where it had made him dizzy to see the birds fly in the day; cut off from all good people, who at such an hour were safe at home and sleeping in their beds" [3, 120–22]. The bells show him his own mangled body at the bottom of the tower.

Despite this hint of peril—of knowledge at the cost of death—Trotty is able to survive what he has heard and seen. He learns the beneficent operations of time. "I know there is a sea of Time to rise one day, before which all who wrong us or oppress us will be swept away like leaves. . . . I know that we must trust and hope, and neither doubt ourselves, nor doubt the good in one another" [*TC*, 4, 151]. He keeps his naïveté and directness, but adds to them a comprehensive understanding of history and society, the sort of grasp that Cute and his friends can only pretend to possess. Trotty has made the vast, inhuman reverberation of the ancient bells his personal affirmation. His personal affirmation takes on the authority of the chimes.

That *The Chimes* recalls Dickens's previous allegories can be quickly demonstrated. Those earlier books study a society where belonging to a group is a sinister, almost an obscene, fate; where collective energies seem to persecute vulnerable individuals; and where agreeing on a center from which to survey the whole is virtually impossible. All of these difficulties reappear in *The Chimes,* which works in its turn towards a now-familiar response. *Oliver Twist* desires that liberating moment when Sikes is seen by the city and therefore proves able to see it (although at the cost of his life). *The Old Curiosity Shop* has as its appropriate epilogue Humphrey's ascent to the top of Saint Paul's; Humphrey remains cloaked by darkness, as does London, yet city and self silently draw together. *Martin Chuzzlewit* reprises the nightmare of *Twist,* adding to it the bells so loved by Humphrey and the interplay between seeing and hearing. *The Chimes* weaves together these situations. Trotty is more like Humphrey than like Sikes or Jonas, yet—no less than the melodramatic villains—he finds that his newly acquired power of sight means also a power of surveillance directed upon himself. It is as though Humphrey had stepped into Sikes's or Jonas's role, except that the protagonist's ordeal issues in forgiveness, survival, and an understanding prolonged beyond the moment of crisis.

Dickens effects a remarkable synthesis—whose issue is none other than a character familiar years before his own career had begun. A contemporary reviewer noted, "The mysterious affection and attraction between the bells and Trotty Veck may be traced to Quasimodo, in Victor Hugo's *Notre-Dame de Paris.*"[5] This comment implies a complaint on grounds of unoriginality, but Dickens's allusion to Quasimodo demands a different sort of evaluation. Ainsworth's attempt to write a novel of the modern city had centered on the unfortunate Auriol, a minor-league Faust who seduced his Gretchen but otherwise got nowhere. Quasimodo (whom Ainsworth calls Flapdragon) remains on the periphery of the story—as he does throughout Dickens's early novels, with the possible exception of *The Old Curiosity Shop.*[6] *The Chimes* in this context attempts something rather surprising. It suggests that the modern novel of city life has a central role for the misbegotten hunchback. A seemingly archaic harmony can work for modern London as it did for medieval Paris. It can supply an organizing consciousness and conscience for society.

Could a critical reader of *The Chimes* be made to believe this? Recall the pattern of the previous novels, where storytelling is concentrated on forming and reforming figures of urban life. The appropriate character for unriddling the figures seems to come into being as the result of a sustained narrative inquiry, as when Jonas and Mrs. Gamp draw together in a suddenly common dilemma, as when Sikes assumes Oliver's scapegoat role just in the nick of time, as when Master Humphrey takes Nell's image into himself, grasping London through her death and perhaps through Quilp's. Such intricate ways of designing a story emphasize how difficult it is to imagine an intelligence—individual on the one hand, connected with a community on the other—that could comprehend London without being destroyed by it. Trotty is no less artificial a production than were his predecessors; his experience, as has been seen, is a synthesis of materials from previous novels by Dickens, a synthesis that issues in a summoning up of Quasimodo. But the reliance on Hugo is not a useful device, not in this form. Trotty's affinity with the bells remains a "Great Mystery." The mystery is no more than an elaborate literary reference.

The Chimes introduces a new Quasimodo without providing grounds for belief in his possible existence, much less for his ability to guide us from the "sea of Thought" to the "sea of Time" [*TC*, 3, 120; 4, 151] (i.e., from an imagined human consciousness back to a sense of history and perhaps historical design). Let it be supposed, all the same, that Quasimodo's resurrection is desirable; that this character rather than some other is appropriate to Dickens's purposes. The problem then persists of how Quasimodo might be brought up to date, of how this kind of agent might play an effective role in the novel of urban mysteries.

The original Quasimodo lost his affinity for bells when the bell rope became the hangman's noose, which tightened around the neck of Esmeralda. Perhaps the obscene image of the gypsy dancing upon nothing should have canceled, once and for all, the vision of a community assembled by this means—that is, by the overmastering performance of the deaf bell ringer. In other words, *The Chimes* may embody one of the sins that it satirizes. Almost without realizing it, Dickens indulges in Toryism at its most unthinking, nostalgia in a picturesque but question-begging form. He relies on a Gothic[7] church—and on the forms of authority it embodies—to provide him with a deus ex machina.[8] Imagine, by contrast, the possibility of a Quasimodo-like hero separated from his cathedral and his bells but nonetheless capable of heroic thought leading to heroic action. Such a character could be made plausible through isolating some special quality in the modern city, a nightmare that might inflict suffering on this hero (as the bells took Quasimodo's hearing) but would, at least, allow him a new sense of purpose and understanding. Thus the question: If the bells will no longer speak for Quasimodo or reveal the city to him, what will?

Notre-Dame contains the germ of an answer. The novel presumes that nineteenth-century Paris is defined by the movement on paper of data and opinions rather than by articulated physical space. Hugo realized that this shift had its sinister side. His hunchback dies with the old, monumental Paris; a creature who finds his identity inside the frame of the Gothic cathedral is thus spared modernity. However, an unrealized ending jostles against this actual one. Quasimodo and old Paris are memorialized by the book we hold in our hands. The book could replace the cathedral, if only one knew how to use it.

Here I approach a difficulty, to be elaborated by succeeding chapters. In *Notre-Dame,* it was Frollo who knew about reading. And it is characters more like Frollo than like Quasimodo who dominate the popular serials, works roughly contemporaneous with *The Chimes.* For the intriguers of Sue or Reynolds, words on paper are a means to power. Those who can manipulate information—particularly recorded information—control urban life. Hugo and Dickens institute a critique of this idea; the critique makes it possible to imagine a hero who can live humanely on the terms set by the city. The hero in question will not bear much resemblance to Frollo or the urban intriguers—in important ways he will be defined *against* them—but neither will he be a faux naïf Quasimodo like Trotty Veck.

The books where this possibility is developed most completely are *Bleak House* and *Les Misérables.* I will not insist that these novels are identical under the surface. Especially in their treatment of crime, they are opposite or antagonistic works. Jean Valjean's flight from the city of documents forces him into an underworld of illiterates. Esther Summerson's only meeting with society's ultimate outcasts comes when she takes in the urchin Jo and subsequently catches smallpox from him. Though Esther is literally marked by Jo's stay with her, neither she nor any other respectable person enters his world for more than a few moments. The realm of *misérables* remains mostly out of bounds for Dickens, partly, perhaps, because he is reluctant to dwell further on those myths of crime analyzed in *Oliver Twist;*[9] mainly, I think, because he is more concerned to link crime with literacy and the power conferred by professional status than with the relative powerlessness of Hugo's "underclass." In this respect he has learned positively from Reynolds, whereas Hugo almost completely rejects Sue's myths of the city.

Despite such differences, there remains the essential similarity, the drive to conceive a certain kind of hero. The triumph of Trotty Veck was represented through his affinity with church bells, an affinity declared rather than explored. Literacy, so distrusted in *The Chimes,* offers a more precise means for linking hero and society. The document city is initially represented as an oppressive and terrorizing structure that denies basic human needs. The new Quasimodo—call him Jean or, however odd it may seem, call him Esther—tries to live apart from this horror, to create by domestic busyness or sheer willpower a sheltering space of his own. At first his best efforts are made to little avail: paper, the darkest of urban figures, comes close to annihilating this inarticulate protagonist; it speaks for him, it overwhelms him, it assimilates him into a system of communication where no one's word and no one's identity could possibly be his own. The very idea of meaningful intent is challenged, a development that reflects back on the powers and status of the novelist. Then this situation modifies itself. The document city becomes the means by which the new Quasimodo communicates and by which he locates himself within the world he previously evaded.

8. Mystery and Revelation in *Bleak House*

"The bill is indeed beautifully executed," re-marked Maxwell, with a sigh, after he had care-fully examined the note. "I will take a package of fifty of them."

George
Thompson,
*The Brazen
Star*

A VICTORIAN NOVELIST could be titillated by the very idea of property and power without land: as was G. W. M. Reynolds in *The Mysteries of London*, as was Dickens (a few years later) in *Bleak House*. Dickens, at least, got beyond titillation. Influenced by Reynolds's critique, he discovered a London where the most coveted possession was knowledge: where words on paper were more real than real estate. From this encounter there followed two further thoughts.

1. Once the idea of property is separated from tangible assets like land, ownership becomes infinitely problematic. No one can say what it means to own knowledge, a dilemma that strikes at the basis of social relations, and through such relations at the basis of human identity.
2. There is perhaps a way to live in such a world. If knowledge cannot be controlled, at least it can be passed on. Under the tutelage of Allegory, the painted Roman on Mr. Tulkinghorn's ceiling, *Bleak House* moves toward a gesture of this kind: a motion of release in which heroine, author, and reader all participate and from which emerges an under-standing—though not a mastery—of a city filled with documents.

Documents and Fear

One pleasure of the Gothic novel is that secrets are always changing status. First they are carefully guarded, then they begin to get out, then they are no longer secrets. What starts as a "mystery" is divested of exclusiveness, shared among author, reader, protagonist, villain, and the rather scanty supporting cast that an isolated castle, for example, affords. At least in Ann Radcliffe's novels, the dissolution of secrets is terrifying but finally reassuring. *Udolpho's* heroine walks into danger ignorantly, then realizes that she must discover the true nature of her situation. Eventually she is in danger because she knows too much. "Thus compelled to bear within her own mind the whole horror of the secret that oppressed it, her reason seemed to totter under the intolerable weight."[1] At this point there is no going back; she must try to find out yet more. Her inquisitiveness will save her. At the end, when the secrets of Udolpho are exhausted, the world is restored to normal and the survivors can move on.

Radcliffe's scheme was old news by the 1840s. Revived in the urban novel of that decade, it took on a fresh significance: it developed, I will suggest, into a fantasy of documents,[2] a fantasy extravagant and horror-charged but answering to workaday social considerations. G. W. M. Reynolds's *The Mysteries of London,* perhaps the period's greatest best-seller, suggests how this situation came about.[3] The first series of *Mysteries* (October 1844–September 1846) is the story of two brothers, Richard and Eugene Markham. (The choice of *Eugene* must be a tribute to Sue.) Eugene goes off to seek his fortune in the city, having been too stubborn to settle a quarrel with his father. He promises to meet Richard again twelve years from the day of their parting, at which time the brothers will compare their respective fortunes. The narrative then follows alternately the careers of Richard and Eugene. After being duped by a gang of forgers and im-prisoned for two years in the Old Bailey, Richard leads a revolution in an Italian state and wins the hand of a princess. Under the name Montague Greenwood, Eugene becomes an accomplished financial swindler and a member of Parliament. Eventually he is driven to moral and financial desperation, dying repentantly a few moments after he is reunited with Richard. Meanwhile the reader has made his way through the huge accumulation of characters who have gathered around these two: Gypsies, faithful and unfaithful retainers, criminals, victimized working girls, men of fashion, politicians, bankers, and many others. Reynolds constantly expands the world he is writing about, taking care, every few chapters, to describe new characters and scenes. The reassuring tale of the good brother and the bad becomes the framework for a more elaborate and elusive narrative, fifty or sixty interlocking stories presenting "all that is most refined in elegance, or most strange in barbarism" [*ML,* 2: 240, 347]. London is perceived as a gigantic web of secrets.

At first they accumulate gradually. A London bank that seems wealthy has little or no money within its coffers, and its officers must organize their lives around this uncomfortable fact. The wife of an aristocrat is having an affair with a financier, a matter likely to be of interest to others besides the lovers. The bond between a young man aspiring to respectability and a desperate criminal is the latter's knowledge of the former's prison record. A potboy (like the notorious Boy Jones, who lurked about Queen Victoria quite uninvited) is drawn back repeatedly to Buckingham Palace to eavesdrop on ladies-in-waiting who are gossiping about madness and marital problems in the Hanoverian dynasty. By the time the serial reaches its halfway point, these situations and many others have accumulated; they weigh on the mind all at once. " 'Lord, sir!' said the constable, 'if we took up all persons that we know to be imposters, we should have half London in custody' " [*ML,* 2: 137, 4]. More than half of Reynolds's characters are imposters, and so one falsehood constantly confronts or creates another. The Reverend Reginald Tracy is reputedly pure but has lusted after women and fallen. Ellen Monroe is reputedly a chaste young woman but has had an illegitimate child by "Montague Greenwood." When Reginald and Ellen meet, the relationship immediately centers on secrets guessed at or known. A balance of power is temporarily established. " 'Yes—go,' said Ellen: 'you are punished sufficiently. You possess the secret of my frailty—I possess the secret of your hypocrisy: beware of the use you make of your knowledge of me, lest I retaliate by exposing you' " [2: 149, 36]. This kind of deadlock often punctuates the action in *The Mysteries of London.* Situations never become completely static, however. Reginald and Ellen may have maneuvered themselves into a brief standoff; on the other hand, they have managed in the course of a few pages to reveal important secrets to other characters. In this way, further plans are set in motion; there is a gradual piling up of motives and perceptions among a widening circle of plotters.

Everybody gets into the act, but some plotters prove more accomplished than others. Eugene Markham/Montague Greenwood has directed his whole career toward learning the ways of power, first as a kind of Pierce Egan character—"A few years ago, when I first entered on a London life, I determined to make myself acquainted with all the ways of the metropolis, high or low" [*ML,* 1: 49, 149]—then, anticipating Trollope's Melmotte or Dickens's Merdle, as an apparently respectable financier. In the latter role, he displays real flair for juggling secrets. Chapter 48 shows him working at the height of his powers, negotiating with one and then another visitor to his West End quarters, always attempting to extract, use or create secrets. He inquires after the whereabouts of an Italian prince in hiding: " 'That remains a secret' answered the count" [1: 48, 142]. The impending resignation of an MP from Rottenborough, though also a "profound secret," is known to both "Greenwood" and Tremordyn. "Greenwood" makes it clear to Tremordyn that he wants the seat. Soon after, he consults with Lady Cecilia Harborough and then seduces her; there follows immediately a financial discussion with Sir Rupert, her impecunious husband. " 'I shall hold him in iron chains,' said Greenwood to himself, when he was again alone. 'This bill will hang constantly over his head. Should he detect my intrigue with his wife, he will not dare open his mouth' " [1: 48, 146].

"London is filled with Mr. Greenwoods," i.e., with busy entrepreneurs whose sense of self emerges from the theft and manipulation of secrets [*ML,* 1: 49, 148]. By the same sort of logic, secrets become objects—letters to be opened surreptitiously, scribbled messages dropped accidently by the road, certificates of insanity covering evil intentions.[4] In the Black Chamber of the Post Office, one of Reynolds's favorite places, industrious servants of the Crown steam open the correspondence of suspected persons; the Spanish Inquisition of the Gothic novelist has here its modern equivalent, except that letters rather than human bodies are being violated. This transgression of social decency alarms the narrator, prompting him to remark of the Chief Examiner: "Can we be astonished if he gloated, like the boa-constrictor over the victim that it retains in its deadly folds, over the mighty secrets stored in his memory?" [1: 72, 221]. Similar though even more terrifying intrusions are accomplished by the Tax Office, at least as it is described in Reynolds's *London Journal.* (See fig. 20.) Intrigue, typically, is a recorded fact as well as a state of mind. Hear George Saintsbury on the novel of urban mysteries: "When you have got an ivory casket supposed to be full of all sorts of compromising documents, somebody produces another, exactly like it, but containing documents more compromising still." *The Mysteries of Constantinople,* Edward Gorey's pastiche-parody, makes a similar point: "The ambassador is compulsively going over some documents with his secretary when a bogus message is brought by an urchin mute."[5] Saintsbury and Gorey satirize a convention by which secrets at their most virulent must be imagined as written down. In Reynolds's London also, one good document deserves another.

Little of the obsession with paper is invented by Reynolds: his immediate and acknowledged source is *Les Mystères de Paris* (for which, see chapters 9 and 11, below). All the same, his use of the fearsome document

LONDON JOURNAL;

And Weekly Record of Literature Science, and Art

No. 7. Vol. I.   FOR THE WEEK ENDING APRIL 12, 1845.   [Price One Penny.

THE SECRET CHAMBER IN THE TAX OFFICE, SOMERSET HOUSE.

In a preceding number we gave an engraving representing the interior of the Secret Chamber of the General Post Office, Saint Martin's Legrand, accompanied with a letter-press description of the entire process of opening, examining, and resealing letters. We now come to the second act of the Spy-system of the English Government, and introduce our readers to the Secret Chamber in the Tax Office, Somerset House.

The object of this second department of the English Inquisition may be described in a few words. The Dividend Books of the Bank of England are at certain times removed to Somerset House, and placed in the hands of the Commissioners of Taxes. Three clerks belonging to the Bank preside over the proceedings in the Secret Chamber at Somerset House; and upwards of twenty clerks are employed under the guidance of those three persons, in making extracts from the books. By these means the names of all stock-holders, with the amount of landed property standing to their accounts upon the books, are copied and subsequently placed at the disposal of the Commissioners of Taxes and the Lords of the Treasury. The Government and its authorities can thus ascertain not only whether individuals holding stock return correct statements of their pecuniary resources, in respect to the operations of the Income-tax, but also what sums of ready money are at the disposal of any persons

concerning whom the Government, for its own political purposes, may wish to obtain such information.

The clerks who are employed in the Secret Chamber at Somerset House, are all sworn not to divulge the nature of the proceedings. It is however clear to any one at all acquainted with human nature, that implicit secrecy cannot be ensured amongst so many persons. There must always be one at least, if not more, who will be found of a garrulous disposition, and who will reveal the mysteries of that Chamber. Many of the clerks are very young men, and are therefore prone to be induced by sentiments of pride to boast to their friends and acquaintances of the confidential employment entrusted to them. A mere vaunt of this kind, however vague, leads to questioning and cross-questioning; and an endearing sweetheart or a much-loved sister can soon wheedle the young clerk out of his secrets. Then the ladies gossip amongst each other,—for we hope it is no sin to say that ladies *are* fond of a little chit-chat; and what becomes of the secret? Seriously speaking, it is impossible to keep such a system long quiet; and, in plain terms, the pecuniary circumstances of every fund holder are at the mercy of those clerks and the friends, acquaintances, and relations of the clerks.

People have a great dislike to any publicity

being given to their financial means. No person ever asks his friend to let him have a peep at his banking book. It would be a strange salutation were one to say to another, "How do you do to-day, my dear sir, or madam?" (as the case may be): "pray what is the amount of your income?" It may be through pride, or it may be through weakness, but it is nevertheless a fact that most people are anxious to appear better off than they really are. Indeed, such appearance is the vitality of many millions of tradesmen's commercial existence. There are moreover thousand of families and individuals who possess a certain little income derived from property in the funds, and who maintain a far better appearance than the world would imagine to be consistent with their resources, were the amount of those resources known. And yet those families and individuals pay their way, wrong no one, owe no one a penny. What matters it to the world if the leg of mutton be served up three days running in the domestic circle, to enable the members of the family to appear decently in public;—what matters it to the world how much economy is practised privately,—to leave means for a comfortable aspect publicly,—so long as no debts are incurred, no tradesmen made to suffer, no friends applied to for loans which are never refunded? Many—many families, with incomes of two hundred a year, sustain an appearance—aye,

20. *The Secret Chamber in the Tax Office, Somerset House.* The first page of the *London Journal*, 12 April 1845. (From a copy in a private collection.)

is quite different from that of his French master. Sue's manipulator of secrets is the benevolent aristocrat Count Rodolphe. Not only is Reynolds less attracted than Sue to fantasies of noblesse oblige, he situates his secret entrepreneur in a markedly different way. He appears to have been stimulated by Pierre Proudhon's *Qu'est-ce que la propriété?* (First Memoir, 1840), where Proudhon equates property with thievery, then classifies increasingly impalpable and abstract forms of theft.[6] Much like Proudhon, Reynolds categorizes crime in ascending levels of sophistication from direct violence to theft by talent, labor, and possession; and much like Proudhon also, he is eager to have the more sophisticated varieties of crime condemned along with the primitive ones. This leads him to provide the following justification for his narrative:

L, 1: 49,
3—a
apter ap-
propriately
ed "The
cu-
nt"]

> *The more civilization progresses, and the more refined becomes the human intellect, so does human iniquity increase.*
>
> *It is true that heinous and appalling crimes are less frequent;—but every kind of social, domestic, political, and commercial intrigue grows more into vogue . . . hypocrisy is the cloak which conceals modern acts of turpitude, as dark nights were trusted to for the concealment of the bloody deeds of old: mere brute force is now less frequently resorted to; but the refinements of education or the exercise of duplicity are the engines chiefly used for purposes of plunder. The steel engraver's art, and the skill of the caligrapher, are mighty implements of modern misdeed . . . he who gambles at a gaming-table is a scamp, and he who propagates a lie upon the Exchange and gambles accordingly, and with success, is a respectable financier.*

This passage defines the whole range of villainy in *The Mysteries of London*. Reynolds displays "every kind of social, domestic, political, and commercial intrigue." There are also "heinous and appalling crimes," the "bloody deeds" of proletarian malefactors, as well as the traditional exploitations of vile aristocrats. But twits and thugs do not have it all to themselves. Writing for an audience close to illiteracy,[7] Reynolds highlights "modern acts of turpitude"—crimes based on education and fundamentally middle-class in character.[8]

At least in its own day, *The Mysteries of London* had a considerable impact. The ultimate purpose of Reynolds's polemic remains ambiguous, however, especially in light of his own contribution to the scheme of things he describes. "Haply the reader may begin to imagine that our subject is well-nigh exhausted—that the mysteries of London are nearly all unveiled?" [*ML*, 2: 240, 347]. The answer is that London is inexhaustible; so many strange people and institutions thrive in the great city that there will always be more mysteries to uncover, more documents to decipher. It follows that there can be no satisfactory method for ending *The Mysteries of London*. Arguably, this was true of any serial proceeding by the accumulative means of Reynolds. His case is (at the least) a particularly hard one. He wants to be the obverse of his blackmailers and intriguers: to unveil mysteries for the benefit of an anxious and vulnerable audience instead of concealing them, mastering them, for his own purposes. And yet, though his book is bold in its preachy manner, the whole is less than the sum of its lively parts. *The Mysteries of London* recalls a London genre familiar from preceding generations, the guidebook designed to warn hicks of urban perils. To what end does Reynolds's unveiling of secrets proceed, besides this exploitative one? Not revolution: revolutions happen in Italy, where Richard makes his illustrious career. Reform seems equally distant. Even success on the city's terms is dubious. Eugene/Montague dies a broken man, breathing his last under a tree inscribed with the exposed secret of his identity. He becomes himself, his best self, only at the moment of his defeat—following which the veil drops again as Reynolds promises "a SECOND SERIES" of mysteries. Telling a secret is harder than might be supposed, particularly when the teller supposes that his interest lies in an eternal game of peekaboo.

Corporeal Enemies, Spiritual Friends

Claiming that Dickens wrote like G. W. M. Reynolds would have seemed pointless during the 1830s or 1840s. The lesser author began as an imitator—almost a plagiarist—of the greater, concocting such now-forgotten works as *Pickwick Abroad*. Later, when Reynolds had his success with *The Mysteries of London*, Dickens kept his distance. *Dombey and Son* ridiculed the craze for the novel of urban mysteries; the silly schoolteacher Mr. Feeder "spoke of the dark mysteries of London," which he planned to experience on his vacation in the city [*DS*, 14, 187]. Mr. Feeder's aspirations were hardly to be taken seriously, but within a few years Reynolds seemed more of a threat. On 30 August 1849 (Chartism was still alive and Reynolds lately one of its leaders) Dickens made a stern, somewhat prissy comment to his friend W. C. Macready: "If 'Mr. G. W. Reynolds' be the Mr. Reynolds who is the Author of the *Mysteries of London*, and who took the chair for a mob in Trafalgar Square before they set forth on a window-breaking expedition, I hold his to be a name with which no lady's, and no gentleman's, should be associated."[9] Dickens may have consorted with Hugo and even Sue, but clearly Reynolds was beyond the pale.

Then comes *Bleak House*, a novel of which one Victorian critic—George Brimley—wrote that it was "meagre and melodramatic, and disagreeably reminiscent of that vilest of modern books, Reynolds' *Mysteries of London*."[10] Brimley is right. Specific plot resemblances to *Bleak House* can be found in Reynolds's *The Seamstress; or, The White Slaves of England*, which ran as a serial in *Reynolds's Miscellany* from 23 March to 10

August 1850 (not long before *Bleak House* began appearing, in March 1852). This work features a duke who resides often in London, his somewhat younger duchess who has a secret love affair in her past, the blackmailing French lady's maid of the duchess, a scheming lawyer who has worked his way into the confidences of the duke—"just the man to push his way successfully onward amidst the mazes of an artificial world and a vitiated condition of society," writes Reynolds [*Reynolds's Miscellany,* 27 April 1850, 210]—as well as various lower-class characters who become entangled with the aristocratic group. While *The Seamstress* is much less wide-ranging than either *The Mysteries of London* or *Bleak House,* it demonstrates superbly the degree to which both writers had converged on the same group of motifs.

Perhaps it could be denied that there is a puzzle here: since Reynolds borrowed heavily from Dickens in works of the 1830s, it is hardly surprising that he and Dickens still sound alike in the middle of the century. However, this observation cannot explain how Reynolds got ahead of Dickens, how, in Brimley's formulation, Dickens came to sound like Reynolds rather than vice versa. Nor will it do to note Dickens's relish for melodrama and popular literature generally. It is true that Dickens was—culturally at least—no snob, that like Shakespeare he learned from all sorts of disreputable materials (and was himself disreputable in certain circles), but the particular similarities between *Bleak House* and Reynolds's serials remain an anomaly: no one writes a novel echoing the work of someone he despises socially and politically. At least no one does this without a good reason. The challenge is to discover that reason, to seek the terms on which Dickens choose to stray into Reynolds's territory.

The best clue I have to this matter lies in the work of the philosopher Georg Simmel, whose *Soziologie* (1908) provides a guide to urban secrecy. Since Simmel was not born until 1858, since his most influential work appeared between 1890 and World War I, he might at first seem an odd guide to London in the mid-nineteenth century—especially if one takes with a grain of salt his various claims to have constructed a sort of archetypal sociology valid at many times and places. (Cf. Karl Mannheim's criticism of Simmel: he has "abstracted in a completely unhistorical manner, the capitalistic money form from its capitalistic background and imputed the characteristic structural change to 'money as such' "; cf. also this dry summary: according to Simmel's "tragic" view, "the humanistic impulse must . . . be forced back into an inner subjectivity, into the *intérieur,* and society must remain as it is.") For my purposes, however, these reservations are secondary. Simmel's friend Karl Joël pointed out that the philosopher's work—specifically his *Philosophie des Geldes*—could only have been written "in these times and in Berlin." Since Berlin's urban growth began late, the city bore, at the turn of the century, more than a slight resemblance to the London of fifty or sixty years before. What Simmel learned from Berlin is not quite the "unhistorical" lesson with which Mannheim identified him—nor, as shall be seen, does Simmel preach so easy a message of passive withdrawal from an overwhelming world as his critics have suggested.[11]

In the *Soziologie,* Simmel argues that nineteenth-century democratic governments established new possibilities for individual fulfillment while also prompting an extension of the public domain. "Politics, administration, and jurisdiction . . . have lost their secrecy and inaccessibility in the same measure in which the individual has gained the possibility of ever more complete withdrawal, and in the same measure in which modern life has developed, in the midst of metropolitan crowdedness, a technique for making and keeping private matters secret, such as earlier could be attained only by means of spatial isolation." In brief, "what is public becomes ever more public, and what is private becomes ever more private" [Simmel, 336–37]. Simmel is describing a highly charged situation. Publicity and privacy both acquire new momentum; society's dependence on information and the desire for an existence apart from prying eyes flourish simultaneously. This seems to be a case of complete polarization. Under pressure, however, polarization can produce some surprising reversals. Every "good" trend—good according to Enlightenment values—creates a fearful regression. Through what are basically property transactions, the private becomes the public and vice versa.[12]

Simmel explains in detail the nature of this double transformation, which he traces in each direction. On the one hand, great quantities of information are becoming accessible or significant for the first time. A good way to achieve power is to discover methods for reversing this trend, for shrouding, once again, public affairs in secrecy. There are two advantages thus gained. If one can act secretly in a society that is presumed to operate publicly, all kinds of illicit opportunities open up. Money (for example) has an "abstractness and qualitylessness, through which transactions, acquisitions, and changes in ownership can be rendered hidden and unrecognizable in a way impossible where values are owned only in the form of extensive, unambiguously tangible objects" [Simmel, 335]. Even more important, secrecy within an expected context of public action creates a special aura of prestige. What the ordinary man cannot understand, cannot even gain access to, he respects. "Formally secretive behavior"—above and beyond the mere shielding of a secret content—is a way for elite groups to affirm their eliteness. "For many individuals, property does not fully gain its significance with mere ownership, but only with the consciousness that others must do without it" [332]. Secrecy of behavior is perhaps the best example of this general principle: what the expert knows he must know exclusively, even when he appears to be sharing knowledge with others.

As public institutions can turn to secrecy, so, on the other hand, can private life be exposed or annihilated. This danger is wrapped up with the function of the personal letter. Not only is the letter "subjective, momentary, solely-personal" [Simmel, 353], but it asserts the importance of these categories; transient states of feeling are put down in permanent form and thus given a new significance. The letter embodies an affirmation of subjective life and its rewards. It is a form of what Simmel calls "intellectual private property" [322]. Unfortunately, there is a major weakness involved in phenomena like letters. A letter will tend to betray itself, for it is among the most vulnerable forms of communication: it can, for instance, be opened by the wrong person. "It is extremely difficult to trace the legal limit" of such trespasses into "intellectual private-property" [323]. When Simmel studies this dilemma, he approaches a favorite theme: "the difficulty of asserting [one's] own personality within the dimensions of metropolitan life." The individual "can cope less and less with the overgrowth of objective culture." "It is the function of the metropolis to provide the arena for this struggle and its reconciliation" [353; 420–23]. Given the context of the city, letters suggest perfectly both the need for privacy and the constant difficulties in trying to keep it. Betrayal is implicit in this effort to maintain a separate space for one's mind away from the "overgrowth of objective culture" that typifies the urban scene [353; 422].

In Simmel's analysis intellectual thefts can threaten either the world's rationality or the integrity of an individual person: what one strives to be and what one strives to know may thus be connected in all sorts of treacherous ways. This manner of thinking bears more than a passing relation to *The Mysteries of London;* Reynolds, however, circumvents a contrast crucial to Simmel, between the desire to make mysteries and the desire to expose them. These two opposing forces—the one subjective and surreptitious, the other demystifying and rational—could be shown as interrelated only in a narrative of great sophistication. How could this perception be expressed or activated in fiction? Suppose that a novelist were to depict some great London institution that had retreated from general accessibility back toward obscurity and at the same time to depict the buried love affair of a great lady hovering on the edge of exposure. Suppose, further, that these two stories were to twine inextricably. This plan governs *Bleak House*. Taken together, the postponements of Chancery and the struggles to uncover Lady Dedlock's past constitute Dickens's version—I should say Dickens's transformation—of the Reynoldsian serial story.

Chancery: Fatal Transfers

According to Maitland, medieval England was unique less for Parliament or trial by jury than for legal reports; such reports made possible the common law, which emerged by a process of preserving, interpreting, and reapplying judicial opinions. The emphasis on recorded precedent lost its priority at one point only. In the Court of Chancery, decisions were originally made on the merits of the case at hand—on the basis, in other words, of equity. Not until the seventeenth century did the decisions of chancellors begin to be recorded regularly, and when they did, Chancery moved closer to the methods of common law. By the early nineteenth century, it was as bound up in precedent as other courts. Equity, theoretically, can be determined by any right-thinking man. Once a decision turns on the technical interpretation of previous judicial opinions, opinions that accumulate because they are written down, only a lawyer can judge. Under these circumstances, Chancery was inevitably professionalized. After Shaftesbury, no layman has ever been chancellor.[13]

When Dickens makes the chancellor of *Bleak House* ineffective and vague, the characterization is more historical than personal. By itself, at this late hour, the chancellor's moral authority means little. He must administer a complex system that had its source in an attempt to establish objective criteria for judgment, but evolved into a muddle of inexplicable technicalities. Though the lawyers make "a pretence of equity with serious faces" [*BH*, 1, 2], Gridley "mustn't go into Court, and say, 'My Lord, I beg to know this from you—is this right or wrong? . . .' My Lord knows nothing of it. He sits there, to administer the system" [15, 215]. Gridley speaks out boldly; he speaks out to no effect because the rules of the court declare him a nonentity. The historical accumulation of documents overpowers his verbal challenge, just as it renders pointless the orations of barristers. Mr. Jarndyce refers to "property of ours, meaning of the Suit's, but I ought to call it the property of Costs" [8, 96]. This sentence dramatizes a process that continues throughout the book. The learning of the law and the uses to which it is put are the basis of a nightmare whose keynote— of course—is that people are always writing. Attorneys and their underlings produce piles of paper, "bills, cross-bills, answers, rejoinders, injunctions, affidavits, issues, references to masters, masters' reports, mountains of costly nonsense," above all "the entanglement of real estate in meshes of sheep-skin. . . . Over which bee-like industry, these benefactors of their species linger" [1, 2; 32, 443]. This oppressively cumulative paperwork becomes the hallmark of a corrupt civilization that includes characters outside the legal hierarchy proper, such as Krook ("It's a monomania with him, to think he is possessed of documents," 32, 453) or Mrs. Jellyby ("it's quite impossible that I can put my papers away," 30, 419), but centers on the lawyers themselves. Chancery "knows no wisdom but in Precedent" [39, 555]—with the result that what might seem a property dispute (a dispute over trusts in a will) becomes instead a dispute over written words, "masterly fictions, and forms of procedure"[14] on which the law expends all its "ability, eloquence, knowledge, intellect" [8, 146; 65, 923].

Dickens's notion of Chancery is an exaggeration with a purpose. Legal pedantry existed long before the mid-nineteenth century, and elsewhere than in cities like London, but for the novelist it is this time and place that make the abuses of the court so important. Chancery is at the heart of the fog because it exemplifies a frightening reversion: the eruption of mystery out of rationalizing, bureaucratic organization; the disappearance of public eloquence into endless piles of recorded information. The journalism of *Household Words* (much of it written by Dickens himself) praises those archival systems just then becoming prominent. Modern society is so complex, so vast, that it really does need acres of paperwork; there must be ways to index bankruptcies, analyze the population, count dividends and deposits, or sort the mail. *Household Words* tends to reassure its readers about the London institutions that accomplish these ends—hardly a Reynoldsian approach.[15] *Bleak House* can confront possibilities that the magazine chooses to suppress for its own polemical purposes. Letting himself go, Dickens asks: What if all of London were to develop as Chancery has? What if all London *is* so developing?

Arguably this would be just fine. On reading *Bleak House,* Bernard Shaw suggested that "given our property system . . . the Court of Chancery is inevitable. . . . Indeed, the swallowing up of an estate in costs is by far the most satisfactory ending of a chancery suit, since the parties who get it have had to do at least some sort of professional work for it."[16] Dickens would have agreed that where property law is efficient, those with property benefit; in certain moods, he would have cheered this result: as *All the Year Round* was to put it, "facility of transfer is a very precious element in the value of any commodity."[17] Nonetheless, Shaw's gibe misses a crucial point. The larger significance of Chancery is summed up by a passage about Jo, the crossing sweeper—a vital passage, evidently, since it is illustrated in the novel's title-page vignette. "It must be a strange state to be like Jo! To shuffle through the streets, unfamiliar with the shapes, and in utter darkness as to the meaning, of those mysterious symbols, so abundant over the shops, and at the corners of streets. . . . what does it all mean, and if it means anything to anybody, how comes it that it means nothing to me?" [*BH*, 16, 221]. These sentences define a moment in modern, urbanized culture when "ignorance is turning into a kind of social handicap"[18]—and when (a shocking discovery) the handicap turns out to afflict a wide variety of people, including many far more educated than Jo. Dickens signals the pertinence of the sweeper's situation by a shift in point of view: "how comes it that it means nothing to *me*," where the reader becomes Jo or illiterate Jo the reader, where either way the barriers are eerily thrown down. This effect is repeated elsewhere: legal writing is like "that kindred mystery, the street mud . . . we only knowing in general that when there is too much of it, we find it necessary to shovel it away" [10, 135]. "We" act out the crossing sweeper's dilemma, just as the crossing sweeper acts out ours.

The influence of the court does not erase distinctions between classes: for many purposes Jo continues to be a remote figure, cut off not only from Lady Dedlock or Esther but from a lowly person like Snagsby (How disoriented is the law stationer when Bucket conducts him to Jo's haunts in Tom-All-Alone's—*BH*, 22, 310). All the same, the omnipresent fog of the law in one sense links the city's inhabitants together. Anyone terrorized by a London where lawyers preside—Dickens's educated audience as well as Reynolds's uneducated one—will reside in "utter darkness" among "mysterious symbols," that is, among self-propagating and rule-bound documents whose result is "mystification" [8, 96]. As the novel develops, even the lawyers, the master obfuscators, will be afflicted by the darkness from which their power has grown. Chancery, then, threatens both more and less than "facility of transfer" in property; it effects a slow, obscure, grindingly effective transfer involving *intellectual* property—involving, that is, an ability to comprehend the world and to articulate one's comprehension. This ability is transferred from laymen to lawyers, from lawyers to . . . nowhere at all. Along with both the Lord Chancellor and Jo, the modern Londoner knows nothing, nothink.

A Sheet of Paper with Two Sides

Contemporary critics of *Bleak House* tended to see the Chancery plot as the novel's organizing center. Though this insight can be defended, it involves us in a difficulty. H. F. Chorley—a favorable reviewer, soon to become a personal friend of Dickens—praises what he takes to be the supplementary Dedlock plot but suspects that the novelist "has been thereby led away from his great Chancery case further than may have been his original intention" [Collins, 278]. Brimley suggests that the tale of Lady Dedlock could be dropped altogether, without "perceptible effect upon the remaining characters" [284]. Granted that the former comment is a bit condescending and the latter not so sympathetic as it might be, both observations raise a vexing question. The solution of one plot is not the solution of the other;[19] how then can Dickens base his narrative on strands of action associated so tenuously?

The answer lies in two incidents from the novel's opening installment. Both incidents involve Nemo, Lady Dedlock's former lover, who works at the most impersonal of literate trades: he is a copyist of legal documents. He has withdrawn from society, but while engaged in the eternal, mind-numbing task of copying (the next best thing to opium), he inadvertently communicates with his mistress and daughter. Without meaning to do so, he sets in motion the novel's principal intrigues. When Mrs. Snagsby refers to Nemo as Nimrod, the error is appropriate [*BH,* 11, 142]. Like the builder of Babel, the unfortunate copyist generates a confused gibberish of claims and surmises, of recognitions and disappearances; he transports us from the public to the private realm.

One document copied by Nemo becomes a communication with his former mistress. "The only property" Lady Dedlock brought her husband, Sir Leicester, was her part in the Chancery suit of Jarndyce vs. Jarndyce. Sir Leicester, who approves of the suit as a "slow, expensive, British, constitutional kind of thing," is listening to the solicitor Tulkinghorn present the latest news from the great court—while his lady is busy examining Nemo's handwriting [*BH,* 2, 13]. The piece of paper begins its journey at a desk described as "a wilderness marked with a rain of ink" [10, 136] and ends it at Chesney Wold, also rainy and also "a view in Indian ink" [2, 9]. Within this frame it precipitates a complex sequence of causes and effects. Tulkinghorn notes Lady Dedlock's interest, setting him on Nemo's track. Nemo dies shortly before Tulkinghorn arrives, leaving a pack of incriminating love letters, to be pilfered by Krook just before the lawyer can get his hands on them. Tulkinghorn then goes after a letter written by Nemo and owned by the shooting-gallery proprietor George, who must be pressured through the Smallweed family. The elusive love letters will again and again create battles for control of information.

This is the most conspicuous but not the only manifestation of the law writer's presence. Immediately after narrating My Lady's scene of recognition, Dickens introduces Esther Summerson—who tells how she got a note inviting her to join Mr. Jarndyce's household. The importance of the note is emphasized by its prominent position on the page (laid out for inspection apart from Esther's narrative) and by its distinctive typography, imitating legal handwriting [*BH,* 3, 26].[20] The note's role is further underlined by Esther's words about it. "Oh, never, never, never shall I forget the emotion this letter caused in the house! It was so tender in them to care so much for me; it was so gracious in that Father who had not forgotten me, to have made my orphan way so smooth and easy, and to have inclined so many youthful natures towards me; that I could hardly bear . . . the pain of it, and the pride and joy of it, and the humble regret of it" [3, 27]. Whether or not the letter is ordained by her Father, it has been written by her father, a fact Esther cannot realize.[21] Esther enters the realm of law where the law clerk Guppy will discover the relationship between her and Lady Dedlock. No less than the incriminating love letters, Esther will become an element in the struggle to conceal or unearth her mother's past.

In chapters 2 and 3, a Chancery action is linked with the buried love affair; this connection is kept up throughout the novel. Dickens seems to be examining the "mysteries" of the court [*BH,* 51, 751 and passim]. Sometimes he is, for the story of Richard Carstone genuinely centers on them. At certain other moments, the mysteries of the suit yield to the "mysteries of great houses" [36, 567]. The public mystification and the private battle over secrets will never become identical, a seamless unity; nonetheless, they take on a relation to one another, a relation sustained and emphasized in the actions of certain enterprising lawyers. Tulkinghorn need not concentrate on the Chancery suit of whose developments he is informing Sir Leicester; he can afford to observe My Lady, to analyze her reactions under the guise of his official duties. Guppy's situation permits him the same choice. Think of the restless law clerk sitting around in the long summer holidays, bored with Jarndyce and Jarndyce, all his passions concentrated on finding a packet of lost letters. He knows that affairs like Jarndyce are lucrative yet futile—that way lies "confusion" [20, 272]. Affairs like Lady Dedlock's are something else again. Redirected from a world of bureaucratic inanition, legal energy proves able to uncover substantive mysteries. Such mysteries are handled in good lawyerly style; the battle over secrets becomes pretty much what Chancery would be, were Chancery to exploit people without intolerable delays. It is a suit immensely speeded up, thereby rendered more explicitly destructive than in its official, plodding form, where at least costs take a long time to consume estates. The only legal habit dispensed with in such moments is that burdensome reliance, so conspicuous in Chancery, on "masterly fictions" and intricate "forms of procedure"; action tends to be brutally direct, even where the pretense of sticking to form persists. "He gets plainer as he gets on," writes Dickens of Tulkinghorn's negotiations with Lady Dedlock [41, 580]. So do they all. When the "property" in question is a compromising document [39, 559] rather than a obfuscatory one, archaic usage goes by the boards. Ruthlessly efficient action becomes the order of the day.

Dickens's Simmel-like contrast—between a mystified public realm and a private realm probed by inquisitive opportunists—might seem to break a narrative deadlock. On the one hand the novelist condemns the eloquence of Chancery; he maintains that the pomp and ceremony of law are a meaningless show. On the other, he seems to suggest that pomp and ceremony can be circumvented: under the glittering, ornamental surfaces of the court or similar institutions, lawyers are working busily to ferret out valuable secrets. The reader who follows the battle over secrets is able to grasp situations instead of taking it on faith that they last forever or anticipating a judgment far in the future (the conclusion of a suit, the crumbling of England). The ignorance of Jo and of everybody else is replaced by a new, substantial knowledge.

All this is true. However, replacing mystified eloquence with furtive knowledgeability is not in itself a satisfactory response to London. This treatment of the novel's two strands of action is more a starting point or a provocation than a solution. If Dickens begins by exploiting such contrasts, he eventually tries to dissolve them: his effort takes its crucial form in the central—literally central—chapters of *Bleak House,* where Esther Summerson's life reaches a crisis point.

Esther Written

Ambitious Guppy, an emulator of Tulkinghorn, has been on a tour of the Dedlock estate, where he saw a portrait of Lady Dedlock. He soon realizes that My Lady and Esther (whom he knows from her visit to the offices of Conversation Kenge) are uncannily alike. Acquiring a lead to the letters once owned by Nemo and presently hoarded by Krook, Guppy goes to My Lady with the joyful news that she possesses a hitherto unknown relation. Would she approve of his continuing his investigations? Guppy's plan—apparently aimed at blackmail—is clever, but it is stymied on two counts. Twice his quest after secrets becomes the prelude to an uncontrollable explosion. One explosion can be traced back to the churchyard, "pestiferous and obscene, whence malignant diseases are communicated to the bodies of our dear brothers and sisters who have not departed" [*BH*, 11, 151]. Nemo's resurrection occurs when his putrid essence is "communicated" to Jo; from Jo—who is fleeing Tulkinghorn and his kind—to Esther's maid Charley; and from Charley to Esther herself. "You're getting quite strong. . . . Strong enough to be told a secret, I think, Charley?" [31, 440]. The competition for secrets has produced the useless "secret" of Esther's fever and more permanently the ravaging of her face, a pattern of destruction immediately repeated. The scene this time is the rag-and-bottle shop where Mr. Weevle and Mr. Guppy prepare for a rendezvous with Krook. Krook is to deliver to them Nemo's letters, but they must wait for midnight before this transaction can take place. Meanwhile the old man makes one last attempt to wring the letters' secret from them, to read them without being able to read. He combusts, permeating his shop with yellow grease and soot. As Dickens writes, "this from which we run away, striking out the light and overturning one another into the street, is all that represents him" [32, 455]. Like those kindred mysteries the street mud and the law, Krook is reduced to all-pervasive gunk.

Mr. Snagsby's trembling expectation that a secret might "take air and fire, explode, and blow up" has come to pass, first in the fever and pustular eruptions of smallpox, then in the inflammable putrescence of a body filled with alcohol [*BH*, 25, 354]. These counterpointed disasters belong to the established design of the novel, the design set in chapter 2 when Lady Dedlock recognized Nemo's handwriting. Once again Dickens describes events that have a Chancery surface. On the one side, Krook's shop is compared to Chancery, Krook is called the "Lord Chancellor" [5, 51], and Guppy belongs to Kenge and Carboy, the firm that handles the Dedlock interest in Jarndyce and Jarndyce (when he sees Lady Dedlock, he must make a point of denying that he has come on Chancery business). On the other side, Jo arrives at Bleak House as Charley is learning to copy, so that there is a reference back to the copyist, Nemo, and the legal milieu where he found work: "Writing was a trying business to Charley, who seemed to have no natural power over a pen, but in whose hand every pen appeared to become perversely animated, and to go wrong and crooked" [31, 427], a Chancery dilemma if ever there was one. In both these cases, furthermore, there is a plunge beneath the surface of Chancery-like paperwork. To adapt Mr. Weevle's helpful terminology, the novel's interest shifts from smouldering to spontaneous combustion, from the invisible and infinitely prolonged disintegration of England to the immediate crises created by the threatened exposure of Lady Dedlock's past [39, 556].

This much said, there is a difference between the present constellation of events and the earlier scenes where Lady Dedlock and Esther read documents written by Nemo. The pursuit of secrets has spread further; in spreading, it has involved a greater range of people; given new scope it has shown its destructive capacity, not just in regard to the victims such as My Lady and her daughter but in regard to victimizers such as Guppy or Krook. One sign of a change in emphasis is that the letters start to become an object of repulsion; there is something dangerous about them, some power that may rebound upon their aspiring manipulators. Much the same may be noted of Esther. Though her face remains "imprinted" on Guppy's "art" to the very end of the novel [*BH,* 29, 406; 64, 861], "that image is shattered" [39, 556]; Esther's usefulness as a manipulable secret, a kind of document in the flesh, seems to be at an end. Guppy shuns her— citing, of course, "circumstances over which I have no control" [38, 543]. Tulkinghorn, "high-priest of noble mysteries" [42, 583], still presides untouched over London, but beneath his august level the would-be Tulkinghorns start to come to grief. And even so *knowing* a fellow as the high priest himself may not know as much or be so invulnerable as he thinks.

To say that the hierarchy is shaken up—that manipulator and manipulated exist on newly even terms—is to raise the possibility of other fresh developments. If brash Guppy can be reduced to such abject terror that he won't even go back into Krook's house alone, might not the opposite occur with Esther? Before her illness she was usually an object of other people's schemes. Many of her acquaintances seemed to know more about her than she did. People whispered in her presence, frowned at her as though she had done something wrong, or hinted at unspeakable possibilities. Esther has put all such peculiarities out of her mind, but she finds it increasingly difficult to do so. Describing Chancery, Mr. Jarndyce notes that "all through the deplorable cause, everything that everybody in it, except one man, knows already, is referred to that only one man who don't know it, to find out" [*BH,* 8, 95]. Esther's life seems to possess the same monstrous, grinding, and overwhelming inefficiency, but here inefficiency has unexpected results. The case is being referred to her, whether she likes it or not: she *must be* a party to it [paraphrase of Jarndyce on Chancery, 8, 96]. Perhaps she might begin to understand, to brave the terrors of this undesired affiliation.

Esther is understandably reluctant to take any action concerning her own position in the mystery. During her nightmare she prays to be removed from the burning necklace on which she is one of the beads [*BH,* 35, 489]. Father/father fulfills her prayer; he helps her become literally self-effacing. (This transformation is emphasized by Phiz's illustrations where never, after Esther's illness, is her countenance exposed.) Soon after, My Lady confesses everything to Esther, whereupon she feels "a burst of gratitude to the providence of God that I was so changed as that I never could disgrace her by any trace of likeness" [36, 509]. She is the daughter of parents quite different in status, one called Nemo or Nobody (an "anonymous character, his name being unknown" [29, 408]), the other virtually a celebrity [20, 285; 39, 561], not to mention a woman "perfectly self-possessed" [18, 255]. The more Esther learns of mother, the more she resembles father. Afraid that she might betray Lady Dedlock, she embraces the anonymity Nemo inadvertently communicated; always shy, she is now tempted to will herself into nothingness (even while she continues her charitable projects). Down the hall at Bleak House, Mr. Jarndyce tries by a similar means to accommodate Chancery. He would live outside the suit even though he bears its name, would do good deeds without seeming to do them—a blundering strategy that enrages Richard, his ward. Jarndyce will never learn how to cope with the court; Esther is more fortunate in her analogous struggle. The question of who owns the secret haunts her and others as the property dispute haunts the parties in the great suit: it is Lady Dedlock's secret, of course . . . it is Mr. Tulkinghorn's . . . it is Mr. Tulkinghorn's "in trust for Sir Leicester and the family" . . . at all events it is "not mine," (i.e., not Esther's), with the paradoxical result that Esther has to "bear [it] alone" [48, 659; 37, 518].[22] However, though this tangled dispute shows signs of becoming interminable, not to mention inexplicable, its obscurities are eventually clarified. Dickens's heroine is compelled to admit her "secret interest" in the events developing around her [52, 702; cf. Mr. Vholes on "interests," 60, 821: "It is a term we use"]. Having admitted it, she moves toward the production of a document more effective than any other in *Bleak House,* a document that— combining eloquence with secrets—grants the elusive secret to its final, rightful owner, and thus reconstructs the "shattered image" of a face.

Esther Writing

My discussion has so far centered on Dickens's divided subject, his attempt to combine a story of private with a story of public life. At least since the time of E. M. Forster and *Aspects of the Novel* (1927), it has been customary to treat *Bleak House* in terms of a different division, the sharing of the story between two contrasted narrators. I'm going to agree that this is a crucial topic—crucial, however, mainly insofar as it throws light on that other, more basic split between public and private realms. Esther's excursions into wit and eloquence are kept to a minimum; a common first impression is that she is upstaged by her unnamed counterpart, a clever authority on everything within his broad purview. However, this evaluation is not quite accurate. The unnamed narrator gains much of his ease (in articulation, in perception, in combining public with private address, something he accomplishes beautifully in much of *Bleak House*) by means of his evident detachment: his safety, so to speak. So far as can be established, he is not part of the situation that he describes; one doesn't know where or how to locate him. His accusations against England and the English—for example, on Jo's death[23]—are therefore delivered securely. He can speak in a public voice without peril. Esther, by contrast, writes from an engaged position. She's not going to become *like* her colleague, the elusive social commentator and comic; it would be more accurate to say that she will learn to match his accomplishment on her own, perilous terms.

That she does so with the aid of Allegory—that is, of a half-imaginary character who appears only on the unnamed narrator's pages—adds to the peculiarly divided excitements of *Bleak House*. Dickens develops this collaboration carefully. He has his unnamed narrator work out an analytic and abstruse approach to Allegory; then he suggests that it applies to Esther—in fact, that it could resolve some of her difficulties about telling secrets while keeping them. More exactly yet: the caustic, protected narrative's treatment of Allegory strengthens one's understanding of Esther's potential power, of what a vulnerable narrator located inside London's social systems might accomplish; then Esther herself puts the understanding to use. As this last sentence implies, the relation between the two narratives is a great deal like that between theory and practice. The narrator is *theoretical* because he can't be touched, because he is, in effect, tinkering with a model of reality that can't strike back at him, because he exploits the advantages of unfettered and unrestricted thought; Esther is *practical* in the specific sense that the consequences of her words are going to devolve upon her, and that she must thus be very careful about anything she writes for an audience larger than herself. Under Allegory's aegis, she manages to write a great deal, revealing secrets that would otherwise have remain hidden. Here, therefore, is a more productive version than usual of that nasty dialectic, that nasty exchange between public and private, that governs so much of *Bleak House*. The way the narrators play off against each other helps establish a vital form of public commentary, which in Esther's apparently hopeless case supersedes a deadly hoarding of secrets. A secretive and retiring narrator goes public—revealing, in the last analysis, more than could that confident voice she learned from.

Esther's opening chapter demonstrates some of her initial perplexities, as she begins to work toward a public form of writing: "I have a great deal of difficulty in beginning to write my portion of these pages, for I know I am not clever. . . . It seems so curious to me to be obliged to write all this about myself! As if this narrative were the narrative of *my* life!" [*BH*, 3, 15 and 26]. What might be of interest here is less Esther's coyness— irritating though it proves—than the extensive difficulties that lie just behind it. Dickens makes her conscious of setting pen to paper and of contributing to a larger unit ("my portion of these pages") over whose shape she does not possess final authority. Esther, it seems, is not the usual first-person narrator who tells a story by established literary convention (such a narrator can easily be represented as speaking rather than writing, which would have been a simple and elegant way out for Dickens); nor is she a compulsive diarist like Clarissa; nor, so far as can be determined, is she a contributor to a commissioned document of the sort posited in *The Moonstone* (the reader is teased with this alternative, but teased only). Most problematic: from the way she flounders about, one could almost suppose that there had been no alteration in Esther, that the girl who wilted under Miss Barbary's hand and the woman who looks back on a terrible childhood were the same person, without substantial development interceding. Impossible—an Esther who had remained unchanged would not have agreed to produce an ambitious manuscript designed for many unknown eyes, recording the horrible, in some cases shaming, fates met by parents and friends. It would take a bold or original person to write these things down under any circumstances. What, then, is the means by which the child becomes the adult, the victim a narrator of such sufferings—even though a reluctant one?[24]

Into the chapter where these perplexities are crowded—and where Esther's connection with Chancery and its infernal writing machine is also established—Dickens pauses over one story about writing that seems particularly suggestive. Esther quotes from the Gospel of John, "how our Saviour stooped down, writing with his finger in the dust, when they [the Pharisees and scribes] brought the sinful woman to him. 'So when they continued asking him, he lifted up himself and said unto them, He that is without sin among you, let him first cast a stone at her!' " [*BH*, 3, 19]. Christ's writing in the dust has long been a controversial topic among biblical interpreters.[25] Dickens's *Life of Our Lord* (a children's book written in 1849) attempts several bold clarifications of an ambiguous tale:

> *Jesus looked upon the noisy crowd attentively, and knew that they had come to make Him say the law was wrong and cruel and that if He said so,*

*they would make it a charge against Him and would kill Him. They were
ashamed and afraid as He looked into their faces, but they still cried out,
"Come! What say you Master? what say you?"*

* * * * *

*Jesus stooped down and wrote with his finger in the sand on the
ground, "He that is without sin among you, let him throw the first stone
at her." As they read this, looking over one another's shoulders, and as He
repeated the words to them, they went away ashamed, until not a man of
all the noisy crowd was left there; and Jesus Christ, and the woman,
hiding her face in her hands, alone remained.*[26]

In Dickens's version, the prophet neither doodles distractedly nor conceals
what he has deliberately written; he writes in order to speak, he speaks in
order to take a position on a topic full of dangers for himself (questions like
the one asked of him are an inquiry into his nature as well as into the law's).
Even where writing looks like a withdrawal into solitude, the claim to a
private space, it can thus serve a public function. Far from indicating a
desire to elude a difficult situation, this message is an act of commitment: it
lasts long enough to serve as a tool for teaching the crowd mercy, or in the
terms of English law, equity; it makes readers of actors and auditors of
readers, thus blurring the line between those who participate in the story
and those who learn about it at a distance; it creates a momentary but
powerful community where the justice of a new order can be proclaimed.
(This community is not a court, but it substitutes for a court.) Most
intriguing of all, it ends with a confrontation between a practitioner of
purposeful writing and a woman who "hides her face in her hands." (The
latter detail is Dickens's addition.) In one way that woman anticipates the
figure of Lady Dedlock, the adulteress hounded by the law; in another, she
anticipates Esther, the daughter of the adulteress, reduced to facelessness
by pressure from both within and without. A gospel text recast by the
novelist gives us a preview of perhaps his greatest novel.

A preview only. When Dickens places the tale from John in Esther's
narrative—indeed, places it almost at the start, where she is especially
awkward—he suggests a possible answer to her difficulties; he sketches
something of an inward-outward movement, a movement that begins
with a seeming retreat from view but then achieves unexpected force and
conviction. Dust, that "universal article" of London and *Bleak House,* into
which papers, self and "all things of earth, animate and inanimate, are
resolving" [*BH,* 22, 305], becomes the medium of a communication both
truthful and effective.[27] On the other hand, this does not means that the
biblical story can transmit its message simply. The retelling in the *Life of*

Our Lord contains two striking ellipses: the asterisked pause at the tale's middle, the point where writing must begin, and the unspoken (or unwritten) aftermath, where the woman hiding her face must be counseled, consoled, or helped to learn some valuable lesson. Articulating the lesson, passing it on, will be difficult, to say the least: as Dickens immediately establishes, it cannot be transmitted through mere reiteration of a biblical text. Esther reads John's words to her aunt Miss Barbary; caught up in repressed guilt and the throes of legalism (of fear concerning "what is written" 3, 17), the latter falls down in a fit that soon kills her. Words of mercy become words of judgment. *Bleak House* must further define the sense in which Christ's writing could be reinvented for the metropolis.

Nine chapters after this dilemma is formulated, Esther's fellow narrator describes Allegory, the painted Roman who gesticulates from Mr. Tulkinghorn's ceiling.[28] The ceiling is part of a "former house of state"; it belongs to a mansion whose public spaces are no longer used to a public end (a kind of reversal met elsewhere in *Bleak House*). As might be expected, the grandiloquent rhetoric of this place is perfectly irrelevant. Once Allegory may have been an allegory of something in particular; now he is nothing more than a habit of personification.[29] The joke, then, is to personify the habit—a regression into figures about figures that bars Allegory from any referential capacity or any possible audience. The Roman occupies what could be a crucial borderline position between a public world receding into mystery and a private one about to be exposed. All the same, his sole remaining capacity is to make the head ache [*BH*, 10, 130]. Lost among Tulkinghorn's secretive manipulations, "foreshortened Allegory [stares] down at his intrusion, as if it meant to swoop upon him, and he [cuts] it dead" [10, 131]. This brilliantly phrased comment, combining the language of social manipulation with that of physical action ("swoop"/"cut"), equating an optical effect ("foreshortened") with a disastrous cultural decline, sums up the unnamed narrator's attitude toward the London he describes: he is wonderfully witty and exact about a place where witty exactness is either difficult or impossible—where Allegory, most especially, is . . . nothing.

Allegory's status starts to change in chapter 16. The unnamed narrator— in a passage cited above—describes Jo's puzzlement at being surrounded by visible but mysterious language. His enforced vagrancy as he is constantly "moved on" is juxtaposed with the behavior of Lady Dedlock, who has "flitted away to town, with no intention of remaining there, and will soon flit hither again, to the confusion of the fashionable intelligence." These two restless beings are about to meet. It is Allegory who directs us to their confrontation. Tulkinghorn sits working in his chambers, while "Allegory, in the person of one impossible Roman upside down, points with the arm of Samson (out of joint, and an odd one) obtrusively toward the window" [*BH,* 16, 222]. The pointing gesture is noted for the first time, then dismissed. "Why should Mr. Tulkinghorn, for such no reason, look out of window? Is the hand not always pointing there?" Tulkinghorn misses Lady Dedlock, who is passing by at that moment; she in her turn catches up to Jo, commissioning him to show her all the places associated with Nemo. Last and most awful is the "place of abomination" where he is buried. Lady Dedlock veils her face, recoiling in disgust; the crossing sweeper "thrusts the handle of his broom between the bars of the gate, and, with his utmost power of elaboration, points it out" [16, 225: the moment is illustrated by Phiz under the title "Consecrated Ground"].

This account—verbal and graphic—has exploited a peculiarity of any pointing, that it draws attention *to* the pointer, then *away* from him. One is inveigled into scrutinizing an image as though for some hermetic message, yet the closer this scrutiny becomes, the more one is encouraged to search in widening circles: to search (in this case) through the city until the gesture finds an appropriate context.[30] This sequence of events suggests Allegory's unique strength. A "masterly fiction," Allegory is powerless in himself, but so far as he is applied or directed, even by unsuspecting agents, he helps revive a public speaking/writing more truthful than that represented by the Court; he links eloquence with a pursuit of knowledge otherwise possible only to furtive intriguers. Allegory is not Christ. The Roman suspended in air will never become a Palestinian prophet squatting on the ground; his extended digit will never touch any markable surface— and yet, if hardly so down-to-earth as the protagonist of John's tale, he presides over a transformation of the word and its possibilities.

Allegory's metamorphosis occurs in several stages, each noted in turn by the unnamed narrator. Though the Roman is released from Tulking- horn's chambers, his pointing finger acquires only a limited significance when it is passed to Jo. Jo points with the handle of his broom, an instrument whose other end is reserved for sweeping street mud. The latter substance is "kindred" to the law in that London contains excessive quantities of it; the boy thus clears away the sort of obstruction that lawyers typically accumulate. This accomplishment has little impact. If the broom's brush is insufficient to clarify the "unintelligible mess" of London, then so is its handle. Like sweeping, pointing is more the asser- tion of an intention than its fulfillment. Jo's mistake is to believe that "I don't know nothink!" [*BH*, 16, 225]. He points at the right place; if only she gave him a chance and he persevered, he could tell Lady Dedlock the story of her lover's last days (that story never got into the newspaper because Jo was barred from testifying at the inquest). Instead the two of them stare at the blessed or perhaps damned ground of the churchyard. "I should think it was t'othered [damned] myself," says Jo [16, 225]. When he looks around, Lady Dedlock is gone and so is his opportunity to speak.

This first unfolding of Allegory's possibilities will have to be succeeded by another. His pointing will again be decoded and again lead to the churchyard—by a means more fully described and to an end more fully understood. The journey begins when Tulkinghorn is murdered by the irate lady's-maid Hortense. Just before the fatal shot, "every noise is merged, this moonlight night, into a distant ringing hum, as if the city were a vast glass, vibrating" [*BH*, 48, 663]. The energies of nocturnal London achieve an ominous unity, then are concentrated to one spot when Hortense fires her pistol. It is this spot toward which Allegory newly points.[31] "He is pointing at an empty chair, and at a stain upon the ground before it that might be almost covered with a hand. These objects lie directly within his range. . . . It happens surely, that every one who comes into the darkened room and looks at these things, looks up at the Roman, and that he is invested in all eyes with mystery and awe, as if he were a paralysed dumb witness" [48, 665]. Allegory's "mystery" is much greater than before: how inaccessible, how cut off from any possible interrogation, seems this potential witness. That Allegory lives in his own unreachable world—which all the same contains a vital, hidden significance—has become more than the narrator's conceit. "Everyone" who enters the room shares this striking thought.

To Allegory's hermetic withdrawal corresponds his unfolding into the world outside the window. His gesture is made meaningful by a succession of agents: preeminently, Bucket the detective, Sir Leicester Dedlock, and Esther (arguably Alan Woodcourt belongs in this list too). I should note that Bucket is often taken to be the guiding figure of knowledge in the novel's later chapters. It is certainly true that when he first appears he seems to have supernatural powers; however, once put to the test, these powers prove flawed, no less than those of the novel's legal investigators. Bucket is a highly problematic character; it is in combination with others that he makes his contribution to the action over which Allegory more distantly presides.[32] The sequence of events is as follows. Arriving to investigate the murder, Bucket compares his forefinger with the Roman's. "The fat forefinger seems to rise to the dignity of a familiar demon"; it not only "whispers information," as Jo's finger did, it "charms" the guilty party to her destruction [*BH*, 53, 712]. Bucket's pointing allows him to establish a "dreadful right of property" in Hortense [54, 741]; nonetheless, he cannot control her ability to pass on information. Before she is taken away Hortense reveals to Sir Leicester My Lady's affair with Nemo. Sir Leiceister collapses, paralyzed and dumb like a certain Roman. "After vainly trying to make himself understood in speech, he makes signs for a pencil. . . . he writes, 'My Lady.' . . . He points . . . in great agitation, at the two words. They all try to quiet him, but he points again with increased agitation" [56, 761–62]. Sir Leicester's pointing conveys "full forgiveness" for his wife, a message that can be relayed only by Bucket— who thus arrives once more on the scene.

As Bucket remarks, "the cat's away, and the mice they play; the frost breaks up, and the water runs" [*BH*, 54, 736]. According to Bucket's account, it is not just small fry like the well-named Guppy who relinquish control over the circulation of documents. In the current situation—and especially now that the high priest Tulkinghorn is dead—everyone faces new constraints, new limitations on their power. The result is a reordering of energies attributable to no single character in this novel but devolving upon Esther. Bucket recruits her to accompany him in the pursuit of My Lady ordained by Sir Leicester. If the detective is deputed the husband's spokesman, then Esther in her turn will speak for the detective. The case is referred to her once again, but on new terms. Allegory and his agents point her toward the churchyard where her mother lies cold and dead.

Esther's approach to the churchyard is narrated with extraordinary vividness. She moves among "clogged and bursting gutters and water-spouts;" she feels "great water-gates . . . opening and closing in my head" [*BH*, 59, 811]. There may be a reference back to the "curious sense of fulness" that she felt when she was getting sick [31, 440]; there are probably connections with Bucket's observation that "the frost breaks up, and the water runs" [54, 736], Lady Dedlock's anticipation of an "unim-agined flood" [55, 758], and her husband's complaint that "the floodgates of society are burst open, and the waters have—a—obliterated the land-marks of the framework of the cohesion by which things are held to-gether!" [40, 570–71]. The current perception, however, is different from any of these earlier ones. Esther's words suggest a curious parity between "clogged" and "bursting," "opening" and "closing." Her situation is retarded and driven forward at the same time: she shrinks back as she inches forward under Allegory's distant, passive, but ultimately effective sway. She experiences the abrupt rearrangement of a complex pattern, suffering the biggest headache the Roman ever gave anybody.

The last moments of Esther's journey are also the most telling. She makes one final effort to dissociate herself from her difficult circumstances, for when they discover a woman lying at the churchyard gate and Bucket explains that the woman is Lady Dedlock, she refuses to comprehend. What she thinks she sees is "the mother of the dead child" (i.e., the serving-maid of Lady Dedlock). Then, when she "turn[s] the face" of the woman, she finds "my mother, cold and dead" [*BH*, 59, 812]. Mr. Guppy remarks of Nemo's death, "It was supposed . . . that he left no rag or scrap behind him by which he could possibly be identified. But he did. He left a bundle of letters" [29, 408–9]. Lady Dedlock tries to die even more anonymously than her lover: "I have nothing about me by which I can be recognized. This paper I part with now" [59, 808]. Like him, however, she leaves one thing behind her, one compromising secret—passed on when Esther confronts her mother's corpse. Recognizing Lady Dedlock's face, Esther resumes an identity that she supposed herself to have lost. What father/Father destroyed by his death, mother ("my mother," *mine* by the physical resemblance that reverberates through the book) restores in hers. Esther Summerson lays claim—not to My Lady, not even to "my mother," really, but to Esther Summerson.

The concluding chapters of *Bleak House* clarify this action: clarify, that is, the terms on which it succeeds. The reader is asked to keep in mind two very different treatments of the scandalous secrets over which so many battles have been fought. Tulkinghorn had predicted to Lady Dedlock that her "flight . . . would spread the whole truth, and a hundred times the whole truth, far and wide. . . . the wall-chalking and the street-crying would come on directly" [*BH*, 41, 579–80]. Lady Dedlock flies her home on the assumption that "her shame will be published—may be spreading while she thinks about it" [55, 758]. The "truth" of her "shame" proves harder to publish than either of these antagonists would have supposed. My Lady never becomes more than "vaguely the town talk" [58, 787]. The rumor of the hour subsides, neither clarified nor understood, obscured in part by Bucket's negotiations with the Smallweeds, but even more by the fickleness of fashion. According to the last of the unnamed narrator's chapters, how Lady Dedlock died remains "all mystery" [66, 872]. Dickens thus establishes the limits of what the unnamed narrator can accomplish; however much he may tell us, he is oddly powerless over the world he describes.

The case is different at the end of Esther's narrative:

H, 67,
o]

> *"My dear Dame Durden . . . do you ever look in the glass?"*
> *"You know I do; you see me do it."*
> *"And don't you know that you are prettier than you ever were?"*
> I did not know that; I am not certain that I know it now. But [my
> children, friend, husband, and guardian] can very well do without much
> beauty in me—even supposing——.[33]

Esther the writer has seemed much like Esther the child, as though no
significant action had intervened between her girlhood and the composition of her manuscript. A significant action does intervene but has its effect
primarily when it is written, when it is made into a document associated
with the name of Esther Summerson. Apart from Esther's fleeting hint,
there is no way of judging whether her countenance has actually been
restored (i.e., accepted from mother, where it was previously rejected).
Nor can it be determined to whom she thinks she writes, except that it is an
"unknown friend" ("he or she"). Attention is thus focused on the facts that
can be known. Given the constraints of Victorian biography and autobiography, it is hardly imaginable that a memoir such as Esther's could
have been issued in the 1850s or for some time afterwards. Set against the
city of documents created in *Bleak House,* the fiction that she has published
her account, and published it under her name, nonetheless makes sense.
"Looking up from my desk as I write," Esther completes her narrative,
then lets it go: releases it under circumstances where uncertainty of audience, like uncertainty of ownership, is inevitable. The prophet controlled the meaning of the writing in the dust by reciting and explaining it
to those around him. Though Esther can do no such thing, she moves
toward a related end by a less certain means. She *publishes* Lady Dedlock's
"shame" and her own; she writes from an engaged, located, and therefore
threatened position to a readership out of sight—situated in some ambiguous region between the society described by *Bleak House* and the novel-
loving public that Dickens had helped create. To borrow a phrase from
Mr. Turveydrop, her words have now become "the general property" [14,
193]: for better or worse, they are granted to everyone.[34] Like Allegory's
pointing, her writing goes out to the world—confirms her identity while
testing its truth. She owns up to what she cannot, and never could, own.

Are there other such actions in the book? Many, I would say—but one
especially close. I refer to the release of Miss Flite's birds, whose position in
the Chancery plot matches the position of Allegory in the story of Lady
Dedlock and her daughter. Miss Flite will not tell the birds' names when

the wards first visit; later Krook reveals that the names constitute—what else?—a personification allegory [*BH,* 14, 200]. Here are "Hope, Joy, Youth, Peace, Rest, Life, Dust, Ashes, Waste, Want, Ruin, Despair" and many others: qualities of a feather, caged together. It is not until the missing will is discovered, the suit "melts away" [65, 867], and Richard finally dies that they are freed. Like other allegorical gestures of release, this letting-go has a mixed significance. Perhaps (as Krook predicts) the tame birds will be killed by wild ones. They could never survive in the open, for they have never known it. On the other hand Krook is not the wisest character in *Bleak House,* and allegory has greater powers than even Miss Flite—Miss Flight—may happen to realize. To tell the names of the birds is to indicate rather little about these powers, as it happens. To free them at the moment of another's demise is to confront one's own imprisonments: the beginning of knowledge about where one stands. Perhaps Miss Flite's ceremony is the nearest the Chancery tale can come to the relinquishments associated with Esther Summerson after Lady Dedlock's death. At this moment, she too is able to combine eloquence with truth. The world of public mystifications repeats in a minor key what has been worked out more fully in the world of domestic scandal. The two worlds vibrate together, as they have from the opening chapters of *Bleak House*—though now Chancery repeats a compromise effected in the private intrigue, whose nature and logic it had originally shaped.

"The secret," says Simmel, "contains a tension that is dissolved in the moment of its revelation. . . . The secret, too, is full of the consciousness that it *can* be betrayed; that one holds the power of surprises, turns of fate, joy, destruction—if only, perhaps, of self-destruction. For this reason, the secret is surrounded by the possibility and temptation of betrayal; and the external danger of being discovered is interwoven with the internal danger, which is like the fascination of an abyss, of giving oneself away." This passage from the *Sociology* [333–34] is matched by one from the later *Philosophie des Geldes* where Simmel says almost the same thing about property: "The fascination of owning is so intensified at the moment of giving property away—painfully or joyfully—that it is not possible to do so [i.e., to realize possessive ties] without paying this price. . . . The ability of the personality that ownership represents appears visibly intensified by disposing of what is owned."[35] The point of the closing words of *Bleak House* is to combine—to merge—these closely related sensations. Retrospectively, Esther's entire narrative, a tale not just whispered to a confidant but written down, day after day, *deliberately,* must seem a confession of almost erotic abandon—as well as the biggest potlatch of all time, a giving-away party where what might seem self-destruction has at last become a usable and socially proper self-possession.

For D. A. Miller, *Bleak House's* fluctuation between private and public spheres suggests the generic nature of novels; a novel is "a drill in the rhythms of bourgeois industrial culture."[36] Miller is amusing, at times rigorous. His judgment is overly reductive: first in the assumption that home is the environment par excellence for novel reading (a novel, certainly a Dickensian parts-issue, is attractive for its portability—for the fact that it can be taken almost anywhere); second, in the proposal that a strict and broadly applicable division limits the ethos of *Bleak House* (for Miller, private is to public as domestic to institutional and leisure to work, a dubious set of equations; moreover, these contrarieties can only be merged by a process of "imbrication," like tiles overlapping on a roof, not by a process of interchange and mutual transformation); third, in the pervasive assumption that novels inculcate, indoctrinate, propagandize, without ever confronting (bringing to consciousness) the ethos that underlies them. Novels are not only objects of study but instruments by which analytic thought can occur. Novels are not only the voice of society but voices that speak to and speak about society. Through Esther, Dickens locates himself within a system in order to anatomize it. By settling his place within the system, he can think beyond the limits that it sets. This activity—this fluctuation, if you will, between private and public, between home and the world at large—is not much like the sort of disciplinary exercise assumed by the term *drill*.

At the end, *Bleak House's* kind of clarification remains perilous: it asks for a trust that it may not get; it therefore runs the risk of being assimilated back into the perverse systems of a city that is also a document. Only in one sense are the tensions of London mitigated. The novelist has managed to specify within the reality of the novel a fellow writer whose activities work to a positive if perilous end. Moreover, he has done so without violating the argument of his book, the sense of a metropolis at once vast and claustrophobic, where public institutions are riddles maintained by a priesthood of experts and where private selves are always capable of exploding into the murky general atmosphere. Documents create the terror of such a world; documents also create a perspective on it, but only if one knows oneself well enough to let them go.

Gone they are: once they are released, it becomes clear that they were never the property of any individual. While this thought is perhaps comforting, while it may help stop the vicious competition for secrets, note that it implicitly admits the preeminence of Simmel's "objective culture."

Objective culture belongs to everyone or no one. The discovery of such a category may be the most important fact about *Bleak House*. It might be argued that most of Dickens's novels are concerned with culture of this kind, as embodied in the physical shape or social arrangements of the city. After *Bleak House* and its scrutiny of documents, however, the concern is more precisely focused. Dickens starts to worry about something unpossessable even in an act of mind. I may claim myself (on qualified but genuine terms). I may not claim London. What then is my relation to the city?

9. Mystery and Revelation in *Les Misérables*

IT IS SAID that urban society dissolves traditional ties, abandoning the individual within an impersonal and dwarfing environment. That same society prompts him to make himself heard. Not only Gavroche the street urchin but the other inhabitants of Paris are isolated atoms,[1] hurried on from disguise to disguise or passion to passion. Under these circumstances, people are led to articulate their beliefs by any means available, becoming ever more ingenious as the conflicts of class or the possibilities of revolution provoke them. Little wonder, then, that *Les Misérables* deals so plentifully in curses, codes, jargons, and inscriptions or that these various means of communication often seem isolating. As Hugo notes: "Dieu livre aux hommes ses volontés visibles dans les événements, texte obscur écrit dans une langue mystérieuse. . . . il y a déjà vingt traductions sur la place publique. De chaque traduction naît un parti, et de chaque contre-sens une faction; et chaque parti croit avoir le seul vrai texte, et chaque faction croit posséder la lumière" (God grants men a vision of his will in unfolding events, an obscure text written in a mysterious language. . . . There are already twenty translations offered in the marketplace. From each translation is born a party, and from each misreading a faction; and each party believes that it has the only true text, and each faction that it possesses the light) [*LM,* 4.1.4, 403–4]. Hugo's comments pose a difficulty for any city novelist, but especially for his own endeavor: How is a metropolis caught among premature translators to be apprehended; is there any substantive sense in which it can be described as a whole or in which its inhabitants can be imagined as sharing the same world? So far as *Les Misérables* is concerned, the integrity of Paris is discovered by those who *decipher* slowly ("déchiffre lentement," 4.1.4, 403), making their way through a profusion of linguistic mysteries until they reach—the sewers. Perhaps this goal is not so dubious as it appears. The sewer is the realm of argot: slang as crime; it is also a place where literacy and illiteracy mix, where the book is freed by license, where the energies of urban speech and urban writing in all their varieties combine at last. In fact, the sewer is much like the city above, except that those conflicting translations can now be understood, each in its own terms and each as it contributes to an evolving whole. If this subterranean community reforms communication, communication in its turn underlies a new understanding of community.

Melancholy, 1845

The dilemma addressed by *Les Misérables* has sources in the visionary preachments of *Notre-Dame*. The earlier novel insists that the public word—above all, the word of the printing press—determines Western history. It formulates a theory of urban life according to which the harmonies of medieval Paris are replaced by the melancholic mixtures of the modern city. Nietzsche evokes "those extraordinary broad towers of society which distinguished the Middle Ages," and which enforced a belief that the individual gains fulfillment as *"a stone in a great building."* "Democratic ages" foster a very different notion of human identity; man believes that he *"can play almost any role."*[2] Hugo's figures define a similar shift. "Adieu le mystère, le mythe, la loi. Voici la fantaisie et le caprice. . . . Le livre architectural n'appartient plus au sacerdoce, à la religion, à Rome; il est à l'imagination, à la poésie, au peuple" (Goodbye to mystery, myth and law. Fantasy and caprice have arrived. . . . The architectural book no longer belongs to the priest, to religion, to Rome, but to imagination, poetry, and the people) [*ND*, 5.2, 202]. This revolution is seen as the basis for the social, political and aesthetic forms of democracy. Cities, like human minds, participate in the chaos of free expression whose founding invention was the movable type of Gutenberg.

"Adieu le mystère," but as "mystère" in a theological sense withdraws from a dominant position it gives way to mysteries far less comprehensible. The Hugo of *Notre-Dame* is of two minds about this change. On the one hand, he suggests that the victory of alphabet over edifice opens up essential opportunities for the human race. A society based on words freed from theocratic authority creates "activité incessante, labeur infatigable, concours acharné de l'humanité tout entière, refuge promis à l'intelligence contre un nouveau déluge" (incessant activity, indefatigable labor, the strenuous competition of all humanity, a refuge promised to intelligence against a new flood) [*ND*, 5.2, 211]. On the other hand words so freed may lose the power that they originally possessed; it is no longer clear what stands behind them, except the possibility of infinite replication. Replication may not be enough, a thought Hugo skirts but fails at this stage to confront.

Reaching middle age, he could no longer avoid certain doubts. By the 1840s, his literary career had reached a point of crisis. The failure of *Les Burgraves* (1843) was in some respects the deathblow of French romanticism. A few months after, the drowning of Hugo's daughter Léopoldine left him in a depression from which he would never entirely recover. Though he went on writing, he shunned publication during the next nine years. Literature had become a private matter. Hugo wished to remain a part of the strenuous competition of all humanity, but he would do so not as a poet, dramatist, or novelist: instead he would become a politician. Promoting himself by any means necessary—above all, by flattering the duchesse d'Orléans—he worked his way toward a peerage. On April 13, 1845, he attained this goal. "Alphonse Karr observed that, if Hugo owed some gratitude to Louis-Philippe, 'perhaps he owed even more to the Duchesse . . . who, it was said, carried off the nomination almost by assault.' "[3]

In retrospect it is easy to see how and why the political career failed. Hugo was no more suited to a legislature or cabinet than Dickens to the daily editorship of a newspaper. In 1845 this cannot have been so clear. Hugo would continue his literary work but, feeling in these years of crisis what literature alone cannot accomplish, would attempt to combine it with political words, whose impact was presumably direct and unmistakable. It is against this background that we can understand a reminiscence recorded by his surviving daughter, Adèle. She recalls Hugo reading his poem "Melancholia" on Christmas Day, 1855. "La pièce que je vais vous lire, nous dit-il, m'est venue à la chambre des pairs en 1845, et même je l'y avais déjà commencée, sur ce papier, et mon père nous montre le papier vénérable qui s'était installé à la chambre des pairs et mon père nous lut la pièce de vers" (The piece that I am going to read to you, he told us, came to me in the chamber of peers in 1845, and I had already started it there, on this piece of paper—whereupon my father showed us the venerable paper that had been installed in the chamber of peers, and read us the poem). After *installé,* at least one editor has placed a *sic.*[4] Adèle seems to be making a pun; she speaks as though the paper itself had been installed in the chamber; as though, in fact, the paper *were* her father. This liberty suggests much of Hugo's dilemma. As Adèle goes on to tell us, Hugo was attempting to push through the chamber a law regulating child labor. The law never came to anything; the chamber itself was dispersed to the four winds (Adèle's Hugolian phrase) with the abdication of Louis-Philippe in February 1848. What survived was the poem, whose poetic "installation" proved more lasting than Hugo's political one.

"Melancholia" begins with the command "Ecoutez," as though to summon an increasingly elusive audience to the poet. This gesture has a certain pathos. According to contemporaries, Hugo was a poor public speaker, incapable of thinking on the spur of the moment: he *writes* "Ecoutez," converting the orator's situation back into the poet's—retreating, in this act, from the world of political power he had supposedly entered. What will be "heard" under these equivocal circumstances is a series of word pictures, each displaying some form of social injustice. In 1854, not long before the reading to his family, Hugo would finally finish this sequence. During the mid-forties, when he belonged to the chamber of peers, only half of "Melancholia" was actually completed. It is these initial passages of "Melancholia" that are most instructive for my purposes. Hugo describes (in sequence) a prostitute with a child mocked by people in the street (the demon, misery, has forced her to this shame); a man who, having stolen a loaf of bread to feed his starving family, now faces trial; and a man of genius, either an orator and politician or a poet, who suffers for his opinions: he describes, to look forward to *Les Misérables,* Fantine, Jean Valjean, and himself, their creator.[5] Adèle confirms this similitude; in the reminiscence already quoted, she notes, "mon père nous dit que c'était elle [cette pièce] qui contenait le germe du roman inédit *Misérables* (my father told us that this piece contained the germ of the unpublished novel *Misérables*). "Melancholia" is an early version of *Misérables*—or, more exactly, it alludes to the situation from which *Les Misérables* had its origin.

I have already described something of this situation. At its center was a man whose capabilities lay with language but who yearned for action instead; who plotted a move from literature to politics, but found that the words of the peer did not come so easily as the word of the poet, and might be less efficacious. Lingering among these doubts, Hugo recalled an image of knowledge much admired by his own literary circle: Dürer's *Melencolia I.* (See fig. 10; on the influence of this engraving in the nineteenth century, see chapter 5, above.) He had already written at least one poem describing a Dürer engraving ("A Albert Dürer," in *Les Voix intérieures,* 1837). Unlike the earlier work, "Melancholia" is not ekphrastic: i.e., it does not describe the image to which its title alludes, a fact that has puzzled some commentators.[6] The title makes sense, nonetheless. It underlines Hugo's interest in a character unable to make use of great intellectual powers, a character whose frustrations are defined by the play of light and dark. This frustrated genius is first described as though he were a sun-god:

Il est doux,
Il est fort, il est grand; il est utile à tous;
Comme l'aube au-dessus de l'océan qui roule,
Il dore d'un rayon tous les fronts de la foule;

[*P,* 1: 672, Il luit; le jour qu'il jette est un jour éclatant.
lines 61–65]

He is mild,
He is strong, he is great; he is useful to all;
Like the dawn which rolls up from beneath the sea,
He gilds with a ray the brows of the multitude;
He shines; the daylight he casts is brilliant.

Then his radiance dims. Poetry and politics are equally futile for such a person. He gathers insults from all sides (from "ceux qui flattent le roi, ceux qui flattent l'égout"; those who flatter the king, those who flatter the sewer, l. 74). And though he continues to illuminate those around him, times become black ("Si le temps devient noir," l. 103). When the genius dies, Envy bends over him in a somber night—admitting his genius, confirming its apparent uselessness. Hugo evokes the unforgettable glowing darkness of *Melencolia I,* which the melancholic's inspiration (manifested by a luminescent face) only partially offsets.[7] As with Dürer, a visual effect presses home a powerful doubt. Despite knowledge, inspiration, and eloquence, words may be no more than the playthings of the idle or the meretricious (in *Melencholia I* it is the thoughtless putto who scribbles away busily). Inspiration may not have yet found a medium through which to express itself—in which case, the brilliant sun remains shadowed, the face, however bright, veiled. This antithesis between light and dark becomes a keynote. Toward the end of "Melancholia," Hugo describes an infernal city of the damned, "noir paradis dansant sur l'immense cachot!" (black paradise dancing on an immense prison!) [l. 306]. In an "Eden étrange fait de lumière et de nuit" (strange Eden made of light and night) [l. 302], fevered, futile activity points toward death. Nothing is solved by the chronicling of this extraordinary vision, which ends with an appeal to "forêts! bois profonds! solitudes! asiles!" (forests! deep woods! solitudes! retreats!) [l. 336]. Left to the reader's consideration are the problems of what words, literary *or* political, can accomplish amid the injustices of modern life and of how the intellectual's "misery," highlighted in the title of the poem, relates to the misery of those more severely downtrodden victims whose stories both precede and follow his own.

Once concluded, "Melancholia" found a place in the closely integrated collection *Les Contemplations* (1856, 3.2). Here, Hugo's mourning for Léopoldine and her husband, Charles (who died trying to save her, in an act of "willing self-immolation"), leads to a vision of messianic redemption. The means of redemption is the poet's language—once again affirmed. Hugo is able to have it both ways, to meditate on the meaning of a personal crisis, his daughter's death, while simultaneously moving toward the resolution of a collective human dilemma. Drawing on the grand traditions of elegy, he endows autobiography with universal meaning.[8] *Les Contemplations* does not reach its conclusions easily or slickly; on the other hand, "Melancholia" defines a problem which that great sequence, considered as a whole, forgets. The poem questions the author's unique power; it imagines him as just another of the *misérables;* privileging his introspections is thus a dubious move. An occult revelation of universal harmonies may not be available, after all, not at least through poeticized autobiography. In its form and its reference to Dürer, "Melancholia" intimates that "la génie de la mélancolie et de la méditation, le démon de l'analyse et de la controverse" (the genius of melancholy and meditation, the demon of analysis and controversy) [*PC,* 49]—the energies, in fact, of the intellectual—may not be the solution but, until further notice, one of the problems.

Language can redeem only when it has been redeemed. Answering to the problem set in "Melancholia"—its own "germ"—*Les Misérables* will imagine the immolation and ultimately the redemption of words. One key poem from *Les Contemplations,* "Réponse à un acte d'accusation," (*P,* 1: 641–44; written 1854), seems to pursue a similar goal, but there it is Hugo, the all-powerful author—Danton and Robespierre rolled into one!—who brings about the change: who manages on his own a linguistic revolution in which different sorts of language are mixed and made equal.[9] It is possible to have reservations about the intoxicating eloquence of "Réponse" because Hugo gets all the credit; the possibility of an author who might learn from the words of others is evaded or even ignored here. The magus, the magician of language, can accomplish miracles by himself. His translation is the true one: end of discussion. The situation defined by "Melancholia," where the genius is subjected to the same strains as everybody else, affords a more interesting starting point. Working from this beginning, Hugo recalls that language is a social product. He seeks a version of Paris that includes many different sorts of linguistic behavior, each with its own character, each making its contribution to a larger and finally comprehensive undertaking. In the novelistic conventions of *Les*

Mystères de Paris he finds a way to imagine such a city—a "paradise" whose blackness assists communication rather than suppressing it.[10]

Rodolphe to the Rescue

Sue's serials must have afforded a sensation of déjà vu, drawing as they did on Hugo's early fictional innovations. But Sue had his own original points, or at least he was thought to have them. So widespread was the rage for *Les Mystères de Paris,* its author was paid the compliment of philosophical interpretation. From the involutions of *Les Mystères,* the young Hegelians abstracted an *idea* of mystery—an idea that they then claimed was the organizing principle of the narrative. This approach was too elaborate for its own good, yet it contained a kernel of truth. Sue understood the mysteries of Paris to be mysteries of intrigue. Paris becomes a giant conspiratorial mechanism, describable on the assumption that everyone is scheming against someone else. The conventions of intrigue—the secret, the document, the conspiracy—are combined and recombined to provide a succession of thrills. (For a related version of these conventions, see chapter 8, above.) In this way, Sue can mirror, assimilate, or redefine much of that actual Paris that he and his readers knew from personal experience.

To present poverty within a framework of intrigue posed difficulties that the author may not have foreseen. Louis Chevalier tells us that Sue's readers pushed him away from the depiction of crime per se and toward a literary involvement with the suffering poor of Paris.[11] According to Chevalier, this change can be pinpointed; it occurs during the adventures of Rodolphe, the philanthropist-prince, in the rue du Temple, where Madame Pipelet's apartment house is the meeting place for a bewildering myriad of citizens, all pursuing intrigues of the most dangerous nature. As Rodolphe tours the house, secrets literally drop into his hands. He begins by receiving from the postman two letters of fearful import; of the first Sue tells us: "La prétention héraldique de ce casque et de cette croix fit sourire Rodolphe et le confirma dans l'idée que cette lettre n'était pas écrite par une femme. Mais quel était le correspondant musqué, blasonné . . . [ellipsis in text] de madame Pipelet?" (the heraldic claim of this helmet and cross made Rodolphe smile and strengthened in him the idea that the letter was not written by a woman. But who was the bemusked, emblazoned correspondent . . . of Madame Piplet?), while of the second he remarks, "fantaisie de son imagination ou réalité, cette lettre parut à Rodolphe d'une triste apparence" (deludedly or not, Rodolphe thought the letter looked sad) [*MP*, 1: 23, 175]. Each of the letters—and this is typical of Sue's art—leads into a grand conspiracy, marked by the frantic back-and-forth movement of suspicion and speculation. Moving up through the building, Rodolphe walks into one intrigue after another; his function as master of secrets is to intervene at key moments so that justice may be done. This pattern culminates in a chapter titled "Misère" [2: 4, 60–76]. The porter has confided to Rodolphe that there is a sort of exterior closet—a cabinet of melodrama—through which he can observe the huddled and shivering Morel family. When Rodolphe finds time, he spends an instructive morning of eavesdropping. Ultimately the spy hole allows Rodolphe to effect a grand coup; when Morel is about to be imprisoned for debt, he is watching and so is able to step in and save the unfortunate lapidary.

Morel is eminently worthy of the reprieve. He is the type of the oppressed workingman, doomed to endless poverty but struggling to survive, without a serious thought of turning to crime. (See fig. 21.) Sue's attitude toward this situation is ambivalent: Morel's misery is a dead-weight inertness, "si écrasante, mais si désespérée, que l'homme anéanti, dégradé, ne sent plus ni la volonté, ni la force, ni le besoin de sortir de sa fange" (so crushing, yet so hopeless, that the destroyed and degraded man no longer felt that he had the will or the strength or the need to get out of the mud) [*MP*, 2: 4, 60–61], but it also suggests a miraculous forgivingness at the foundations of society: "ce n'est pas la force, que ce n'est pas la terreur, mais le *bon sens moral* qui seul contient ce redoutable océan populaire dont le débordement pourrait engloutir la société tout entière" (it is not strength or terror but the moral sense that alone contains the dangerous popular ocean, whose overflowing could completely drown society) [2: 4, 62]. Either way, Morel is shaped by his inability to act, or even speak. His dilemma is summed up in the contradictions of his job: because he is working with valuable jewels, he cannot let his employer suspect that he is desperately poor, and because everyone else thinks the jewels are false, he gets no credit at all for self-control. Morel *needs* Rodolphe, not just to save him but to articulate his goodness. Rodolphe, the intriguer with a social conscience, fathoms the "secret" of the deserving but necessarily silent poor.

The Morel chapters were extraordinarily popular among Sue's lower-class readers, who saw in the jeweler's double bind an image of their own situation. There was no more famous incident in nineteenth-century fiction. Not until Marx and Engels wrote a polemic against the young Hegelians were the less attractive aspects of the Morel episode acknowledged. "Herr Szeliga [observe Marx and Engels] does not know that

21. *Morel le lapidaire.* Wood engraving [?] for the chapter "Misère" [2: 4] in *Les Mystères de Paris,* nouvelle édition, 1843. (From The University of Chicago Library.)

Eugène Sue commits an *anachronism* out of courtesy to the French bourgeoisie when he puts the motto of the burghers of Louis XIV's time '*Ah! si le riche le savait!*' into the mouth of the working man Morel who lived at the time of the *Charte vérité.* In England and France, at least, this *naive* relation between rich and poor has ceased to exist."[12] Sue leaves himself open to such an attack, for the revelation of *misère* is staged, as though it could not come about *except* through Rodolphe's uncanny percipience. This idea is absurd. Far from providing that hidden principle of order on which Paris is founded, intrigue is incapable of "revealing" or defining poverty. *Misère* is a known fact, one of those "mysteries which are a mystery to no one."[13]

Sue must half realize the feebleness inherent in this, his central presentation of poverty; he keeps guilty secrets and incriminating documents at the periphery of the scene, even while he allows the gratuitous, awkward eavesdropping. The Morel chapters might actually be more effective if written with the bravery of excess, the confidence of the writer who trusts his figures not at all but can indulge them nonetheless. It is this sort of attitude that Hugo adopts in his own philanthropic fantasy, at the midpoint of *Les Misérables*.

Jean Valjean at the Gorbeau Tenement

Cast out from society after he steals the famous loaf of bread, Jean Valjean finds his heart misshapen by ugly deformities, like a spinal cord growing under too low a roof. During his nineteen-year imprisonment, "chaque fois qu'il tournait le cou et qu'il essayait d'élever son regard, il voyait, avec une terreur mêlée de rage, s'échafauder, s'étager et monter à perte de vue au-dessus de lui, avec des escarpements horribles, une sorte d'entassement effrayant de choses, de lois, de préjugés, d'hommes et de faits, dont les contours lui échappaient, dont la masse l'épouvantait, et qui n'était autre chose que cette prodigieuse pyramide que nous appelons la civilisation" (each time he turned his head and tried to look up, he saw with mingled terror and rage, rising above him, extending out of his view, an endless structure with horrible escarpments, a terrifying accumulation of things, laws, prejudices, men, and facts whose outlines evaded him and whose mass panicked him, and which was nothing else than the prodigious pyramid that we call civilization) [*LM*, 1.2.7, 96–97]. These phrases recall Quasimodo, like Valjean a deformed pariah lurking within a great building. However, Quasimodo's physical flaws can be alleviated by his affinity for the cathedral: inside it and in relation to it his ugliness makes sense, his body can accomplish wonders. No such possibility is open to Valjean. He wanders within that social darkness for which the novel is named. "Il y a un point où les infortunés et les infâmes se mêlent et se confondent dans un seul mot, mot fatal, les misérables" (There is a point at which the unfortunate and the infamous mix and become confused with each other in a single word, a fatal word, *misérables*) [3.8.5, 304].

Hugo observes elsewhere that ideas have indefinable boundaries, but that words are exact in form.[14] *Misérables* is an exception. "Se mêlent et se confondent" suggests the disorienting obscurity that characterizes the concept, the ambiance that accompanies this word. The bishop's treatment of Valjean leads to great changes: it separates light and darkness in the convict's mind, it clears the turgid chaos that obscures his vision [*LM*,

1.2.13, 117]. But in one way things are gloomier than before. While Valjean's spiritual flaws can be corrected by Bishop Myriel's forgiveness, the convict has no refuge like Notre-Dame. Since the social pyramid is made of laws, prejudices, and facts rather than of stones, our hero must continue to wander at large without any saving context. Valjean has learned to distinguish good from evil, he has moved up into light—and yet he is always in danger of undergoing a horrible change. Even looking at a chain gang seems to turn him for a moment into one of the *misérables*. He trembles on the edge of that horrible metamorphosis where anger transforms poverty into crime.

Jean Valjean seeks refuge from this threatened transformation by assuming the role of M. Madeleine, pillar of Montrueil-sur-Mer. This turns out to be a false start. Circumstances drive him out of his fine position; he is arrested for the second time and after his second escape goes to Paris, a city that (cf. *Notre-Dame*) is said to contain all history, all historical possibilities [*LM,* 3.1.10, 130]. Quasimodo was stymied by this kind of clashing and contradictory environment. Valjean learns to thrive on it. Here it is easier to assume new roles or discard old ones than anywhere else in the world.[15] Here Valjean can choose to live one way or another as events dictate, without people observing any suspicious discontinuities. It is true that Valjean is tempted to assume a permanent identity: he considers staying at the convent of Petit-Picpus, where by an extraordinary turn of events he has become assistant gardener and Cosette a novitiate. But though the convent is a genuine community, in the sense that certain values and laws are shared within it, its lack of liberty makes it unattractive; a medieval survival, a cousin, as it were, to the cathedral of Notre-Dame, it is nonetheless inferior to the cathedral because it cannot combine freedom with authority. Cosette, decides her father, must have the choice of how she is to live. After gardening for many years with a warning bell absurdly tied to his knee (as though he were a sort of Quasimodo in training), Valjean leaves the convent. He always abandons one life for another, constructing and reconstructing his world and Cosette's, avoiding by this means a fall back into the abyss beyond or beneath all social identities.

By the midpoint of *Les Misérables*—halfway through part 3—Valjean has become a practiced Parisian and a practised quick-change artist. Marius knows him as respectable M. Leblanc (a name given in jest by the humorous Courfeyrac), a strangely elusive old gentleman who can show up one day strolling through the Luxembourg Gardens in middle-class gear and another prowling meaner streets in workman's garb. Marius hardly knows what to make of this peculiar behavior. He can never figure out just where Leblanc lives, and so has no chance to investigate—until Leblanc visits the room next door to his own.

Marius lives in the Gorbeau tenement, where Valjean happened to reside on his first entry into Paris. Hugo takes great care to describe the neighborhood of this decaying house. It lies near the old horse market, in a region where Paris seems to disappear; this area is neither wilderness nor town but—Hugo's paradox—an inhabited place where there is no one. The novelist admits a little later in *Les Misérables* that he has a special affinity for such places: "Le lieu où une plaine fait sa jonction avec une ville est toujours empreint d'on ne sait quelle mélancolie pénétrante. La nature et l'humanité vous y parlent à la fois. Les originalités locales y apparaissent" (The place where open country blends into town is always impregnated with an undefinable but penetrating melancholy. Nature and humanity speak at the same time. The originalities of place become visible) [*LM*, 3.1.5, 122]. The *barrières* (gates, border areas) are special locales because hardly locales at all; their melancholy comes from straddling many boundaries, between squalor and splendor, modernity and ancient times, man's intent and nature's, poverty and crime (the fatal intersection that produces *misérables*). The Gorbeau tenement is thus the perfect spot for a confrontation with limits or boundaries, social and rhetorical as well as geographical.

The first step toward such a confrontation occurs when Marius catches a glimpse of a young girl, Eponine Thénardier, fleeing from gendarmes. Eponine and her sister lose the packet of begging letters with which her father has entrusted them. Shortly afterwards she appears on the doorstep, handing Marius himself a begging letter. She wanders around the room, demonstrating—as if to assert her dignity and competence—that "je sais écrire. . . . Et avant qu'il eût eu le temps de répondre, elle écrivit sur une feuille de papier blanc qui était au milieu de la table: *Les cognes sont là*." (I know how to write. . . . And before he had had time to respond, she scribbled on a sheet of white paper lying on the table: *Cheese it, the cops*) [*LM*, 3.8.4, 299]. After penning this note she sings a song and falls in love with Marius, who then presents the lost documents.

Marius has been living "dans la pauvreté, dans le dénûment, dans la détresse même" (in poverty, in destitution, in distress even), but he now perceives "qu'il n'avait point connu la vraie misère. . . . Cette jeune fille fut pour Marius une sorte d'envoyée des ténèbres" (that he had scarcely known true misery. . . . This young girl was for Marius a sort of messenger from the darkness) [*LM*, 3.8.5, 303]. He decides, then, to track Eponine back to her source—an ambition easily fulfilled since the Thénardiers live next door and there is a convenient crack in the wall. Marius peers through the crack. Thénardier is sitting at a table, "vêtu d'une chemise de femme qui laissait voir sa poitrine velue et ses bras nus hérissés de poils gris" (dressed in a woman's chemise that revealed his hairy chest and his exposed arms bristling with grey hair) [3.8.6, 307]. His wife—"une espèce de géante à coté de son mari" (a giant by the side of her husband, 3.8.6, 308)—squats next to a fireplace containing a grotesque assortment of objects, while a sickly daughter slouches listlessly on a pallet. Among the "constellations de vieux chaussons, de savates et de chiffons affreux" (constellations of old slippers, worn-out shoes, and frightful rags), Marius observes a variety of Napoleonic icons: an engraving, a propagandistic novel, and "une espèce de panneau de bois" (a sort of wooden panel) that turns out to be an inn sign representing Thénardier at the battle of Waterloo [3.8.6, 306–7].

At first the room shows the stamp not so much of fate, of an abstract social injustice, as of Thénardier's own awful mind. Indeed, Thénardier begins at once to voice his hatred. If he lacks Morel's infinite patience, he also lacks his productivity, or at least this productivity changes nature drastically. "Il ne se révélait dans ce logis la présence d'aucun travail; pas un métier, pas un rouet, pas un outil" (Nothing could be seen that suggested work was ever done in the room, no loom, spinning wheel, or machine tool) [*LM*, 3.8.6, 308], and yet there is an incessant process of creation: Thénardier is writing his begging letters, writing them so audibly that Marius can hear the scratching of his pen. Sue's Morel works with real jewels, which—for security—he must pretend are false. Thénardier is the falsifier par excellence, whose ludicrous lies are expected to earn him a living.

Perhaps this expectation is reasonable. As Thénardier writes, his daughter bursts into the room, heralding the arrival of "Le philanthrope." At that moment, "On eût dit un général qui fait les derniers préparatifs au moment où la bataille va commencer" (One might have said that Thénardier was a general making his last preparations before the battle began) [*LM*, 3.8.7, 312]. Thénardier is just like his hero Napoleon, except that his preparations consist of putting out the fire and forcing the younger daughter to smash a pane of glass in the window. She cuts her hand, and this pleases him greatly as a further picturesque addition to the poverty of the room. Thénardier is a general, but even more a stage manager, busy rearranging the scene that Hugo has already set. When Jean Valjean makes his entrance, he become the straight man in an elaborate and deadly farce.

This farce he apparently has little ability to control since—as Thénardier remarks—he has something or other to hide: "vous n'avez pas crié, c'est mieux, je vous en fais mon compliment, et je vais vous dire ce que j'en conclus: . . . c'est que vous ne vous souciez pas plus que nous de voir arriver la justice et la police" (you have not cried out, just as well, my regards, and I am going to tell you what I deduce from this: . . . that you don't want the police here anymore than we do) [3.8.20, 364]. Thus begins the battle between an almost mute Jean Valjean and an increasingly loquacious Thénardier.

At this point in the drama the reader has seen enough to remember a previous incident quite a bit like the one under way. Jean Valjean and Thénardier first met at Montfermeil, where their confrontation began with another of Thénardier's confidence games. "Après un bon quart d'heure et quelques ratures, le Thénardier produisit ce chef-d'oeuvre" (After a good quarter of an hour and various erasures, Thénardier produced this masterpiece [Jean Valjean's exorbitant bill]), contemplated by its creator with "l'accent de Castlereagh rédigeant au congrès de Vienne la carte à payer de la France" (the tone of Castlereagh drafting for the Congress of Vienna a list of the debts owed by France) [*LM*, 2.3.9, 424]. The bill, which appears to Thénardier an imposition of genius, is merely a start. When Jean Valjean attempts to repossess Cosette, Thénardier observes soulfully, "Vous l'emmèneriez, je dirais: eh bien, l'Alouette? où donc a-t-elle passé? Il faudrait au moins voir quelque méchant chiffon de papier, un petit bout de passeport, quoi!" (If you take her away, I'll be asking: where have you gone, little lark? I've got to see a crummy scrap of paper anyway, a piece of passport, something like that!) [2.3.9, 428].

So commences an extraordinary battle. "Le Thénardier se perdait en suppositions. Il entrevoyait tout, et ne voyait rien. Quoi qu'il en fût, en entamant la conversation avec l'homme, sûr qu'il y avait un secret dans tout cela, sûr que l'homme était intéressé à rester dans l'ombre, il se sentait fort; à la réponse nette et ferme de l'étranger, quand il vit que ce personnage mystérieux était mystérieux si simplement, il se sentit faible" (Thénardier was getting lost among his own guesses. He had a glimpse of the truth; he saw nothing. When he started talking with the man—sure that the fellow wanted to keep things in the dark—he had felt powerful. On the clear and steady response of the stranger, when he saw that this mysterious person was so simply mysterious, he felt weak) [*LM*, 2.3.9, 429]. A secret can be manipulated; a mystery—at least, a mystery of a certain sort—cannot. It is this distinction that Thénardier fails to grasp, for he thinks shortly after he has allowed Cosette and Jean Valjean to leave,

"Et puis ce paquet d'habits préparés d'avance pour la petite, tout cela était singulier; il y avait bien des mystères là-dessous. On ne lâche pas des mystères quand on les tient. Les secrets des riches sont des éponges pleines d'or; il faut savoir les presser" (And then the bundle of clothes prepared beforehand for the child, all this was singular; there w re quite a few mysteries under this surface. One does not let go of mys:eries when one gets hold of them. The secrets of the rich were sponges full of gold; they had to be squeezed just so) [2.3.10, 432]. The upshot is that Thénardier pursues them and confronts Jean Valjean once more, declaring "je ne puis rendre l'enfant qu'à une personne qui m'apporterait un écrit signé de la mère comme quoi je dois remettre l'enfant à cette personne-là. Cela est clair" (I can give up the child only to someone who brings me a piece of paper signed by the mother, saying that I must release the child to the person in question. That is clear) [2.3.10, 434]. He is left wordless when Jean Valjean actually produces such a document: Thénardier has been defeated on his own ground.

Thénardier's flair for intrigue and nose for secrets are associated with a battle over documents. In Paris, this battle is magnified to a degree hitherto undreamt of. The exchange of letters, whereby Marius returns the one packet and receives not only a letter from Thénardier but one from Eponine, sets a pattern that reappears once the eavesdropping has begun. When Thénardier reveals his name, it is by offering to sell his visitor the Waterloo signboard (inscribed: AU SERGENT DE WATERLOO) [LM, 1.4.1, 150]. The signboard means little to Valjean, whose memories of Thénardier have nothing to do with Waterloo, but everything to Marius, for the name of Thénardier "il l'avait porté sur son coeur, écrit dans le testament de son père! il le portait au fond de sa pensée, au fond de sa mémoire, dans cette recommandation sacrée: 'Un nommé Thénardier m'a sauvé la vie. Si mon fils le rencontre, il lui fera tout le bien qu'il pourra.' . . . quelle dérision que d'avoir si longtemps porté sur sa poitrine les dernières volontés de son père écrites de sa main pour faire affreusement tout le contraire!" (he had carried over his heart, written in the testament of his father! He carried it in the depths of his thoughts, in the depths of his memory, in this sacred injunction: 'A man named Thénardier saved my life. If my son ever meets him, he will do him all the good that he can.' . . . What a sick joke to have carried next to his heart for such a long time the last wishes of his father written in his own hand and then so horrifyingly go against them!) [3.8.20, 355–56]. Any doubts Marius may attempt to nurse on the question of Thénardier's identity are finally squelched by the man's proud explication of his signboard. A circuit is established; what

Marius knows from the will is confirmed, then revised by the sign and the accompanying boast. This show of egotism, irrelevant to the blackmailing of Jean Valjean, saves Thénardier's life; Marius is reluctant to fire his pistol and blow off the man's head, as he would otherwise be eager to do.

As power flows back and forth, its changes are signaled time and again by the appearance and interpretation of inscriptions: the signboard (answering to the will), the initials on Jean Valjean's handkerchief (U.F., duping Thénardier and making it possible for Jean Valjean to falsify a letter he is forced into writing), then, at a culminating moment, Jean Valjean's branding of his own arm. Writing becomes flesh, prompting Thénardier to the point of murder, when Marius suddenly remembers Eponine's demonstration letter and throws it into the room. This causes a general panic. Eponine's scribble advances a developing confusion, not to receive its final elaboration until Jean Valjean escapes from Javert as the latter is writing his police report.

Hugo subjects the conventions of intrigue to a sustained analysis. He elaborates, indeed exaggerates, these conventions until they begin changing into something radically different. The confrontations in the Gorbeau tenement remind us that intrigue presupposes a coherence of motives and goals on which the plotters can base their scheming. As the scene unfolds, there is a desperate attempt to maintain such an order. Javert composing his police report, Thénardier gesturing at the inn sign, Marius worshipping the will and last wishes of his father, above all Jean Valjean burning the stamp of the brand into his arm: all are fascinated by the magic of writing, which deceives others but more importantly oneself. If, as in *Notre-Dame,* the book has splintered the form of Paris, then the message, the scrawl, the brand, reestablish the illusion that men are stones in a great building: that they can assume, by an act of will, the fixed identities that modern life has annihilated. The extremity of this attempt underlines its failure. Marius "était replongée dans ce mystère où il errait à tâtons" (was immersed once more in that mystery where he had to wander on gropingly) [*LM*, 4.2.1, 428]. Javert is left with the doubtful prize of Thénardier and assorted henchmen, but he cannot hold on to them for long. Valjean disappears into the covering anonymity of Paris, where—as Hugo observes later—"l'identité qui lie un individu à lui-même se rompt d'une rue à l'autre" (the identity that connects an individual with himself is broken when you turn from one street to another) [4.6.1, 522].

The dynamics of intrigue, defined by the spy hole or the document, gradually collapse. The character who *knows,* who survives in Paris as a clever manipulator, is a possibility raised and then rejected. Rodolphe never has a chance. His entrance would be irrelevant because the materials of his vocation, while plentiful, turn out to be largely factitious: "écrire nos noms! les mettre dans un bonnet!" (write our names! put them in a hat!) yells Thénardier incredulously, just before he is arrested [*LM*, 3.8.20, 376]. What counts in the scene is not strategy or documents but a state of mind: a mode of perception formulated in book 8, "Le Mauvais Pauvre," but crucial to *Les Misérables* from the moment when Jean Valjean steals the fatal loaf of bread. Thénardier inches from poverty to crime, from the unfortunate to the unspeakable. He takes it for granted, initially, that he can exhibit his suffering only by faking it, a paradox that pushes him into an increasingly elaborate conspiracy until the climactic moment when he reveals his intentions. Having begun in an abject oppression that meshes absurdly with intrigue, Thénardier now discovers an integrity beyond all his scheming and planning. "Il y avait dans toutes ces paroles . . . dans l'accent, dans le geste, dans le regard qui faisait jaillir des flammes de chaque mot . . . dans ce mélange de fanfaronnade et d'abjection . . . dans cette conflagration de toutes les souffrances combinées avec toutes les haines, quelque chose qui était hideux comme le mal et poignant comme le vrai." (There was in all these words . . . in the accent, in the gestures, in the look that made flames leap from each word . . . in this mixture of bragging and abasement . . . in each blaze of cumulative suffering combined with cumulative hate, something hideous like evil and thrilling like truth) [3.8.20, 360]. Hugo does not say that Thénardier's hatred is truth, but he does admit, in a kind of fascinated reverie, that it is *like* the truth. Thénardier, that is to say, is part of some larger puzzle, in which he finds his place by an unconscious turn of intention.[16]

Nowhere else in the novel does Thénardier reach this level, or depth, of inspiration. He reaches it here because he is straining after an elusive opponent, who forces him out of his blackmailing role and to the verge of murder. Jean Valjean's strength is suggested later in a comment of Grantaire: "Oh! si les bons coeurs avaient les grosses bourses! comme tout irait mieux! Je me figure Jésus-Christ avec la fortune de Rothschild!" (Oh! if good hearts only had big purses! how wonderful everything would be! Think of Jesus Christ with the fortune of Rothschild!) [*LM*, 4.12.3, 143]. Valjean is less a psychological portrait than a living oxymoron.[17] He and Thénardier confront each other not as men but as figures—of speech, of society—each attempting to categorize the other and thus dissipate his power. "Pardon, monsieur," observes Jean Valjean, "je vois que vous êtes un bandit" (Excuse me, sir, I see that you are a bandit). To which Thénardier returns: "Bandit! oui, je sais que vous nous appelez comme cela, messieurs les gens riches!" (Bandit! yes, I know that you call us that, you rich men!) [3.8.20, 358]. The case is more complicated than either of them is likely to admit, for they are both looking into a sort of fun house mirror, which presents a threatening distortion of self. Thénardier raves; Jean Valjean is mostly silent. Thénardier, the poor man as criminal, encounters the poor man as saint, the saint as millionaire, who for his part is faced with a nightmare version of what he once was and what he could still become. The tensions so generated will require the remainder of the novel to be resolved, for if *misérables* is a potential act, a moment in which poverty and crime "se confondent," then Valjean's sainthood is a potential cessation of will. Jean Valjean offers a vacuum—a mystery—into which Thénardier's inchoate malice can rush and be reshaped.

Argot, or Secrecy in Common

Sue, it will be recalled, makes the philanthropist speak for the poor man; we understand his logic even if we do not accept it. That the poor man should speak for the philanthropist—a process just beginning in the Gorbeau tenement—is an anomaly unexplainable by any simple reversal of intentions. Hugo's city is a highly specialized structure that nonetheless encourages a progressive breakdown of categories. When Thénardier the schemer meets Valjean the sufferer, they have not only traded the roles defined by Morel and Rodolphe, they have also stumbled into a kind of unwilling conspiracy, which begins where the conscious manipulations of intrigue leave off. Quite against his intentions, Thénardier is drawn toward Jean Valjean to the point that his maniacal hostility will become his enemy's voice. This is not just, or not merely, the irony of the melodramatist. Hugo is preparing the way for an excursion into the most difficult of urban subjects: the relationship, in the city, of individual consciousness and the deepest—literally the deepest—communal identity.

Les Misérables, a novel of miraculous escapes, pushes its characters to a point of dissolution where mystery is less a manipulable condition than an abyss in which to lose oneself. The abyss is reached by a series of releases: from intrigue, from identity, from a secrecy of the self that surrenders to a deeper, communal secrecy. An inadequate but useful figure of this condition is what can be called thieves' language: "la langue laide, inquiète, sournoise, traître, venimeuse, cruelle, louche, vile, profonde, fatale, de la misère" (the ugly, restless, cunning, treacherous, poisonous, cruel, crosseyed, vile, profound, fatal language of misery) [LM, 4.7.1, 10]. Thieves' talk has a complex literary ancestry; perhaps the most important points of reference are Hugo's own *Notre-Dame* and Sue's serials. Gringoire is initiated into the kingdom of argot under compulsion; he has strayed too near the Court of Miracles where he is first assaulted by demands in every language from a crawling mass of beggars ("O tour de Babel") and then made the center of a lively spectacle in which he gives up philosophy for thievery. It need not be argued that *Notre-Dame*'s use of argot is systematic and thoughtful; *Les Mystères de Paris,* like the Newgate novel in England, kept the whole notion of thieves' language in the public eye, but used it, too often, as no more than decoration. Rodolphe visits argot from time to time (as in the opening sequence of *Les Mystéres,* at the Tapis-Franc) but he is magically capable of moving through that world without adopting its manners, without being marked by it. When, in *Les Misérables,* Hugo writes an extended essay on thieves' language, he acknowledges Sue's contribution (also Balzac's), then reclaims the subject for his own. "L'étude et l'approfondissement de cet étrange idiome mènent au mystérieux point d'intersection de la société régulière avec la société maudite" (The study and the excavation of this strange idiom leads to the mysterious point of intersection between respectable society and the society of the damned) [4.7.2, 21]. The reader of *Les Misérables* has visited this point of intersection many times before—but always in the company of Jean Valjean, whose efforts to transcend the condition of *misérables* have formed Hugo's central subject. Now the perennial conflict is approached from the perspective of the essayist rather than that of the novelist. Distanced from the particular case of Valjean, one can understand his dilemma in a more comprehensive manner than before.

The proliferation of documents throughout *Les Misérables* creates a network of relationships connecting the characters of the novel. The Gorbeau foursome of Marius-Thénardier-Valjean-Javert is as elegant an example as could be wished. The tangle of loyalties and lies is virtually irresolvable, while possessing a strange, floating irrelevancy. To descend from Thénardier's begging-letter operation into the communal and violent world of argot is to cast off as much of this baggage as possible. "Tous les mot de cette langue sont perpétuellement en fuite comme les hommes qui les prononcent" (All the words of this language are perpetually in flight like the men who speak them) [*LM,* 4.7.2, 18]. These terms "qui masquent et qui montrent" (which hide and reveal) [4.7.2, 17] live and die and are reborn in a process of incessant, fertilizing corruption:

> *PIGRITA est un mot terrible.*
>
> [4.7.1, 7]   *Il engendre un monde,* la pègre, *lisez:* le vol, *et un enfer,* la pégrenne, *lisez:* la faim.

> *Ainsi la paresse est mère.*
> *Elle a un fils, le vol, et une fille, la faim.*
> *Où sommes-nous en ce moment? Dans l'argot.*

> PIGRITA *is a terrifying word.*
> *It breeds a world,* la pègre *[the thief, masculine], for which read: robbery, and a hell,* la pégrenne *[the thief, feminine], for which read: hunger.*
> *Thus laziness is a mother.*
> *She has a son, robbery, and a daughter, hunger.*
> *Where are we at this moment? In argot.*

So far as one exists in argot, his commitments are either primitively to himself or mysteriously to an invisible and omnipresent body of comrades. The secrecy of the letter tends to enforce or control one-to-one relationships; the secrecy of argot creates a whole universe of darkness in which one can move ambiguously and at will. "Dans ce monde des actions sombres, on se garde le secret. Le secret, c'est la chose de tous" (In this world of dark deeds, secrets are kept. The secret belongs to all) [4.7.2, 21], argot being the hermetic instrument of communication among thieves and protection from respectable society.

Argot is "une énigme où se réfugie le voleur qui complote un coup, le prisonnier qui combine une évasion" (an enigma that offers itself as a refuge to the robber who plots a blow, to the prisoner who plans an escape) [*LM*, 4.7.2, 17]. In the distant past its "sombre esprit symbolique" (sombre symbolic spirit) had a "caractère impuissant et accablé" (impotent and exhausted character); by the eighteenth century it embodied "une gaîté diabolique et énigmatique" (a diabolical and enigmatic gaiety) [4.7.3, 22–23]. This shared secret of society's outcasts has changed its nature according to the politics of various periods: what is its function now? Hugo maintains that the French Revolution has made an irreversible difference—no more Restif de la Bretonnes, no more Jacqueries (i.e., no more subversive, widely read sophists and no more people's revolts powered by material deprivation). "Le grand ressort du spectre rouge est cassé." (The great spring of the red specter is broken) [4.7.3, 26]. It is hard to put much confidence in Hugo's assurance; just because France has had its revolution, other countries are not barred from following suit. The red specter might well show up somewhere else than Paris. Nonetheless Hugo is making a coherent argument. He suggests that after the French Revolution a new means will be necessary for achieving social progress. He suggests that argot in its contemporary guise might help us define this means.

What happens, then, to those who desert, or are expelled from, or have never reached the literate levels of civilization? By studying argot one can begin to understand the exiles of society: how they become exiles, how they reach an understanding with the world from which they have been banished. To speak this language is to enter an "édifice souterrain bâti en commun par tous les misérables" (a subterranean edifice built in common by all the *misérables*) [*LM*, 4.7.2, 15]. The subterranean edifice is the manifestation of a historical "law" introduced in *Notre-Dame*, that an architecture of the people follows an architecture of caste [*ND*, 5.2. 201]. The architecture of the people conceived by *Les Misérables* is hardly an architecture at all: ad hoc, chaotic, it is created or adopted at a moment's notice—more like spitting out slang than building a cathedral or a convent. Of Gavroche, his quintessential gamin and an embodiment of popular Paris, Hugo writes: "ce génie énorme qu'on appelle Paris, tout en transfigurant le monde par sa lumière, charbonne le nez de Bouginier au mur du temple de Thésée et écrit *Crédeville voleur* sur les pyramides" (while transfiguring the world by its light, the immense genius called Paris can charcoal the nose of Bouginier on the wall of the Temple of Theseus and write *Crédville the thief* on the Pyramids) [*LM*, 3.1.11, 133]. Gavroche would presumably accept such a characterization. In the midst of breaking streetlights, he notices the Archives and declares, "Comment est-ce que vous appelez ce monument gigantesque que vous avez là au bout de la rue? C'est les Archives, pas vrai? Il faudrait me chiffonner un peu ces grosses bêtes de colonnes-là, et en faire gentiment une barricade" (What do you call the huge monument that you have at the end of the street? It's the Archives, right? They ought to crack up some of those big stupid pillars and make them a barricade, very nicely) [4.15.2, 209]. This is the spirit in which the physical city is loved or abused by its *misérables*. The forms of Paris are adapted to the exigencies of instantaneous expression. The city becomes a mutter or a shout; its most monumental structures are transformed by a scrawl.[18]

In the last third of the novel, Hugo repeatedly shows a character or group of characters committing themselves to the subterranean edifice of *misérables*. The paradigmatic case is that of the two Thénardier children, abandoned in the streets of Paris, their evanescent claim to a "parent" lost with the piece of paper that flutters away from them in the wind. The children meet Gavroche [*LM*, 4.6.2, 526], who introduces his newfound charges to *his* Paris. "Il y a vingt ans, on voyait encore dans l'angle sud-est de la place de la Bastille. . . . une sorte de symbole de la force populaire. C'était sombre, énigmatique et immense" (Twenty years ago, one could still see at the southwest corner of the place de la Bastille. . . . a sort of symbol of the popular will. It was gloomy, enigmatic, and huge) [4.6.2, 534]. This monument is the Elephant, in which Gavroche has set up housekeeping.[19] Now it is true that the symbols of this passage are pressed home rather relentlessly in this passage, but they should not on that account be scorned: within the Elephant occurs an initiation—counterpart and successor to the initiation of Gringoire. The children have entered the belly of the people (Rabelaisian conceit) and must therefore learn its language, which Gavroche most willingly teaches them:

> —*Dame, fit l'enfant, nous n'avions plus du tout de logement où aller.*
> —*Moutard! reprit Gavroche, on ne dit pas un logement, on dit une*
> [4.6.2, 542]   *piolle.*

> —*Well, said the child, we hadn't anymore a lodging to go to.*
> —*Urchin! responded Gavroche, we don't say a lodging, we say a dive.*

Much later Hugo describes the children on their own, wandering through the Luxembourg Gardens, at which point a pun scorned by the novelist as a feeble bourgeois effort (cygnes/signes) is contrasted to the wisdom of the vagrant children. "Colle-toi ça dans le fusil" (Stick that in your gun), says the older to the younger, having rescued a piece of bread from the swans [*LM*, 5.1.16, 280]. "Ces êtres appartenaient désormais à la statistique des 'Enfants Abandonnés' que la police constate, remasse, égare et retrouve sur le pavé de Paris" (These beings belonged henceforth to the statistics of "abandoned children" that the police ascertain, gather, lose, and find again on the pavements of Paris) [5.1.16, 273]. They have entered the belly of the people, a condition prefigured when they sleep in the Elephant. Hugo claims to fear argot—he analyzes it in the vocabulary of Gothic horror—but this language of darkness, to the Thénardier children, is equally a language of love. The impersonality of their suffering—from the viewpoint of the police, they are statistics—allows an inspired improvisation, an addiction to the life of the streets as a fragmentary and exhilarating immediacy.

From the Barricade to the Sewer

In narrating a descent to argot, Hugo approaches the resolution of an emotional and political dilemma belonging to the nineteenth-century societies of Europe that lived on the edge of democracy. He enacts with increasing point a fear that is also an aspiration: the prospect of merging with the *misérables*—of throwing off class or social categories to enter that ambiguous realm of the disinherited—becomes a reiterated motif. The Elephant is a reminder of Napoleonic glory, now reduced to beggary. Even more than Thénardier, the Elephant suggests both the decay of willed, individualistic, self-made power and transformations that might occur from within its collapse, as it were. This appropriate symbol of the post-Revolutionary masses and their dilemma is succeeded by a pair of drastically polarized variations on the initial theme. The barricade is an idealized version of the Elephant, the sewer a gothicized and sublimated version. The kind of commitment called forth by each of these structures suggests the difference between them. As Hugo is at pains to suggest, the utterances of the people make a wide variety of claims.

The barricade is created purposely as a political statement and a military stratagem. The group supervising its construction is the Friends of the ABC—the *abaissé* (the abased). This pun is problematic. Learning the ABC's should help the *abaissé*—so the Revolutionary doctrines inherited by the Friends insist.[20] Unfortunately for these ardent young men, their status as renegade intellectuals puts them ahead of their times: *abaissé* or not, the Paris of 1832 is reluctant to follow their lead and rise against Louis Philippe. Hugo admits that the barricade has some popular support: he locates its headquarters at the wineshop of Corinth. Hugo's "Histoire de Corinthe depuis sa fondation" (History of Corinth since its foundation) [chapter title, *LM*, 4.12.1] plays with all sorts of comic moments in which literacy can emerge from illiteracy, the Latin of Horace, for example (*Carpe horas*, seize the hour), from a cook's misspelled scrawl advertising stuffed carp: CARPES HO GRAS. (Hugo tells a similar joke in *Notre-Dame*, but reverses the direction of the transformation: the inscribed injunction TU, ORAS—YOU, PRAY—becomes *Trou aux Rats*, the Rat Hole [*ND*, 6.2, 227–28].) The wineshop of Corinth seems to be a location where abased and alphabet might fruitfully meet. Perhaps the barricade is not doomed. There comes a moment in its defense when Enjolras, the selfless leader, can declare, "il me semble que Paris s'éveille" (it seems to me that Paris is awakening). Soon after this moment, however, "les insurgés sentirent retomber sur eux cette espèce de chape de plomb que l'indifférence du peuple jette sur les obstinés abandonnés" (the insurgents felt the pall of indifference that the people let fall on abandoned zealots) [*LM*, 5.1.13, 265–66]. The comrades prove friends of the ABC but cannot conceive how to be friends of the *abaissé*. They die heroically because they are premature translators, with a loyalty to principle and philosophy rather than an instinct for mass feeling. Unable to benefit from Horace's advice (or the long-deceased cook's carp), they fail to seize the hour.

Hugo uses the barricade, "le lieu de jonction de ceux qui pensent et de ceux qui souffrent" (the place where thinkers and sufferers cross paths) to raise the question of intellectuals and politics in modern French history [*LM*, 5.1.5, 246]. Far from simplifying this question, he is capable of turning it around, of situating a counter example at an essential moment in his cautionary demonstration. The aged bibliophile M. Mabeuf enters the fight as a suicidal gesture. He is ready to enter it only after an excruciating time of deprivation, in the course of which he must sell the plates to his masterwork of botanical studies, then a collection of rare books. The last book goes on July the fourth; the next day, Mabeuf dies at the top of the barricade, replanting the standard that no one else dares raise. For Mabeuf, this action is based not on principle or philosophy but, in the most literal sense, on a painful separation from bookish consciousness. The significance of Mabeuf's heroism is revealed only in the long run. Though he shares a death with the Friends of the ABC, he remains in their eyes an anomaly: he is certainly not the regicide for which one fighter takes him. On the other hand, Mabeuf's relinquishment of the book will turn out to have greater possibilities, more potential meaning, than the Friends' bookish attempt at revolution.

The barricade is a place to lose the self in the glory of revolutionary action. The sewer is both an escape from the barricade and a commentary on it, as Hugo implies by his crisscrossing of motivations. The controlling device—the mechanism that creates a meeting between Jean Valjean and Marius, then pushes them into the climactic underground flight—is a letter from Cosette to her lover. Eponine delivers the letter to the barricade and then dies in the fighting; Marius sends Gavroche back with an answer. Meanwhile Jean Valjean has discovered the letter by what must be the most elaborate means imaginable: "L'écriture s'était imprimé sur le buvard" (The writing was imprinted on the blotting-pad); next, "Le miroir reflétait l'écriture" (The mirror reflected the writing) [*LM*, 4.15.1, 203], so that a reversed image is corrected by being reversed once more. The conceit of a double negative producing a positive—new understanding arising from the twists and turns of an enigma—suggests something of what follows, for since Marius and Jean Valjean are forced into the fighting together, each is finally compelled to survive. What binds them to each other is the letter, in its multiplying forms and effects. When Gavroche delivers Marius's reply (intercepted by Jean Valjean, who is thus enabled to locate the barricade), he declares: "Ne vous imaginez pas que c'est là un billet doux. C'est pour une femme, mais c'est pour le peuple." (Do not imagine that this is a love letter. It is for a woman, but it is for the people) [4.15.2, 210]. This is a misinterpretation. The letter is not for the people.

Cosette's original note has distinguished Marius from the other combatants, prompting him to write a memorandum requesting that his body be carried to his grandfather's. Marius still has urgent personal ties, and they can be affirmed or preserved at this moment only by the written identification. He cannot help but feel the pull of the darkness in which all ties dissolve: "La logique se mêle à la convulsion. . . . il n'avait pu resister longtemps à ce vertige mystérieux et souverain qu'on pourrait nommer l'appel de l'abîme" (Logic was lost in the midst of the upheaval. . . . it was impossible to resist for long that mysterious and sovereign vertigo that could be named the call of the abyss) [4.13.2, 173; 4.14.4, 184). All the same, he lacks the desire to perish anonymously for the émeute. Writing within the barricade brings Jean Valjean to him, beyond his intention but not his desire. Thus Hugo prepares for the escape into the sewers.

We must not, Hugo exhorts his readers, "flatter, pas même un grand peuple . . . Paris contient Athènes, la ville de lumière . . . il contient aussi Lutèce, la ville de boue" (flatter, not even a great people . . . Paris contains Athens, the city of light . . . it also contains Lutèce, the city of filth) [LM, 5.2.1, 316]. The apology is a boast: Hugo loves the sewer, on which he pauses to provide an extensive commentary.[21] One expects to associate this dark and formless abyss with the cave of crime, of *misérables*. Hugo will encourage such links, but he also writes of the Paris sewer that "c'est la conscience de la ville. Tout y converge, et s'y confronte. Dans ce lieu livide, il y a des ténèbres, mais il n'y a plus de secrets. Chaque chose a sa forme vraie. . . . Cette sincérité de l'immondice nous plaît, et repose l'âme" (it is the conscience of the city. Everything converges and meets there. In this ghastly place there are shades, but nothing is secret any longer. Everything has its true form. . . . This sincerity of sewage pleases us, and sets the soul at ease) [5.2.2, 318–19]. Here at the biological base of life, excrement turns out to harbor, even to articulate, the pleasures of politics and art. The reader should remember what Hugo says of the *barrières*, and by implication of all indeterminate areas, that they bring out the originalities of place. The sewer brings out the originalities of muck. There was an old story that, after its removal from the Pantheon, Marat's body had been thrown into the sewers. According to Hugo, the great revolutionary's winding-sheet is still there; bearing a half-effaced inscription (no more Hugolian detail could be imagined), the winding-sheet is understood to embody art, aristocracy, revolution, and death, all at once [5.2.4, 325]. Such objects give up their secrets; they exist in a splendid uniqueness, an afterlife or shadow life where what was thought worthless is freshly valued.

Along with the Friends of the ABC, Hugo intermittently assumes that literacy (education) will eliminate the darkness of *misérables*. "Diminuer le nombre des ténébreux, augmenter le nombre des lumineux, voilà le but. . . . Apprendre à lire, c'est allumer du feu; toute syllabe épelée étincelle" (Lessen the number of people in darkness, increase the number in light—this is the goal. . . . To learn how to read is to kindle a fire; every spelled syllable sparkles) [*LM*, 4.7.1, 13–14]. All the same, the conviction that "cette cave . . . n'a aucun rapport avec la noirceur sublime de l'écritoire" (this cave [the cave of crime] . . . has no connection with the sublime blackness of ink) [3.7.2, 278] does not entirely ring true. Hugo notes that "de cette cave sort Lacenaire" (from this cave emerges Lacenaire) [3.7.2, 278]. This can hardly be; one of the main reasons for Lacenaire's fame as a criminal was his dandified literacy, which became a general object of admiration.[22] The need for such distinctions ends when one reaches the sewers, which are an inclusive and reconciling receptacle, a world where conflicts become mixtures. The metamorphosis of conflict into mixture is enacted first by Hugo's rhetoric (in a few pages his narrative will follow the same path). Thus, alphabet and sewer mutually transform one another. There is a hint of this shift in Hugo's treatment of Marat's winding-sheet: first it seems nothing more than a filthy rag; then—identified by its inscription, its destiny imprinted ("empreinte") upon it, it can be seen anew. From the caves of argot, of filth, writing reemerges; as Hugo presents it, the sewer itself becomes a kind of alphabet. "On se fera une image plus ressemblante de cet étrange plan géométral en supposant qu'on voie à plat sur un fond de ténèbres quelque bizarre alphabet d'orient brouillé comme un fouillis, et dont les lettres difformes seraient soudées les unes aux autres, dans un pêle-mêle apparent et comme au hasard, tantôt par leurs angles, tantôt par leurs extrémités" (One can form an image closer to this strange geometric plan by supposing that one sees against a background of darkness some weird alphabet of the orient, jumbled as in a medley, and of which the deformed letters would be joined, sometimes by their corners, sometimes by their extremities, evidently pell-mell)[23] [5.2.2, 317]. The unfathomable abyss yields up writing—first an oriental alphabet but later on in this description the familiar Roman one, broken, then rejoined.[24]

"Il n'y a plus de secrets," or more precisely the secrets, disguises, and bluffs that do remain are no longer the stuff of intrigue even when they seem to be. This change is brought home on a narrative level as, for the second time, Javert, Thénardier, Valjean, and Marius meet. Thénardier guards the exit to the sewer with Javert waiting outside. Jean Valjean is tired and filthy ("si défiguré, si fangeux et si sanglant qu'en plein midi il eût été méconnaissable"; so disfigured, so muddy, and so bloodstained that at full noon he would have been unrecognizable) but luckily "cette inégalité de conditions suffisait pour assurer quelque avantage à Jean Valjean dans ce mystérieux duel qui allait s'engager entre les deux situations et les deux hommes. La recontre avait lieu entre Jean Valjean voilé et Thénardier démasqué" (this inequality of condition sufficed to give Jean Valjean the advantage in the mysterious duel that was about to start up between the two situations and the two men. The encounter took place between Jean Valjean masked and Thénardier unmasked) [*LM,* 5.3.8, 360–61]. "Ce mystérieux duel" is mostly on Thénardier's side, for "plus Thénardier était loquace, plus Jean Valjean était muet" (the more Thénardier was talkative, the more Jean Valjean was silent) [5.3.8, 363]. In fact, the only positive statement that Valjean makes is a curt "c'est vrai," in response to Thénardier's observation that he must get out of the sewer. Even more than at the Gorbeau tenement, Thénardier speaks words recalling the truth, but whose claim to truth eludes exact definition. He assumes that Jean Valjean has murdered Marius. Who else would be lurking in the sewers, carrying what is obviously a corpse, but one of the *misérables*—one of those in whom poverty can so easily turn to crime? Thénardier's assumption is apt: Jean Valjean hates Marius (he has just looked at him with implacable hatred) and has let *misérables* become the determining factor of his life. Thénardier's assumption is beside the point: Jean Valjean is saving Marius's life and has struggled all his days to escape the category of *misérables.* Thénardier fills the silence around him with the negotiations of an intrigue neither fact nor altogether fiction.

One of the best commentaries on Jean Valjean's experience in the sewers is Michelet's *Le Peuple,* which speaks eloquently and hopefully of the connection between genius and simplicity. Michelet writes against the lurid representations of crime he remembers from *Les Mystères de Paris* and similar productions.[25] To this vision he opposes his own, in which the birth of genius is a model for the birth of society. According to Michelet, "l'esprit de simplicité qui fait que les divisions n'entravent jamais [the genius's] esprit, qui sur une partie, un signe, lui fait voir, prévoir un être entier, un systéme que personne ne devine encore, cette faculté merveilleuse est justement celle qui fait l'étonnement, le scandale presque, du vulgaire. . . . La trace qu'il y laissera, ce n'est pas seulement l'oeuvre de génie. C'est cette vie même de simplicité, d'enfance, de bonté et de sainteté, où tous les siècles viendront chercher une sorte de rafraîchissement moral" (the spirit of simplicity that never permits division to shackle [the genius's] spirit, that through a part, a sign, makes him see—foresee—a whole being, a system that no one yet anticipates, this marvelous faculty is exactly what shocks, what scandalizes almost, the vulgar. . . . The mark he leaves is not only the work of genius. It is that life of childlike simplicity, of goodness and sanctity, to which all the centuries will come, seeking moral refreshment).[26] This phenomenon, observes the historian, is "un mystère du coeur" (a mystery of the heart); more explicitly, "s'il y a dans l'homme de génie trêve et pacification, cela tient à un beau mystère, aux sacrifices intérieurs que ses puissances opposées se font les unes aux autres. Le fond de l'art, comme celui de la société, ne l'oubliez point, c'est le sacrifice" (if there be truce and peace in the man of genius, that is due to a beautiful mystery, the mystery of those sacrifices that his opposed powers make to one another. Never forget: the basis of art, as of society, is sacrifice).[27]

Rejecting the morality of *Les Mystères,* Michelet imagines a situation in which the self-sacrifice of genius—its submission to transformation by social forces outside itself—becomes the basis of national rebirth. Hugo works through the conventions refined by *Les Mystères* to his own version of this program. There is a moment in *Les Misérables* when Jean Valjean lectures the petty thief Montparnasse on the horrors of the criminal life. "Tomber au hasard, dans le gouffre, d'une hauteur quelconque, sur quoi? sur ce qui est en bas, sur l'inconnu. Ou tu grimperas par un tuyau de cheminée, au risque de t'y brûler; ou tu ramperas par un conduit de latrines, au risque de t'y noyer. . . . Une serrure se présente; le bourgeois a dans sa poche sa clef fabriquée par un serrurier. Toi, si tu veux passer outre, tu es condamné à faire un chef-d'oeuvre effrayant" (To drop at random into the abyss, from an unknown height, on what? on that which is below, the unknown. Or you clamber by way of a chimney flue, at the risk of getting burnt; or you crawl through a sewer pipe, at the risk of drowning. . . . A lock presents itself; the respectable man has in his pocket the key, made by a keymaker. If you want to get by the lock, you are condemned to create a frightful masterpiece) [*LM,* 4.4.2, 496]. This anticipates his own dilemma, hauling Marius through the sewer. He must create one frightful masterpiece after another, until one understands his situation to require nothing less than a spirit-breaking effort of imagination. At the barricade, the Friends of the ABC want to fuse suffering and thought, which are poverty and crime on an abstract, a *willed* level. There is genius in the barricade [4.12.1, 135; 5.1.1, 224], but not, perhaps, the right kind. When the émeute breaks down—when the sewer replaces the barricade—the attempt at synthesis is renewed, except that Jean Valjean's denial of self is metaphorically and literally on a different level than Enjolras's. He has used his genius to succor those within *misérables* while himself participating in its metamorphoses, its rejuvenations. Descending to an underworld strangely like the one he has so valiantly resisted, he finds it newly inclusive. The sewer is by its nature what the barricade aspires to become. It is a part that stands for the whole: alternately the mysterious subgroup of *misérables* and Paris comprehensively understood. It is said of the criminal underworld that "ce qui rampe dans le troisième dessous social, ce n'est plus la réclamation étouffée de l'absolu; c'est la protestation de la matière" (what crawls in the third substage is no longer the stifled demand for the absolute; it is the affirmation of matter itself) [3.7.2, 278]. At the much-feared material base of things, Valjean and his creator encounter the substance that connects us all: genius finds a medium in which it is truly unshackled by division, where the part is neither isolated from the whole nor forcibly imposed upon it but—Michelet's term—*foretells* it.

Three Exits

There have been some good long arguments over whether Victor Hugo possessed a sense of humor. Dare one laugh at a novelist who affirms progress and God while his hero almost drowns in shit? Bakhtin once complained that Hugo tried to moralize everything, even Rabelais, thus losing all feeling for the life-giving power in profanity, debasement, and filth: when Hugo says of "Rabelais's world, *totus homo fit excrementum* [all men make shit], he ignores the regenerating and renewing element of the images."[28] *Les Misérables* suggests otherwise. Hugo may not be Rabelais, but in his own moralistic, nineteenth-century manner he acknowledges the power of carnival, of the world turned upside down. He admits that it is necessary to grasp society through categories and equally necessary to elude the same categories if we are to find any basis for a modern and democratic kind of community. Particularly after Hugo's account of the sewer, a reader should be capable of muttering *Totus homo . . .* and of placing the novel's passages of high, humanistic seriousness within this context of comic aspiration. The same reader should also be capable of appreciating three appropriate exits, by Javert, Thénardier, and Jean Valjean.

   "Pour Javert, les incidents habituels de la voie publique étaient classés catégoriquement, ce qui est le commencement de la prévoyance et de la surveillance, et chaque éventualité avait son compartiment; les faits possibles étaient en quelque sorte dans des tiroirs d'où ils sortaient, selon l'occasion, en quantités variables; il y avait, dans la rue, du tapage, de l'émeute, du carnaval, de l'enterrement" (For Javert, the everyday incidents of the public way were classified categorically, this being the beginning of foresight and close observation, and each contingency had its compartment; possible facts could, in a manner of speaking, be brought out from drawers, according to the occasion and in appropriate quantities; there were, in the street, rows, emeutes, carnivals, and funerals) [*LM,* 5.3.10, 370]. This approach can no longer carry him through; Jean Valjean will not fit under the legal code, as Javert finally recognizes, and if the code goes—if "tout ne s'encadrait pas dans le texte du code" (all is not included in the text of the code) [5.4.1, 385]—then Javert must die. He writes a last report, whose nonsensical orderliness reveals this breakdown, then drops into the rapids of the Seine, "cette redoutable spirale de tourbillons qui se dénoue et se renoue comme une vis sans fin" (that dangerous spiral of eddies that unravel and then knot together again like an endless screw) [5.4.1, 392]. The river replicates the machinery of order in which Javert has lived and which now grinds him to pieces.

Thénardier makes his exit in an equally revealing spirit. Following Cosette's wedding Jean Valjean confesses to Marius that even his name is stolen. "Des lettres de l'alphabet, cela s'escroque comme une bourse ou comme une montre" (The letters of the alphabet can be stolen like a purse or a wristwatch) [*LM,* 5.7.1, 466]. Valjean's past has caught up with him— not in Javert's person but as an aftereffect of his descent to the sewers and Cosette's entry into respectable life. This rift is healed by the former innkeeper. When Valjean tries writing Cosette a last note, "comme la plume ni l'encre n'avaient servi depuis longtemps, le bec de la plume était recourbé, l'encre était desséchée, il fallut qu'il se levât et qu'il mit quelques gouttes d'eau dans l'encre, ce qu'il ne put faire sans s'arrêter et s'asseoir deux ou trois fois, et il fut forcé d'écrire avec le dos de la plume" (as pen and ink had not been used for a long time, the quill was bent back, the ink was dried up, it was necessary that he get up and put several drops of water in the ink, which he could only do after stopping and resting two or three times, and he was forced to write with the back side of the pen) [5.9.3, 506]. More or less simultaneously, a Thénardier begging letter arrives at Marius's home: "l'odorat, ce mystérieux aide-mémoire, venait de faire revivre en lui tout un monde. . . . c'était bien là l'écriture connue" (the sense of smell, that mysterious aide-mémoire, had just revived in him a world. . . . it was indeed the familiar handwriting) [5.9.4, 508], and it is indeed Thénardier, that "brocanteur de secrets, marchand de mystères, fouilleur de ténèbres, misérable!" (secondhand dealer in secrets, merchant of mysteries, excavator of darkness, *misérable!*) [5.9.4, 523], who follows the letter into the room. Thénardier seems not to have grasped that everything in the sewer assumes its true form, that the secret he brings from the depths, intending to sell it, can do Jean Valjean only good: it is not at all one of those exploitable secrets which he takes it for. Nor is this the last of Thénardier's errors. He tells Marius, "quand je parle, c'est que j'ai des preuves. Non des preuves manuscrites, l'écriture est suspecte, l'écriture est complaisante, mais des preuves imprimées. . . . Deux faits, deux preuves" (when I speak, it is because I have evidence. Not evidence in manuscript, writing is doubtful, writing is malleable, but printed evidence. . . . Two facts, two pieces of evidence) [5.9.4, 519]. This tour de force of proof is to rest on indisputable fixities and definites—whereupon he presents his customer with two newspaper clippings plus "un lambeau de drap noir déchiqueté, tout couvert de taches sombres" (a jagged scrap of black cloth, all covered with dark stains) [5.9.4, 522]. The clippings confirm Valjean's innocence of murder. The scrap of cloth does this and more. Like Marat's winding-sheet, "une sorte de loque informe et souillée" (a sort of formless and soiled rag) [5.2.4, 325], it appears worthless at first, but on closer examination can be interpreted: it proves to be part of the coat that Marius had worn in the sewer (almost, therefore, another winding-sheet for a revolutionary). Thénardier is so concerned with the mechanisms of proof—he has assembled his jigsaw puzzle beautifully— that his comprehension of substance lags seriously behind. Unbeknownst to him, he is not Jean Valjean's prosecutor but his defender. At the moment in the novel when Jean Valjean has most definitively retired—at the moment when his attempt merely to write a farewell has collapsed— Thénardier becomes his voice. Thénardier's brooding potency of speech, first discovered in the Gorbeau tenement, finds a content beyond itself.

Jean Valjean's final appearance is hardest of the three to analyze. He dies in the grand nineteenth-century manner, blessing his two "children" and announcing that he sees a light; then Hugo conducts us to a grove in Père Lachaise, where stands an unadorned stone on which—many years ago—"une main y a écrit au crayon ces quatre vers qui sont devenus peu à peu illisibles sous la pluie et la poussière, et qui probablement sont aujourd'hui effacés" (a hand had penciled four lines of verse that gradually, under the rain and the dust, became unreadable, and that have probably, at this day, been completely effaced) [*LM,* 5.9.6, 536]. This kind of twist is familiar from *Notre-Dame.* At the moment that all traces of the self-effacing hero are wiped away, his memory is restored in the consciousness of this book, *Les Misérables.* Hugo complicates the old paradox when he situates a poem within the novel: an epitaph penciled not by Cosette—not conceivably!—not by Marius, but by a someone identifiable mainly with Victor Hugo. These lines have "probably" vanished but here they are, memorializing a disappearance that has and has not occurred.[29] Valjean's stone is situated near but not on the communal grave. He enters the subterranean anonymity of *misérables;* at the same time he remains a hero whose singularity is guaranteed by the power of the word inscribed, the word written. In the imagery of the fading epitaph, the word both chronicles and arrests the fading of day to darkness.

Misérables is the subject of Hugo's novel and also its generating principle. The concept of poverty as a meeting place between state and act suggests the power of mystery: especially that kind of mystery that cannot be manipulated, that breaks down categories rather than confirming them. From his conversion onward, Valjean is threatened by what he takes to be an absolute separation between day and night, between responsible society and *misérables. Misérables*—or argot—is more comprehensive than it seems. When Valjean actually enters this world, an extraordinary process is set in motion. The desperate communications of Paris—Javert's, Thénardier's, Valjean's, even Hugo's—speak to an end beyond any one intention. Drawing on the energies thus released, the book—*this* book— becomes a means through which a city is imagined. I have already suggested that Hugo had a sense of humor. Perhaps I can go a step further: at times he had humility too. The grandest of nineteenth-century novels admits the value of an abyss that its author and hero both aspire to bridge. Knowledge of Paris grows from a darkness shared by many, linking Hugo with Valjean, Valjean with Thénardier, Thénardier with countless others. They meet underground; they meet on the page.

One of my favorite illustrations to *Les Misérables,* originally commissioned for the national edition of Hugo's works that began publication in 1885, shows a winding path somewhere down in the sewers. (See fig. 22.) We observe the slightly bloated shapes of rats, note the textures of wood, masonry, and mud, follow a glimmering path of liquid. In one absurdly lavish edition for the American market, this etching is printed four times: on Japanese vellum in black and in bistre; on papier de chine, mounted on Dutch handmade paper; on India paper. An excessive gesture, if there ever was one: an instructive gesture also. The etching is a study in many qualities of darkness (not unlike Phiz's "dark plates" for *Bleak House;* not unlike the black light of *Melencolia I).* To examine it in four different versions is to have the variety of these gradations emphasized almost insanely. Even seeing it in one version, the viewer can sense the demon-

22. Pierre Georges Jeanniot, Parisian sewer with rats. Etching for *Les Misérables*, 5.2.1, *Edition de Grand Luxe of the Novels, Drawings, and Selected Poems of Victor Hugo*, ca. 1892–97. (From a copy in a private collection.)

strative, didactic ambition of the image. Ink, it would seem, is peculiarly adaptable to evoking the subtleties and distinctions of a world far from the light of day. Much the same conclusion can be drawn from the study of *Les Misérables*. Struggling with his longtime habit of thinking in grand oppositions, Hugo seeks a moment when the darkness of ink and the darkness of the sewer are one.

IV

Figures and Knowledge

"I have eyes in my head, and use them," returned Meliboeus with dignity. *"I know more about London than any other man in the world . . ."*

"Meliboeus," cried I, with sudden vehemence, *"you are a gross imposter; your 'great habits of observation' are all moonshine. I see it all now: you have been getting up the Commercial Directory."*

James Payn, "Meliboeus on the Commercial World of London"

10. Meryon's Hybrid Monster: Failed Knowledge

JEAN VALJEAN'S CAREER, like Esther Summerson's, defines an awkward condition of urban allegory: the closer its agents come to conceiving comprehensive truths, the nearer they are to facing the sternest necessities—including, perhaps, their own deaths. Submission to defacement or immersion in an abyss is not an appealing prospect. Is it inevitable? Traditional allegories elude this question by putting the final burden of knowledge on God. A human protagonist interprets dark figures; dies, literally or symbolically; is subsequently transformed. An infinite Mind saves this protagonist by holding in consciousness what he or she cannot. Urban allegory seeks a less ambitious formula. It recognizes that comprehensive knowledge must be distinguished from knowledge as a basis for everyday life: otherwise the sheer oppression of trying to understand a city and its figures leads to madness in the form of referential mania. I will illustrate such perils by reference first to Charles Meryon, then to Michel Foucault—whose association of knowledge with power recalls Meryon's most damaging, exhausting visions.

During the early 1850s, Meryon produced his *Eaux-fortes sur Paris* (*Etchings of Paris*). The best known among them is a panorama that includes its own viewer; it depicts a chimeralike gargoyle staring out over the city from the summits of Notre-Dame. (See fig. 23.) The artist commented to his father that he "thought [he] saw" in the gargoyle an embodiment of *luxuria*. In other words, he wanted to localize a sense of the city's corruption. He would do so by means of a personification allegory, a modern emblem of a kind I have touched on in previous chapters.[1] The gargoyle would signify in one way what the view signified in another; to interpret the gargoyle was thus to interpret the view. Meryon states his intentions clearly enough; on the other hand, he does not assume that the etching carries them out. "I *thought* I saw," he writes—not "I saw." Elsewhere he hedges further. He first called his creature *La Vigie* (The lookout), as though it were the figurehead of a ship. A related version of the same design—accompanied by a sonnet—transforms the chimera-gargoyle

23. Charles Meryon, *Le Stryge*. Etching, 1853. (Yale University Art Gallery.)

into *Le Singe de Notre-Dame* (The monkey of Notre-Dame). An inscription beneath the image tells another story yet. "Insatiable vampire l'eternelle Luxure / Sur la Grande Cité convoite soi pature" (Insatiable vampire eternal Luxuria / Coveting the great city as its feeding place). Late versions of Meryon's etching pick up this hint and rename the chimera-gargoyle-lookout-monkey *Le Stryge* (The vampire).[2]

One clue to the puzzle of *Le Stryge* comes from its association with *Notre-Dame*. This pairing will not surprise anyone who has studied Meryon and Hugo; a look through the Burke catalog of Meryon's work reveals one instance after another of his admiration for the eminent man of letters, his consistent attraction toward *Notre-Dame* in particular. (In 1853, the year of *Le Stryge,* he also produced *La Galerie Notre-Dame,* a variant on the bird's-eye view whose Hugolian links were emphasized in the artist's own memoir.) All the same, it seems to me that Meryon's affinity for Hugo hasn't been taken seriously enough. I work from the simple proposition that Meryon could read, and the more complex proposition that he read *Notre-Dame* to excellent if frightening advantage. His images can be understood fully only if we also know Hugo's words.

Among these words, three have special importance: *stryge, chimère, sphinx.* The first term is a favorite throughout Hugo's work; notable in this regard is a poem of 1835, "Le Poète," eventually published in *Les Contemplations,*[3] which describes the poet's situation as follows:

> Le monde tout entier passe à travers son crible; . . .
> Les sujets monstrueux qu'il a pris et vaincus
> Râlent autour de lui, splendides ou difformes;
> Il étreint Lear, Brutus, Hamlet, êtres énormes,
> Capulet, Montaigu, César, et, tour à tour,
> Les stryges dans le bois, le spectre sur la tour.

[P, I: 689, lines 22–26]

> The entire world passes through his sieve [or riddle]. . . .
> Monstrous subjects that he takes prisoner and conquers,
> Splendid or deformed, give out death rattles around him;
> He embraces Lear, Brutus, Hamlet, gigantic beings,
> Capulet, Montague, Caesar, and, by turns,
> The vampires in the wood, the specter on the tower.

The artist who experiences reality comprehensively—dominating it, simultaneously dissolving into it, catching it in a sieve or a riddle (or a riddlelike sieve: in any case, a less than trustworthy receptacle)—and who identifies with vampires and specters on towers to the point of embracing them, seems close already to the central figure of *Le Stryge.*

Hugo's fascination with chimeras is even more instructive. As Yves Vadé has shown, *Notre-Dame* characterizes these curious composite monsters by contrasting them with sphinxes, an opposition that recurs throughout nineteenth-century French literature. "The . . . sphinx speaks the language of the absolute: it assumes that the world is ordered by mystery and revealed by symbols at once universal and necessary."[4] The chimera, on the other hand, suggests a sort of knowledge typically embodied in uncontrolled or uncontrollable expressions. The cathedral of Notre-Dame is a sphinx in its fundamental structure, a chimera in its ornamentation and extravagance. (Cf. *ND*, 5.1, 197 with *ND*, 3.1, 136.) A similar antithesis is suggested by the contrast between sphinxlike Frollo and chimeric Quasimodo. In Hugo's conception, the Quasimodo side of Notre-Dame anticipates the cultural future of Europe. "Adieu le mystère, le mythe, la loi. Voici la fantaisie et le caprice" (Goodbye to mystery, myth, law. Here come fantasy and caprice) [*ND*, 5.2].

Meryon's chimera is explicable within the same context. The sculpture is literally modern; it was constructed by the architect/historian Viollet-le-Duc, whom Louis-Philippe had commissioned to restore Notre-Dame (a task the architect began in 1844).[5] At first there seems to be no opposing sphinx, the sphinx one might expect from Meryon's Hugolian enthusiasms; however, the viewer who looks toward the middle distance of the etching will focus on the tower of Saint-Jacques-de-la-Boucherie, a dominant feature of the view as of the print. *Notre-Dame* pays particular attention to this building:

> *Il y avait aussi de beaux édifices qui perçaient l'ondulation pétrifiée de cette mer de pignons. . . . C'était le riche clocher carré de Saint-Jacques-de-la-Boucherie, avec ses angles tout émoussés de sculptures, déjà admirable, quoiqu'il ne fût pas achevé au quinzième siècle. Il lui manquait en particulier ces quatre monstres qui, aujourd'hui encore, perchés aux encoignures de son toit, ont l'air de quatre sphinx qui donnent à deviner au nouveau Paris l'énigme de l'ancien; Rault, le sculpteur, ne les posa qu'en 1526, et il eut vingt francs pour sa peine.*

[*ND*, 3.2, 152]

> *There were also some handsome edifices that ran through the petrified undulations of this sea of gables. . . . There was the rich, square belfry tower of Saint-Jacques-de-la-Boucherie, its corners rounded with sculptures, already admirable, though it was not finished in the fifteenth century. It lacked in particular those four monsters that, even today, perched at the four corners of its roof, look like so many sphinxes presenting new Paris with a riddle of the old. Rault, the sculptor, did not put them there until 1516, and got twenty francs for his trouble.*

In *Le Stryge*, the sphinxes are tiny but finely etched: one can make out three of them "perched" at corners of Saint-Jacques's roof. By a perspectival illusion, they seem quite close to the gargoyle (in terms of the flat surface of the etching, about half an inch to its left, at exactly the same height as its wings). Both species, moreover, rest upon medieval elements raised above a modern cityscape. On these heights, the etching implies, nineteenth-century Gothic meets medieval Gothic. The two possibilities are weighed within the one view.

It is not immediately obvious, however, what this presentation of alternatives might mean for Meryon: it has *some* relation to Hugo's historical conception, but the exact point is hard to pin down. One possible agenda is articulated in a conversation between the artist and Jules Andrieu. Here *Le Stryge* becomes an example of how to get an *authentic* Gothic revival going; Meryon claims that he is the heir of the builders of Saint-Jacques, which makes his chimera and their sphinxes monsters of the same kind.[6] On the other hand this interpretation has several ambiguous points. It not only ignores Viollet-le-Duc's creation of the gargoyle—a peculiar omission—but ends by contradicting itself.[7] Furthermore, the motto's identification of the gargoyle as an "insatiable" vampire sets up a parasitical relation between the revival piece and the late medieval structure a few hundred yards away. A vampire is not resurrected from the dead; he is one of the undead, and he sucks life from those upon whom he feeds (from "la Grande Cité," to quote Meryon's sonnet again, socially or architecturally conceived). The relation between sphinx and chimera thus remains problematic. It is perhaps unpleasant, but then what? One seeks an additional hint as to how the meeting of sphinx and chimera might operate in this particular frame of reference, as to how absolute knowledge might contrast with its chimeric descendant.

I turn to the birds. There are thirteen of them. There seem to be many more. Apparently they are eagles. (Arguably they might be ravens: see below for Meryon's comments on Edgar Allan Poe.) They swoop through the space defined by Notre-Dame on the right and Saint-Jacques on the left, lending the scene a vertiginous feeling. This sort of effect is often found in the *Eaux-fortes*. Even at his most precise, his most topographical, Meryon liked to depict erratic flights of winged creatures, sometimes biologically plausible fowl, sometimes unclassifiable nightmare creatures. One precedent is a well-known Delacroix etching for Goethe's *Faust,* where Mephistopheles flaps lewdly over a darkening cityscape.[8] Given the subject matter of *Le Stryge,* however, a second possible source (literary rather than visual) appears more significant.

Notre-Dame 5.2, the famous chapter "Ceci tuera cela," includes the following passage: "Sous la forme imprimerie, la pensée est plus impéris-

sable que jamais; elle est volatile, insaisissable, indestructible. Elle se mêle
à l'air. Du temps de l'architecture, elle se faisait montagne et s'empa-
rait puissamment d'un siècle et d'un lieu. Maintenant elle se fait troupe
d'oiseaux, s'éparpille aux quatre vents, et occupe à la fois tous les points de
l'air et de l'espace" (In the form of print, thought is more imperishable than
ever; it is volatile, elusive, indestructible. It loses itself in the air. In the time
of architecture, it became a mountain, and took hold of a century and a
region. Now it has been transformed to a flock of birds, scattering to the
four winds and filling all air and space) [*ND*, 5.2, 205]. A bit further on
Hugo adds, "le nouveau monde qui sortira de ce chaos verra en s'éveillant
planer au-dessus de lui, ailée et vivante, la pensée du monde englouti" (the
new world that emerges from this chaos will see, when it awakens,
hovering over it, winged and alive, the thought of the world that has been
swallowed up) [206]. The writer continues to believe in progress—even if,
as in *Notre-Dame* and *Les Misérables,* his belief must be frequently reformulated. Note that books (or birds) preserve the thought of the old world
while transforming its import. Hugo's formulation implies that—even in
the most chimerical age—thought is a whole. What changes is the way it is
manifested. Knowledge positions itself all over the map.

To some extent, *Le Stryge* evokes a similar action—refining it, however, in a wonderfully dizzying fashion. At three points on the left-hand
side, obtruding wing or tail feathers seem to puncture the cameo-style
oval frame. The gargoyle's own wings are neatly folded, just inside a curve
on the right side. This chimera will not fly, no more than can the stone
sphinxes. The flock acts out the energies of both. To some extent, it
dramatizes a transfer of energy from one of these stationary icons to the
other, yet we cannot simply say: "This will replace that, sphinx will yield
to chimera." Looping along wind currents, sailing easily, the thirteen birds
head away from the sphinxes and (almost all) toward the vampire of
Viollet-le-Duc—then, lazily, around it. The birds suggest a continuous,
spiraling line but also mark a dispersion; they embody a directed force
working *through* a dispersion, a concept easier seen than expressed in
words.

The birds enliven the sphinx-chimera opposition, especially its status
as a kind of historical discourse. One is made aware of a change that is
under way, or perhaps of a change that has already occurred. However, it
is even more to the point that the flock dislocates this structuring antithesis. Meryon's chimera would seem to be an allegory of knowledge as it
exists in the modern world, inheriting the energies of the old but in a
newly malleable, newly elusive form: everything I have argued up to this
point confirms such a conclusion. Nonetheless, once the role of the flock is

underlined, once that third element enters the antithesis, any neat conclusion is upset. Holcomb discusses "the derivation of *Stryge* from the Latin *striga,* or predatory night-bird" ["Le Stryge," 152]. If the viewer (alerted by the pun, by the probable reference to "Ceci tuera cela," by the cutting power of those wings) concentrates on the birds, then *they* become the subject of *Le Stryge;* as in Hugo, it is the flock rather than the stationary monster that embodies the powers of knowledge in the modern world.

This is the heart of the matter: the chimera is not a new kind of knowledge—Meryon at once encourages and denies that attractive conclusion—so much as the consciousness that suffers from it. To quote Hugo once more: "the new world that emerges from this chaos will see, when it awakens, hovering over it, winged and alive, the thought of the world that has been swallowed up." The gargoyle is the witnessing "new world," but what he witnesses, above all, is an act of surveillance directed against himself. Meryon, then, goes beyond illustrating Hugo's thought. He makes it a good deal more disturbing than it is in the predictions of "Ceci tuera cela." He elides the Utopian implication that—after the unspoken deluge—an enlightened survivor will realize that nothing has perished, that nothing could possibly perish. The gargoyle is neither enlightened nor elated: he awakes to a staring madness, persecuted rather than saved by the world that surrounds him. This is a bird's-eye view that would turn the most prehensile monster to stone, freeze him in his place with fear.[9]

Meryon shared this fear. James Yarnall has studied those writings of the artist where he "imagines himself in a role of authority similar to that of Napoleon III."[10] One imagines a competition between emperor and artist, each seeking in his own way to master the city, to stamp it with his mark: the former by his improvements, the latter by his etchings. Meryon's rulership was troubled, as well it might have been; it's hard to become an emperor by spending one's day in such lonely and painstaking work. The artist's sense of sway easily disintegrated into feelings—chimeric feelings—of omnipresent persecution. On one occasion these feelings are explicitly linked to a flock of birds hovering in the skies of Paris. *Le Pont-au-Change,* etched a year after *Le Stryge,* includes a threatening ornithological visitation that—Meryon told Baudelaire—represented a conspiracy of the government, a conspiracy that had been noted even in the newspapers. Which is not to say that birds are the only sign of conspiracy: Meryon, wrote Baudelaire, "sees intrigue everywhere."

> He asked me if I had read the novels of a certain Edgar Poe. I told him I know them better than anyone—and justifiably so. Then he asked me in

a very insistent tone, whether I believe in the reality of this Edgar Poe. Naturally, I asked him to whom, then, he would attribute the novels. He answered me: "To a Society of literary men who were very clever, very powerful, and very knowledgeable in all matters." And here is one of his reasons: "La Rue 'Morgue.' I made a design of the Morgue. An 'Orang-utang.' I have often been compared to a monkey. This monkey killed two women, a mother and her daughter. And I, too, have morally assassi-nated two women, a mother and her daughter. I have always taken the story to be an allusion to my misfortunes. You would do me a favor if you could discover the date when Edgar Poe (assuming he had been helped by no one) composed this tale, to see if the date coincides with my exploits."[11]

As noted above, a supplementary version of *Le Stryge* transforms the gargoyle into a monkey. Meryon's conversation with Baudelaire empha-sizes how personal this alteration was. "I have often been compared to a monkey." It is as if, by producing a pendant, the artist had wished to highlight the biographical relevance of his etching. The pendant might seem to restore his focus on a single, dominating figure. No Saint-Jacques is juxtaposed with the gargoyle; only a few inconspicuous birds drift in the background. Paris hardly shows itself . . . and yet, appearances are deceptive. Meryon's delusion—that an all-knowing secret society had encoded his own deeds in "Poe's" fiction—created a situation where he had to fear everything without exception, where fleeting notions of his authority over what he saw, what he knew, were perennially overthrown.

The sonnet printed with *Le Singe de Notre-Dame* addresses the gar-goyle, asking him what he perceives. "Que contemples-tu donc, hideux monstre de pierre, / Dans ce gouffre béant où ton oeil est plongé?" (At what do you gaze, hideous stone monster, / In this gaping abyss where your eye is cast?). No certain answer is given, unless by the original plate. It is Paris itself that the gargoyle or Meryon must survey, Paris that irretrievably haunts him, pursuing his beleaguered mind through a mil-lion diverse forms. The monster that seemed the personification of a contemporary, romanticized knowledge has become the helpless onlooker to an eternal plot against him. The viewer of the etching is similarly trapped. From tower to gargoyle I glance and from gargoyle to tower, and between them trace the swooping eagles, and below them face a world that embodies a greater variety of intentions and accomplishments than an individual could ever comprehend. Conspiracy, illusionary or real, is identified with the urban landscape—the landscape of modernity itself.

Le Stryge grows out of *Notre-Dame* in textually specific ways. A close reading of certain passages from the novel makes possible an accurate analysis of the etching. This affinity might also be defined in social or historical terms. *Notre-Dame* is very much a book of its moment; the exhilaration of 1830, when Charles X was dethroned, soon died down; the reign of Louis-Philippe, the bourgeois king, soon showed that the uprising against Charles had not accomplished as much as might have been hoped. The best work in the arts tended to be frenetic, morbid, or self-enclosed; what could not be accomplished in the realm of politics might still, it was thought, be acted out through the power of imagination. If these tendencies were evident before 1830, afterwards they were drastically intensified.[12] None of this would have much to do with Meryon, an artist of a later generation—except that the uprising of 1848 and the coup d'état of Napoleon III created a second moment when fantasy and caprice seemed an attractive alternative to the world as it was. At midcentury, realism dominates the arts, not the dark romanticism of the thirties: *Le Stryge,* however, manages a throwback to a well-established pattern. For all their surface realism, his *Eaux-fortes* manifest a sort of self-torture familiar from the earlier debacle; a failed revolution precedes and perhaps prompts a descent into private and almost absurdly morbid fantasy— fantasy as a delusive resistance against official cooptation.[13] In both periods, the chimera/vampire is an appropriate icon for postrevolutionary depression and for a consequent effort to insulate art from society—as though it could be its own self-supporting raison d'être, thus preserving poetic sensibilities from a disappointing, bourgeoisified reality.

These similarities noted, I would add that the imaginative indulgence of *Le Stryge* is purer and perhaps more dangerous than that of *Notre-Dame*. Hugo's novel appropriates three distinct methods for protecting art from the banality of bourgeois life under Louis-Philippe. First, the embrace of Quasimodo and Esmeralda at Montfaucon asks us to be disgusted yet exalted by a tale of love's martyrdom: the thrill of decay and loss are to ennoble both readers of the scene and actors within it. Second, that same embrace evokes the attractions of a morbid but wonderfully self-enclosed world—art for art's sake . . . death for death's sake . . . a story not known, so preserved from the desecrations of everyday inquisitiveness. Hugo thus uses the aesthetic to qualify the frenetic and vice-versa, much as though he had combined Dumas's ghastly *Tour de Nesle* with Gautier's hymn to artistic beauty, *Mademoiselle de Maupin.*[14] There is, as it were, a balance of power between terror and formalism. Finally, as I argued in chapter 2, a third alternative to these choices is present by implication; Montfaucon is not only a colorful place in a morbid historical novel but a notorious site for waste disposal in Paris, 1831: we can read this story's conclusion as pointing toward an ongoing public discussion. By contrast, the choices with which Meryon leaves us are limited. He is arguably something of an aesthete and he certainly has political and social obsessions, but neither the political-social concerns nor formal ones modify the nightmare of *Le Stryge*. Meryon draws out the frenetic possibilities of his amazing Parisian reverie—refining them to the stage where they become a form of paranoia, a state of mind often called referential mania.

The latter term needs a solid definition. Referential mania is endemic in big cities, environments produced by multitudinous but often enigmatic intentions. G. K. Chesterton writes as follows: "there is no stone in the street and no brick in the wall [of a city] that is not actually a deliberate symbol—a message from some man, as much as if it were a telegram or a post-card." He goes on to praise "this romance of detail in civilisation," for "anything which tends . . . to assert . . . [an] unfathomably human character in flints and tiles, is a good thing."[15] Many observers have disagreed (as Chesterton might well have done in another mood: cf. his *Man Who Was Thursday*). To be sure, "such sensations . . . may be experienced as a source of tranquillity and assurance, by filling us with the sense that our own life, too, is involved in this hidden meaning of the world." On the other hand: where they do not, as in traditional allegory, converge "upon the absolute One, whence all things emanate," they are likely to produce a "morbid oppression, so that all things seem to be charged with a menace or riddle which we must solve at any cost."[16] Intrigue of this chimeric kind is exemplified by the activities of Mr. Tulkinghorn, say, or of the postal examiners in Reynolds's Black Chamber. It is also related to the sensation of the tourist who reaches the roof of Todgers's (a sensation that Dickens eventually tries to equate with a murderer's fevered suspicions of observation). But in one respect it is worse than any of these cases. The sufferer works out the pattern of an intrigue that can never end. Although the sum of human culture is objective, it imprisons city dwellers within a radical subjectivity verging on nothingness.

This problem is neither specialized nor esoteric. I am reluctant to go as far as Julia Kristeva and associate paranoia with interpretation as such.[17] On the other hand, even the most adept interpreter can become a paranoiac. Michel Foucault's *Discipline and Punish* offers a pertinent instance. Foucault argues that power was once exercised through such ceremonies as executions, where the king's majesty was displayed to the people: displayed publicly and materially, in front of a large audience and by particular actions inflicted on a particular body. During the last two centuries, power operates on a new model. It is located within totalizing systems of knowledge; it is no longer exercised by a human agent but upon him, so that relations of sovereignty give way to relations of discipline [208]. One of Foucault's clearest examples is a city struck by the plague, a city therefore under quarantine: "this enclosed, segmented space, observed at every point, in which . . . the slightest movements are supervised, in which all events are recorded, in which an uninterrupted work of writing links the centre and periphery, in which power is exercised without division. . . . all this constitutes a compact model of the disciplinary mechanism. . . . [Order] lays down for each individual his place, his body, his disease and his death, his well-being, by means of an omnipresent and omniscient power that subdivides itself in a regular way even to the ultimate determination of the individual" [197]. Foucault calls this new power "panopticism," after the model of Jeremy Bentham's Utopian prison, the Panopticon.

One need only enter a drugstore monitored by conspicuous cameras, fill out an income-tax form, or inspect a child's report card to see that much of what Foucault claims is plausible, even where his history of prison discipline leaves much to be desired.[18] Still, he neglects a crucial dilemma.[19] At what point does the hypothesis of omnipresent power create a kind of referential mania—and how is this state to be resisted or controlled? Foucault is attracted to the same motifs as Meryon; moreover, he uses them in much the same way as the artist. The malign "lookout" whose existence as a horror apart seems certain but who then is revealed as one of . . . us; the panoramic observers—birds or books, documents with wings—who scatter this way and that, apparently far more mobile than a human spy could ever be; the difficulty of locating power in any one place; above all the link between modern structures of knowledge and the omnipresent infliction of discipline: these overlaid fascinations demonstrate that this philosopher functions within a well-established tradition of French culture, that his particular originality has deep roots. There is even the similarity that Foucault, like the romantics of the 1830s and the Meryon of the fifties, worked in an era of post-revolutionary burnout where there was ample opportunity for tortured compensations. Perhaps for this very reason, he proves incapable of analyzing the weakness in his own nightmarish images.

Others have attempted such an analysis. Two lines of criticism strike me as fruitful. One, formulated most fully in a study by Allan Megill, accuses Foucault of "lack of interest in the past." Where all forms of objectivity are undercut, there is nothing left but interpretation, feeding on itself in a void: as Megill puts it, " 'historical reality' [becomes] a mere projection of present needs and interests."[20] Foucault is in danger of trivializing his "projection of present needs and interests" by failing to build upon any usable theory of fact, of the otherness that his own investigations reveal. The second critique is Charles Taylor's. Where Megill argues that Foucault turns history into myth, Taylor maintains that he fails to provide his reader with any incentive for action. "He dashes the hope, if we had one, that there is some good we can *affirm,* as a result of the understanding his analyses give us."[21] The era of the old power and the era of the new are what they are. The notion of judging between them is absurd. To be sure, Foucault seems always on the edge of making such a judgment, but it is not quite articulated. The stance of neutrality persists throughout his later writings, negating the forms of evaluation his work seems designed to provoke.[22]

Megill and Taylor might almost seem to be writing about different philosophers. Megill's Foucault turns history into myth in order to change the present. Taylor's Foucault denies any basis for moral discrimination; he denies, in other words, the *possibility* of effective change based on rational judgments. Nonetheless, these two critiques originate in the same dissatisfaction. Foucault articulates the logic of cultural systems with wonderful flair; he uses wide reading and a superb eye for detail to build hypotheses about how societies hold together. Then, in an almost invisible shift, these hypotheses become premises: they are treated as axioms applying uniformly. An act of description, an act that began as an ambitious and subversive unmasking, begins to function as part of the mechanism it apparently condemns. The describer finds himself inventing new powers, new oppressions. He contemplates them with disgust. He contemplates them fatalistically. It is Meryon all over again—but Meryon in the guise of a learned polemic.[23]

Dickens offers a contrasting response to modern pathologies of knowledge. His immersion in that French invention, the novel of urban mysteries, makes him sensitive to both of the Hugolian indulgences described above—freneticism and aestheticism. Like Meryon, he puts more emphasis on the first alternative, intensifying it into referential mania—but the second alternative is also present, largely as a *reaction* to the first, even as a sort of proposed solution to it. Dickens's fascination with the *Arabian Nights* provides one point of entry into his engagement with the dilemmas of referential mania and self-contained aestheticism; his consideration of omniscience provides another. In each of these cases a threatening personality—the oriental despot, the omniscient Shadow—is perceived as a formidable influence on London, an influence that seems to reach everywhere through one disturbing dispersal or another. Dickens tries to grasp the significance of despot and Shadow, to gauge the omnipresence of their conspiracies. Then he measures his own limitations against a force that has no obvious boundaries. He is tempted to surrender himself to referential mania à la Meryon; he is also tempted by the aesthetic/linguistic approach: as though language *of itself,* language without social or ethical context, could be a refuge against the threat of universal intrigue. I find it an advantage of Dickens's work that he sustains a system of reference rather than a system of referential mania or a flight from reference altogether: because he resists these debilitating forms of fantasy, because he uses paper, writing, and words as a way of granting agents access to a broadly understood social world, he can create a productive, active relationship with London—and is able, moreover, to imagine such relationships for his characters. Reference as conceived by Dickens allows him to confront, then abolish, self-tormenting fantasies like those so wonderfully imagined in *Le Stryge.* Analyzing despot and Shadow, following their dissemination into the form and fabric of London, celebrating their disappearance or transformation, he reaffirms the worth—in fact, the possibility—of understanding cities.

11. Dickens's *Arabian Nights*

THE FRAMING DEVICE OF THE *Arabian Nights* is that Scheherezade must tell stories to keep her sultan-husband Shahryar from decapitating her; since her stories are invariably unfinished at dawn, he always postpones her execution just one night more, thus eliciting more stories. Authority and tale telling are at war in this difficult marriage, a point often noted by nineteenth-century readers. Hazlitt observes that the "serious and marvellous stories in [the *Arabian Nights*], which have been so much admired and so greedily read, appear to me monstrous and abortive fictions, like disjointed dreams, dictated by a preternatural dread of arbitrary and despotic power."[1] The form of the tales, as well as the content, is "dictated" by "arbitrary" decree. Coleridge makes a similar argument when he notes of his *Rime of the Ancient Mariner* that it "ought to have had no more moral than the Arabian Nights' tale of the merchant's sitting down to eat dates by the side of a well, and throwing the shells aside, and lo! a geni starts up, and says he *must* kill the aforesaid merchant *because* one of the date shells had, it seems, put out the eye of the geni's son."[2] The date merchant in question embarks upon a defensive telling of tales. He is a version of Scheherezade—as is the Mariner, struggling against a world of warring, inexplicable forces until he achieves his power of speech and creates from his plight a tale.

The tales of Scheherezade imitate the arbitrariness that made them necessary. The *Arabian Nights* is a mechanism for turning power into story, fate into words, and so neutralizing these threatening forces. On these terms, Scheherezade saves herself. At first this fantastical interpretation is expressed indirectly, in the outpouring of tales within tales of which the *Ancient Mariner* is an early example (1798). Jan Potocki's *The Saragossa Manuscript* (1804) and Gérard de Nerval's *Smarra* (1821) provide further cases. Later, in Jorge Luis Borges, the *Arabian Nights* becomes a point of departure for extended speculations about reality and its relationship to narrative form. Borges's "Partial Enchantments of the *Quixote*" describes the great tale collection as "infinite and circular," "like a Persian carpet." His impression is confirmed by recent commentaries, among them Edward Said's: "Stories like those in *The Arabian Nights* are ornamental, variations on the world, not completions of it; neither are they lessons, structures, extensions, or totalities designed to illustrate either the author's prowess in representation, the education of a character, or ways in which the world can be viewed and changed."³ The *Arabian Nights* is devoid of psychology and social concern. Freed from the tyrant, the story escapes reality too, telling the tale only of itself. As James Merrill writes of Scheherezade and Shahryar:

> They wept, then tenderly embraced and went
> Their ways. She and her fictions soon were one.
> He slept through moonset, woke in blinding sun,
> Too late to question what the tale had meant.⁴

Such is the *Arabian Nights* that has been a presence in Western literature of the nineteenth and twentieth centuries. The book has been treated as our preeminent antirealistic work, the account of a stormy marriage followed by an inevitable divorce. One can easily see why this approach has persisted. It has often been strengthened by a widespread tendency to view the orient as a field of fantasy and play, a field that exists, somehow, outside the strictures and demands of everyday reality. (Most Americans or Europeans would have an easier time imagining an extravagant sexual adventure in Alexandria, say, than in Manchester.) Furthermore, it dovetails neatly with the most widely accepted theories of language in our time: like Hazlitt and other interpreters of the *Arabian Nights*, Saussure tends to treat arbitrariness as threatening or canceling referentiality and the mimetic capacity of language. If language is arbitrary, so the reasoning goes, it cannot be very firmly connected with the world.⁵ Where popular opinion and the higher linguistics confirm a strong romantic inheritance, there are bound to be certain effects on the general cultural understanding of a text; when we consider the *Arabian Nights,* the Hazlitt version, so to speak, is likely to prevail. Nonetheless, there are—and always have been—other possibilities worth considering. Dickens never faltered in his fascination with Scheherezade's tales. He used them in letters, speeches, essays, stories, and novels throughout his career; he alluded to them more often than any of his contemporaries; and he almost always managed to connect them with his own society. In Dickens's works, more than in anyone else's, the divorce between story and power is postponed, perhaps even called off. The arbitrary tyrant and the arbitrary tale teller work together toward a common end: the presentation of modern, urban realities. Mimesis wins the day—though not without a struggle.

Can This Marriage Be Saved?

A few cross-references will suggest some of the difficulties Dickens faced when he tried to reconcile Scheherezade and Shahryar. In *Les Mystères de Paris,* Eugène Sue made his own attempt to novelize the book, and he did so without any inspiration at all from the Coleridge-Hazlitt type of insight. Sue was taken with the *Arabian Nights* figure of Harun al-Raschid, the melancholy sultan who wanders Baghdad in disguise. Harun indulges kingly whims with a sudden and passionate enthusiasm; pursuing his often inexplicable appetites, he brings judgment on himself and others. Sue realized that this character was more attractive than the bloodthirsty Shahryar; he must have appeared the perfect vehicle to bring the *Arabian Nights* in touch with modern society. From some such starting point emerged the Harun-like protagonist of *Les Mystères.* He is, of course, the redoubtable Prince Rodolphe, sovereign of Gerolstein.

Gerolstein is a tiny kingdom full of sober and obedient Germans, hardly a suitable challenge for a cocky fellow like Rodolphe. Consequently he spends most of his time in Paris, where his avocation is to stroll around disguised, righting wrongs. Rodolphe is the flaneur as moralist, the aesthete as man of action. He comments to Clémence d'Harville (the woman he loves, but who is unfortunately married to another), "si vous vous *amusiez* comme moi à *jouer* de temps à autre *à la Providence,* vous avoueriez que certaines *bonnes oeuvres* ont quelquefois tout le piquant d'un roman" (if you would *amuse* yourself, as I do, at *playing* from time to time, *at the game of Providence,* you would acknowledge that occasionally our *good deeds* acquire the piquancy of a novel) [2.3, 53]. Rodolphe's journeys between the Paris of the rich and of the poor provide him with the adventures of "des *Milles et une Nuits*" (a *thousand and one nights*) [1.26, 219]. Despite the distance from his literal power base, Gerolstein, Rodolphe exercises a princely sway over Paris. As "Th. Burette" wrote in his open letter to Sue (printed at the beginning of the 1843 "nouvelle édition" of *Les Mystères*), "Quant à Rodolphe, que ce soit Haroun-al-Raschid demandant à la nuit les secrets de Bagdad, ou tout autre prince de fantaisie, redresseur de torts, je ne m'informe pas d'où il vient, mais . . . je ne lui conteste pas le droit de faire le bien à sa manière, ou de juger en dernier ressort à son tribunal exceptionnel" (As for Rodolphe—he who was Haroun al-Raschid, asking of the night the secrets of Baghdad, or who was any other prince of fantasy, righter of wrongs—I have not informed myself where he came from, but . . . I do not argue with his right to do good in his manner, or to judge in the last resort at his extraordinary tribunal) [*MP,* iv].

At first the appeal of Rodolphe seems obvious. He allows a wonderful daydream in which the gratifications of desire and the workings of justice merge. His heroism survives a technological, bureaucratized age. Sue appears to have resolved the struggle between tyrant and storyteller altogether, for instead of hearing stories, Rodolphe (like Harun) is in them: Paris (like Baghdad) is used for a potentially endless series of entertaining encounters. Nobody has to flee from reality; under the auspices of the tyrant, world and story converge. The pattern of the oriental carpet is adapted to the purpose of moral reform, a reconciliation on which Sue's "thousand and one nights" are based.

Only gradually does the reconciliation betray its weak points.[6] No matter how hard he tries, Rodolphe cannot really duplicate Harun's fine carelessness. "Then said Harun," when making up a lottery for the poor fisherman whose destiny is intwined with his, " 'As Allah lives, I must do justice upon him to-day and let him have his due. If Allah wishes to send him pains and penalties through me, it must be so; if he wishes to send him rank and fortune, it must be so.' "[7] Harun appears as the instrument of Providence, yet at the same time Providence is his plaything. As a corollary, he is alternately the tale's servant and its master. It is this shimmering uncertainty—a sort of Möbius strip between tyrant and tale—that eludes Sue when he narrates Rodolphe's exploits.

Especially notable in this regard is the scene where Rodolphe punishes the Schoolmaster, arch-villain of the Parisian underworld, "insouciant d'une vie misérable" (careless liver of the life of poverty and crime). According to Rodolphe, "tout crime s'expie et se rachète, a dit le Sauveur; mais, du tribunal à l'échafaud, le trajet est trop court, il faut le loisir de l'expiation et du repentir. . . . si je te plonge dans une nuit impénétrable . . . [ellipsis in text] seul . . . [ellipsis in text] avec le souvenir de tes forfaits . . . [ellipsis in text] c'est pour que tu contemples incessamment leur énormité" ("All sin may be forgiven," said our blessed Savior, "but from the tribunal to the scaffold the passage is too short, time is necessary for atonement and repentance. . . . if I plunge you into impenetrable night . . . alone . . . with the memory of your abominable crimes . . . it is that you may incessantly contemplate their enormity") [*MP*, 1.17, 131–32]. The more he talks, the more outrageous becomes his blinding of the Schoolmaster. For the dandy he aspires to be, Rodolphe preaches too much. He does not so much play at the game of Providence as work at it. Winning is everything to this reactionary vigilante.

Sue tries, with dubious results, to moralize the tyrant's actions. Several of Robert Louis Stevenson's early fictions promote a different approach, nearer (though not identical) to the romantic one. In Stevenson's *New Arabian Nights* (1882), London and Paris are a backdrop for extravagant narratives, often revolving around Prince Florizel of Bohemia. Florizel's name and kingdom are lifted from "The Winter's Tale." His nature is lifted from the *Arabian Nights* as filtered through romancers like Sue and Dumas—but Stevenson is trying for a somewhat different effect than these predecessors. His Florizel would be indistinguishable from a character like Rodolphe, were it not that he displays little concern either for righting wrongs or for policing society.[8] If Rodolphe is a Harun who preaches morality and thus tries to claim his place within the modern world, Florizel adopts a more offhand approach. As he says of himself and his faithful retainer Colonel Geraldine, "We pass our lives entirely in the search for extravagant adventures; and there is no extravagance with which we are not capable of sympathy" [*Works*, 3: 17].

After a reading of the *New Arabian Nights,* it might seem that Stevenson himself is the most determined of aesthetes, prepared to inhabit forever Scheherezade's (supposed) realm of escapist narrative and even to pretend that London or Paris is identical with that realm. Several contemporary reviewers declared that the pretence was unsatisfactory, that Stevenson, in effect, was more like Sue than he thought—a writer of penny dreadfuls rather than of oriental fantasies.[9] A gesture at the end of the *Nights* suggests that the writer understood this unresolved tension. "In consequence of his continued absence and edifying neglect of public business," Florizel loses his kingdom; he is reduced to reigning over a London tobacco shop, where he becomes the handsomest of tobacconists [*Works*, 3: 247]. The deliberate shattering of an illusion no one ever believed demonstrates, I think, a sort of penance: Florizel is reduced to living on the level of the reality he has weightlessly and effortlessly denied.

The eponymous hero of *Prince Otto* (1885) will suffer a similar end more thoughtfully examined. Otto rules the little state of Grünewald, "an infinitesimal member of the German Empire" [*Works*, 5: 339]. Stevenson begins by placing his "infinitesimal" state within a purely literary geography: Grünewald borders Rodolphe's Gerolstein on one side and on another Florizel's "Seaboard Bohemia." The novelist thus signals that his Green Wood is a never-never land whose connection to historical Europe is minimal. He seems to be working to avoid the discrepancy so obvious in the *New Arabian Nights,* between familiar city and fantastical adventure. He seems to have located a setting where aesthetic tale telling can be indulged in without reality making any claims at all. In Grünewald—to quote the title of chapter 2—"the Prince Plays Haroun-al-Raschid" to his heart's desire. Then, just as he appears to have established what kind of

book *Prince Otto* will be, Stevenson shifts his ground. Adopting anonymity to circulate among commoners, irresponsible Otto learns that
people despise him because he chooses not to govern. He also hears that his
wife and his Prussian minister Gondremark (a sort of small-time Metter-
nich) are planning war on Gerolstein. Finally he comes to realize the
strength of a revolutionary conspiracy against him. Stevenson mocks the
convention by which the princes of small central-European states can
spend their time amusing themselves anonymously and abroad. More
ambitiously, he begins to explore the kinds of power available to rulers
after the French Revolution.

The exploration is largely negative. Stevenson mocks Otto, the failed
Harun, who begins to think like a king but never learns to govern like
one—and in any case has little taste for the arbitrary exercise of power; he
mocks Otto's wife Seraphina for trying to rule behind the scenes (much as
Glencora tries to rule behind the scenes in Trollope's *The Prime Minister*);
he mocks Gondremark for trying to rule through Seraphina even while
fomenting the republican conspiracy he publically opposes; he mocks,
though more mildly, the rebels who eventually take over Grünewald.[10]
One character alone is allowed any effectiveness as a political operator: the
countess von Rosen, Gondremark's mistress. Not only does she assume
the Harun-like function of "Providence"—she is constantly referred to as
"Providence von Rosen"—but she also becomes a manipulator of documents, a character type familiar from the novel of urban mysteries: at one
point, she tremblingly holds "the paper by which all depended" [*Works*, 5:
520]. Von Rosen, however, has such mixed motives that she could never
become an effective ruler.

The most notable feature of Stevenson's comic romance is the impact
of all these failures taken together. Grünewald is a fiction advertised as
such. And yet, as the novelist chronicles successive losses of power, as he
narrates the blunders of Otto, Seraphina, Gondremark, and the countess
von Rosen, as he anticipates the ultimate defeat of the republicans and the
extinction of the motherland, Grünewald starts to acquire an actuality
inappropriate for storybook countries. The power of the tyrant and the
power of the tale fall apart simultaneously. Otto does not even consider
writing his own memoirs, a task he leaves—with dubious results—to
others. Stevenson leaves him "ageing peaceably at the court of [his] wife's
father, jingling French rhymes and correcting joint proofs" [*Works*, 5: 616].
The slim volumes he coauthors with his wife will be read by no one. Tale
and tyrant have suffered not so much a divorce as a mutual descent into
premature senility.

Double takes

Formally, Dickens's use of the *Arabian Nights* is quite different from Stevenson's or Sue's. Dickens neither faces the *Arabian Nights* fully nor fully dispenses with it. It persists on the periphery of his work, in spur-of-the-moment citations, as if its energies could be tapped without its anti-realistic bias confusing the novelistic project.[11] All the same, these references add up. The key to Dickens's success with the *Arabian Nights* is the now-familiar motif of "summary and arbitrary power."[12]

Power is defined, not in a single figure, but through a kind of delayed reaction experienced by novelist, reader, and sometimes hero: double take, I shall call it.

1. *Double take* implies first that Dickens's references to the *Arabian Nights* assume the form of awkward jokes, where the awkwardness is in figuring out what he means. It is often said that he reverts to the tales so often because they connote childhood imagination; he engages therefore in a game of wit, demonstrating his ability to invoke the book on any given occasion.[13] This playful spirit will be found in the examples that follow. Dickens admits the *Arabian Nights* into his works as a disruption that he indulges for the moment—a disruption, moreover, whose relevance is strained.

2. In the short run, the awkwardness of Dickens's *Arabian Nights* references may seem like vaudeville wrongly timed. For the reader who works his way through large quantities of Dickens, this will not be the case. The double take allows a discovery: Dickens finds repeatedly that power and authority reside somewhere else than he thought and so must be newly described. Such shocks prompt the exploration of reality even while setting in motion a regression, a search for the origins and nature of narrative that threatens not just to disrupt the novel but to eliminate all possibility of meaningful action.

Thus described, Dickens's approach will seem much nearer to Stevenson's than to Sue's; on the other hand, he is less despairing than the author of *Prince Otto* about the possibility of acting purposefully. He looks for a fruitful compromise between tale and tyrant, a compromise that will allow for education about reality, representation of reality, and acts that change reality—without the silly brutalizations promoted by *Les Mystères*. The double take helps him achieve this end. It creates a moment of floating doubt but is seldom paralyzing: there are ways to control the regression into tales about tales. One needn't end up producing slim volumes only.

Knowledge begins in passivity but leads to representation and education, even to action. Something of this pattern is suggested by three of the novelist's favorite Nights and one crucial chapter from *Great Expectations*.

In the simplest version of the double take, Dickens tests the tyrant's power and finds it wanting. Among the Christmas stories is an unusually elaborate account of the process. The young hero of "The Haunted House" desires "a Seraglio. . . . It was the custom of the East, it was the way of the good Caliph Haround Alraschid . . . the usage was highly laudable, and most worthy of imitation." Thus begins a fantasy of tyranny, the child playing the role of caliph and appointing his friends to positions about the court. His "Moosulmaun responsibilities" swell until he learns that his father has died, whereupon "Haroun Alraschid took to flight." Haroun is now no more than "the ghost of my own airy belief" ["The Haunted House: The Ghost in Master B's Room," *CS*, 246, 251–52].

What is assumed to be a reality turns out to be a ghost. Similar jolts occur elsewhere, often expressed in just a few words. On tour in America, Dickens wished "I could have remained longer in Philadelphia, but I am forced onward by my poverty of time—not by my will—and in some sort following the example of that renowned Sultan to whose despotism we are indebted for so much delight, must go on making friendships overnight, and cutting their heads off, every morning" [*Pilgrim Edition*, 3: 114]. The sultan is Shahryar, not Harun, but the point is the same. Dickens would seem to be exclaiming on his own unwanted despotism over the American public, but at a second glance he proves to be doing something else. He is making an excuse about his slavery to time; he is dramatizing powerlessness through an image of power.

As in the tale and the letter, so in the novels: within the space of a paragraph, Dickens can evoke the glamor of an imagined despotism and puncture it. The world proves unresponsive to tyrannic aspirations. Cast out by Mr. Pecksniff, Tom Pinch fails to realize that "it would have been a strictly rational and eminently wise proceeding to have revenged himself upon mankind in general. . . . Indeed this piece of justice, though it is upheld by the authority of divers profound poets and honourable men, bears a nearer resemblance to the justice of that good Vizier in the Thousand-and-one-Nights, who issues orders for the destruction of all the Porters in Bagdad because one of that unfortunate fraternity is supposed to have misconducted himself, than to any logical, not to say Christian system of conduct, known to the world in later times" [*MC*, 36, 556]. There is no basis for despotic behavior within a "Christian system of conduct." Perch the messenger "might have laid himself at Mr Dombey's feet, or might have called him by some such title as used to be bestowed upon the Caliph Haround Alraschid"; Mr. Skimpole imagines what he might have achieved "if he had been a Sultan, and his Grand Vizier had said one morning, 'What does the Commander of the Faithful require at the hands of his slave?' " [*DS*, 13, 170; *BH*, 15, 217]. Dombey and Skimpole commit the blunder Tom Pinch avoids, of flirting too thoughtlessly with fantasies of sultanhood.

The limits of tyrannical power are revealed a moment after its assertion. Sometimes the revelation occurs by itself, but it is often associated with another: a turn of attention from personal gesture to impersonal situation. Arbitrariness comes from places. One of the best tales for illustrating this second double take is "Aladdin and the Wonderful Lamp," where social climbing—the attempt to become a king—is both facilitated and foiled by Providence.

Dickens's references are less to Aladdin than to the instruments of his power (jewels and lamp) discovered in the magic cave. This emphasis makes sense. While it is Aladdin's sorcerer-"uncle" who discovers the cave, he can possess its treasures only through his so-called nephew, a naive and shiftless street urchin. The fates have written that the lamp and the jewels are Aladdin's. Not that he gains them automatically: Aladdin must find the wherewithal to live up to his destiny. He must learn, that is, to use the talismans of Providence and to hold on to them. Until such time as he does, they float through the story almost with a will of their own.[14]

Money, according to Dickens, is a good deal like these tantalizing jewels of Aladdin's. In Dickens's youth, "The City was to me a vast emporium of precious stones and metals. . . . Baring Brothers had seen Rocs' eggs and travelled with caravans. Rothschild had sat in the Bazaar at Bagdad with rich stuffs for sale; and a veiled lady from the Sultan's harem, riding on a donkey, had fallen in love with him" ["Gone Astray," *HW* 7 (13 August 1853): 555]. The evident corollary of this premise is that "any iron ring let into stone is the entrance to a cave which only waits for the magician, and the little fire, and the necromancy, that will make the earth shake" ["A Christmas Tree," *CS*, 8]. Money materializes out of nowhere: the Cheeryble brothers rub their hands as Aladdin his lamp, shedding cash and benevolence all around.

The dangers of so supposing that riches will rain from heaven, and the advantages too, are treated in a essay Dickens wrote with Henry Morley, "Discovery of a Treasure Near Cheapside." "Aladdin sent his mother to propose for the Sultan's daughter, with a tolerable present of jewels, but still with no more than could be spread forth on a china dish and tied up in a napkin" [*HW* 6 (13 November 1852): 193]; Dickens, on the other hand, knows a London firm that refines three tons of gold a day. "After hearing of those tons of gold, I should not have been very much surprised if [my guide] had proceeded according to the precedents in the thousand and one nights; if he had desired me to collect a few dried sticks and leaves in Cheapside; if he had made a fire, cast in some powder from his vest, caused the earth to shake and open, a trap-door with a ring in it to appear" ["Discovery of a Treasure near Cheapside," 194]. The writer exits from the crowded street and finds himself in a world of unlimited, palpable wealth. Under the spell of so much gratuitous money, he is at first fulfilled. In the present case, money is not earned but simply discovered. This arbitrariness of fortune becomes a chance for him to fantasize, to appropriate a treasure possessed by no one in particular. In the "golden fables" of the *Arabian Nights,* "there was never enough gold for me. . . . When imagination does begin to deal with what is so hard of attainment in reality, it might at least get out of bounds for once in a way, and let us have enough." Under Cheapside, this "old sense of injury" can be healed ["Discovery of a Treasure near Cheapside," 193].

But perhaps it can't. The evident purpose of the article, as of so much in *Household Words,* is to "help make daily life more imaginative and therefore more bearable."[15] The imaginative appropriation of a vast impersonal process has its limits, however. When at length he emerges from the gold-refining factory, Dickens feels (another reference to the *Arabian Nights*) "like the man who found his charmed money changed into leaves" ["Discovery of a Treasure near Cheapside," 197]. The point is just the opposite of what it first appeared to be: he has finally found something he cannot imagine. His thirst for gold is quenched, with the unexpected result that his sense of possessing his own experience seems diminished: dwarfed by the incomprehensible.

Like the Christmas story about an infant Harun, this tale does elaborately what is elsewhere accomplished in a paragraph. The desire for money or magic is fulfilled, then overfulfilled. Neither lamp nor jewels prove much in our control—or where they are, they don't do much good. One of the *Sketches by Boz* includes a proposal that "If Bedlam could be suddenly removed like another Aladdin's palace, and set down on the space now occupied by Newgate, scarcely one man out of a hundred, whose road to business every morning lies through Newgate Street, or the Old Bailey, would pass the building without bestowing a hasty glance" ["A Visit to Newgate," *SB,* 201]. London, that "one perpetual stream of life and bustle" [201], suggests an urgent question: by what gesture could the moving crowd be stopped, its attention compelled? Immediately Dickens reverts to Aladdin, whose ascent from street urchin to imperial intriguer provides an equivocal answer. Aladdin's career is dazzling enough to flabbergast a dozen crowds, except perhaps this metropolitan one. When the original Aladdin's palace appeared, "the slaves and porters fell back aghast. . . . Their eyes followed beyond the carpet and saw the palace blazing with jewels, its crystal dome appearing above the roofs like the rising of the sun. They reported these things to the grand wazir, who carried news of them to the King."[16] Dickens elicits from his imagined passersby only a "hasty glance." The deed is swallowed up by London, becoming part of a city where discontinuities—sharp and sudden severances—are the stuff of everyday life. They apparently exist by virtue of a power, a gesture, but they blend in so well with London that they might as well be invisible.

Another reference to Aladdin's palace presses this point to absurdity. *Our Mutual Friend* describes the suburban outskirts of London, where "the schools were newly built, and there were so many like them all over the country, that one might have thought the whole were but one restless edifice with the locomotive gift of Aladdin's palace. They were in a neighbourhood which looked like a toy neighbourhood taken in blocks out of a box by a child of particularly incoherent mind, and set up anyhow . . . rank field, richly cultivated kitchen-garden, brick viaduct, arch-spanned canal, and disorder of frowziness and fog. As if the child had given the table a kick and gone to sleep" [*OMF*, 2.1, 218]. This palace is manipulated by inscrutable economic and bureaucratic forces, paralleling the whims of an infant whom we can neither control nor avoid. Power is right there in the landscape but nonetheless inscrutable, inaccessible. It is conceived as a human intention that dissipates itself in destruction and boredom.

Dickens's references to Aladdin depersonalize power; the tyrant's arbitrary decree is replaced by the will of the world. This shift in emphasis reflects the author's lifelong concern with the comprehensibility of modern life. "Aladdin," it happens, suggests a response to this problem. In the "Preliminary Word" to *Household Words,* Dickens asserts that "the traveller whom we accompany on his railroad or his steamboat journey, may gain, we hope, some compensation for incidents which these later generations have outlived, in new associations with the Power that bears him onward . . . even with the towering chimneys he may see, spurting out fire and smoke upon the prospect" [*HW* 1 (30 March 1850), 1]. Which is to say: no matter how alienated the traveler may feel from the industrialized and urban landscape, its powers will eventually seem his. Reading Dickens, he will come to feel that he possesses them—as Aladdin earned the magic rightfully his. Dickens now brings up that very tale, instructively distorting it. "The swart giants, Slaves of the Lamp of Knowledge, have their thousand and one tales, no less than the Genii of the East; and these, in all their wild, grotesque and fanciful aspects, in all their many phases of endurance, in all their many moving lessons of compassion and consideration, we design to tell" [1]. This rhapsodic sentence marks a shift in emphasis. So described, *Arabian Nights*–style magic is a power that must be narrated and perhaps a power of narration. The Slaves of the Lamp of Knowledge undertake, not to chop off heads (like the tyrant), not to move palaces (like Aladdin's magic), but to tell a thousand and one tales. There is only one person in the *Arabian Nights* who does that. Turned upside down and inside out, the tale of Aladdin reveals Scheherezade.

"A Preliminary Word" thus introduces Dickens's third, most inclusive use for the *Arabian Nights*. Arbitrary power is a will-o'-the-wisp: once located in the tyrant's gesture or the world's force, it migrates yet again. It becomes an attribute of story. This final double take is the most intricate of the series. Its import can be illustrated through Dickens's interest in "The Tale of the Hunchback," a model for all tales about tales.[17]

At the beginning of the story, the king's deformed jester—a distant relation of Quasimodo and perhaps a third cousin of Triboulet (*Le Roi s'amuse*)—apparently chokes to death on a bone. All sorts of people try to revive him; each fails, and each is left with the mistaken impression that he has actually killed him. The "corpse" and the whole pack of would-be resuscitators end up in front of the king, trying to talk their way out of being decapitated or boiled in oil. The king, imitating the example afforded by Shahryar, agrees to let everyone go—on condition that someone will tell a story better than the one they're all in. This familiar situation produces no Scheherezades until a tailor relates the story of the barber, "the inimitable story of the Impertinent Barber himself," as Hazlitt puts it, "his pertinacious, incredible, teasing, deliberate, yet unmeaning folly."[18] The barber is one of the great nonstop talkers in literature, perhaps the first whom Dickens encountered. He takes over the tale in which he appears, ruining a client's rendezvous, then narrating the almost endless misfortunes of his six maimed brothers. When the tailor has finished his account of all this talk, the king—in wonderment—summons the barber himself.

He babbles as much as could be wished; he also removes a bone from the hunchback's throat, restoring to him simultaneously life and the power of speech.

The barber can talk. In the manner of a Dickensian character, he performs an "amazing feat of oratorical jugglery on which the main foundation of his celebrity has from time immemorial reposed. In other words, he has talked for hours together without the slightest intermission, and, at the end of the time, has said—nothing."[19] Not only does the barber say nothing; he proves able to cancel the death of the hunchback and thus to retract the event out of which the story grows.

These surprises were appreciated by Dickens. The tales of "The Thousand and One Humbugs"—a series of leading articles he wrote for *Household Words*—has as a climax "The Story of the Talkative Barber" [*HW* 11 (5 May 1855): 313–16]. The Thousand and One Humbugs is an adaptation of the *Arabian Nights* for Victorian England. The young man victimized by the barber is in love with Fair Guvawnment, and the barber represents English aristocracy, bent on gulling "the unhappy Publeek." Dickens's barber (anachronistically) is Dickensian, not least because his follies produce a pleasure irrelevant to the satirical purpose of the tale. "Barber of mischief, Barber of sin, Barber of false pretence, Barber of froth and bubble, said I, stamping my foot upon the ground." The barber answers, "I am not like Dizzee, who draws blood; nor like Darbee, who claps on blisters; nor like Johnnee, who works with the square and rule; I am the easy shaver, and I care for nobody, I can do anything" ["The Story of the Talkative Barber," 314].

The story of the hunchback yields metaphors evoking a comic potency and a comic emptiness of imagination. The barber's fifth brother attended the Barmecide Feast, where he was coerced into praising nonexistent dishes: "hasten to set before my good friend, Guld Publeek, the rare stew of colonial spices, minced crime, hashed poverty. . . . But, you don't eat with an appetite, my brother, said the Barmecide. I fear the repast is hardly to your liking? Pardon me, my benefactor, returned the guest, whose jaws ached with pretending to eat, I am full almost to the throat" ["The Story of the Talkative Barber," 315]. Besides this version in the Thousand and One Humbugs, there are several other Dickensian adaptations of the Barmecide Feast. At Tellson's Bank, "Your lighter boxes of family papers went up-stairs into a Barmecide room, that always had a great dining-table in it and never had a dinner" [*TTC*, 2.1, 50]. "To the admirer of cities," Washington, D.C., "is a Barmecide Feast: a pleasant field for the imagination to rove in; a monument raised to a deceased project, with not even a legible inscription to record its departed greatness" [*AN*, 8, 117]. The dinginess of the English capital and the grandiose pretensions of the American one have this metaphor in common. "The Tale of the Hunchback" creates such images in one anecdote after another; it would seem to embody a kind of tantalized disappointment, but then there is that last reversal in which the comic side of the situation reveals itself, in which the instigator of so much chaos brings the hunchback to life once more. The barber is both a ludicrous figure and a powerful one; he suggests the potency of words, which might almost be confused with reality—as if the Barmecide Feast really did exist.

The narrative organization by which death, life, and stories are so closely interconnected—by which imagination is alternately powerless and all-powerful—amuses Dickens. His imitating the example is another matter altogether. Periodically, Dickens experiments with devices by which the modern world might be self-consciously conceived as a story. The *Arabian Nights* format appears in *Master Humphrey's Clock* and in the Christmas tales of the 1840s; it is discernible elsewhere too, almost always as a failure. The subject of Dickens's frame-tale narrations has been treated thoroughly, so I need not dwell on it.[20] I will only reiterate the essential fact, that Dickens acknowledged the futility of each such venture and finally gave them up. Despite his admiration of such tales as the hunchback's, he tried to avoid being drawn into the infinite regression implied by the tale-within-a-tale. He avoided that sense of stories releasing stories releasing stories: of authority receding from tyrant to world to narrative and then spiraling ever inward. The logic that has led from Harun to Aladdin to the hunchback in a real sense leads no further, for the last step of the series this author rejects.

Pip and the Power of the Arabian Nights

Dickens's involvement with the *Arabian Nights* seems both intense and superficial. It is associated with a glorious irresponsibility: giving the table a kick and going to sleep, rounding up small girls for a harem, clowning about in politics. Puzzling out these examples, one may come to suspect that the irresponsibility is Dickens's own, that he is caught in the intractable dilemma of the novelist flirting with literature's great anti-realistic work. For the most part, of course, this bind does not weigh heavily. Only the compulsive, long-term reader of Dickens will notice it very often— nor is he encouraged to do so by the novelist, whose dispersion of the *Arabian Nights* throughout his works is an evasive strategy, not a confrontational one. On the other hand, there are a few occasions when the problem of the *Arabian Nights* comes to a head, as evidenced by moments of crisis in *The Old Curiosity Shop, A Tale of Two Cities,* and *Great Expectations.*[21] A paragraph from the last of these novels offers the most instructive case. In this passage the powers of tyrant, world, and narrative are all evoked, all linked together. The effect is dizzying, but not by virtue of any infinite regression; the oriental story becomes a new kind of tool. A tale is told, a deed is done, to dazzle a king. The consequent redistribution of authority facilitates the understanding of a city and a life.

First a preliminary word about a character who needs one. Dickens told John Forster that he "became famous in his childish circle for having written a tragedy called *Misnar, the Sultan of India,* founded (and very literally founded, no doubt) on one of the *Tales of the Genii.*"[22] His tragedy has not survived, which is probably just as well, but by going to James Ridley's *Tales of the Genii,* we can discover much about Misnar and the young boy's interest in him. In "The Inchanters; or Misnar, the Sultan of India," Misnar does not have an easy time of it, suffering many hardships in the attempt to secure his government. His adventures, which are concerned obsessively with disguise and secrecy, culminate in a hard-won victory, after which he muses on the nature of power. "In a well-regulated city . . . every one is known. . . . it is no infringement on the freedom of the honest to oblige them, by their dress and appearance, to show forth their manner of life." He elaborates on this futile vision of the well-ordered city, only to conclude that "till my capital is better regulated, I mean to take advantage myself of the confusion of the city, and examine in disguise those private outrages which are screened from the eye of justice."[23]

Ridley, author of the tales, is usually a dogged imitator of the *Arabian Nights.* He has enough wit to exaggerate his sources or shift them around, but not to change them fundamentally. Here, in the tale of Misnar, he does effect a significant transformation. Because his word is law, Harun can afford extravagant whims. Misnar, by contrast, must fight for his throne and his authority. Having won them, he is only too aware of the limits on the power of a sultan. His move from the public arena to Harun's special province of disguise and anonymity stems not at all from boredom—When has he had time to be bored?—but from doubts about how thoroughly a king can hold sway over his city. Where Harun revels in confusion, always assuming that he can return instantly to the role of sultan, Misnar hopes to take advantage of confusion—to turn it against itself. His approach to power is that of a doubter and a skeptic who sees the best hope for order in a calculated retreat.

It is this aspect of Misnar to which Dickens recurs in *Great Expecta-*

tions, chapter 38. Pip has been courting Estella, who holds Miss Havisham, Bentley Drummle, and the world at arm's length. Having devoted his "one chapter" to the subject of love, Pip—very consciously the writer— announces a change of subject. He will now deal with "the event that had impended over me longer yet":

> *In the Eastern story, the heavy slab that was to fall on the bed of state*
> *in the flush of conquest was slowly wrought out of the quarry, the tunnel*
> *for the rope to hold it in its place was slowly carried through the leagues of*
> *rock, the slab was slowly raised and fitted in the roof, the rope was rove to*
> *it and slowly taken through the miles of hollow to the great iron ring. All*
> *being made ready with much labour, and the hour come, the sultan was*
> *aroused in the dead of the night, and the sharpened axe that was to sever*
> *the rope from the great iron ring was put into his hand, and he struck with*
> *it, and the rope parted and rushed away, and the ceiling fell. So, in my*
> *case; all the work, near and afar, that tended to the end, had been*
> *accomplished; and in an instant the blow was struck, and the roof of my*
> *stronghold dropped upon me.*

[GE, 38, 297]

The question is raised how people perceive crises; how they recognize them as such. Pip comes to a revelation whose turns are linked with the surprises of *Arabian Nights*–style narrative. The point in Misnar's adventures to which Pip refers is the moment just before the deposed monarch will accomplish his return to power. Misnar does not know that by wielding the axe he will crush his enemies. He chides his vizier, whom he feels has betrayed him. " 'Is there deceit in Horam . . . that he cometh like a thief in the night.' "24 Misnar cuts the rope: a severance like, yet also unlike, those of the *Arabian Nights* and those of Pip's treacherous life. Misnar is no Shahryar, not even a Harun. Only after he acts does Horam reveal to him the significance of what he has done. It is as if the vizier wanted to take the guilt and responsibility on his own shoulders, while allowing the glory to Misnar. The story becomes stranger still when we think seriously about the parallel with Pip's situation. Magwitch is Horam, who comes like a thief in the night—untrusted, yet a faithful servant preparing the triumph of a master kept in the dark. Pip, then, is the lucky master . . . but no, that is not quite the case: Pip is lucky only from Magwitch's viewpoint. According to his own standards Pip is the victim, an unfortunate conspirator whose pretensions must be crushed by the fall of his expectations. However, this second account is also inadequate. Pip must suffer the fall of the rebels in order to gain a mastery like Misnar's *after* the cataclysmic moment when he trustingly let the axe fall. This mastery is associated with recognizing the limits of one's authority—one's need for help, as it were, amongst the surprises of narrative and of society. Pip *is* like Misnar, though not as Magwitch would have understood the likeness; this analogy works only because Pip has suffered a victim's fate and is therefore brought to a moment of self-consciousness, a moment that will enable him to tell the tale of these slippery, twisting events. He is thus a storyteller—and thus a king. Through repeated double takes, Shahryar and Scheherezade are enabled to meet in a single character.

Pip's need to leave his dead selves behind is amply suggested by the analogy with Ridley's narrative, whose revelations are made to double back on themselves and then to double back again . . . and again. Appropriately, the double take emerges from a series of doublings, multiplication of texts to match the multiplication of Pips. The *Arabian Nights* acquires its shadow self in *Tales of the Genii,* both these books—under the rubric of oriental tale—setting off *Great Expectations.* As a consequence, the implications of the crisis must be continually rethought. The rethinking is done through correlations among literary works yet the embedding of the *Arabian Nights* within the *Tales of the Genii* within *Great Expectations* does not create an infinite regression. There is none of that wonderful, locked-in neatness that typifies "The Tale of the Hunchback" and similar productions. There is little of the resigned plangency that enwraps deposed rulers like Prince Otto. Although *Great Expectations* is the narrative of how a narrative came to be, the potentiality of self-reference—of self-enclosed subjectivity—is redirected. Dickens narrates the merging of story and world, at the moment the tyrant's image of self is destroyed. Like Esther Summerson—but in a more concentrated way—Pip is revealed as that hero to whom things happen and who finds, in his apparent passivity, a new means of action. Storyteller, tyrant, victim of his own narratives, narrator of his own power, he suggests how his creator can reconcile the conflicting forces within the intricate tales of Scheherezade.

If I can reverse a judgment cited earlier, the *Arabian Nights* as conceived by Dickens is used "to illustrate . . . the author's prowess in representation, the education of a character . . . [and] ways in which the world can be viewed and changed." Did the novelist understand what he was doing; could he have explained the impact of his transformed *Arabian Nights* in anything like these terms? A month after the "Misnar" episode appeared in *Great Expectations, All the Year Round* published another evocation of oriental story, an article detailing the "Adventures of Ali Mahmud" ["Adventures of Ali Mahmud," *AYR* 5 (8 June 1861): 258–60].[25] This essay spells out certain premises, accepted, I believe, by Dickens and many of his imitators. The writer begins, "Nothing surprises readers of Oriental stories, such as the Arabian Nights, more than the rapid changes of feeling exhibited by the chief actors, and the frequent inadequacy of the motives assigned to produce such changes." The first example proffered is naturally that of "the tyrant," who "suddenly relents on his hearing his intended victim recite some moving lines from a Persian poem, or some moral text from the Koran." Genies, burglar, and lovers prove susceptible to the same arbitrariness—that of an entire world, for "all kinds of vicissitudes . . . change the current of a life in the turning of an eye." This observation leads the essayist to "the story which we are now proceeding to relate . . . a story of actual Persian life at the present day . . . it has many of the features of the *Arabian Nights*" [258–59]. Fantastic arbitrariness links tyrant, circumstances, and story, all of which become figures for daily life.

There could be no better summary of Dickens's *Arabian Nights*. His allusions to it produce a sense of the movement from tyrant to storyteller across the perilous space of the everyday world. The novelist details certain readjustments contingent upon this elusive flight of power; in certain privileged cases he suggests that power can be redefined—as though the tyrant and the storyteller had met in one person and achieved a reconciliation fuller than any hinted by the ancient compendium. Upon a synthesis like this one, I suggest, the representation of the modern world, the chance of a usable connection between writing and city, depends.

12. Dickens's Omniscience

OMNISCIENCE IS A LITERARY CONVENIENCE. It shows up everywhere in fiction, even in stories that seem to be told from a limited point of view, but it is seldom on that account understood literally.[1] Claims to absolute knowledge are made playfully, withdrawn coyly, or implied without direct commitment by a massive piling-up of narrations and descriptions. No one concludes from such claims that human beings can grasp reality all at once. The novelist's omniscience is seldom equated with a capacity for godlike understanding. Omniscience "is a generative proposition," which is to say a premise on which novel writing is almost unavoidably based, rather than a subject for discussion or a wonder requiring a special act of belief.[2]

Among the Victorian novelists there are two prominent exceptions to this rule, George Eliot and—my present concern—Dickens.[3] From the early stages of Dickens's career he is fascinated by abnormal states of consciousness, moments when the mind seems to sweep across a world, a life, or both. Oliver Twist is the first of his characters to have this experience. Inadvertently exposed to privileged knowledge—watching Fagin unearth and count his money—Oliver feels himself supernaturally engaged "with almost everybody he had ever known" [*OT*, 9, 58]. He has no further moments of just this sort, but other Dickensian people carry on the tradition: they blunder into visions whose power seems beyond them.

Why omniscience in this second, oddly fantastical vein? I begin with some explorations of mid-Victorian journalism, a field where it is relatively simple to define the issues in the omniscience debate. The discussion of journalism leads to comments on three late Dickens novels: *Little Dorrit, Great Expectations,* and finally *Our Mutual Friend.* Given this range of cases, I can work toward what is perhaps a surprising conclusion: omniscience is less an extreme than a middle term, less an ultimate Faustian grab for power than an effort to avoid relinquishing such little power, such few decisions, as the urban citizen may still be capable of making.

The Shadow Knows

From its inception *Household Words* strove for lucid, entertaining presentations of potentially dry material. "One Man in a Dockyard," by Dickens and R. H. Horne, explains how ships are built [*HW* 3 (6 September 1851): 553–57]. It does so not merely superficially and by the aid of local color but with a serious attention to how the huge mills and saws actually operate. The supposed narrator of "One Man" is John Strongitharm, a commonsensical Englishman. By implication, if he can grasp such things, others like him can also. The gulf between expert and casual observer, technician and layman, is to some extent spanned. At the end of the article, when Strongitharm expresses some strong political opinions, the reader is meant to feel that he has earned the right to them.

The John Strongitharm approach is used by many writers for *Household Words* and later *All the Year Round:* "The law of supply and demand is not to fall under my critical eye. It is my simple business to keep my eyes wide open." "Per-centages, averages, and all the hocus-pocus of statistics are only mists, fogs, curtains, and sleeping-draughts."[4] Alas, this attitude often proves insufficient for anyone who wants to explain the modern world. A visit to the shipyard is one thing. But is visualization the most useful technique for understanding finance or the spread of cholera? Despite his desire for vivid effects, for the sense of a plain man looking at things and seeing them as they are, Dickens suspected otherwise. When occupied with planning *Household Words,* he suggested that the magazine should have a a persona "a certain Shadow, which may . . . be supposed to be cognisant of everything, and go everywhere. . . . I want him to loom as a fanciful thing all over London."[5] The Shadow is more than a convenient narrative device; Dickens imagines him a supernatural being. It is notable that he blocks the ability to see—he looms over London as though the city were under a gigantic cloud—yet is evidently supposed to further human knowledge. He is "cognisant of everything"; he holds everything in his mind, implacably, calmly. Whatever the Shadow's precise nature, he is not John Strongitharm. Perhaps because he embodies a problem as well as its presumed solution, he seems more a threat than a comfort; the intended effect is not the one produced.

At the urging of John Forster, Dickens dropped the Shadow from his plans. All the same, variations on the theme of omniscience recur throughout *Household Words* and *All the Year Round* (not to mention Dickens's contemporaneous fiction). Despite the novelist's respect for John Strongitharm, despite his limited love for authoritative experts, despite Esther Summerson's rejection of property or possession as a model for knowledge, he finds it difficult to dismiss such fantasies.[6] He says of the apocryphal "Best Authority" that "in respect of getting into the Queen's Palace, the Boy Jones was a fool to him. He knows everything that takes place there," and (in his role as the Uncommercial Traveller, a far from omniscient flaneur) he asks similarly of "The Dentist's Servant": "Is that man no mystery to us, no type of invisible power? The tremendous individual knows (who else does?) what is done with the extracted teeth. . . . The conviction of my coward conscience when I see that man in a professional light, is, that he knows all the statistics of my teeth and gums, my double teeth, my single teeth, my stopped teeth, and my sound" ["The Best Authority," *HW* 15 (20 June 1857): 577–78; "The Uncommercial Traveller: London out of Season," *AYR* 3 (29 September 1860): 591]. The jokiness is uneasy. Dickens both mocks and emphasizes a dilemma of real importance. Science, government, business, and journalism try to discover as much as they can about the human hive, down to the last organizational nuance; however, no one person can absorb such knowledge: "When a Reviewer or other Writer has crammed himself to choking with some particularly abstruse piece of information, why does he introduce it with the casual remark, that 'every schoolboy knows' it? . . . If there were a run against the monetary system of the country to-morrow, we should find this prodigy of a schoolboy down upon us with the deepest mysteries of banking and the currency" ["Why," *HW* 13 (1 March 1856): 145].[7] The disturbing point about the mysteries of banking is not that information about them is inaccessible but that the total amount of information is disproportionate to any individual mind: not just the schoolboy's but the journalist's, not just the journalist's but (most likely) the banker's. One reacts to this anomaly by pretending otherwise. Dickens mocks the trend, but he is implicated in it. He is as caught up as anyone else by the notion of a mind that could conceive a world like modern London. His very rejections intensify further the mythology of omniscience.

The theoreticians of knowledge can provide words to gauge Dickens's dilemma. By the end of the nineteenth century, Simmel had focused on the gap between what he called "subjective" and "objective" culture. (See chapter 8.) More recently, Ian Hacking has observed, "knowledge, once possessed by individuals, is now the property of corporations." Hacking is also interested in "corporate products of the more physical sort," among which cities could be included, but his main focus—rightly, I think—remains on knowledge itself, without which the cities could not have been fabricated. Inspired by some rather disparate sources (Karl Popper, French Marxism of the 1960s, evidently not Simmel), Hacking argues that "a demonstration used to be a showing: a showing to the eye, the only eye, the inward eye. . . . the thing to do with proofs [was] not to check the formal steps slowly and piecemeal, but to run over the proof faster and faster until the whole thing [was] in one's head at once, and clear perception [was] guaranteed." He then suggests that the situation has changed. Gradually there evolves a theory of "meaning," that is, of public communication as opposed to private ideas. As a further development from this emphasis on the public and the shared, knowledge is thought of as truly autonomous, separate from any given mind. "Although a product of human endeavour, [it] has its own existence and perhaps its own laws."[8] Autonomous knowledge exists in print or on the circuits of a computer; it is not held in the mind, as proofs once were; it is not even shared discourse, as was meaning. In one sense a burden is removed from the citizen, a burden of responsibility for what is known; at the same time the citizen's freedom of choice and action is threatened, unless there are effective means for working around—or working with—the autonomy of knowledge.

Hacking suggests that autonomous knowledge came into its own during the nineteenth century—for example, with the founding of institutions like the British Association for the Advancement of Science (1831). If so, then it is no wonder that Victorians could find themselves struggling to retain the concept of the knowing subject: could posit Knowing Subjects still human but more and more like God, as if somehow to create a M(m)ind that *saw* the modern world. Dickens's Shadow and his other knowledgeable men answer to this dilemma. They register the uneasiness verging on panic with which people felt the humanized world of the city recede from human view. They show that people can react to such panic by upping the stakes. A process once called "proof" is exaggerated, satirized, declared to be a miracle, implied to be implausible—all as it continues to seems desirable. Finally, only a formidable personage indeed can be conceived to hold "proofs" in his mind. What then? First, one could resign any questions about modern society to that genius of order who presides—who *must* preside—over the urban scene.[9] Second, one could imagine the great genius as an inescapably malevolent force, and choose to combat him on those terms.[10]

A third alternative proves difficult of attainment. Among those who fumbled after it were George Sala and Andrew Wynter, minor Dickensians from the perspective of our time but eminent Victorians in theirs. Sala and Wynter want to give "meaning" its due, but they fear slipping over into autonomous knowledge. They want to grasp the metropolis all at once, but to grasp it through such figures as the street or the view: not through that world of writing that denies human experience but can also (like the Shadow) be personified as a superhuman knower. I will try to gauge what degree of success they had in this endeavor.

How George Sala Lost the Key of the Street

Sala's first piece for *Household Words* was "The Key of the Street," an account of a night spent wandering London after being locked out of a boardinghouse [*HW* 3 (6 September 1851): 565–72]. He observes the chaos of the Opera crowd, meets an unfriendly policeman, tries to sleep in a fourpenny lodging house but is driven away by the bugs, gains a penny from one passerby, gives it up to another, gawks at a fire in a Soho pickle shop, and falls asleep at last on a bench in St. James's Park. He claims that at this point he could have slept on a slab in the Paris morgue. Waking from his counterfeited death, he visits Covent Garden Market and after that spends his last fourpence on breakfast in a coffee shop. Here he first dreams of his adventures, then reads about the fire in a newspaper. Finally the hour arrives when Sala can reassume his identity as a respectable citizen. He goes home to his own bed, leaving the key of the street to "its proper custodian, whoever he may be—and, whoever he may be, I don't envy him" [572].

"The Key of the Street" made a stir: Thackeray said it was one of the best things he had ever read, and his reaction was not untypical.[11] As Sala's biographer notes, this enthusiasm is hard to understand today. With Mayhew's investigations only a few years old, it could have come as no surprise that many Londoners were homeless. Perhaps the article's fascination lay more in its rhetorical organization than in any information it contained. By becoming a vagrant for a single night, Sala gives the *impression* of making great discoveries. He is able to circulate quickly among many well-known localities, experiencing each newly because of the role he has assumed. If this much is true, then the figure of the crowded street becomes the crucial organizing principle. Once Sala commits himself to it, the street is a territory of intensified mobility and intensified perception, not so much a place as a way of reimagining his relation to places. Though he keeps explaining how humbling his experience is, his loss of social status is only temporary; moreover, his gain in the power to write, and through writing to imagine the city, is enormous. While this kind of point had been made previously—for example, by novels like *The Old Curiosity Shop*—finding it in a sketch, that briefest of urban literary forms, is bracing. Sala's telegraphic narrative of his experiences seems to cram them all together, an effect underlined when he has his coffee-shop dream, "a dreadful vision . . . of bugs, and cabbages, and tramping soldiers" ["Key," 571]. Some 140 sketches later, almost at the end of his *Household Words* period, he declares, "I have ridden a tall horse in the park, and drawn up at Achilles' statue among the dandy horsemen, and taken off my hat as the Queen went by. And I have gone up Holborn Hill—in a cart—though I have not yet exactly taken my gill at St. Giles's, or made my will at Tyburn. For I have had the key of the street, and have known the secrets of the gas, and have communed with the paving-stones" ["Curiosities of London," *HW* 11 (23 June 1855): 499]. Sala's "for" suggests a relation of cause and effect. At this moment he looks back to the essay that began his journalistic career, paying it the sort of tribute that is owed transforming experiences. He recognizes that the key of the street has been an "open sesame," just as he anticipated: a key to the sort of knowledge that ends up whirling all at once in one's head.

In Sala the street allows a combination of immediacy and omniscience. But there are many occasions on which this illusion of compromise fails. A typical danger sign is an extraordinary thickening of style. Sala often writes ponderously, piling sentence on sentence as though he were engaged in investigations of mind-boggling difficulty. Like the Levantine postmaster described in one of his essays, I want to scream at Sala, "Troppa scrittura!" ("Too much writing!") ["Curiosities," 496]. It would be possible to demonstrate that such an overflow occurs most frequently in the London sketches. The reader is spared this demonstration because Sala several times makes the connection on his own. He observes that London—more broadly, urban civilization—is the cause of too much writing. Starting from this complaint, he shows how the fantasy of human omniscience fades away, to be replaced by institutions like the newspaper and the directory.

One place where *Troppa scrittura!* would be an appropriate refrain is in Sala's masterpiece, *Twice Round the Clock* (1858–59). This work is dedicated to describing London localities, each at a successive hour of the day or night. Sala cites the usual literary precedent. "I know that the part which I have proposed to myself in these papers is that of a chronological Asmodeus; . . . you must, perforce, hold on by the skirts of my cloak as I wing my way from quarter to quarter of the immense city, to which the Madrid which the lame fiend showed his friend was but a nut-shell."[12] Generally, Asmodeus grants "his friend" an overview; Sala's Asmodeus flies closer to earth than most, no higher—as he later tells us—than the top of an omnibus.[13] Just as *Twice Around the Clock* is an attempt to expand "The Key of the Street," to wander the city for twenty-four hours rather than for eight, so is Asmodeus the fantasy of an effortless and superhuman circulation through London traffic.

When he identifies with "the lame fiend" Sala seems close to getting all of London whirling in his head at once, but a sudden twist suggests other possibilities. The essayist gets caught up in a digression on modern authors, especially those who function as literary factories, then—expressing puzzlement that his subject has drifted away from him—returns to the realm of mythology: "I should be Briareus multiplied by ten thousand, and not Asmodeus at all, if I could set down in writing a tithe of London's sayings and doings, acts and deeds, seemings and aspects, at seven o'clock in the morning."[14] Sala tries to imagine what Briareus would see at seven o'clock—see *all at once,* with his many heads. He subsequently returns to his Asmodeus incarnation, winging, walking, or riding his way "from quarter to quarter," but his detour is nonetheless instructive. London pushes him toward a yearning for an omniscience that belongs to a many-headed giant—a creature far more powerful than a mere Asmodeus. The city is so systematically complex that he wishes to see it with many eyes—or barring this impossible desire, to write about it as if with many hands. (Cf. that odd digression on overprolific authors.) Sala fears yet seeks to become this Briareus of writers.

And he knows that he never can. If Briareus has a modern incarnation, it is not in any individual but in certain semimythical institutions. Consider the offices of the *Times,* where "at the rate of twelve thousand an hour, the damp broad sheets roll from the grim iron instrument of the dissemination of light throughout the world." Sala's feelings about the *Times* are mixed. "Nothing is wanting: city correspondence, sporting intelligence, markets, state of the weather," and so on, yet this comprehensiveness is fostered by an odd fiction of authorship: "Absolutely necessary is it that . . . the 'awful, shadowy, irrresponsible, and yet *puissant* we' should dominate over the columns." "Will a strange day of revolution ever arrive, when the mystic 'we' shall be merged into the responsible, tax-paying, tangible, palpable, shootable, suicidable, and kickable 'I?' "[15] Perhaps not. Functionally and rhetorically, the *Times*'s omniscience is dependent on its assertion of corporate identity. Only many writers together could produce this publication that seems to know all. This "we" is sometimes a mask for the kickable I; just as often it intimates an inescapable truth, that knowledge has become distinct from human consciousness.

Under these circumstances, Sala assumes extraordinary mental postures. In one series of sketches he describes "Imaginary London." Here he complains, "Not a small local journal but it possesses some pigmy pseudo-Dickens, who thinks that he can describe Seven Dials and Monmouth-street as accurately as did the author of *Sketches by Boz.* . . . We have become slaves to facts filtered through much verbiage, and the Blue-book has entered into our soul."[16] Sala deplores the excessive written coverage of familiar locales; he defies it by writing some more, but writing of places to which he alone has access, a London that he has created. An alternative to this solipsistic gesture is to forget about direct contact with the city, concentrating instead on its written reflections: thus the "Akbar newspaper" becomes "a magic mirror of Algiers in itself," and in "Want Places" observation of street life gives way to speculative scrutiny of the *Times's* advertising columns ["Yadacé," *HW* 11 (5 May 1855): 319; "Want Places," *HW* 7 (27 August 1853): 601–8]. Either way Sala's goal is to assert a kind of mastery. What the key of the street cannot open, the key of the book will— so he hopes. His expectations are most explicitly tested when he comes to study Kelly's *Post-Office London Directory:*

> *An accurate Directory of almost every London subject indeed. The age of the moon; the Princess Helena's birthday; the commencement of grouse-shooting; information relative to sauce manufacturers, commissioners for taking affadavits, adhesive postage stamps, Archidiaconal Courts, provincial hotels, post-office receiving-houses, waxwork exhibitions, bankrupts' letters, Foreign-office passports, Newgate, bottles containing liquid not to be sent by post, clubs, the Court of Peculiars. [And so on, through a long paragraph!]*[17]

For the endless moment of an endless list, Sala appears to have absorbed the directory's comprehensiveness, to have taken it into himself. But he knows that this absurdly impressive heap of facts cannot be visualized,[18] cannot even be held in mind; it is designed to remain on the page for consultation one bit at a time (thus the paradoxical quality of his willfully assembled catalog) and it is produced by yet another fictional "we," the directory's seventy researchers: "What can [the researcher] be besides a 'Courier and Enquirer?' I shudder to think. He must know more about people and their whereabouts than a postman, a detective policeman, a sheriff's officer, an income-tax schedulist, or a begging-letter writer" ["The Great Red Book," 408]. Sala's joke makes a disturbing point. Although the book can be celebrated as a substitute for comprehensive observation, this substitution raises a question about who is doing the

observing. Sala fears that the book itself is the observer. In that case he can
no longer claim to be the subject in whom knowledge of London resides;
on the contrary, he becomes one more object of inquiry. He is thus unable
to regain the prerogative that he lost when the key of the street slipped out
of his hands. Human omniscience is no longer conceivable, not even as a
premise for exploration.

How Andrew Wynter Met the Man of the Mirror

Andrew Wynter was a prominent London doctor, the only medical man of
any eminence to indulge in the Dickensian city sketch.[19] Wynter seldom
lets the reader forget his training. His account of Hyde Park, in the second
of two essays he wrote for *Household Words*, begins by describing a frog's
lung as observed under the microscope: "Distinctly within the narrow
field of vision I could see the dark red blood globules, rushing in a
tumultuous tide along the transparent veins. . . . With that curious
spectacle fresh in my recollection [i.e., the process by which blood absorbs
air] I will, in imagination at least, change 'the field' of the microscope for
that of air, and suspend myself in a balloon over this mighty city of
millions. . . . A little adjustment of the sand-bags and the escape-valve, and
I can focus London as the physiologist does the frog's lung in the microscope." As the lung to the frog, so Hyde Park to London; as the microscope to the frog, so the balloon's-eye view to Hyde Park and the surrounding city alike. The city is "focused" by controlling the height of the
balloon; we trace—"in imagination at least"—the passage of riders and
pedestrians through the park. Their constant circulation accomplishes for
London what the circulation of blood globules accomplishes for the frog.
Hyde Park is "an aërator to the race, as [the lung] was to the individual!"[20]

Wynter loves to treat social collectivities as though they were organ-
isms: in various essays he studies the lungs, heart, stomach, and nervous
system of the metropolis. Sometimes such analogies are illuminating;
even when they are murky, they have an imaginative resonance that
derives from the author's close acquaintance with medicine. For example,
though riders on Rotten Row are not functionally comparable to blood
globules, Hyde Park turns out to be quite literally a lung. The park is the
location of "the boat house belonging to the Royal Humane Society"
where people who have attempted suicide by jumping into the Serpentine
are resuscitated. "Over the door is the bas-relief of a child attempting to
kindle with his breath an apparently extinguished torch. . . . Baths, hot-
water beds, electrifying machines, and mechanism[s] by which artificial
breathing can be maintained, are ranged around the rooms."

However, Wynter's organic metaphors are not primarily notable for their substance. Their purpose is orientational: they posit a relationship between writer and city. Wynter thinks of himself as a practicing, inquiring scientist (his other article for *Household Words* describes an operation at St. George's Hospital). He finds this role transferable to his studies of London. His panorama of the park encourages him to scrutinize the metropolis in a manner at once intrusive and detached. After that initial moment in which he is still getting his sights fixed, he is able to shift his point of view instantly: "Let me descend to a more minute anatomy of this great pulmonic space," "Let me constitute myself (for the nonce) a young man about town," etc. But it is the opening view—the view under the microscope—that seems to make these metamorphoses possible. Wynter can go where he wants because, when he starts, he has the whole in his mind. The panorama opens to him a world where he can see anything he desires, where he can pass any restricting gate—as long as he exercises proper surgical delicacy.[21] So did the student examine the lung of the frog; so does the doctor guide his students through Hyde Park.[22]

Wynter's panoramas are the equivalent of Sala's phantasmagorias: they function as a declaration of mastery. The logic by which the panorama begins to undermine itself can be traced through many of the doctor's sketches. "If, early on a summer morning before the smoke of countless fires had narrowed the horizon of the metropolis, a spectator were to ascend to the top of St. Paul's, and take his stand upon the balcony . . . he would see sleeping beneath his feet the greatest camp of men upon which the sun has ever risen . . . the mighty map of the metropolis. . . . At such a moment the thought would naturally arise in his mind,—in what manner is such an assemblage victualled? By what complicated wheels does all the machinery move?"[23] Wynter would have his reader ascend St. Paul's on one of London's rare clear mornings, yet the view is not observed so much as studied. "Naturally" one thinks of food distribution and the systems by which it is carried through: an appropriate subject for this diagrammatic London on which the functional routes can be traced. The sights of London are to be enjoyed as the signs of a hidden economic and technological power—a power brought to the surface by explanation and paralleled, as so often in Wynter, with a physiological process (digestion). What is familiar or localized is not expanded into a comprehensive spectacle but reasoned into an endless network of data. Far from remaining picturesque, the panorama becomes a means to information, so that the spectator is inclined toward seeing *through* the sights.

No less than Sala, Wynter reaches a periodic moment of crisis in his use of urban figures. While the panorama seems like a means to knowledge, the knowledge it reveals has less and less connection with the necessary limits of human consciousness. As Henry James notes, "We are oppressively reminded as we turn his pages of the vast and daily increasing number of things that demand to be known about, and what a serious matter it is constantly becoming to attempt to appear well-informed." Wynter has the same fear but takes it more seriously. "In this age . . . when the boy has to go through an examination for a clerkship of a more severe character than was demanded for an University degree of old . . . is it to be wondered at that the mental fibre, in cases where there is hereditary taint, becomes weakened, and unable to resist the strain of any great excitement?" Or more specifically yet: "We see no reason to doubt that mere disordered functions of the brain may be converted by the same undue attention into positive disorganization and mental disease." Inclusive seeing—instantaneous omniscience—is thus connected with insanity. "Dr. Elliotson mentions a patient who, previous to an attack of Meiplegia, felt such an extraordinary acuteness of hearing, that he heard the least sound at the bottom of his house. His vision was also exaggerated to that degree."[24]

Given such fears, why does Wynter persist with his panoramas and persist with the approach to London that they facilitate? Perhaps like that "irrepressible, instructive monomaniac" Mr. Barlow—who "invested largely in the moving panorama trade"—Wynter cannot stop teaching.[25] More broadly, I think, he is hampered by traditional beliefs about knowledge—just those beliefs that Ian Hacking has summarized. *Of course* knowledge and experience are connected: once he admits that the link between them has weakened, there is no telling where he will be. And yet the fear of madness persists. The idea that "mental ruin springs . . . from mental stimulation" goes against Wynter's strong belief in progress—but if the growth of knowledge drives men mad, there is little use in celebrating "the Chisel-Marks of our Industrial and Scientific Progress"[26]

Little use—unless the Shadow is on hand, for the Shadow can conceive any structure of knowledge at all. While Shadow-like personages appear in Wynter's essays on London,[27] his most memorable character along these lines is the product of a patient's hallucination. Wynter is not the first to report the Man of the Mirror hallucination, whose persistence through the Victorian period suggests its status as a kind of urban folklore, but his account (I will suggest) has special pertinence to his own dilemma as a writer. An idle wanderer through London (later Wynter's patient) meets an old gentleman who persuades him to visit the top of St. Paul's. Once they are there, the old gentleman mutters some words over a mysterious compass, then asks his companion "If he should like to see any friend at a distance, and to know what he was at that time doing." The request is irresistible. Granted a magical vision of his sleeping father, the wanderer falls into an immitigable terror, becoming "the slave of the Man of the Mirror." This sinister character—apparently identified with the old gentleman—lives at the top of Saint Paul's. From the Man of the Mirror, "there is no concealment. . . . He sees us and hears us now." Moreover, he controls "all those within the circle of his hieroglyphics . . . 'signs and symbols, which you, in your ignorance of their true meaning, have taken for letters and words, and read, as you have, *Day and Martin* and *Warren's Blacking!*' "28

A sentence in the middle of this narration provides a key to the dream. "Remember," says the gentleman to the patient, "you are the slave of the Man of the Mirror." The catoptromantic mirrors possessed by Prester John, Dr. Faustus, Nostradamus, and other seers revealed everything that was going on in the world.29 The Man of the Mirror tempts the unfortunate narrator with this magical omniscience, produced by (and restricted to) "the circle of his hieroglyphics." He gives in to the temptation, and the hugeness of London is counterpointed by the image of his father, a frail sleeping man who is blissfully unaware. Contrastingly, his own awareness is horribly transformed. Wynter points out that this transformation is "absurd," but it is equally like a nightmarish version of his own London journalism. The city calls forth the ubiquity of a masterful observer, then counterpoints it with the experience of a man who *feels* that his environment is all of a piece but is trapped rather than freed by the perception. He cannot live without the panorama, nor can he live with it. The unifying vision of omniscience turns into an irresolvable struggle, a battle between the Man of the Mirror and his slave. The encompassing view constricts, generating the panic of those who have experienced and are therefore imprisoned by it. The city becomes the embodiment of autonomous knowledge—knowledge expressed through anonymous, omnipresent, and all-powerful writing.

The Suspensions of Mystery

Sala and Wynter crave a middle ground that proves largely unavailable; they then make their failure to find it the subject of some wayward but striking essays. A reader absorbed by their work—by its density of fact, by its use of urban figures, by its interest in the presumed autonomy of knowledge—will be all the better prepared to trace the more elusive fate of omniscience in Dickens's novels of the period. These novels are concerned with a failure too, and at first it may appear to be the same one that Sala and Wynter suffered: a collapse of nerve that allows the Shadow to take over, to loom at will. I will suggest, however, the failure in this case ultimately is the Shadow's rather than the human viewer's.

Dickens's novelistic use of omniscience can be introduced by a passage from *Little Dorrit*: book 2, chapter 10, "The Dreams of Mrs Flintwich Thicken." Here Arthur Clennam journeys to "his mother's dismal old house" by the Thames. "His imagination was sufficiently impressible to see the whole neighborhood under some dark tinge of its dark shadow."[30] Having spent his day at the Circumlocution Office in an attempt to unravel his present, Clennam is returning to his childhood home and his past, an equally alienating territory of mystery. Clennam meditates on "deserted counting-houses, with their secrets of books and papers locked up in chests and safes," on other secrets contained in "banking-houses," on yet others hidden away by "dispersed grinders in the vast mill," including "trust-betrayers of many sorts;" next he thinks of the dead, "of the lonely church-vaults, where the people who had hoarded and secreted in iron coffers were in their turn similarly hoarded, not yet at rest from doing harm." These lines suggest a general problem of the novel. Certain phrases imply that secrets are fascinating and powerful because a solitary person knows them but fails to divulge them; many more phrases, however, presume that the power of secrets lies beyond any mind: secrets are located in "papers," "in strong rooms," above all in those coffins where a final closing up of consciousness is time and again confirmed [*LD*, 2.10, 542]. Death is understood as a form of autonomous knowledge, and, I think, autonomous knowledge as a kind of death. Dickens's words confront the slippage of the city beyond what Arthur Clennam could possibly grasp. To quote Affery Flintwich on her marriage: "It was no doing o' mine. *I'd* never thought of it" [1.3, 38]. In the London of *Little Dorrit*, many experiences are like this: even if they putatively belong to oneself, they often seem based on nothing but a kind of staring at locked doors, closed caskets. It is not only Mrs. Flintwich whose dreams thicken about her.

To this difficulty there is an immediate reaction. Having evoked Clennam's peculiar ignorance, the novelist discovers within it a moment of comprehensive vision. We should recall that Dickens is drawn to the nocturnal Thames; he remarks in his account of another night walk that "the very shadow of the immensity of London seemed to lie oppressively upon the river," and elsewhere yet that "this river looks so broad and vast, so murky and silent, seems such an image of death in the midst of the great city's life."[31] The river is an escape from the humanized world of the city, yet it also reflects that depository of secrets. This mirroring tantalizes Clennam, who imagines "the secrets of the river, as it rolled its turbid tide between two frowning wildernesses of secrets, extending, thick and dense, for many miles, and warding off the free air and the free country swept by winds and wings of birds" [*LD*, 2.10, 542]. Even as the prose evokes imprisonment, its perspective changes to that of a bird's-eye view. The phantasmagoria, the panorama—figures linked *together*, as though mutually reinforcing—preserve the mind's ability to locate itself within a surveyable world. Darkness thus comes to imply a kind of enlightenment: the intuition of inaccessible secrets has led us on toward a hallucinatory sense of freedom.

All this occurs within one paragraph, a condensation that is crucial; it is as though London has been focused to a very small point indeed. Through an effect stylistically local, the whole of the city is summoned up.[32] The evocation is a partial victory for Clennam. His suspension between mystery and revelation helps him to retain for human experience, for the knowing subject, what would otherwise be given up to the Shadow. But a fiction of this sort proves hard to sustain. "The Dreams of Mrs Flintwich Thicken" is in fact a turning point between the two most important acts that Clennam performs before the concluding chapters of *Little Dorrit*. And taken together these acts—these investments of capital—test the usefulness of Clennam's ignorant knowledge.

His first investment is with Daniel Doyce, inventor. Doyce is reassuring on account of his modesty: "There was something almost ludicrous in the complete irreconcilability of a vague conventional notion that he must be a visionary man, with the precise, sagacious travelling of his eye and thumb over the plans. . . . He never said, I discovered this adaptation or invented that combination; but showed the whole thing as if the Divine artificer had made it, and he had happened to find it. So modest he was about it" [*LD*, 2.8, 515–16]. The insistence that attention and alertness are enough for creating new knowledge or for understanding it recalls *Household Words*'s faith in explanation. However, there is something "vague," "conventional," about Dickens's presentation of the inventor (whose invention remains largely unspecified, though the novelist constantly insists what a good idea it is). Doyce belongs in some other world than the London of *Little Dorrit*.[33] Characters and novelist alike admit this archaic quality about him; he becomes therefore a lovable but distant presence.

The same complaint cannot be made about Mr. Merdle, whose name (Dickens notes) has become the name of the age. Merdle is the opposite of Doyce, in that his accomplishments, his field of endeavor, and even his profession are so large, so abstract, as to be virtually indescribable (with Doyce, at least, we can fill in the gaps for ourselves; so far as we take Merdle straight, it's impossible to imagine how he functions). The greatness of this financial "Deity" [*LD*, 2.12, 556] must be taken on faith. If one wants to understand why faith in Merdle is such an attractive prospect, the Circumlocution Office—that other great satirical target of the novel—provides a point of reference. At the office, Nobody presides. Under Nobody's reign, paper seems to circulate on its own. "There was an imposing coming of papers . . . an imposing going of papers, almost constantly; wherein another gentleman, number four, was the active instrument" [1.10, 115]. Seldom has an active instrument been placed this passively. So enraged is Dickens at the autonomy of paperwork that he goes a step further and blames bureaucracy on insouciant, parasitic aristocrats (the Barnacles). This is rash of him, as he would have admitted in another mood,[34] but the important point has been established. People need a human personality to fill this kind of void; if they have to make up a personality, so be it. Somewhere in modern life, a mind that *knows all* must be seen to emerge. That mind is Merdle's. Merdle is created by a society that is not only greedy but lacking in reassuring "proofs": I intend Hacking's sense of the word.

Although Clennam is among the last to be swept up in the excitement, he finally transfers his capital to Merdle after consultation with Pancks, who advises him to be *as rich as he honestly can*, "not for your sake, but for the sake of others. . . . You don't know what depends upon you" [*LD*, 2.13, 584]. Remembering the "gathering shadows" of 2.10 (especially the blackmailing Blandois, whom he encounters immediately after his night walk), Clennam agrees: his knowledge is a knowledge of gaps, he is surrounded by mysteries—and therefore he must rely, not on Doyce's competence (Doyce is now another among his dependents), but rather on that omnipresent Shadow, Merdle.

Doyce or Merdle? Clennam is drawn to the first, then to the second. One might be tempted to say: he makes a good investment that is Dickens's nostalgic fantasy, then a bad investment that is Dickens's nightmare of his own cultural moment. The situation is ultimately more equivocal because neither character, neither investment, answers to a prominent feature of Clennam's own nature: his ability to live among doubts that take on the substance of knowledge. Clennam's middle territory is reestablished only when Merdle slits his wrists. The supposedly infallible financier, who seemed to be weighted with the foreknowledge of all things, who seemed resistant to every "mental strain" that burdened him in his omniscience [*LD*, 1.21, 253], was actually conscious of little more than his falsity. But the novelist is intent on more than destroying myths about all-powerful capitalists. Although the narrative now shifts away from Clennam—he is one among thousands of Merdle's victims—it renews the approach to London with which he is associated.

Dickens prepares for the renewal by focusing on two otherwise minor characters, members of the London professional elite who have attended Merdle throughout his career. "Few ways of life were hidden from Physician. . . . Many wonderful things did he see and hear . . . yet his equality of compassion was no more disturbed than the Divine Master's of all healing was"; whereas "Bar's knowledge of that agglomeration of Jurymen which is called humanity was as sharp as a razor. . . . [he] picked up all sorts of odds and ends about Westminster Hall" [*LD*, 2.25, 702–3]. The comparison prefaces Physician's discovery of the Merdle suicide, an event instantly communicated to Bar. "Before parting at Physician's door, they both looked up at the sunny morning sky . . . and then looked round upon the immense city, and said, If all those hundreds and thousands of beggared people who were yet asleep could only know, as they two spoke, the ruin that impended over them, what a fearful cry against one miserable soul would go up to Heaven!" The consciousness of Merdle's crime seals a bond between them. They look "round upon the immense city" as if the view from Physician's door were an endless circle of a panorama, which it almost certainly is not [2.25, 708]. Dickens has used this meeting of minds, which is like a reconciliation within his own mind, to suggest a miracle of collaboration. Momentarily, these representatives of the urban power structure achieve a sense of London's wholeness, shared between them so that they seem to meditate in chorus. Neither sharpness nor equality of compassion, knowingness nor wisdom, predominates in this strange mixture.

Dickens does not want his readers to miss his prospect that is not a prospect. In case they do, he repeats it. The rumor of Merdle's ruin is passed from Physician to Bar, from Bar to some friend in court. Dickens describes the spread of the news over London, until finally "the talk, lashed louder and higher by confirmation on confirmation, and by edition after edition of the evening papers, swelled into such a roar when night came, as might have brought one to believe that a solitary watcher on the gallery above the Dome of St. Paul's would have perceived the night air to be laden with a heavy muttering of the name of Merdle, coupled with every form of execration" [*LD*, 2.25, 710]. London itself speaks with one voice; the city fades into night but leaves behind it a "heavy muttering" that a hypothetical viewer "would have perceived," had he reached the gallery of St. Paul's.

I have already noted *Little Dorrit*'s tendency toward lyric concision. Merdle's downfall is compressed into a smaller space than was originally planned,[35] but within that space Dickens works miracles. It is worth comparing a similar incident from *Bleak House:* the occasion (chapter 11) when "the news [of Nemo's death] got into the court." Here, the rumor of death allows Dickens to explore the convivial and profuse workings of a microcosmic society, Cook's Court. Merdle's ruin, on the other hand, must strike all of London within a day. A leisured profusion of incident is beside the point—precisely because the territory to be covered is so large, the news to be revealed so universally sensational. A few paragraphs, then, are made to do the work of a chapter. Within those paragraphs, Merdle's crime is discovered three or four times: by Physician, by Physician and Bar together, by Merdle's household (the chief butler in particular), by London as a collective presence. The sequence of realizations reaches its fulfillment in the two impossible panoramas, the first in the wrong place, the second at the wrong time. That the city is surveyed in the dark or from Physician's door is an artful contradiction. No one in the metropolis could perceive the reality of Mr. Merdle. His career called forth elaborate genuflections from every level of society. Although this "uncouth object of such wide-spread adulation" has been revealed for what he "simply" is, the revelation—in all its simplicity—begins to disappear as it is unveiled. The concision of the passage works to suggest the transience of an apparently obvious perception, and the elusive grounds on which even this preeminent truth about Merdle can be held in mind by the people of Victorian London.

Merdle's suicide, with its aftermath, refines the interplay of ignorance and knowledge established by earlier sections of *Little Dorrit*. Having destroyed the Shadow/financier (who hardly believes in his own precarious existence), Dickens finds it necessary to invent an all-seeing witness of a different sort: a mind composed from the divergent impulses of Bar and Physician and then passed on, as it were, to the "solitary watcher" of a visible muttering. The brief existence of these beings is justified by the occasion of London's ruin. The downfall of Merdle provokes a vision of a city united by disaster and an onlooker who can bear the vision—but suffers it, like Clennam, as a kind of groping ghost, with certainties dissolving around him and such knowledge as he possesses emerging out of the collapse that is always in progress.

The omniscience of Bar and Physician recreates rather than resolves the atmosphere that pervades Clennam's night walk. Taken together, these passages suggest a great deal about *Little Dorrit*. This is a strange book. It seems to press past Clennam's halting diffidence to one violent unmasking after another. Merdle's death can stand for all these apocalyptic scenes. Ultimately, however, the crises of the novel leave its mysteries suspended.[36] The quality of this suspension is exemplified by a phrase from Clennam's encounter with bureaucracy. In the Circumlocution Office, he reiterates the phrase "I want to know," receiving an equally formulaic reply: "You mustn't come into the place saying you want to know, you know" [*LD*, 1.10, 113]. The exchange parodies a permanent condition of life in London. Only by a postponement of understanding can one who is part of the pattern retain a feeling for his own place in it. His sense of London's wholeness remains an intuition of mystery, of the separateness of human minds. "To know, you know" is an activity that—like the phrase, or like the Thames mirroring the city—doubles itself into a mysterious meaninglessness. Thus it is that when the secrets of the Clennams and the Dorrits are finally unveiled, in a confrontation between Mrs. Clennam and Rigaud, the novel's hero is not even present. Clennam may take those extraordinary night walks forever: feeling, guessing, but never pinning down the links of guilt that bind him to London. Perhaps he likes it this way. The distance he keeps from the metropolis is only partial, yet it gives him a view of the city and—despite lapses—a separation from the crowd's consuming energy. "To know, you know" is a consummation wished for and also avoided by that Clennam who finally goes "down into the roaring streets" [2.34, 826].

Dickens's mixed feelings toward omniscience are expressed by a developing vocabulary of perception: the panorama and the night walk are opposed to autonomous knowledge; autonomous knowledge is represented either by a person or a self-regulating process (e.g., paperwork). Among these proliferating possibilities, the reader is encouraged to weigh finite against infinite understanding, and somehow to remain at ease between the two. Even, however, if it is feasible to work around Dickens's Shadows, they remain a cultural threat: Merdle will return because the systems of modern life call him into being. And this temptation to personify what cannot be held in mind—to make of the unknowable a kind of fictional knower—is not altogether harmful. It allows someone like Arthur Clennam to be taken in by Merdle (to get rid of responsibility while pretending that he is doing something positive, like exercising trust or providing for dependents). But it also prevents such people from relying too much on verities that no longer apply.

Guilty Pursuits

Like Clennam, the Pip of *Great Expectations* is surrounded by secrets that he fails to comprehend. Unlike Clennam he eventually grasps the mysteries of modern London; rather than holding them in suspension, he identifies them with the secrets of his own life. To appreciate Pip's accomplishment, the reader should keep in mind some famous scenes from Dickens's earlier fiction. A malefactor is brought to judgment by a mass outcry aroused at the last moment. A solitary pursuer—often reminiscent of a previous victim—dogs the footsteps of a fugitive, touching off the vengeance of the London crowd.[37] This denouement suggests something of conscience, and something as well of society. Dickens's most eloquent comment on the connection is in *Bleak House*. Lady Dedlock's "murderous perspective, before the doing of the deed, however subtle the precautions for its commission, would have been closed up by a gigantic dilatation of the hateful figure, . . . those consequences would have rushed in, in an unimagined flood, the moment the figure was laid low—which always happens when a murder is done" [*BH*, 55, 758]. Guilt is a turning point from the hateful figure (all the murderer can think about) to the rush of accusers; it connects the fugitive with the condemnation of the society, the "unimagined flood," around him.

Dickens's fascination with crime has many sources, one of them being that the vivid experience of guilt makes run-of-the-mill assumptions difficult. Clennam, Bar, and Physician feel, in their various ways, an involvement with the wickedness of the city, but it is unclear where the wickedness resides: the responsibility for it is diffused, and on this diffusion rests the possibility of a humanized omniscience. Bill Sikes, Jonas Chuzzlewit, or perhaps even Mrs. Clennam, knows that judgment is to fall on him personally. Even though he perish, the fugitive must reimagine his relationship to the city, whose wholeness is called forth as a kind of delirium—an experience containing the extremes of private agony and public condemnation. Focused guilt produces the obsessionally *condensed* city of accusation. This phenomenon simulates but also mocks the capacity "to see a world" [*TTC*, 3.2, 249]. It is as though omniscience were imaginable only as a kind of punishment.

The guilty pursuit of *Great Expectations* moves beyond its predecessors, for Pip—unlike Sikes or Chuzzlewit—is a redeemable character. We can see Dickens trying out this turn of the screw as early as 1851 (a decade before he publishes the story of Pip). "Bill-Sticking," a *Household Words* essay, is a kind of miniature bildungsroman; a half-concealed subtext celebrates the writer's survival of city life and the imaginative potency he supposes that he has gained [*HW,* 2 (22 March 1851): 601–6]. Dickens first proposes that a hypothetical enemy "had surreptitiously possessed himself of a key. I would then embark my capital in the lock business, and conduct that business on the advertising principle. In all my placards and advertisements, I would throw up the line SECRET KEYS. Thus, if my enemy passed an uninhabited house, he would see his conscience glaring down on him from the parapets, and peeping up at him from the cellars" [601]. As the eyes of Nancy tracked Sikes, so Dickens's enemy will be tracked by SECRET KEYS. The idea is too good to let go. Having impersonated the accuser who is translated into the whole geography of London, Dickens then turns these energies *against* himself: "Have I sinned in oil? CAB-BURN pursues me. Have I a dark remembrance associated with any gentlemanly garments, bespoke or ready made? MOSES AND SON are on my track" [601–2]. Dickens elsewhere reminds us that he has a "dark remembrance" associated with WARREN'S BLACKING—one of the commonest London trademarks: "The blacking warehouse was . . . a crazy, tumble-down old house. . . . My work was to cover the pots of paste-blacking: first with a piece of oilpaper, then with a piece of blue paper; to tie them round with a string; and then to clip the paper. . . . When a certain number of grosses of pots had attained this pitch of perfection, I was to paste on each a printed label. . . . No words can express the secret agony of my soul as I sunk into this companionship."[38] The "secret agony" of the warehouse is recalled to Dickens not only by the trademarks but by the affinity between label pasting and billsticking. In turn, both these activities suggest that purely businesslike function of literacy which Dickens escaped by becoming a successful novelist. The blacking warehouse may or may not be identifiable as a childhood trauma, but it is certainly a powerful image: a memory of which Dickens is strangely fond, as embodying the mysterious link between words and imagination, or between London and the novelist's triumph.[39] These connections are confirmed in Dickens's confession that "the foregoing reflections presented themselves to my mind, the other day, as I contemplated . . . an old warehouse which rotting paste and rotting paper had brought down to the condition of an old cheese. . . . Here and there, some of the thick rind of the house had peeled off in strips, and fluttered heavily down, littering the street; but still, below these rents and gashes, layers of decomposing posters showed themselves, as if they were interminable" ["Bill-Sticking," 601]. Thus the wanderer's past presents itself: the warehouse, so vivid in mind, is rotting now, yet even more powerful for that: "interminable," as though all the pasting of labels, or all the billsticking, only made the memory indestructible. London encodes Dickens's life by the impersonal techniques of modern commerce, techniques not likely to die unless with the city itself, "pulled down . . . in one adhesive heap of rottenness and paper." The dilemma recalls the delusion of the Man of the Mirror, but it is a conscious fabrication of art: a way of masking a personal truth that can be articulated by the SECRET KEY of Dickens's autobiographical fragment. Turning the fragment into a melodrama of escape suggests London's pursuit of him and his of London. The novelist has discovered a point at which a city and his own biographical history can merge. This equivalence is at once revealed and withheld, as though the writer were eternally in the moment of telling a cherished secret.

London is not coterminous with the life of Charles Dickens, nor need one be edified by supposing it is. *Great Expectations* works from an identification of city and autobiography but acknowledges the constraining elements in the equation, makes them, in fact, part of its developing drama. Pip's great expectations and his chance to live in London are announced to him by the lawyer Mr. Jaggers. Jaggers has already been presented as possessing "a manner expressive of knowing something secret about every one of us that would effectually do for each individual if he chose to disclose it" [*GE*, 18, 128]. However, this seemingly omniscient functionary is more the specialist, less the god, than he seems. It is one of the (morbid) jokes of the novel that Pip's expectations are opened to him by a man whose exclusive practice—with the peculiar exception of Miss Havisham—lies in the defense of small-time murderers and thieves. Pip's problem is that he fails to get the joke. When he takes the coach to London, "the mists had all solemnly risen now, and the world lay spread before me" [19, 152]. The mists may have risen, but the world so Miltonically spread out is also closing in. "While I was scared by the immensity of London, I think I might have had some faint doubts whether it was not rather ugly, crooked, narrow, and dirty" [20, 153]. Pip continues to live in a Jaggers-like London that is claustrophobic, penny-pinching, and permeated by guilt even while it pretends to be much larger than it is; *immensity* in this case refers to nothing more than the existence of many mean streets together. His lack of a more comprehensive view is signaled after his first visit to Jagger's office in Little Britain, when he tries to look out over the metropolis; he is nearly guillotined under a falling window, an incident that suggests that his understanding of city and self will have to be acquired through some more difficult process [21, 163].

As in "Bill-Sticking," Dickens now plays on connections among memory, snobbery, and guilt. Pip thinks "how strange it was that I should be encompassed by all this taint of prison and crime; . . . Newgate in my breath and on my clothes" [GE, 32, 249–50]. He will have to learn why there is so much Newgate in his life and London; he will have to realize, in fact, what Jaggers has done: helped him exchange one sponsor or father (Joe) for another (the convict Magwitch). And as he tries to come to terms with this discovery, the city will first close in on him even further, then open out beyond Jagger's narrow omniscience.

At an early stage of Pip's London sojourn, Joe comes up for a visit; Pip's humble life has returned upon him at a moment when he can least bear a reminder of it. "Have you see anything of London, yet?" he asks, to which his guest replies: "Why, yes, Sir . . . me and Wopsle went off straight to look at the Blacking Ware'us. But we didn't find that it come up to its likeness in the red bills at the shop doors" [GE, 27, 210]. Joe is to Pip what the warehouse is to Dickens: an embarassing reminder of a working-class past that can neither be denied nor forgotten. It is thus appropriate that all Joe can grasp of London is the building that is the novelist's hidden past. Joe is attracted to the warehouse whose function in Dickens's life he himself duplicates within the narrative. And he finds it a disappointment, not nearly so compelling as its printed representations. Joe speaks for his creator on this occasion; at the same time, his opinion of London helps set the terms on which Pip—Dickens's fictional counterpart—will receive him. Pip suffers guilt for feeling shame at Joe's ignorance. This is to put the matter awkwardly, but awkwardness is the essence of the scene, for Joe, for Pip, and I think for Dickens too.

Pip is burdened by an anxiety he wouldn't be feeling, were he not a hopeless snob. (Dickens implicitly criticizes his own class prejudices.) Not so long after Joe's visit, this dilemma recurs. When the shining possessor of great expectations realizes that Magwitch, a former convict, is his benefactor, "all the truth of my position came flashing on me; and its disappointments, dangers, disgraces, consequences of all kinds, rushed in in such a multitude that I was borne down by them and had to struggle for every breath I drew. . . . With these fears upon me, I began either to imagine or recall that I had had mysterious warnings. . . . for weeks gone by, I had passed faces in the streets which I had thought like his. . . . these likenesses had grown more numerous, as he, coming over the sea, had drawn nearer" [GE, 39, 303 and 308]. Like Dickens's previous revenants, Magwitch precipitates the onrush of the London crowd, which grows in Pip's imagination until he, more than Magwitch, becomes the fugitive. Pip is running from Magwitch (whom he indeed perceives as his pursuer [40,

319]); from Compeyson (who wants to destroy Magwitch); from the justice that will hang Magwitch and thus make him—Pip—the convict's "murderer" [41, 325]; but above all from the implications of a social standing founded on money earned by a mere convict.

Pip starts out in a small London that then gets smaller and smaller. Whatever "immensity" the metropolis may have had at the beginning is gradually expunged from his mind. The secrets or merely the awkwardnesses of the past—which stem from "the provinces mostly" [*GE*, 40, 312]—are reenacted in a city whose appropriate center is a blacking warehouse, Newgate, or Jagger's Little Britain. The reader can discover for himself how the last stage of Pip's expectations becomes a series of awakenings; even the lamps are "red eyes [opening] in the gathering fog" [48, 367]. Finally, his own eyes opened, he can speak to Jaggers without treating him as an oracle.[40] Pip has made too many connections to consider the lawyer all-knowing; Jaggers is merely one participant in a drama involving a few obsessed people: the *same* people over and over, even though they may have seemed like all of London. After this crucial episode, the sense of instantaneous revelation, of pieces falling tightly into place, is something that he can carry with him, back to the scenes of childhood:

[53, 405]

> It was not only that I could have summed up years and years and years while [Orlick] said a dozen words, but that what he did say presented pictures to me, and not mere words. In the excited and exalted state of my brain, I could not think of a place without seeing it, or of persons without seeing them. It is impossible to over-state the vividness of these images, and yet I was so intent, all the time, upon him himself— who would not be intent on the tiger crouching to spring!—that I knew of the slightest action of his fingers.

On the verge of "perishing out of all human knowledge" [53, 407] Pip knows his life. London has *prepared* him for this experience, but he now leaves the city behind, to face Orlick in the solitary marsh until that moment when the rush of the crowd ("responsive shouts . . . voices and tumult" [53, 407]) preserves rather than annihilates him. The first face he sees on regaining consciousness is that of Trabb's boy. It is as though the "years and years and years" that he instantaneously remembered have come to life and also come to his aid. Pip's past no longer dogs or mocks him (as Trabb's boy once did); it is his salvation rather than his burden. The accusing crowd, a figure of memory and guilt, is transformed, reminding the reader that the knowledge Pip has achieved is not of a whole society but only of a few particular follies within it. And then this action creates its opposite reaction. Freed from the misunderstanding that began when he saw London through Jagger's trade and Jagger's narrow path, Pip begins to think within a larger context. When he returns to London he can *see* it:

> The winking lights upon the bridges were already pale, the coming sun was like a marsh of fire on the horizon. The river, still dark and mysterious, was spanned by bridges that were turning coldly grey, with
[53, 411] here and there at top a warm touch from the burning in the sky. As I looked along the clustered roofs, with church towers and spires shooting into the unusually clear air, the sun rose up, and a veil seemed to be drawn from the river, and millions of sparkles burst out upon its waters. From me, too, a veil seemed to be drawn, and I felt strong and well.

This is the first and I think the only moment in Dickens when an urban panorama permits such an affirmation. Pip loses one "brilliant look-out" [24, 190: Wemmick referring to Pip's expectations], but in the process he gains another. The world lies all before him, after all. He realizes—just before he must return to a final and literal flight, with Magwitch down the river—that he comprehends the metropolis, not just the Jaggers-like city of guilt and judgment but a lucid and wholly composed London: a city intimately connected, but not identified, with the understood pattern of his life.

A Mysterious Currency

Dickens's plans for John Harmon are announced on the opening page of *Our Mutual Friend*, where (in the original parts-issue for May 1864) there appears an inset slip announcing: "*The Reader will understand the use of the popular phrase* OUR MUTUAL FRIEND, *as the title of this book, on arriving at the Ninth Chapter (page 84).*" At page 84 Mr. Boffin designates the disguised Harmon "Our Mutual Friend," the capital letters signaling that a "popular phrase" has become a proper name. Nor is Harmon's importance established only through this one procedure. Formally as well as nominally he is crucial. His seeming death is supposed to generate, then to knit together, the diverse actions of the novel. His survival is supposed to allow a unique perspective on the chaos that it causes; Dickens wants to comprehend the struggles of Harmon and the other characters of *Our Mutual Friend* from outside the cultural compulsions of London. At every step, it would appear, Harmon's death-created *mutuality* is presented as the shaping device of the narrative.

Although Dickens felt he had carried through with his plan to make Harmon's death centrally important (see the postscript to *Our Mutual Friend*, dated 2 September 1865), many readers have disagreed with his evaluation. By consensus the detached perspective is achieved marginally at best, and the unity of cause is arguable only if—following Harmon's example—one can place a "very broad and free construction" in "tracing out affairs for which John's fictitious death was to be considered . . . responsible"—e.g., if one considers Jenny Wren part of the Harmon tale because of her association with Lizzie Hexam and Lizzie part of the Harmon tale because she assisted her father in retrieving what was supposed to be Harmon's corpse [*OMF*, 4.16, 803]. This is all rather strained. And even Harmon's nominal importance finally comes to seem doubtful: "Our Mutual Friend" is a relative phrase, whose meaning is dependent on context; therefore it cannot refer to him exclusively, despite the inset, despite the capital letters (Dickens's unsuccessful struggle against an inevitable dissemination of meaning). So far as one assents to these and similar observations, *Our Mutual Friend* turns out to be the least omniscient of books. Dickens's fascination with coincidences and hidden but traceable lines of connection has broken down. No room here for moments of encompassing vision: no room for the all-knowing author whose conventional presence lay behind the treatment of omniscience as a topic. *Our Mutual Friend* is composed in "different voices" whose incoherence—whose fundamental lack of connection—is the most significant point about them.[41]

I make this case briefly because others have made it at length.[42] Its merits—and limits—will become clearer in relation to those figures of spectacle that so often for Dickens underlie a humanized omniscience. John Harmon tries returning to the scene of his presumed death in the twelfth and thirteenth chapters of book 2. Harmon appreciates "the power of knowledge; the power derivable from a perfect comprehension of his business" [*OMF*, 1.16, 193]. Interrogating Rogue Riderhood, who helped bring the deed about, he asserts (very much in character) that "I alone know . . . the mysteries of that crime [his murder]. I alone know that your trumped-up story cannot possibly be true. . . . I came here to-night to tell you so much of what I know, and no more" [2.12, 361]. Excepting the odd echo by which "know" becomes "no," Harmon's rhetoric is masterful: he claims both exclusive knowledge and control over it (he will tell only so much as appropriate to the circumstances). But a few moments later, when he exits Rider's den "into the darkness and dirt of Limehouse Hole," his sense of his own position becomes more elusive.

" 'Thus much I know,' he murmured. 'I have never been here since that night, and never was here before that night, but thus much I recognise. I wonder which way did we take when we came out of that shop.' . . . walls, dark doorways, flights of stairs and rooms, were too abundant. And, like most people so puzzled, he again and again described a circle, and found himself at the point from which he had begun" [*OMF,* 2.13, 365]. This passage recalls the moment in *Notre-Dame* when Gringoire got lost among the circling streets of Paris; but where Hugo was opening up the possibilities of knowing and knowledge in urban figures, Dickens appears to be closing them off. An initial sign of closure is that the "too abundant" walls and doors comprise not even the same place over and over (as with Gringoire) but no place at all. A more complete alienation from one's own experience could hardly be imagined. Describing his presumed death, Harmon remembers that "there was no such thing as I, within my knowledge" [2.13, 369]. He has got the "I" back when he wanders around Limehouse—so, at least, the form of his words implies—but he has not recovered the memories to which it should be attached. Under these circumstances, the topography, much less the meaning, of London is unavailable.

Every denial may conceal an affirmation. So—it might seem—with Harmon. Following the lines I have quoted, he has the wonderful thought that his perambulations constitute a guilty pursuit, and that for him as for other escapees "the little track of the fugitives in the night" could well "take the shape of the great round world." However, though this "secret law" illuminates the experience of previous Dickensian heroes, in Harmon's case its encouraging implications are immediately ruled out. There may be a hidden pattern to Harmon's frustrated night walk; the miniaturized adventure may replicate the encompassing globe, even though the much smaller territory of Limehouse remain incomprehensible. But Harmon or Dickens only teases us with such possibilities. As if in parody of the logic that governs the figures of *Little Dorrit* and *Our Mutual Friend,* Harmon relinquishes his wanderings through Limehouse Hole and looks up at "the high tower [of Limehouse Church] spectrally resisting the wind" [*OMF,* 2.13, 366]. Though Harmon is "dead," though the night walk has led him to the verge of a panoramic view, though the bells toll, still he knows nothing. The "high tower" (solid enough to resist the wind but spectral all the same) is as much a false clue as was his search of the streets. Phantasmagoria and panorama are juxtaposed but no longer reinforce one another, no longer enter into that intimacy that confirmed a humanized omniscience.

Harmon's frustration throughout his "solo" confirms the consensus on *Our Mutual Friend;* now follows my demurral. Two years after Dickens completed the novel, he boasted that "I know London better than any one other man of all its millions."[43] These are not the words of a writer who has decided to dwell on limits or has fallen into skepticism. Perhaps, then, his last complete book is not so withdrawn or specialized a performance as it has sometimes seemed. Of a minor character in *Our Mutual Friend* it is said that "the more he himself knew, in his little, limited human way, the better he could distantly imagine what Omniscience might know" [*OMF*, 2.10, 331]. Even at their humblest, Dickens's characters want to know inclusively. However absurd their desire, however implausible, the writer leaves means for its satisfaction—and I suggest that these means share much with a line of scientific thought that begins around the middle of the nineteenth century.

The age of Dickens's Shadow is also the age of James Clerk Maxwell's demon: a tireless worker who tries to distinguish fast from slow molecules and get them sorted into separate compartments. Can he only succeed in his task, the system he governs will be able to do work. According to Maxwell's version of this parable, the demon is unsuccessful. Every time he tries to create order, he finds himself stymied by the second law of thermodynamics. The system, along with the demon, decays irreversibly. A being who clarifies the cosmos by gathering information about it would thus appear to be an impossibility. Any knowledge he gathered—and any actions he took on the basis of that knowledge—would be ineffective, at the least. The demon remained an irritation to Victorian science, but in our own century his dilemma has been reconsidered. To quote Jeremy Campbell, "as the theory of thermodynamics progressed, the focus of interest shifted from what it is possible for a system to do, to what it is possible for an observer to know about the system." This change, in its turn, made possible a fresh consideration of what omniscience might mean. On the one hand, certain kinds of information have come to seem inaccessible. Nobody occupies a "privileged, special place" in the cosmos; if the universe is a stack of cards, "it is meaningless to say that you are at such and such a place in the stack, even when you have full information about the order of cards at that place." On the other hand, "the meaningful properties of the cosmos . . . are all statistical, dealing with great collections of small particles." As the old, certain, and largely deterministic kinds of knowledge have receded from view, they have been replaced by a probabilistic understanding. One knows as much as ever—indeed there is more to know as time goes by, pace the second law of thermodynamics—but this knowledge has changed in character.[44]

Although Dickens was certainly interested in the science of his time—witness his correspondence with Michael Faraday[45]—I do not mean to raise questions of influence. My interest at the present moment is in analogies (an approach of which Maxwell would certainly have approved).[46] It is useful to think of *Our Mutual Friend* as working with the dilemma dramatized by the demon. The demon's desired omniscience is unavailable to the characters or perhaps to the writer of the novel. But they can still gain a usable kind of comprehensive knowledge. On these new terms, comprehension has little to do with the Man of the Mirror and his totalitarian survey, or indeed with the traditional Dickensian aesthetic of coincidence and connection, where everything ultimately fits together.[47] London is not unlocked by a single key, nor is it a puzzle where every piece has its place. Our experience of London is more like this:

> *Every street was a sawpit, and there were no top-sawyers; every passenger was an under-sawyer, with the sawdust blinding him and choking him.*
>
> *That mysterious paper currency which circulates in London when the wind blows, gyrated here and there and everywhere. Whence can it come, whither can it go? It hangs on every bush, flutters in every tree, is caught flying by the electric wires, haunts every enclosure, drinks at every pump, cowers at every grating, shudders upon every plot of grass, seeks rest in vain behind the legions of iron rails. In Paris, where nothing is wasted, costly and luxurious city though it be, but where wonderful human ants creep out of holes and pick up every scrap, there is no such thing. There, it blows nothing but dust. There, sharp eyes and sharp stomachs reap even the east wind, and get something out of it.*
>
> *The wind sawed, and the sawdust whirled.*

[OMF, 1.12, 144]

Dickens turns from the "sawing" wind, then, after a brief space, returns to it. The interpolated paragraph treats a "mystery" far removed from the fiction of Sue or Reynolds. This novelist's conceit, that the metropolis is possessed by enigmas of the everyday rather than of the melodramatic and extraordinary, was invented as a response to the novel of urban mysteries, probably by Alfred Crowquill. Later it was picked up by many London journalists (including Sala and Wynter).[48] It is part of the convention that questions about small mysteries are never answered. Perhaps they are more amusing if left in the form of questions. Or perhaps no pertinent information is available: surely not even Henry Mayhew in his maddest statistical moments would attempt to trace the origins of all wastepaper. For one of these reasons or some other, "whence can it come, whither can it go?" remains an interruption. The reader is encouraged to meditate the query—then to pass it by.

Just this once I will linger over it: Dickens's everyday mystery may prove to have its rewards; the scrutiny of such enigmas may be less idle, less the parlor game, than it seems. Consider a discrepancy. Paris is said to be the city where nothing is wasted, "London, Londres, London" [*OMF*, 1.12, 145], the city of waste. Does Dickens intend a hymn to the efficiency of the Gallic ragpicker? This seems unlikely. Later in *Our Mutual Friend* the honor of British scavengers is upheld; they are depicted gathering the "papers and pins" that here go neglected [2.15, 393]. And waste generally is supposed to be valuable: thus the Harmon fortune, thus Gaffer Hexam's living from the Thames. I become more puzzled when I observe that wastepaper is being compared to money. The machinations of the City's financial institutions have become a pervasive standard, extending into such areas of life as marriage or adoption of orphans. But now I have paper that is not only ubiquitous but unclaimed, a different matter. *Our Mutual Friend* alternately celebrates and condemns the pursuit of waste.[49] In describing his "mysterious currency," Dickens gets past the category of waste as usually understood, or so it would appear. How is this irritating crux to be treated?

It could be that Dickens is only stating a fact; that wastepaper did float around the metropolis, which may be true. There is no moneyless Utopia hidden within the ugliness of this urban spring, a limitation that will be recognized even during the most fantastical moments of Dickens's happy ending. Nonetheless, his wastepaper neglected by scavengers, blowing outside the terms of the market, has a power of its own, aside from the literal fact of its existence. Like the Shadow, it looms all over London, blinding in its omnipresence. Unlike the Shadow (and unlike Maxwell's demon), it cannot be given a singular human identity or a single privileged position. It haunts, cowers, shudders—all very anthropomorphic—but it does these things erratically and in bits. Rather than a knower—or an object of knowledge—these flying scraps are a medium in which knowledge can occur. An agent both totalizing and infinitely scattered, Dickens's "mysterious currency" moves through a dance of incalculable complexity, accommodating the wind, the fences, the electric wires, the sewers—and takes us with it too.

One passage does not a novel make; one passage, nonetheless, can invite a rethinking of familiar readings. Harmon's ineffectiveness as an organizing center, etc., has been taken to imply that *Our Mutual Friend* withdraws into subjectivity or textuality. But it might also imply that the novelist is recasting the conventions by which urban life can be usefully represented. Silas Wegg hates "to be what I may call dispersed, a part of me here, and a part of me there" [*OMF*, 1.7, 82]. Dickens insists that dispersal of a certain sort is advantageous: especially in a London ungoverned by occult patterns of coincidence and connection, and where no one hero, however mutual, can organize a narrative. Say that London really is a city of this sort. Making the admission forces a readjustment. It "turns out that the [city] itself has certain unexpected properties, setting it apart from the smaller, local systems it contains."[50] A cosmos of a kind, London cannot be known detail by detail, place by place, or event by event. There remain gaps in all narratives and descriptions of it, gaps that can never be filled. A John Harmon can trace the pattern of the great world as often as he likes and still not pin down his own location within it. Panorama and phantasmagoria are useless. However, it is this sense of missing information that compels one to adjust, to think about what one knows less as an accumulation of facts and more as the report of a dialogue with an unpredictable whole. Knowledge then becomes a product of organized guessing: necessarily so, since it is directed to a world that is random rather than providential, definable by statistics but not with "mathematical certainty."[51] Knowledge is macroscopic rather than microscopic, comprehensive as one person's experience can never be, yet comprehensible too, even if not organized around the privileged center of the self. Its "meaningful properties" deal "with great collections of small particles,"[52] probable patterns from which new features may emerge. To mention a crucial example from the concluding chapters of *Our Mutual Friend:* Think of Eugene Wrayburn's marriage to Lizzie Hexam. It develops—if that is the word—from the discovery of a corpse in the novel's first chapter. What counts about this branching of the plot is its erratic quality, the way that it can be traced to a source with which it has little connection at first and none later on. Freedoms like this one do not deny omniscience: they further it. A difficult union across classes is marked by a willfully awkward narrative turn. Fragmentation is a condition for grasping more or doing more. Wastepaper scatters. The reader is blinded, and sees.

Fifteen years after *Our Mutual Friend,* Ruskin's "Fiction, Fair and Foul" would delineate another urban landscape covered with "remnants, broadcast, of every manner of newspaper, advertisement or big-lettered bill, festering and flaunting out their last publicity in the pits of stinking dust and mortal slime."[53] Ruskin was seeking a way to preserve human choice and human integrity among metropolitan pressures. One reason that Dickens gets further in this endeavor—one reason that he can contemplate Croxted Lane less bitterly than the sage—is that he changes his mind about a few things. When he makes omniscience a topic as well as an enabling device, when he studies its shifting relation to urban figures, he is able to refine his notions of knowledge and how it is attained. Knowledge is a fluctuation between Doyce and Merdle; or perhaps it emerges from the guilty pursuit, where a hero flees from self and society only to confront both; or perhaps—most inclusively—it is the recognition that mind knows most when it works through what it can never fully grasp. Dickens had toyed with this latter conclusion by the early fifties, in the resolution of *Bleak House;* the irruption of the Shadow out of those projects kept the matter usefully in doubt for many years afterward. *Our Mutual Friend* represents a return to the convictions of midcentury and a refinement of them: not because it is about record keeping (it isn't), not even because it represents a world pervaded by institutionalized writing (though it does), but because it denies the fantasy of all-knowingness. And at the moment that fantasy is destroyed, the human reality nearest to it can begin taking shape more effectively than ever before. Like Esther Summerson many years previously, the novelist both relinquishes and accepts. Goodbye Shadow: goodbye Asmodeus, Briareus, the *Times,* the Man of the Mirror, Mr. Merdle, Jaggers, and Maxwell's tireless demon. After all that has been written, Dickens assumes the burden of his own omniscience.

V

Writing in the Depths

The jaspers of Oregon are probably un-
rivaled for the almost morbid complexity of their
curved designs and their range of contrasting or
merging colors: a graphic madness attained by no
other mineral. Each one, however small, looks
like a colored lithograph, crammed and tumul-
tuous as a picture by a schizophrenic.

Roger
Callois,
The
Writing of
Stones

13. The City and the Cosmos, or, Digging Your Own Grave

THE NOVEL OF URBAN MYSTERIES never died—not in the nineteenth century anyway. In 1911 Gaston Leroux's novel *Le Fantôme de l'Opéra* was published and the first showings of Feuillade's film serial *Fantomas* occurred. In spinning their fantasies of Paris, these works acknowledged a debt to *Notre-Dame;* subsequent movies (adaptations of Leroux and Hugo among them) have repeated, if not deepened, this tribute.[1] The literary line has also continued, particularly among the surrealists and their heirs; to mention one prominent example, Aragon's *Le Paysan de Paris* assumes and exploits a knowledge of the urban Gothic writers.

The tradition flourished long after the deaths of Victoria or Napoleon III. On the other hand, if Hugo and Dickens did not exhaust the novel of mysteries, they took it as far as it would go in one possible direction. A proof of this claim is afforded by *Les Travailleurs de la mer* and *The Mystery of Edwin Drood:* the former first published in 1866, the later in 1870. There are systematic correspondences between *Notre-Dame* and *Travailleurs:* the great rock formation, the Douvres, answers to the cathedral; Gilliat to Quasimodo; and so forth.[2] While *Drood*'s debt to *Notre-Dame* is less often noted, it could once be taken for granted. In 1911 (with Leroux and Feuillade busy across the channel), J. A. Nicklins observed of the cathedral crypt at Rochester that "Jasper and Durdles revisit these haunts by the glimpses of the moon as persistently as Quasimodo and the sinister Priest beset with their ghostly presences the belfry of the great Paris minster."[3] Such associations seemed obvious enough in their day; once they are acknowledged, however, an anomaly comes up. *Drood* is set on the Channel Islands and in the surrounding waters, *Travailleurs,* in a little cathedral town—a "city" by ancient right but hardly a metropolis. It would seem that the mysteries novel has deserted the great centers of civilization that gave it its raison d'être. It turns from artificial environments to natural ones. It positions itself on a wavering borderline between nature and art.

Despite appearances, this puzzling development is best understood as an outcome of urban allegory rather than as a deviation from it. I will recall four points that have shaped my argument thus far:

1. The metropolis is an artifact whose inhabitants cannot seem to grasp what it is that they have made. As a means of understanding, they turn to allegorical figures.
2. Such figures demand interpretation; furthermore, they ask to be compared with one another.
3. Interpretation of figures—a process enacted through stories with elusive but determined heroes—proceeds toward a knowledge that is useless or even maddening unless it is treated as autonomous: as existing fundamentally apart from human consciousness and human experience.
4. Comparison among figures suggests that one among them is privileged: the labyrinth opens out on panoramas and crowds, which dissolve into paperwork; paperwork is identified with the power of that same, maddening knowledge—independent of consciousness and of experience—that plagues the interpreter.

I proceed to a fifth supposition: It is tempting to suppose that writing can lead beyond all the figures. Disassociated from paperwork, its social embodiment, perhaps the power of the written word could open up access to the natural. In other words, there are circumstances under which the book of the city might be assimilated back into the book of nature. Goethe would have been comforted by this thought: recall his letter to Zelter (see chapter 1, above) where he criticizes *Notre-Dame* for destroying a sense of the natural; moreover, he would have realized the inevitable direction of such a journey. To Zelter (once more) he observed: "All the Arts . . . seem to me like towns, the ground and soil of which, the foundations in fact, can no longer be made out. . . . Where the earth gave way, it was intrenched and walled up; perhaps by the very side of the primary rock, a bottomless piece of swamp was met with, where stakes and pile-work had to be driven in; when all is at last completed and made habitable, what part of it can be called Nature, and what, Art?"[4] The borderline between city and earth is subterranean (or subaqueous); arriving here, one can no longer distinguish between what is natural, given, and what is made. If human beings are only responsible for what they have made or had a hand in making, this fantasy of Goethe's is arguably reactionary. It suggests what might be called the chthonian side of his social thinking, where all prospects of critical thought and action give way before the embrace of the great earth mother. At the same time, going underground can have a very different outcome. Confronting nature—most especially, *reading* what one finds there—could be a way of returning to city life, of analyzing the claims of a constructed human environment as opposed to a given or natural one.[5]

Several previous chapters have described the mystery novel's country excursions. Throughout the genre there are firm reminders that the city can be defined in terms of the country and vice versa.[6] The more specific motif I will be describing here, where one digs or descends beneath remnants of urban life to discover a naturalized writing, is less frequent. After Quasimodo's disinterment under Montfaucon, perhaps the richest examples occur in *Drood* and *Travailleurs*. Dickens's John Jasper discovers a golden ring in the tomb where he has stowed his nephew's body; written on the ring is Jasper's guilt. Hugo's Gilliat faces an octopus at home in his glittering grotto; the octopus's tentacles form the letters V. H. while plaguing Gilliat with unforgettable nightmares. These cases share a good deal. Buried—hidden away among the stuff of nature—writing displays a decaying yet attractive universe of death. This revelation is enough to encourage suicide; all the same, it has a more invigorating side. Hugo and Dickens have journeyed outward to read the cosmos so that they might return to the close and blotted text of the metropolis—might learn to treat it as a refuge rather than an alien horror. Turned back on itself, the quest for nature and the natural makes possible an affirmation of city life.

A Singular Worker, A Singular Work

Hugo's introductory note to *Travailleurs* includes the following observation: "Un triple anankè pèse sur nous, l'anankè des dogmes, l'anankè des lois, l'anankè des choses. Dans *Notre-Dame de Paris,* l'auteur a dénoncé le premier; dans *Les Misérables,* il a signalé le second; dans ce livre, il indique le troisième" (A triple fatality weighs on us, the fatality of dogmas, the fatality of laws, the fatality of things. In *Notre-Dame de Paris,* the author has exposed the first; in *Les Misérables,* he has pointed out the second; in this book, he condemns the third) [*LT,* 89]. By *anankè* or fatality (cf. the introductory note to *Notre-Dame,* where *anankè* is an inscription discovered on the cathedral), Hugo means the most fundamental necessities; to paraphrase another passage from the introductory note, it is *necessary* that man believe (thus dogma), that he create (thus the city, thus law), that he work (thus the plough and the ship). I find the schema striking—first, for its double presentation of necessity, at once the scourge and the saving feature of humanity; second, for its placement of the city, an area of ordered creation that is located between ideology and material need. At the end of *Travailleurs* these two points will merge; metropolitan environments will be understood as a refuge from the negative features of necessity, a refuge created by work, positive necessity. To anticipate my conclusion: if Hugo does not reaffirm Enlightenment notions of progress, neither does he subside into his protagonist's eventual fatalism.

At the beginning of the novel, the question of progress is specifically raised. Hugo reminds his reader that he writes from an age in which the world has been urbanized; culturally, the Guernsey of 1868 has more in common with Paris than it does with the Guernsey of the 1820s. Light has replaced darkness, except perhaps "dans les campagnes." Everywhere but in distant rural outposts the old ways are gone. They have become "des temps historiques," so that "ce livre" alone can recapture them [*LT*, 1.5.3, 193]. In this particular narrative, the leading agent of urbanization is the mechanized ship *Durande,* invented by Mess Lethierry; there could be no more promising image of progress through city life. A wonder and a rarity in the twenties, the ingeniously designed vessel makes possible "sécurité de voyage, régularité de communication, va-et-vient facile et prompt, agrandissement de circulation, multiplication de débouchés, extension de commerce" (safe traveling, regular communication, prompt and easy passages to and fro, an increase of circulation, an extension of markets and of commerce) [1.3.4, 141]. *Durande* is a novelty because, carrying a steam engine, it depends much less than other ships on weather, tides, and seasons. It is "cette machine où l'homme met sa volonté, cette chaudière toute-puissante" (that machine embodying human will, that all-powerful steam boiler), a ship that laughs at winds and tides [3.1.1, 476; 3.2.2, 499]. It seems the perfect example of human independence from nature; or more exactly of human ability to manipulate the forces of nature: it looks like a ship on fire, yet the fire is controlled; it is regarded as a living being, but life is given by mortal rather than divine decree. *Durande* is no substitute for Paris, but it was conceived there—inspired by a newspaper article, that is, by the world of writing on which urban culture is based—and it evokes the Utopian aspirations with which the city is often associated [3.2.1, 495].

The first shadow falls on this bright picture when, because of a dishonest captain's rapacity, *Durande* is left to the whim of the elements. The reef on which the steamboat finally comes to rest is less accessible to mortal labor than anyplace else in the novel. When Hugo first describes the Douvres, he notes that "ce qui se fait là ne regarde plus le genre humain" (what happens there does not concern the human race) [*LT*, 1.6.1, 245]. Even a rock in the English Channel might be expected to bear some mark of humanity; the Douvres bears only the mark of the abyss and its severe inhospitality. The Douvres would hardly be noticed were it not for the "deux roches d'une forme extraordinaire" (two rocks of an extraordinary shape) [1.6.1, 244] that signal its location. These rocks look like they have been consciously carved. If *Durande* is an artifact that assimilates the energy of nature, the reef is just the reverse: a work of nature has apparently appropriated the power and the character of art.

There is a name for the phenomenon of the Douvres. Although it looks like human handiwork, it is natural. It is therefore "cette singularité" [*LT*, 2.1.7, 324], that sort of "bizarre énigme" in the landscape which shocked eighteenth- and nineteenth-century travelers out of their presuppositions, revealing (supposedly) the logic of a material world. In my account of *Martin Chuzzlewit* I discussed one use of singularity. The meeting of *Durande* and the Douvres initiates another. With the ship perched on the rocks—as if by a giant hand, Hugo observes—the singularity of the Douvres is intensified. The work of the elements dominates those artifacts that try to declare their independence from nature. This triumph is all the more powerful because it includes nature's imitation of human work.

Anything Mess Lethierry can do, the sea can do better . . . apparently. Lethierry, however, refuses to give in; for the rescue of *Durande* he offers the hand of Déruchette, his niece. The eccentric loner Gilliat sets out to salvage the steamboat's suspended engine. The suitor replaces the father as hero—and immediately faces the same challenge as his predecessor, only in a more concentrated form. An impression of nature's superiority mocks his quest. It is as if nature wanted to convince him of her consciousness and her possession of intentions superior to his own. The metropolis is already present in the wilderness, not as a fulfillment of the promise held out by *Durande,* but as a field of secrecy and paranoia. This rhetoric, if it can be called that, is not confined to the image of the ship held up by the rocks. Working at an improvised forge above the reef, Gilliat "avait le sentiment singulier d'une attaque latente qu'il réprimait ou qu'il prévenait" (had the singular premonition of an attack that he was somehow repressing or preventing) [*LT*, 2.1.10, 341]. Which is to say: He is tempted to personify the elements, to infer omnipresent conspiracies. The *singular* sense of conspiracy persists, and with it other impressions pointing to masked intentions. Shortly after Gilliat arrives on the reef, he discovers underneath it "un labyrinthe noyé" (a drowned labyrinth) [1.6.1, 244], which is in effect a city created by the elements. "Les écueils, ces maisons de la vague, ces pyramides et ces syringes de l'écume, appartiennent à un art mystérieux . . . l'Art de la Nature. . . . Le fortuit y semble voulu. . . . Une dynamique extraordinaire étale là ses problèmes, résolus. D'effrayants pendentifs menacent, mais ne tombent pas." (Reefs, those houses of the waves, those pyramids and spouts of the foam, belong to a mysterious art . . . the Art of Nature. . . . Here the fortuitous seems planned. . . . An extraordinary dynamic displays its problems ready-solved. Frightful pendentives threaten but do not fall) [2.1.11, 343]. Hugo's sea city is full of solutions to problems that mortal intelligence can barely intuit. Gilliat is fascinated by the marine metropolis; he is particularly drawn to a grotto where—"sous une archivolte cyclopéene d'une coupe singulièrement correcte" (under a Cyclopean archivolte singularly exact in form) [2.1.13, 352]—he spies a sort of altar with a vague female presence hovering in the background. The novelist describes the same kind of threatening atmosphere as when Gilliat works at his forge; the combination of anxiety, gratuitous personification, and incomprehensible vastness is stronger than ever.

These pressures would wear most people down. Gilliat survives the mocking presence of so many singularities by a means that the novelist is careful to display. Although Hugo ranks his hero among "les opiniâtres" (the self-willed) and celebrates "sa volonté" (his will), Gilliat remains a dreamer: there is something essentially passive in his nature. "Le penseur veut, le songeur subit" (The thinker desires, the dreamer submits) [*LT*, 2.2.4, 368; 1.1.6, 114]. And how does the dreamer, the naif, this pastoral yet opinionated hero, save the wrecked steamship? The answer is that Gilliat mixes his efforts with the sea's. "Gilliat rêveur amalgamait à son propre travail le prodigieux travail inutile de la mer" (Gilliat the dreamer blended his own work with the prodigious, useless work of the sea) [2.1.10, 341].

This process is at first nothing more than a consciousness of the churning motion all around him. Gradually it becomes more. When Hugo discusses elemental forces (sea, wind, and darkness), he emphasizes what he calls a complex unity:

> La mer. . . . est compliquée; sous ses vagues d'eau, qu'on voit, elle a ses vagues de forces, qu'on ne voit pas. Elle se compose de tout. De tous les pêle-mêle, l'océan est le plus indivisible et le plus profond.

[*LT*, 2.1.5, 317–18]

> The sea. . . . is complex; under its waves of water, which we see, it has its waves of force, which we do not see. It is made up of everything. In all this promiscuous jumble of things, the ocean is the most indivisible and the most profound.

L'ombre est une; de là l'horreur. En même temps elle est complexe;
de là l'épouvante. Son unité fait masse sur notre esprit, et ôte l'envie de
.2.5, 371–   *résister. Sa complexité fait qu'on regarde de tous côtés autour de soi.*
•]

The dark is one, thus horror. At the same time it is complex, thus
terror. Its unity weighs on the spirit, removing the desire to resist. Its
complexity makes us look all around us.

Le vent est multiple, mais l'air est un.
.3.3, 402]   *De là cette conséquence: tout orage est mixte. L'unité de l'air l'exige.*

The wind is complex but the air is one.
It follows that every storm is mixed. The unity of the air demands
this.

In these vatic statements (and in others like them), Hugo fluctuates between contrasting views; he wants to suggest the overwhelming wholeness of air, darkness, water; he wants to suggest the myriad interpenetrat-
ing forces by which that wholeness is enlivened. So far as Gilliat can attend
to both views simultaneously, he can manipulate the elements; what he
cannot accomplish by his independent strength perhaps they will accomplish for him. The prodigious wasted efforts of the sea, that parodic city,
can be redeemed.

Gilliat's salvage operation depends on his changing his relationship to
the Douvres, on making the reef and through it all nature work with him.
The cosmos is not to be treated as a divinity but as an insentient, manipulable force composed of discrete units. His first success in this project
comes when he sets up an elaborate pulley system; the pulleys redistribute
the weight of *Durande* so that the remains of the ship can be lowered safely
into the sea. Hugo's point is not that Gilliat has suddenly become a learned
man, a scientist, but that his ignorance gives him a special power: the
power of discovery, Hugo calls it, rather than of invention [*LT,* 2.2.2,
359]. Discovery comes in a flash ("en bloc" [2.2.2, 358]—cf. *Notre-Dame*);
nonetheless, as *Travailleurs* shows, discovery depends on analysis as well
as synthesis: "Cette combinaison contraignait les quatre palans à travailler
ensemble, et, véritable frein des forces pendantes, gouvernail de dynamique sous la main du pilote de l'opération, maintenait la manoeuvre en
équilibre. . . . fait par un seul homme, [this machine] était surprenant. . . .
Disons ici que les fautes même les plus grossières n'empêchent point un
mécanisme de fonctionner tant bien que mal. Le carrose du czar Pierre était
construit de telle sorte qu'il semblait devoir verser à chaque pas; il roulait

pourtant" (This combination compelled the four pulley blocks to work together, and, a virtual bit upon the suspended forces, a dynamic rudder under the pilot's hand, kept the maneuver in equilibrium. . . . constructed by one man alone [this machine] was surprising. . . . Let us say here that faults just as bad do not prevent a mechanism from functioning pretty well. The carriage of the Czar Peter was made in such a way that at every step it seemed it must overturn; it rolled along nonetheless) [2.2.3, 361–62]. By reapportioning the ship's weight, Gilliat creates a surprising equilibrium. The ropes above modify gravity, as does the water below, the difference being that a lone, guiding intention is in control of the ship's descent, whereas the marine city is the product of impersonal forces, a chance that only looks like design. The pattern is confirmed in Gilliat's fight against the tempest that follows his salvage operation. Here the breakwater (with the Douvres backing it up) acts on the wind-stirred sea as the pulley system had acted on gravity. Once again, Gilliat's labors resist the elements by dividing and thus redirecting them: an accommodation of the natural subtler, more yielding, and more effective than the *Durande*'s proud independence in its heyday. To sum up, Gilliat has encountered a natural imitation of the human and appropriated it for genuinely human purposes; collaborating with the elements, he himself becomes a fabricator of singularities, the pulley system ("quelque chose de singulier," 2.2.3, 360) and the breakwater ("un cul-de-sac singulier," 2.3.6, 419). The analytical capacities of human intelligence—the ability to break down a whole into constituent parts—is valued fully, as is the ability to reassemble those parts for new ends.

Circulation, Personification, and Writing

Nature imitates art; in response, Gilliat conceives a sort of art that imitates nature. By this means he saves the steam engine, not to mention his own sanity. Before he can leave the reef, however, nature has one more word with him. None of her peculiar blandishments have reduced him to the passivity that (as a dreamer) is properly his. A last effort succeeds where the rest have failed. Waking after the storm, Gilliat is hungry—and his hunger drives him back to the drowned labyrinth underneath the Douvres. He is looking for a crab to eat; he finds more. The novel reaches a point of crisis that brings it into its most meaningful conjunction with *Notre-Dame* and *Les Misérables*.

Throughout his career, Hugo is obsessed with the possibility of a magical place where figures form a totalizing field of discourse. The conflict in *Notre-Dame* is between a labyrinth unified by Esmeralda's dance and a labyrinth unified by the view from the cathedral. Apparently the two are irreconcilable, a dilemma brought into the open when Quasimodo descends to the tomb and to Esmeralda's lifeless arms. He encounters a third kind of wholeness, a third labyrinth deriving from the others but boasting its own deathly coherence. Hugo evokes a mysterious unity revealed in an underworld hostile to human comprehension yet *readable,* graspable, as the book we hold in our hands. This realm is explored further in *Les Misérables.* While the barricade is being subdued above ground, the sewer below becomes the semblance of a democratic community—whose darkness can be assimilated to the sublime blackness of ink. Writing in general and novels in particular are taken to be the instrument by which people recognize what they have in common. Jean Valjean's descent to a material stratum makes possible the imagination (and possibly the redemption) of an elusive social whole. Like Quasimodo, Valjean is oppressed, then memorialized by a world of writing that he never altogether understands.

The drowned labyrinth is a further version of Hugo's visionary underworld. There are early clues to this effect: the waves and the rocks seem to be in eternal conflict (like the crowd and the cathedral of Paris, with which they are correlated), but beneath the sea they attain a weird harmony. Nothing actually happened to Gilliat on his first visit there; after he has finished his labors, however, he undergoes a transforming experience in the sea city. He meets the monster at the center of the maze. An octopus—that hovering presence in the grotto visited earlier—becomes the agent of an extraordinary change in his state of mind.

The physical struggle between hero and monster does not take much time. Gilliat kills the beast, but is left to ponder its intricate embrace. The octopus brings with it a ludicrous surplus of associations. Listing them gets to be a chore, even if a funny one.[7] The important thing to realize is that the accumulation of meanings has rhetorical results. Gilliat suffers from the circulation of images, pictures generated by his recent fight and thereafter linked.[8] Hugo has had an interest all along in things that go round and round: mechanically *Durande*'s paddle wheel or Clubin's revolver; elementally the "circulation mystérieuse" [*LT,* 2.1.11, 344] that shapes the architecture of the sea city and is thus expressed in its forms; economically the effort to put an inaccessible object (a stranded ship, a stolen fortune) back into human hands and the resulting advancement of "des affaires, et de la circulation, et du commerce" (business, circulation, and commerce) [3.2.1, 494]; socially the circulation of news, whether through gossip, journalism, books, or letters; biologically the cycle that guides organic life through such activities as sex, eating, excreting, and dying: "Pourriture, c'est nourriture" (rotting is feeding) [2.4.2, 441], observes Hugo, and even the words turn round on themselves. Circulation so imagined is nowhere near that orderly vision of metamorphosis that theorists such as Goethe found inscribed in the logic of the cosmos. Circulation means a constant blending of one form into another—a process of fateful violation where everything is consumed, nothing preserved but the pictures that circulate through human minds.

Gilliat does not realize that in the octopus he has confronted this formidable principle. He is still an ignorant genius, a natural philosopher susceptible to visions but hardly aware that he is having them. For this reason Hugo communicates his hero's horror subliminally—that is, through the patterning of a narrative rather than through the exploration of a consciousness. In one of the land-sea doublings that enliven *Travailleurs,* the undersea cave is foreshadowed by a ruined house on a cliff at one end of Guernsey. This house—connected with the grotto by many telling details[9]—creates a certain psychology of fear. "Les effrayés se sentent dans leur tort d'avoir été effrayés, ils s'imaginent avoir surpris un secret, ils craignent d'aggraver leur position, mystérieuse pour eux-mêmes, et de fâcher les apparitions" (The terror-stricken feel in the wrong for having felt terror, they imagine themselves to have unveiled a secret, they have a fear inexplicable even to themselves of making their position worse, of angering the apparitions) [*LT,* 1.5.4, 199]. To sum up, the house inspires people "se confesser en sens inverse" (to confess in an inverted sense) [1.5.4, 200]. The victims of this pathology at the house are three little boys, bird-nesters who eavesdrop there on a conversation between smugglers. Gilliat, Hugo reminds us, has done his best to discourage the activities of urchins like these as harmful both to themselves and to the birds. Nonetheless, his adventure follows a similar course: the perilous ascent of a cliff to retrieve a delicate object, the accidental meeting with demons after the deed is done, the consequent guilty terror. After all his labors seems to be over, Gilliat is stricken with a fear that he has encountered the horror at the heart of things.

The parallel between grotto and ruined house articulates Gilliat's fate. It remains a little unclear *why* the octopus in particular should have this persuasive power over him. With its five lashes attached to it like spokes to the hub of a wheel [*LT,* 2.4.1, 434], the beast is a remarkable image for the maleficent unity of the world—but previously Gilliat has resisted such images (e.g., the terrifying King of the Auxcriniers, 1.1.4, 105–6). He has been the object of other people's Gothic fantasies, rather than the perpetrator or sufferer of his own. How is it then that this monster—which, after all, he has slain—should lodge in his mind so irresistibly?[10]

There are hints throughout *Travailleurs* that the sea contains writing. *Durande* on the Douvres forms a giant H (tantalizingly, *Douvres* suggests *oeuvres,* the word that names a writer's *works* as opposed to the kind of work, *travail,* that nature accomplishes—cf. a usage like "le travail de l'érosion" [the work of erosion]); the grotto is full of mock arabesques and apparent runic inscriptions; a post office in the midst of the waves allows sailors to send mail from ship to ship. The most striking hint comes later than any of these, and will suggest the reasons for Gilliat's vulnerability. In a wonderful drawing by Hugo—one of those illustrations on which the novel itself is arguably a commentary—the octopus faces the viewer head-on, its tentacles swirling around in a manner not only threatening but literate: as Roger Caillois notes, "les deux tentacules supérieurs représentent les initiales de V. H" (the upper two tentacles represent the initials V. H.).[11] The octopus seems like an unlettered thug from some marine equivalent to the kingdom of argot, but here it is all the same, signaling its author's name. Among the mock artifacts that keep showing up in nature, this one stands out. The nature that keeps getting in ahead of art turns out to be the fabrication of Victor Hugo.

To say that Hugo has put his mark on the octopus is not an idle pun. A canceled passage from *Travailleurs* anticipates a success that followed the book's publication: the novelist popularized the term *la pieuvre* as signifying the fearsome monster octopus in opposition to the timid beast otherwise chronicled by science.[12] Hugo creates *la pieuvre*—creates it, moreover, to finish a job that his own words have begun. Throughout the novel no one but Victor Hugo has spoken (or written) for nature; no one but he has articulated the sense of a hostile will brooding on the waters. The octopus picks up where Hugo leaves off; it is his ultimate persuasive device because it acts out the integrative power of writing in an underground world like Montfaucon or the sewers.

Readers usually see Gilliat as his author's alter ego; more precisely, Gilliat is Hugo without the kind of knowledge that literacy and urbanization make possible (but do not automatically bring into being). This is one reason that the rhetorical power of the octopus works against, rather than with, Gilliat. He is unusual among the islanders in possessing books and perusing some of them. But he is hardly a reader par excellence. When, in the novel's first chapter, Déruchette traces his name in the snow, he understands the letters and the gesture differently than he should. The journey that leads to the octopus begins at this moment. Caught between the archaic, superstititious culture of Guernsey and the new world embodied in *Durande,* Gilliat is at ease nowhere. Hugo toys with the idea that the salvaging of the steamship's engine is a masterpiece—an act of imagination—comparable to the works of Aeschylus and Shakespeare combined. It is nothing of the sort. Gilliat cannot bear the burden of comprehensive knowledge that his labors bring upon him. When he is compelled to make a vast number of connections all at once, he becomes incapable of analysis: he loses the controlled skepticism that any good reader needs—especially in this treacherous sea metropolis where reason and the irrational so easily become one.

If Gilliat is different from Aeschylus and Shakespeare, then he is also different from Hugo. This point is worth emphasizing because the novelist is often identified with his lugubrious, self-sacrificial heroes. The equation is never less plausible than in *Travailleurs.* One difference is that Hugo, unlike Gilliat, strains to make a theodicy out of the confrontation with the octopus. Hugo's imagined conversion of circulation into progress can seem ludicrous, particularly when stated explicitly. His arguments historicize Pope's declaration that whatever is, is right. One ascends to the best through the better, and if lots of dead bodies occur along the way, so be it [*LT*, 2.4.2, 442]. On the other hand Hugo's effort to accept the whole of the universe has a basis more compelling than eloquent self-mystification. Part 3 of *Travailleurs* establishes the terms on which one can escape from the writing of nature to the writing of that urban world that Gilliat has helped usher in.

After he returns the ship to harbor one night, Gilliat overhears a young pastor propose to the enthusiastic Déruchette. He is spying again: looking where he should not, and burdened with more unwanted knowledge on that account. In reaction he speeds the marriage of Déruchette and her new lover. The major bar to the marriage is Mess Lethierry, who has determined on uniting his adopted niece with the rescuer of *Durande.* Mess Lethierry is described by Hugo as a rock in the sea and a child of the sea; the sponsor of civilization, he is also an unstoppable natural force. Gilliat gets around him by deceptive use of a letter the old man has written. The letter orders an immediate marriage between Déruchette and some unnamed person, who is presumed by an officiating ecclesiastic to be the pastor.

Gilliat arranges the marriage of his beloved, then chooses to end his life sitting on a singular rock at the edge of the peninsula, the Bû de la Rue, where his house is situated. The rock is characterized by "une sorte de niche dans la façade à pic du rocher" (a sort of niche in the peaked façade of the rock) [*LT*, 1.1.8, 121]. This niche forms a natural seat, like a recess for a statue on a Gothic cathedral. Gilliat sits here quietly, watching the ship that carries the happy couple dip below the horizon as the waves close above his head. Hugo observes that his hero has relinquished all desires. He returns to that passive state of the dreamer, a state that the novelist calls reverie; he is fixed there permanently until the sea blots him out.

Though Hugo is not renowned for his wit, these episodes are witty. Both offer diminished, almost parodistic versions of the epic labors that precede them. The arrangement of Déruchette's marriage is one last triumph over a rock in the sea: a rock (like the Douvres) both friend and foe, controllable by Gilliat's diffusion of its power. Again he wins a sea combat—sea combat on land and in a social rather than an elemental mode. The pathos of the episode is upset by this odd echo. Similarly, Gilliat's self-immolation completes the sacrifice begun on the singular altar of the grotto. Gilliat merges with the material universe. The natural world swallows up his labors, even, in an optical illusion, the happy young couple for whom he has recently schemed. That the ship's disappearance is only visual—and occurs only from Gilliat's perspective— might give a reader pause. Although Gilliat gives into the sea, nature's absorption of art is hardly complete. Hugo's introductory description of the Bû de la Rue clarifies the point. He notes that "toute cette crête d'écueils est depuis longtemps partie pour Londres" (all that ridge of the reef has long ago been conveyed to London) and also that "elle est devenue quai, église et palais, dans la capitale" (it has gone into the quays, churches, and palaces of a great capital city) [*LT,* 1.1.8, 120]. The urbanization of nature is able to proceed because the seat of Gilliat's annihilation (nature outdoing art and thus taking on an anthropomorphic power) is in its own turn transformed by human work: a reiteration of this novel's action as well as of its title. One is hardly surprised to learn that, in 1862, Hugo had written to a correspondent that for a place to write he had "une espèce de fauteuil naturel dans un rocher" (a kind of natural armchair in a rock) [quoted in *LT,* p. 598, note 16, Yves Gohin's extended commentary on the fun Hugo had naming rocks]. This book is replete with workers of the sea, the novelist himself among them. Not all such workers are liable to be swallowed up; those who write, rather than allowing themselves to be written, are, I surmise, safer than the others.

Treating part 3 of *Travailleurs* in this way suggests both the merits and the limits of Gilliat's accomplishment. Figural thinking has encouraged him to equate octopi with women and women with ships. One has to know how to use these correspondences—which also means knowing when to stop believing them. Wit is useful for this purpose because it makes people aware of differences at the same time that it acknowledges similarities. Wit thus becomes the appropriate weapon against mesmerizing phantoms like *la pieuvre*. It makes sense to say that all circulations blend into a single, vast, devouring cycle. It also makes sense to say that some of the smaller cycles are less relentless than that large and encompassing one, and some of their parts distinct, functionally and ethically. A fight with the octopus is different from a wedding night with Déruchette, and the wedding night in its turn is different from a ride on *Durande*. Up to a point Gilliat acknowledges the principle: How else could he use analysis so effectively when he disassembles the giant H formed by *Durande* and Douvres? When he stops analyzing, the reader has to start, an effort that Hugo's narrative encourages.

The city remains unknowable—almost in the way that nature is, almost as though it had nothing to do with human intention. On the other hand, the saving *almost* has weight. Hugo transports his reader from art to nature so that the same reader may recoil from nature to art. The novelist's writing enacts what Gilliat's salvage operation could not accomplish: it allows a view of the whole that admits a possibility for significant action on the part of human beings. Two years before the appearance of *Travailleurs*, Hugo had affirmed this possibility somewhat overconfidently. "Nous disons l'Art comme nous disons la Nature; ce sont là deux termes d'une signification presque illimitée. . . . L'Art est la branche seconde de la Nature. . . . nature et art sont les deux versants d'un même fait" (We say Art as we say Nature; these two terms both have a limitless signification. . . . Art is the second branch of Nature. . . . nature and art are the two sides of the same fact) [*WS*, 3.2, 81–82]. Nature manifests the kind of creativity associated with a great writer, while Shakespeare shares vastness and sublimity with natural phenomena like the ocean.[13] The proper conclusion is that art—writing most especially—can harness the power of nature, thus contributing to civilization. *Travailleurs* not only repeats but refines such assertions. It points toward a hero who could accomplish what Gilliat does but who could also go the one step further: extricate himself from the last phantom entanglement, the false reading of the octopus's embrace. Hugo seeks and does not find this protagonist. Division of labor rules in *Les Travailleurs de la mer*, as it did in *Notre-Dame* and *Les Misérables*. The epic hero begins an undertaking that the author and his audience must finish.

Sublimity in Miniature

Edwin Drood is a tale of two cities, London and Cloisterham (the latter a fictional town based on Rochester). The characters of the novel travel frequently between these places and no others. John Jasper travels from a London opium den to the door of Cloisterham cathedral, Mr. Honeythunder and his wards from the former's London headquarters to Minor Canon Corner, Edwin (and later Rosa) from Cloisterham to Mr. Grewgious's chambers at Staple Inn, Mr. Grewgious to Miss Twinkleton's in Cloisterham, Neville up to London (with Jasper stalking him), the Princess Puffer down to the cathedral (following Jasper). As Dickens emphasizes, it is not easy to get back and forth this way: there is no railway to Cloisterham (and Mr. Sapsea says there never will be). The London-Cloisterham shuttle becomes all the more conspicuous—as does the stark contrast between the cities in question. London is dirty, noisy, and immense, a place where you can lose youself or practice your favorite perversion while remaining perfectly respectable back home (Jack in town and Ernest in the country). Most inhabitants of Cloisterham seem to know one another. To any traveler returning from the outside world after a long absence, the cathedral city will seem "wonderfully shrunken in size"—and so on until the quaintness, cuteness, and nostalgic mood of Cloisterham seem its primary characteristics, especially when it is compared with the metropolis.[14]

Dickens goes out of his way to establish this contrast. It is true (as John Nicklin wrote in the early part of our century) that "amid the rather sordid encroachments of a modern industrialism, Rochester still keeps something of the air of an old-world country town."[15] But modern industrialism was right down the road, even in the era of Mr. Pickwick's visit—if not in Rochester itself, then in the "almost indistinguishably overlapping towns" of Chatham (whose shipbuilding industry was much chronicled by Dickens), Strood ("a long, disagreeable, narrow, ill-built town" that catered to "shipping and seafaring persons") and Brompton.[16] When Dickens insists on Cloisterham's remoteness from modern urban life, he is altering the Rochester of fact to suit the purposes of fiction. His pair of cities—for both of them have a right to that ancient title—must for some reason be kept separate, conceived as opposed worlds, even while every twist of the plot reveals that they are intimately involved.[17]

Why set up the novel this way? Dickens develops his approach to Cloisterham in order to resolve a problem raised by the metropolis, or more precisely by its imaginative presence. He avers throughout his career that London is a city of death, but is not always certain what this claim implies. From passages in many of the novels (*Edwin Drood* included) it might be inferred that death consists of separation from nature: rowing up the Thames, a Londoner on an outing will reach an "everlastingly-green garden"; returning, that same Londoner will see "the great black city cast its shadow on the waters, and its dark bridges [span] them as death spans life" [*ED*, 22, 253–54]. The formula will not do for all occasions, though. Reside long enough in the green garden and one finds death there also, as does Little Nell in the picturesque village where she ends her days. The suspicion arises that Nell has never left London, that the city's presence has been obscured only by an implausible pastoral surface.

If it is this hard to escape London, if nature keeps turning out to be second art, then a new approach is needed. Dickens is committed to the link between London and death and its corollary that death is the revealer of urban secrets; there are nonetheless moments when he explores a different possibility. In a nocturnal perambulation from *All the Year Round,* he speculates as follows: "it was a solemn consideration what enormous hosts of dead belong to one old great city, and how, if they were raised while the living slept, there would not be the space of a pin's point in all the streets and ways for the living to come out into. Not only that, but the vast armies of dead would overflow the hills and valleys beyond the city, and would stretch away all round it, God knows how far." Once Dickens has this thought he cannot very easily let it go. His vision of London's dead blends into an equally desolate, if more abstract thought. A church clock strikes "in the dead of the night" and "the spreading circles of vibration" move out forever into "eternal space."[18] Both these fantasies associate death with inclusive knowledge, not an unusual connection for Dickens to make. What is unusual is the kind of knowledge involved. The underlying thought is that death might reveal more than the city; might restore a sense of the continuity between artificial environments and the cosmos. Why should not the armies of death direct attention beyond the metropolis—or why should not a tolling bell articulate the infinity of space? Either way one is reminded of a world larger than this urban one. London no longer seems so all-absorbing. If it is impossible to restore a "judgment based on nature" in Goethe's sense—if it is impossible to flee from London and forget it permanently—at least there might be a way to mitigate those shifting and elusive judgments that are based on city life.

Such thoughts are an undercurrent in much of Dickens's writing: for example, in *Bleak House,* where documents are repeatedly identified with fog and mud (a human product becomes a natural one, and in this guise reveals a new perspective on London); or in *Our Mutual Friend,* where the river rolling through the city clears the space for a metaphorical dying—a deathly exit from an oppressive social framework. In these cases, however, the city never opens out for long. Perhaps a drastic move like summoning up the armies of the dead is necessary to suggest that the phenomenon of London is not all-inclusive. Or perhaps a smaller city, where humanity and nature were equally weighted, would provide a less strained reminder. Such a city could stand apart from London and also stand in for it. Concentrating on it would involve no pretense of permanently evading the metropolis; one would only be looking for those passages to nature obscured by London but still present there had one the power to locate them. Undistracted by London's immensity, a speculative explorer could follow to its end the dissolution of human purpose and the reintegration of nature with urban culture.

In his first sustained description of Cloisterham, Dickens calls it "a monotonous, silent city, deriving an earthy flavour throughout from its Cathedral crypt, and so abounding in vestiges of monastic graves, that the Cloisterham children grow small salad in the dust of abbots and abbesses, and make dirt-pies of nuns and friars. . . . In a word, a city of another and a bygone time is Cloisterham" [*ED*, 3, 18–19]. These sentences set the tone for much that follows. Cloisterham's inhabitants live on familiar terms with the human past. The past accumulates constantly, but is never confronted all at once because it pops up almost at random, and is absorbed bit by bit into the earth: it has an earthy flavor. If the living and the dead mingle on such intimate terms, if "the most agreeable evidences of progressing life . . . are the evidences of vegetable life," which themselves spring directly from human death, then Cloisterham requires a certain agility of response [3, 19]. The sum of material culture is imagined as constantly returning to nature, as decaying into an encompassing natural world that then provides objects or substances for human beings to work upon. Nature and culture are so closely intertwined as to be inextricable.

This kind of point is made throughout *Edwin Drood,* never so persistently as when Dickens describes the cathedral. Those introductory sentences quoted above suggest the determining influence of the crypt on Cloisterham's earthiness. Dickens frequently notes the cathedral's ubiquity—bits and pieces of it extrude or gradually collapse all over Cloisterham—as well as its involvement with the natural scene. He describes the building in autumn, mobbed by the leaves that fall from its own Virginia creeper; in winter, when it seems like an angry sea or the mouth of old Time; and in spring, when the light filtered through its windows preaches the Resurrection and the Life. The cathedral is the most monumental artifact of Cloisterham and also a kind of camera obscura through which the changing seasons can be discerned. No less than the city with which it is identified, the cathedral suggests that point in human endeavor when ambition and accomplishment fall into ruin—but somehow persist in retaining a distinct or a *shaped* identity.

Readers have responded to Dickens's depiction of Cloisterham and its cathedral in an almost comical variety of ways.[19] The lack of agreement is instructive. It points us to Dickens's own uncertainty about whether or not he likes this sort of place. "A drowsy city, Cloisterham" (he writes, in the introductory paragraph already quoted) "whose inhabitants seem to suppose, with an inconsistency more strange than rare, that all its changes lies behind it, and that there are no more to come" [*ED*, 3, 18]. Thus the satirist of the Circumlocution Office and the Chinese Junk—but another Dickens also has his say. In describing Minor Canon Corner, the novelist praises "that serenely romantic state of the mind—productive for the most part of pity and forbearance—which is engendered by a sorrowful story that is all told, or a pathetic play that is played out" [6, 50–51]. It is partly on the level of ideas that these comments contradict one another: the author assumes that history and progress provide the appropriate context for understanding the city, and then he implies that they do nothing of the sort (the play really is played out, death has won and everyone is somehow the better for it). Similarly, there is an affective contradiction. Dickens is enraged by fusty, reactionary Cloisterham; Dickens is charmed (in the old sense of the word) by earthy, decaying Cloisterham. These confusions signal a deadlock. The little cathedral city may be the appropriate site for breaking through from a human to a natural order, yet it is still unclear how the breakthrough could occur. Might one not metamorphose into a reactionary jackass before discovering the appropriate means? Avoiding this all-too-plausible fate, might one not simply keel over and be resumed into nature all too thoroughly? Dickens cannot make up his mind about tradition, that is, about Cloisterham's dying into the earth. An additional power must be tapped if he is to discover a usable passage between city and nature.

Adornment and the Cosmos

Angus Fletcher reminds us that the "oldest term for ornamental diction" is *kosmos*, a word whose meanings connect a decorative detail with the overarching frame of the universe. (Cf. the Babylonian belief that precious stones can tap the power of the planets and are *inscribed* therefore with the appropriate planetary virtue.) Fletcher concludes that a jewel or *kosmos* is the quintessential allegorical image, designed for the revelation of macrocosmic order through obsessive ornamental images. To state the matter differently, jewels are the kind of art nearest to nature and to natural forms (a cut jewel is not so different from a crystal, that natural singularity).[20] It might be supposed that beliefs of this kind disappeared with magic and divine right; however, they often survived in a transmuted shape appropriate to the age of Victoria or Edward. When Georg Simmel writes on adornment as a social phenomenon, he provides a modernized version of the lore analyzed in Fletcher. Jewels—most likely worn by women—compel other people to look and admire. A jewel places its wearer, assigning him a rank in a social hierarchy. Simmel is writing about a time in which social orders are no longer thought to have any necessary natural basis; he is fascinated with the process by which human beings make the world they live in. Despite this bias, he uncovers an ideology of jewels not dissimilar to the traditional one. The biggest difference is that Simmel assumes no inevitable jump from the social to the natural or the universal; if this latter dimension continues to exist, it is only as a ghost of its former self. Jewels project not occult but social magic, creating a space for the ego to flourish and (by the same token) linking the possessor of a jewel with other people [Simmel, 338–44].

Like many other nineteenth century novelists, Dickens is sensitive to the social function of jewels and other ornaments. Occasionally he ventures further and hints at their latent cosmic significance. Previous to *Edwin Drood,* there are strict limits to what he allows himself to do with this theme. The most instructive example comes from *Bleak House,* whose fashionable world is "wrapped up in too much jeweller's cotton and fine wool, and cannot hear the rushing of the larger worlds, and cannot see them as they circle round the sun" [*BH,* 2, 8]. A world of this kind is itself nothing more than an ornament, with Lady Dedlock the cold, flashing stone—the lifeless sun—at its center. Jewelry thus evoked suggests the workings of a self-absorbed clique that is not so important as its members suppose.

Most members of the fashionable world will never learn any better—but what about the rest of us? In one key episode, Dickens shows that the affinity between jewels and stars can be used to a different effect. Recalling her bout with smallpox, Esther Summerson describes "a flaming necklace, or ring, or starry circle of some kind, of which *I* was one of the beads!" [*BH,* 35, 489]. The ring or necklace *flames* because Esther is afflicted by the pustules of smallpox, a crisis that parallels Krook's spontaneous combustion (see chapter 8, above). Two incriminating documents, Esther's face and a packet of love letters, seem to be destroyed in these conflagrations—yet, by the end of the novel, it appears that both have survived. Some documents burn like stars and survive their burning with a kind of clarified brightness, twinkling and wavering but persisting through the dark. The starlike jewel or the jewellike star is an image of writing, transcribed human experience, changed by suffering into a hard, shining, and apparently indestructible surface. The transience of socially defined jewels gives way to the durability of cosmic jewels.

These compacted associations go by—dare I say it?—in a flash. They are, after all, part of a dream only. And their significance is in some ways obscure: from her sojourn in "great black space," Esther learns that she does not transcend society, that she is affected by its corruption whether she will or no. She cannot escape by straightening up the house. While the signals are unclear even in *Drood,* Dickens is bolder here than before. A *kosmos* becomes cosmic. The jewel in question does not possess magical powers (as it might, for example, in a Christmas fable or a fairy tale), but it functions *as though* it had them. There are precedents for a social novelist structuring a story around such an object, the nearest example being Wilkie Collins's *Moonstone.* But no influence of this kind explains what Dickens is attempting. I think that he is willing to risk a sustained regression into something like magic for the simple reason that he feels it will get him what he wants. He has concentrated his narrative powers on Cloisterham; escape from the urban obsession seems near but remains blocked unless a bit of magic can be used. The jewel is the last necessary touch, not powerful enough in itself to open a true escape from the city but powerful enough when combined with other elements: just those elements established so carefully by the early scene-setting efforts of *Edwin Drood.*

The chapters where the ring's power is first defined are 11 and 13. In chapter 11 comes a London prelude: a dinner between Edwin and Mr. Grewgious, the lawyer-guardian of Edwin's wife-to-be. Edwin and Rosa Bud will wed by the wish of now-deceased parents; Grewgious is the overseer of this arrangement. It is his duty to ascertain whether the marriage would be a satisfactory one. From "a little secret drawer" in his "bureau or escritoire" he produces the ring, then embarks on an impassioned description of it. "This rose of diamonds and rubies delicately set in gold" belonged to Rosa's mother, who drowned many years before. "See how bright these stones shine! . . . And yet the eyes that were so much brighter . . . have been ashes among ashes, and dust among dust, some years! . . . I might imagine that the lasting beauty of these stones was almost cruel" [*ED*, 11, 124]. Before Edwin leaves with the ring, Grewgious charges him to think about what he is doing before doing it. He should not marry Rosa merely because he has "long been accustomed to look forward to" this event; his placing the ring on her finger "will be the solemn seal upon your strict fidelity to the living and the dead." Grewgious implores him, should he have second thoughts, "by the living and by the dead, to bring that ring back to me" [11, 125]. And Dickens has the old lawyer, a few lines down, wonder whether the ring *will* return.

Grewgious's comments and actions contain in germ most of the crucial facts about the ring. It belonged to a beautiful woman, whose eyes outshone it. It is thus identified with eyes, but in a qualified and reluctant way. The ring's power is not really its brilliance but its capacity for signification. Taken from its owner's hand and hidden away, it gains rather than loses power. When it finally emerges from Mr. Grewgious's escritoire—which is to say, his writing desk—it has come to embody not so much the brilliance of a momentary impression as the weight of a memory long considered. The ring is a "solemn seal," the mark of a contracted agreement. It is not literally a signet ring but according to Mr. Grewgious it functions like one. It will be associated with the paper that Dickensian lawyers hoard or hold in trust, as much as with items of display. It will prepare John Jasper's journey underground, to a deathly, totalizing world where a cosmic (natural) document can be appropriately deciphered.

After the prelude of chapter 11, chapter 13 provides an illustration of the ring's ultimate power. "But for the ring," Edwin would have married Rosa; once put "on his truth to the living and the dead," he finds his "way of action" "narrowed." He has to "consider," instead of plunging ahead [*ED*, 13, 145]. By mutual assent he and Rosa break their engagement. Edwin cannot fully credit "those sorrowful jewels" with what they have done for him, but he grasps their similarity to "old letters or old vows" (i.e., he knows that they mean as well as sparkle) [13, 151]. And at one moment he starts to grasp what this bejeweled writing might accomplish. Walking outside the city, Edwin and Rosa agree to cancel their engagement. He ponders whether to show her the ring; he decides that the gesture would be pointless, then finds this suppressed subject of the conversation conditioning their panoramic grasp of the scene that now encircles them: "The bright frosty day declined as they walked and spoke together. The sun dipped in the river far behind them, and the old city lay red before them, as their walk drew to a close. The moaning water cast its seaweed duskily at their feet, when they turned to leave its margin; and the rooks hovered above them with hoarse cries, darker splashes in the darkening air" [13, 152]. Because Edwin and Rosa have been true to it, the ring need not be mentioned. Their "truth to the living and the dead" both parts them and draws them together. Dickens's phrasing is noteworthy. Cloisterham lies "red before them," this faintest of Miltonic echoes recalling a couple more painfully disillusioned. Unlike Adam and Eve, Edwin and

Rosa are not stuck with one another in guilty, permanent complicity. All the same, they have learned more than they expected to; truth can be almost as wearing as falsehood. In this sense the two of them have come to share a good deal. Their mutual—collaborative—relation with the landscape becomes suddenly intimate, as though every movement they made found its response elsewhere. They turn, and in a superb ornamental sentence (the nearest Dickens ever came to Tennyson's great style), the world shimmers with them on the verge of darkness. It is wonderful that the *darker* rooks should enter the mind and the sentence before the *darkening* air that serves as a comparative standard: the dusk has come before anyone realizes its presence.[21] The picture of brightness disappearing has something of the memento mori about it: along with consciousness of mortality, it yields awareness of the world. The small shift toward the city—with the panorama a single, fortunate glance—and the small shift back to elemental things contribute equally.

The ring pushes Edwin to a negative decision; he declines an irrevocable step. Moreover, he resolves his dilemma quickly. He discovers in his perambulation away from Cloisterham and back to it that sometimes one can best honor ancestors by declining their dearest wishes: on these terms he and Rosa have their single, fading glimpse of the city, of the living and the dead subsisting together in a glow that is almost darkness and that combines the red of the sun with the red of Cloisterham rooftops and by implication the red of the ruby ring. Edwin discovers that moment which Dickens has so often sought, where mortal arrangements (here a city and an engagement) crumble gently, thereby revealing a larger order than the human one. His uncle, on the other hand, has only started to grasp how life and death might link up and what their meeting might produce. Jasper goes to London, smokes opium, and dreams repeatedly of Edwin's murder; he returns home, chafes at the narrowness of his "niche," and makes spasmodic preparations whose significance he himself (in *one* of his "phases") must hardly understand.[22] Whereas Edwin's story is finished— finished, indeed, whether he is murdered or not—Jasper's remains a question mark. His involvement with the ring—on which this book will turn—is yet to come.[23]

The True Secret of Mixing

Jasper's name suggests an intricate and disturbing connection with jewels. *Jasper* is an opaque variety of crystal; at one point the stone's namesake complains to Canon Crisparkle, "You are always training yourself to be, mind and body, as clear as crystal, and you always are, and never change;

whereas I am a muddy, solitary, moping weed" [*ED, 14, 166*]. His comment makes it likely that Dickens is thinking of a passage in Revelation; as John Beer observes, that vision includes a figure sitting on a throne who "to look upon [was] like a jasper and a sardine stone." Moreover, the New Jerusalem is twice associated with jasper: its light is "even like a jasper stone, clear as crystal" and its wall "was of jasper: and the city was pure gold, like unto clear glass" [Rev. iv, 3; xxi, 11 and 18].[24] A comparison suggests itself. The Jasper of Cloisterham should be clear (like the sparkling canon), but remains a mystery to everybody. When Jasper finally bursts into apocalyptic light, the results may horrify even him. Jasper repeatedly dreams himself a sultan who goes to his palace with scimitars flashing sunlight (a malign splendor unveiled, concealed no longer). By the sultan's orders Turkish robbers are impaled on spikes, and behind the spikes—behind one particular figure who writhes in agony—rises the tower of Cloisterham cathedral. This dream predicts how the muddy Jasper may eventually shine, arising (or better, descending) to rule his inverted New Jerusalem. He will glow (as it were) in the dark.

So much for Jasper's state of mind. However, it is not only the wordplay of names and biblical references, or the splendor of oriental fantasy, that determines the direction of the narrative. The ring comes to figure in Jasper's fate as it did in Edwin's. His career as a murderer will be transformed by a crystal more hidden, more obscure than himself—and also capable of fuller revelations. To borrow a phrase from the Princess Puffer (Jasper's opium supplier), the choirmaster does not yet know "the true secret of mixing" [*ED, 22, 263*]. The princess's best mixture is sucked from an ink bottle [1, 2]. So, in effect, will Jasper's be. In his murder of Edwin he learns (I surmise) to read the ring and thereby to pass from an artificial order to an encompassing natural one, a synthesis both illuminating and fatal.

One crucial clue to Jasper's relation with the ring occurs in a passage where he is introduced to Durdles. Mr. Sapsea, the self-important auctioneer of Cloisterham, has commissioned the stonemason to inscribe an elaborate epitaph on his wife's tomb in the churchyard:

> *Mr. Sapsea, with an Author's anxiety to rush into publication, replies that it cannot be out of hand too soon.*
>
> *"You had better let me have the key, then," says Durdles.*
>
> [*ED, 4, 39*]   *"Why, man, it is not to be put inside the monument!" [Durdles avers that he likes to look at his work "all round"; Mr. Sapsea gives him the key to the tomb, which Durdles stores in a pocket—whereupon Jasper exclaims]*

> *"You are undermined with pockets!"*
> *"And I carries weight in 'em too, Mr Jasper. Feel those!" producing*
> *two other large keys.*
> *"Hand me Mr Sapsea's likewise. Surely this is the heaviest of the*
> *three."*

These (and several subsequent lines) imply that Jasper leaps at an opportunity to identify one particular key with one particular monument. In other words, he has already identified the Sapsea tomb as an appropriate resting-place for Edwin's remains. Jasper's nocturnal tour of the cathedral confirms and perhaps enlarges his plans for hiding the corpse. The would-be murderer drugs Durdles so that he can filch Mr. Sapsea's key and make a copy. During that same tour (it seems likely) he transfers some loose quicklime to the Sapsea tomb, perhaps to Mrs. Sapsea's coffin. For the quicklime to consume a body, Durdles has told him, only "a little handy stirring" is necessary [12, 132]. Jasper strangles Edwin, then quietly inters whatever remains of him. He stirs away until nothing is left, having previously removed his nephew's shirt pin and watch. He does not, of course, know about the ring, since Edwin told Rosa nothing of it when his uncle was eavesdropping on them. The ring therefore stays. Edwin has figured among the "golden youth of England" craved by the girls in Miss Twinkleton's seminary. [13, 142] Now gold becomes his distinguishing characteristic.[25] It stands for his absent corpse.

I can—and will—continue a discussion of the plot that Dickens conceived, but not before considering a crucial point: that the ring ends up in the Sapsea tomb and *there* of all places gains its power to change Jasper's life as thoroughly as it changed Edwin's and Rosa's. Why should the ring in the tomb have such potency? If one reads *Edwin Drood* as though it had been written by Agatha Christie, the answer is clear enough: located in this place, the ring is the only substantial evidence concerning the identity of Edwin's murderer.[26] If one reads the novel as though it had been written by Dickens, an additional approach is also required. Here as elsewhere the novelist has done his best to construct a "mystery" that requires all the mental faculties, not just the puzzle-solving ones.

Dickens suggests the tomb's importance in connection with a pair of representative Cloisterham personalities. The first of these is Mr. Sapsea, who begins the novel as a generally acknowledged "credit to Cloisterham" and becomes by chapter 18 "The Worshipful the Mayor," still a credit to a "city which is under his beneficent sway" [*ED*, 4, 31; 18, 211]. The tomb he commissions memorializes Mrs. Sapsea, but only—the planned epitaph suggests—for her single heroic characteristic: boundless admiration of a husband

> Whose Knowledge of the World
> Though somewhat extensive,
> Never brought him acquainted with
> A SPIRIT
> More capable of
> LOOKING UP TO HIM.

Sapsea loves to be flattered on this supposed "knowledge of the world"; when Jasper claims an interest in his "reputation for that knowledge," the auctioneer obligingly explains: he has acquired his grasp of reality by touching, describing, and selling objects from diverse countries (a French clock, an Eskimo spear, and so forth). "A very remarkable way, Mr Sapsea, of acquiring a knowledge of men and things" [4, 33; cf. 12, 129]. The epitaph, then, celebrates a special kind of knowledge, better called knowingness. Mr. Sapsea is the last and perhaps the least pleasant of Dickens's *knowing* characters, capable of getting on in the world and of pretending great understanding—but taking in little of significance. He feels that nothing has changed since he was a child (and Dickens means us to understand that he is ridiculously wrong). He feels, even thinks, that he has invented the cathedral on his own, another ludicrous conviction [18, 213]. Mr. Sapsea is the man who worships tradition because he believes that he embodies it.

The tomb expresses much of this; at the same time, it is connected with a personality different from Sapsea's but just as certainly representing the city. Dickens writes of Durdles that "no man is better known in Cloisterham"; even his dinner is "a Cloisterham institution" [*ED*, 4, 38]. Durdles is "material producer and perpetuator" of the epitaph on the Sapsea tomb [18, 214]. He must have carved other epitaphs as well, for he compares himself to "a poplar Author" "surrounded by his works" [5, 43]. Like Sapsea, he is famed as the possessor of extensive knowledge, if not of the world than of the cathedral and its crypt. Jasper (flattering again) pays tribute to "the remarkable accuracy with which [Durdles] would seem to find out where people are buried" [5, 46]. He exercises this skill through a power that the novel elsewhere associates with bells: he works through vibrations, which tell him what lies behind walls and under floors. His knowledge is not of surfaces, then; he "comes by *his* knowledge through grubbing deep for it"—and long too, as his frequent "Tombatism" (a Durdlism coined from "rheumatism") indicates [5, 47; 4, 38]. The peculiar quality of Durdles's knowledge is indicated by an anecdote that the stone-mason tells. Speaking of himself in the third person ("perhaps . . . a little misty as to his own identity," in contrast to egoistic Sapsea), he describes how " 'Durdles came upon the old chap,' in reference to a buried magnate of ancient time and high degree, 'by striking right into the coffin with his pick. . . . And then he turned to powder' " [4, 37]. *Notre-Dame's* last chapter contains a similar incident—but there it is the grotesque who turns to powder, despite his previous harmony with the cathedral, whereas here he confronts along with us the dilemma of a spectacle simultaneously uncovered and destroyed. Durdles is a Quasimodo who has learned to cope with the burden of underground revelations: what Hugo would call reverie or knowledge by digging.

The ring accomplished much for Edwin just by staying in his pocket while he took a walk with his girlfriend. It mediated such difficult categories as death, nature, and the city. Located in the Sapsea tomb its capacity for mediation grows. Here—on a site where different kinds of knowledge make their claims, where reactionary Cloisterham and earthy Cloisterham meet, where mixing is a principle of being—the ring itself creates a form of understanding. It suggests more Durdles's than Sapsea's view of the world but coincides with neither. The ring works through writing, through death, and ultimately through a moment when human plottings dissipate into a natural order. This delicate conjunction of forces helped direct Edwin's stroll with Rosa; it will start to reshape Jasper's life when he holds the clue to the mystery in his hand. (See Dickens's cue for this denouement at 16, 188.) The crucial scene when the ring arrives there does not exist; despite the best endeavours of many enterprising scribes, no one has succeeded in composing it for Dickens. One can consider the portions of text evidently designed to prepare it. Mr. Sapsea (see above) assures Durdles that no inscription is to go inside the monument. Dickens thus implies that sooner or later an inscription will be discovered in that location and will record when it is found a great deal more than Mr. Sapsea's magnificence.[27] Another passage suggests the same twist. After Edwin's murder, Mr. Grewgious stares at the stars "as if he would have read in them something that was hidden from him" [*ED,* 17, 205]. The alphabet of the sky is not yet known, Dickens avers. By implication the ring is a star that could be read, if only the appropriate reader knew where to find it. Will its alphabet prove to be human or natural? It hardly makes sense any more to speak of these alternatives; the ring fills the gap that opened up in *Bleak House* between Lady Dedlock's necklace and the astronomical necklace on which Esther found herself strung. In other words, it embodies knowledge materially, but cannot be engulfed by either society or nature: by those social conventions that Jasper above all hates (e.g., Mr. Sapsea and his epitaph) or those forces of natural decay that encircle Cloisterham (e.g., Durdles and his exploits in the crypt). The ring is not a mere bauble, but neither is it one of those "jewels, cast upon the pavement of the nave from stained glass" that decline and perish with the setting sun [9, 93]. It is composed of diamonds and rubies—as Gaston Bachelard says, "les pierres les plus objectivement sûres de leurs qualités" (stones that are the most objectively certain of their attributes)—and precisely because of this objectivity it prompts imagination all the more, it takes up its real existence in the mind or on the page. (Cf. Bachelard on "La Rêverie cristalline": "L'image de la pierre précieuse *s'écrit*": the image of the precious stone *writes itself.*)[28] An object of this kind becomes substance and idea alike, a Platonic form stirred in with human institutions or quicklime and surviving both handily. For Jasper even more than for Edwin, the ring so understood will persist in recording the truth, even if it is a truth from which he recoils.[29]

In discussions of *Edwin Drood,* there often arrives a stage when the critic forgets that the novel is unfinished and plunges ahead regardless. " 'I like,' says Mr. Datchery, 'the old tavern way of keeping scores. Illegible except to the scorer. The scorer not committed' " [*ED*, 23, 276]. The scorer remains uncommitted and will forever, but one last link to his stated plans remains for consideration. Sometime after Jasper recovered the ring, he would have confessed the murder of Edwin Drood.[30] These two events, I propose, would have stood to one another as cause and effect. Jasper denies that he has any aspirations toward authorship: in this respect as in others he stands apart from Sapsea and Durdles, those other connoisseurs of Mrs. Sapsea's tomb [12, 128]. Author or no, he would at least have become a reader—would have scrutinized the inscription inside the tomb as he had the inscription outside. And his scrutiny would have had drastic consequences. The ring would have compelled him to admit a crime that he had previously blocked from consciousness. "When the wicked man turneth away from his wickedness that he hath committed and doeth that which is lawful and right, he shall save his soul alive."[31] Jasper has tried to turn away from wickedness by splitting his personality: the ring has revealed the futility of the split. Holding the ring in his hand, Jasper would have realized that he could turn away from wickedness only by acknowledging it as part of himself.

When the ring catches Jasper out, it supports a perennial hope: that somewhere *within* the human-made world a natural one persists, and with it a law that is given instead of made. It is too late for Jasper to avoid an irrevocable mistake, as Edwin did earlier; it is not too late for him to feel remorse before his suicide or execution. And with the painful, necessary healing of his consciousness will come another reconciliation—between London and Cloisterham. Jasper has strained to keep these cities apart, almost as though they *were* the two sides of his mind; the novel itself has conspired to postpone any synthesis between them. Ultimately their imaginative union is necessary. My sense that Dickens craves this conclusion is strengthened by the late chapters of *Drood*, where so many of the good characters flee the cathedral city to gather about Mr. Grewgious in the great metropolis. All of a sudden, in spite of various coy denials, London starts seeming a rather friendly place, more hospitable, in fact, than the ersatz Rochester that has been standing in for it. Perhaps the strange evasions of the novel have started to work the magic that Dickens desires. Perhaps one can come back to London after a sojourn in the provinces and find the metropolis informed by the law of the *kosmos*.

This (hypothetical) resolution suggests a kind of mirror inversion between what the ring accomplishes for Jasper and what it can do for other—more conventional—readers. London is where Jasper has gone to dream when he can stand Cloisterham no longer. Cloisterham is where Dickens and his audience have come to dream, to solve a problem that London blocks. Cloisterham has been a displacement of London; it has permitted a hope of lightening the imaginative burden imposed by the metropolis—but sooner or later the two cities must be acknowledged as one. Writing in a world of death creates a vision of the whole—and keeps insisting on its wholeness, in larger and larger ways. Perhaps what is fatal for Jasper could preserve the rest of us, including Dickens.

Or perhaps it will be necessary to start all over again, to admit the limitations of the human framework and to function within them. The afternoon of his death, Dickens was working at Gadshill, his home (since the mid-fifties) outside Rochester. He composed a beautiful paragraph about Rochester (or Cloisterham) Cathedral in the spring: "Changes of glorious light from moving boughs, songs of birds, scents from gardens, woods, and fields—or, rather, from the one great garden of the whole cultivated island in its yielding time—penetrate the Cathedral, subdue its earthy odour, and preach of the Resurrection and the Life." No more bountiful interpenetration of nature and art is imaginable—and death is not even the necessary passage, the earthy odor is subdued. Here, it might seem, is the sort of reassurance that Dickens needed to return and face the metropolis once more. At dinner, a little while later, the novelist seemed ill. "Suddenly he said he had to go to London at once. Pushing back the crimson-damasked chair in which he had been sitting, he rose, but would have fallen where he stood if Georgina [his daughter] had not hurried around the table to support him. . . . 'On the ground,' he murmured faintly."[32] The earthy odor returns. So does the obsessive need for the city, where there is unfinished business. At the moment of his death Dickens tries to return one last time, and less in a spirit of renewal than of panic: *at once*.

To confront Hugo's octopus is to be absorbed by it, pulled past the glitter of the grotto into the cycle of eating and decaying. To find the ring in Mrs. Sapsea's tomb is a different experience: the ring is that which cannot be absorbed, which persists when everything else is swallowed. Although the ring and the octopus are objects that demand to be read, the readings they provoke are not completely alike, nor are the visions of the whole that they produce. Hugo is much more confident than Dickens about assuming a prophetic role: his monster causes a horrifying, inclusive, and instantaneous vision of the cosmos, whereas the ring transports its reader discreetly to a kind of edge, a precipice from which one can view nature and decay but cling to a last remaining bit of art. It might be concluded that the octopus performs the same function as Mrs. Sapsea's tomb, while the ring's real affinity is with the bejeweled cave where the octopus hides out. In the one novel, after all, the container promises annihilation and the thing contained prevents it; in the other, the container is attractive while the thing contained threatens instant destruction.

An accurate thought, I hope—except that it casts Dickens in the role of optimist and presents Hugo as a sort of cosmic naysayer, far too simple a contrast. In both cases, last-minute reversals are possible. In neither case does affirmation or despair predominate. Perhaps the crucial link between *Drood* and *Travailleurs* has less to do with attitudes adopted or beliefs assumed than it does with a sort of necessary admission. The lonely visionary on his island (Victor Hugo pretending to be Victor Hugo) and the busy man of affairs on his country estate (Charles Dickens failing to be anyone but himself) recognize that the city is where they belong. Human beings live in a world fabricated largely, if not exclusively, by themselves: no matter how deeply it is buried or submerged, a written law cannot be identified purely with nature but points its persistent readers back toward the metropolis—which is to say, toward the problem of the artificial. Commentaries upon the mysteries tradition rather than exemplary members of it, *Travailleurs* and *Drood* enact this realization. They reveal in a new light a moment, central to the novel of urban mysteries, when writing can be identified as an inescapable attribute of city life.

Notes
Bibliography
Index

Notes

Preface

1. Alfred Crowquill [Alfred Henry Forrester], "Outlines of Mysteries," *Bentley's Miscellany* 17 (1845): 529. This essay was followed by others titled "Glimpses of Mysteries"; see especially "Glimpses and Mysteries," *Bentley's Miscellany* 17 (1845): 632, and *Bentley's Miscellany* 18 (1845): 91. Cf. "Real Mysteries of Paris and London," *AYR* 4 (27 October 1860): 69–72, and "Mysteries of London," *Punch*, 19 June 1880: 282.
2. Richard R. Wohl and Anselm L. Strauss, "Symbolic Representation and the Urban Milieu," 531. This article begins with a quotation from Robert Park's *The City* (1925), which makes the claim that a city is "a state of mind." Wohl continues: "Not only does the city dweller develop a sentiment of place gradually, but it is extremely difficult for him even to visualize the physical organization of his city, and, even more, to make sense of its cross currents of activity. Apparently an invariable characteristic of city life is that certain stylized and symbolic means must be resorted to in order to 'see' the city." Wohl and Strauss quote extensively from nineteenth- and twentieth-century journalism, where such figures as the panorama flourish.

Chapter 1. "Allegory and City Life"

1. William Hazlitt wrote of "that *knowing* character which [the Cockney] so much affects"—which he is bound to affect, living "in a go-cart of local prejudices and positive illusions." See "On Londoners and Country People," in *Complete Works*, 12: 71, 69. *SB* is stocked with knowing types; the most sympathetically treated is Mr. Bung of "The Broker's Narrative." Among later characters whom Dickens describes as knowing are Jobling the doctor [*MC*, 27, 438], Tulkinghorn the lawyer [*BH*, 41, 574], and that lovely couple the Lammles [*OMF*, 3.12, 557], all attempting to dominate society or rise in it through a certain manipulative skill. In chap. 2 of *The Ravenswing*, "Who in London did not know little Tom Dale? . . . He was everywhere at once. Everybody met him every day, and he knew everything that everybody ever did. . . . he knew what you had for dinner the day before he met you, and what everybody had for dinner for a century back almost. That is, he never knew anything really" [William Makepeace Thackeray, *The Ravenswing*, in *Complete Works*, 4: 216]. In chap. 1 of *The Idiot*, Lebedyev makes his debut. "Such omniscient gentlemen are to be found pretty often in a certain stratum of society. . . . the words "they know everything' must be taken in a rather limited sense" [Dostoyevsky, *The Idiot*, 6]. A good example of a *knowing*

novelist might be Theodore Hook in a book like *Maxwell*—or Dickens himself in some of his lesser moments.

2. Isaiah Berlin has studied the history of the idea that a maker is in a privileged position to know the thing he has made. See his *Vico and Herder*, 13 ff. A countercase is enunciated by several crucial modern thinkers. Marx's ideas about commodities and alienation are pertinent here; so are Georg Simmel's studies of urban life.

3. The novel of urban mysteries is seldom studied *as such*, but a few recent critical and historical studies work in this direction: see Donald Fanger, *Dostoyevsky and Romantic Realism;* Louis Chevalier, *Laboring Classes and Dangerous Classes in Paris during the First Half of the Nineteenth Century;* Alan Trachtenberg, "Experiments in Another Country"; Leslie Fiedler's Introduction to George Lippard, *The Monks of Monk Hall;* Christopher Prendergast, *Balzac: Fiction and Melodrama;* and Peter Brooks, "The Mark of the Beast," in his *Reading for the Plot,* where links between the mysteries novel and the sensation novel of which Wilkie Collins was master are discussed. My own essay "City Life and the Novel" attempts a brief genealogy of the genre.

4. A note concerning usage: the "he" of this paragraph is literally male; to the best of my knowledge, there are *no* female novelists in the mysteries tradition (female protagonists are another matter: Esther Summerson will provide a case of special interest; so—more distantly—will Scheherezade). However, I do not imply that female novelists contemporary with Dickens and the others were uninterested in dilemmas of knowledge; George Eliot's achievement, though directed largely to rural life, in some ways parallels the novel of urban mysteries. (On Eliot and modern structures of knowledge, see chap. 12, n. 3.)

5. The definition of *figure* ("predisposes us," etc.) is quoted from Aldo Scaglione, "Rhetorical Factors as Clues to Meaning," 352. Further analysis might distinguish between figures of thought and of language, but for my purposes this division is unnecessary. The importance of inspiration in allegory is underscored by Michael Murrin in *The Veil of Allegory,* 71–73. Mark Caldwell studies "incessant, cumulative transformation" in "Allegory: The Renaissance Mode," 597 ff. In *The Language of Allegory,* Maureen Quilligan develops a related point at much greater length: she emphasizes the "horizontal," accretive action of allegory, the attempt to unfold the meaning of figures sequentially, rather than the "vertical," one-on-one correspondences of meaning. My comments on language and divine wisdom rely on Michel Foucault, *The Order of Things,* 58, 56. Edgar Wind's book is *Pagan Mysteries in the Renaissance;* for "composite gods," see 199 ff. "Absolute and shattering as death" is Murrin's phrase: see *Veil of Allegory,* 53.

6. Angus Fletcher's comment should perhaps be quoted at length. Allegory "allows for instruction, for rationalizing, for categorizing and codifying, for casting spells and expressing unbidden compulsions, for Spenser's "pleasing analysis,' and, since aesthetic pleasure is a virtue also, for romantic storytelling, for satirical complications, and for sheer ornamental display. To conclude, allegories are the natural mirrors of ideology" [*Allegory,* 368].

7. In English literature, a good point of reference for the decline of allegory would be the meeting of Satan, Sin, and Death in book 2 of *Paradise Lost.*

Stephen Fallon, "Milton's Sin and Death," surveys much of the long-standing controversy over this passage; Fallon suggests that "Milton's genius is to have reserved allegory, the reality of whose characters was more than suspect, for . . . non-beings" [342].

8. On the revival of allegory that occurred in the late eighteenth century and the nineteenth century, see Murrin, *Veil of Allegory;* E. S. Shaffer, *"Kubla Khan" and the Fall of Jerusalem;* Theresa Kelley, "Proteus and Romantic Allegory"; and Tobin Siebers, *The Romantic Fantastic.* Alexander Welsh's *The City of Dickens* discusses allegory and city life, especially with reference to Dickens's domestic angels.

9. Paul de Man, "The Rhetoric of Temporality," in his *Blindness and Insight,* 222. This essay is extremely careful to qualify the association between allegory and irony. (Cf. Murrin, *Veil of Allegory,* chap. 3.) Later, de Man is less cautious; for example, his essay on Pascal in *Allegory and Representation,* ed. Stephen Greenblatt, ends by implying aphoristically that allegory is ironic at all times and in all places. Though de Man once promised that "at the far end of this ongoing enterprise [rhetoric], the question of history and of ethics can be seen to reemerge," I cannot believe that his work encouraged such a development [quotation from de Man's Introduction to *Studies in Romanticism,* special issue on "The Rhetoric of Romanticism," 499]. Walter Benjamin's thinking offers a notable contrast: like de Man, Benjamin casts a critical eye on the allegory-symbol distinction formulated by Goethe and others; unlike de Man, he gives a sustained account of a kind of allegory more or less peculiar to the nineteenth century. Compare, for example, Benjamin's description of baroque allegory in *The Origin of German Tragic Drama* with his commentary on Baudelaire's allegories in *Charles Baudelaire.*

10. "Mimesis of death" is quoted from Benjamin, *Charles Baudelaire,* 83. Whether Benjamin's application of this notion to Baudelaire is convincing remains an open question. Michael Jennings, *Dialectical Images,* gives a powerful account of the negative emphases in Benjamin's thought; his argument is disputed by Susan Buck-Morss, *The Dialectics of Seeing.*

11. Cf. Louis Althusser: "Human societies secrete ideology as the very element and atmosphere indispensable to their historical respiration and life" ["Marx and Humanism" in *For Marx,* 232]. If this is true, then ideologies are not going to disappear; all knowledge, however scientific, will be *in part* conditioned by them. As a consequence, there is no point in anticipating the arrival of an uncorrupted or absolute knowledge.

12. Could de Man or Benjamin have conceived such a possibility? The former writes, "The growth of the spirit is a tragic growth, which implies ever-increasing pain and destruction, but it nevertheless is a movement of becoming that marks a kind of progression. The failures are not just an alignment of identical absurdities; each one is enriched by the knowledge of the one that precedes it and the spirit grows by reflecting upon its successive aberrations. At the limit, the total accomplishment of the spirit will also be a total annihilation, but this event . . . remains in the future as long as there remains a language able to express it" ["The Double Aspect of Symbolism," 14]. These finely phrased sentences, evoking a sort of austere Hegelianism, are intended

as a description of Mallarmé; they might also suggest something of the urban allegorist's project, in which negative energies enable a positive creation while postponing the advent of nothingness. On the other hand: urban allegory explicitly defies the idealism as well as the locked-in energies of something like Hegel's *Phenomenology;* it puts much more emphasis on contingency and arbitrariness than would any Hegelian system. (For further thoughts concerning Hegel and the novel of urban mysteries see chap. 9, below, on Hugo and the young Hegelians.) Benjamin's "mandarin optimism" [Jennings, *Dialectical Images,* 37] as well as his concept of criticism as a kind of transforming alchemy [Jennings, *Dialectical Images,* chap. 4; cf. my own chap. 3, below] could also be associated with urban allegory. However, there is once again an important difference. As Benjamin writes in his essay on Karl Kraus, "Work as a supervised task . . . is attended by dirt and detritus, intrudes destructively into matter, is abrasive to what is already achieved, critical toward its conditions. . . . the monster stands among us as the messenger of a more real humanism. . . . He feels solidarity not with the slender pine but with the plane that devours it, not with the precious ore but with the blast furnace that purifies it" [*Reflections,* 272]. The point is that a destructive work can also be constructive; nonetheless, Benjamin's obsession with *purity* (for this is his obsession rather than Kraus's) separates him decisively from the allegories of the mysteries novel—where purity of any sort is out of the question, where the social and aesthetic implications of *mixing* become crucial.

13. Goethe, *Maximen,* nos. 1112 and 1113, quoted in the translation of Hazard Adams, *Philosophy of the Literary Symbolic,* 54–57; I have also drawn upon Adams's accompanying discussion.

14. For a sympathetic treatment of personification, see Morton Bloomfield, "A Grammatical Approach to Personification Allegory." Personification, notes Bloomfield, "is a method of presenting generalized and idealized notions" [170]. Personification is perhaps the clearest example of the antiexperiential "allegory" condemned by Goethe; as such it will figure importantly in succeeding chapters, both on its own merits and as a starting point or provocation leading to related forms of allegory.

15. See Eudo Mason, *Goethe's Faust,* 110–78, for the best discussion of the earth spirit and its place in the plan of *Faust.* Mason works from the traditional distinction between the contemplative and the active life, identifying the earth spirit with the latter.

16. *Antezedentien* is Goethe's word. See Wolfgang Binder, "Goethe's Classical Conception of *Faust,*" in Cyrus Hamlin's edition of Goethe's *Faust,* especially 583. Goethe's "Die Metamorphose Der Pflanzen" (1798) studies transformation in Nature, discerning a "heiliges Rätsel" (holy riddle) and a "geheimes Gesetz" (secret law) behind what seems to be the chaotic profusion of forms [Goethe, *Selected Verse,* p. 147, ll. 6–7]. Goethe was not always so optimistic, but I have chosen to emphasize the side of his thought that bears most directly on his use of allegory. "Der schönste Besitz . . ." is quoted in Harold Jantz's translation (for which, see Jantz's *The Mothers in Faust,* 82); the passage originally appeared in Goethe's 1823 essay "Bedeutende Fordernis durch ein

einziges geistreiches Wort" (Significant advancement through a single sagacious word).

17. *Phantasmagory* appears in Thomas Carlyle's "Goethe's Helena," first published
in the *Foreign Review*, no. 2, in 1828: "*Helena* is not an Allegory, but a Phantasmagory; not a type of one thing, but a vague fluctuating fitful adumbration of
many" [*Critical and Miscellaneous Essays*, 191]. "Durch einander . . ." is quoted
from Goethe's letter to Iken (23 September 1827), where he is commenting
specifically on the *Helena;* the translation is Jantz's [*Mothers*, 82–83]. "Ein
beginnendes Vorbild" is quoted from "Die Metamorphose," p. 148, l. 15.

18. George Henry Lewes's commentary on *Faust II* is in his *Life and Works of
Goethe:* "the kiss of Gretchen is worth a thousand allegories" [565]. Lewes
explicitly challenges Carlyle's more sympathetic account.

19. See A. D. Coleridge's translation of *Goethe's Letters to Zelter*, no. 356, 28 June
1831. (The next letter in this collection, dated a month later, notes Goethe's
pleasure in an elaborate allegorical ornament dispatched by English admirers.)
On Goethe and Hugo, see also Eric Blackall's discussion in *Goethe and the
Novel*, 217–19.

20. Martin Green, *Cities of Light and Sons of the Morning*, 146–47. Green also has
some striking comments on *Faust II* and its equivocal relationship to Weimar
culture [159].

21. "Greatness of Style" is chap. 3 in Ruskin's *Modern Painters*, pt. 4; sincerity is
one of five qualities by which Ruskin characterizes stylistic greatness [*Works of
John Ruskin*, 5: 58–63].

22. Ibid., 60.

23. John Ruskin, "Grotesque Renaissance," from *The Stones of Venice*, vol. 3, in
Works, 11: 180–81.

24. Ibid., 181–86. Jacob's Ladder reappears in "Fiction, Fair and Foul"—where
Ruskin cites "the stories continually told [Walter Scott] of the executions at
Carlisle . . . issuing, he himself scarcely knows how, in the unaccountable
terror that came upon him at the sight of statuary . . . especially Jacob's
Ladder" [*Works*, 34: 280].

25. Ruskin, "Grotesque Renaissance," 172–73.

26. Ruskin, "Fiction, Fair and Foul," 271–81. The public association between
Hugo and the Paris morgue was longstanding: see [Julia Pardoe], "Pilgrimages
in Paris. No. 1. La Morgue," *Fraser's Magazine* 27 (March 1843): 260. For
Dickens on the Paris morgue, see "The Uncommercial Traveller: The Paris
Morgue," *AYR* 9 (16 May 1863), where the narrator finds "that my feet,
straying like my mind, had brought me to Notre-Dame" [276]—and from
there wanders into the nearby morgue, to view the bodies on display.

27. Ruskin, "Fiction, Fair and Foul," 266–67, 271.

28. Ruskin, "Grotesque Renaissance," 180.

29. Ibid., "Grotesque Renaissance," 185; Ruskin, "Fiction, Fair and Foul," 278–
79. Such cityscapes are nothing new; Descartes observes that cities often grow
at random, that they appear more the product of chance than of human will
operating rationally [*Discours de la méthode*, part 2, in *Oeuvres et lettres*, 132–33].
However, not only does Ruskin lack Descartes's faith in "simple reasoning";

he concludes that any form of interpretation will be defeated by sights like this one.

30. Ruskin, "Peace," chap. 12 from *Modern Painters,* pt. 9, in *Works,* 5: 441.

31. "The gods hid" is quoted from Ovid, *Metamorphoses,* bk. 5, l. 326; cf. Eric Auerbach, "Figura," in his *Scenes from the Drama of European Literature,* 22.

32. I should anticipate one likely objection to this line of thought. Much of Hugo's work—especially the long poems—seems to depend on a seerlike, inspired model of literary composition. There are times at which Hugo apparently wills himself back into the old forms of allegory. How does this fact square with the case I am making? First, I don't doubt that Hugo is capable of divine allegory. Looking at *La Légende des siècles* recently, I came across the passage in "Puissance égale bonté" where God and Eblis have a creation contest. God turns a spider into a sun: a perfect example of Goethean image metamorphosis—divinely rather than humanly controlled, at least in the fiction of the poem. It is clear, then, that Hugo's poetry (no less, say, than the work of the American Transcendentalists) works in the old modes. On the other hand: his novels *as distinguished from* his poems use allegory of the new kind; this is the argument advanced by subsequent chapters. On the difference between divine and human allegory in Hugo, see especially the section in chap. 9, below, where I compare *Les Contemplations* and *LM.*

33. Phantasmagorias have a prehistory in romantic literature. The earth spirit of *Faust* was to be produced by a magic lantern; *Nacht,* the scene in which it appears, is imitated by Coleridge: see "The Landing-Place," essay 2, 136–43, in *The Friend,* where he gives an account of Luther's bout with the devil. Here Luther himself becomes a magic lantern, projecting the devil in front of him after his efforts to allegorize an obnoxious biblical passage fail. All this before the word itself was coined. No wonder Goethe and Coleridge picked it up when it did appear—for which, see Neil Flax, "Goethe's *Faust II,*" and Mark Cumming, "Allegory and Phantasmagory in the French Revolution." For the history of phantasmagorias, see Richard Altick, *The Shows of London,* 141–62, 217–19 (citing Carlyle's reference in *The French Revolution* to "loud-gibbering Spectral Realities"). The citation from *Howitt's Journal* appears in Louis James, *Print and the People,* 25. The Hazlitt remark is from "On Londoners and Country People," in *Complete Works,* 12: 68–69. Thomas Pynchon brings up the phantasmagoria (cheek to cheek with "a Eugène Sue melodrama") in *Gravity's Rainbow,* 12–13; he uses it to describe the career of a man who dreams other people's dreams in London during World War II. "La pousée obscure . . . ," a citation from *L'Homme qui rit,* is among many gathered in George Poulet's essay on Hugo in *The Interior Distance,* 153–81. Poulet shows how "Hugolian poetry" begins in a vision of crowds. For epistemological questions see Max Milner, *La Fantasmagorie.* For nineteenth-century ideas of reality as ghostly, see Jonathan Arac, *Commissioned Spirits;* Robert Caserio, "Joseph Conrad, Dickensian Novelist of the Nineteenth Century"; and Terry Castle, "Phantasmagoria." Note also that *phantasmagoria* became a crucial term in Marx and later in the cultural analyses of the Frankfurt School.

34. Dolf Sternberger's *Panorama of the Nineteenth Century* (first published in 1938) offers an early and extraordinary analysis of panoramas, situating them among

other nineteenth-century cultural items (including allegory, evolution, and interior decoration). In *The Shows of London,* Altick recounts at length the history of the London panoramas. Arac, *Commissioned Spirits,* provides the important recent account of panoramas and nineteenth-century fiction.

35. Carlyle, "The Paper Age," vol. 1, bk. 2, in *The French Revolution.*

36. On the book of the world, see Ernst Robert Curtius, "The Book as Symbol," chap. 16 of his *European Literature and the Latin Middle Ages.* Dickens writes of London almshouses as "gaps in the busy life around them, parentheses in the close and blotted texts of the streets." See "The Uncommercial Traveller," [Titbull's Almshouses,] *AYR* 10 (24 October 1863): 206. Henri Lefebvre's comment is quoted from *Everyday Life in the Modern World,* 152 ff., Claude Lévi-Strauss's from *Tristes Tropiques,* 299.

37. The vexed connection between allegory and interpretation is the subject of Gerald Bruns, "The Hermeneutics of Allegory."

38. Louis Aragon, *Le Paysan de Paris,* 18 (my translation); cf. the English version in *Paris Peasant,* which has the dreamer projecting his "absence of mind" [28] toward the sphinxes. Aragon's surrealist promenades through Paris are heavily influenced by the line of urban mysteries; at the same time, this late flaneur is more concerned with remythologizing city life than with achieving a rational understanding of it.

39. The question of "metropolitan readership" will be treated in chapters 3 and 8, below, but a preliminary word might be helpful. Both Dickens and Hugo aimed at a national or even an international audience, but both had a particular fondness for—and sensitivity toward—the readers of their great imperial capitals. On occasion a metropolitan audience could seem the equivalent of a national one. Hugo, especially, tended to equate Paris with France, Parisians with the French. The dithyrambs of *Paris,* his introduction to the *Paris-Guide* published in connection with the Universal Exposition of 1867, press home this point with an eloquence unusual even for him.

40. Charles Taylor offers a suggestive definition of agents in terms of responsibility; see "What is Human Agency?" in his *Human Agency and Language.* The subtlest account of the relation between will and nature is perhaps Benjamin's, in *The Origin of German Tragic Drama.*

41. "Useful knowledge" is the Utilitarian program for promoting practical science and economic liberalism to the end of increased efficiency in production. If here and elsewhere I speak of usable knowledge, it is to suggest that there might be other ways of using knowledge besides those envisioned by Brougham, Mill, etc. On the Useful Knowledge movement, see Richard Altick's *The English Common Reader,* chap. 6.

42. The idea that cities tend to cancel out experience, to substitute for it an abstracted order of information, runs (at the least) from Wordsworth to such philosophers of city life as Georg Simmel and Benjamin. (See Jonathan Arac, "Benjamin and Materialist Historiography," in his *Critical Genealogies,* 177–83.) I am agreeing that this substitution often occurs, but dissenting from the further thought that its consequences are necessarily bad: there may well be ways to live with it and use it positively. Such a claim puts me in direct conflict with a great continental theorist (René Girard has demonstrated the corrup-

tions of mediation in practically all of his works) as well as with a quintessen-
tially British line of Dickensian criticism, initiated by people like Walter
Bagehot but running down to the present day: cf. John Carey's argument, in
Here Comes Dickens, that Boz is remarkable as a man who lives through his
senses but has virtually no mind to speak of. I suggest, on the contrary, that
Dickens is an excellent guide if one wants to learn to think beyond one's
senses.

Chapter 2. *"The Labyrinths of* Notre-Dame*"*

1. On labyrinths, dances, and the founding of Troy in classical and popular
   tradition, see John Heller, "Labyrinth or Troy Town?" C. Kerenyi makes his
   comment in *Dionysos,* 100. "Endlessly repeated meander or spiral line" is also
   quoted from Kerenyi, 92.
2. J. B. Carol gives a helpful general definition of *mediator*: "A mediator is one
   who interposes his good services between two physical or moral persons. . . .
   In most cases, the mission of a mediator is to bring about a reconciliation
   between parties at variance" ["Mary, Blessed Virgin II: Mediatrix of All
   Graces," in *The New Catholic Encyclopedia,* 9: 359]. Classical and Christian
   conceptualizations of the labyrinth, and particularly of the mediating woman
   who helps a traveler through it, are studied in Penelope Reed Doob, *The Idea of
   the Labyrinth from Classical Antiquity through the Middle Ages,* which includes
   informative commentaries on Ariadne in Greek myth, Philosophy (in Boe-
   thius, *The Consolation of Philosophy*), and Beatrice (in Dante, *The Divine
   Comedy*). The history of the doctrine of Mary as mediatrix is given in Jaroslav
   Pelikan's *The Christian Tradition,* especially 3: 160–74. Pelikan notes that "the
   title itself seems to have appeared for the first time in Eastern theology, where
   [Mary] was addressed as 'the mediatrix of law and of grace.'" The term
   mediatrix was widely accepted in the West during the eleventh and twelfth
   centuries as "a means of summarizing what had come to be seen as [Mary's]
   twofold function: she was 'the way by which the Savior came' to mankind . . .
   she was also the one 'through whom we ascend to him who descended
   through her to us'" [Pelikan, 3: 165]. The modern form of this doctrine (with
   emphasis on Mary as co-redemptrix and Mary as essential to salvation) was
   established by St. Alphonsus Liguori, whose *The Glories of Mary* (1786) was,
   for many decades, enormously popular.
3. Robert Nisbet, *Sociology as an Art Form,* 101.
4. *PC* hints at such a twist. For the third age's inclusiveness—its potential ability
   to turn back on history and absorb the others—see a crucial passage in *PC,* 58.
   From the phrase "tenons-nous-en aux faits" onward, Hugo emphasizes the
   power of mixed styles and genres to cut *across* orderly chronological development. "Le drame est la poésie complète" (The drama is poetry complete). On
   the other hand, without *ND* the full meaning of this power would not be
   evident—not to the reader and perhaps not to Hugo himself.
5. I quote from John Dryden's translation of *The Aeneid,* in Dryden, *Works,* 5:
   513–14, ll. 769–80 (Latin phrase and accompanying translation from the Loeb
   Virgil, translated by H. Rushton Fairclough, 1: 485). Virgil draws on the *Iliad*
   (bk. 18, ll. 590–93, comparing the dancing ground incised on Achilles' shield

to the Minoan labyrinth); it is through Homer (whom Hugo claims to have enshrined—like a jewel!—in Sir Walter Scott: see his essay, "Sur Walter Scott, à propos de *Quentin Durward*" [On Walter Scott, with regard to *Quentin Durward*], first published in 1823, republished in *Littérature et philosophie melées,* 1: 37), through Virgil's expansion of Homer, or perhaps through oral tradition that the lore of the labyrinth dance was transmitted to modern Western culture. Postclassical examples of this figure are legion. In *Pagan Mysteries in the Renaissance,* Edgar Wind analyzes an unusually explicit Renaissance instance of the labyrinth as knot dance [206]. See also chap. 37 of *Kenilworth,* one of Hugo's favorites among Scott's novels, where a dance of "mazy evolutions" represents "the conflicts which had taken place among the various nations which had anciently inhabited Britain" [461]; the dance is succeeded by Queen Elizabeth's symbolic reconciliation of these conflicts.

6. Philip West, "The Redundant Labyrinth," 70.
7. Heller, who has worked out the patterns of the drill described in Virgil, notes that it is characterized by "succeeding phases when the same operations will occur in the same order" ["Labyrinth or Troy Town?" 132]. The labyrinth is thus a recursive phenomenon, created by deliberate repetitions of (relatively) simple rules. On labyrinths, recursion, and repetition, see Douglas Hofstadter, *Gödel, Escher, Bach,* especially chap. 5, and Alexander Tzonis and Liane Lefaivre, *Classical Architecture,* which takes up the influence of a rhetorical architecture—"countless redefinitions of the game of interspacing and termination, superimposition and repetition" [287]—on the history of city planning.
8. Gringoire is not utterly disoriented. He recognizes Les Halles, the great food market of Paris; he circles around Les Innocents, that "immense Necropolis . . . which for six centuries swallowed up half the dead of Paris" [Thomas Okey, *The Story of Paris,* 417–18]. He moves, in other words, through a territory defined by familiar architectural landmarks as by the biological functions of eating and death.
9. On argot and Gringoire's initiation, see also Jeffrey Mehlman, *Revolution and Repetition,* 76–77.
10. The Minotaur's original name was Asterion, Star. "In Minoan Crete the star whose early rising was celebrated in connection with honey, wine, and light was Sirius. Here a duality and parallelism may be observed. The star appeared in the sky; the light emerged from a cave. The festival of the light in the cave was a mystery rite" [Kerenyi, *Dionysos,* 117–18]. Presumably Hugo was not familiar with these details; however, there is no doubt that he was fascinated by the cathedral's cultic role. Note especially his citation of Cenalis's comparison between Notre-Dame and the Temple of Diana at Ephesus, *ND,* 3.1, 135.
11. "Paris à vol d'oiseau" is the title of *ND,* 3.2. In "Le Vieux Paris dans *Notre-Dame,*" Max Bach argues that this chapter is based on Hugo's study of two maps. One, dating from the mid-sixteenth century, "est dessiné *à vol d'oiseau*" (is drawn as a bird's-eye view). Bach notes that this phrase refers to the simultaneous use of two cartographical conventions. On the one hand, a "bird's-eye view" map shows us a geometrical diagram of streets; on the other,

it shows us buildings in perspective. He then demonstrates some specific parallels between this work and Hugo's *vol d'oiseau*. I would add that the *vol d'oiseau* technique, as defined by Bach, produces a sense of immediacy combined with comprehensive knowledge—an impression also given in Hugo's description, quite aside from the identifying phrase. The second map from which Hugo (probably) drew dates from the seventeenth century; it was engraved in 1818 by a mediocre antiquary named Mauperché. Mauperché's engraving declares itself to be a reproduction of "Le Plus Ancien Plan de Paris éxécuté en tapisserie" (the oldest map of Paris executed as a tapestry), suggesting one source of Hugo's conceit (see below in text) that a view might be *knitted* together. For a recent discussion of early bird's-eye views of Paris, see Hilary Bullon, *The Paris of Henri IV*, especially figs. 151 and 159, with accompanying commentary.

12. The Ficino quotation is from Rudolph Wittkower, "Hieroglyphics in the Early Renaissance," in his *Allegory and the Migration of Symbols*, 116; see also Wind, *Pagan Mysteries*, 208.

13. In his edition of *ND* [17], Léon Cellier notes the parallel between the 1830 barricades and the assault of the Truands on the cathedral. Perhaps one could go a step further. The Victorian architectural journal *The Builder* observes in its lead article for 15 March 1856: "Between the south side of [Notre-Dame] and the Seine stood the episcopal palace. . . . All that remained of it . . . was sacked and destroyed in 1831." (*The Builder* cites as its source M. Guilhermy's *Itinéraire*, a work I have not been able to consult.) *ND* was first published on 16 March 1831—too early for Hugo to have been inspired by this particular destruction of a monument. On the other hand, the augmented issue of the novel, where "Ceci tuera cela" first appears, was not published until 17 December 1832. In the meantime Hugo would have had ample confirmation of the inverse relation between the circulation of free thought and the respect granted to ancient buildings. He would also have had occasion to observe a practical demonstration of the difference between printed books and unique manuscripts: many of the latter, according to *The Builder*, were ripped apart and thrown into the Seine by the mob that destroyed the palace. The double antithesis by which books are opposed to buildings and printed books to manuscripts reappears throughout *ND* (see especially Hugo's comments on the destruction of the Palace of Justice in 1618: 1.1, 40), but events that occurred between *ND*'s first edition and its second would have made a passage already written seem much more than a variation on Scott.

14. On the sort of labyrinth associated with downward movement, see West, "The Redundant Labyrinth," which links labyrinthine descent with the myth of a hero's visit to the underworld. If the hero can return from this journey, he gains the authority to found a city, state, or empire; coming up out of the earth, it seems, one acquires the authority of the earth and the earthborn [70 ff.]. Frollo's strategy is like a mangled remnant of this large-scale narrative. It suggests an unsuccessful descent, from which no satisfactory return will be possible.

15. Dostoyevsky, quoted in Natalie Brown, *Hugo and Dostoyevsky*, 15.

16. I have followed in part the analysis of George Lakoff and Mark Johnson in *Metaphors We Live By*, chap. 8.
17. Mehlman, *Revolution and Repetition*, 83.
18. Nicholas Perry and Loreto Echeverría, *Under the Heel of Mary*, 85. The argument of *Under the Heel* is that reactionary forms of Christianity in the nineteenth and twentieth centuries have used Mary as a kind of figurehead. In "Devotion and Distortion," his review of *Under the Heel*, Thomas Kselman suggests that "the anti-Marian hostility of the authors leads them to neglect the popular and subversive strains that can also be discerned in Marian apparitions" [Kselman, 867]. Maurice Agulhon's *Marianne into Battle* analyzes the most secular of these "subversive strains"; Agulhon argues that Marianne, the allegorical figure of the Republic, was designed to replace the Virgin [Agulhon, 27, 33, 57; see also 60–61, for Agulhon's comments on Hugo's treatment of the Marianne theme in *LM*].
19. John Ruskin, "Fiction, Fair and Foul," in *Works*, 34: 277.
20. Eva Cantarella works out these connections in learned detail. She concludes that "by hanging themselves (and by being hanged) women reproduced in the city an archaic, pre-city image which—while at this point deprived of its original meaning—remained in the memory of the Greeks. The link between women and the noose, which is so frequent in literature and in iconography, is founded on a quasi-institutional link" ["Dangling Virgins," 65].
21. A phrase of argot familiar from *DJ:* see especially the sixteenth paper, p. 304, where a young girl sings a song about a hanging ("J'li ferai danser une danse / . . . Où il n'y a pas de plancher"; I will make him dance a dance / . . . where there is no floor). *ND*, 9.1, 377, contains a song almost as pointed. Hugo's interest in the lore of hanging as dancing derives partly from Scott—e.g., from *Quentin Durward*, chap. 6, and perhaps from *The Fair Maid of Perth* (first published 1828, translated into French the same year, at a time when Hugo and his friends were reading Scott avidly), where, in chap. 24, the assassin Bonthron dances "a pavise in mid-air to the music of his own shackles" [340]. Such images were to remain with Hugo for life; cf. "Puente de los contrabandistas," a pen-and-ink sketch of 1868, where a smuggler's body hangs by a rope over a convincing Hugolian abyss. Hugo wrote of his work: "I'm sending you this gloomy dance. . . . We must rub the executioners' noses in their own work." See further commentary in Pierre Georgel, *Drawings by Victor Hugo*, no. 71.
22. See Marta Weigle, *Spiders and Spinsters*, especially chap. 1.
23. One adaptation of Quasimodo develops this unsettling analogy with particular point. In *ML* Reynolds treats us to several scenes between the London hangman, Smithers, and his son Gibbet, whom he has transformed into a hunchback by beatings. The hunchback's only joy in life is his beautiful cousin Katherine, for whom he "cherished a profound love [as for] his guardian angel" [2: 143, 20]. Reynolds develops his beauty-beast situation over the course of several chapters.
24. For Quasimodo as Astolfo, the monster as knight, see *ND*, 4.3, 176, where (in a passage already quoted) the hunchback is "une espèce d'Astolphe horrible

emporté sur un prodigieux hippogriffe de bronze vivant" (a sort of horrible Astolfo carried away on a prodigious hippogriff of living bronze). The hippogriff transports Astolfo to the moon; the bells move in ever-repeated arcs. Quasimodo is going nowhere, unless to Montfaucon. *Orlando Furioso,* where Astolfo is a principal character, is (like *ND*) an allegory with a powerfully realistic dimension.

25. I am paraphrasing *WS,* 2.2.5 and *LT,* 2.2.5 (the latter passage is also discussed in chap. 13, below).

26. The quotation is from p. 186 of an unattributed review, "French Romances" [*Fraser's Magazine* 27 (February 1843): 184–94]. The novel under discussion is not *ND* but George Sand's *Spiridion* (1839)—concerning a hero who "has been already dead for more than a century when the story commences." As the reviewer notes, "this Spiridion had, we are told, been in his lifetime a Jew by birth, most learned, devout, and intolerant. He afterwards becomes, by reading Bossuet's works, a Roman Catholic. . . . He builds a monastery, and is himself its abbot. Pursuing his studies, however, he in his heart, abjures Romanism, and embraces the doctrines of the Reformation. But he does not stop here. The Reformation and Christianity itself appear to him but partial, broken bits of truth. . . . He discovers at last the great truth he has so perseveringly sought after. . . . he directs the manuscript on which he has recorded his great *Eureka* to be buried with him, and bequeaths it to the person who, after a century, shall have the anxiety to seek it in his tomb" [186–87]. The fascination with broken and partial truth, the expectation of a great revelation, the association between revelation and exhumation: Sand writes more in the spirit of Hugo than, with her generally skeptical attitude toward him, she might have wished to acknowledge.

27. The phrase is quoted from Victor Brombert's "The Rhetoric of Contemplation: Hugo's 'La Pente de la rêverie,' " 59.

28. Gerald Mast on the ending of *Citizen Kane* (where a similar narrative paradox is used): see his *Film • Cinema • Movie,* 76.

29. In *Laboring Classes and Dangerous Classes in Paris during the First Half of the Nineteenth Century,* Louis Chevalier comes close to suggesting that the lore of Montfaucon is a locus for accounts of the relation between crime and poverty in nineteenth-century France. *ND* (not treated in *Laboring Classes*) would then represent an early, perhaps the earliest, fictional contribution to this discussion. Chevalier's discussion at 210–13 contains the quote from Parent-Duchâtelet used here; "the setting of horror par excellence" is Chevalier's own phrase. For further details on Montfaucon, see Donald Reid's *Paris Sewers and Sewermen.* For a discussion of analogies between sewers and prostitution (i.e., a conspicuously nonvirginal institution), with accompanying comments on Montfaucon, see Charles Bernheimer, *Figures of Ill Repute,* chap. 2, "Parent-Duchâtelet: Engineer of Abjection." I use Reid's translations (72; 203 n. 6) of an eyewitness account by Henri Joseph Gisquet, prefect of police during the 1830s ("totally nude men . . . objects of value") and of Roux's extraordinary polemic. The enthusiastic description of "fat white worms" is borrowed from Eugen Weber, "From Ordure to Order." A postscript: During the Second Empire, Baron Haussmann transformed Montfaucon and the surrounding

area into the Parc des Buttes-Chaumont—a change for the better that did not, however, end this locale's association with urban Gothic frissons: see Louis Aragon's extraordinary evocations and studies of the Suicides' Bridge at Buttes-Chaumont, in part 3 of *Le Paysan de Paris*.

30. Georg Lukács, *The Historical Novel*, 81–85.

31. At least through the eleventh edition of the *Encyclopedia Britannica*, the article on Hugo is by A. C. Swinburne, who describes *ND* as "the greatest of all tragic or historic or romantic poems in the form of prose narrative." Even considering the bias of this particular author, I take his comment as a locus classicus on *ND*'s cultural status during the decades before World War I. Regarding the special uses for the novel listed above: I have examined an undated copy of *The Hunchback of Old St. Paul's;* it is a serial publication bound in this case with two school stories, so must have been conceived—at least by the binder!—as a work for older children. The evidence for *ND* as a source of picturesque scenes lies in such artifacts as the *Edition de Grand Luxe* of Hugo, a limited-edition production that contains 1,724 extravagantly produced plates, each reproduced in four different shadings, covering every aspect of the author's career but reaching a delirious height in Luc Olivier-Merson's scenes from *ND*. (The *Edition de Grand Luxe* was published in Philadelphia, for what must have been a well-heeled American market; the illustrations are reproduced from the formidable *Edition nationale* of Hugo published in Paris in 1885: See fig. 22.) The *Annals of Opera* lists eighteen versions of *ND* (some called *Quasimodo* or *Esmeralda,* one written for Patti) between 1831 and the early twentieth century. The sadistic aspects of *ND* are emphasized by John Ruskin (see chap. 1, above) and perhaps more surprisingly by Robert Louis Stevenson in his *Familiar Studies of Men and Books* ("Victor Hugo's Romances"). A memorable recent commentary on Hugo and sadism is offered in James Ellroy's *film noir*-style detective story *The Black Dahlia*, where a copy of *L'Homme qui rit* is a crucial clue.

32. See Flaubert's *Madame Bovary*, 1.7, 32 and 2.5, 76 ("she accompanied her caresses with lyrical outbursts that would have reminded any one but the Yonvillians of Sachette in 'Notre Dame de Paris.'") Djali, of course, is Esmeralda's goat; Sachette, her mother. A more sustained fictional critique of *ND* is given in Emile Zola's *Le Ventre de Paris* (1873). According to Zola, "Il me faudrait dans l'oeuvre un personnage épisodique, qui fût le Quasimodo de mes Halles" (It would seem necessary for me to have in this work a character who could appear from time to time and be the Quasimodo of my Halles) [quoted in *Ventre,* 1620]. Zola's adaptation is analyzed by Ilianca Zarifopol-Johnston, " 'Ceci tuera cela': The Cathedral in the Marketplace."

33. See the introductory note to *LT*.

34. Sue's admiring letter to Hugo on the occasion of *ND*'s publication is printed in Adèle Hugo, *Victor Hugo raconté par Adèle Hugo,* 486. I have not completely restricted myself to the study of novels influenced by *ND*. In some cases other works, less directly connected with Hugo's historical romance but addressed to the problems it raises, will also be discussed (see especially chap. 12, below).

35. For the attractions of such syntheses, see Lionel Gossman's "History as Decipherment: Romantic Historiography and the Discovery of the Other."

As Gossman writes, "the historical imagination of the nineteenth century was drawn to what was remote, hidden, or inaccessible: to beginnings and ends, the archive, the tomb, the womb." This seems like a perfect description of Montfaucon, archive, tomb, and womb all at once, in which—to quote Gossman once more—the intrepid explorer might expect to discover "hidden mediating links . . . between forces . . . visibly in conflict" [258–59]. From hidden, mediating sources—imaginary or actual, as we may like it—came the yearning for a great romantic vision that would reveal the injustices of the past, yet incorporate them within a harmonious present. A wonderful, if dangerous, program: Hegel, Michelet, and Freud knew its attractions, as did Hugo himself. Montfaucon is not such a place, however close it may come. No one could take the union of Quasimodo and Esmeralda as a whole. There is wholeness here—wholeness of a kind—but we know it, so far as we do, through its collapse, frequently reenacted.

36. Adèle Hugo, *Victor Hugo,* 484. Cf. the title (and action) of *LM,* 5.9.4, "Bouteille d'encre qui ne réussit" (A bottle of ink that only whitens).

37. For a detailed treatment of connections between Montfaucon and writing (among other subjects), the reader should consult Gilbert D. Chaitin, "Victor Hugo and the Hieroglyphic Novel."

Chapter 3. *"Ainsworth's Revelations: Failed Narrative"*

1. "The illusion . . ." is quoted from Noël Carroll, *Mystifying Movies,* 162. Carroll surveys the dispute over narrative with reference to film theory; he argues that the view of narrative as *essentially* conservative is incorrect. Frederic Jameson's *The Political Unconscious* suggests that narrative is "the central function or *instance* of the human mind" [13].

2. The German influence continued, of course—and occasionally seemed to speak from *behind* the French. W. H. Ainsworth's preface to his *Rookwood* summarizes a typical overlay: "Romance, if I am not mistaken, is destined shortly to undergo an important change. Modified by the German and French writers—by Hoffmann, Tieck, Hugo, Dumas, Balzac, and Paul Lecroix (*Le Bibliophile Jacob*)—the structure commenced in our own land by Horace Walpole, Monk Lewis, Mrs. Radcliffe, and Maturin, but left imperfect and inharmonious, requires, now that the rubbish which choked up its approach is removed, only the hand of the skilful architect to its entire renovation and perfection" [*Rookwood,* in Ainsworth, *Collected Works,* xxxviii]. To get a sense of how much Dickens shares with a German tradition that existed well before *ND,* see Kenneth Ireland, "Urban Perspectives."

3. J. W. Croker's *Quarterly* essay [56 (April 1836): 65–131] is quoted in Patricia Thomson, *George Sand and the Victorians,* 14 ff. A later essay in the same mode is "French Romances," quoted and discussed in chap. 2, both text and note 26.

4. Perhaps it is a misnomer to refer to Chartism as a socialist movement; at any rate, there was considerable communication between English and French left-wing groups of the 1830s and 1840s, with literary interchanges often accompanying political ones.

5. Thackeray worked on his translation of *MP* during a brief period in 1844. Because he was not paid, he abandoned the project—though not before

composing a puff that he described as a "remarkable manifesto." As Gordon Ray notes in his edition of Thackeray's *Letters*, the translation was finished by others and issued in weekly illustrated parts by Chapman and Hall (Dickens's publishers also). Thackeray proposed an article on Sue in a letter of 16 July 1845 to Macvey Napier, editor of the *Edinburgh Review*. He noted at this time his distaste for Sue's novels. The Sue essay was eventually published in the *Foreign Quarterly Review;* see R. S. Garnett's edition of Thackeray's *The New Sketch Book*. For pertinent passages from the letters, see Thackeray's *Letters*, 2: 140, 141, 159, 202.

6. On Reynolds's admiration for and use of French literature, see chap. 8, nn. 3 and 4. Victor Brombert's comments on *ND* are pertinent here: Hugo in this novel "only dimly perceived the full thrust of his own ideas" [*Victor Hugo and the Visionary Novel*, 68]. The dependence of Sue and Reynolds on a putatively monarchist work, indeed their admiration for that work, thus makes better sense than we might suppose. Reynolds's dependence on Sue is perhaps more problematic; in retrospect, the French work seems reactionary rather than radical, while Reynolds continues to scare conservatives. See chapters 8, 9, and 11 for further discussion of these points.

7. See Louis James, *Fiction for the Working Man*. James is particularly instructive in his accounts of Dickensian fiction aimed at readers who had not achieved middle-class status. The implication is that Dickens himself was *not* for such readers. Dickens associated with Sue in Paris—for which, see below in this chapter—but (addressing his British readers) emphasized the distance between his tastes and this fellow novelist's work; see *AN*, "From Verona . . . ," where he sets out for Mantua repeating passages from *Romeo and Juliet* while the conductor of his omnibus reads *MP*, as strict a division of taste by class as could be imagined [340].

8. W. H. Ainsworth, *Old Saint Paul's*, bk. 2, chap. 6, in *Collected Works*, 118.

9. The background to this development includes one curious false turn. Several times during the 1830s, Ainsworth had attempted to interest Dickens in collaborating on a project he called "The Lions of London." "The Lions" would have appeared in monthly parts, combining scenes of past and present city life. Dickens stalled, probably refusing the offer outright, but Ainsworth was not discouraged permanently.

10. The original serial version of *Revelations of London* began in *Ainsworth's Magazine* for October 1844. The tale was suspended for several months in 1845 during a dispute between Ainsworth and his publisher; the later chapters were published in the *New Monthly Magazine* between August 1845 and January 1846 under the eventual book title, *Auriol*. First book publication was in 1850. *Auriol's* publishing history is described in John Sutherland's *Stanford Companion to Victorian Fiction*, which includes a separate entry on the novel.

11. Ludwig Goldscheider quotes a letter of Goethe's where he assumes, somewhat cavalierly, that Rembrandt too was trying to envision an earth spirit. Goethe seems to forget that this creature is largely his own invention. A copy of the Rembrandt etching appears as title page to the first edition of *Faust* 1790. See Goldscheider's catalog, *Rembrandt*, commentary on no. 74.

12. Mircea Eliade bases this observation on several sources; e.g., he quotes a

sixteenth-century alchemical treatise, the *Summa Perfectionis:* "what Nature cannot perfect in a vast space of time we can achieve in a short space of time by our art." See Eliade's *History of Religious Ideas,* 3: 257.

13. Among the more telling examples: between the first and second series of *ML,* Reynolds wrote *Faust, a Romance;* Sue followed *MP* with *Le Juif errant;* an incident of "spontaneous combustion" occurs at the center of *BH.* For an extended study of Dickens and the occult (though not of Dickens and alchemy), see Fred Kaplan, *Dickens and Mesmerism.*

14. Walter Benjamin, too, notes an affinity between alchemy and allegory: "It must not be assumed that there is anything accidental about the fact that the allegorical is related in this way to the fragmentary, untidy, and disordered character of magicians' dens or alchemists' laboratories familiar above all to the baroque. Are not the works of Jean Paul, the great allegorist in German literature, just such children's nurseries and haunted rooms?" However, Benjamin puts more emphasis than I do here on the frustrating side of such images, their affinities with a mood of "desolate, sorrowful dispersal." Dickens's kind of relish for such scenes would be foreign to Benjamin's allegorist; even the old curiosity shop, as will be seen in chap. 5, offers possibilities of life and energy, as opposed to penance and violence—if only it can be understood properly, a task that Master Humphrey finally achieves. In other words, not all allegories are self-flagellating. See Benjamin, *The Origin of German Tragic Drama,* 188.

15. Ainsworth's criminals, like Sue's, have colorful nicknames: the Sandman and the Tinker. Also as in the French tradition they become entangled with a dandified young man (Auriol) who is involved in intrigues all over a large city.

16. Ainsworth made small changes between the serial and the book text. The changes made the passage a little less droll in tone than it was originally, suggesting (I think) the author's regard for his devastated London landscape. That the Vauxhall Road area appeared roughly as Ainsworth describes it is confirmed by the testimony of numerous contemporary Londoners, e.g., Thomas Carlyle, equally impressed but less enthusiastic: "I have also walked [from Chelsea] to Westminster Hall by Vauxhall Bridge-end, Millbank, &c.; but the road is squalid, confused, dusty and detestable, and happily *need* not be returned to." The comment is from a letter to John Carlyle, 17 June 1834 (see Carlyle's *Collected Letters,* 6: 215).

17. Percy Fitzgerald, *Memories of Charles Dickens,* 284.

18. Forster, *Life,* 1: 442–54.

19. *Pilgrim Edition,* 5: 15.

20. For which, see Kenneth Hooker, *The Fortunes of Victor Hugo in England,* 32–33.

21. For "of all the literary men," see *Pilgrim Edition,* 5: 42. Dickens adds, "If you would like to hear the French language spoken in its purity, you'd better come to London and enquire for me." The letter of four years later appears in *Pilgrim Edition,* 6: 434. Speculation about Hugo's feeling for Dickens proceeds on less certain ground, but Kathryn Grossman, " 'Angleterre et France melées,' " suggests some fruitful lines of inquiry.

22. Not many people have made extended comparisons between Hugo and Dickens, but see comments scattered through Mario Praz, *The Hero in Eclipse in Victorian Fiction.*

23. Barrett's comments can be found in *Elizabeth Barrett to Miss Mitford*, 147; cf. E. A. Poe's comparison of *Barnaby Rudge* (a novel I do not discuss here) with *ND*, in *Graham's Magazine*, 1842, reprinted in Collins, 110.

Chapter 4. *"Knotting the Maze in* Oliver Twist*"*

1. According to the Vicar of Wakefield, those who exercise power should not "draw hard the cords of society" [Oliver Goldsmith, *The Vicar of Wakefield*, chap. 27, p. 163]. On the Atuot and "phenomena which bind," see John Burton, "Figurative Language and the Definition of Experience: The Role of Ox-songs in Atuot Social Theory," *Anthropological Linguistics* 24 (Fall 1982): 263–79.

2. John Bayley, *"Oliver Twist,"* in John Gross and Gabriel Pearson, *Dickens and the Twentieth Century*, 57, and Stephen Marcus, *Dickens from Pickwick to Dombey*, 63–65.

3. Dickens, "The Uncommercial Traveller: A Visit to a Dockyard," *AYR* 10 (29 August 1863): 16. This Gothicized version of industrial process frightened others also. Cf. the unattributed "A Physician's Dreams," *AYR* 2 (26 November 1859): "Often, as a boy, I have felt myself toiling on through some palpable obscure, through the whole of which, infinite spiders' webs and infinite threads from infinite looms were endlessly weaving about me—no, not *me*, but about some other identity into which I was half converted" [112].

4. Twist = verb, to hang; hence "twisted" = hanged, as in "he was twisted for a crack." See John Farmer and W. E. Henley, *Slang and Its Analogues*.

5. The term *dreadful enclosure* is used by E. V. Walter in "Dreadful Enclosures." Walter notes that "despite their intentions to demystify and demythologize social life, social scientists generate stereotypes that fashion urban myths and make the lives of the poor more difficult." In this connection: Might the nineteenth-century distinction between the deserving and the undeserving poor illuminate current studies of the "underclass"? *Underclass* may be a new term, but its filiations with Victorian lore seem to me significant. Cf. the prose of Peter Collier and David Horowitz in "Slouching towards Berkeley," 67: "To visit People's Park now is to see the radical dream revealed for what it is: a place ruled by the desperate and the derelict—not just the beaten and disoriented homeless, but an underclass of predators who appear especially after nightfall." For a firsthand account of life in a dreadful enclosure, see Raphael Samuel, *East End Underworld*, and Peter Keating's review of this volume. Arthur Harding observed to Samuel that "Oliver Twist could never have existed because he wasn't able to help himself." But Oliver Twist is not the whole book. Dickens has contributed more than the sociologists to the process of demystification that Walter advocates—a point I hope to demonstrate.

6. On hanging and handkerchiefs, see also Dianne Sadoff, "Locus Suspectus." Here the (Lacanian) emphasis is on anxious father-son relationships and the threatening phallic mother. Sadoff is particularly interesting at 222, where she discusses Fagin's trial and his perception of the court artist who is sketching him.

7. On the interplay between word and image in Blake, see W. J. T. Mitchell, *Blake's Composite Art*. Goya's illustrated books are treated by Ronald Paulson

in *Representations of Revolution.* Bewick is discussed by Charles Rosen and Henri Zerner in *Romanticism and Realism.* On the illustrated novels of the Victorian era, two modern volumes are particularly useful: John Harvey, *Victorian Novelists and Their Illustrators,* and Jane Cohen, *Charles Dickens and His Original Illustrators.* An important landmark for the understanding of Cruikshank's status as artist and illustrator is Robert Patten's essay collection, *George Cruikshank: A Revaluation.* Also instructive is J. Hillis Miller, *"Sketches by Boz."* Many of the works just cited comment on allegory as a mode that includes both visual and verbal elements and that, in the interplay between these elements, defines an area of comprehension belonging neither to literal nor to figurative understanding as they are normally conceived. This kind of effect goes back (at least) to the emblem books of the seventeenth century; I believe that it has also thrived in the last two hundred years, in some of our great illustrated books. On the subject of figures in this special sense (but without reference to the illustrated books), Ann Kibbey's *The Interpretation of Material Shapes* offers a suggestive etymological perspective: Kibbey notes that "in its earliest usage *figura* meant a dynamic material shape, and often a living corporeal shape such as the figure of a face or a human body"; she goes on to offer the twentieth-century example of the mobile, in which "the motion of material shapes continually reconstitutes different figures (or *figurae*) without ever producing a shape that one would distinguish from the others as distinctly literal in opposition to figurative" [3]. Among figures of this kind, the labyrinth is perhaps the most prominent. On "the problem of how such an eminently visual sign can be realized in the medium of language at all," see Werner Senn, "The Labyrinth Image in Verbal Art," 219.

8. Cf. the analysis of Michal Ginsburg in "Truth and Persuasion," especially 229, where Oliver's understanding of Fagin's game is described. To simplify, Ginsburg's interest is in middle-class (context-free) language versus lower-class (context-bound) language. I would add to this account that the trickiness of the scene emerges from an unpredictable shifting back and forth *among* contexts.

9. Umberto Eco, "The Myth of Superman," 121, and "Rhetoric and Ideology in Sue's *Les Mystères de Paris,*" 130–40, in *The Role of the Reader.*

10. For further stages in the labyrinthine collaboration of Dickens and Cruikshank, see chap. 22 and accompanying plate (*The Burglary*) as well as chap. 38 and accompanying plate (*The Evidence destroyed,* with its implied equation between hanging and suppression of knowledge: a lantern hangs from a knotted rope, above an open trapdoor, into which Monks casts an incriminating document—he "drew the little packet from his breast, where he had hurriedly thrust it; and tying it to a leaden weight, which had formed a part of some pulley, and was lying on the floor, dropped it," *OT,* 38, 285).

11. Most persuasively, Bayley, *"Oliver Twist,"* in Gross and Pearson, *Dickens and the Twentieth Century,* 51. *"Oliver Twist* is not a satisfying novel—it does not liberate us." But at least one important kind of liberation does occur in the novel, ours from the figure of the maze or the dreadful enclosure.

12. This is a not infrequent complaint. Cf. the *Dublin Literary Gazette,* 8 May 1830, 289: "We well remember of what a singularly fanciful and erroneous

character were all the notions (notions which we mistook for knowledge) that we entertained of London, before the fatiguing reality of the mighty city was known to us. . . . the very name of Downing-street, brought with it recollections of treaties and dispatches . . . insomuch that the *res ipsa,* the passage bounded by certain edifices of brick mortar, scarcely ever occurred to our thoughts."

13. The handkerchief reappears in the next chapter. Struck by Sikes, Nancy "staggered and fell . . . [and] raising herself, with difficulty, on her knees drew from her bosom a white handkerchief—Rose Maylie's own" [*OT,* 47, 362]. The novel's last transfer of a handkerchief from rich to poor is tendentious but expressive. It opposes that previous moment when the Dodger lifted a handkerchief from Mr. Brownlow, setting in motion the ultimate revelation of Oliver's identity. By revealing Monk's whereabouts (the crime for which she must die), Nancy completes the process that Dodger began; she also initiates a further sequence of events, in which relations between rich and poor will be examined more broadly.

14. J. Saunders, "Bermondsey," in *London,* edited by Charles Knight, 3: 3.

15. The quote is from the issue of 1 April 1890 (a date that gives pause for thought) of the *South London Chronicle.* This clipping is from an extraordinary scrap-book—the "Chronicles of Bermondsey," compiled by Canon Frank Allingham—kept in the Southwark Local Studies Library. In one section of the "Chronicles," a range of late nineteenth-century and early twentieth-century clippings from local newspapers chronicles the gradual disappearance of Dickens's Jacob's Island. After the publication of *OT,* the island was identified with Dickens—but in several fundamentally different ways. A wall poster of 1846, addressed "To The Inhabitants of Dockhead," invites people to a celebration of the repeal of the Corn Laws "on that highly interesting Spot, described by Charles Dickens." The site of crime has become a site of radical activity: *les misérables* live! A clipping from the 1920s (newspaper unidentified) notes of the area that "the only visitors it receives from the outer world are the Dickensians . . . it is hardly the sort of place that even the most enthusiastic Dickensian would desire to be kept in being." The interest here seems bookish rather than political. The end for "Bill Sikes's house" came in 1934 (*Daily Mirror:* "LAIR IS DOOMED / TWO HOUSES WITH A HISTORY / LONDON TO LOSE LINK WITH DICKENS / DEMOLITION"). So far as I can determine, the site of the house where Sikes supposedly hung himself is now occupied by London Council housing—with buildings named after various Dickens characters, not including Bill Sikes. On Jacob's Island in the Victorian mythology of the city, see also Anne Humpherys, *Travels into the Poor Man's Country,* 191–92, contrasting Henry Mayhew's description of the island with that in *OT.*

16. See, for example, Dickens's own letters on capital punishment, the *Daily News,* 9, 13, and 16 March 1846.

17. For the conflict between artist and novelist in the later stages of the work, see especially Cohen, *Charles Dickens,* 21.

18. In "Bull's-eye's 'Eyes,'" Sarah Solberg argues that Bull's-eye should not be visible on the roof, since we are likely to take him as a stand-in for the avenging

ghost, thus suppose it is he, not Nancy, who makes Sikes fall. Cruikshank is
therefore an insensitive and willful interpreter of Dickens's text. I disagree.
Collaboration of the best kind (as well as the worst) depends on differences as
well as similarities. Cruikshank brings the dog into view, whereas Dickens
has him crouch down—but both are interested in the dynamics of a self-
destructing social system. Loyalty no longer holds the gang together. Loyalty
in this peculiar world might just as well split it up . . . and that is Cruikshank's
point.

19. See Larry Andrews, "Dostoevskij and Hugo's *Le Dernier Jour*." Dickens's "A
    Visit to Newgate," from *SB*, had been compared to *DJ* by his future father-in-
    law, George Hogarth. Keith Hollingsworth suggests that Hogarth's comment
    may have sent Dickens to Hugo and thus influenced the depiction of Fagin's
    last days. See Hollingsworth's *The Newgate Novel*, 117–18.

Chapter 5. "Creating the Crowd in The Old Curiosity Shop"

1. William Howitt's comment is from the *People's Journal*, 3 June 1846 [Collins,
   206]; the praise of *Pickwick* is from the *Literary Gazette*, 24 November 1838
   [Collins, 79]; the American illustration is reproduced on the back cover of
   Hartford Studies in Literature 8 (1976); Robert William Buss's *Dickens's Dream* is
   reproduced on the cover of Angus Wilson, *The World of Charles Dickens*, and in
   Luke Fildes's *The Empty Chair* on 297; "a genius rich" is quoted from R. H.
   Hutton's obituary in the *Spectator*, 18 June 1870 [Collins, 519]; the quotation
   from the *Sunday Times* is for 12 June 1870 [Collins, 512].
2. See Erwin Panofsky, *The Life and Art of Albrecht Dürer*, 156 ff.
3. As Panofsky says, "the influence of Dürer's *Melencolia I*—the first representation in which the concept of melancholy was transplanted from the plane of
   scientific and pseudo-scientific folklore to the level of art—extended all over
   the European continent and lasted for more than three centuries . . . reinterpreted according to the taste and mental habits of the day" [170]. In the cases
   of Fuseli, Goya, and Cruikshank (all discussed at subsequent points in this
   chapter), I suggest mediated rather than direct influence: i.e., these artists
   probably looked at works shaped by *Melencolia I* rather than at *Melencolia I*
   itself. The crucial points are (1) their link to a tradition of speculation about
   artistic or more generally imaginative inspiration and (2) their loyalty to a
   much-used composition that surrounds a dreaming-imagining figure with a
   swarm of beings that define the dominant figure's mood. A full discussion of
   this iconography would take in visualizations of Saint Anthony's temptation,
   the Nativity, the mocking of Christ, and Renaissance dream lore: here I
   simplify the story.
4. On *The Nightmare* (including a discussion of Burton's *Anatomy*, partition 2,
   section 2, member 5 ["Waking and terrible Dreams rectified"], see Nicholas
   Powell, *Fuseli*. Links between *The Nightmare* and the tradition of melancholy
   are also suggested by several of Fuseli's later works. *The Dream of Belinda*, a
   painting (1780–90), is "an improvisation on themes in [*The Rape of the Lock*]
   mingled with symbols from Fuseli's own world of dreams and fantasy"; *The
   Cave of Spleen* [spleen is melancholy], an engraving of 1799, illustrates a scene

from the fourth canto of *The Rape*. Both images feature a semirecumbent female figure reminiscent of the dreamer in *The Nightmare;* both surround this figure with a variety of bizarre or threatening creatures, much as in the Goya *capricho* discussed immediately below. Fuseli's *Rape* illustrations are analyzed in Robert Halsband, *The Rape of the Lock and Its Illustrations*, 44–53.

5. William Hazlitt, "On the Old Age of Artists," in *Complete Works*, 12: 90: "His ideas are gnarled, hard, and distorted, like his features—his theories stalking and straddle-legged, like his gait—his projects aspiring and gigantic, like his gestures—his performance uncouth and dwarfish, like his person. His pictures are also like himself, with eye-balls of stone stuck in rims of tin, and muscles twisted together like ropes or wires." Powell's monograph [*Fuseli*, 60] suggests the autobiographical basis for identifying the *marra* with Fuseli: the female sleeper may be a portrait of a woman with whom the artist was fruitlessly in love and whose portrait (evidently) occupies the back of the canvas on which *The Nightmare* is painted.

6. On Goya's debt to the iconography of melancholy—transmitted, it would seem, largely through emblem books—see George Levitine, "Literary Sources of Goya's *Capricho* 43"; Folke Nordstrom, *Goya, Saturn, and Melancholy*, especially 16–20, 138–40; and Alfonso E. Pérez Sánchez and Eleanor A. Sayre, *Goya and the Spirit of Enlightenment*, 69–71. Sánchez and Sayre also discuss *Goya Attended by Doctor Arrieta*, a late painting (1820) in which Goya depicts an awakening *contra* melancholy.

7. For a detailed treatment of *El sueño*, see Paul Illie, "Goya's Teratology and the Critique of Reason." Ilie notes at least two corruptions of Reason to which Goya may be referring: "speaking historically about Spain, the Enlightenment produces a burgeoning knowledge that degenerates into extracts and compendia" [54]; speaking historically about Europe, the Enlightenment produces the abuses of the French Revolution, where irrational actions follow from presumably rational precepts (e.g., in the Terror). See also the related treatment in Ronald Paulson, *Representations of Revolution*.

8. On Goya's fortunes on the Continent, specifically among the French in the 1820s and 1830s, the most thorough study is Ilse Lipschutz, *Spanish Painting and the French Romantics*. Lipschutz establishes that the *caprichos* were by far the best known of Goya's works in France during this decade; she reproduces one anonymous travesty of *El sueño* (*Le Cauchemar de Louis Philippe*, 1832) but states that she has discovered no others. While French artists sometimes rationalized Goya's extravagant fantasies (as in Louis Boulanger's orderly witches' sabbath [1828], an illustration to Hugo's "La Ronde du sabbat" [1825, *Odes et ballades*]), they did not often use him for the purpose of mockery as the English so often used Fuseli. Perhaps this difference is explained by the greater power of Goya—after all, it is hard to ignore that Fuseli's *Nightmare* verges on the ludicrous—perhaps by the lateness of French romanticism, a movement just reaching its height in the 1830s. On the Goyaesque theme of the *ronde* (i.e., a circling dance of witches and demons) in French romanticism, see Lipschutz, *Spanish Painting*, 175–80; on the connection between *Los Caprichos* and *ND*, ibid., 181–84. Charles Nodier's *Smarra ou les démons de la nuit* (in the *Contes*, 1821) combines references to *El sueño* and *The Nightmare*, perhaps the preemi-

nent occasion on which these images appear (more or less) together; for details see Powell, *Fuseli*, and Nodier's *Contes*, 3 and 65. Powell also catalogs the many English travesties of *The Nightmare*.

9. For historians and critics (most German) of the early nineteenth century Dürer was an artist characterized by naive strength: Goethe (*Erklärung eines alten Holzschnittes, vorstellend Hans Sachsens poetische Sendung;* Explanation of an old woodcut, introducing Hans Sachs's poetic mission) eulogizes the painter's "festes Leben und Männlichkeit" (firm life and manliness); W. H. Wackenroder (*Herzensergiessungen eines kunstliebenden Klosterbruders;* Effusions of an art-loving monk) and Ludwig Tieck (*Franz Sternbald*) expand on this theme. In 1835, C. G. Carus's *Briefe über Goethe's Faust* (Letters on Goethe's Faust) proposes a different evaluation. A few years before the vogue of *OCS*, Carus compares *Melencolia I* to *Faust:* both works are characterized by "agonizing yearning," "dark demonic musings." The same point is made visually by T. M. von Holst, a German-English artist: *Ein Traum nach dem Lesen von Goethes Walpurgisnacht* (1827) is a typical creator-tormented-by creatures image. (On Dürer's posthumous reputation, including the remarks by Goethe cited above, see Keith Andrew's essay, "Dürer's Posthumous Fame," in C. R. Dodwell, ed., *Essays on Dürer;* another essay in the same volume, Ulrich Finke's "Dürer and Thomas Mann," quotes Carus [127], and Holst is treated by Gert Schiff, "Die Faust-Illustrationen Des Malers Theodor Matthias von Holst," 74–88.) Jules Michelet's *Histoire de France au seizième siècle* (1855) includes a whole chapter structured around *Melencolia I;* Michelet too emphasizes the Faustian or romantic strand. Charles Baudelaire's "L'art philosophique" (published posthumously: see Baudelaire's *Oeuvres complètes*, 1099–1107) defines a type of regressive didactic art influenced by Dürer, using allegory, etc., and discusses the problems for art of this kind in an age of the mass audience. Baudelaire gives the example of Alfred Rethel's "Dance of Death" woodcuts (1848), which he interprets as a preachment against revolution. Other—perhaps less reactionary—explorations in this mode (each using *Melencolia I* as a kind of icon) are Gérard de Nerval's dream-vision *Aurélia* (1855), James Thomson's poem "The City of Dreadful Night" (1870–74), and Lucien Levy-Dhurmer's painting *Quiétude* (1896, depicting a modern angel of melancholy against the background of Dürer's engraving). William Vaughan's *German Romanticism and English Art* includes many crucial and otherwise unavailable materials on Dürer's influence on English artists during the midnineteenth century. My chap. 9 considers the relation of *Melencolia I* and *LM*.

10. In addition to being published as a separate print, *Napoleon Dreaming in His Cell at the Military College* appears in [William Combe], *The Life of Napoleon* (1815), facing p. 6 (from which I have quoted a few lines of the relevant verses).

11. On the identity of the figures who make up the triumphal procession presided over by Cupid, see William Feaver's "Cruikshank: The Artist's Role," 5. Blanchard Jerrold's biography (*The Life of George Cruikshank*, 1894) prints *The Triumph of Cupid* as its frontispiece; on the cover of this handsome volume the image of artist with meerschaum is stamped in gold. This choice suggests an orthodox Victorian assessment of Cruikshank's accomplishment. Jerrold's laudatory description of *The Triumph of Cupid* is at pp. 210–11 of his biogra-

phy; he also tells the tale of *The Triumph of Bacchus,* a teetotaling preachment of 1863, produced more or less simultaneously in the form of engraving and oil painting, which was supposed to revive Cruikshank's fashionableness but didn't. "He [Cruikshank] was confident that crowds would flock to see it. He had visions of policemen at the door of his gallery to keep off the tumultuous throng" [288]. Alas, Cruikshank could paint throngs but was no longer so capable of drawing them. No doubt his antialcohol line was harder to popularize than his protobacco line: imagination in this crowded Victorian mode seems to benefit from certain kinds of indulgence.

12. Benjamin Roubaud's caricature of Hugo is reproduced in Priscilla Clark, *Literary France,* 147, with Clark's commentary. A work striking the same, slightly ambiguous tone is imagined by Eugène Sue. In *MP,* Sue describes a painting by the insolvent artist Cabrion: "on voyait une palette, entouré d'êtres bizarres, de figures grotesques, dont la spirituelle fantaisie eût fait honneur à Callot" (one saw a palette surrounded with bizarre beings, grotesque figures whose conception would have done honor to Callot—1: 24, 196, with illustration closely matching this text). References to Jacques Callot, the seventeeth-century etcher, are common in French literature of the fantastic variety; Lipschutz [*Spanish Painting,* 118] suggests that Théophile Gautier's "Albertus" (1831) set a fashion of evoking Callot and Goya together when there was a swarming, demonic scene to be described. In Sue's case, however, the swarming demons are too lovable, too cozy, to be Goyaesque. Like Roubaud, Sue slides into Cruikshankian territory almost despite himself.

13. Following Karl Giehlow and others, Walter Benjamin argues that Dürer was trying to transform a long-established mythology of melancholy, to see this condition as a blessing for the artist rather than as a disease. See Benjamin's *The Origin of German Tragic Drama,* 145 ff. and Michael Camille, "Walter Benjamin and Dürer's *Melencolia I.*" Philip Sohm tends to confirm Benjamin's interpretation of *Melencolia I:* "planning disparate ideas within each object, Dürer has created a *coincidentia oppositorum* which conveys the transfigured vision of an enlightened Melancholy" ["Dürer's *Melencolia I,*" 32].

14. Julius Charles Hare's was the first English translation of *Sintram:* it appeared in 1820. William Blake, who admired *Melencolia I* and once or twice adapted it for his own purposes, remarked that *Sintram* was "better than my things" [quoted in Vaughan, *German Romanticism,* 114, citing Henry Crabb Robinson's testimony]. A representative Victorian edition of *The Four Seasons* (*Sintram* and three related tales) was published in London by Edward Lumley in 1853, with a Dürer frontispiece to *Sintram* and excellent supplementary illustrations by John Tenniel. The quotations from Charlotte Yonge, *The Heir of Redclyffe,* appear at 53, 90, 224.

15. Dickens's change of mind regarding the woodcut is documented. He specifically requested George Cattermole to provide the woodcut: "I want to know whether you would object to make me a little sketch for a woodcut—in indian-ink would be quite sufficient—about the size of the enclosed scrap; the subject, an old quaint room with antique Elizabethan furniture, and in the chimney-corner an extraordinary old clock—the clock belonging to Master Humphrey, in fact, and no figures." Master Humphrey, then, disappears; only

the clock in the empty room remains. See Frederic Kitton, *Dickens and His Illustrators*, 82–83, 122–25.

16. Letter to Forster, 30 August 1846, in *Pilgrim Edition*, 4: 612.

17. The early publishing history of *OCS* is complex. The serial version of *MHC* began publication on 4 April 1840. The first chapter of what was to become *OCS* appeared in this periodical on 25 April 1840. Soon Dickens began using *MHC* exclusively as an outlet for the tale of little Nell. At the end of that tale (p. 223 of the serial *Clock*), there is a vignette of Nell being drawn up to Heaven by angels and the announcement "End of 'The Old Curiosity Shop'"; then occurs an episode (discussed below, in this chapter), titled "Master Humphrey from His Clock Side in the Chimney-Corner," a kind of epilogue to the narrative just concluded. Immediately following this section the text of *BR* begins. Dickens published a hardbound issue of *MHC*, with a newly composed preface (dated September 1840) recounting the history of *MHC* thus far. The first separate volume publication of *OCS* occurred about half a year later: the preface to that volume (largely printed from stereotype plates of the serial *MHC*) is dated March 1841. A number of significant alterations in the text occurred between the serial *MHC* and the two subsequent versions of Nell's story; some of these are discussed in the present essay. Passages that only appear in *MHC* are quoted from a bound issue of that periodical; passages in *OCS* from the Oxford Illustrated, except where otherwise noted.

18. This is the version given in *MHC* and the 1841 separate issue of *OCS*, among other places. Reprints from some later texts, including the Oxford Illustrated Edition, preface Humphrey's opening remark with the words, "Although I am an old man." Here Dickens insists on a distance between himself and Humphrey. I prefer the early reading, where, though Humphrey's age has been established by previous chapters of *MHC*, it is momentarily downplayed—where, in effect, Humphrey and Dickens merge. (This effect is stronger in the separate issue than in *MHC*.)

19. John Harvey, *Victorian Novelists and Their Illustrators*, 123. Harvey discusses the influence of a review by Thomas Hood on Dickens's decision to add this passage.

20. The drawing of Nell asleep was first assigned to Phiz. "It should have the girl in it, that's all," wrote Dickens to his publisher, Edward Chapman (25 March 1840). Williams got the job soon after; on 31 March Dickens returned his first attempt, explaining that it was too "pretty," "the object being to shew the child in the midst of a crowd of uncongenial and ancient things." Dickens encouraged Williams to work from the paragraph that his woodcut now precedes. A few "pretty" things remain; in keeping with Dickens's words, the element of horror is emphasized. See *Pilgrim Edition*, 2: 46–49.

21. Forster [*Life*, 1: 123] insists that it was he who showed Dickens the implications of his own narrative premise. On Victorian emblem reading—of which Forster's comments, offer, informally, an example—see Karl Josef Höltgen, *Aspects of the Emblem*, especially chap. 4, "The Victorian Emblematic Revival."

22. Cf. John Kucich's remarks in *Excess and Restraint in the Novels of Charles Dickens*, especially 23–25. For an argument disassociating Nell from death, see Nina Auerbach, *Woman and the Demon*.

23. I note a possibly sinister side to the argument pursued here: Ruskin comments famously that Nell "was simply killed for the market as a butcher kills a lamb" [Ruskin, "Fiction, Fair and Foul," in *Works*, 34: 275]. This comment raises a disturbing possibility. Ruskin suggests that, much like the show people with whom the novel is populated, Dickens makes "extraordinary efforts to stimulate the popular taste, and whet the popular curiosity" [*OCS*, 32, 243]; he drains the life from his creatures as a declaration of mastery over the only crowd that truly counts, the crowd out there clamoring for his books. On the other hand: I will try to show that Ruskin's "simply" begs the question; though Dickens is responsible for Nell's death in the sense that any novelist is responsible for the fate of a character, his motive is not to pander to his audience but—*with their support*—to explore fully the significance of his own figures for London.

24. For a short history of "Beauty and the Beast" in its various versions, see Iona and Peter Opie, *The Classic Fairy Tales*, 137–38.

25. Cf. Forster, *Life*, 1: 453, where Forster quotes from Dickens's letter of 12 February 1847. Here the novelist narrates an anecdote about a drunken coachman. Visiting Dickens after some contretemps between himself and the novelist, this personage "seemed to be troubled with a phantasmagorial belief that all Paris had gathered around us that night." Phantasmagorias and the shocking semi-illusionary sense of the city crowd's presence are once again associated. Cf. also the 1846 letter from Lausanne (quoted above) where the busy street is a "magic lantern."

26. Occasionally Quilp can be understood in other terms, his bizarre behavior traced to sexual or financial motives, his malice explained by hatred toward those who mock his physical appearance. However, given the frame of the novel (Humphrey's introductory tale) and given Quilp's narrative function (driving Nell away from her one retreat within London), the social allegory is most significant.

27. Stephen Marcus, *Dickens from Pickwick to Dombey*, 149–50.

28. Walter Benjamin, writing not about allegory but about the stories of novelists in contrast to traditional storytelling: see "The Storyteller," in his *Illuminations*, 101.

29. See Garrett Stewart, *Dickens and the Trials of Imagination*, especially 105, where Stewart shows that in contrast to Quilp—Humphrey is not important to this reading—Swiveller "is a truly creative agent."

30. Cf. Benjamin's *The Origin of German Tragic Drama*: "the only pleasure the melancholic permits himself, and it is a powerful one, is allegory. It is true that the overbearing ostentation, with which the banal object seems to arise from the depths of allegory is soon replaced by its disconsolate everyday countenance; it is true that the profound fascination of the sick man for the isolated and insignificant is succeeded by that disappointed abandonment of the exhausted emblem, the rhythm of which a speculatively inclined observer could find expressively repeated in the behaviour of apes. But the amorphous details which can only be understood allegorically keep coming up" [185].

31. Kitton, *Dickens and His Illustrators*, 81. In *MHC*, the plate appears at 2: 228 and features characters from both *OCS* and *BR*. Like the section of text that

precedes it, it serves as a connecting point between the two novels. *BR* will feature a quite different interrogation of crowds, focusing on their revolutionary potential rather than on their everyday existence.

32. The passage quoted from the Preface is partly about Master Humphrey's audience: Dickens "thinks how Jack Redburn might incline to poor Kit, and perhaps lean too favourably even towards the lighter vices of Mr. Richard Swiveller." But Master Humphrey's audience is analogous to Dickens's own; if he cannot envision the one, how is he to envision the other, which despite its greater substance is equally invisible? Problems of this kind were mitigated— though not necessarily solved—by Dickens's public readings, where contact with an audience was more immediate. On invisible audiences, see also chap. 8, below.

33. John Bayley, review of Max Hayward, 25.

Chapter 6. *"Repeating the Singular in Martin Chuzzlewit"*

1. See Suzanne Graver, *George Eliot and Community*, especially 150–53. Graver lists definitions of *consensus* by Auguste Comte, John Stuart Mill, Herbert Spencer, and George Eliot; she points out that each of them highlights the organic connotations of the word: e.g., Mill writes (1843) that in a *"consensus . . .* nothing which takes place in any part of the operations of society is without its share of influence on every other part" [*Collected Works*, 8: 900]. Graver sees the fascination with consensus as a "corrective" to the "individualist values" often expressed by these same, largely positivistic writers. For a treatment of consensus in literary terms see Elizabeth Ermarth, *Realism and Consensus in the English Novel*, especially comments in chap. 1 on perspective, detail, and the creation of a "common horizon." Finally, Victoria Kahn's "Habermas, Machiavelli, and the Humanist Critique of Ideology," gives "an account of Habermas's early affiliations with the 'consensus' party in Renaissance humanism and of Machiavelli's criticisms of this party [465]"; in her account of fact-value separations and her emphasis on "disinterestedness" as a constitutive problem of humanism from the Renaissance through most of the twentieth century, Kahn provides a helpful frame of reference for exploring the ideological implications of consensus.

2. The relation between panoramas and periods of (relative) social harmony is discussed, for example, by Deborah Nord in "The City as Theater."

3. Hornor's Panorama took form in the 1820s, with Dickens growing up not far away. Hornor himself is mentioned in a sketch of 1835, "Greenwich Fair." On the illusionistic means by which the Panorama was constructed, see Richard Altick's *Shows of London*, chap. 11.

4. Cf. Patrice Thompson's argument that panoramas construct a special kind of relation between viewer and spectacle: "Essai d'analyse des conditions du spectacle dans le Panorama et le Diorama." The advantage of artificial viewing conditions in panoramas is also noted by some Victorian observers: see [Joseph Charles Parkinson], "All Round St. Paul's," *AYR* 19 (4 April 1868): 392; cf. the note to "London at Night, Seen from the Summit of St. Paul's," where "F. W. N. B.," presumably the author of "London at Night," writes as follows: "Of

course it [is] not permitted to the community at large to find, *at night,* the opportunity of inspecting *'marvellous London'* from the real St. Paul's; but this favour was accorded, in a spirit of art-patronage, to Messrs. Danson and Telbin, two gifted artists, who were thus enabled to carry out the worthy project of Mr. Bradwell, in that wonderful picture of *'London at Night'* now [July 1845] to be seen at the colosseum, and the beautiful illusions of which, it is only fair to say, furnished the inspiration of this poem" [86]. "London at Night" is a description of a panorama by artists, not of the view from St. Paul's itself; the fiction involved is not only admitted but *gratefully* admitted by the poet—a writer under no delusions as to the immediacy of his vision. Also see David Masson's memoir, "Dead Men Whom I Have Known; or, Recollections of Three Cities: London from the Top of St. Paul's, Part I," published in 1865, which makes play with the necessity of "*à priori*" (*sic*) assumptions when viewing London from above [275–76]. A tentative conclusion: The importance of fictions and structuring premises for understanding or even describing panoramas becomes a frequent theme in nineteenth-century popular journalism.

5. I quote Elie Halévy, *A History of the English People in the Nineteenth Century,* 4: 77. As for specific "alliances and rivalries," one might mention: Feargus O'Connor's order to his Chartist followers to vote for Tory candidates in the elections of 1841; the shifting contentions between the Chartists and the Anti-Corn Law League; the failure of the factory bill of 1843, shattering "the delusion of High Church enthusiasts that the country was once more in their hands" [Halévy, 4: 68]; the rivalry-collaboration of Cobden and Peel; ultimately, Peel's decision to support the repeal of the Corn Laws (1846).

6. This phrase is quoted from Wordsworth's description of London, in *The Prelude,* bk. 7, l. 573, (1805 version).

> Folly, vice,
> Extravagance in gesture, mien, and dress,
> And all the strife of singularity,
> Lies to the ear, and lies to every sense,
> Of these, and of the living shapes they wear,
> There is no end.

Wordsworth claims to have maintained a near-indifference toward singularities, to have observed them with a "curious" but "quick" eye.

7. The summary of Bacon in the previous five sentences (and the first of the next paragraph) relies heavily on Lorrain Daston, "The Factual Sensibility"; Daston's review-essay is essential to an understanding of *singularity, curiosity,* and *fact* as these terms figure in the early history of science. My quotations are all from the *Novum organum,* bk. 2, pts. 28–29 [on the adjoining but distinct categories of the singular and the monstrous], in Bacon, *Works,* 236–38. Bacon notes in this section of the *Novum organum* that singularities manifest "an apparently extravagant and separate nature": he offers as instances quicksilver, the sun, the moon and—a nice touch—the letter *S,* for its ability to combine phonetically with other letters. On freakish natural specimens as jokes (a topic closely connected to, though not identical with, Baconian singularity) see Paula Findlen, "Jokes of Nature and Jokes of Knowledge."

8. Barbara Stafford, "Toward Romantic Landscape Perception," 96, 112–17. In "Now, Voyager," a review of Stafford's *Voyage into Substance*—her subsequent book on illustrated travel accounts—Charles Rosen attacks what he takes to be "a facile opposition between metaphorical style and plain description . . . tradition and unprejudiced, objective experience" [55]. Rosen makes some valuable points in his critique; however, his apparent desire that we see all the travel books as falling within the set categories of romanticism remains disturbing. He is surely correct that metaphor and description are somehow related—but when he gives his own version of travel books and their influence, it comes to seem that everything leads up to something like Proust's experience with the madeleine. "Unprejudiced, objective experience" is assimilated by the activities of the individual mind. The tension between particularized acts of seeing and objective description is therefore lost. Stafford's account of "singularity" has the virtue of sustaining this tension.

9. For Darwin on singularity, see the *Origin of Species,* 72, 122. His (particularly apposite) quotation from Whewell's *Bridgewater Treatise* reads: "But with regard to the material world, we can at least go so far as this—we can perceive that events are brought about not by insulated interpositions of Divine power, exerted in each particular case, but by the establishment of general laws." Toward the end of the nineteenth century, according to the *OED,* the scientific use of *singular* penetrates even the higher mathematics: by 1893, one can refer to the "point at which a function takes an infinite value" as a singularity.

10. I am thinking especially of Robert Young's conclusion in *Darwin's Metaphor* that "Darwinism and Anglicanism were able to accommodate to each other rather readily" [22]. Young gives an excellent account of how consensuses were formed in Victorian England.

11. For the *News*'s daguerreotype panorama, see Priscilla Metcalf, *Victorian London,* chap. 2. Some other typical Victorian descriptions of the London panorama are listed in my essay "City Life and the Novel," 164.

12. Hugo's description of the coat of arms with singular details appears in *Choses vues,* 1: 65–66, *Oeuvres complètes* (1904–52), pt. 4.

13. Later in *MC* [38, 590], there is one striking reference to St. Paul's, where Nadgett is compared to the cross on the cathedral. But Nadgett (I would argue) is much more a Todgers's than a St. Paul's sort of spy, a lurker in odd corners rather than on traditionally authoritative summits. And *MC* is a Todgers's sort of novel.

14. The blank left by the window is the most maddening feature of the view from Todgers's because windows are such evocative icons in the nineteenth century. See "The Open Window and the Storm-Tossed Boat," where Lorenz Eitner discusses treatments of views through windows in the period 1810–30; he notes that "the typical picture of this kind shows an interior of fairly ordinary character, with a figure quietly at work or absorbed in meditation near a window" [284]. Dickens, of course, describes window and figure from the outside; he makes a frame of reference into a source of disturbance.

15. Cf. Georg Simmel in his *Soziologie:* "Someone who sees without hearing is much more uneasy than someone who hears without seeing. In this there is something characteristic of the sociology of the big city. Interpersonal rela-

tionships in big cities are distinguished by a marked preponderance of the activity of the eye over the activity of the ear." Simmel is quoted in Walter Benjamin's *Charles Baudelaire,* 37–38. If only by an exercise in evocation, Hugo attempts to reverse this tendency.

16. Dickens notes the presence of "many a ghostly little churchyard" at *MC,* 9, 128; he first describes the ringing of the bells at 10, 155: "Shaking off his incertitude as the air parted with the sound of the bells, [Martin Chuzzlewit, Sr.] walked rapidly to the house." Though the passage has no allegorical import, certitude and bells are linked—an anticipation of much to come.

17. The corresponding event in *ND* would be Frollo's fall from the cathedral; this fall, which occurs many chapters after Hugo's extended description of the bird's-eye view, is associated with the destruction of consensus, of that taking things as a whole which Hugo insists was typical of the Middle Ages.

18. Many contemporaries noted the novelist's own longsightedness. The same contemporaries often observed that Dickens's works manifest a fascination with detail. Where do we interpret and where do we hold our peace, enjoying the "irrelevant details" as they come? Is Dickens a hallucinator or an accurate transcriber? Can anyone else besides Dickens be expected to participate in the novel's vision of the world? Read with attention to its allegorical elements, *MC* is the most sophisticated contribution to this long-standing conversation among readers. For Dickens's long sight see Collins' *Dickens: Interviews and Recollections,* 1: 82, 125. On unnecessary detail in *MC,* the earliest statement seems to be that of an anonymous reviewer [Thomas Cleghorn?] in the *North British Review* [Collins, 186–91]. The earliest general statement of the detail controversy is probably Bagehot's in the *National Review,* October 1858 [Collins, 390–401].

19. On partnerships in *MC,* see especially Edward Eigner, *The Metaphysical Novel,* 34–35. Eigner charts the process by which the narrative of the novel keeps collapsing characters into each other—finally leaving us with "Jonas Chuzzlewit, the ultimate self-partner." One of my aims will be to show how Mrs. Gamp fits—and does not fit—into this scheme.

20. J. Hillis Miller, *Charles Dickens,* 111–13, give a related treatment of this point.

21. One other character has some claim to be the protagonist in an allegorical pursuit of singularities. Tom Pinch is much involved with "singular" sensations [*MC,* 39, 614; 40, 620; 45, 693], and his view of the world is drastically altered by the disappearance of a dominating figure, Mr. Pecksniff: see chaps. 37 and 54. Gerhard Joseph has written on Pinch and panoramas, though not on singularity: see his "The Labyrinth and the Library."

22. Like the Anglo-Bengalee Insurance Company, Mrs. Gamp depends on life and death for her business (a nurse for all seasons, "she went to a lying-in or a laying-out with equal zest and relish," *MC,* 19, 313). Like the Anglo-Bengalee she is constantly engaged in building up a list of customers (forcibly recruiting them if necessary). No wonder Bailey Junior, servitor at the Anglo-Bengalee, considers her to be a fine figure of a woman.

23. In fuller form, Faulkner's comment was: "My favorite characters are Sarah Gamp—a cruel, ruthless woman, a drunkard, opportunist, unreliable, most of her character was bad, but at least it was character; Mrs. Harris, Falstaff,

Prince Hal, Don Quixote, and Sancho of course. Lady Macbeth I always admire. And Bottom, Ophelia, and Mercutio—both he and Mrs. Gamp coped with life, didn't ask any favors, never whined." The interest in *paired* characters is striking; Mrs. Harris is mentioned as a necessary afterthought. See *Writers at Work,* edited by Malcolm Cowley, first series, 137.

24. For H. F. Chorley's discussion, see the *Athenaeum,* 17 September 1853 [Collins, 277] on Dickens's weakness for depicting "the minutest singularities of so many exceptional people" and on "the sense of fatigue which the manoeuvres of such singular people cannot fail to cause." Chorley's observations—like those of G. H. Lewes in the *Fortnightly Review,* February 1872 [Collins, 574]—raise the issues that subsequent readers have struggled with. Neither Chorley nor Lewes makes the connection between singularity of character and city life; neither makes the distinction between life and fiction (it is evidently assumed that characters who are boring in the one context must be boring in the other). "Strikingly characteristic" is quoted from Simmel, 421: "The temptation to appear 'to the point,' to appear concentrated and strikingly characteristic, lies much closer to the individual in brief metropolitan contacts than in an atmosphere in which frequent and prolonged association assures the personality of an unambiguous image of himself in the eyes of the other." J. Hillis Miller (*Charles Dickens,* 104 ff.) gives a related but distinct account of Mrs. Gamp and similar urban types.

25. Cf. Marvin Mudrick's Afterword to the Signet Classic *MC* (1965), especially 888. Mudrick is one of the few readers to allow the Gamp-Prig confrontation its full weight.

26. I quote from *Friar Bacon and Friar Bungay* in Robert Greene's *Works,* 13: 77–82.

27. "The same mimesis that is conflictual and divisive as long as it focuses on objects of appropriation must become reunitive as the very intensity of the escalation substitutes one single scapegoat for many disputed objects" ["An Interview with René Girard," in Girard, *"To double business bound,"* 202].

28. As its name implies, the diorama is first cousin to the panorama. See Altick's *Shows of London,* especially chap. 12. Baudelaire's comments are from his essay on the Salon of 1859. He goes on to note that, rather than dioramas, he prefers dreams, which because they are false are infinitely nearer the truth. It seems likely that neither Dickens nor Hugo would share this preference. See Baudelaire's *Oeuvres complètes,* 1085.

Chapter 7. *"The Hunchback of Saint Dunstan-in-the-West: Failed Heroism"*

1. The idea that narrative produces agents is suggested in Vladimir Propp's studies of Russian folktales. I have been particularly influenced by Frank Kermode's adaptation of Propp in his work on New Testament narratives. See Kermode's *The Genesis of Secrecy,* especially 84–85, where Kermode argues that "Betrayal becomes Judas."

2. I take this phrase from Alex Callinicos, *Making History,* 5.

3. See Karl Marx, *Grundrisse,* 83: "Smith and Ricardo still stand with both feet on the shoulders of the eighteenth-century prophets, in whose imaginations this eighteenth-century individual—the product on one side of the dissolution of

the feudal forms of society, on the other side of the new forces of production developed since the sixteenth century—appears as an ideal." Callinicos [*Making History*, 64 ff.] discusses recent versions of Marxism in which this individual is more than an "idea." Most particularly he quotes Sartre's *Critique of Dialectical Reason:* "if we do not wish the dialectic to become a divine law again, a metaphysical fate, it must proceed first *from individuals* and not from some kind of supra-individual ensemble."

4. Other works besides *TC* suggest the centrality of questions about agency and identity at this stage of Dickens's career—most obviously the autobiographical *David Copperfield* (1849–50), written after *TC* and immediately before *BH*. (For instance, note David's opening speculation on whether he will turn out to be the hero of his own life.)

5. Quoted from "Modern Novels," an anonymous review of *TC* in the *Christian Remembrancer* (January 1845), reprinted in Collins, 161. The reviewer also perceives influences from Schiller, Carlyle, Reztsch (for the illustrations), and *MP*.

6. In *OT*, a "hump-backed man" or "hunchback" with a vile disposition makes a cameo appearance—rather as if trying to elbow his way into the novel—but Dickens can do nothing with him [32, 234].

7. I take it that Dickens and his architectural illustrator, Daniel Maclise, had a *common* understanding that the church of *TC* was Saint Dunstan-in-the-West. On the Gothicism of this building see, for instance, Karl Baedeker (*Baedeker's London*): "Between Fetter Lane and Chancery Lane rises the church of *St. Dunstan* . . . erected by *Shaw* in 1832 on the site of a more ancient building; it has a fine Gothic tower" [169]. The cultural connotations of Gothic architecture differed from decade to decade. Ian Nairn suggests that Saint Dunstan belongs to the earlier, frivolous phase ("the consequences of Horace Walpole and his like," *Nairn's London*, 91) but also admits the church's religious power. To this extent, anyway, Saint Dunstan belongs in the later, earnest phase of the Gothic Revival movement and thus can be said to carry the connotations I attribute to it. One of the ironies here is that the literary Gothicism of Sue and Reynolds (to be discussed at some length in succeeding chapters) functions so differently than the architectural Gothicism of roughly the same years.

8. In "Dickens, 'The Chimes,' and the Anti-Corn Law League," Michael Shelden situates the view of history expressed by *TC* within an early Victorian political context. He shows that Dickens's millenarian predictions should be associated with the free-trade movement of the forties. Shelden's argument is convincing, but I do not think he has told the whole story. Many forms of millenarianism can be progressive and regressive at the same time. Dickens's is one of them. He is nearer to his hated Sir Joseph Bowley than he would care to suppose; even at his most radical, he flirts with that particular kind of Toryism. Later novels by Dickens are considerably less optimistic about bells: see *LD*, 1.3, 67–69, for a particularly devasting passage: "In every thoroughfare . . . some doleful bell was throbbing, jerking, tolling, as if the Plague were in the city and the dead-cart were going round." On bells and historical nostalgia, see also J. K. Huysmans's extraordinary *Là-Bas* (1891) where Durtal's conversations in a church tower with the bell ringer Carhaix serve (among other functions) as a gloss on

ND. After a busy day of bell lore, Durtal has a vision of a city permeated—articulated—by the ringing of bells. He then reluctantly concludes, "Maintenant les cloches parlaient une langue abolie, baragouinnaient des sons vides et dénués de sens" (Nowadays the bells speak a suppressed language, jabbering sounds that are empty and stripped of sense) [chap. 3, p. 64]. Later he considers going up to the top of the tower for a view of Paris "à vol d'oiseau," but concludes that he would perceive only a mechanically regular order and not that labyrinthine one of the Middle Ages [chap. 17, p. 223]. Durtal himself is an interesting study in the connections between aestheticism, satanism, and nineteenth-century medievalism.

9. A few years after Dickens published *BH*, Augustus Mayhew did his own modernized version of *OT. Paved with Gold* (London: Chapman and Hall, 1858) finds no role for Fagin. His place has been taken by lore drawn from *London Labour and the London Poor*, the work of Augustus's brother Henry. The Newgate myths have at this point outlived their attractiveness. Another approach to poverty—or to the link between poverty and crime—is required. *BH* acknowledges much the same necessity.

Chapter 8. "Mystery and Revelation in Bleak House"

1. Ann Radcliffe, *The Mysteries of Udolpho*, 350.
2. The *OED* gives four meanings for *document* as a noun; only the fourth and most recent (first citation, 1727–51) specifies that a document must be written. Written documents of the mid-eighteenth century seem to be legal by definition, a convention to which Dickens proves more sensitive than Reynolds.
3. For a good biographical sketch and bibliography of G. W. M. Reynolds, see E. F. Bleiler's edition of *Wagner the Wehr-Wolf*, including some interesting if not altogether certain circulation figures: Bleiler suggests that *ML* sold a million copies over ten years and attributes a circulation of 600,000 copies to *Reynolds's Weekly Newspaper*. (By comparison, *BH* sold about 35,000 in parts-issue format: it appeared in a bound version later, but naturally the parts-issue reached the greater number of people.) For Reynolds's conscious use of the Gothic novel, see his *Robert Macaire in England*, 1: 97–98, where a farcical-sinister scene "at the house of a British merchant" is compared to an incident from *The Old English Baron*; for his sense of Hugo's importance to his own work, see *The Modern Writers of France*, 2: 4. "Though the ages of romance have yielded to brighter ones, in which facts are less darkened by the shadows of gloom—of terror—and of mystery, which the votaries of the Radcliffe and the Maturin school, following the examples of their German predecessors, were delighted to mingle amongst the incidents of their tales—though Hugo revived the exploded style, and introduced fresh horrors to the world . . . he nevertheless gathered a mighty audience around him." It would have been just a year or two later that Reynolds discovered Sue's adaptation of Hugo.
4. Reynolds was fascinated with this kind of situation. *Robert Macaire in England* begins with the robbery of a mail coach: "What have we here? A lengthy document from a mercantile house in Paris to its correspondent in London. Let us read this attentively: any attempt to obtain useful knowledge cannot be

considered a crime" [1: 13–14]. During 1845 Reynolds returned once more to the theme of opening letters, not only in *ML* but simultaneously in front-page articles for the *London Journal:* "The Secret Chamber in the General Post Office," 15 March 1845; "The Secret Chamber in the Tax Office, Somerset House," 12 April 1845.

5. George Saintsbury, *A History of the French Novel,* 2: 299–300; Edward Gorey, installment of *Les Mystères de Constantinople,* 37.

6. Pierre Proudhon, *Qu'est-ce que la propriété?* in *Oeuvres complètes,* 4: especially 131–61. Reynolds's sympathy with Proudhon is substantiated by Bleiler (in Reynolds, *Wagner the Wehr-Wolf,* xiii), who notes that *Reynolds's Political Instructor* (published for six months beginning in November 1849) looks forward to the day when "all property shall be national, and consequently no property is robbery." Whether this statement reflects an accurate understanding of Reynolds is unclear. *Caveat lector.*

7. Proving the precise nature of Reynolds's public is difficult. Louis James's *Fiction for the Working Man* offers a useful context; also helpful are certain more or less contemporary sources, such as Henry Mayhew's *London Labour and the London Poor* (itself largely reprinted from newspaper reports of the late 1840s), where Mayhew describes the popularity of Reynolds among London costermongers. He quotes passages from Reynolds particularly relished by this audience; he emphasizes the importance of illustrations for engaging the attention of the illiterate [1: 25–26]. "The Unknown Public," Wilkie Collins's lead article for *HW* 18 (21 August 1858) surveys a later phase in literature for the working classes. Collins makes the striking observation that translations of *MP* have not done well in penny journals, a point he attributes to ignorance of French customs and nomenclature (for example, the term *mademoiselle*). More generally, he emphasizes the unknown public's lack of assurance about its own knowledge and literacy.

8. The reader should be warned that my account of Reynolds is unorthodox. In most discussions of his work, the emphasis is on a split between high life and lowlife, each in its way becoming a Gothicized fantasy. The middle classes are left out altogether. The most interesting version of this schema is advanced by Gertrude Himmelfarb, who suggests that Reynolds's "idea of poverty was nihilistic rather than compassionate or heroic"; she substantiates her argument by an account of the Resurrection Man. Her conclusion is that in Reynolds, violence and depravity are a crucial means of redemption or resurrection for the poor. (Perhaps getting carried away, she adds that John Stuart Mill might have changed his mind about liberty and freedom of expression had he known what writers like Reynolds were really up to.) I agree with Himmelfarb that there is a sadomasochistic strain in Reynolds, even though it is hardly confined to his advice, implicit or explicit, to the poor. Calling this "nihilism," however, stretches the boundaries of an already much-abused word. Himmelfarb seems closer to the mark when she discusses Reynolds's tangled fascination with the "cool and calculating" criminal and his deserts. Cool calculation is Reynolds's specialty. We are all potentially middle-class manipulators— traders on the Board of Exchange—if only we knew where to put our energies. Reynolds cannot quite make up his mind whether he is happy or

horribly indignant about this condition of urban man. See Himmelfarb's *The Idea of Poverty*, 445, 449, 451–52.

9. See *Pilgrim Edition*, 5: 603.

10. [George Brimley], review of *BH* in *Spectator*, 24 September 1853 [Collins, 284].

11. The contemporary comments of Karl Mannheim and Karl Joël are analyzed in the Introduction to Georg Simmel's *Philosophy of Money*, where Tom Bottomore also provides the "dry summary," a paraphrase of criticisms made by H. J. Lieber [6–8, 28, 34]. "Large-scale industrialization" did not begin in Berlin until 1838, when a railroad line between Berlin and Postdam was completed. Only after the foundation of the German Reich, in 1871, did the town become a major European metropolis. See Eberhard Roters, *Berlin*, 15.

12. Later Edward Shils (*The Torment of Secrecy*) was to discriminate among three distinct categories, the private, the public, and the secret—and to argue that the three were related such that in times when the public domain invades the private, the desire for secrecy increases. This is helpful. But the basic idea is there already in Simmel.

13. See Frederick Maitland, *The Constitutional History of England*, 221–26.

14. The association of equity with legal fictions, noted so disparagingly in Dickens's critique, has a history worth noting. Blackstone defended such fictions as a means of getting through potentially cumbersome procedures: he instanced the action of *ejectment,* by which people wishing to prove a freehold title claimed they were leasing land that they actually owned, thus allowing their cases to be treated under the relatively rational law of leases. This sort of pretense increased "the power of the court . . . to prevent fraud and chicane." In the 1820s, Bentham was more suspicious of equity and its fictions: he saw them as "the elaborately organised, and anxiously cherished and guarded products of sinister interest and artifice." Dickens seems to take up a Benthamite position, but a little too late in the day: while *BH* was being issued, the fictions were in the process of being abolished. One recalls Fitzjames Stephens's gibe that Dickens's efforts at reform were always half a step behind the times. See "The Licence of Modern Novelists," *Edinburgh Review,* July 1857 [Collins, 372]. On the other hand, Dickens's Chancery is not so much a satirical target as it is a structural necessity. It is less the particular abuses of Chancery that are at issue than a certain relationship between individuals and institutions. For Blackstone and Bentham on fictions, see Harrison's discussion in *Bentham;* see also Marjorie Stone, "Dickens, Bentham, and the Fictions of the Law."

15. As a note to the *Pilgrim Edition* observes, Dickens "undoubtedly had Reynolds in mind when he wrote of the 'Panders to the basest Passions of the lowest natures' whom he sought to 'displace' with *Household Words*." If implied criticism were not enough, the *Household Narrative* that supplemented *HW* directed the attack specifically to Reynolds—whereupon Reynolds called Dickens a "lickspittle hanger-on to the skirts of Aristocracy's robe—originally a dinnerless penny-a-liner" [*Reynolds's Miscellany*, 8 June 1851]. See *Pilgrim Edition,* 5: 603, also 6: 790. For a fuller account of the relationship between the early numbers of *HW* and the novel of urban mysteries, see my "G. M.

Reynolds, Dickens, and the Mysteries of London," especially 198, noting two early *HW* articles on Chancery, and 199–203, noting Dickens's sustained interest in commissioning essays on recording-keeping systems (with only one lapse from the prevailing, sunny tone, in Dickens's own "Valentine's Day at the Post Office," *HW* 1 [30 March 1850]), where joviality is briefly superseded by a memorable Gothic fantasy): 6–12.

16. George Bernard Shaw, "From Dickens to Ibsen," printed (for the first time) in *Shaw on Dickens*, 19.

17. Dickens continued to follow abuses and reforms in the treatment of real property long after finishing *BH*; see "Economy in Sheepskin," *AYR* 2 (3 December 1859): 133–35, on reforms of "the mysteries of conveyance" in South Australia [132]; and "Portable Property in Land," *AYR* 6 (26 October 1861): 114–17, on proposed reforms to the Incumbered Estates Act. The grounds for increased efficiency in transfers of property are most specifically set out in "Portable Property," from which the remark about "facility of transfer" is quoted [114]. For "transfer" in *BH*, see 42, 583, where Mr. Tulkinghorn transfers *himself* (an ever more valuable repository of secrets) from Chesney Wold to London.

18. On the connections among law, writing, and ignorance as a "social handicap," see François Furet and Jacques Ouzouf, *Reading and Writing*, 313–14. Furet contributes to the line of historically specific studies of writing and society; this line seems more pronounced in French than in English scholarship, but in any case provides a useful supplement to Simmel and to *BH*.

19. In his Introduction to the Penguin *BH* (Harmondsworth: Penguin Books, 1971), J. Hillis Miller notes: "Lady Dedlock's mystery and the mystery of Chancery are so closely intertwined that the reader may be enticed into thinking that the solution of the one is the solution of the other" [34]. As Miller immediately observes, this is not so.

20. See Furet and Ouzouf, *Reading and Writing*, 310: "Right up to the mid-19th century, the technique of writing retained its bewildering formal complexity, with the variety of handwritings testifying to its status as a rare and learned art."

21. When Esther reaches Krook's shop, she notices that the inscriptions over the shop "were written in law-hand, like the papers I had seen in Kenge and Carboy's office, and the letters I had so long received from the firm. Among them was one, *in the same writing* [my emphasis: note that she does not say, "in the same kind of writing"], having nothing to do with the business of the shop, but announcing that a respectable man aged forty-five wanted engrossing or copying" [*BH*, 5, 50]. *Engrossing* is a technical legal term for copying; it implies the official preparation of a document. Engrossment also signifies the state of being absorbed or monopolized: Nemo, no man, will use engrossment as a means to engrossment, copying as a road to oblivion. Nonetheless, he remains (barely) perceptible within or through the document he transcribes.

22. On trusts cf. *BH*, 45, 625, where Woodcourt promises to accept Richard Carstone as a trust from Esther. (Chap. 45, titled "In Trust," plays on the legal and everyday meanings of the word, as do many other passages in *BH*.) The institution of "trust," which has its sources in land law and its appropriate

home in Chancery, reverberates through English culture. See Frederick Maitland's "Trust and Corporation," in *Maitland: Selected Essays*. Cf. George Spence, *Equitable Jurisdiction of the Court of Chancery*, 2: 6: "Every kind of property may be the subject of a trust."

23. On most occasions the anonymous narrator is imperturbable; however, at the moment of Jo's death and a few others he chooses to change his tone, to put a conspicuously public rhetoric at the service of substantive accusations: "Dead, your Majesty. Dead, my lords and gentlemen. Dead, Right Reverends and Wrong Reverends of every order. Dead, men and women, born with Heavenly compassion in your hearts. And dying thus around us every day" [*BH*, 48, 649]. The eloquence of these words on Jo's death is rhetorical in two senses: there is a strictly deployed stylistic pattern (anaphora, a kind of repetition) that reveals meaning; there is a defined audience (majesty, reverends, etc.) to which the words are addressed. To the extent that Dickens's words stay on the page, this audience must in some ways be a fiction. Nonetheless, it has a greater claim to reality than the flesh-and-blood audience of Chancery. The anonymous narrator does not always orate so strenuously as at Jo's death—he would be insufferable if he did—but he does manage to integrate eloquence with thought, to elude the separations that scramble so much communication within *BH*.

24. This kind of formula brings *BH* close to what Stephen Kellman calls "the self-begetting novel": "it is an account, usually first-person, of the development of a character to the point at which he is able to take up his pen and compose the novel we have just finished reading." Although Esther composes only half a novel (and is unconcerned with thinking of her manuscript as *art*), it might be tempting to include Dickens's work as one of the relatively few nineteenth-century examples of this genre—were it not for another defining remark by Kellman; the self-begetting novel creates "a fantasy of Narcissus become autogamous" [*The Self-Begetting Novel*, 3]. Esther has no such fantasy; she is concerned not only with her parents but with other, broadly social sources of her life and her writing. On the problematic nature of Esther's struggle to write, the reader can consult Robert Newsom in *Dickens on the Romantic Side of Familiar Things*, 14, and Jeremy Hawthorn, *Bleak House*, 27 and 58 (shrewd on the difference between secrets spoken and secrets written).

25. There is a Middle Eastern custom of doodling when distraught. On the other hand, "in Roman legal practice the judge first wrote the sentence and then read it aloud." The question thus arises: Is Christ's writing the deliberate tracing of a decision or a kind of preliminary stalling for time? Given the general tone of John's Gospel—to which this story is an early addition—and given the Greek term used for the act of writing (*kategraphen*), the first alternative seems promising. One nineteenth-century commentator who favors it is Thomas Scott (*The Holy Bible*, 1823, 5: 509). I have drawn from two modern commentaries: Raymond Brown, ed. and tr., *The Gospel According to John*, 1: 333, on Roman legal practice and Middle Eastern doodling; John Marsh, *The Gospel of St John*, 686, on *kategraphen*.

26. *The Nonesuch Dickens*, 1: 872–73.

27. The *Life of Our Lord* has Christ writing in the sand; *BH* has him writing in the

dust. This change links the biblical story with the events of the novel—with Jo's sweeping, with the filth in the streets (the Victorian sense of "dust" is, of course, more inclusive than ours, sometimes connoting "refuse" rather than "minute particles"), with the law (which is explicitly compared to the mess of the streets), and, as witness the wonderful remark about dust as "universal article," with the general sense of entropy so important throughout. Dickens's problem is to imagine a positive form of writing that could occur in this context—or rather in this medium.

28. Phiz's illustration of Allegory appears at the end of chap. 48; this image has Allegory pointing in the wrong direction (away from the window rather than toward it, pace chap. 16) but gives an impression (verging on caricature) of the kind of baroque spatial construction Dickens must have had in mind. A deconstructionist reading of Allegory is given in J. Hillis Miller's introduction to the Penguin *BH* [29]. See also Michael Ragussis, "The Ghostly Signs of *Bleak House*." Comments perhaps nearer in spirit to mine may be found in Albert Hutter, "The High Tower of His Mind," 304, where the subject is the referential quality of Dickens's prose at certain key junctures; in Michael Steig, *Dickens and Phiz*, informative on Allegory's gesture of pointing and its reverberations throughout the novel, as well as on Phiz's preliminary sketch of Allegory (*too* facetious; subject, therefore, to revision); and in Nancy Metz, "Narrative Gesturing in *Bleak House*," 17.

29. A habit still much respected by many Victorians, though attempts to link it with substantive thought tended to fall flat. Of particular interest at midcentury: William Dyce, under Prince Albert's sponsorship, is at work on the most prominent Victorian attempt at a public personification allegory, the Arthurian paintings in the queen's robing room at Westminster. On the failure of this ambitious cycle, see Debra Mancoff, *The Arthurian Revival in Victorian Art*, 117 ff.

30. Several recent discussions of *pointing* offer a suggestive context for thinking about *BH*'s Allegory. Claude Gandelman's *Reading Pictures, Viewing Texts* studies "the gesture of demonstration." In quattrocento painting, this gesture is associated with John the Baptist, who points—typically to his left—at a figure of Christ, thus announcing Christ's divinity to the viewer. Baroque painting offers a variation; for instance, "Carracci's *Quo Vadis?* has the hand of the pointing Christ jutting out toward the viewer. . . . [It projects] the space of representation onto the space of observation" [30, 34]. Wolfgang Giegerich also identifies pointing of this latter kind with Christianity, which "bursts through the 'canvas' of the 'painting,' the 'screen' of the 'movie' that it presents or the 'text' of the 'mythos' it has to tell. By exploding the plane of the 'picture,' it leaps out of the sphere of imaginal reality and into the outer space of literal reality—a reality which however is originally created only by this very act of an archetypal, primordial leap" ["The Rocket and the Launching Base," 66]. Dickens's classical variant, the pointing Roman, is connected with a similar projection, a similar leap.

31. In his Introduction to the Penguin *BH*, J. Hillis Miller quotes the number plans for the novel as confirmation that Dickens intended the connection between Jo's pointing and Allegory's. Steig suggests (rightly, I think) that the link

would be clearer had novelist and illustrator coordinated their efforts more efficiently, i.e., had Allegory's gesture been given visual as well as verbal emphasis at an earlier point in the novel [*Dickens and Phiz,* 146].

32. Hutter, "High Tower," argues at length for a high valuation of Bucket: Bucket is "identified with the other artist of this novel, the omniscient narrator," he "accurately perceives Lady Dedlock's flight toward self-destruction," "reader, omniscient narrator, and detective all seem to share a common perspective and, for the moment at least, a common identity" [Hutter, 303–4]. I am reluctant to grant these claims without considerable qualification. Note particularly that in a passage central to Hutter's argument ("he mounts a high tower in his mind"—*BH,* 56, 767), Dickens qualifies the identification between detective and third-person narrator: "*If,* as he folds the handkerchief and carefully puts it up, it were able, with an enchanted power, to bring before him the place . . ." (my emphasis). The "if" is crucial. I persist in supposing that Bucket is not infallible, certainly not capable in himself of healing the novel's various rifts—just as he is incapable of finding Lady Dedlock before she has died. On Bucket, see also Michael Steig and A. C. Wilson, "Hortense versus Bucket," where it is argued that Dickens's treatment of the detective reflects his own bewilderment: "He is caught in the toils of a confused dialectic, which he would like to disguise as purposive, but where no progression of any kind is achieved" [297]. However, Steig does not believe that Allegory contributes to the clarification of this "confused dialectic," only to further obscuring it.

33. In the parts-issue and the first bound edition of *BH,* the text of the last chapter ends with a long dash, ——, the equivalent of two em dashes run together, followed by a period. (This long dash is used earlier in these editions as a sign that a statement or speculation is being interrupted.) The Norton Critical Edition and the Oxford Illustrated Edition use the same long dash followed by nothing. In the Penguin edition, there is a short dash followed by a period. This is a very small matter; nonetheless, it could stand investigation. On the whole, I prefer the long dash plus period: it communicates a hesitation not so much coy as prolonged beyond reason (Esther is interrupting herself), and then throws in the period for good measure. Even *this* self-willed pause must have its resolution.

34. In 1852–53, during the writing of *BH,* Dickens was closely involved with the negotiations for an Anglo-American copyright agreement. Among the "necessary expenses" of the agreement was a sum for bribing Congress. Dickens had serious misgivings about the bribe but contributed to it. Here was an exercise in secrecy and publicity that touched very closely indeed on control of intellectual property. The results were unsatisfactory. No copyright agreement was reached until 1891. Dickens's writings remained "the general property," at least in the United States, an unsatisfactory outcome for a novelist always in need of cash. On the social origins of the idea of literary property, see Joseph Loewenstein, "For a History of Literary Property." For an account of the relation between property and copyright in English law—focusing on the transformation of text into commodity—see N. N. Feltes, *Modes of Production*

of Victorian Novels, 7. I have also consulted Thomas Barnes, *Authors, Publishers and Politicians,* especially chap. 11.

35. Simmel, *Philosophy of Money,* 322. Robert Merton has shown how this same ethic governs modern dispositions of "intellectual property": "I propose the seeming paradox that in science, private property is established by having its substance freely given to others who might want to make use of it" ["The Matthew Effect in Science," 606].

36. D. A. Miller, *The Novel and the Police,* 83.

Chapter 9. *"Mystery and Revelation in* Les Misérables*"*

1. The title of *LM,* 3.1, on Gavroche as gamin, is "Paris étudié dans son atome."

2. Nietzsche, *The Joyful Wisdom,* in *Complete Works,* 10: 302–3, section 356.

3. Joanna Richardson, *Victor Hugo,* 103. Richardson's account of Hugo's political career is more savage than most, but few students of the subject suppose that he would have made a good politician, even had events not taken the turn they did.

4. Adèle Hugo's words, from her *Journal de l'exil,* are quoted and commented upon by Bernard Leuilliot in *P,* 1: 671.

5. Hugo comes to a standstill in the process of describing this latter figure; the completed poem follows the genius's story with an indictment of child labor (the subject on which Hugo was trying to influence the peers), then with many other vignettes of futility and persecution.

6. As Bernard Leuilliot comments in *P,* 1: 671: "Le rapport avec la célèbre gravure de Dürer . . . est assez lointain" (The connection with the celebrated engraving of Dürer . . . is quite distant). Gautier had already composed an elaborate descriptive poem on Dürer's engraving ("Melancholia," written 1834, published 1845), a fact that helps explain Hugo's avoidance of ekphrasis.

7. Erwin Panofsky's description is pertinent: "The face [of Dürer's melancholic] is overcast by a deep shadow. It is not so much a dark as a darkened face, made all the more impressive by its contrast with the startling white of the eyes" [*The Life and Art of Albrecht Dürer,* 163]. Panofsky also cites Milton's *Il Penseroso:*

> [His] saintly visage is too bright
> To hit the sense of human sight,
> And therefore to our weaker view
> O'erlaid with black, staid wisdom's hue.

The background of *Melencolia I* has something of this quality too; a rainbow and a comet shine eerily through an indeterminate dusk, magnificent but (as yet) suppressed.

8. My description of *Les Contemplations* draws heavily on Suzanne Nash, *"Les Contemplations" of Victor Hugo,* from which I quote the phrase about "willing self-immolation" [146].

9. See Hugo, "Réponse," ll. 26–29, in *P,* 1: 641:

> je suis ce monstre énorme,
> Je suis le démagogue horrible et débordé,

Et le dévastateur du vieil A B C D;
Causons.

I am this enormous monster,
I am the demagogue, horrible past all conception,
And the destroyer of the old A B C D;
Let's chat.

—the casual invitation to chat both confirming and mocking the admission that precedes it. See also ll. 68–70, *P,* 642:

Je fis une tempête au fond de l'encrier,
Et je mêlai, parmi les ombres débordées,
Au peuple noir des mots l'essaim blanc des idées.

I raised a tempest at the bottom of the inkwell,
And I mixed among the overflowing shadows,
The black people of words with the white swarm of ideas.

The difference between "Réponse" and *LM* is the difference between descending to a flood in an inkwell and descending to a flood in a sewer. "Réponse" is one of Hugo's most-studied poems; a good recent commentary on some of its difficulties is given in Wendy Greenberg, *The Power of Rhetoric,* where the emphasis is on Hugo's simultaneous rejection of rhetoric and reliance upon it.

10. "Melancholia," the early fragments of *LM* (see the timetables in the third volume of Leuilliot's edition), and Sue's great serials (*MP,* 1842-43, *Le Juif errant,* 1844–45) all date from the mid-forties. That there was a connection between *LM* and Sue was understood quickly: see Baron Ernouf's essays in the *Revue contemporaine* for 1862 (written as parts of the novel were published), especially 26: 587 and 28: 112.

11. Louis Chevalier, *Laboring Classes and Dangerous Classes in Paris during the First Half of the Nineteenth Century,* 403 ff. While I do not fully agree with Chevalier's analysis of "diffused" crime in Hugo and Sue, my debt to his work is considerable, both in details (see discussion of the criminal Lacenaire, later in this chapter) and in general orientation.

12. Karl Marx, *The Holy Family,* in Marx and Engels, *Collected Works,* 4: 56. Cf. James Allen's discussion in "History and the Novel," especially 250–52.

13. *The Holy Family,* 72. To put this another way, "it is just as great a Critical mystery that locked doors are a *categorical necessity* for hatching, brewing and perpetrating mysteries" [73].

14. "L'inconvénient des mots, c'est d'avoir plus de contour que les idées. Toute les idées se mêlent par les bords; les mots, non" (The inconvenience of words is that they have better-defined outlines than ideas. All ideas mix around the edges; words, no) [Hugo, *L'Homme qui rit,* 2: 196].

15. In *LM,* 1.2.2, 73, Bishop Myriel is said to be working on a book about duties of the community as a whole and duties of the individual "selon la classe à laquelle il appartient" (according to the class to which he belonged). Alas, Hugo notes, the bishop never finished this work.

16. Using a phrase invented by the romantic painter Washington Allston and popularized by T. S. Eliot, one might say that Thénardier seeks, but fails to find, an "objective correlative" for his emotion. "Ce tableau que vous voyez,

et qui a été peint par David à Bruqueselles, savez-vous qui il représente? il représente moi. . . . Je ne lui en ai pas moins sauvé la vie au danger de la mienne, et j'en ai les certificats plein mes poches!" (This painting you see, which was executed by David at Brussels, do you know what it shows? It shows me. . . . I saved his life [the life of Marius's father] at the risk of my own and my pockets are stuffed with documents that prove it!) [*LM*, 3.8.20, 359]. The painting and the certificates, in which Thénardier attempts to ground his hatred, are pathetically beside the point.

17. See especially Frances Vernier, *"Les Misérables:* Ce Livre est dangereux,*"* and Jeffrey Mehlman, *Revolution and Repetition,* 112–13. See also two articles by Anne Ubersfeld: "Le Rêve de Jean Valjean" and "Nommer la misère."

18. On Gavroche, Renée Winegarten offers some provocative words: this character "was inspired by the pistol-waving youth who moves beside bare-breasted *Liberté* in Delacroix's great painting of the 1830 barricades. . . . Hugo did not heed the warning of his one time master Chateaubriand, against encouraging the emulation of such dangerous armed children." More generally, Hugo justified revolutionary excesses by fallacious arguments—e.g., the "burning of the great Louvre library [in 1871] . . . was seen as the action of one who had never been taught to read," though in actuality the rioters probably *could* read [32, 33]. Winegarten's detailed, often careful essay ends by presenting us with Hugo the mythologist of progress-as-violence; in other words it gives us a Hugo who supports violent political acts without fully understanding their implications. Gavroche is taken to be a typical example, since his violence is sentimentalized (he never actually kills anyone, dies a martyr, etc.) The argument of *LM* on violence, illiteracy, and revolutionary is subtler, more capable of supporting intelligent distinctions, than Winegarten implies. Hugo is not the political dunce that even his admirers often take him to be—least of all when he is engaged in writing a novel.

19. See Fréderic Bouchot's lithograph of that notorious Napoleonic monument, the Elephant (1844), reproduced in Bonnie Grad and Timothy Riggs, *Visions of City and Country,* pl. 51. Bouchot shows the rats (also featured in Hugo) running all over the miserable beast; one rodent is half in, half out of an elephantine eyeball.

20. See François Furet and Jacques Ouzouf, *Reading and Writing,* especially 315: "it was the French Revolution which most intransigently insisted on the benefits of written culture as opposed to the pernicious influence of oral tradition. . . . The written word is conceived of as instrumental in breaking with the everyday life of the *Ancien Régime.*" See also David Vincent, *Literacy and Popular Culture* (about the English scene rather than the French, but—because it is excellent on the social complications of working-class literacy—a useful supplement and occasionally a useful corrective to the presentations of this subject in nineteenth-century novels).

21. The voluminous nineteenth-century literature about sewers points up both Hugo's conventionality and his originality. Donald Reid, *Paris Sewers and Sewermen,* provides an excellent survey of this immense subject. For the English background see Christopher Hamlin's survey, "Providence and Putrefaction"; Hamlin focuses on the reclamation of putrefying matter (a subject

Hugo also considers). See also Thomas Knox, *Underground, or Life below the Surface* (1875), where the controlling rubric, "underground," includes an instructive span of topics (and where Jean Valjean's sewer adventures are quoted generously).

22. On Lacenaire and Hugo, see Chevalier, *Laboring Classes and Dangerous Classes*, 113–14.

23. The rhetorical mixtures of this passage could be treated at greater length. The sewer is already a cross between the figures of crowd and labyrinth (it is what becomes of the crowd when the crowd descends into a maze); furthermore it has the inclusiveness of the panorama: e.g., Hugo presents us with a bird's-eye view that could be seen by no bird but that somehow takes in Paris. Add the imagery of writing and it appears that Hugo has crammed together the four figures through which the action of *ND* developed some thirty years before. Cf. my treatment of the Douvres, the oceanic rock formation of *LT*, in chap. 13, below.

24. A cross-reference is afforded by the horrible procession of the chain gang, whose members "avaient été liés et accouplés pêle-mêle, dans le désordre alphabétique probablement, et chargés au hasard sur ces voitures. Cependant des horreurs groupées finissent toujours par dégager une résultante; toute addition de malheureux donne un total" (had been bound and coupled together pell-mell, probably in alphabetical disorder, and loaded at random on the carts. However, massed horrors always end by displaying an outcome; every accumulation of misfortune yields a total) [*LM*, 4.3.8, 483]. An overlay of literate thinking—"alphabetical disorder" in Hugo's phrase—leaves all in the chaos of argot, of criminal and anti-literate thinking, out of which grows a new and almost incomprehensible order, "un total." (A comment on my translation of this passage: Norman Denny's *Misérables* gives "alphabetical order" instead of "alphabetical disorder." Denny may have fathomed something of Hugo's meaning, but the French wording is confusing in just the right way; we are not quite sure whether the grouping by alphabet yields order or disorder, or interacts with the power of *misérables* to produce something that requires a new way of thinking altogether.)

25. Jules Michelet, *Le Peuple*, viii.

26. Ibid., 197, 196. To the best of my knowledge, the first extended comparison of Hugo and Michelet occurs in Réné Journet and Guy Robert, *Le Mythe du peuple*, 73–76. See also 81: "Comme Eugène Sue, comme Michelet, Hugo ne peut admettre l'opposition des classes. Il a, comme eux, confiance dans la bonne volonté des riches" (Like Eugène Sue, like Michelet, Hugo cannot admit the conflicting interests of classes. Like them, he puts his confidence in the good will of the rich). My own analysis is partly an attempt to show that the "truths" embodied by *LM* are not so simple as some of Hugo's own statements might seem to suggest.

27. Michelet, *Le Peuple*, 209.

28. Mikhail Bakhtin, *Rabelais and His World*, 152.

29. In *The Human Condition*, Hannah Arendt observes, "Goodness can exist only when it is not perceived, not even by its author. . . . Only goodness must go

into absolute hiding and flee all appearance if it is not to be destroyed" [74–75]. Hugo accepts this premise but with the crucial qualification I am describing.

Chapter 10. "Meryon's Hybrid Monster: Failed Knowledge"

1. Meryon's letter to his father (dated 17 April 1854) is quoted in James Burke's catalog, *Charles Meryon* (hereafter cited as Burke, Cat.), 35. Meryon retains one of the crucial features of the emblem, its link between word (verse motto, implicit reference to Hugo) and image. Cf. Dürer's *Melencolia I*, Goya's *El sueño* (both iconographically connected with *Le Stryge*), and some of the original illustrations for *MHC*.

2. For the basic documents and information concerning *Le Stryge*, I have relied on Burke, Cat., especially the entries on various states of the etching, 34–39, and on Adele Holcomb, *"Le Stryge de Notre-Dame."*

3. See also, from *La Légende des siècles*, "Eviradnus," *P*, 2: 55, l. 15, and 65, l. 756; "L'Italie—Ratbert," 81, l. 169.

4. Yves Vadé, "Le Sphinx et la chimère," 6.

5. Viollet-le-Duc himself was attracted to Gothic architecture for what he took to be its structuring, orderly qualities. In technical terms, he argued that modern architects could learn from the Gothic style because of its system of rib construction—to which would correspond iron-skeleton buildings like the Crystal Palace. One might say: Viollet-le-Duc wanted to rationalize the sphinx rather than to indulge the chimera. Meryon's attitude is as usual harder to specify.

6. Meryon's technical procedure implies the same point: in early sketches for *Le Stryge*, the space for gargoyle and tower is left blank, as though these Gothic elements inhabited a single cultural dimension. See Burke, Cat. 9.

7. Jules Andrieu writes:

> Taking up the etching which did not then bear the name of "Le Stryge," Meryon said to me, "You can't tell why my comrades, who know their work better than I do, fail with the Tower of St. Jacques? [The church itself had been destroyed during the French Revolution.] It is because the modern square is the principal thing for them, and the Middle Age tower an accident. But if they saw, as I see, an enemy behind each battlement and arms through each loophole; if they expected, as I do, to have the boiling oil and the molten lead poured down on them, they would do far finer things than I can do. For often I have to patch my plate so much that I ought indeed to be a tinker. My comrades," added he—striking the *Stryge*—"my comrades are sensible fellows. They are never haunted by this monster." "What monster?" I asked, and, seeing a reproachful look, corrected myself; "or, rather what does this monster mean?" "The monster is mine and that of the men who built this Tower of St. Jacques. He means stupidity, cruelty, lust, hypocrisy—they have all met in that one beast."

[Andrieu quoted in Frederick Wedmore, *Meryon and Meryon's Paris*, 44–5]

Meryon dwells on the demonic force that, in his opinion, links his own work to that of the Gothic builders (rather than to the modern restorers of Saint-

Jacques, or, indeed to bumblers like Louis Philippe or Napoleon III). Then, toward the end of his explanation, there comes a change in mood: the gargoyle now suggests neither fear of besiegement nor artistic inspiration, the readings ventured up to this point, but "stupidity, cruelty, lust, hypocrisy." The relation between gargoyle and the medieval past—a relation that Meryon has up to this point insisted on—is thus thrown into doubt. Meryon approaches a satiric theme related, in his oeuvre, more to contemporary Paris than to its medieval past. He condemns the decadence of the imperial capital, in which he feels himself implicated. On Meryon and decadence, see Holcomb, *Le Stryge*.

8. The Delacroix work dates from 1828. Burke, *Cat.*, links it to Meryon's *Ancienne Porte du Palais de Justice*—another of the *Eaux-Fortes*, executed a year after *Le Stryge* (cf. *ND*, 1.1, 38–39)—Holcomb (a little less convincingly) to *Le Stryge* itself.

9. Other passages from *ND* might provide more appropriate parallels: think of Quasimodo on Notre-Dame watching Esmeralda die by hanging in the square beneath. (This incident is discussed in chap. 2, above.)

10. Meryon begins one such document, "If I were Emperor or King of some powerful state (which I would not wish nor be able to be)" and then, after this inevitable disavowal, proceeds to outline an elaborate system of improvement for city life, a system based on "Solar Law" [James Yarnall, "Meryon's Mystical Transformations," 294]. Cf. Elias Canetti's comments on "Rulers and Paranoiacs" (in the section so named of *Crowds and Power*, 411–64). Particularly illuminating is Canetti's analysis of Daniel Paul Schreber—his sense of universal persecution and his simultaneous sense that he is the only person in the universe, that *nobody else exists*. According to Canetti, rulers and paranoiacs share this sense.

11. Baudelaire quoted in Burke, *Cat.*, 63–64.

12. This is to register a partial disagreement with Yves Vadé, who (quoting Cellier) puts more emphasis on French romanticism's fascination with unity, with total science, a science of totality ["Le Sphinx et la chimère," 7].

13. On cooptation of the arts in the reigns of Louis Philippe and Napoleon III, see Michael Marrinan, *Painting Politics for Louis Philippe*, and Albert Boime, "The Second Empire's Official Realism."

14. Each of these works is slightly later than *ND:* Dumas's *La Tour de Nesle* was first performed in 1832, Gautier's *Mademoiselle de Maupin* first published in 1835.

15. See G. K. Chesterton's "Defence of Detective Stories," 4–5. *The Man Who Was Thursday* was first published in 1908. An important later account of urban paranoia—the romance of detail gone strange—is given by André Breton in *L'Amour fou*, where the Tour Saint-Jacques is celebrated as "the world's great monument to the hidden" and where "paranoiac interpretation" of riddle images is a crucial way of imagining Paris. M. A. Caws's translation of the Breton text is titled *Mad Love:* see especially 47 and 87 ff. Vladimir Nabokov's memorable story "Signs and Symbols" and Thomas Pynchon's novels offer postwar, perhaps "postmodern" variants on the closely related themes of urban paranoia and paranoiac interpretation.

16. I quote from J. Huizinga, *The Waning of the Middle Ages*, 194, on the great

systems of medieval symbolism and their threatened disintegration into a "chaotic phantasmagoria."

17. In an attempt to "specify some of the modalities of signifying dispositions," Julia Kristeva suggests that "metalanguage and text-practice" (roughly speaking the activities of the critic) are "practices allied with psychotic (paranoid and schizoid) economies." A disturbing statement: partly for its tone (so austere, dispassionate), partly for its implication that built into the reader's or viewer's desire for ordering pattern is a delusionary, ultimately destructive impulse. See Kristeva's *Revolution in Poetic Language*, 89.

18. The panopticon model is most pertinent to the early nineteenth century; midcentury forms of prison discipline (particularly in England) are in some respects worse than panopticism; however, they are also quite different. Sean McConville spoke on the peculiarities of midcentury prison discipline at the annual meeting of the Midwest Victorian Studies Association, spring 1990; his talk was titled "System and Sentiment: A Clash of Views on Crime and Criminals in Late Victorian England." I know less about French developments at this time, but suspect equal variance from the early part of the century.

19. Foucault's last works are perhaps less vulnerable to the criticisms I will register here. See the discussion of Alex Callinicos in *Making History*, 22–25.

20. Alan Megill, "Foucault, Structuralism, and the Ends of History," 494, 498.

21. Charles Taylor, "Foucault on Freedom and Truth," in *Philosophy and the Human Sciences*, 152.

22. At 179–80, Taylor (ibid.) notes one partial exception to his general presentation: in Foucault, "unmasking can only [or at least!] be the basis for a kind of local resistance within the regime." Taylor allows a certain credit to the notion of local resistance—which is after all a form of action—but concludes: "this [strategy] by itself does not determine one to adopt the Nietzschean model of truth, with its relativism and its monolithic analyses. Just because some claims to truth are unacceptable, we do not need to blow the whole conception to pieces."

23. Cf. James Holstun, "Ranting at the New Historicism": "If the alternative to a metaphysical and trans-historical conception of the sovereign self is to be something other than the specter of sheer instrumental domination, or the inversion and celebration of that specter as the 'decentered subject,' then it seems to me it must be a vision of a new, more humane collective life" [225]. To me, Holstun offers the strongest recent critique of the Foucauldian historicism I criticize here.

Chapter 11. *"Dickens's* Arabian Nights*"*

1. William Hazlitt, *Lectures on the English Comic Writers*, in *Complete Works*, 6: 13.

2. S. T. Coleridge, *Selected Poetry and Prose*, 488–89. In the same bit of table talk, Coleridge calls the *Ancient Mariner* a work of "pure imagination."

3. For comments on the *Arabian Nights'* pervasive presence throughout nineteenth-century literature, see Margaret Annan, "The Arabian Nights in Victorian Literature"; Donald Stone, *The Romantic Impulse in Victorian Fiction*, 285–86; and Peter Caracciolo, *The "Arabian Nights" in English Literature*. The phrases quoted from J. L. Borges's "Partial Magic in the *Quixote*" appear in his

Labyrinths, 195. The quotation from Edward Said can be found in his *Beginnings,* 81; cf. Tzvetan Todorov, "Narrative-Men," in *The Poetics of Prose.* Generalizations about the *Arabian Nights* are difficult to make because the book contains such a variety of stories; for an introduction to this subject, see Andras Hamori, *On the Art of Medieval Arabic Literature,* chapters 6 and 7. Generalizations about the book's image in the West—my primary concern here—are perhaps easier to formulate.

4. James Merrill, "The Thousand and Second Night," in *From the First Nine,* 132. Quoted by permission.

5. "The bond between the signifier and the signified is arbitrary. Since I mean by sign the whole that results from the associating of the signifier with the signified, I can simply say: *the linguistic sign is arbitrary*" (French *arbitraire*) [Ferdinand de Saussure, *Course in General Linguistics,* 67]. For difficulties with Saussurean arbitrariness, and an argument for the related but distinct concept of conventionality, see Margaret Deuchar, "Are the Signs of Language Arbitrary?"

6. The great critique of Sue is in Karl Marx's *Holy Family* (see chap. 9, above). For a witty commentary on Sue (among other things), see Isak Dinesen's "A Consolatory Tale," in her *Winter's Tales,* where the young Persian prince Nasrud-Din, who has been reading the *Arabian Nights* and hearing *MP,* attempts to become Harun and Rodolphe at once—with mixed results.

7. "Khalifah," *The Book of the Thousand and One Nights* (hereafter cited as *Book*), 3: 135. This erratic but readable version is usually considered the best so far in a European language. Dickens may have read the *Book* in any of numerous translations, but the auction catalog of his library lists Jonathan Scott's 1811 edition.

8. Remembering—perhaps—this lack of moral earnestness, Stevenson's wife claimed that the character of Florizel was inspired by the example of the Prince of Wales. See Stevenson's *New Arabian Nights* in Robert Louis Stevenson's *Works,* 3: 6. This edition is cited hereafter in brackets in text as *Works.*

9. See the complaint in the *Westminster Review* (January 1883), reprinted in Paul Maixner, ed., *Robert Louis Stevenson,* 119: "Mr. Stevenson's tales are Arabian only in name, the suicides, robberies and murders, which form their subject matter are perpetrated in our own day, not further off than London or Paris, and the treatment and colouring are essentially modern and realistic. Consequently in our opinion they much too nearly resemble glorified and mundane 'Penny dreadfuls'—with royal princes, general officers, physicians, and clergymen for *dramatis personae*—to be regarded as legitimate successors of 'The Arabian Nights.'"

10. The Trollope-Stevenson connection is discussed in Edward Eigner, *Robert Louis Stevenson and Romantic Tradition,* 54–58. Eigner is also interested in the Stevenson hero's difficulty with action, a topic he treats more broadly than I do here.

11. No one believes the novel to be a pure form. All sorts of things get into it: on the same principle that whatever Miss T. eats turns into Miss T., everything that the novel assimilates apparently turns into the novel. The *Arabian Nights* must be assumed to be digestible, but there is a special challenge involved—

especially for the writer who is concerned to explore, describe, and analyze a vast social world like Dickens's London and England. On the novel as an unstable compound, emphasizing both the familiar and the romantic, see Robert Newsom, *Dickens on the Romantic Side of Familar Things,* chap. 5.

12. For "summary and arbitrary power," see *OT,* 11, 74: "the presiding Genii in such an office as this, exercise a summary and arbitrary power . . . enough fantastic tricks are daily played to make the angels blind with weeping."

13. For the *Arabian Nights* and imagination, see Harry Stone, *Dickens and the Invisible World,* 24–26 and passim. Also pertinent is a comment by Angus Wilson: "The *Arabian Nights,* indeed, is a sort of exotic original Mrs Harris, as useful as an authority in all cases where imagination is at work as that mythical lady was a general aid to Mrs Gamp when her rich fancy needed substantial support" [!]; see *The World of Charles Dickens,* 24.

14. This point is made with particular brilliance when Aladdin oversteps the bounds of his power, asking the genie for a roc's egg from the highest peak of Mount Caucasus; the genie then announces that he is the servant of the roc, that his first allegiance is to this mighty Father of Eggs, and that he would like to stomp on Aladdin for even thinking of such a theft. See "Ala Al-Din and the Wonderful Lamp," in *Book,* 3: 435.

15. Harry Stone's comment in his edition of *Uncollected Writings from "Household Words,"* 2: 443.

16. "Ala Al-Din," in *Book,* 3: 415.

17. "The Tale of the Hunchback with the Tailor, the Christian Broker, the Steward and the Jewish Doctor; What Followed after; and the Tales Which Each of Them Told," in *Book,* 1: 174–232.

18. Hazlitt, *Lectures,* in *Complete Works,* 6: 1.

19. [Charles Dickens and Wilkie Collins], "Doctor Dulcamara, M.P.," *HW* 19 (18 December 1858): 49. This description refers to Dulcamara in Donizetti's *L'elisir d'amore,* not Scheherezade's barber.

20. See Ruth Glancy, "Dickens and Christmas."

21. See *OCS,* 64, 475–76 and *TTC,* 2.24, 231. There are magnetic mountains in both the *Persian Tales* (1714) and the *Arabian Nights.*

22. Forster, *Life,* 1: 8. *Tales of the Genii,* an eighteenth-century pastiche of the *Arabian Nights* seems to have influenced Dickens quite as much as its great original. Oddly enough, Victor Hugo's *Le Chateau du diable,* a melodrama that Hugo claimed to have written when ten years old, offers a parallel instance. The plot of *Le Chateau* is borrowed from Pixérécourt's *Les Ruines de Babylone, ou Giafar et Zaïda,* first given in Paris in 1810, and relating the almost incomprehensibly intricate rivalry between Haroun al-Raschid and his vizier, Giafar. For *Le Chateau, Les Ruines,* and a third play that may be Pixérécourt's source and/or Hugo's, see Richard Fargher, "Victor Hugo's First Melodrama."

23. [James Ridley], "The Inchanters; or Misnar, the Sultan of India. Tale the Sixth," in *Tales of the Genii,* 2: 16.

24. Ibid.

25. Chap. 38 of *GE* was published on 4 May 1861. Cf. Walter Thornbury's running comments on East vs. West—especially Constantinople vs. Lon-

don—in his series of Turkish dispatches in *AYR* 2. My thanks to Philip Collins for identifying Thornbury as the author of these articles.

Chapter 12. *"Dickens's Omniscience"*

1. Wayne Booth makes this case in *The Rhetoric of Fiction*, 161: "Many modern works that we usually classify as narrated dramatically, with everything relayed to us through the limited views of the characters, postulate fully as much omniscience in the silent author as Fielding claims for himself."

2. J. Hillis Miller, *The Form of Victorian Fiction*, 88. In Victorian novels, he argues, such narrators "are one form or another of a collective mind."

3. George Eliot often devotes attention to the dilemmas of omniscience, but see especially her novella *The Lifted Veil* (1859), where the subject is supernaturally inclusive vision, a more than conventional omniscience. On Eliot and knowledge generally, the reader can consult Alexander Welsh, *George Eliot and Blackmail*.

4. "Master and Man," *AYR* 3 (26 May 1860): 159; [John Hollingshead], "A New Chamber of Horrors," *AYR* 4 (2 March 1861): 500.

5. The idea of the Shadow was confided to Forster in an awkward, almost embarrassed outpouring: see *Pilgrim Edition*, 5: 622–23, for more on this "previously unthought-of Power."

6. *BH*, with its contrast between Esther and pseudo omniscient characters like Tulkinghorn, provides a prelude to the later stages of Dickens's struggle over omniscience. See chap. 8 above, and—for a line of thought from the Shadow to *BH* specifically—"Charles Dickens, Hans Christian Andersen, and 'The Shadow,'" where Irene Woods traces the Shadow mythology back to a story by Hans Christian Andersen and forward to Tulkinghorn. Gradgrind of *HT* may also belong in this company, though his uses for knowledge are different from Tulkinghorn's.

7. Dickens would have been quite familiar with journalistic cramming, since he encouraged so many of his writers to do it. In his autobiography John Hollingshead records the following words of his erstwhile chief: "Let Hollingshead do it. . . . He's the most ignorant man on the staff [of *HW*], but he'll cram up the facts, and won't give us an encyclopaedical article" [Hollingshead, *My Lifetime*, 1: 190].

8. Georg Simmel's clearest exposition of "objective culture" is in *The Philosophy of Money*, 449. Ian Hacking's discussion is in *Why Does Language Matter to Philosophy?*, 50–51, 157–87. The old notion of "proof"—where perception is used as a metaphor for knowledge—has precedents in the memory systems of the Middle Ages and the Renaissance (themselves based on Platonic traditions).

9. See chap. 60 of *The Prime Minister* where—in a passage much-beloved of Trollopians—the great railway junction outside London becomes an image of modern society: "It is a marvellous place, quite unintelligible to the uninitiated, and yet daily used by thousands who only know that when they get there, they are to do what someone tells them. . . . Not a minute passes without a train going here or there . . . the spectator at last acknowledges that over all this apparent chaos there is presiding a great genius of order." While

Trollope is a bit vague about the identity of his "great genius" (the only informed people we see at the junction are officials appropriately called "pundits"), it is implied that the genius is society itself. Trollope is praising the accumulated wisdom of tradition—but this Burkean notion has been strangely recast in modern industrial and scientific terms. Tradition has become autonomous knowledge in its conservative version.

10. Cf. Karl Marx, *The Eighteenth Brumaire of Louis Napoleon:* "the state enmeshes, controls, punishes, superintends bourgeois society from its most comprehensive manifestations of life down to its most insignificant stirrings . . . this parasitic body acquires a ubiquity, an omniscience, a capacity for swifter motion and an elasticity which has an analogy only in the helpless dependence . . . of the actual body of society" [in *The Marx-Engels Reader*, 470].

11. See Ralph Straus's *Sala*, 95.

12. George Sala, *Twice Round the Clock*, 49.

13. In *Commissioned Spirits*, Jonathan Arac surveys many of the Victorian references to Asmodeus: see especially 22 and 111–13. It is not until 6 P.M. that Sala's Asmodeus ends up on the omnibus, "unroofing London in a ride from the White Horse Cellar to Hammersmith Gate" [*Twice Around the Clock*, 220]—but the informed reader will have expected this descent, such is our author's love for the city streets!

14. Sala, *Twice Round the Clock*, 50.

15. Ibid., 35, 28–29.

16. [Sala], "Imaginary London: A Delusive Directory. I. Ticonderoga Square, E.C.," *Belgravia* 16 (February 1872): 437.

17. Sala, "The Great Red Book," *HW* 10 (9 December 1854): 408. Sala was not the first to write this kind of article—cf. "A Look into a Directory," *Chambers's Edinburgh Journal* (1848): 280–82—but no previous example has quite this tone of wavering, facetious hysteria. Perhaps Dickens, with his compulsive desire to popularize or transform "useful information" subjects, was partly to blame here. Another of Dickens's journalistic disciples was to treat the *London Directory* almost as tensely, just a few years later: [James Payn], "Meliboeus on the Commercial World of London," *Chambers's Edinburgh Journal* 17–18, 3d ser. (1 February 1862), where Meliboeus protests that "I have eyes in my head and I use them. . . . *I know more about London than any other man in the world.*" However, it turns out that he has only been "getting up the Commercial Directory" [79]. In "London Directories," P. J. Atkins offers a highly illuminating guide to the accuracy (or inaccuracy) of these volumes: so far as Meliboeus trusted to them *exclusively*, he would have deluded himself on many important points.

18. The appropriate point of reference would be those precursors of the Victorian *London Directory*, compilations like *Tallis' Street-Views*, where major London streets are diagrammed shop by shop: elevations are given for each side of the street, with a little engraving of the "street-view" tucked away at the far end of the sheet. This sort of directory is still closely connected with the visible appearance of London. By contrast, alphabetical or analytical order establishes an abstract, conceptual space: the city is recreated in the image of the book, rather than the book attempting to imitate the city.

19. It is certain that Andrew Wynter had read some of Dickens's work, because he published a slightly altered version of "Shops and Their Tenants" (*SB*) under his own name. See "A Chapter on Shop-Windows," in Wynter's popular *Our Social Bees*, 123–33; this anthology also collects Wynter's essays from other periodicals (*Once a Week, Fraser's,* etc.). Another Wynter imitation or even plagiarism of Dickens is "The Post-Office," in *Our Social Bees,* 1–23: cf. [Dickens with W. H. Willis], "Valentine's Day at the Post-Office," *HW* 1 (30 March 1850): 6–12.

20. "Hyde Park" appeared in *HW* 5 (12 June 1852): 302–4, and later in *Our Social Bees,* 43–51.

21. Cf. Wynter, "St George and the Dragon," *HW* 5 (12 June 1852): "The surgeon has broken into the house of life, and every eye [in the operating theater] converges towards his hands . . . those fingers that *see,* as it were, where vision cannot penetrate" [78]. In his autobiography Sala expressed a particular admiration for this passage.

22. Wynter's powers of perception are not just self-proclaimed. The rhetorical assertion of panoramic powers corresponds to an actual accomplishment. The writer manages to observe the variety of people around him, something highly uncommon in sketches of Hyde Park. A judgment here must necessarily be a comparative one. From the 1820s through the end of the century, there are many descriptions of the park complaining that the fashionable promenade has been ruined by intruders, and often looking back nostalgically to a moment *just a few years ago* when the intruders stayed away. For example, set "Hyde Park on a Sunday," in *The Hermit in London,* 1: 35–36 (1822), against Mallock's *Memoirs of Life and Literature,* 94 (on Hyde Park in the 1890s). Are we dealing here with a combination of distorted memories and distorted class perceptions—or did the exclusiveness of Hyde Park rise and fall like the stock market? My guess is that focusing on all the classes who actually used the park was difficult for most of those who wrote about this subject. Even Sala in the brilliant mid-Victorian description of *Quite Alone* [chapter 1 serialized as "Seule au Monde," *AYR* 11 (13 February 1864): 1–9], treats the fact that unfashionable intruders were included in the "everybody" of Hyde Park as a kind of melodramatic revelation: it is the old Eugène Sue trick (see chap. 9, above). By comparison with the other nineteenth-century treatments of Hyde Park (at least those that I have studied), Wynter's is calmly probing. He understands that *everybody* comes through the park.

23. Wynter, "The London Commissariat," in *Curiosities of Civilization,* 200–201. For an example a little nearer to Dickens, cf. [John Hollingshead], "All Night on the Monument," *HW* 17 (30 January 1858): 145–48, where Hollingshead views London during a nighttime sojourn on the Monument, perceiving the city first as a sensory experience, then as a technological and economic marvel, "the whirling vortex of work, of speculation, and of trade" [148].

24. [Henry James], review of Wynter's *Fruit between the Leaves,* 15; Wynter, "The Borderlands of Insanity," in *Borderlands,* pp. 7, 22, 23. In *Madness in Society,* 182–93, George Rosen shows that similar concerns are typical of Victorian medical men.

25. [Charles Dickens], "New Uncommercial Samples: Mr. Barlow," *AYR*, n.s. 1 (16 January 1869): 157—another satire on the man who knows everything.
26. For "mental ruin," see Timbs, *Curiosities*, 194; *Chisel-Marks* is the subtitle of Wynter's *Subtle Brains and Lissom Fingers*.
27. Two examples from *Our Social Bees*: (1) the Commissioner of Police "spider-like, sits in the centre of a web [of telegraphic wires] co-extensive with the metropolis, and is made instantly sensible of any disturbance that may take place at any point" ["The Nervous System of the Metropolis," 287]; (2) Mr. Reuter (of the wire-service) is "a man like ourselves, having 'feelings, organs, dimensions,' etc.," but could easily be conceived as "an institution or a myth" ["Who Is Mr. Reuter?" 297]. Typically, Wynter is suspended between two possibilities: he can either demystify Reuter's apparent omniscience (by demonstrating how autonomous knowledge functions) or he can mythicize it further—and typically the second alternative becomes a subtext to the first.
28. The indefatigable compiler John Timbs—whose *Curiosities of London* Sala admired (see text above for his review)—included the story of this hallucination, the Man of the Mirror, in his *Romance of London*, reviewed in *AYR* 14 (14 October 1865): "London in Books," 270–76, where again the tale of the Man of the Mirror is given special billing [276]. Timbs attributes the story to a Doctor Arnould of Camberwell (whereas Wynter cites "Dr. Prichard"). Timbs's Arnould-derived version includes a touch by which Hugo or the Dickens of *The Chimes* might well have been struck: the Man of the Mirror hears all that is going on through his "organ of hearing" [*Romance* 2: 17], a great bell at Saint Paul's that is in communication with all the other bells "within the circle of hieroglyphics, by which every word spoken by those under my control is made audible to me." Here ringing and writing work together, can indeed be hardly distinguished. Wynter's version of the story appears in his "Hallucinations and Dreams," in *Borderlands*, 261–65.
29. For catoptromantic mirrors, see Theodore Ziolkowski, *Disenchanted Images*, 163–68.
30. On shadows in this novel, see also Elaine Showalter, "Guilt, Authority, and the Shadows of *Little Dorrit*."
31. [Charles Dickens], "Down with the Tide," *HW* 6 (5 February 1853): 481; [Charles Dickens], "The Uncommercial Traveller: Houselessness," *AYR* 3 (21 July 1860): 349, an essay that strongly recalls Sala's "The Key of the Street."
32. This effect might be compared to a lyric interpolation in an epic, a space where narrative stops so that a sustained action can be clarified through pithy summary. Economy is here the grandest gesture possible. There are similar moments earlier in Dickens—particularly in *MHC*—but they seem much more like accidents than does the present example. Cf. *BR*, 3, 71.
33. In "Community and the Limits of Liability," N. N. Feltes discusses the historical conflation of *LD*, where a business world typified by partnerships (like Doyce and Clennam) is combined with one typified by joint-stock companies (from which Mr. Merdle's capital proceeds). Partnerships mandate "personal knowledge, direct involvement and full responsibility" [365]. Joint-stock companies shape a world where capitalism and production are more and

more distant from one another, where nobody (or Nobody?) is completely responsible (liable), and where neither investors, financiers, nor those involved in production have a full picture of what is going on. Feltes notes that the 1850s, the period when *LD* was written, were a turning point in the emergence of the modern joint-stock company.

34. When Dickens responded to Fitzjames Stephens's slashing attack on *LD*, he cited the career of Rowland Hill; see "A Curious Misprint in the *Edinburgh Review*," *HW* 16 (1 August 1857): 97–100. Hill was perhaps appropriately cast as the isolated but brilliant organizer who struggled against the odds to establish the modern post office. But cf. an article from *AYR*, "Strong Guns" [13 (15 September 1860): 544–49], which offers the following supposition: "If there arose in this country a great magician who, by the magic of genius joined to intense labour, solved every unsettled question that now stands in the way of our knowing how to make an absolutely strong and serviceable field gun, what would his chance be with the Ordnance Select Committee?" This imaginary inventor is in the position of Daniel Doyce or Rowland Hill, except that the Ordnance Select Committee "consists of specially informed men." Through nobody's fault—nobody's fault truly—"the subject [of field guns] is one about which the wiser a man is, the more numerous are his uncertainties" [545]. The writer goes on to describe a process of invention and decision making perfectly institutionalized, where nobody is in a position to grasp the whole picture—where there is, in fact, no picture to be grasped. Autonomous knowledge rears its invisible head. It is not a con job (though it might encourage con jobs) but a condition of modern life.

35. Paul Herring, "Dickens's Monthly Number Plans for 'Little Dorrit,'" 52–54.

36. On the conclusion to *LD*, see Randolph Splitter's "Guilt and the Trappings of Melodrama in *Little Dorrit*": "Dickens gives us an imitation of liberation, an elaborate sleight of hand" [133].

37. So—with variations—in *OT*, 50, 442; *MC*, 51, 866; *DS*, 55, 871. The nearest equivalent in *LD* is at 2.31, 856, when Mrs. Clennam makes her mad dash from her "cell," but here "the turbulent irruption of this multitude of staring faces" issues only in mental and architectural collapse.

38. Forster, *Life*, 1: 21–22. The bitter pun ("pitch of perfection") perhaps needs underlining. For memory and London posters, cf. "Astley's," in *SB*, 104.

39. According to Fitzgerald, Dickens delighted in designing eye-catching posters to publicize his work. Billsticking itself translates the pasting of labels into a dream of omnipresent power.

40. See *GE*, 51, 423–26, a passage discussed in more detail by Anthony Winner in "Character and Knowledge in Dickens."

41. It is Betty Higden who famously announces of Sloppy, "He do the Police in different voices" [*OMF*, 1.16, 246]. T. S. Eliot used this line as the original title of the poem that became *The Waste Land*, and *The Waste Land*, of course, is another work that emphasizes the incomprehensible (newspaperlike) fragmentation of London. However, it is worth noting that even Eliot depends on a fiction of human omniscience in the person of his all-seeing Tiresias.

42. The peculiarities of *OMF* were noticed by J. Hillis Miller in *Charles Dickens*, 291–93; here he emphasizes the limits of the narrator's knowledge. In *Dickens*

and Reality, John Romano treats the novel as a gateway to all of Dickens's work; the book is seen as dwelling on what lies beyond the boundaries of our understanding. "Reality is forever escaping our grasp" [47]. Arac's *Commissioned Spirits* disputes Romano in crucial ways—but Arac too believes that *OMF* rejects the ambition of omniscient overview, overview having become "suffocatingly all-enveloping" [64]. For Arac what replaces overview is writing, words liberated from usable meaning: he quotes Henry James's extraordinary comment that the novel is not "seen, known, or felt" but *"written"* [185]. Rosemary Mundhenk, "The Education of the Reader in *Our Mutual Friend,"* suggests a reader-response explanation of Dickens's frustrating play with point of view. In *Charles Dickens,* Stephen Connor examines the problem of John Harmon's identity; he mentions shifters (but not the inset) and he has some striking comments on Harmon's anomalous position as "secretary" to his own autonomous affairs [157, 154]. Among recent treatments, Albert Hutter's "Dismemberment and Articulation in *Our Mutual Friend"* is particularly interesting: according to Hutter, "so powerful are the elements of dismemberment in the novel that they continue to act on us, just as we might look at the reconstituted corpse of Hannah Brown [victim of a notorious murder] . . . and yet always have before us the vision of her dismemberment" [158]. Willed unity is thus one more form of incoherence; things constructed are reminders of disintegration. For the ubiquity of paper in *OMF,* Richard Altick offers broad documentation and commentary: see his "Education, Print, and Paper."

43. Philip Collins, *Dickens: Interviews,* 2: 326.
44. I am working from Jeremy Campbell's popular account of information theory, *Grammatical Man,* especially 48–49 (on the demon and on Leo Szilard's reconsideration of him) and 88–90 (on David Layzer's Cosmological Principle: the stack of cards is Layzer's example). For another critique of omniscience in science, see Ilya Prigogine, *Order Out of Chaos,* a volume more technical than Campbell's but still popular: especially 75–77, "LaPlace's Demon." On the use of demons as "sophisticated rhetorical figures," see Helen Trimpi's "Demonology," in *The Dictionary of the History of Ideas,* 1: 670.
45. See Ann Wilkinson, *"Bleak House:* From Faraday to Judgment Day."
46. James Clerk Maxwell's "Analogies in Nature" was presented to the Apostles Club at Cambridge in February 1856. Maxwell writes, "That analogies appear to exist is plain in the face of things, for all parables, fables, similes, metaphors, tropes, and figures of speech are analogies, natural or revealed, artificial or concealed" [Maxwell, "Essay for the Apostles on 'Analogies in Nature,' " in *The Scientific Letters and Papers of James Clerk Maxwell,* 376].
47. See Neil Forsyth, "Wonderful Chains: Dickens and Coincidence."
48. On Alfred Crowquill, etc., see my preface. Andrew Wynter's exploration of small mysteries is "Palace Lights, Club Cards, and Bank Pens" (*Our Social Bees,* 226–28). However, it is Sala who used this conceit most frequently. See especially "The Precinct," *AYR* 3 (12 May 1860): 115–20, and *Twice Around the Clock,* where Sala's mysterymongering reaches a kind of climax. (Evidently it reaches another sort of climax in the pornographic *Mysteries of Verbena House,* a work I have not been able to examine.)

49. Nancy Metz, "The Artistic Reclamation of Waste in *Our Mutual Friend*," emphasizes the side of the book that values the transformation of unusable into usable things (e.g., Jenny Wren making her dolls); Arac, *Commissioned Spirits*, 183, suggests more unusually that "we do not want to be in the grotesque shop of Venus, or out on the river with Gaffer, or stumping in the mounds." These readers (publishing at the same moment) are both correct, I think, but they leave us with a little difficulty about waste in *OMF*.

50. Campbell, *Grammatical Man*, 88. I have replaced "universe" with "city."

51. Thus the statistics of *TC* [171 and 178] or of *HT*. Among Dickens's less deterministic accounts of statistical thinking there is Montague Tigg's reliance on probabilities in the con game of his insurance racket [*MC*, 27, 514]—but Montague is of course a scamp, a villain, and his calculations no more than a form of gambling.

52. Campbell, *Grammatical Man*, 88. I think that we can understand *meaningful* not just in the casual sense but with Hacking's denotation, by which "meaning" is shared discourse: more public than "ideas" but less cut off from mind than is autonomous knowledge. Cf. the difficulty—discussed by Campbell—in deciding whether probability is an "objective" or a "subjective" phenomenon.

53. John Ruskin, "Fiction, Fair and Foul," in *Works*, 34: 267.

Chapter 13. "The City and the Cosmos, or, Digging Your Own Grave"

1. Richard Roud, "Feuillade," in *Cinema: A Critical Dictionary*, 1: 350–51, discusses the connection between *Fantomas* and the novel of urban mysteries. On surrealism, film, and city life (i.e., on a twentieth-century version of urban Gothic fiction), see Anne Michelson, "Dr. Crase and Mr. Clair." Hollywood films (not Michelson's subject) also help revive the tradition of urban mysteries. William Dieterle's extraordinary *Hunchback of Notre Dame*, starring Charles Laughton (1939), has never faded from the minds of American moviemakers and moviegoers: recent production—*The Fly, Batman, Gremlins II, Darkman*, are particularly intent on evoking its wonders. My "Return of Quasimodo" treats the case of *The Fly*. For an excellent filmography of Hugo (beginning with an *Esmeralda* of 1906 and ending with a *Les Misérables* of 1982), see Pierre Georgel, Jean-Paul Boulanger, and Geneviève Renisio, *La Gloire de Victor Hugo*, 778 ff.

2. The parallels are explored in Jeffrey Mehlman, *Revolution and Repetition*, 130–32. See also chap. 5 of Victor Brombert's *Victor Hugo and the Visionary Novel*.

3. J. A. Nicklin, *Dickens-Land*, 19. Dickens's use of *ND* in *ED* has been studied by Wendy Jacobson in *The Companion to "The Mystery of Edwin Drood."* Jacobson demonstrates the links between certain specific scenes: Frollo bursting into laughter in front of Quasimodo is like Jasper bursting into laughter in front of Durdles; the panorama from Rochester Cathedral is like the panorama from Notre-Dame Cathedral; Frollo declaring his passion to Esmeralda is like Jasper declaring his passion to Rosa [Jacobson, *Companion*, 117, 119, 156]. I would add: the slight oddity of Dickens imitating *ND* this closely, so long after the novel's publication (might one not have expected a Dickensian Gothic cathedral novel in the 1830s or 1840s?) is paralleled by a theatrical revival of interest

in *ND,* at roughly the same time. In 1871, the year after *ED* (and the year after Dickens's death), there were three separate dramatic productions of *ND* running in London—one written by Andrew Halliday, Dickens's friend and a frequent *AYR* contributor (up until that time there had been only two such productions, one in 1834, one in 1852, both apparently, by the same author, Edward Fitzball). See Victor Bowley, "*Notre-Dame* and *Les Misérables* on the English Stage."

4. Goethe, letter of 22 June 1808 [*Goethe's Letters to Zelter,* 60].

5. In "Walter Benjamin's Chthonian Revolution," Ned Lukacher shows that Benjamin's fascination with a chthonian mythology has both right-wing and left-wing implications. One can see Benjamin as a revolutionary or a "neo-romantic fascist" depending on how one interprets his interest in "subterranean mysteries" [Lukacher, "Revolution," 48, 55]. This sort of ambiguity is not peculiar to Benjamin; it can also be found in Hugo and Dickens, among other nineteenth-century authors.

6. See especially chap. 5, above, on *OCS*.

7. Morphologically, the octopus recalls Gilliat's bagpipe, his major means of expression when courting Déruchette. Putting aside bagpipes (so far as I can), the octopus is an emblem of hypocrisy; it is the zoological counterpart of two-faced Sieur Clubin, who was originally responsible for scuttling *Durande* and who has recently been slain by this same animal. The octopus also doubles for *Durande* and for Gilliat's intended. Devilfish, devil boat, and Déruchette is a trinity that the novelist chooses to emphasize. Not to stop here, the octopus embodies that complex unity with which Gilliat has struggled—only it uses his own methods against him, something no other natural force has done. ("Nous l'avons dit, on ne s'arrache pas à la pieuvre. . . . Son effort croît en raison du vôtre. Plus de secousse produit plus de constriction" (We have already said, one does not struggle against the octopus. . . . Her effort increases as yours does. Every jolt produces another constriction) [443]. Finally, the octopus confirms the voracity of nature; blessed with an extraordinary cavity (both mouth and anus, Hugo insists, against all anatomical evidence), the octopus kills, eats, voids—and then goes through the same routine again.

8. On circulation, see particularly Wolfgang Giegerich, "Deliverance from the Stream of Events," where Giegerich studies "the conception of a water continuously streaming back into its source, in unending circulation." This water is linked with the Greek primal ocean, Okeanos; with urban sewers; with the circulation of the blood; and with such phenomena as "band, tie, cord, ring, girdle, noose, knot" [119, 123]. These—conspicuously Hugolian—associations define a realm of necessity that can be conceived to exist either outside human beings or within them. Of *LT,* one might say that Gilliant's descent into the ocean compels him to internalize circulation; in one sense this is a deliverance, in another an introduction to a set of problems that he has not previously faced. While Giegerich's schema can hardly provide the last word on *LT*—Gilliat is situated too equivocally between an archaic and a modern world for that—it confirms both Hugo's sensitivity to the implications of long-established mythical images and his willingness to use such images for his own particular purposes.

9. See Yves Gohin's introduction to *ND* and *LT,* 1289. Both house and grotto are "demeures délabrées et creuses comme des antres, fermées de hauts murs, ouvertes cependant à la pluie, au froid et aux vents; gîtes où se rejoignent les êtres des bas-fonds; points de convergence des activités nocturnes du désir; habitacles de Satan" (abodes dilapidated and hollowed out like caves, closed off by high walls, open nonetheless to the rain, the cold and the winds; lairs where beings of the underworld caught up with one another; meeting points for nocturnal acts of desire; habitations of Satan)—and so forth.

10. Hugo's books contain many spiderlike monsters, but there is an especially striking parallel between the octopus and the dream tarantula of *PS,* whose bite causes people to dance an unending dance—until all that is left of them are dancing heads surrounded by fragments of ribs "Cette ronde de têtes use la terre, y creuse un cercle horrible et disparaît" (This ring of heads wears away the earth, hollows out a horrible circle there and disappears) [472]. *PS* was written in late 1863. The legend of the tarantula is part of what Hugo calls the Gothic phantasmagoria. The octopus of *LT* bites Gilliat with much the same effect as the tarantula bites its victims (note both the susceptibility to going around in circles and the disappearing head). The spiderish monster creates (even embodies) a mad circle of self-destruction.

11. From the caption to an unnumbered plate following 120 in Roger Callois, *La Pieuvre.*

12. The passage is quoted, and the aftermath narrated, in Caillois, *La Pieuvre,* 82 ff.

13. Is there also a Gilliat-like death wish implicit in the notion of the great author? Hugo was fond of punning "Shakespeare" and "j'expire"; even at its most affirmative, his mind remained antithetical.

14. *ED,* 14, 154. Cf. Angus Wilson's sharp remark: "The oddest aspect of *The Mystery of Edwin Drood* as we have it is the degree to which England has shrunk to a cathedral town and its classes to the upper-middle professional class" [*The World of Charles Dickens,* 291]. Wilson's comment does not acknowledge Durdles, an important figure. But he is right about the oddness of England's shrinkage. Something new is going on here, something Dickens has not tried before.

15. Nicklin, *Dickens-Land,* 14. It is unclear at what time in the past *ED* is set, but see the Penguin edition, where Arthur Cox summarizes the reasons for supposing the story to take place before the 1840s [*The Mystery of Edwin Drood* (Harmondsworth: Penguin Books, 1974), 306 n. 3].

16. The towns were "indistinguishably overlapping" to Nicklin in 1919 [*Dickens-Land,* 13–14]; so were they in 1830 to W. H. Ireland, who describes Chatham, Rochester, and Strood as sharing "one long street, more than two miles in length, [the resulting conurbation] commonly called the Three Towns" [*A New and Complete History of the County of Kent,* 4: 347]. Just a few years later Mr. Pickwick writes of "the four towns" (i.e., he includes Brompton in the reckoning).

17. Dickens consistently refers to Cloisterham as a "city." In this context the word implies, not size, but status: "Under the Norman kings, the episcopal sees, which were formerly often established in villages, began to be removed to the

chief borough or 'city' of the diocese. . . . there grew up a notion of identification between 'city and 'cathedral town' " [*OED*].

18. Dickens: "The Uncommercial Traveller: Houselessness," *AYR* 3 (21 July 1860): 351. Michel Ragon chronicles the removal (or closing) of urban cemeteries during the late-eighteenth and early-nineteenth centuries. He is particularly interesting on the phenomenon of mortuary stations, first built in England around 1850 and conducting the traveler from London to special pastoral cemeteries. Historically, then, Dickens's armies of the dead were being conducted out of the metropolis by one means or another for decades before the years of *AYR* and *ED*. See Ragon's *The Space of Death*, 202–3.

19. The classic points of reference are Edmund Wilson's essay on "Dickens: The Two Scrooges," especially 83–94, and Philip Collins, *Dickens and Crime*, 290–319. My sympathies are more with Wilson than with Collins, but an adequate reading of *ED* would have to come to terms with both sides of Cloisterham and of the novel, something I try to do here.

20. Angus Fletcher, *Allegory*, 128–46. On the Babylonian belief see Joan Evans, *Magical Jewels*, 14.

21. Before one gets to "darkening," the "splashes" of the rooks seem to be juxtaposed with the "moaning water . . . at their feet"; once "darkening" enters the sentence, the verbal echo compels one to rethink this association. "Darker" anticipates rather than recalls. The style of *ED* is characterized by such wheels-within-wheels, boxes-within-boxes effects. See William Burgan, "The Refinement of Contrast."

22. This is familiar territory for critics of *ED;* I will point only to the crucial passage at 3, 20, where Dickens explains that Miss Twinkleton has "two distinct and separate phases of being." The implication is that she's not the only one.

23. At an early stage of thinking about *ED*, Dickens wrote to Forster, "what should you think of the idea of a story beginning in this way?—Two people, boy and girl, or very young, going apart from one another, pledged to be married after many years . . . the interest to arise out of the tracing of their separate ways, and the impossibility of telling what will be done with that impending fate." A month later the novelist had "laid aside the fancy I told you of and have a very curious and new idea . . . not a communicable idea" [Forster, *Life*, 2: 365–66]. What happens at the end of chap. 13 is that Dickens completes his telling of the original idea, the one he had supposedly "laid aside"—even while he lays the foundation for a transmuted and much more elaborately developed version of it. In other words, the novel mimes its own process of conception, so that we can observe—if we know the letter to Forster—one premise metamorphosing into another. And we can also pinpoint better the concerns common to the two narrative lines. One other (speculative) connection is worth the mention. The night after Edwin's murder, the hands of the cathedral clock have been torn off and there is evidence of damage up on the tower. It is possible that the damage is evidence of a struggle and that Edwin has fallen to his death—*into* the panorama of chap. 12—after trying to break away from Jasper, slipping, and grabbing the clock hands. Of the many attempts to finish *ED*, the most thoughtful as a detective solution is Forsyte's

The Decoding of Edwin Drood; Forsyte [193] connects the writhing slave on the spear, Jasper's fear of the abyss in his journey toward murder, and the evidences of damage on the tower the night after the murder to suggest how the crime was actually committed.

24. See John Beer's "*Edwin Drood* and the Mystery of Apartness," 163.

25. I proceed by inference, but most of my surmises reflect the consensus on *ED*. For Edwin's burial in Mrs. Sapsea's monument see especially Richard Baker, *The Drood Murder Case*, 47. (Baker is brilliant here, but later [61 ff.] he gets Mrs. Sapsea's tomb confused with another, less capacious one and is thus encouraged to press his case too far.)

26. This is substantially the position of Philip Collins in *Dickens and Crime*, 308: the novel is a detective story first and foremost.

27. The reader is directed to Forsyte's completion of *ED*, especially 138 ff. Here will be found Forsyte's continuation of the "Sapsea fragment" originally published in Forster's *Life*. Forsyte has the Poker of that episode praise Mr. Sapsea's epitaph for his wife as "a deathless page written in stone!" "This Crown Jewel, the Inscription," he avers, "must be seen in all the perfection of its setting." Forsyte is on to something.

28. Gaston Bachelard, *La Terre et les rêveries de la volonté*, 322.

29. Bert Hornback writes of *ED* that "the primary focus is on a larger kind of knowing, a comprehensive and comprehending kind of 'watching' that those who are grown up take on as their role, their duty." This comment suggests the sort of mixture that the ring helps create ["*The Hero of My Life*," 139]. Forsyte [*Decoding*, 177] and Leon Garfield [*The Mystery of Edwin Drood Concluded*, 298 ff.] both suggest that after its involvement in Drood's murder, the ring is somehow defiled. It is hard to imagine Rosa happily wearing it on her wedding day—even before the murder this jewel is a sorrowful one!—but after all, the ring is consistently presented as a creator and reminder of truth, and truth (it would seem) can survive the most corrosive substance.

30. Forster, *Life*, 2: 366: "all discovery of the murderer was to be baffled till towards the close, when, by means of a gold ring which had resisted the corrosive effects of the lime into which he had thrown the body, not only the person murdered was to be identified but the locality of the crime and the man who committed it." Moreover, the murderer was to review his "career by himself at the close, when its temptations were to be dwelt upon as if, not he the culprit, but some other man, were the tempted." The murderer's wickedness would be "all elaborately elicited from him as if told of another."

31. According to Dickens, Ezekiel 18:27 is a keynote of his novel [*ED*, 1, 4 and n. to 1, 40].

32. Edgar Johnson, *Charles Dickens*, 2: 1153–54.

Bibliography

THE FOLLOWING BIBLIOGRAPHY is designed to be used in conjunction with the list of works frequently cited at the beginning of this volume. Materials are listed under seven headings (no item is listed twice, though some could have been).

1. *Works on or by Dickens, Hugo, and Other Writers of Fiction or Poetry*
2. *City Life*
3. *Allegory*
4. *Literary and Linguistic Theory*
5. *The History of Art, Architecture, and Film, with Associated Works on Images and Iconography*
6. *Cultural, Social, Intellectual, and Political History*
7. *Nineteenth-Century Periodicals*

Works on or by Dickens, Hugo, and Other Writers of Fiction or Poetry

Adams, D. J., and A. R. W. James. "Bibliographie sommaire des oeuvres de Hugo traduites en Anglais de son vivant." In *Victor Hugo et La Grande-Bretagne,* edited by A. R. W. James. Paris: Francis Cairns, 1986: 203–16.

Ainsworth, W. H. *Collected Works.* Author's Copyright Edition. 14 vols. London: The Waverley Book Company, n.d.

——— [attributed to]. *Nell Gwynne, or the Court of the Stuarts: An Historical Romance.* Philadelphia, 1847.

Allen, James Smith. "History and the Novel: *Mentalité* in Modern Popular Fiction." *History and Theory* 22, no. 3 (1983): 233–52.

Altick, Richard. "Education, Print, and Paper in *Our Mutual Friend*." In *Nineteenth-Century Literary Perspectives: Essays in Honor of Lionel Stevenson,* edited by Clyde de L. Ryals, 237–54. Durham, N.C.: Duke University Press, 1974.

Andrews, Larry. "Dostoevskij and Hugo's *Le Dernier Jour d'un condamné*." *Comparative Literature* 29 (Winter 1977): 1–16.

Angenot, Marc. "Roman et idéologie: *Les Mystères de Paris*." *Revue des langues vivantes* 38 (1972): 392–410.

Annan, Margaret. "The Arabian Nights in Victorian Literature." Ph.D. dissertation, Northwestern University, 1945.

Arac, Jonathan. *Commissioned Spirits: The Shaping of Social Motion in Dickens,*

Carlyle, Melville, and Hawthorne. New Brunswick, N.J.: Rutgers University Press, 1979.

Ariosto, Ludovico. *Orlando Furioso,* translated by Barbara Reynolds. 2 vols. Harmondsworth: Penguin Books, 1975.

Auerbach, Nina. *Woman and the Demon: The Life of a Victorian Myth.* Cambridge, Mass.: Harvard University Press, 1982.

Bach, Max. "Critique et politique: La Réception des *Misérables* en 1862." *PMLA* 77 (December 1962): 595–608.

———. "Le Vieux Paris dans *Notre-Dame:* Sources et ressources de Victor Hugo." *PMLA* 80 (September 1965): 321–24.

Baker, Richard. *The Drood Murder Case.* Berkeley: University of California Press, 1951.

Baldick, Chris. *In Frankenstein's Shadow: Myth, Monstrosity, and Nineteenth-Century Writing.* Oxford: Clarendon Press, 1987.

Barrère, Jean-Bertrand. *La Fantasie de Victor Hugo.* 3 vols. Paris: Editions Klincksieck, 1973.

Barrett, Elizabeth. *Elizabeth Barrett to Miss Mitford,* edited by Betty Miller. London: J. Murray, 1954.

Baudelaire, Charles. *Oeuvres complètes,* edited by Y.-G Le Dantec and Claude Pichois. Paris: Editions Gallimard, 1961.

Bayley, John. "The Upper Depths," review of Max Hayward, *Writers in Russia: 1917–1978. New York Review of Books.* 22 December 1983: 22–25.

Beer, John. "*Edwin Drood* and the Mystery of Apartness." *Dickens Studies Annual* 13 (1984): 143–91.

Blackall, Eric. *Goethe and the Novel.* Ithaca, N.Y.: Cornell University Press, 1976.

The Book of the Thousand and One Nights, rendered into English by Powys Mathers from the French translation of J. C. Mardrus. 4 vols. New York: St. Martin's Press, 1972.

Borges, Jorge Luis. *Labyrinths: Selected Stories and Other Writings,* edited by Donald Yates and James Irby. New York: New Directions, 1964.

Bowley, Victor. "*Notre-Dame* and *Les Misérables* on the English Stage." *French Quarterly* 11 (December 1929): 210–21.

Breton, André. *Mad Love,* translated by M. A. Caws. Lincoln: University of Nebraska Press, 1988.

Brochu, André. *Amour/Crime/Révolution. Essai sur "Les Misérables."* Montréal: Les Presses de l'Université de Montréal, 1974.

Brombert, Victor. "Hugo's *William Shakespeare:* The Promontory and the Infinite." *Hudson Review* 34 (Summer 1981): 249–57.

———. "The Rhetoric of Contemplation: Hugo's 'La Pente de la rêverie.'" In *Nineteenth-Century French Poetry: Introductions to Close Reading,* edited by Christopher Prendergast. Cambridge: Cambridge University Press, 1990: 48–61.

———. *The Romantic Prison: The French Tradition.* Princeton, N.J.: Princeton University Press, 1978.

———. "*Les Travailleurs de la mer:* Hugo's Poem of Effacement." *New Literary History* 9 (Spring 1978): 581–90.

————. "V.H.: L'Auteur éffacé ou le moi de l'infini." *Poétique* 52 (November 1982): 417–29.

————. *Victor Hugo and the Visionary Novel.* Cambridge, Mass.: Harvard University Press, 1984.

Brooks, Peter. *Reading for the Plot: Design and Intention in Narrative.* New York: Knopf, 1984.

Brown, Nathalie Babel. *Hugo and Dostoyevsky.* Ann Arbor, Mich.: Ardis, 1978.

Burgan, William M. "The Refinement of Contrast: Manuscript Revision in *Edwin Drood.*" *Dickens Studies Annual* 6 (1977): 167–82.

Burns, Wayne. *Charles Reade: A Study in Victorian Authorship.* New York: Bookman Associates, 1971.

Caracciolo, Peter, ed. *The "Arabian Nights" in English Literature: Studies in the Reception of "The Thousand and One Nights" into British Culture.* New York: St. Martin's Press, 1988.

Carey, John. *Here Comes Dickens: The Imagination of a Novelist.* New York: Schocken Books, 1974.

Carrera, Rosalina de la. "History's Unconscious in Victor Hugo's *Les Misérables.*" *MLN* 96 (May 1981): 839–55.

Caserio, Robert. "Joseph Conrad, Dickensian Novelist of the Nineteenth Century: A Dissent from Ian Watt." *Nineteenth-Century Fiction* 36 (December 1981): 337–47.

————. "The Name of the Horse: *Hard Times,* Semiotics, and the Supernatural." *Novel* (Fall 1986): 5–23.

————. *Plot, Story, and the Novel: From Dickens and Poe to the Modern Period.* Princeton, N.J.: Princeton University Press, 1979.

Chaitin, Gilbert D. "Victor Hugo and the Hieroglyphic Novel." *Nineteenth-Century French Studies* 19 (Fall 1990): 36–53.

Coleridge, Samuel Taylor. *Collected Works,* general editors Kathleen Coburn and Bart Winer. Princeton, N.J.: Princeton University Press, 1971– .

————. *Selected Poetry and Prose,* edited by Stephen Potter. London: The Nonesuch Press, 1950.

Collins, Philip. *Dickens: Interviews and Recollections.* 2 vols. Totowa, N.J.: Barnes and Noble, 1981.

————. *Dickens and Crime.* Bloomington: Indiana University Press, 1968.

————. "Dickensian Errata." *TLS,* 20 November 1987: 1278.

————. "Little Dorrit: The Prison and the Critics." *TLS,* 18 April 1980: 445–46.

Connor, Stephen. *Charles Dickens.* Oxford: Basil Blackwell, 1985.

Cowley, Malcolm, ed. *Writers at Work.* 1st ser. Harmondsworth: Penguin Books, 1983.

Craig, David. *The Real Foundations: Literature and Social Change.* New York: Oxford University Press, 1974.

Curtius, Ernst Robert. *European Literature and the Latin Middle Ages,* translated by Willard Trask. New York: Harper and Row, 1953.

Decaux, Alain. *Victor Hugo.* Paris: Libraire Académique Perrin, 1984.

Dédéyan, Charles. *Victor Hugo et L'Allegmagne.* Paris: Minard, 1964.

Dickens, Charles. *Bleak House,* edited by George Ford and Sylvère Monod. New York: Norton, 1977.

———. *The Nonesuch Dickens.* 23 vols. Bloomsbury: The Nonesuch Press, 1937–38.

Diedrick, James. "The 'Grotesque Body': Physiology in *The Mill on the Floss.*" *Mosaic* 21 (Fall 1988): 27–43.

Dinesen, Isak. *Winter's Tales.* New York: Random House, 1942.

Dostoyevsky, Fyodor. *The Idiot,* translated by Constance Garnett. New York: Random House, Modern Library, 1925.

Dryden, John. *Works.* Berkeley: University of California Press, 1956– .

Egan, Pierce, Jr. *The Waits.* London, 1884.

Eigner, Edward. *The Metaphysical Novel in England and America: Dickens, Bulwer, Melville, and Hawthorne.* Berkeley: University of California Press, 1978.

———. *Robert Louis Stevenson and Romantic Tradition.* Princeton, N.J.: Princeton University Press, 1966.

Eliot, T. S. *The Complete Poems and Plays.* London: Faber and Faber, 1969.

Ellroy, James. *The Black Dahlia.* New York: The Mysterious Press, 1987.

Ermarth, Elizabeth Deeds. *Realism and Consensus in the English Novel.* Princeton, N.J.: Princeton University Press, 1983.

Fanger, Donald. *Dostoyevsky and Romantic Realism: A Study of Dostoyevsky in Relation to Balzac, Dickens, and Gogol.* Chicago: University of Chicago Press, 1967.

Fargher, Richard. "Victor Hugo's First Melodrama." In *Balzac and the Nineteenth Century,* edited by D. G. Charlton, J. Gaudon, and Anthony R. Pugh, 297–310. New York: Humanities Press, 1972.

Feltes, N. N. "Community and the Limits of Liability in Two Mid-Victorian Novels." *Victorian Studies* 17 (June 1974): 355–69.

———. *Modes of Production of Victorian Novels.* Chicago: University of Chicago Press, 1986.

[Féval, Paul]. *The Mysteries of London: or Revelations of the British Metropolis,* translated by R. Stephenson. London, 1847.

Fitzgerald, Percy. *Memories of Charles Dickens.* Bristol: J. W. Arrowsmith, 1913.

Flaubert, Gustave. *Madame Bovary,* translated by Paul de Man. New York: Norton, 1965.

Fleishman, Avrom. "The City and the River: Dickens's Symbolic Landscape." In *Studies in the Later Dickens,* edited by Jean-Claude Amalric, 111–24. Montpéllier: Université Paul Valéry, 1973.

———. *Fiction and the Ways of Knowing.* Austin: University of Texas Press, 1978.

Ford, George. *Dickens and His Readers: Aspects of Novel-Criticism since 1836.* New York: Norton, 1965.

Forsyte, Charles. *The Decoding of Edwin Drood.* London: Victor Gollancz, 1980.

Forsyth, Neil. "Wonderful Chains: Dickens and Coincidence." *Modern Philology* 83 (November 1985): 157–65.

"French Romances." *Fraser's Magazine* 27 (February 1843): 184–94.

Garfield, Leon. *The Mystery of Edwin Drood Concluded.* New York: Pantheon Books, 1980.

Garret, Peter. *The Victorian Multiplot Novel: Studies in Dialogical Form.* New Haven, Conn.: Yale University Press, 1980.

Georgel, Pierre, Jean-Paul Boulanger, and Geneviève Renisio. *La Gloire de Victor Hugo.* Paris: Editions de la réunion des musées nationaux, 1985.

Gillet, Michel. "Machines de roman-feuilletons." *Romantisme* 41 (1983): 79–90.

Ginsburg, Michal Peled. "Truth and Persuasion: The Language of Realism and of Ideology in *Oliver Twist.*" *Novel* 20 (Spring 1987): 220–36.

Glancy, Ruth. "Dickens and Christmas: His Framed-Tale Themes." *Nineteenth-Century Fiction* 5 (June 1981): 53–72.

Goethe, Johann Wolfgang Von. *Faust: Der Tragödie erster und zweiter Teil.* Munich: Verlag, 1969.

———. *Faust,* edited by Cyrus Hamlin. New York: Norton, 1976.

———. *Goethe's Letters to Zelter,* translated by A. D. Coleridge. London: George Bell and Son, 1887.

———. *Selected Verse,* with an introduction and prose translations by David Luke. Harmondsworth: Penguin Books, 1969.

Goldsmith, Oliver. *The Vicar of Wakefield,* edited by Stephen Coote. Harmondsworth: Penguin Books, 1982.

Graver, Suzanne. *George Eliot and Community: A Study in Social Theory and Fictional Form.* Berkeley: University of California Press, 1984.

Greenberg, Wendy. *The Power of Rhetoric: Hugo's Metaphor and Poetics.* New York: Peter Lang, 1985.

Greene, Robert. *Frier Bacon and Frier Bongay,* edited by Alexander Grosart in Grosart's edition of Greene's *Works.* 15 vols. New York: Russell and Russell, 1964.

Grimaud, Michel, ed. *Victor Hugo,* vol. 1: *Approches critique contemporaines.* Paris: Minard, 1984–   .

Gross, John, and Gabriel Pearson. *Dickens and the Twentieth Century.* London: Routledge and Kegan Paul, 1966.

Grossman, Kathryn. " 'Angleterre et France melées': Fraternal Visions in *Quatre-vingt-Treize* and *A Tale of Two Cities.*" In *Victor Hugo et La Grande-Bretagne,* edited by A. R. W. James, 105–20. Paris: Francis Cairns, 1986.

———. *The Early Novels of Victor Hugo: Towards a Poetics of Harmony.* Geneva: Librairie Droz, 1986.

———. "Hugo's Romantic Sublime: Beyond Chaos and Convention in *Les Misérables.*" *Philological Quarterly* 60 (Fall 1981): 471–86.

Hamori, Andras. *On the Art of Medieval Arabic Literature.* Princeton, N.J.: Princeton University Press, 1974.

Harvey, W. J. *Character and the Novel.* Ithaca, N.Y.: Cornell University Press, 1965.

Hawthorn, Jeremy. *Bleak House.* Atlantic Highlands, N.J.: Humanities Press International, 1987.

Herbert, Christopher. "DeQuincey and Dickens." *Victorian Studies* 17 (March 1974): 247–63.

Herring, Paul D. "Dickens's Monthly Number Plans for 'Little Dorrit.' " *Modern Philology* 64 (August 1966): 22–63.

Hoggart, Paul. "Travesties of Dickens." *Essays and Studies* 1987 (special issue on "Broadening the Context"): 32–44.

Hollingsworth, Keith. *The Newgate Novel*. Detroit: Wayne State University Press, 1963.

Hollington, Michael. *Dickens and the Grotesque*. Totowa, N.J.: Barnes and Noble, 1984.

Hook, Theodore. *Maxwell*. 3 vols. London: Henry Colburn and Richard Bentley, 1830.

Hooker, Kenneth. *The Fortunes of Victor Hugo in England*. New York: Columbia University Press, 1938.

Hornback, Bert. *"The Hero of My Life": Essays on Dickens*. Athens: Ohio University Press, 1981.

House, Humphry. *The Dickens World*. London: Oxford University Press, 1971.

Howard, Edward. *Rattlin the Reefer*, edited by Arthur Howes. London: Oxford University Press, 1971.

Hugo, Adèle. *Victor Hugo raconté par Adèle Hugo*, edited by Annie Ubersfeld and Guy Rosa. Paris: Plon, 1985.

Hugo, Victor. *Edition de Grand Luxe of the Novels, Drawings, and Selected Poems of Victor Hugo*. 41 vols. Philadelphia, ca. 1892–97.

———. *L'Homme qui rit*. 3 vols. Paris, 18–?.

———. *The Hunchback of Notre-Dame*, translated by Walter Cobb. New York: Signet Classics, 1965.

———. *Littérature et philosophie melées*, edited by A. R. W. James. 2 vols. Paris: Editions Klincksieck, 1976.

———. *Les Misérables*, translated by Norman Denny. Harmondsworth: Penguin Books, 1976.

———. *Les Misérables*, translated by Charles Wilbour. New York: Random House, Modern Library, n.d.

———. *Notre-Dame de Paris 1482* and *Les Travailleurs de la mer*, edited by Yves Gohin. Paris: Gallimard, 1975.

———. *Oeuvres complètes*. 45 vols. Paris: Librairie Ollendorf, 1904–52.

Hume, Kathryn. "Views from Above, Views from Below: The Perspectival Subtext in *Gravity's Rainbow*." *American Literature* 60 (December 1988): 625–42.

Humpherys, Anne. "The Geometry of the Modern City: G. W. M. Reynolds and *The Mysteries of London*." *Browning Institute Studies* 11 (1983): 69–80.

The Hunchback of Old Saint Paul's: Or, A Romance of Mystery. London, n.d.

Hutter, Albert. "Dismemberment and Articulation in *Our Mutual Friend*." *Dickens Studies Annual* 11 (1983): 135–75.

———. "The High Tower of His Mind: Psychoanalysis and the Reader of 'Bleak House.'" *Criticism* 19 (1977): 296–316.

Huysmans, J. K. *Là-Bas*, edited by Pierre Gorny. Paris: Garnier-Flammarion, 1978.

Ireland, Kenneth. "Urban Perspectives: Fantasy and Reality in Hoffmann and Dickens." *Comparative Literature* 30 (Spring 1978): 133–56.

Jacobson, Wendy. *The Companion to "The Mystery of Edwin Drood."* London: Allen and Unwin, 1986.

Jaffe, Audrey. " 'Never Be Safe but in Hiding': Omniscience and Curiosity in *The Old Curiosity Shop.*" *Novel* 19 (Winter 1986): 118–34.

James, Louis. *Fiction for the Working Man, 1830–50.* Harmondsworth: Penguin Books, 1974.

———. *Print and the People, 1819–1851.* London: Allen Lane, 1976.

Johnson, Edgar. *Charles Dickens, His Tragedy and Triumph.* New York: Simon and Schuster, 1952.

Jordan, John. "The Purloined Handkerchief." *Dickens Studies Annual* 18 (1989): 1–17.

Joseph, Gerhard. "The Labyrinth and the Library: A View from the Temple in *Martin Chuzzlewit.*" *Dickens Studies Annual* 15 (1986): 1–22.

Journet, René, and Guy Robert. *Le Mythe du peuple dans Les Misérables.* Paris: Editions Sociales, 1963.

Kaplan, Fred. *Dickens and Mesmerism: The Hidden Springs of Fiction.* Princeton, N.J.: Princeton University Press, 1975.

Keating, Peter. *The Working Classes in Victorian Fiction.* New York: Barnes and Nobles, 1971.

Kellman, Stephen. *The Self-Begetting Novel.* New York: Columbia University Press, 1980.

Klancher, John. *The Making of English Reading Audiences, 1790–1832.* Madison: University of Wisconsin Press, 1987.

Kucich, John. "Death Worship among the Victorians: *The Old Curiosity Shop.*" *PMLA* 95 (January 1980): 58–72.

———. *Excess and Restraint in the Novels of Charles Dickens.* Athens: University of Georgia Press, 1981.

LaCapra, Dominick. "Ideology and Critique in Dickens's *Bleak House.*" *Representations,* no. 6 (Spring 1984): 116–23.

Larson, Janet. *Dickens and the Broken Scripture.* Athens: University of Georgia Press, 1986.

Lesser, Wendy. "From Dickens to Conrad: A Sentimental Journey." *ELH* 57 (Spring 1985): 185–208.

Lewes, George Henry. *Life and Works of Goethe with Sketches of His Age and Contemporaries.* London: J. M. Dent, 1924.

Lippard, George. *The Monks of Monk Hall,* with an introduction by Leslie Fiedler. New York: Odyssey Press, 1970.

———. *Writings of an American Radical,* edited by David Reynolds. New York: Peter Lang, 1986.

Lukacher, Ned. *Primal Scenes: Literature, Philosophy, Psychoanalysis.* Ithaca, N.Y.: Cornell University Press, 1986.

Lukács, Georg. *The Historical Novel,* translated from the German by Hannah and Stanley Mitchell. Boston: Beacon Press, 1963.

Maixner, Paul, editor. *Robert Louis Stevenson: The Critical Heritage.* London: Routledge and Kegan Paul, 1981.

Mann, Thomas. *Doctor Faustus,* translated by H. T. Lowe-Porter. New York: Random House, Modern Library, 1966.

Marcus, Stephen. *Dickens from Pickwick to Dombey.* New York: Simon and Schuster, 1965.

Maxwell, Richard. "City Life and the Novel: Hugo, Ainsworth, Dickens." *Comparative Literature* 30 (Spring 1978): 157–71.

———. "Dickens, the Two *Chronicles,* and the Publication of *Sketches by Boz.*" *Dickens Studies Annual* 9 (1981): 21–32.

———. G. M. Reynolds, Dickens, and the Mysteries of London." *Nineteenth-Century Fiction* 32 (September 1977): 188–213.

Mehlman, Jeffrey. *Revolution and Repetition: Marx/Hugo/Balzac.* Berkeley: University of California Press, 1977.

Mercié, Jean-Luc. "*Les Travailleurs de la mer* ou les avatars du roman parisien." In Victor Hugo, *Oeuvres complètes,* edited by Jean Massin. 18 vols., 12: 485–512. Paris: Club du Livre Français, 1967.

Merrill, James. *From the First Nine: Poems, 1946–1976.* New York: Atheneum, 1982.

Metz, Nancy Aycock. "The Artistic Reclamation of Waste in *Our Mutual Friend.*" *Nineteenth-Century Fiction* 34 (June 1979): 59–72.

———. "Narrative Gesturing in *Bleak House.*" *Dickensian* (Spring 1981): 13–22.

Miller, D. A. *The Novel and the Police.* Berkeley: University of California Press, 1988.

———. "Under Capricorn." *Representations,* no. 6 (Spring 1984): 124–29.

Miller, J. Hillis. *Charles Dickens: The World of His Novels.* Cambridge, Mass.: Harvard University Press, 1958.

———. *The Form of Victorian Fiction.* Notre Dame, Ind.: University of Notre Dame Press, 1968.

———. "*Sketches by Boz, Oliver Twist,* and Cruikshank's Illustrations." In *Charles Dickens and George Cruikshank,* 1–69. Los Angeles: William Andrew Clark Memorial Library, University of California, 1971.

Mudrick, Marvin. Afterword to *Martin Chuzzlewit.* New York: Signet Books, 1965.

Mundhenk, Rosemary. "The Education of the Reader in *Our Mutual Friend.*" *Nineteenth-Century Fiction* 34 (June 1979): 41–58.

Nabokov, Vladimir. "Signs and Symbols." In *Nabokov's Dozen: A Collection of Thirteen Stories,* 67–74. Freeport, N.Y.: Books for Libraries Press, 1969.

Newsom, Robert. *Dickens on the Romantic Side of Familiar Things: "Bleak House" and the Novel Tradition.* New York: Columbia University Press, 1977.

———. "The Hero's Shame." *Dickens Studies Annual* 11 (1983): 11–24.

Nicklins, J. A. *Dickens-Land.* Blackie and Son Ltd. [1911].

Nodier, Charles. *Contes,* edited by Pierre-Georges Castex. Paris: Editions Garnier Frères, 1961.

Opie, Iona, and Peter Opie. *The Classic Fairy Tales.* London: Oxford University Press, 1974.

Ousby, Ian. "The Broken Glass: Vision and Comprehension in *Bleak House.*" *Nineteenth-Century Fiction* 29 (March 1975): 381–92.

Porter, Laurence M. *The Literary Dream in French Romanticism: A Psychoanalytic Interpretation.* Detroit: Wayne State University Press, 1979.

Praz, Mario. *The Hero in Eclipse in Victorian Fiction,* translated by Angus Davidson. London: Oxford University Press, 1956.

Prendergast, Christopher. *Balzac: Fiction and Melodrama*. London: Edward Arnold, 1978.

Prickett, Stephen. *Victorian Fantasy*. Bloomington: Indiana University Press, 1979.

Pynchon, Thomas. *Gravity's Rainbow*. New York: Viking Press, 1973.

Radcliffe, Ann. *The Mysteries of Udolpho*, edited by Bonamy Dobrée. Oxford: Oxford University Press, 1970.

Ragussis, Michael. "The Ghostly Signs of *Bleak House*." *Nineteenth-Century Fiction* 34 (December 1979): 253–80.

Reynolds, G. W. M. *Faust: A Romance*. In the *London Journal*, 4 October 1845–18 July 1846.

———. *Master Timothy's Book-Case, or The Magic Lanthorn of the World*. London, 1841.

———. *The Modern Writers of France*. 2 vols. London, 1839.

———. *Robert Macaire in England*. 3 vols. London, 1840.

———. *The Seamstress, or The White Slaves of England*. In *Reynolds's Miscellany*, 23 March 1850–10 August 1850.

———. *Wagner the Wehr-Wolf*, edited by E. F. Bleiler, with bibliography of Reynolds. New York: Dover, 1975.

Rice, Thomas Jackson. "The End of Dickens's Apprenticeship: Variable Focus in *Barbaby Rudge*." *Nineteenth-Century Fiction* 30 (September 1975): 172–84.

Richardson, Joanna. *Victor Hugo*. New York: St. Martin's Press, 1976.

[Ridley, James]. *Tales of the Genii: or, the Delightful Lessons of Horam, the Son of Asmar, translated from the Persian by Sir Charles Morell*. 2 vols. London, 1799.

Riffaterre, Michel. "La Poésie metaphysique de Victor Hugo: Style, symboles, et thèmes de *Dieu*." *Romantic Review* 51 (December 1960): 268–76.

Rigby, Brian. "Victor Hugo and the English Secularists and Republicans." In *Victor Hugo et La Grande-Bretagne*, edited by A. R. W. James, 75–101. Paris: Francis Cairns, 1986.

Rimbaud, Jean. *Complete Works, Selected Letters*, edited by Wallace Fowlie. Chicago: University of Chicago Press, 1966.

Romano, John. *Dickens and Reality*. New York: Columbia University Press, 1978.

Sabin, Margery. *English Romanticism and the French Tradition*. Cambridge, Mass.: Harvard University Press, 1976.

Sadoff, Dianne F. "*Locus Suspectus:* Narrative, Castration, and the Uncanny." *Dickens Studies Annual* 13 (1984): 207–30.

Saintsbury, George. *A History of the French Novel (to the Close of the Nineteenth Century)* 2 vols. New York: Macmillan, 1917–19.

Scott, Walter. *Waverley Novels*. 24 vols. Edinburgh: Adam and Charles Black, 1852.

Seebacher, Jacques. "Gringoire, ou le déplacement du roman historique vers l'histoire." *Revue d'histoire littéraire de la France* 75 (March–June 1975): 308–20.

———. "Le Système du vide dans 'Notre-Dame de Paris.'" *Littérature*, February 1972: 95–106.

Serlen, Ellen. "The Two Worlds of *Bleak House*." *ELH* 43 (Winter 1976): 551–66.

Shaw, George Bernard. *Shaw on Dickens*, edited by Dan H. Laurence and Martin Quinn. New York: Ungar, 1985.

Shelden, Michael. "Dickens, 'The Chimes,' and the Anti-Corn Law League." *Victorian Studies* 25 (Spring 1982): 329–53.

Showalter, Elaine. "Guilt, Authority, and the Shadows of *Little Dorrit*." *Nineteenth-Century Fiction* 34 (June 1979): 20–40.

Splitter, Randolph. "Guilt and the Trappings of Melodrama in *Little Dorrit*." *Dickens Studies Annual* 6 (1977): 119–33.

Starkie, Enid. *Petrus Borel the Lycanthrope: His Life and Times*. New York: New Directions, 1954.

Starobinski, Jean. "Windows: Rousseau to Baudelaire," translated by Richard Pevear. *Hudson Review* 40 (Winter 1985): 551–60.

Steig, Michael, and F. A. C. Wilson. "Hortense versus Bucket: The Ambiguity of Order in *Bleak House*." *Modern Language Quarterly* 33 (September 1972): 289–98.

Stevenson, Robert Louis. *Familiar Studies of Men and Books*. London: Chattos and Windus, 1882.

———. *The Works of Robert Louis Stevenson*, edited by L. Osbourne and F. Van de G. Stevenson. 26 vols. Vailima Edition. London: William Heinemann, 1922–23.

Stewart, Garrett. *Death Sentences*. Cambridge, Mass.: Harvard University Press, 1984.

———. *Dickens and the Trials of Imagination*. Cambridge, Mass.: Harvard University Press, 1974.

———. "The New Mortality of *Bleak House*." *ELH* 45 (Fall 1978): 443–87.

Stoehr, Taylor. *Dickens: The Dreamer's Stance*. Ithaca, N.Y.: Cornell University Press, 1965.

Stone, Donald. *The Romantic Impulse in Victorian Fiction*. Cambridge, Mass.: Harvard University Press, 1980.

Stone, Harry. *Dickens and the Invisible World: Fairy Tales, Fantasy, and Novel-Making*. Bloomington: Indiana University Press, 1979.

———, ed. *Charles Dickens' Uncollected Writings from "Household Words": 1850–1859*. 2 vols. Bloomington: Indiana University Press, 1968.

Stone, Marjorie. "Dickens, Bentham, and the Fictions of the Law: A Victorian Controversy and Its Consequences." *Victorian Studies* 29 (Autumn 1985): 125–54.

Sue, Eugène. *Le Juif errant*. 10 vols. Paris: Paulin, 1844–45.

———. *The Mysteries of Paris*. 4 vols. in 2. London: Chapman and Hall, 1845.

Sutherland, John. *The Stanford Companion to Victorian Fiction*. Stanford, Calif.: Stanford University Press, 1989.

Swinburne, A. C. "Hugo, Victor." *Encyclopedia Britannica*, 11th ed. (1910–11).

Thackeray, William M. *Complete Works*. 20 vols. New York: George D. Sproul, 1899.

———. *The Letters and Private Papers of William Makepeace Thackeray*, edited by Gordon Ray. 4 vols. Cambridge, Mass.: Harvard University Press, 1946.

———. *The New Sketch Book, Being Essays Now First Collected from the Foreign Quarterly Review*, edited by R. S. Garnett. London: Rivers, 1906.

Thibaudet, Albert. *French Literature from 1795 to Our Era*, translated by Charles Lam Markmann. New York: Funk and Wagnalls, 1967.

Thomas, Marilyn. "*Edwin Drood:* A Bone Yard Awaiting Resurrection." *Dickens Quarterly* 2 (March 1985): 12–18.

Thomas, Ronald. "Dickens's Sublime Artifact." *Browning Institute Studies* 14 (1986): 71–96.

Thompson, George. *The Brazen Star: or, The Adventures of a New-York M.P. A True Tale of the Times We Live In.* New York, 1853.

Thomson, Patricia. *George Sand and the Victorians: Her Influence and Reputation in Nineteenth-Century England.* New York: Columbia University Press, 1977.

Tillotson, Kathleen. *Novels of the Eighteen-Forties.* London: Oxford University Press, 1961.

Tombeau de Victor Hugo: Le 22 Mai 1885. Paris: Editions Quintette, 1985.

Trollope, Anthony. *The Prime Minister.* London: Oxford University Press, 1961.

Ubersfeld, Anne. "Nommer la misère." *Revue des Sciences Humaines* 39, no. 4 (1974): 581–96.

———. "Le Rêve de Jean Valjean." *L'Arc* 57 (1974): 41–50.

Vadé, Yves. "Le Sphinx et la chimère." *Romantisme* (1977), no. 15, pp. 2–17, and no. 16, pp. 71–81.

Van Ghent, Dorothy. "The Dickens World: A View from Todgers's." *Sewanee Review* 58 (1950): 419–38.

Vernier, France. "*Les Misérables:* Ce Livre est dangereux." *L'Arc* 57 (1974): 33–39.

Virgil. *Works,* edited and translated by H. Rushton Fairclough. 2 vols. Rev. ed. Cambridge, Mass.: Harvard University Press, Loeb Classical Library, 1965.

Welsh, Alexander. *The City of Dickens.* Oxford: Clarendon Press, 1971.

———. *George Eliot and Blackmail.* Cambridge, Mass.: Harvard University Press, 1985.

———. *The Hero of the Waverley Novels.* New York: Atheneum, 1968.

Wilkinson, Ann Y. "*Bleak House:* From Faraday to Judgment Day." *ELH* 34 (June 1967): 225–47.

Wilson, Angus. *The World of Charles Dickens.* New York: Viking Press, 1970.

Wilson, Edmund. "Dickens: The Two Scrooges." In his *The Wound and the Bow: Seven Studies in Literature,* 1–104. New York: Oxford University Press, 1947.

Wilt, Judith. "Confusion and Consciousness in Dickens's Esther." *Nineteenth-Century Fiction* 32 (December 1977): 285–309.

Winegarten, Renée. "Victor Hugo: On the Legacy of Myth." *Encounter,* September–October 1987: 25–35.

Winner, Anthony. "Character and Knowledge in Dickens: The Enigma of Jaggers." *Dickens Studies Annual* 3 (1974): 100–121.

Woods, Irene. "Charles Dickens, Hans Christian Andersen, and 'The Shadow.'" *Dickens Quarterly* 2 (December 1985): 124–29.

Wordsworth, William. *The Prelude: A Parallel Text,* edited by J. C. Maxwell. Harmondsworth: Penguin Books, 1971.

Yonge, Charlotte M. *The Heir of Redclyffe.* London: Duckworth, 1964.

Zarifopol-Johnston, Illianca M. "'Ceci tuera cela': The Cathedral in the Markplace." *Nineteenth-Century French Studies* 17 (1989): 355–66.

Zola, Emile. *Les Rougon-Macquart: Histoire naturelle et sociale d'une famille sous le second empire.* 3 vols. Paris: Editions Gallimard, 1960.

City Life

Allingham, Frank, compiler. "Chronicles of Bermondsey," unpublished scrap-book. The Southwark Local Studies Library, London.

Aragon, Louis. *Paris Peasant,* translated by Simon Watson Taylor. London: Pan, 1980.

———. *Le Paysan de Paris.* Paris: Gallimard, 1926.

Atkins, P. J. "London Directories." *London Journal* 14, no. 1 (1989): 17–28.

Baedeker, Karl. *Baedeker's London and Its Environs: Handbook for Travellers.* Leipzig, 1898.

———. *Paris and Environs with Routes from London to Paris: Handbook for Travellers.* Leipzig, 1891.

Benjamin, Walter. *Charles Baudelaire: A Lyric Poet in the Era of High Capitalism,* translated by Harry Zohn. London: NLB, 1973.

Berman, Marshall. *All That Is Solid Melts into Air: The Experience of Modernity.* New York: Simon and Schuster, 1982.

Blanchard, Marc Eli. *In Search of the City: Engels, Baudelaire, Rimbaud.* Saratoga, Calif.: Anma Libri, 1985.

Briggs, Asa. *From Iron Bridge to Crystal Palace: Impact and Images of the Industrial Revolution.* London: Thames and Hudson, 1979.

———. *Victorian Cities.* New York: Harper and Row, 1965.

Buck-Morss, Susan. *The Dialectics of Seeing: Walter Benjamin and the Arcades Project.* Cambridge, Mass.: MIT Press, 1989.

Bullon, Hilary. *The Paris of Henri IV: Architecture and Urbanism.* Cambridge, Mass.: MIT Press, 1991.

Byrd, Max. *London Transformed: Images of the City in the Eighteenth Century.* New Haven, Conn.: Yale University Press, 1978.

Chast, Roz. "Stores of Mystery" [cartoon]. *New Yorker.* 13 January 1986, 25.

Chesterton, Gilbert Keith. "A Defence of Detective Stories." Reprinted in *The Art of the Mystery Story,* edited by Howard Haycraft. New York: Grosset and Dunlap, 1946: 3–6.

Chevalier, Louis. *Laboring Classes and Dangerous Classes in Paris during the First Half of the Nineteenth Century,* translated by Frank Jellinek. New York: Howard Fertig, 1973.

———. *Montmartre du plaisir et du crime.* Paris: Editions Robert Laffont, 1980.

Cohen, Margaret. "Mysteries of Paris: The Collective Uncanny in André Breton's *L'Amour fou.*" *Dada/Surrealism,* no. 17 (1988): 101–10.

Corry, John. "About New York." *New York Times,* 4 October 1974, 36.

Le Diable à Paris: Paris et les Parisiens. Mœurs et coutumes, caractères et portraits des habitants de Paris, tableau complèt de leur vie privée, publique, politique, artistique, littéraire, industrielle, etc., etc. Paris, 1845.

Dickens, Charles, Jr. *Dickens's Dictionary of London, 1879: An Unconventional Hand-book.* London, 1879.

Doré, Gustave, and Blanchard Jerrold. *London: A Pilgrimage.* New York: Dover, 1970. (Originally published 1872).

Dyos, H. J., and Michael Wolff. *The Victorian City: Images and Realities.* 2 vols. London: Routledge and Kegan Paul, 1973.

Engels, Friederich. *The Condition of the Working Class in England,* translated by W. O. Henderson and W. H. Chaloner. Stanford, Calif.: Stanford University Press, 1968.

Gorey, Edward. Installment of *Les Mystères de Constantinople. New York Review of Books,* 3 April 1975: 37.

Grad, Bonnie, and Timothy Riggs. *Visions of City and Country.* Worcester, Mass.: Worcester Art Museum and the American Federation of Arts, 1982.

Green, Martin. *Cities of Light and Sons of the Morning: A Cultural Psychology for an Age of Revolution.* Boston: Little, Brown, 1972.

————. *Travels into the Poor Man's Country: The Work of Henry Mayhew.* Athens: University of Georgia Press, 1977.

Hyde, Ralph. *Printed Maps of Victorian London, 1851–1900.* London: Wm. Dawson and Sons, 1975.

[James, Henry]. Review of Andrew Wynter, *Fruit Between the Leaves. The Nation* 21 (1 July 1875): 15–16.

Keating, Peter. "In the Heart of the Nichol," review of Raphael Samuel, *East End Underworld. TLS,* 15 May 1981: 533–34.

Knight, Charles. *London.* 4 vols. London, 1842.

Knox, Thomas. *Underground, or Life below the Surface: Incidents and Accidents beyond the Light of Day; Startling Adventures in All Parts of the World; Mines and the Mode of Working Them; Under-currents of Society; Gambling and Its Horrors; Caverns and Their Mysteries; the Dark Ways of Wickedness; Prisons and Their Secrets; Down in the Depths of the Sea; Strange Stories of the Detection of Crime.* Hartford, 1875.

Kuberski, Philip. "Unconscious Cities." *Georgia Review* 44 (Winter 1990): 678–89.

Landa, Louis. "London Observed: The Progress of a Simile." *Philological Quarterly* 54 (Winter 1975): 275–88.

"London at Night: Seen From the Summit of St. Paul's" (poem), *Ainsworth's Magazine* 8 (July 1845): 86–89.

McGann, Jerome. "Rome and Its Romantic Significance." In *Roman Images,* edited by Annabel Patterson, 83–104. Baltimore: Johns Hopkins University Press, 1984.

Marcus, Stephen. *Engels, Manchester, and the Working Class.* New York: Random House, 1974.

Masson, David. "Dead Men Whom I Have Known; or, Recollections of Three Cities: London from the Top of St. Paul's, Part I." *MacMillan's Magazine* 12 (1865): 275–88.

Maxwell, Richard. "Henry Mayhew and the Life of the Streets." *The Journal of British Studies* (Spring 1978): 87–105.

Mayhew, Augustus. *Paved with Gold.* London, 1858.

Mayhew, Henry. *1851: or, the Adventures of Mr. and Mrs. Sandboys and Family, Who Came up to London to Enjoy Themselves and to See the Great Exhibition.* London, 1851, original parts-issue monthly between February and October.

————. *London Labour and the London Poor.* New York: Dover Publications, 1968, facsimile edition of the 1860–61 version.

————. *The Unknown Mayhew,* edited by Eileen Yeo and E. P. Thompson. New York: Schocken Books, 1972.

Metcalf, Priscilla. "A to Z as was," review of Ralph Hyde, *Printed Maps of Victorian London, 1851–1900. TLS,* 8 August 1975, 904.

———. *Victorian London.* New York: Praeger, 1972.

Nairn, Ian. *Nairn's London.* Harmondsworth: Penguin Books, 1967.

Nord, Deborah Epstein. "The City as Theater: From Georgian to Early Victorian London." *Victorian Studies* 31 (Winter 1988): 159–88.

Okey, Thomas. *The Story of Paris.* Medieval Towns Series. London: J. M. Dent, 1911.

Olsen, Donald. *The City as a Work of Art: London, Paris, Vienna.* New Haven, Conn.: Yale University Press, 1986.

———. *The Growth of Victorian London.* Harmondsworth: Penguin Books, 1979.

[Payn, James]. "Meliboeus on the Commercial World of London." *Chambers's Journal* 17–18, 3rd ser. (1 February 1862): 79–80.

Pike, Burton. *The Image of the City in Modern Literature.* Princeton, N.J.: Princeton University Press, 1981.

Pinkney, David. *Napoleon III and the Rebuilding of Paris.* Princeton, N.J.: Princeton University Press, 1958.

Raban, Jonathan. *Soft City: The Art of Cosmopolitan Living.* New York: Dutton, 1974.

Ragon, Michel. *The Space of Death: A Study of Funerary Architecture, Decoration, and Urbanism,* translated by Alan Sheridan. Charlottesville: University Press of Virginia, 1983.

Reid, Donald. *Paris Sewers and Sewermen: Realities and Representations.* Cambridge, Mass.: Harvard University Press, 1991.

Roters, Eberhard. *Berlin, 1910–1933,* translated by Marguerite Mounier. New York: Rizzoli, 1982.

Sala, George. *Paris Herself Again in 1878–79.* 2 vols. London, 1880.

———. *Twice Around the Clock, or the Hours of the Day and Night in London.* Leicester: Leicester University Press, 1971.

Samuel, Raphael. *East End Underworld: Chapters in the Life of Arthur Harding.* London: Routledge and Kegan Paul, 1981.

Schwarzbach, F. S. *Dickens and the City.* London: Athlone Press, 1979.

———. "'Terra Incognita'—an Image of the City in English Literature, 1820–1855." *Prose Studies* 5 (May 1982): 61–84.

Smith's Indicator Map of London with a List Containing 4000 Streets. London, 1862.

Straus, Ralph. *Sala: The Portrait of an Eminent Victorian.* London: Constable and Co., 1942.

Summerson, John. *Georgian London.* Harmondsworth: Penguin Books, 1969.

Tallis's London Street Views, Exhibiting Upwards of One Hundred Buildings in Each Number, Elegantly Engraved on Steel: With a Commercial Directory Corrected Every Month, the Whole Forming a Complete Stranger's Guide through London. Text by William Gaspey, Elevations by [Charles?] Bigot. London, 1838.

Timbs, John. *The Romance of London.* London, n.d.

Trachtenberg, Alan. "Experiments in Another Country: Stephen Crane's City Sketches." *Southern Review* 10 (Spring 1974): 265–85.

Walter, E. V. "Dreadful Enclosures: Detoxifying an Urban Myth." *European Journal of Sociology* 28, no. 1 (1977): 151–59.

Weber, Eugen. "From Ordure to Order," review of Donald Reid, *Paris Sewers and Sewermen*. *The New Republic* 1 July 1991: 40–42.

Wechsler, Judith. *A Human Comedy: Physiognomy and Caricature in Nineteenth Century Paris*. Chicago: University of Chicago Press, 1982.

Williams, Raymond. *The Country and the City*. New York: Oxford University Press, 1973.

Wohl, Richard R., and Anselm L. Strauss. "Symbolic Representation and the Urban Milieu." *American Journal of Sociology* 63 (March 1958): 523–32.

Wynter, Andrew. *Curiosities of Civilization. Reprinted from the "Quarterly" and "Edinburg" Reviews*. London, 1860; reprint, Detroit: Singing Tree Press, 1968.

———. *Our Social Bees: or, Pictures of Town and Country Life, and Other Papers*. London, 1861; reprint, Detroit: Singing Tree Press, 1969.

———. *Subtle Brains and Lissom Fingers. Being Some of the Chisel-Marks of Our Industrial and Scientific Progress*. London, 1860; reprint, Detroit: Singing Tree Press, 1968.

Yates, Edmund. "London by Night." *The Train* 2 (1856): 371–74.

Allegory

Applewhite, James. "Postmodernist Allegory and the Denial of Nature." *Kenyon Review*, n.s. 11 (Winter 1989): 1–17.

Benjamin, Walter. *The Origin of German Tragic Drama*, translated by John Osborne. London: NLB, 1977.

Bloomfield, Morton. "A Grammatical Approach to Personification Allegory." *Modern Philology* 60 (February 1963): 161–71.

Blum, Claude. "Recherches sur les fonctions d'une représentation allégorique: L'Exemple de la mort en squelette." *Journal of Medieval and Renaissance Studies* (Spring 1985): 13–27.

Bruns, Gerald. "The Hermeneutics of Allegory and the History of Interpretation." *Comparative Literature* 40 (Fall 1988): 384–95.

Caldwell, Mark. "Allegory: The Renaissance Mode." *ELH* 44 (Winter 1977): 580–600.

Camille, Michael. "Walter Benjamin and Dürer's *Melencolia I:* The Dialectics of Allegory and the Limits of Iconology." *Ideas and Production*, no. 5 (History of Art): 58–79.

Cumming, Mark. "Allegory and Phantasmagory in *The French Revolution*." *Journal of English and Germanic Philology* 86 (July, 1987): 332–47.

de Man, Paul. *Allegories of Reading: Figural Language in Rousseau, Nietzsche, Rilke, and Proust*. New Haven, Conn.: Yale University Press, 1979.

———. *Blindness and Insight: Essays in the Rhetoric of Contemporary Criticism*. 2d ed. Minneapolis: University of Minnesota Press, 1983.

———. "The Double Aspect of Symbolism," *Yale French Studies*, no. 74 (1988): 3–16.

———. Introduction to *Studies in Romanticism* 18 (Winter 1979), special issue on "The Rhetoric of Romanticism": 495–99.

Fallon, Stephen. "Milton's Sin and Death: The Ontology of Allegory in *Paradise Lost*." *English Literary Renaissance* 17 (Autumn 1987): 329–50.

Fletcher, Angus. *Allegory: The Theory of a Symbolic Mode.* Ithaca, N.Y.: Cornell University Press, 1964.

———. *The Prophetic Moment: An Essay on Spenser.* Chicago: University of Chicago Press, 1971.

Foucault, Michel. *The Order of Things: An Archaeology of the Human Sciences, a Translation of "Les Mots et les choses."* New York: Vintage Books, 1973.

Glidden, Hope H. "Babil/Babel: Language Games in the *Bigarrues* of Estienne Tabourot." *Studies in Philology* 79 (Summer 1982): 242–55.

Greenblatt, Stephen, ed. *Allegory and Representation.* Baltimore: Johns Hopkins University Press, 1981.

Huizinga, J. *The Waning of the Middle Ages.* Harmondsworth: Penguin Books, 1968.

Jameson, Frederic. "*La Cousine Bette* and Allegorical Realism." *PMLA* 86 (March 1971): 241–54.

Jantz, Harold. *The Mothers in "Faust": The Myth of Time and Creativity.* Baltimore: Johns Hopkins University Press, 1969.

Jennings, Michael. *Dialectical Images: Walter Benjamin's Theory of Literary Criticism.* Ithaca, N.Y.: Cornell University Press, 1987.

Kahn, Victoria. "Habermas, Machiavelli, and the Humanist Critique of Ideology." *PMLA* 105 (May 1990): 464–76.

Kelley, Theresa. "Proteus and Romantic Allegory." *ELH* 49 (Fall 1982): 623–52.

Kibbey, Ann. *The Interpretation of Material Shapes in Puritanism: A Study of Rhetoric, Prejudice, and Violence.* Cambridge: Cambridge University Press, 1986.

McFarland, Thomas. *Romanticism and the Forms of Ruin: Wordsworth, Coleridge, and Modalities of Fragmentation.* Princeton, N.J.: Princeton University Press, 1981.

Mason, Eudo. *Goethe's "Faust": Its Genesis and Purport.* Berkeley: University of California Press, 1967.

Mazzeo, Joseph. "Allegorical Interpretation and History." *Comparative Literature* 30 (Winter 1976): 1–21.

Murrin, Michael. *The Veil of Allegory.* Chicago: University of Chicago Press, 1969.

Nash, Suzanne. "*Les Contemplations*" of Victor Hugo: An Allegory of the Creative Process.* Princeton, N.J.: Princeton University Press, 1976.

Quilligan, Maureen. *The Language of Allegory: Defining the Genre.* Ithaca, N.Y.: Cornell University Press, 1974.

Siebers, Tobin. *The Romantic Fantastic.* Ithaca, N.Y.: Cornell University Press, 1984.

Wind, Edgar. *Pagan Mysteries in the Renaissance.* Harmondsworth: Penguin Books, 1967.

Wittkower, Rudolph. *Allegory and the Migration of Symbols.* London: Thames and Hudson, 1977.

Literary and Linguistic Theory

Aarsleff Hans. *From Locke to Saussure: Essays on the Study of Language and Intellectual History.* Minneapolis: University of Minnesota Press, 1982.

Abrams, M. H. *Natural Supernaturalism: Tradition and Revolution in Romantic Literature.* New York: Norton, 1971.

Ackbar, Abbas. "Walter Benjamin's Collector: The Fate of Modern Experience." *New Literary History* 20 (Autumn 1988): 217–37.

Adams, Hazard. *Philosophy of the Literary Symbolic.* Tallahassee: University Presses of Florida, 1983.

Althusser, Louis. *For Marx,* translated by Ben Brewster. New York: Vintage Books, 1970.

Arac, Jonathan. *Critical Genealogies: Historical Situations for Postmodern Literary Studies.* New York: Columbia University Press, 1987.

———. "Reading the Letter." *Diacritics* 9: (Summer 1979): 42–52.

Aristotle. *Rhetoric,* translated by W. Rhys Roberts, and *Poetics,* translated by Ingram Bywater. New York: Random House, Modern Library, 1954.

Auerbach, Eric. *Mimesis: The Representation of Reality in Western Literature,* translated by Willard Trask. New York: Doubleday Anchor, 1957.

———. *Scenes from the Drama of European Literature.* New York: Meridian Books, 1959.

Bachelard, Gaston. *La Terre et les rêveries de la volonté.* Paris: Librairie José Corti, 1948.

Bahti, Timothy. "History as Rhetorical Enactment: Walter Benjamin's Theses 'On the Concept of History.'" *Diacritics* 9 (Fall 1979): 2–17.

Bakhtin, Mikhail. *Problems of Dostoyevsky's Poetics.* Minneapolis: University of Minnesota Press, 1984.

———. *Rabelais and His World,* translated by Helene Iswolsky. Cambridge, Mass.: The MIT Press, 1968.

Benjamin, Walter. *Illuminations,* edited by Hannah Arendt and translated by Harry Zohn. New York: Schocken Books, 1969.

———. *Reflections: Essays, Aphorisms, Autobiographical Writings,* translated by Edmund Jephcott. New York: Harcourt, Brace, Jovanovich, 1978.

Berlin, Isaiah. *Vico and Herder: Two Studies in the History of Ideas.* New York: Viking Press, 1976.

Booth, Wayne. *The Rhetoric of Fiction.* Chicago: University of Chicago Press, 1967.

Brown, Marshall. "The Logic of Realism: A Hegelian Approach." *PMLA* 96 (March 1981): 224–41.

Deuchar, Margaret. "Are the Signs of Language Arbitrary?" In *Images and Understanding: Thoughts about Images, Ideas about Understanding,* edited by Horace Barlow, Colin Blakemore, and Miranda Weston-Smith. Cambridge: Cambridge University Press, 1990: 168–79.

Eco, Umberto. *The Role of the Reader: Explorations in the Semiotics of Texts.* Bloomington: Indiana University Press, 1979.

Girard, René. *"To double business bound": Essays on Literature, Mimesis, and Anthropology.* Baltimore: Johns Hopkins University Press, 1978.

Gossman, Lionel. "History as Decipherment: Romantic Historiography and the Discovery of the Other." In his *Between History and Literature,* 257–84. Cambridge, Mass.: Harvard University Press, 1990.

Greisman, H. C. "'Disenchantment of the world': Romanticism, Aesthetics, and Sociological Theory." *British Journal of Sociology* 27 (December 1976): 495–507.

Hacking, Ian. *Why Does Language Matter to Philosophy?* Cambridge: Cambridge University Press, 1975.

Hesse, Carla. "Enlightenment Epistemology and the Laws of Authorship in Revolutionary France, 1777–1793." *Representations* 30 (Spring 1990): 109–37.

Hofstadter, Douglas. *Gödel, Escher, Bach: An Eternal Golden Braid.* New York: Basic Books, 1979.

Holstun, James. "Ranting at the New Historicism." *English Literary Renaissance* 19 (Spring 1989): 189–225.

Hunter, Linda. "Silence Is Also Language: Hausa Attitudes about Speech and Language." *Anthropological Linguistics* 24 (Winter 1982): 389–409.

Jameson, Frederic. *Marxism and Form: Twentieth-Century Dialectical Theories of Literature.* Princeton, N.J.: Princeton University Press, 1971.

———. *The Political Unconscious: Narrative as a Socially Symbolic Act.* Ithaca, N.Y.: Cornell University Press, 1982.

Jay, Martin. *The Dialectical Imagination: A History of the Frankfurt School and the Institute of Social Research, 1923–1950.* Boston: Little, Brown, 1973.

Kenshur, Oscar. "(Avoidable) Snares and Avoidables Muddles." *Critical Inquiry* 15 (Spring 1989): 658–68.

———. "Demystifying the Demystifiers: Metaphysical Snares of Ideological Criticism." *Critical Inquiry* 14 (Winter 1988): 335–53.

Kermode, Frank. *The Genesis of Secrecy: On the Interpretation of Narrative.* Cambridge, Mass.: Harvard University Press, 1979.

Kristeva, Julia. *Revolution in Poetic Language,* translated by Margaret Waller. New York: Columbia University Press, 1984.

Lakoff, George, and Mark Johnson. *Metaphors We Live by.* Chicago: University of Chicago Press, 1980.

Loewenstein, Joseph. "For a History of Literary Property: John Wolfe's Reformation." *English Literary Renaissance* 18 (Autumn 1988): 389–412.

Lukacher, Ned. "Walter Benjamin's Chthonian Revolution." *Boundary 2* 11 (1983): 41–57.

Lukács, Georg. *The Theory of the Novel: A Historico-Philosophical Essay on the Forms of Great Epic Literature,* translated by Anna Bostock. Cambridge, Mass.: MIT Press, 1971.

McGann, Jerome. *The Romantic Ideology: A Critical Investigation.* Chicago: University of Chicago Press, 1983.

———. *Social Values and Poetic Acts: The Historical Judgment of Literary Work.* Cambridge, Mass.: Harvard University Press, 1988.

Markley, Robert. "What Isn't History: The Snares of Demystifying Ideological Criticism." *Critical Inquiry* 15 (Spring 1989): 647–57.

Martin, Andrew. *The Knowledge of Ignorance: From Genesis to Jules Verne.* Cambridge: Cambridge University Press, 1985.

Moretti, Franco. *Signs Taken for Wonders: Essays in the Sociology of Literary Forms,* translated by Susan Fischer, David Forgacs, and David Miller. London: NLB, 1983.

Said, Edward. *Beginnings: Intention and Method.* New York: Basic Books, 1975.

Saussure, Ferdinand de. *Course in General Linguistics,* edited by Charles Bally and

Albert Sechehaye in collaboration with Albert Riedlinger, and translated by Wade Baskin. New York: McGraw-Hill, 1966.

Scaglione, Aldo. "Rhetorical Factors as Clues to Meaning." *Comparative Literature* 32 (Fall 1980): 337–54.

Senn, Werner. "The Labyrinth Image in Verbal Art: Sign, Symbol, Icon?" *Word and Image* 2 (July–September 1986): 219–30.

Shaffer, E. S. *"Kubla Khan" and the Fall of Jerusalem: The Mythological School in Biblical Criticism and Secular Literature, 1770–1880*. Cambridge: Cambridge University Press, 1975.

Speier, Hans. "The Communication of Hidden Meaning." *Social Research* 44 (Autumn 1977): 471–501.

Tave, Stuart. *The Amiable Humorist: A Study in the Comic Theory and Criticism of the Eighteenth and Early Nineteenth Centuries*. Chicago: University of Chicago Press, 1960.

Todorov, Tzvetan. *The Poetics of Prose,* translated by Richard Howard. Ithaca, N.Y.: Cornell University Press, 1979.

Turner, Mark. *Death Is the Mother of Beauty*. Chicago: University of Chicago Press, 1987.

West, Philip. "The Redundant Labyrinth." *Salmagundi* 46 (Fall 1979): 58–83.

Wolin, Richard. *Walter Benjamin: An Aesthetic of Redemption*. New York: Columbia University Press, 1982.

The History of Art, Architecture, and Film, with Associated Works on Images and Iconography

Agulhon, Maurice. *Marianne into Battle: Republican Imagery and Symbolism in France, 1789–1880,* translated by Janet Lloyd. Cambridge: Cambridge University Press, 1981.

Allderidge, Patricia. *The Late Richard Dadd*. London: The Tate Gallery, 1974.

Altick, Richard. *The Shows of London: A Panoramic History of Exhibitions, 1600–1862*. Cambridge, Mass.: Belknap Press of Harvard University Press, 1978.

Babcock, Barbara, ed. *The Reversible World: Symbolic Inversion in Art and Society*. Ithaca, N.Y.: Cornell University Press, 1978.

Boime, Albert. "The Second Empire's Official Realism." In *The European Realist Tradition,* edited by Gabriel Weisberg, 31–123. Bloomington: Indiana University Press, 1982.

Burke, James. *Charles Meryon: Prints and Drawings*. New Haven, Conn.: Yale University Art Gallery, 1974.

Carroll, Noël. *Mystifying Movies: Fads and Fallacies in Contemporary Film Theory*. New York: Columbia University Press, 1988.

Castle, Terry. "Phantasmagoria: Spectral Technology and the Metaphorics of Modern Reverie." *Critical Inquiry* 15 (Autumn 1988): 26–61.

Clark, T. J. *The Painting of Modern Life: Paris in the Art of Manet and His Followers*. New York: Knopf, 1985.

Cohen, Jane. *Charles Dickens and His Original Illustrators*. Columbus: Ohio State University Press, 1980.

[Combe, William]. *The Life of Napoleon: A Hudibrastic Poem in Fifteen Cantos, by*

Doctor Syntax, Embellished with Thirty Engraving by G. Cruikshank. London: T. Tegg, 1815.

Conrad, Peter. *The Victorian Treasure-House.* London: Collins, 1978.

Crary, Jonathan. "Techniques of the Observer." *October* 45 (Summer 1988): 3–35.

Dodwell, C. R., ed. *Essays on Dürer.* Manchester: Manchester University Press, 1973.

Eitner, Lorenz. "The Open Window and the Storm-Tossed Boat: An Essay in the Iconography of Romanticism." *Art Bulletin* 37 (December 1955): 281–90.

Evans, Joan. *Magical Jewels of the Middle Ages and the Renaissance particularly in England.* 1922; reprint, New York: Dover, 1976.

Feaver, William. "Cruikshank: The Artist's Role." In *George Cruikshank,* 5–30. London: Arts Council of Great Britain, 1974.

Flax, Neil. "Goethe's *Faust II* and the Experimental Theater of His Time." *Comparative Literature* 31 (Spring 1979): 154–66.

Fouqué, Friedrich Freiherr de la Motte. *The Four Seasons,* with illustrations by Albrecht Dürer and John Tenniel. London, 1853.

———. *Sintram and His Companions* and *Undine,* with an introduction by Charlotte M. Yonge and illustrations by Gordon Browne. London, 1896.

Gandelman, Claude. *Reading Pictures, Viewing Texts.* Bloomington: Indiana University Press, 1991.

Georgel, Pierre. *Drawings by Victor Hugo.* London: Victoria and Albert Museum, 1974.

Goldscheider, Ludwig. *Rembrandt: Paintings, Drawings, and Etchings.* Greenwich, Conn.: Phaidon, 1960.

Gombrich, Ernst. *Aby Warburg: An Intellectual Biography.* London: The Warburg Institute, 1970.

Halsband, Robert. *The Rape of the Lock and Its Illustrations, 1714–1896.* Oxford: Clarendon Press, 1980.

Harvey, John. *Victorian Novelists and Their Illustrators.* New York: New York University Press, 1971.

Heller, John. "Labyrinth or Troy Town?" *The Classical Journal* 42 (December 1946): 122–39.

Holcomb, Adele. "*Le Stryge de Notre-Dame:* Some Aspects of Meryon's Symbolism." *Art Journal* 31 (Winter 1971–72): 150–57.

Höltgen, Karl Josef. *Aspects of the Emblem: Studies in the English Emblem Tradition and the European Context.* Kassel: Edition Reichenberger, 1986.

Hyman, Timothy. "From Siena to London." In *The Subjective City: Fifteen Artists Respond to the City.* Exhibition catalog. Middlesbrough: The Cleveland Gallery, 1989.

Ilie, Paul. "Goya's Teratology and the Critique of Reason." *Eighteenth-Century Studies* 18 (Fall 1984): 35–56.

Jerrold, Blanchard. *The Life of George Cruikshank in Two Epochs,* new edition. London, 1894.

Kemp, Wolfgang. "Death at Work: A Case Study on Constitutive Blanks in Nineteenth-Century Painting." *Representations,* no. 10 (Spring 1985): 102–23.

Kerenyi, C. *Dionysos: Archetypal Image of Indestructible Life,* translated by Ralph Mannheim. Princeton, N.J.: Princeton University Press, 1976.

Kilbansky, Raymond, Erwin Panofsky, and Fritz Saxl. *Saturn and Melancholy: Studies in the History of Natural Philosophy, Religion, and Art.* New York: Basic Books, 1964.

Kitton, Frederic G. *Dickens and His Illustrators.* London, 1899.

Landow, George. *Victorian Types, Victorian Shadows: Biblical Typology in Victorian Literature, Art, and Thought.* Boston: Routledge and Kegan Paul, 1980.

Levitine, George. "Literary Sources of Goya's *Capricho* 43." *Art Bulletin* 37 (March 1955): 56–59.

Lipschutz, Ilse Hempel. *Spanish Painting and the French Romantics.* Cambridge, Mass.: Harvard University Press, 1972.

Lynton, Norbert. "Timothy Hyman." In *Timothy Hyman: Recent Work.* Exhibition catalogue. London: Austin/Desmond Fine Art, 1990.

Mancoff, Debra. *The Arthurian Revival in Victorian Art.* New York: Garland, 1990.

Marrinan, Michael. *Painting Politics for Louis-Philippe: Art and Ideology in Orléanist France, 1830–1848.* New Haven, Conn.: Yale University Press, 1988.

Mast, Gerald. *Film · Cinema · Movie: A Theory of Experience.* Chicago: University of Chicago Press, 1983.

Matthews, W. H. *Mazes and Labyrinths: Their History and Development.* 1922; reprint, New York: Dover Publications, 1970.

Maxwell, Richard. "The Return of Quasimodo." *Cresset* (March 1987): 16–18.

Michelson, Annette. "Dr. Crase and Mr. Clair." *October* 11 (Winter 1979): 30–53.

Milner, Max. *La Fantasmagorie: Essay sur l'optique fantastique.* Paris, P.U.F., 1983.

Mitchell, W. J. T. *Blake's Composite Art: A Study of the Illuminated Poetry.* Princeton, N.J.: Princeton University Press, 1978.

———. *Iconology: Image, Text, Ideology.* Chicago: University of Chicago Press, 1986.

Nordstrom, Folke. *Goya, Saturn, and Melancholy: Studies in the Art of Goya.* Stockholm: Almqvist and Wiksell, 1962.

Panofsky, Erwin. *The Life and Art of Albrecht Dürer.* Princeton, N.J.: Princeton University Press, 1955.

Patten, Robert, ed. *George Cruikshank: A Revaluation.* Special issue of the *Princeton University Library Chronicle* 35 (Autumn, Winter 1973–74).

Paulson, Ronald. *Representations of Revolution: 1789–1820.* New Haven, Conn.: Yale University Press, 1983.

Powell, Nicolas. *Fuseli: "The Nightmare."* New York: Viking Press, 1972.

Ray, Gordon. *The Illustrator and the Book in England from 1790 to 1914.* New York: Pierpont Morgan Library, 1976.

Rosen, Charles. "Now, Voyager," review of Barbara Stafford, *Voyage into Substance. New York Review of Books.* November 6, 1986: 55–60.

———, and Henri Zerner. *Romanticism and Realism: The Mythology of Nineteenth-Century Art.* New York: Viking Press, 1984.

Roud, Richard. "Feuillade." In *Cinema: A Critical Dictionary. The Major Filmmakers.* 2 vols. New York: Viking Press, 1980, 1:348–59.

Sánchez, Alfonso E. Pérez, and Eleanor A. Sayre, *Goya and the Spirit of Enlightenment.* Boston: Museum of Fine Arts, 1989.

Schiff, Gert. "Die Faust-Illustrationen Des Malers Theodor Matthias von Holst." *Jahrbuch des Wiener Goethe-Vereins* 66 (1962): 74–88.

Sohm, Philip L. "Dürer's *Melencolia I:* The Limits of Knowledge." *Studies in the History of Art* 9 (1980): 13–32.

Solberg, Sarah. "Bull's-Eye's 'Eyes' in *Oliver Twist.*" *Notes and Queries,* June 1980: 128–37.

Stafford, Barbara. "Toward Romantic Landscape Perception: Illustrated Travels and the Rise of 'Singularity' as an Aesthetic Category." *The Art Quarterly,* n.s. 1 (Autumn 1977): 89–124.

——. *Voyage into Substance: Art, Science, Nature, and the Illustrated Travel Account, 1760–1840.* Cambridge, Mass.: MIT Press, 1984.

Steig, Michael. *Dickens and Phiz.* Bloomington: Indiana University Press, 1978.

Sternberger, Dolf. *Panorama of the Nineteenth Century,* translated by Joachim Neugroschel. New York: Urizen Books, 1977.

Stevens, Joan. "'Woodcuts Dropped into the Text': The Illustrations in *The Old Curiosity Shop,* and *Barnaby Rudge.*" *Studies in Bibliography* 20 (1967): 113–34.

Thompson, Patrice. "Essai d'analyse des conditions du spectacle dans le Panorama et le Diorama." *Romantisme,* no. 38 (1982): 47–64.

Trapp, Frank Anderson. *The Attainment of Delacroix.* Baltimore: Johns Hopkins University Press, 1971.

Tzonis, Alexander, and Liane Lefaivre. *Classical Architecture: The Poetics of Order.* Cambridge, Mass.: MIT Press, 1986.

Vaughan, William. *German Romanticism and English Art.* New Haven, Conn.: Yale University Press, 1979.

Vincent, Howard. *Daumier and His World.* Evanston, Ill.: Northwestern University Press, 1968.

Wedmore, Frederick. *Meryon and Meryon's Paris.* 2d ed. London: Deprez and Gutekunst, 1892.

Weigle, Marta. *Spiders and Spinsters: Women and Mythology.* Albuquerque: University of New Mexico Press, 1982.

Yarnall, James. "Meryon's Mystical Transformations." *Art Bulletin* 61 (June 1979): 289–300.

Ziolkowski, Theodore. *Disenchanted Images: A Literary Iconology.* Princeton, N.J.: Princeton University Press, 1977.

Cultural, Social, Intellectual, and Political History

Altick, Richard. *The English Common Reader: A Social History of the Mass Reading Public, 1800–1900.* Chicago: University of Chicago Press, 1963.

Annan, Noel. *Leslie Stephen: The Godless Victorian.* New York: Random House, 1984.

Arendt, Hannah. *The Human Condition.* Chicago: University of Chicago Press, 1958.

Bacon, Francis. *The Works of Francis Bacon,* edited by James Spedding, Robert Leslie Ellis, and Douglas D. Heath. 15 vols. Boston, 1863.

Barnes, James. *Authors, Publishers, and Politicians: The Quest for an Anglo-American Copyright Agreement, 1815–1854.* Columbus: Ohio State University Press, 1974.

Beniger, James. *The Control Revolution: Technological and Economic Origins of the Information Society.* Cambridge, Mass.: Harvard University Press, 1986.

Bernheimer, Charles. *Figures of Ill Repute: Representing Prostitution in Nineteenth-Century France.* Cambridge, Mass.: Harvard University Press, 1989.

Brown, Raymond E., ed. *The Gospel According to John.* Garden City, N.Y.: Doubleday, 1966.

Burton, Richard. *The Anatomy of Melancholy.* 3 vols. Everyman Library. London: J. M. Dent, 1932.

Callinicos, Alex. *Making History: Agency, Structure, and Change in Social Theory.* Ithaca, N.Y.: Cornell University Press, 1988.

Callois, Roger. *La Pieuvre: Essai sur la logique de l'imaginaire.* Paris: La Table Ronde, 1973.

Campbell, Jeremy. *Grammatical Man.* New York: Simon and Schuster, 1982.

Canetti, Elias. *Crowds and Power.* New York: Continuum, 1973.

Cantarella, Eva. "Dangling Virgins: Myth, Ritual, and the Place of Women in Ancient Greece." In *The Female Body in Western Culture: Contemporary Perspectives,* edited by Susan Rubin Suleiman, 57–67. Cambridge, Mass.: Harvard University Press, 1985.

Carlyle, Thomas. *Critical and Miscellaneous Essays Collected and Republished.* Chicago: Hooper and Clarke, n.d.

———. *The French Revolution: A History.* London: Chapman and Hall, 1837.

———, and Jane Welsh Carlyle. *Collected Letters of Thomas and Jane Welsh Carlyle,* edited by Charles Richard Sanders and Kenneth Fielding. Durham, N.C.: Duke University Press, 1970–

Clark, Priscilla Parkhurst. *Literary France: The Making of a Culture.* Berkeley: University of California Press, 1987.

Cockshutt, A. O. J. *Truth to Life: The Art of Biography in the Nineteenth Century.* New York: Harcourt Brace Jovanovich, 1976.

Collier, Peter, and David Horowitz. "Slouching Towards Berkeley: Socialism in One City." *Public Interest* 94 (Winter 1989): 47–68.

Darwin, Charles. *The Origin of Species by Means of Natural Selection, or, The Preservation of Favoured Races in the Struggle for Life,* edited by J. W. Burrow. Harmondsworth: Penguin Books, 1968.

Daston, Lorrain J. "The Factual Sensibility." *Isis* 79 (September 1988): 452–66.

Descartes, René. *Oeuvres et lettres.* Paris: Editions Gallimard, 1953.

Doob, Penelope Reed. *The Idea of the Labyrinth from Classical Antiquity through the Middle Ages.* Ithaca, N.Y.: Cornell University Press, 1990.

Eliade, Mircea. *A History of Religious Ideas.* 3 vols. Chicago: University of Chicago Press, 1978–85.

Farmer, John, and W. E. Henley. *Slang and Its Analogues.* New York: Kraus Reprint Co., 1974.

Findlen, Paula. "Jokes of Nature and Jokes of Knowledge: The Playfulness of Scientific Discourse in Early Modern Europe." *Renaissance Quarterly* 43 (Summer 1990): 292–331.

Foucault, Michel. *Discipline and Punish: The Birth of the Prison,* translated by Alan Sheridan. New York: Vintage Books, 1979.

Freud, Sigmund. *The Standard Edition of the Complete Psychological Works of Sigmund Freud,* edited by James Strachey. 24 vols. London: Hogarth Press and the Institute of Psycho-Analysis, 1981.

Furet, François, and Jacques Ozouf. *Reading and Writing: Literacy in France from Calvin to Jules Ferry.* Cambridge: Cambridge University Press, 1982.

Giegerich, Wolfgang. "Deliverance from the Stream of Events: Okeanos and the Circulation of the Blood." *Sulfur* 21 (Winter 1988): 118–40.

———. "The Rocket and the Launching Base, or: The Leap from the Imaginal into the Outer Space Named 'Reality.'" *Sulfur* 28 (Spring 1991): 63–78.

Halévy, Elie. *A History of the English People in the Nineteenth Century.* 6 vols. New York: Barnes and Noble, 1961.

Hamlin, Christopher. "Providence and Putrefaction: Victorian Sanitarians and the Natural Theology of Health and Disease." *Victorian Studies* 28 (Spring 1985): 381–411.

Harrison, Ross. *Bentham.* London: Routledge and Kegan Paul, 1983.

Hazlitt, William. *Collected Works of William Hazlitt,* edited by P. P. Howe. 21 vols. London: Dent, 1930.

Henderson, James. "Agency or Alienation? Smith, Mill, and Marx on the Joint-Stock Company." *History of Political Economy* 18, no. 1 (1986): 111–31.

The Hermit in London: or Sketches of English Manners. London, 1822.

Himmelfarb, Gertrude. *The Idea of Poverty: England in the Early Industrial Age.* New York: Knopf, 1984.

Hollingshead, John. *My Lifetime.* 2 vols. London: S. Low, Marston, and Co., 1895.

Ireland, W. H. *A New and Complete History of the County of Kent: Embellished with a Series of Views from Original Drawings.* G. Virtue: London, 1830.

Kselman, Thomas. "Devotion and Distortion," review of Nicholas Perry and Loreto Echeverría, *Under the Heel of Mary. TLS.* 11 August 1989: 867.

Lefebvre, Henri. *Everyday Life in the Modern World,* translated by Sacha Rabinovitch. New York: Harper and Row, 1971.

Lesser, Wendy. *The Life below the Ground: A Study of the Subterranean in Literature and History.* Boston and London: Faber and Faber, 1987.

Lévi-Strauss, Claude. *Tristes Tropiques,* translated by John and Doreen Weightman. New York: Atheneum, 1975.

Loewenberg, Alfred, ed. *Annals of Opera.* Geneva: Societas Bibliographica, 1955.

Ludz, Peter. "Ideology, Intellectuals, and Organization: The Question of Their Interrelation in Early Nineteenth-Century Society." *Social Research* 44 (Summer 1977): 260–307.

McConville, Sean. "System and Sentiment: A Clash of Views on Crime and Criminals in Late Victorian England." Lecture at meeting of the Midwest Victorian Studies Association, spring 1990.

Maitland, Frederick William. *The Constitutional History of England,* edited by H. A. L. Fisher. Cambridge: Cambridge University Press, 1968.

———. *Maitland: Selected Essays,* edited by H. D. Hazeltine, G. Lapsley, and P. H. Winfield. Cambridge: Cambridge University Press, 1936.

Mallock, W. H. *Memoirs of Life and Literature.* New York: Harper and Row, 1920.

Marsh, John. *The Gospel of St John.* Harmondsworth: Penguin Books, 1968.

Martin, Henri-Jean, and Roger Chartier, eds. *Histoire de l'édition française.* 4 vols. Paris: Centre national des lettres, 1982–86.

Marx, Karl, and Frederick Engels. *Collected Works.* New York: International Publishers, 1975–

————. *Gundrisse: Foundations of the Critique of Political Economy,* translated by Martin Nicolaus. New York: Vintage Books, 1973.

————. *The Marx-Engels Reader,* edited by Robert Tucker. New York: Norton, 1972.

Maxwell, James Clerk. *The Scientific Letters and Papers of James Clerk Maxwell,* edited by P. M. Harman. Cambridge: Cambridge University Press, 1990.

Megill, Alan. "Foucault, Structuralism, and the Ends of History." *Journal of Modern History* 51 (September 1979): 451–503.

Merton, Robert. "The Matthew Effect in Science, II: Cumulative Advantage and the Symbolism of Intellectual Property." *Isis* 79 (December 1988): 606–23.

Michelet, Jules. *Histoire de France au seizième siècle,* edited by Robert Casanova. 4 vols. Paris: Flammarion, 1978.

————. *Le Peuple.* Paris, 1877.

Mill, John Stuart. *Collected Works of John Stuart Mill,* general editor, John W. Robson. 33 vols. Toronto: University of Toronto Press, 1963–91.

New Catholic Encyclopedia. 18 vols. San Francisco: Catholic University of America, 1967.

Nietzsche, Friederich. *Complete Works of Friederich Nietzsche,* edited by Oscar Levy. 18 vols. New York: Russell and Russell, 1964.

————. *The Philosophy of Nietzsche,* edited by Geoffrey Clive. New York: New American Library, 1965.

Nisbet, Robert. *Sociology as an Art Form.* London: Oxford University Press, 1976.

Pelikan, Jaroslav. *The Christian Tradition: A History of the Development of Doctrine.* 5 vols. Chicago: The University of Chicago Press, 1971–89.

Perry, Nicholas, and Loreto Echeverría. *Under the Heel of Mary.* London: Routledge, 1988.

Poulet, George. *The Interior Distance,* translated by Elliott Coleman. Baltimore: Johns Hopkins University Press, 1959.

Prigogine, Ilya, and Isabelle Stengers. *Order out of Chaos: Man's New Dialogue with Nature.* New York: Bantam Books, 1984.

Proudhon, Pierre Joseph. *Oeuvres complètes,* edited by C. Bougle and H. Moysset. 15 vols. Paris: M. Rivière, 1923–59.

Rosen, George. *Madness in Society: Chapters in the Historical Sociology of Mental Illness.* Chicago: University of Chicago Press, 1968.

Ruskin, John. *The Works of John Ruskin,* edited by E. T. Cook and Alexander Wedderburn. 39 vols. London: George Allen, 1903–12.

Schiffman, Zachary. "Montaigne and the Rise of Skepticism in Early Modern Europe: A Reappraisal." *Journal of the History of Ideas* 45 (October–December 1984): 499–516.

Scott, Thomas. *The Holy Bible.* Boston, 1823.

Shils, Edward. *The Torment of Secrecy: The Background and Consequences of American Security Policies.* Carbondale and Edwardsville: Southern Illinois University Press, 1956.

Simmel, Georg. *The Philosophy of Money,* translated by Tom Bottomore and David Frisby. London: Routledge and Kegan Paul, 1978.

Simon, Herbert. *The Sciences of the Artificial.* Cambridge, Mass.: MIT Press, 1970.

Spence, George. *Equitable Jurisdiction of the Court of Chancery.* London, 1849.

[Stephen, Leslie]. "Useless Knowledge." *Cornhill Magazine* 20 (July 1869): 41–51.

Stone, Lawrence. "Down the Tube," review of John Carey, *Eyewitness to History*. *New Republic*, 24 October 1988: 40–43.

Taylor, Charles. *Philosophical Papers*. 2 vols.: *Human Agency and Language* and *Philosophy and the Human Sciences*. Cambridge: Cambridge University Press, 1985.

Thompson, E. P. "The Crime of Anonymity." In *Albion's Fatal Tree: Crime and Society in Eighteenth-Century England*. New York: Pantheon Books, 1975: 255–308.

Trimpi, Helen. "Demonology." In *The Dictionary of the History of Ideas,* edited by Philip Wiener. 5 vols. New York: Charles Scribner's Sons, 1973.

Vincent, David. *Literacy and Popular Culture: England 1750–1914*. Cambridge: Cambridge University Press, 1989.

Wellek, René. *Confrontations: Studies in the Intellectual and Literary Relations between Germany, England, and the United States during the Nineteenth Century*. Princeton, N.J.: Princeton University Press, 1965.

Welsford, Enid. *The Fool: His Social and Literary History*. New York: Doubleday Anchor, 1961.

Wynter, Andrew. *The Borderlands of Insanity and Other Allied Papers*. London, 1875.

Yates, Frances. *The Art of Memory*. Chicago: University of Chicago Press, 1966.

Young, Robert M. *Darwin's Metaphor: Nature's Place in Victorian Culture*. Cambridge: Cambridge University Press, 1985.

Nineteenth-Century Periodicals

Belgravia
Bentley's Miscellany
The Builder
Chamber's Edinburgh Journal
Cruikshank's Comic Almanac
George Cruikshank's Omnibus
London Journal
Punch
Revue contemporaine
Revue de Paris
Reynolds's Miscellany

Index